# THE MUSICAL COMPANION

A marvel of mediæval British music—the Round, "Sumer is icumen in," made about 1225. For six voices, it sounds as spontaneous as it is scientific. From that period, and for centuries on, comes nothing to approach it, either in the number of voices used or in the skill of the composition. (*The MS. is "Brit. Museum, Harley No. 978."*)

# The MUSICAL COMPANION

*A Compendium*
*For All Lovers of Music*

By

W. R. ANDERSON     JULIUS HARRISON
EDWARD J. DENT     FRANCIS TOYE
DYNELEY HUSSEY     EDWIN EVANS
F. BONAVIA & ERIC BLOM

*Edited by*
A. L. BACHARACH

London
VICTOR GOLLANCZ LTD

*First published November 1934*
*Second impression December 1934*
*Third impression August 1935*
*Fourth impression October 1936*
*Fifth impression October 1938*
*Sixth impression (first cheap edition) February 1940*
*Seventh impression September 1940*
*Eighth impression November 1940*
*Ninth impression May 1941*

PRINTED IN GREAT BRITAIN BY PURNELL AND SONS, LTD. (T.U.)
PAULTON (SOMERSET) AND LONDON

# ACKNOWLEDGEMENT

Permission to quote musical examples from the works of Arnold Bax and Sir Edward Elgar has been kindly granted by Messrs. Murdoch, Murdoch & Co., and by Messrs. Novello & Co., Ltd., respectively, whom we wish to thank for their courtesy.

# PREFATORY LETTER FROM THE EDITOR TO THE PUBLISHER

Trebetherick,
Cornwall,
*August* 1934.

My dear Gollancz,—

I think you will agree with me that neither of us can claim credit for having first envisaged this book. That we have co-operated in its production is simply the direct result of something that is going on to-day all around us. If it had not been us, it would sooner or later have been "two other chaps"—you remember the story about Buenos Aires ?

Both of us have been for many years lovers of music in all its manifold forms. If you have been the more ardent supporter of opera, and I the more passionate devotee of chamber music, we have had a common meeting ground in the Queen's Hall. Both of us number among our friends composers, performers and musical critics ; both of us, because of our known musical affiliations, must have been asked over and over again by other friends where they could learn more about the art and its exponents.

It was not, therefore, surprising that, when we lunched together nearly a year ago to discuss some quite different matter, a casual remark from me, foreshadowing the possibility of producing a book such as this one, should have elicited from you something more than ready sympathy. The main sketch for THE MUSICAL COMPANION was discussed by us less than two weeks from that day ; by the end of last year we had decided whom we should ask to contribute to it—the most important decision of all.

This question of the contributors, however, was not settled in that fortnight at all. It was settled, in advance and without their knowledge, by the contributors themselves. The rightness of our choice should strictly be judged by the readers of THE MUSICAL COMPANION, yet I cannot refrain from expressing my own conviction that, were I to begin my task of editorship *de novo*, I could not do better than ask the identical eight contributors for their collaboration.

We have to-day in England no shortage of musical authorities—some of them university professors, others heads of musical academies, colleges and conservatoires, others again critics and journalists, still others composers and performers. I concede at once that I could possibly have found sixteen, or twenty-four or thirty-two more among them who would have written this book as well as my eight colleagues, albeit differently; I know that I could not have found eight to do it better. To those among these many experts into whose hands this book may fall, for review or recommendation, I can only say that I know I shall have from them, for the same reasons and to serve the same ends, the same encouragement and ungrudging co-operation that I have had from Mr. Anderson, Mr. Blom, Mr. Bonavia, Professor Dent, Mr. Evans, Mr. Harrison, Mr. Hussey, and Mr. Toye.

It was indeed no small task that I asked from each of them. They are all busy men—very busy men—and it is true to say that two of them are not strictly speaking professional writers at all. But I doubt very much if the reader who does not already know will discover which two !

It is the fact, however, that they all have the closest professional connection with the art of music, while I am only an amateur ; yet every one of them placed himself entirely in my hands when it came to deciding the ground he was to cover and the general outline of his part of the work. All of them have understood that this book is meant first and foremost for the layman, but that it must none the less fail without the support of their fellow musicians. These also, I venture to think, may here find food for thought and, indeed, perhaps some information that may be of use to them, either because they had forgotten it or because it is presented from some new aspect.

THE MUSICAL COMPANION does not, could not, was never conceived able to replace Grove—which is mentioned in its pages more than any other book. But there are some composers named in this volume who find no place even in the great Dictionary—that is, incidentally, my excuse for omitting their dates from the index.

I should not wish to leave the reader with the impression that the eight authors merely had to fill in the names, dates and other facts in a given skeleton scheme. That would be grossly to exaggerate my editorial achievements and, much worse, scandalously to belittle the labours of the contributors. THE MUSICAL COMPANION itself discountenances any such view. Each Book has been treated by its author or authors as a more or less self-contained entity ; my task has merely been the prevention of needless overlapping—purely a demarcatory function. It would have been academic to the point of travesty had I presented every author with a rigorously schematised outline and insisted that every Book should run on lines exactly analagous with those of every other. In any case, I should have insisted in vain, for the authors, being men of character, would naturally have refused to bow down before such hypertrophied dictatorship.

So the reader will find Books I and VII standing apart from the others, by virtue of their subject matter. He will find that Mr. Bonavia's matter, in Book VI, lends itself to a form of sub-division different from Mr. Harrison's in Book II, and more detailed. And he will find Mr. Evans's Book V standing about half-way in scheme and treatment between Mr. Bonavia's on the one hand and Professor Dent's Book III and Messrs. Hussey and Toye's Book IV on the other.

May I conclude with two pieces of advice to the reader ? They are perhaps a little irrelevant in a letter to you, but you will not misunderstand me. First, do not necessarily attempt to read THE MUSICAL COMPANION straight through.

If you are a novice, begin by taking Mr. Anderson's Book slowly and thoughtfully, and then read Mr. Blom's delightful concluding Essay. After that, go as you please. And if you are not a novice, start anywhere you like and read backwards or forwards, as you will, much as the connoisseur reads "Tristram Shandy." The index may help your browsing. Secondly, though I would beg you to read with sympathy, do so with reasoned scepticism. THE MUSICAL COMPANION contains very many facts but by no means a few opinions. The former may be safely held to be as accurate as scholarship and erudition can make them ; the latter deserve the respect due to their holders, all of them musicians and music lovers. But it would be a fatal mistake to take them or accept them as dogmas.

Music is not a science, but an art ; in music an instant of true appreciation and perception is worth an age of learning and lore. You and I have the hope that THE MUSICAL COMPANION may help its readers to add to their musical experience and sensibility, not because its authors are pundits or mandarins, but because they are scholars and musicians, and because for those very authors, learned though they are, the Music's the thing.

I cannot lay down my editorial pen without saying, my dear Gollancz, how much the production of this book owes not only to the superb understanding of its eight authors, but also and at least as much to the perfect sympathy, patience, interest, and encouragement of you, its publisher.

Believe me to be, at the end of this most enjoyable collaboration,

Very sincerely and most gratefully yours,

A. L. BACHARACH

# CONTENTS

## BOOK II. THE ORCHESTRA AND ORCHESTRAL MUSIC
### By JULIUS HARRISON

## BOOK III. OPERA
### By EDWARD J. DENT

# BOOK VI. THE SOLO INSTRUMENT
## By F. BONAVIA

# BOOK I

## THE ABC OF MUSIC

*By* W. R. ANDERSON

# PRELUDE

THIS INTRODUCTORY BOOK of the volume aims at exhibiting the material of the art of music, considered as a language, and the nature of its life and habits. Four chief parts may broadly be headed :

A. How music became a language, how it came to be written down, and how the writing developed into our present notation.

B. The fundamentals of the art—rhythm, melody, harmony, timbre. That is, " How it is done."

C. How these fundamentals are worked into forms— sonatas, fugues, and so forth. That is, " What is made with the means."

D. Instruments. That is, " The means by which the music, when thought out by the composer, comes to life."

Obviously, A and B interweave, but it will be convenient, since music is so complex an art, and a good many of the subtleties of its organisation developed slowly, to take things bit by bit.

Two other things may be mentioned : one, that as there are separate Books, later in this volume, for the large departments of opera, oratorio, chamber music, and the orchestra, I shall only lead up to them, and leave my colleagues to take over. If I happen to say anything about them that overlaps with their sayings, perhaps the reader may amuse himself by comparing our versions.

The second point is that the volume as a whole is not a history of music, so its early treatment by the various peoples of the earth, before about the time when, we may say, the extended composition of " art music " began to be practised, will be very briefly noticed. As with other sides of the art, books will be mentioned that may be read by those who wish to be further informed. Indeed, it is hoped that one of the chief results of anyone's reading this book will be that he will like to know more about this extremely attractive art of music than the covers of one volume can possibly contain ; and a particular little hope of mine is that the reader will be moved to make more music himself. More of that, however, in its place.

There may be occasional divagations which do not fit into the four-square frame of my devising—reflections, opinions, arguments, such as are engendered by a musician's going to and fro for a quarter of a century among all kinds of music-lovers. If any of these are approved, how happy the author will be ! If any be disapproved, maybe there will even be a little profit in pondering why one disapproves.

# A : MUSICAL NOTATION

## CHAPTER I

## THE EARLIEST BEGINNINGS

When we look at the reproductions of the lifelike frescoes and engravings that paleolithic man placed on the walls of his dwelling caves at Altamira, in Spain, it may on first thought seem strange that he should not have possessed an art of sound equally advanced. But of his cultivation of that art we know nothing, and there is no evidence that he ever even achieved a tune. It is pretty clear that man's progress in the art of sound was, first howling, or making vocal his desires and feelings in simple cries, then speaking, and finally singing. But how long it took him to produce even rhythmic pulsations, we do not know. We can observe present-day savage music (the B.B.C.'s " Strange Music " series was valuable : a partial survey of it was printed in the "Listener" for April 19, 1933), and wonder how far it has developed, or whether we are listening to much the same kind of sounds as were heard in the forest primeval. But we know next to nothing of music even among the highly cultured ancient Greeks.

Rhythm comes naturally, since all creation moves to it— the stars, the seasons, all growth ; man's heart throbs rhythmically, his feet march to a lilt. It is not difficult to think that his lips soon began to murmur liltingly likewise. Most savage music is strongest in the rhythmic element. There may have been a good deal of simple invention of snatches of tune, mere fragments, but nobody, probably, could put them together, or thought of trying. Perhaps there was a certain amount of copying, friendly mocking, and some rivalry in the attempted imitation of natural sounds. It does not seem unreasonable that there may have been mimics, not unskilful, of the birds and beasts—moments of relaxation in the dangerous, fierce, devil-take-the-hindmost life of primitive man. But he could have had little time for musical art, even had he conceived it. Artistry needs leisure to burgeon, and music is the most complex of the arts. Most important consideration of all : it only lives by *moving*, and we have to catch it as it flies.

It was a great advance when man learned how to control and direct his breath so as to shape a variety of sounds, each standing for some clear meaning. They were probably decided upon by some individualist, who drove their meaning into his less bright fellows, just suffering for the lack of the right forcible language in which to convey : " Idiot, can't you grasp that when I say ' Whaaa,' I mean ' Fetch me that gourd,' and when I say ' Whoo,' I mean ' Take it away ' ? Haven't you got *any* sense at all ? " . . . We may indulge the fancy that it is not so very different from the taciturn Big Business man of to-day, whose mumbled, semi-articulate questions can be interpreted only by his confidential typist. There may have been occasional ancients with a special little interest in comparing sounds, who amused themselves by putting one over against another : " Whee, whoo, whee, whoo," with maybe a little drop or rise from the one to the other. We may like to think of someone's making up an actual tune-scrap by putting three downward notes together (people sang downward, probably, before upward), and starting " Three Blind Mice " on its long journey. But the appreciation of the *scale*, that tremendous advance, was long ages away ; and nobody got as far as thinking of writing anything down.

Rhythm is the oldest impulse of all, we have noted. Ceremonial dancing is a great outlet for savage emotions—particularly that of fear, which controlled man's dim mind for so long (and still too much masters his maturer one). Elaborate drumming exists—from what distant times we cannot tell—in both savage and cultivated peoples. In India, for instance, two rhythms will be drummed together, with more subtle effects even than those Stravinsky sought in *Le Sacre du Printemps.* That work reminds us of the ritual significance of dancing—a big subject in itself, but outside our present scope.

As the dim ages drew away, and man's intelligence brightened, folk song grew up by word-of-mouth passing on. That was easy, because the memories of simple people are tenacious. Folk singers have learned hundreds of songs by ear, and we remember, in E. Œ. Somerville's delightful Irish reminiscences, the peasant messenger-women who fulfilled numbers of complex orders at the market town, with never a scrap of writing, or a farthing wrong in the addition.

There is much that I should like to say about the development of folk song, but the division of labour in this work rightly places that in Book IV, Part D, to be treated by one of my colleagues ; so I will merely note that the great stream of folk music was quietly taking its course through the world long before art music began to be contrived. It was the learned clerks—the clergy—who mostly ruled music for the first few centuries of its life as an art ; and mighty were the complications they introduced into its scientific handling, whilst the folk went their freer way, unbothered by science, but producing some of the world's truest loveliness. In which reflection there may be a moral somewhere, if we could find it.

## CHAPTER II

# THE RISE OF THE ART OF MUSIC

So we must get on to the other stream of musical invention, which we call art music. There is no separate source for it ; everyone knows, for instance, how Christmas carols began as pagan songs, and were taken over by wise churchmen as means, already familiar to the people, of enforcing religious truths. One finds some such songs with two sets of words, one secular and one sacred. Hence, too, the Latin refrain in the kind of English carol we call " macaronic."

The mediæval monks got their musical system from very distant times. We need to remember always that music as an art is very young, for though we know a good deal about the instruments used in Biblical times, we have very little idea of ancient Greek or Egyptian music. The Egyptians show us plenty of pictures and sculptures of musicians, but they never knew how to use a bow on their strings. They had drums and trumpets for processions and royal magnificence, strings to pluck and pipes to blow : no reeds to give the modern variety of tone-colour, as in the clarinet, oboe and bassoon. Fragments of the music of the Bible remain, probably unchanged, in the services of the Jewish faith. Greek myths delight us with fine imaginative fables, like that of Orpheus who charmed all nature with his music. The Greeks made subtle use of music in their plays, but there was no harmony as we understand it. The big central point on which we take our next stand for a view of the growth of music is their system of notation, a series of Modes, which anyone can hear who starts on each of the white notes of the piano in turn, and plays eight white notes upwards or downwards. Each mode had, for their ears, its own character—one was meet for gay music, others for sad or warlike themes, and so on. In making their actual scales, for use in their songs, they got a good deal of variety by, as we should now say, sharpening (raising) or flattening (lowering) certain notes. But the foundation of the mediæval musical system was the mode. The only one that now sounds perfectly familiar to us is what we call " the major scale of C "—that is, the eight white notes from C to C on the piano. All the others—D to D, E to E, and onwards—have one or two notes that sound odd to us (the reason being, in terms of the piano, that sometimes there is a black note between two adjacent whites, and sometimes there is not ; and the places at which these black-notes or not-black-notes occur are not the same when we start from

C, as when we start from D, and again different when we start from E or any other of the white notes and run up to the eighth note above).

Folk song used the modes too, probably starting by ear, of course, without the theoretical considerations of the Greeks—with three notes only, then extending to four, and later to five, not all of which were next door to each other, as we hear in the " pentatonic " (five-note) scale, common in folk song and dance. A sample of this is easily heard by playing the white notes C, D, E, G, A (" Auld Lang Syne " is pentatonic). Later, the folk's tunes were freer in melody than the churchmen's. They, for long almost the only people who could preserve learning, preserved it with a vengeance. They may be said to have done what the foreign visitor prayed for when, meaning to be complimentary, he addressed his friend : " May the Lord pickle you ! " Music, more than once, was in danger of being pickled.

The problem of communicating music in writing— notation—was for long tangled up, and even now remains, in some of its elements, foolishly illogical and unnecessarily complicated. That is not to frighten anyone from learning it : to read music, even a little, gives one a great advantage as a music-lover, and should be attempted by all amateurs who want to make progress through the many attractive mansions of the art. It should (but even yet does not) go without saying that all children ought to learn to read music at school—the simplest way, of course, being through the Sol-fa notation. It will some day seem yet one other proof that the present was the Age of Confusion, in that young men could leave a University unable to read the simplest song tune : as odd as if one were to profess oneself a lover of books, and be entirely dependent for the enjoyment of literature on hearing somebody else read them. This by the way.

If, forgetting all we know about notation, we had to devise a means of showing the rise and fall of sounds, we should all, I think, do exactly what the first notators did—

listen to speech, and draw a slanting little line up for its rise, and down for its fall. From speech one passes easily to early song. The Church adopted the lines—probably before A.D. 700. The Greeks had used letters, and some "picklers" tried to keep it up, but the sign-system was better, and it was gradually developed into Neumes, as they were called, written over the words, which alone controlled the rhythm. They looked like some of the signs in short-hand, and the alert singer observed, from them, how to express a passage, as well as which notes to sing. There were all sorts of systems, which rambled on in experiment until long after the tenth century. Someone had the notion of using lines for the signs, but it did not at first catch on : its significance was not grasped. But soon it did ; and then the Neumes moved up and down, as notes do now—on lines. On a coloured line, one note's name was fixed by a letter, placed at the start of the line (hence our word " clef "—a " key " to the note-names). Then two lines were used, each differently coloured, and each with its clef-letter. By the fifteenth century, there were four lines, and so they continued for a long time, though the notation was not quickly taken up. The clearest thinker about these things was Guido d'Arezzo, who flourished early in the eleventh century. Then there were the complications of Measured Music, which had to fix the respective lengths of the notes, and find signs for each : and scores of people had each his own idea about that, and set it down in treatises galore, in the fourteenth century. Even the Pope took a hand, with a Bull.

. They were all thinking, at first, of vocal music ; and even now, our system is not ideal for instruments.

About the twelfth century appeared those black lozenges and diamonds, on little poles, which many will have seen in the fine old service-books sometimes shown in the windows of the larger second-hand bookshops—exhibits, often beautifully illuminated, that take one back wonderfully to the ages of faith. Then shorter notes were needed, and the black diamonds had hooks attached, making the equivalent of our modern crotchet. Some black notes gave place to white ones, and so gradually our series of notes was worked out, each half the preceding one—breve, semibreve, minim, crotchet, quaver, semiquaver, demisemiquaver. This was still conceived, of course, in terms of the voice, the most important instrument of praise.

There were complications by the way, as when some of the notes could be either two or three beats long, according to their position in the rhythm. The system had given place to our modern one of notes and rests (which latter had been invented in the thirteenth century) by 1700. Bar-lines, the upright lines drawn across the staff at regular intervals of time, originated as mere guides at *irregular* intervals, to keep the voices together. It is this freer use of the now strait-jacketing bar-line that, in the earlier music, gives such rhythmic suppleness. One needs always to listen to madrigals, for example, bearing it in mind. Bar-lines came in about 1600, and key-signatures (the placing of the key's necessary sharps or flats together at the start of the line) about 1700. The letters used at the beginning of the staff are (now modified forms of) G, F, and C—the first two " treble " and " bass," respectively, the last now used for certain instruments, such as the viola, whose compass is not conveniently notable by the other two. The G clef fixes G as the second of the five lines, and the F clef fixes F as the fourth ; the C clef could be used on *any* line, an obvious convenience for voices or instruments of varying compass.

With the rise of solo song outside the church, and the need for single-instrumental accompaniment other than that of the organ, as well as the interest in playing instruments generally, performers on them, who had to find more than one note at a time, developed a notation of their own, called Tablature, to show when to touch each string or key. It was simpler than the complicated vocal notation. For instance, the important solo and accompanimental instrument the lute, in the fifteenth century, had its special notation—not very different from the sort of thing one gets with the present-day banjulele. You may remember that in the first act of Wagner's great opera, "Die Meister-singer," a sample of this " tablature " notation, on a black-board, usually appears when the young Walter, an aspirant to membership of the worshipful guild of Mastersingers, is to be tested. One of the humorous elements in this scene is that the referee, Beckmesser, delights in marking on his slate, very audibly, the mistakes that Walter makes in composing his song. To us it seems a jolly good song, finely made ; but illustrates a long-besetting weakness of mediæval music-making—the insistence on strict rule.

In the end—say about 1650—our modern staff of five lines was adopted for everything except Plainsong.

While the churchmen and theorists were at their diverse notational labours (and sometimes getting very complicated and dry in their experiments and expositions—missing the beauties of the wood in counting the trees), people outside were enjoying folk song and dance, much freer in its struc-ture. There is one piece—almost it might be called a miracle —of early thirteenth century music, probably put together by a monk of Reading Abbey, that shows a delightful combination of science and humanity. It is a Round (in which one voice starts, and the others come in at intervals, chasing it, with the same tune), and it is called " Sumer is icumen in." You can get a copy from Novello for a penny or two. There is no room to show how much in advance of its time it is, constructively ; the point for the moment is that it brings the freshness of the countryside into the clever, formal, scholarly world. Other examples, it is thought, must have existed, never written down, and now are lost to us : but I doubt if there were many so clever and neat and pretty as this. (See frontispiece.)

For ages, with notational complications of considerable elaboration, music remained limited in scope. There was no harmony for centuries, and little variety in time, the rhythm of the words dictating that of the music, and three-time being used to the exclusion of any other. As might be expected, divers schoolmen (and singers in addition, who liked to try little divagations of their own) had a good deal of solemn fun in playing about with notation. From both mathematical and meddling minds church music suffered. In time the strong man came along who had to put things in order. This was Bishop Ambrose of Milan. From his name we get " Ambrosian chant." Even better remembered is the name of Pope Gregory, who was a strong organiser. " Gregorians " are sung in a great many churches to-day : the Gregorian chant, that is. Well done, nothing takes one out of the hurrying world so sweetly as good Gregorian chanting in a noble church, or a subdued strain from the organ, in a momentary meditation on such a theme. Always most vivid to me is such an impression as, a stranger in a strange land, I turned out of New York's Broadway, with its skyscrapers that hurry the Englishman on to to-morrow before he can conceive to-day, into old Trinity Church, that so significantly faces Wall Street, and heard a few bars of music that took me not only over the water, but back over the centuries. It might be well for us all if we could occasionally secure, whatever our faith or non-faith, some such brief, concentrated sense of the comfort of ageless beauty.

Gregorian chant sought to beautify the psalms as sung in Latin. The music, then, was not to strait-jacket the words, but to take their natural rhythm. Gregory (about A.D. 600) had to overcome the singers' liking for weaving out many notes to a word. He was a beneficent pontiff for music. The themes to which the words were sung were easy for the voices. They did not move up and down more than a few notes. They did not draw attention to themselves. Everybody now sang in unison, and in three-time.

It was a very long time before people began to sing two different notes together. When they did, it was not really harmony, in intention, for they were merely singing the same tune in two different pitches at once—as even now a person with a poor ear might do, if you started a tune that he liked. The ancients did it because they liked it. The pitches were four or five notes apart (i.e., C–G), and the result, to our ears, is, like Joe Gargory's small beer, not

over-stimulating. Try it on the piano. But first impressions
count for much ; and singing in fourths and fifths, which
conveniently suited the natural pitch of a high and a low
voice, was thought beautiful, and taken up. The date for
this is about A.D. 900. The system was called " organum "
or " diaphony," and it in turn was closely discussed and
theorised about by many churchmen, among the best
remembered of them being Hucbald, who came from the
Low Countries, which were in time to be the cradle of a
new art of church music and madrigal singing. It seems
odd that the Bantus of South Africa make very similar
diaphony on a stringed instrument.

This " organum " was at first just the parallelism of two
parts. In time rules and experiment brought about the
individual movement, first of one of the parts and then of
the other, so that ultimately there were two real parts, each
going its own way, and the two working together for good ;
which is what we call " counterpoint "—one " point "
(part) " counter " (over against) another. Counterpoint is
an element in almost all good music—one among several
by which, very often, musicians judge quality. I said that
three-time had been established as basic. Within the limitations of this time, much experiment had gone on in combining the varying rhythms of different sets of words :
ingenious, but getting too precious, as the ingenious went
on. There were other searches for variety, for nothing would
satisfy the aspiring spirit of man (not to forget the perpetual
delight of the singer in his divagatory powers). There was
" descant," in which one part held the theme and another
played about above it. About 1300 two-time provided new
freedoms. A Pope again stepped in—John the Twenty-
Second, in 1322, pared down the indecorums. Other
intervals, as well as the fifth and fourth, found their fruitful
place in the harmony. Nowadays we think a succession of
thirds and sixths sweeter than one of fourths and fifths. In
olden days the reverse was for long upheld.

A mere word must here be given to an art that will be
more fully discussed elsewhere in this volume—that of the

troubadours. For about a couple of hundred years from 1100 these aristocratic artists, arising in the South of France, pursued their charming, chivalrous poesy and minstrelsy. So also did the trouvères, their compatriots of the North ; and the Minnesinger, their counterparts in Germany, starting a little later, practised the same courtly art of making and singing love lyrics. Tannhäuser was a Minnesinger, and in the opera named after him you have a contest of song reproduced. After the Minnesinger came the transition period of German literature, about 1350–1600, in which the guilds and their musical societies allowed the burghers to develop music in their own way—a good deal of it in pious strains. Hans Sachs, greatest of Mastersingers, is a lovable character in " Die Meistersinger," as you will recall.

It was about 1400—the time of the Italian renaissance, roughly—that composition began to find its feet—its wings, rather. It began to be an affair of a man's own notions, not of taking anybody else's as the basis for a work. Music had for long been largely bound to church themes, with their limitations of range and emotion. The idea of freedom, though in some respects toiling in gloom, was growing. Britain led the way, in John Dunstable, and the resourceful folk of the Low Countries, with their clear practicality, wrought mightily in the new art of free composition, building, with characteristic willingness to learn, on what we could teach them. There are notable names, which one need not memorise—Dufay, Okeghem, and Josquin des Prés, makers of many lovely, spirit-freeing worshippieces. A great difficulty used to lie in our getting to hear such music. Radio, that has brought nearly everything to our firesides, gives us but rare hearings of this music of the fifteenth century. Now and again the " Foundations of Music " are dug as deeply as that ; but the best way to hear examples of the first composed music is through gramophone records. There are two collections of historical records readily accessible to us. One is the album and its booklet, "Two Thousand Years of Music," arranged by Dr. Curt

Bc

Sachs (Parlophone). The other is the set of six albums (the fourth has been published quite recently) which, with accompanying booklets, Dr. Percy Scholes is issuing through Columbia. The earliest of these six gives some specimens of the time we have come to, and the Sachs album gives different ones. In addition, the general gramophone catalogues contain a few choice items of church music and madrigals from the fifteenth and sixteenth centuries, well worth looking up.

Students of other arts will find it interesting to consider the history of music alongside theirs, during the years in which the Italian renaissance came to 'its height and sank, in the first quarter of the sixteenth century : to trace how, with Agricola, Melanchthon and Erasmus, the culture was carried North—noting the part that Luther played in the ordering of church music : and to mark the French renaissance, followed by Ronsard's bringing in the classical period there ; and the British, with Linacre, More and Colet, and later Henry VIII. In these movements the inspiration was largely that of ancient culture : so it was when opera was devised, round about 1600, in Italy, developing out of the new feeling for the dramatic treatment of words. Thus we come to the Golden Age, as musicians like to call it, when the contrapuntal style was in its greatest glory.

## CHAPTER III

# THE GROWTH OF MUSICAL FORM

Now emerge a number of musical *forms*, which it will be our business to look at in a moment. Before turning to them, it may be useful to articulate at least the skeleton of the matter of notation by saying that the modern scales, which we broadly designate " major " and " minor," and of each of which everyone knows the characteristic, distinguishing quality, were the result of yet another move for freedom. The ancient modes had for centuries satisfied all needs, largely because they were in the control of churchmen, whose music, after all, moved in a limited round of emotion and made no wide demands upon expressive media. Also, their minds were naturally conservative, and they had generally enough to do in one or other department of experiment or settlement without worrying about the nature of their fundamental material, the scales. With the freedom of the madrigal, and the re-emergence of solo music and the soloist's rise to importance (he had tried to be important in church, but never with full success), the older harmonic and scale contents were felt to be insufficient, but the development of a clear, strong feeling for key, the balance of keys and all that it means to us, was more than could be expected quickly. So in many of the madrigals we feel that the old modes are gently breaking down. There was, in fact, a quiet overlaying of the old by the new scale, and sometimes the one, sometimes the other, was on top. The upshot was that we retained for general use the " major scale," which is simply the old mode that starts on C (C, D, E, F, G, A, B, C) ; and a " minor scale " that (for convenience in untechnical description) may be described as a development of the old mode starting on A (A, B, C, D, E, F, G, A) by sharpening (raising) the seventh to G sharp (the black note immediately to the right of the white G) : this produces what we now call the " harmonic minor scale " ; and then, by sharpening the sixth also (to F sharp) going *up*, and bringing back both seventh and sixth to the normal (A mode) form, in coming *down*, we get a different sort of minor scale, the "melodic." This, like any musical description that has to be mainly untechnical, may sound a bit complicated, but if you try it at the piano (and anyone can find these scales from my description, even if he does not know music), you will quickly get it. This way of showing how the scales differ is, by the way, that in which we teach sight-singers, in those three simple stages : (1) the A mode (" Æolian mode " is its name) ; (2) the " harmonic minor " ; (3) the " melodic minor," so called because it is the smoothest for melody singing, the harmonic minor being, by contrast, not so smooth, but all right for making harmonies.

It may be noted that the modes are much used by certain composers to-day—notably by Vaughan Williams. They come natural to him, but for many imitators modes are merely modish wear. Folk-song idioms are usually worn with them. Only on a few backs do these sit well. A composer in this kind has to be very subtly simple or very crafty if he is not to seem merely art-y. W. McNaught's description of much that was played at the B.B.C.'s six British Music concerts in January, 1934, is true : " The music bespeaks, rather too consciously, a superior mental refinement ; it goes in dread of saying anything common-place ; it is composed in a made language to which ordinary parts of speech are barely admitted ; it is addressed to minds educated in the finer points of texture ; it occupies itself too much with the æsthetics of the studio ; it does not approach the hearer—he has to reach out for it ; it is mighty clever and all that—but it is incapable of setting anyone's pulse beating the faster or of making him forget where he is."

Matters about notation are put in here because, though this is not a history of music, it *is* described as a sort of A B C of it, and the way in which notation has developed is one of the fundamentals of composition. With a little imagination we can understand how worried and annoyed people must for long have felt at not having an easy way of writing down their musical ideas. It is a pity that other developments have not all been cleared up as we went along, and made as simple as the scales. Take the staff, for instance, on which we write our notes. Most people who have attempted the piano remember struggling with the difficulty that, whereas the right hand's five lines (with the treble clef) represented the notes lettered E, G, B, D, F (were you given, as I was, the mnemonic " Every Good

Boy Deserves Favour " ?), the left hand's five (with the bass clef) represented the letters in a different order, G, B, D, F, A (" Good Boys Deserve Favour Always "). Quite early it struck me that we should have been shown a more sensible favour if instead of leaving out one line (middle C's) between the two sets of five, they had left out two, and so made both sets read G, B, D, F, A. It could quite easily have been done, for the lines and spaces are a mere convenient device for showing the rise and fall of notes. The staff built up from the grand, simple idea mentioned a page or two ago—nobody knows who thought of it—that of fixing the position of one note, on a single line, is all very well for voices ; but when we come to the violin, with its big upper range, the double bass, descending into the depths, or the piano, spreading in both directions, we see how little is covered by the two sets of five lines and their spaces—only three out of the piano's seven octaves. For the rest, we have to write on bits of extra staff, written above and below the others—" leger lines," as we call them (from the builder's scaffold poles). The clefs, which fix the note-names of the five lines, were once, we saw, just the letters F, C, and (last to arrive) G, written each on the line which was to have that name. From one name fixed, the others were readily calculable. Sharps and flats, for raising and lowering notes, and the natural, for contradicting either of the other two, have an interesting history of their own, with a twist or two in it for those who expect a straight tale. The business of making a key system was nearly as complex as that of creating the solar system might appear to anybody who set out now to try it. The key-system, in which the composer steers about as comfortably as a fish in a pond, flitting freely in and out of keys so that sometimes the score is covered with sharps and flats in the endeavour to track their wanderings—all this was long in growing. It is still not clear to all of us why it was so slow. Probably the modes gave composers plenty to work with, for long. One of the most useful qualities the listener can develop is the power to hear changes of key, and to remember the original key of a piece. A lot of a composer's subtle effects are lost if one cannot do this. And form, which we shall say more about very soon, depends, to a degree sometimes unremembered, on key—the choice of keys, their balance, the nature and amount of key change (" modulation "), and lots of devices depending on the fact that we can either slide slickly from key to key, or jump with stimulating and even exciting effect among them. The key element is one of the athletic delights of composition, and nothing in the study of form better repays attention. To apprehend key changes, and remember the keynote, means that the ear must be trained to some extent ; the farther the better. Very little musical appreciation can go on until the ear *is* trained ; to get it trained is worth any amount of the music-lover's trouble and time. When it is, he becomes a new man.

Even the tiniest piece of art music can show the shaping influence of key. Without being too long over this, or very technical, I may refer you to a tune such as " Hanover " again (" O worship the King "). It begins in one key (say, in C) and at the middle of its course modulates in a very common, effective way to the key five white notes higher on the piano (G). In the next quarter of its course it modulates for a moment to a minor key (A minor) and then goes back to the root key, C, to finish. There is here the balance not only of the recurring key, C, but of the two that vary things : and one of these two is a new variety, for it is minor : so we have Unity in Variety—a simple instance of musical form depending largely for effectiveness on key. The minor key, by the way, is very powerful for good in hymn-tunes in the major ; and potent, too, are minor *chords*, when well deployed among major ones. There is no better example of this last point than the Doxology " Praise God, from Whom all blessings flow." If you make all its chords major ones, you rob it of half its grandeur.

I am not attempting to define every term I use, because that would lead on to making a text-book on Rudiments, and this section cannot attempt everything. " Minor " and " major," I take it, are well enough understood. A definition need not be sought, if one recognises and distinguishes the effects when heard. In passing, it may be remarked that little dives from major to minor are characteristic of some modern dance music and songs— or *were* characteristic, when this was being written. (In a book on " hot " trumpet playing I read that the author will not write down any particular tricks of such playing, because by the time the book is out they will almost certainly be out too—out of fashion.) One of the little devices I mean is, in a song in a major key, to come to the end of a musical sentence (to the " cadence," as we call it) with a minor-key note as the third from the home-note (that is, in key C major, to have the cadence E flat, D, C, instead of the expected E, D, C. Often the two will be used one after the other, major and minor). Naturally, when this pleasant device has been used a few thousand times, it palls : but as a sentimental element it has its point.

The whole subject of key is a big one, and I stress it a little because even some of the books meant to help beginners do not show its importance. A magical key-change, of the utmost simplicity, is that which leads from the eighth of the variations in Elgar's great " Enigma " set to the ninth, which is the elegiac " Nimrod " variation, written in honour of a dear friend. The eighth, gracious and sweet, has come to an end in the key of G. Violins alone sustain that one note for a moment of musing, and then the ninth, slow variation starts in the key of E flat, in which the G, just now the keynote, is the third of the chord. The effect is perfectly lovely in its quiet unexpectedness and serene certainty. The sudden key-jump, as a relish or lusty gesture, is found in music old and new. Haydn occasionally plays a beautiful late-cut after this manner ; and in that glorious third movement of his fourth symphony Brahms has a key-bang of gusto that brings to the music-lover a smile of pleasure. It comes at bar 199—a little beyond half way through the movement. A good deal of the sport in Dvořák's music comes from his key-jumps. Schubert, too was fond of playing with keys. One of his specialities is sliding from major to minor and back again.

# CHAPTER IV

# THE WRITING OF MUSIC

It will be seen, from this discussion of the main elements making up a musical work, that the chief thing to be cultivated by the listener who wants to get further into music is *memory*. That faculty, in so far as it concerns music, is our naturally weakest quality, and I cannot too strongly urge its persistent development in every possible way. Without memory one misses most of the game. A symphony may last from twenty to fifty minutes : and of most symphonies—at any rate, of the greatest of them—it is true to say that they were conceived as wholes ; so that something is lost if the relation of their (usually) four movements is not appreciated. To take them in properly implies some use of memory, to recall how each movement stands in the scheme, in relation to the others. In some symphonies, and in the works called " symphonic poems " or " tone poems," themes recur, either in simple form or in changed rhythm and harmony—metamorphosed, after the manner of which Mr. Harrison will later be telling. But even if one listens to only one movement of a symphony, which may last from, say, five minutes to fifteen, consider how much is passing—and, passing, does not return, for the present. It is in that cinematic nature of music that most of the listener's difficulties lie. He has to listen to what is passing, remember what has gone, and to some extent anticipate what may be coming ; and he has to relate these things to each other. Repeated hearings, score-reading, analyses, all have their part to play for the keenest listener, but the quality he most of all needs is just memory ; and so I cordially recommend him to practise memorising music with all the concentration he can afford.

Some instruments are transposers : that is, the written notes in their part do not represent the sounds they make. This involves their having a different number of sharps and flats (key signature) from the non-transposing instruments. The use of what we call the C clef for such instruments as the viola is convenient, because of its compass. The treble (G) clef would cause us to write most of the viola's notes on leger lines below the staff, and with the bass (F) clef it only requires about the upper half of the staff, since its lowest note is the C in the midst of it. The C clef, for the viola, is on the third line of the five, and it makes that line middle C. (Note, not the C an octave above that : the fact that there is a treble-clef C next door to the middle line is apt at first to make one think that the C of the C clef is up there. It is actually middle C—the one that, when treble and bass clefs are used, lies on the leger line midway between the two sets of five lines.)

Those who do not happen to have seen an orchestral score would find it interesting to glance at one. I hope that as many as can find or make opportunity will pursue, however gently, the study of reading music. It is best to begin, of course, with a voice part ; and the easiest way of learning to read music is through singing and Sol-fa. Joining a music class is the quickest way to progress. Music teachers are nowadays ready to teach whatever is desired, and it should not be difficult to find one or two others to join in a class. There is nothing like self-activity, and to be able to read a single line of music gives great satisfaction, raising one's spirits in the face of even a formidable orchestral score. A good musical motto for any such learning is " Poco a poco "—little by little. To follow two, three and then the four parts in a part-song is a step approachable by obvious degrees. Here three of the parts—soprano, alto and tenor—will be written with the G clef (the tenor part an octave higher than it is sung : sometimes it has two treble clefs, to indicate that) : only the bass with the F clef. If a hymn-book is opened, the four parts will be found differently arranged, on two staves, soprano and alto on the upper one, and tenor and bass on the lower ; the tenor here will be notated with the F (bass) clef.

Coming to a string quartet, we find the first and second violin parts written with the treble clef, the viola's with the C (alto) clef, and the 'cello's with the bass clef. The viola's clef is the new element to learn, and to place its notes accurately, when switching the mind quickly between treble and bass clefs, will take time ; but its general move-ment is readily traceable. The 'cello, by the way, sometimes, when soaring high, uses the C clef on the *fourth* line (tenor clef), in order to avoid a lot of leger lines. Similarly, the viola may occasionally use the treble clef, for like con-venience.

The step to an orchestral score is a bigger one, and we shall not expect to read everything at once. Here the value of repeatedly going over short sections of a well-known piece of music upon the gramophone, score in hand, will at once be seen. It may be useful to mention that there is one edition (Ricordi's) of the nine Beethoven symphonies in which the actual notes of the instruments are written, the transposing difficulty thus being done away with. I know of no other classical works similarly treated, but the scores of the present-day composer Prokofiev are being issued in that simplified manner.

It is a good thing to begin reading orchestral scores by picking some of those, such as Haydn's, in which the orchestra is small—" two up and two down, with strings," as musicians say : that is, a pair each of wood wind and brass, with the five string parts—two violins, viola, 'cello and double-bass. Though none of the following symphonies has been recorded as I write, all have been broadcast. The number of staves used is indicated after each : Haydn— the " Schoolmaster " (6) ; the " Farewell " (7, except in the finale, which has 8) ; the one named " Maria Theresa " (8). Most such works can be obtained either as Eulenburg or Philharmonia miniature scores, the two largest series of such things. Other publishers issue miniature scores of numerous works, mostly of modern composers. Any good music dealer will look up these things for you.

Messrs. J. & W. Chester, 11 Great Marlborough Street, W. 1, publish an admirable " Reference Book of Miniature Scores " at 1s. It is as complete a list as can humanly be compiled, and includes a Thematic List of symphonies and chamber-music works of the great masters.

# CHAPTER V

# THE DEVELOPMENT OF NOTATION

Musical notation, we have found, is not very logical, and only partially practical. It is perfectly possible to invent a better one, and dozens of people have essayed that. Some of their systems, which I need not detail, are clear improvements on at least several elements in our staff notation : but they have about as much chance of being adopted as I have of becoming Prime Minister. Not only the force of the evolution of the ages is against them : the adoption of any new system would mean the scrapping of millions of pounds' worth of musical plates and copies. Staff notation, after all, is not at all difficult to pick up. It may be noted that the blind are enabled to read music by the adaptation of the Braille dots to the purposes of notation. A considerable library of works for their use exists, and is always being added to by the National Institute for the Blind—a work which, it may be added, is well worth every sighted music lover's support. Much interesting information about this may be had from the N.I.B., Great Portland Street, W. 1. There is even a monthly musical magazine for the blind.

A simpler notation than the staff, easy for beginners, and

a good introduction to the staff, is Tonic Sol-fa, a system invented (as far as anything of this nature can be said to be invented) by Miss Glover of Norwich, and developed by John Curwen, last century. As most people know, it is a letter notation, on the " movable doh " principle (the fixed doh, as used on the Continent, seems to us to lose half the value of the system) ; and its syllables for note-lengths are a simple, logical way of making the learner sound the exact length of the notes he is reading. They are taken from the idea which Guido d'Arezzo, that clever thinker of the eleventh century, adopted from a German source. He used *ut, re, mi, fa, sol, la* for the six notes of the hexachord. Sol-fa changes *ut* to *doh*, for easier singing, and adds the seventh *ti*. Sol-fa divides and conquers. It separates the difficulties of learning rhythm and melody, makes it easy to put the two together, is consistent, and easy enough for very small children to grasp, and for self-teaching sight-readers. It is possible, but difficult, to teach it badly. If properly taught, using not only the syllables doh, ray, me, etc., but the notation as a logical whole, it cannot fail. Nobody with any sense proposes that people should necessarily be restricted to Sol-fa, though I have known excellent aged sight-readers who could read nothing else. Incidentally, my experience as a choirmaster has proved that in a choir where some members read staff and some Sol-fa (intelligence being broadly equal), the Sol-fa readers almost invariably read more quickly and accurately. Sol-fa forms an excellent basis for later (and quite early) staff reading. It can be carried to the length of working orchestration exercises for musical degrees : but few would do that. The best way for anyone who wants to get a sound grasp of musical notation is to begin with Sol-fa, preferably in a small class, and be guided by the teacher, in due course, to staff reading. The use of the Sol-fa time-names makes rhythm-reading sure. The principle is so simple : always " taa " for one beat, with the vowel sound continued as many beats as a note lasts ; " saa " similarly for a silence (rest). The various subdivisions of the beat are shown by an altered vowel, plus (for the smallest) the employment of the initial letter " f " : e.g., a beat divided into four quarters, each with its separate note, would be "tafatefe." When one has tried this simple way of sounding *aloud* the notes read by the eye, its certainty and comfort for the reader are quickly realised. There are primers of Sol-fa published by Curwen's (the descendants of the great propagator of the system) and Novello. The latter firm issues " Tonic Sol-fa," by John Curwen himself, the simplest exposition of the principles. Two good books for learners are John's " How to Read Music " (Curwen, 2s.) and his " The Staff Notation," which is introduced on Sol-fa principles (Curwen, 2s.). I would again kindly urge on music-lovers the very great value of learning to read music. I believe that nothing could be healthier for the generation of respecters and friends of music that we want to grow, than for every child, when he leaves school, to be able to read his part in a chorus or a solo song, and to regard that accomplishment as no more surprising than the capacity to read the newspaper. I do not pretend that reading music comes so easily as reading print, because we are surrounded by print from the start : we hear parents reading, and news and poetry by radio : we can't get away from print ; and we use its language, and hear it, all day long. If we were so surrounded by music, it would come as easily as reading print does. Do not be deceived when a famous musician in his enthusiasm cries that boys should ". catch " reading music as they catch measles. This is just blowing off enthusiastic hot air ; but example counts for much : and would it not be all to the good if every child took learning to read music quite as a natural thing, " because daddy and mummy do it " ?

It is perhaps easy to glow about the glories of the past : but in what musicians like to call the " Golden Age " of English music—the great madrigal period, when we were in the forefront of the world in composition and performance—it was considered part of a gentleman's education to have instruction in music, and often some skill in instrumental performance (you remember, just a little later, Pepys's skill therein). Here is a passage from an entertaining text-book on music which Thomas Morley, one of the madrigalists, wrote in dialogue form; it shows the social implications of a gentleman's musical ignorance at that time. Two friends meet, and one asks the other how he fared at a "banket" last night. He is sore, because he had been put to public shame. Two other guests, arguing about music, had appealed to him for an opinion, and when he honestly said he did not know, the company, presuming that like other educated people he knew enough to give an opinion, thought he was being discourteous. Worse was to come, for, "supper being ended, and musicke bookes, according to the custome, being brought to the table, the mistress of the house presented mee with a part, earnestly requesting me to sing, but when, after many excuses, I protested unfeignedly that I could not, everie one began to wonder, yea, some whispered to others, demaunding how I was brought up : so that, upon shame of mine own ignorance, I goe nowe to seek out mine old friende Master Guorimus, to make myself his scholler."

Shall the twentieth century be beaten by the seventeenth ? Surely not !

———————

Some useful books are : Parry's "Evolution of the Art of Music" (Kegan Paul). This is fairly simply written, and very attractive to the beginning student. Abdy Williams's "Notation" is one of a number of well-illustrated books in the "Music Story" series (W. Reeves, 83 Charing Cross Road, W.C. 1). Besides Grove's "Dictionary of Music and Musicians" (Macmillan), a standard 5-volume encyclopædia, and Cobbett's "Cyclopædic Survey of Chamber Music" (Oxford University Press, 2 vols.), there is the equally authoritative "Oxford History of Music" (originally six volumes : the new Introductory volume concentrates on ancient and mediæval music; Vol. VII goes to the end. of the twentieth century, and Vol. VIII brings the history up-to-date). These works of reference may be found in any public library, and the music-lover cannot do better than start wherever his interest is aroused, and browse in them according to his inclination and opportunity.

About the biggest value for money in one-volume encyclo-pædias is Pratt's (Macmillan, 12s. 6d.). It is, in effect, a boiling down of Grove, with rather more American news. Historically, it is best after 1700—scanty before that. Stanford and Forsyth's " History " (Macmillan, 7s. 6d.) and Colles's (Oxford, 3 vols., 3s. 6d. each, or 10s. 6d., in one) are two good surveys. Rather simpler is P. A. Scholes's " Listener's History " (Oxford, 3 vols., 6s. each : complete in one, with index, 17s. 6d.). A book that aims at showing on a pretty full scale, with pictures and charts, the sort of thing that keen newcomers to music seek, is McKinney and Anderson's "Discovering Music" (Pitman, 12s. 6d.).

Valuable aids to the study of the history of music by means of gramophone records are P. A. Scholes's six albums (Columbia), and Curt Sachs's " Two Thousand Years of Music " (Parlophone, one album). Dr. Dyson's illustrated lectures on " The Progress of Music " are issued by the International Education Society (Columbia) on records D.40118–22, and his talks on " Early Keyboard Music " on D.40137–9.

For handy reference while any part of this book is being read, I have made a short Glossary of Musical Terms.

## CHAPTER VI

# A SHORT GLOSSARY OF MUSICAL TERMS

IT IS OBVIOUSLY impossible to give them all. The smallest pocket dictionary I know is Dr. T. Baker's " Pronouncing Pocket Manual," which can be had from Novello. Dr. Percy

Scholes has a good larger-sized one, " Every Radio Listener's Guide to Musical Terminology " (Oxford). Some
foreign pronunciations can scarcely be given without using
phonetics. But nowadays few people need go for long
without hearing good foreign speech. A little attentive
listening to the radio will teach us much. Like most technical vocabularies, that of music is sometimes illogical or
dubious : one word, e.g., may stand for several things. One
cannot be exhaustive in a line or two : there are reservations
about some of the definitions, and other people might
define differently. I am trying to combine simplicity,
brevity and as much accuracy as possible ; and every
worker knows how difficult it sometimes is to explain shortly
and exactly what the technical terms of his trade mean.
As I have remarked elsewhere, those who are sufficiently
interested in a subject like to learn its terms. I see no point
in elaborate explanatory avoidance of them, which wastes
words and is often confusing. I hope no technical term in
my part of this volume will remain unclear. I have tried either
to explain it when using it, or to catch it and put it in this
list. If any slippery fellow has eluded me, I ask pardon.
Your nearest musical friend will be glad to explain it. I have
omitted words of which anybody knows or can guess the
meaning, such as Ballet, Declamando, Appassionato,
Delicatamente, Lacrimoso, Animato, Ad lib., and many
others. Nor have I defined again things such as Development, or Fugue, which are explained in their proper places
in other chapters. If one is in doubt about some Italian
word not given here, it can not seldom be guessed by thinking what English word is like it. It has been considered
out of the scope of this small list (which does not pretend
to be a musical dictionary) to give more than one or two
German words. A few general notes : *Italian.* Pronounce
every letter. The ending " mente " equals our " ly " ;
" oso " means " in the manner of " ; " issimo," " very " ;
" ino " and " etto " or " etta," " a little " ; " ato " equals
our " ate " (e.g., " passionato "—" passionate " or " impassioned "). Italian vowels : " ah," " eh," " ee," " o,"

" oo " ; " u " is pronounced " oo " ; " z " or " zz " is
" dz." *German.* Final " d " is " t " ; final " ig " is half
" ig " and half " ih " ; " ie " is " ee " ; " ei " is " eye " ;
" e " (final) is " a " (as in " a thing ") ; " u " is " oo " ;
" ä " is nearly " ay," sometimes between that and " eh " ;
" au " is " ow," as in " howl " or very nearly so.

For all terms indicating speed, see *Speeds*.

For all terms indicating loudness, see *Volume*.

For all names of notes, see *Notes*.

# A

A.—The orchestra tunes to this (the A a sixth above middle
C). The oboe generally gives it. " A " (Italian) means
" in the style of " (e.g., " a cappella," in church style—
meaning, usually, unaccompanied part singing).

ABSOLUTE MUSIC.—It has no story behind it : " the music
itself is the meaning." The opposite is Programme
Music, q.v., and also Interlude in this Book, p. 93.

ABENDLIED.—Evening song.

ACCIACCATURA (Ah-chah-ca-too-rah).—Crush note, played
very quickly before the main note.

ACCIDENTALS.—Notes not in the key. They are shown by
sharps and flats (single or double), and naturals, q.v.

AFFETTUOSO.—Affectionately, tenderly.

ALLEMANDE.—An old German dance, used in the Suites of
Bach and Handel's time. English forms also ALMAN(D)
and ALMAIN.

AMORE.—Love. In the form *con* (" with ") *amore*, or
*amoroso*.

ANTIPHONAL.—Usually choral music, in which one section
of the choir answers the other.

APPOGGIATURA (Ap-pod-ja-*too*-rah).—Grace note, usually
taking part of the time of the main note (more than the
*acciaccatura* does).

ARIA.—Air. Usually implies a piece extracted from a longer
work, opera or oratorio.

ARPEGGIO.—" Harp-like." Playing the notes of a chord one
after another.

ASSAI (Ass-*sah*-ee).—Very.

A TEMPO.—" In time (again) " : used after some liberty has been taken with it.

ATONAL.—Discarding the plan of having a fixed key, or series of keys, for a piece.

## B

BAR.—One of the divisions, of so many beats each, that make up a piece. The word is used indiscriminately for the portion of music thus found between two *bar-lines* (the vertical lines that mark off the bars' length), and for the bar-lines. Note that Americans speak of " measures " instead of " bars."

BEAT.—The unit of time-division. Americans call it the " pulse."

BEN.—It. Well. Commonly found in phrases such as *ben marcato*, well marked.

BINARY.—A two-part form : A—B.

BIS.—Twice (i.e., play a particular bar twice). French people call out " Bis ! " when they want an encore.

BRAVURA.—With great spirit, dashing, brilliant. Often used of a difficult aria.

BRIO.—Vivacity, fire. Much the same as *Bravura*.

## C

CADENCE.—The short passage (often only a couple of chords) that brings us to a point of rest, temporary or final.

CADENZA.—A bit of showmanship, usually near the end of a piece, when the soloist interpolates brilliant music that may or may not have been written by the composer. Old Italian airs abounded in this. Musicians, speaking broadly, call it the " curse of the *concerto* " (q.v.).

CANON.—A form in which one or more melodies, begun by certain parts, are copied (usually exactly) by others. Hear, e.g., the start of the last movement of Franck's violin sonata, and the fine series in Bach's Goldberg variations.

CANTABILE (Can-*tah*-bee-leh).—In a singing style.

CANTATA.—A work for one or more soloists and chorus, usually with orchestral accompaniment. Originally, *cantata* was simply a sung work, as differentiated from sonata, a " sounded " (played) one.

CANTILENA.—A little song.

CANTO FERMO.—" Fixed song " : the theme on or round which counterpoint (q.v.) is embroidered.

CANTORIS.—In church, in antiphonal (q.v.) singing, the part of the choir on the North side.

CAPELLMEISTER (or spelt with initial K).—Ger. Master of a body of musicians ; formerly of a choir or orchestra : now used of any conductor. Thus, one sees in a German paper : " Jack Hylton's Kapelle."

CATCH.—A *Round* (q.v.) in which each singer in turn has to catch up the humorous words.

CHAMBER MUSIC : Music for intimate performance : mostly used of music with single performers to each part.

CHORAL, OR CHORALE.—The Lutheran hymn-tune.

CHORD.—Notes sounding together.

CHROMATIC.—" Coloured." A chromatic scale moves by semitones (q.v.). Chromatic notes, chords or intervals are those not belonging to the key in which the music is set. Its opposite is *Diatonic*.

CLASSICAL.—Broadly, music up to Beethoven's time, before the Romantic spirit became so self-conscious. But it is a poor word, especially when used as the opposite to *Romantic*, q.v.

CLAVIER, OR KLAVIER.—Keyboard.

CODA.—Tailpiece : that which rounds off a piece.

COLORATURA.—Showy passage-work ; usually used of singing.

CONCERTO : A work in several (usually three) movements, for soloist(s) and orchestra.

COMMON CHORD.—Consists of a root-note with the third and fifth, in scalic order above it.

COUNTERPOINT.—Melodies woven together. *Polyphony* means the same thing.

CRESCENDO (Creh-*shend*-o).—Gradually louder.

# D

DA CAPO.—From the beginning (head) : i.e., repeat.

DAL SEGNO.—Repeat from the sign :𝄋: (which may be anywhere in the piece).

DECANI (Deck-*ay*-nigh).—Over against the *Cantoris* (q.v.). The South side choir section.

DECISO (Deh-*cheese*-o).—Decisive.

DECRESCENDO (Deh-creh-*shend*-o).—The opposite of *Crescendo* : gradually softer.

DIATONIC.—Of a scale : one that has tones as well as semitones. Of an interval, note or chord : belonging to the key in which the music stands. Its opposite is *Chromatic*.

DIMINUENDO.—Diminishing in volume. The same as *Decrescendo*.

DISSONANCE, DISCORD.—Incomplete sounds, requiring *Resolution*.

DIVISI.—Divided : two notes being written at once for a single part (e.g., the first violin part), the players must divide, half taking the upper and half the lower note. When they come together again, *Unis.* or *Uniti* is written.

DOLCE.—Softly, sweetly.

DOLENTE.—Doleful : sadly.

DOUBLE FLAT.—Lowers a note two semitones. German for "Double Flat," Eses ; It., Bemolle doppia ; Fr., Double bémol.

DOUBLE SHARP.—Raises a note two semitones. Ger., Isis ; It., Diesis doppio ; Fr., Double dièse.

DUMKA.—South Russian : lament, usually impassioned. Dvořák uses it for various movements, with, as opposite number, the *Furiant* (q.v.). The two seem to correspond broadly with the *Lassú* and *Friss* respectively of Hungarian national music.

DUO, DUET.—Piece for two performers.

# E

ECOSSAISE.—Fr. Scots: a dance form used by several older composers, up to Chopin.

ENSEMBLE.—" Together " : used of chamber-music playing, and of its players—e.g., The London Wind Ensemble. A critic might say of a quartet: " Their ensemble was imperfect " or, more rarely, " Their ensemble was perfect."

EXTEMPORISATION.—Making up music on the spur of the moment. The same as *Improvisation*.

# F

FACILE (It., *Fa*-cheel-eh ; Fr., Fa-seal).—Lit., " easy " ; i.e., it must sound so : hence, fluently.

FALSETTO.—Lit., " false." It is. Applied to a peculiar way of producing the notes at the top of the voice.

FANTASIA.—(It., Fan-ta-*zee*-ah : or pronounce in the English way, Fan-*tay*-zee-ah). A piece in free form. The *Fantasy* (*Fancy*) of the 17th and 18th centuries in England was a non-dance piece in free *Imitation* (q.v.). The Dolmetsch family plays much music of this kind.

FERMATA.—A pause.

FIGURE.—A short pattern of notes.

FIGURED BASS.—Bass part only, with figures showing what chords are to be built above it.

FIORITURA.—An ornament. Applied to florid, decorated singing.

FLAT.—♭. Lowers a note a semitone. Ger., Es ; It., Bemolle ; Fr., Bémol.

FORZANDO.—Forceful. *Sforzando* means the same thing, suddenly.

FUOCO.—Fire.

FURIANT.—A fiery Scherzo in Dvořák's works, contrasting with the slow, impassioned *Dumka*, q.v.

# G

GAVOTTE.—Old French dance in four-time, beginning on the third beat.

GEMÜTH.—Ger. With (mit) soul : feelingly.

GLEE.—An English 18th-century invention : vocal piece for three or more solo voices ; secular ; usually in several distinct sections, of varying emotion.

GIGUE.—Jig : a dance ; the finale of many old Suites, such as Bach's.

GIOCOSO.—Jocosely : sportively.

GLISSANDO.—Gliding : sliding from note to note.

GREGORIAN(s).—Chanting, as regulated by Pope Gregory (*c.* A.D. 600). Still in use.

GROUND BASS.—Bass subject, repeated throughout a piece, with varied treatments above.

GRUPPETTO.—Lit., " group " (of ornamental notes). Formerly, either a trill or turn.

GUSTO.—Taste.

## H

HARMONICS.—(Harmonic Overtones, or Partials). Higher notes produced when any note is sounded. The note sounded is called the Prime Tone, or Generator, or Fundamental. Harmonics in string playing are made by touching the string lightly.

HARMONY.—Notes sounding together ; and the science of combining them.

HARMONICA.—Originally, the musical glasses. Now, a mouth-organ.

HAUTBOIS.—Fr. form for " oboe."

HOMOPHONY.—The opposite of *Polyphony*, q.v. Here one melody is the chief, and is accompanied by chordal parts.

## I

IMPRESSIONISM.—Like all " isms," difficult to define. A term borrowed from the 19th-century school of painters who probed effects of light. Though the idea is much older, Debussy may be reckoned its protagonist in music, probing effects of pure sound, not necessarily having anything to do with " stories," fixed forms, or drama in tone.

The clearest explanation and illustration of this and other "isms" is to be found in Percy Scholes's "Listener's History," Book 3 (Oxford Press.)

IMITATION.—One part copying another in melody, or in rhythm, or in both ; not necessarily strictly, or for long.

INCIDENTAL MUSIC.—Here-and-there music in a dramatic piece, used where it will heighten the effect of the stage work, either during or between the acts.

INTERVAL.—The distance in pitch between two notes. Count both starting and finishing notes : e.g., C—E is a third.

INTONATION.—Quality of tone ; also, truth or otherwise of pitch ; also, the beginning of chanting in *Plainsong* (q.v.).

INTONING.—The clergyman's ritual part, chiefly in mono-tone.

INTROIT.—A setting of a short piece of Scripture, sung before Mass or Communion.

## J

JIG.—See *Gigue*.

JOTA.—Northern Spanish dance, after the waltz style, musically.

JUST INTONATION.—Tuning by exact mathematical ratios. The opposite is tuning by *Temperament* (q.v.)—tempering the wind, as it were, to various shorn lambs of intervals, to make them work in all keys tolerably well. *Equal Temperament* is the modern method used.

Those interested might well consult Dr. Alexander Wood's "The Physical Basis of Music" (Cambridge University Press).

## K

KAMMER.—Ger. Chamber. Kammermusik : chamber music. Kammerorchester : small orchestra.

KAPELLE.—See *Capelle*.

KEY.—A system or mode of tones and semitones (q.v.). Also (not very wisely) used to mean the part of an instrument pressed by the finger.

KYRIE.—Part of the Church service, Roman and Anglican :
" Kyrie eleison "—" Lord, have mercy upon us."


## L

LANGSAM.—Ger. Slowly.

LEBHAFT.—Ger. Lively.

LEGATO.—Lit., " bound " : notes smoothly succeeding.
Opposite of *Staccato*.

LEGER LINE (Ledger).—Short bits of line above and below
the staff, continuing it, on which notes are placed.

LEGGIERO (Ledg-*yay*-ro).—Lightly.

LEISE.—Ger. Equals *piano*—soft.

LEIT-MOTIV (Light-mo-*teev*).—Leading theme. A brief,
significant theme that stands for some dramatic element—
person or idea—in a work.

LIBRETTO.—The poem which a composer sets as an opera
or oratorio.

LIED.—Song (Pl., Lieder).

L'ISTESSO.—The same. Common use : l'istesso tempo—at
the same speed (used where there is a change of note-
length, e.g.).

LUSINGANDO (hard " g ").—Coaxingly.

LUSTIG.—Ger. Pleasurably ; joyfully.


## M

MADRIGAL.—See within, Book IV, on Vocal Music.

MAESTOSO—Majestically.

MAJOR—Major Scale : has tones and semitones, the semitones coming 3–4 and 7–8. Major Interval : A semitone
larger than Minor. In a Major Chord or Key, certain
characteristic, distinguishing intervals are major.

MANUAL.—An organ keyboard.

MÄSSIG.—Ger. Moderately.

MAZURKA.—Polish dance, three-in-a-bar, the last usually
accented. Slowish.

MEASURE.—Bar. So called in America, and sometimes in
England.

MESSA DI VOCE (Messa dee *vo*-cheh).—Starting a note softly, swelling to loud tone, and diminishing again.

METRONOME.—Time-keeper, to show so many beats per minute. It is the simplified works of a clock, with the pendulum upside down. Speed indications are often given in this form : " M.M. crotchet 60," the note-unit and number varying. " M.M." means " Maelzel's Metronome." " Crotchet 60 " means sixty crotchets a minute—one a second. With a seconds-hand watch one can quickly estimate speeds. " Minim 90 " (ninety minims a minute) would mean three beats, each a minim long, every two seconds ; " quaver 120 " means two quavers a second ; for the speed 76, count almost exactly five beats to four seconds ; for 80, four beats to three seconds. Any other time may be reckoned on a similar basis.

MEZZA VOCE (Medza *vo*-cheh).—Half-voice power.

M.D.—Contraction for " Right Hand," in Fr. and It. (" Left Hand " is M.G. in Fr. and M.S. in It.)

MINOR.—There are two forms of Minor Scale. In one, the Harmonic Minor, the tone-and-semitone order is T, S, T, T, S, Tone-and-a-half, S. The Melodic Minor has : Upward, T, S, T, T, T, T, S ; Downward (counting from top to bottom), T, T, S, T, T, S, T. A Minor Interval is a semitone smaller than a Major. In a Minor Chord or Key, certain characteristic, distinguishing intervals are minor.

MINUET.—Dignified French dance-form, in three-time. See within, under *Form*, Book I, Part C.

MODES.—Ancient scales.

MODULATION.—Moving from key to key.

MOTET.—Old name of a sacred piece in contrapuntal style, usually unaccompanied : thus allied to the Madrigal, which is discussed in Book IV.

MOTIVE.—A short theme.

MUSIC DRAMA.—The kind of opera that Wagner developed.

MUTE.—A damper for stringed or wind instruments. Ger., Dämpfer.

MUTA.—A direction to the player to change his instrument, its tuning, or its crook.

## N

NATURAL.—♮. The sign that contradicts a sharp or flat. Ger., Quadrat ; It., Quadro ; Fr., Bécarre.

NOCTURNE, NOTTURNO.—Night music : meditative, poetic, sometimes rather melancholy.

NONET.—Piece for nine performers.

NOTES.—Sounds ; and also the symbols representing them. In U.S.A., for our " Sounds," " Tones " is used. Our names for the lengths of the various notes, with foreign equivalents—*Semibreve*: Ger., Taktnote or Ganze Note ; It., Semibreve ; Fr., Ronde ; American, Whole Note. *Minim* (in the same order of languages) : Halbe Note, Minima, Blanche, Half Note. *Crotchet* : Viertel (Note), Semiminima, Noire, Quarter Note. *Quaver* : Achtel, Croma, Croche, Eighth Note. *Semiquaver* : Sechzehntel, Semicroma (or Biscroma), Double Croche, Sixteenth Note. *Demisemiquaver*: Zweiunddreissigstel, Semibiscroma, Triple Croche, Thirty-second Note.

For the English note-names C, D, E, F, G, A, B, C, the Germans use the same letters, but H instead of B. (Their B is our B flat.) Italians use the Sol-fa syllables, almost as we know them : Do, Re, Mi, Fa, Sol, La, Si, Do : the only difference in the French use is that they have Ut instead of Do.

## O

OBBLIGATO (The German has only one " b ").—Indispensable part. But the term is sometimes used, loosely, for a part that *may* be dispensed with—e.g., an additional accompaniment to a song, besides the piano part.

OHNE.—Ger. Without.

OPERA, ORATORIO.—See within, Book III and Book IV.

ORNAMENTS.—Melodic decorations, very few of which are now used.

OVERTONES.—See *Harmonics*.

OVERTURE.—The prelude to an extended work. Concert Overture : a piece of some extent, usually in First Movement form, self-contained, and not infrequently programmatic.

## P

PARTITA (Par-*tee*-tah).—A Suite, of the older kind (e.g., Bach's).

PARTITION—Fr. (Ger., Partitur). Full score.

PASSACAGLIA (Pass-ah-*cal*yah).—Originally, an Italian dance in three-time, written on a Ground Bass (q.v.). A magnificent modern example is the finale of Brahms's Fourth Symphony.

PASSEPIED.—Fr. (pass-p'yay). A sort of quick Minuet.

PAVANE.—A stately song-and-dance piece in two-time, from the 16th century.

PENTATONIC SCALE.—Has five tones. There were many of them. The commonest, often found in folk-tunes, runs (from C) : C, D, E, G, A, C. " Auld Lang Syne " is in this scale.

PIBROCH.—Bagpipe variations.

PIZZICATO.—Plucked (strings).

PLAINSONG.—Early worship song, sung in unison, before harmony was invented. Still used in chanting.

POCO.—Little.

POLONAISE.—Polish processional dance, in three-time. The finest examples in art-music are Chopin's.

POLYPHONY.—The same as *Counterpoint*, q.v.

PORTAMENTO.—Sliding from note to note, through intermediate notes. Its habitual use proves laziness or inartistry.

PROGRAMME MUSIC.—Music that illustrates a story, or has some form of literary background. Its opposite is *Absolute Music*, q.v.

## Q

QUADRUPLET.—Four notes played in the time of 3 (or of 6).

QUARTER TONE.—Half a semitone. Used as a general

term for some modern harmony employing intervals smaller than semitones.

QUARTET (Fr., Quatuor).—A piece for four performers, vocal or instrumental ; usually of Sonata build. Also, the performers (as, the London String Quartet).

QUASI.—As if.

QUINTET (Fr., Quintuor).—As " Quartet," but for five performers.

QUODLIBET.—" What you will " : a stringing together of tunes to make either verbal or musical fun, or both, often due to incongruity. The Bach family was fond of this diversion.

## R

RECITATIVE (It., Recitativo—reh-chee-ta-*tee*-vo).—A free style of declamation, untrammelled by bar-lengths. Much used in opera and oratorio, where it is vocal. Occasionally found in instrumental works. Vocal recitative is known as *Recitativo Secco* (a chord here and there keeping it in the air), or *Recitativo Stromentato* (instrumented, i.e., accompanied, recitative). The two styles are beautifully illustrated in the four recitatives in Handel's "Messiah," beginning " There were shepherds."

REGISTER.—A definite part of the compass in instrument or voice, having characteristic and distinctive quality. Also used of any organ-stop.

REPRISE.—A repeat.

REQUIEM.—Mass for the dead. Also used occasionally for a choral work " in memoriam."

RESOLUTION.—The movement of a discord to a consonance.

RESTS.—Each of the notes has its appropriate rest. In most languages these take their names from the notes (see *Notes*) : e.g., the German for a semibreve rest is Taktpause, for a minim rest, Halbepause, and so on. The Italians use " Pausa della Semibreve," " della Minima," or whatever note is in question. The French list is : Semibreve rest, Pause ; Minim rest, Demi-pause ; Crotchet rest,

Soupir ; Quaver rest, Demi-soupir ; Semiquaver rest, Quart de soupir ; Demisemiquaver rest, Demi-quart de soupir. The American system is to speak of " Whole Note Rest," " Half Note Rest," and so on.

RESULTANT TONES.—Extra notes heard when two notes are sounded.

RHAPSODY.—A declamatory piece, in free form : sometimes based on folk-song (e.g., Vaughan Williams's " Norfolk Rhapsodies ").

RIGAUDON.—Fr. (The Eng. is Rigadoon). Lively French dance, usually in two-time.

RINFORZANDO.—" Reinforced " : special emphasis on particular notes.

RIPIENO.—" Filling up part." In the old concerto, that portion of the orchestra, over against the soloist-section (" concertante "), which filled up the harmonies.

RITORNELLO.—A repeat ; it also means an instrumental interlude in a vocal work.

ROMANTIC.—Used, not very wisely, to mark off, broadly, music of the period of the self-conscious romantic revival in literature, in the early part of the 19th century. It is a mistake, however, to make hard-and-fast distinctions between " classical " and " romantic " music, for the classics were romantics too.

ROUND.—A vocal piece in which each voice copies the last, entering at an arranged distance.

RUBATO.—Lit., " robbed "—which it should not be called, since its essence is the repayment of time borrowed or advanced. In general, swaying the rhythm.

RUHIG.—Ger. Peaceful.


S

SARABANDE.—Stately old dance in three-time, accented on the second beat.

SCALE.—Notes in some settled order. Those in present use developed from the much more numerous *Modes* of older days.

SCHERZO.—" Jest." A development of the Minuet, by Beethoven ; used in sonatas, symphonies, and works of like form.

SCORE.—Parts for performers. When all are laid out beneath each other, they make a *Full Score*. A *Short Score* condenses more than one on a stave, *Open Score* giving each part its own stave. The *Vocal Score*, as its name implies, gives the voice parts in full, with usually a piano accompaniment. The Piano Score condenses the whole work on to two staves.

SCORING.—Writing out all the parts for a work. Also used to mean *Orchestration* or *Instrumentation*.

SEGNO (*Sain*-yoh).—Sign. See above, *Dal Segno*.

SEGUE (*Say*-gweh).—Follows.

SEGUIDILLA.—A Spanish song-dance, in three varieties, from lively to slow.

SEHNSUCHT, MIT.—Ger. (Zain-zucht). With longing, yearning.

SEMITONE.—The smallest normal scale interval. On the piano, the distance from any note (white or black) to that immediately above or below it.

SENZA.—Without.

SEQUENCE.—Repetition of a melodic pattern.

SEPTET (Fr., Septuor).—Piece for seven performers.

SERENADE.—" Evening song." Usually light music : applied also to Suites.

SERENATA.—May mean the same as " Serenade." Applied also to an 18th-century form of cantata (Handel's " Acis and Galatea " is a Serenata).

SEXTET (Fr., Sextuor).—A piece for six performers.

SHARP.—♯. Raises a note a semitone. Ger., Kreuz ; Fr., Dièse ; It., Diesis.

SIGNATURE.—Written at the beginning of a piece, to show (1) key, and (2) time. Sharps or flats (or their absence) show the former ; a fraction, the latter.

SLANCIO (*Slahn*-chee-oh).—Dashingly.

SLENTANDO.—Gradually getting slower.

SMORZANDO (SMORZATO).—Quenching the tone ; dying away.

SONG FORM.—A form in which (almost always) two contrasted sections alternate. Used for many slow movements of sonatas, either in its simplest form as A—B—A, or in simple extension as A—B—A—B—A.

SORDINO.—It. Mute.

SPEEDS.—The Italian terms are given, in order from slow to fast. A batch of words meaning " very slow and broad " includes *Largo*, *Adagio*, and *Grave*. *Lento* is "slow," *Andante* is " getting going " (commonly used to mean " slow," though : and as a general term for the slow movement of a sonata or symphony) ; *Andantino* is a nuisance, because some take it to mean " (only) a little slow," and others, " a little slower than *Andante* " ; *Allegretto* is clear enough —" moderately fast " ; *Allegro* is literally " cheerful "— hence quick, lively. *Presto* is "very quick," and *Prestissimo*, "as fast as possible."

STACCATO.—Detached. Opposite of *Legato*. Used of notes or chords.

STAFF.—Set of five lines used in notation.

STRINGENDO (soft " g ").—Hastening : implies loudening also.

STRING QUARTET.—Two violins, viola and violoncello.

SUITE.—Set (of pieces). Formerly built on dance forms. Later, on some common idea, as alternative (e.g., Countryside Suite).

SUSPENSION.—Holding back one or more notes of a chord, whilst the rest move. Almost always this produces a discord, and then the suspension resolves to make a concord again ; a chain of suspensions may thus be formed.

# T

TEMPERAMENT, EQUAL.—The modern way of tuning, so that acoustic differences are spread over all keys, and all sound tolerable. See also *Just Intonation*.

TEMPO.—Time. Commonly means the speed of a movement.

TENUTO.—Held : sustained.

TESSITURA.—The main range of a part, the amount of the compass which is covered by the music, excluding occasional very high or low notes.

TETRACHORD.—The four scale-tones in the interval of a fourth, used in the Greek system of notation.

THOROUGH BASS.—See *Figured Bass*.

TIMBRE.—Fr. Tone quality : " colour."

TOCCATA.—A brilliant piece to show off the " touch."

TONE.—Two semitones, q.v.

TREMOLO.—Often confused with *Vibrato*, q.v. Strictly, it means a rapid reiteration of a note, the pitch being steady. But it is often used to mean a rapid effect of on-and-off-pitch. Like all legitimate effects, it is either deliberately copied, and heedlessly overdone, by the unskilled ; or it is produced because it cannot be helped : that is, control is lacking. Ninety-nine times out of a hundred it is misused.

TRANSPOSE.—Put into a different key.

TRAURIG.—Ger. Sad.

TRIAD.—Root, third and fifth forming a chord.

TRIO.—Piece for three performers (usually a sonata) ; or, the performers (e.g., London String Trio). It is also used of the middle section of a Minuet or a March.

TRIPLET.—Three notes in the time of two.

TROPPO.—Too much.

## U

UNISON.—Strictly, two parts at the same pitch ; also used of, e.g., male and female voices singing the same tune, and necessarily an octave, or even two octaves, apart.

## V

VELOCE (Vel-*otch*-eh).—Rapid.

VERSE.—A section of an anthem written for one or more solo voices, for contrast with the full choir.

VIBRATO.—Strictly, rapid alternation of a note and one slightly higher or lower. Often used confusingly for *Tremolo*, q.v.

VIOLONCELLO.—Note the spelling (derived from "violone," the large viol, not from "violin").

VOCALISE.—Singing study, sung to Sol-fa or other syllables.

VOLL.—Ger. Full.

VOLUME.—The grading of loudness, beginning at the softest, is : Pianissimo, Piano (Soft), Mezzo Piano (Moderately Soft), Mezzo Forte (Moderately Loud), Forte, Fortissimo. The appropriate abbreviations are pp, p, mp, mf, f, ff. More p's or f's can be added at discretion—three or four. Tchaikovsky uses ppppp at the end of his "Pathetic Symphony."

VORSPIEL.—Prelude.

## W

WELL-TEMPERED.—Equal-tempered. (Cf. Bach's " 48 ").

WHOLE TONE SCALE.—Composed of full tones only. It is of limited value, as there are only two forms—from C : C, D, E, F sharp, G sharp, A sharp (or B flat), C ; and from C sharp : C sharp, D sharp, E sharp (or F), G, A, B, C sharp.

## X

XYLOPHONE.—Tuned wooden bars, struck with wooden sticks.

## Z

ZAPATEADO.—Spanish dance, accompanied by stamping.

ZART.—Ger. Delicate, tender.

ZINGARESE, ALLA.—In gipsy style.

# B: THE FUNDAMENTALS OF MUSIC

THIS IS THE " How it is done " section. We shall look at the elements of rhythm, melody, harmony, timbre, etc., note the parts they play in making up music, and how one may grow to recognise these, or to " appreciate " music (in the simpler meaning of the term : its fuller meaning is to size up, to estimate the value of a thing).

## CHAPTER I

## RHYTHM

AS WE SAW earlier, rhythm comes " by nature." Its meaning is sometimes confused with that of mere time. To jump right up to present-day goings-on, take the clubs that have sprung up for the enjoyment of modern dance music. These are called " Rhythm Clubs," and although of course they do not fail to enjoy the elements of harmony, melody, instrumental timbre or characterisation, and so on, their picking on one element for a title is significant. In passing, it may be said that (putting aside the matter of whether one happens to like or dislike the type of music) the first criticism that musicians make about modern dance music is that " it lacks rhythm." This shows that rhythm, to the musician, is a subtler thing than it is to most makers and " fans " of dance music. The development of certain elements of decoration and extemporisation in " hot music " have increased its rhythmic interest, but in my observation few bands have made an artistic whole out of these new elements. The older type of modern dance music, to the musician, sounded rhythmically uninteresting, because it played with only a few time-patterns, and was tied by the

leg to the banjo's steady clack-clack. That is judged necessary for dancing ; at any rate, I took trouble to hear most
of the admired bands, and none of them had anything to
interest me for more than a few minutes. It may be argued
that such music is not meant for musicians. That is quite
reasonable : it has a definite amusement purpose, and so
long as it remains unpretentious, no musician minds. It was
only when absurd claims were made for " symphonised
syncopation " that musicians had to laugh. The worlds of
amusement-music and serious music move in different
orbits, and each is happiest by itself. It is a pity to try to
mix them up. Remember the Frog and the Ox !

Rhythm, though readily definable as " the legs of music,"
amounts to something much subtler than many people conceive. The basic life of music depends on it, and the root
principle of all structure is in it—Variety in Unity. It com-
prehends the placing of note over against note—short or
long, or in any combination—of phrase over against phrase,
sentence with sentence, until the whole piece is complete.
Many people can keep time, but fewer have rhythm. If,
for instance, the time be swayed, hurrying a trifle here,
slowing up a shade there, that swaying can be done
rhythmically or unrhythmically. The mere correct valuing
of the composer's notes does not make good rhythm. A great
deal of style in this element consists of subtly varying *stresses*.
The commonest thing one has to tell a not very experienced
choir, in adjudicating at a competition festival, is that it
sings " square-toedly," beating out its 1, 2, 3, or 1, 2, 3, 4,
in too evenly stressed steps. In a bar of four beats, for instance, the first beat should have the main stress, the third
the next, slighter, stress, No. 2 and No. 4 having very little :
2, normally, a shade more than 4. But this is only one bar.
The next bar, with its similar general proportions, must be
balanced against bar 1 : and that may mean giving it, as
a whole, a lighter or heavier stress than No. 1 : generally,
lighter. Then bars 3 and 4 have to be considered, each first
as a little entity of four members (beats), and then as over
against the other bar; and then the four bars must be

balanced as a phrase or sentence. Similarly the next phrase or sentence must be considered : then the two together ; and so on throughout the piece.

Now all this careful and happy toil is not usually envisaged by the laymen ; but anyone who thinks that the average person can " learn music " otherwise than by learning how thus to build up a piece is making the biggest possible mistake. A few lucky people just " feel " all this right away, but we are not likely to be high among them. The dusty road for us. The Young Roscius, star of the stage at twelve years old, felt a great deal about drama that others had to be taught to feel, or to simulate feeling ; yet *he* had to be taught how to hold his hands. Fine rhythm is what makes musicians put certain performers higher than perhaps laymen do ; but the musically minded person, ignorant of the mysteries, may yet feel, without knowing why, the superior vitality of a finely rhythmed performance. If you happen to be a performer not very advanced, you will strengthen your rhythm by having fewer stresses in a bar : especially in long bars. If you happen to conduct a choir, make it accustomed to your beating two instead of four in a bar, or one instead of three. It must *feel* the other beats, not have them banged out, in the mind or by the stick. But this is not a treatise on performance.

We saw in our historical introduction that rhythm in music first was guided soberly by that of the words. And in vocal music that is still the ideal. The finest days of rhythmic subtlety were in the madrigalian period (with 1600 as a rough centre-date), about which you will read more in Book IV of this work, on the human voice and the music written for it. One of the readiest ways in which to realise whether the rhythm of words is being beautified by music, or strait-jacketed, is to listen to a choir's chanting. If " Gregorians " are used, the words have a first-rate chance. If " Anglican " chants are used, the words may still be respectfully and affectionately treated : or they may not. It depends on the choir and their master. You may have heard of the bad old " thump " in chanting, as in

" Glory be to the Father and TO the Son, AND to the Holy Ghost." One would not say the words like that. Why sing them so ? There is no need to. The pointing can quite well be arranged so as to preserve the natural rhythm and emphasis of the words, and it is only laziness or shut-ears that ever prevents the following out of the excellent maxim : " Sing as you speak."

The faculty of rhythm is ready to be brought to ample life in nearly everybody. Give it a chance, experiment, and there should be little difficulty in finding out what is right. Even as to speed, some are timid. People write to musical editors to ask " At what pace should I take this piece ? " If they gave their rhythmic sense a chance, they would rarely need to ask.

It is scarcely necessary to define that element in time which has been so much in our ears for almost a generation —syncopation. This disturbance of the normal accent, by carrying a note from a weak to a strong beat, or giving special prominence to a shorter weak beat, is just a relish, and as such has long been used in serious music. Something of its spirit was found in mediæval times, in the Hocket (hiccough), which is clearly exhibited in the article under that heading in Grove's Dictionary (where may be found fuller information on the musical matters here dealt with. The five volumes are in all public libraries, and much benefit may be had by browsing in them, however desultorily). Syncopation is only a device for giving a little shake to the time, and is not necessarily of any value to rhythm : that is, it can be very monotonous, if overdone, just as a meal consisting largely of sauces would be altogether too much of a series of good things. If you want to hear how much syncopation can be used in a short movement, by a composer who knows his job, try the Hornpipe finale of Handel's Concerto Grosso in B flat, No. 18 (called Op. 6, No. 7). The piano duet or solo arrangement of this orchestral work, with a number of others, is published by Breitkopf. It is one of the jolliest movements I know—a perfect little demonstration of the artistic use of syncopation. Another taking instance comes in the finale of the well-liked Schumann pianoforte concerto, where the broad pulsation of twos, in which the movement runs, is changed to one of threes by a method involving syncopation.

Rhythm, then, is not something imposed on music. Whether there be or be not words, the rhythm is inherent in the music. It is not only its legs, but its life. And that life, like ours, is often subtle and complex.

# CHAPTER II

# MELODY

THE OLD definition of melody, " Any agreeable and familiar combination of notes," does not hold good, if we are to include extremist music. There the combination is often certainly not familiar, and sometimes it is not agreeable. Mr. Blom will later have something to say on both of these heads. All I need say, for defining, is that melody (in the old sense) is an element we all enjoy, and most easily take in. It is not often, of itself, either subtle or difficult to grasp. Phrasing—the eloquent articulation of the parts of a melody so that they bear a particular relation to each other—brings us into the element of rhythm. The observance of punctuation in speech broadly corresponds to phrasing : yet there is more in it than that. Some composers' melodies—Berlioz's, for example—need particular care in phrasing if their meaning is to be what the composer intended. This consideration, obviously, depends on knowing what he wrote—being able to read his score. Broadly speaking, then, we all know what we think melody is ; but few can think of it without harmony, as folk-singers do. The main thing to remember is that melody is always going somewhere. Indeed, I once heard an extremist composer define it so : just as a succession of notes going somewhere. The snag may be that only the composer knows where ; and when that is so, he is likely to remain also the only one who cares.

## CHAPTER III

## HARMONY

WE HAVE already seen the genesis of harmony ; but nobody knows who first began to sing " seconds " (musicians would say " thirds," because the accompanying singer usually hits a third below his leader : i.e., the leader is singing the E, D, C of " Three Blind Mice," and the seconder sings C, B, A, which is good enough, as far as it goes—only that A doesn't quite do the job properly. It is only when the second man progresses to the freedom of, say, the C, G, E below that he is really creating something). Modern harmony is often queer, in varying degrees. It can be criticised from a good many points of view : that is, it is not so much a matter of just " liking " or " disliking " as is sometimes thought. *Logic* is the big criterion : partly, " Is it going anywhere, with a purpose ? " But this is too big a subject to go into, depending as it does on a good many technical factors. Harmony and melody must be suited to each other. In the weaker kind of modernism, they notably do not fit. Harmonising " just off the note " is common in such music : as a poor old suit might be made with chemicals to look gay for a night, but would soon turn green and shabby when their effect had worn off. The novelty of the sort of harmonies I mean does not even, now, take in anybody : once, in the happy days round about 1920–25, when nearly anything could be tried with impunity, it did. But really strong modern music does not depend on pepper and salt for its nutriment. Brahms, judging pupils' harmony, used to cover up all but the tune and the bass. If they went well, the work would be further examined, for truth in the inward parts. If not, it was no good.

The values of rhythm and harmony, and our capacity to estimate them, can amusingly be estimated by playing some well known tune in notes of exactly equal length, with no special stress. I have played the National Anthem in this way to members of a University Extension music class, and few spotted it. Still more puzzling is it if the time and rhythm are deliberately altered, only the rise and fall of the notes being unchanged (see (a) below). The other game is to play or sing, on one note, only the rhythm of a tune (see (b) below). Most people score better here than in the other. That shows the strength of rhythms in our minds.

Name the theme

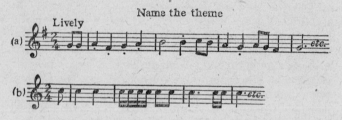

"Counterpoint" (from "point counter point"—one note, in olden times called a "point," against another) explains itself. (The adjective is "contrapuntal.") It is the placing of one melody over against another, each with its individual life. If one person sings a tune, and another sings "seconds" to it, as it is called (three notes below) this second part is not really a counterpoint, because it is just the same tune, sung at the same time. If, however, the second man starts a bit late, and the two continue together, we have counterpoint—and quite likely, a pretty dreadful row. But some tunes will go very nicely in this way. The hymn-tune "Hanover" ("O worship the King") is one. You might try it, starting the second singer off with the tune when the first singer has got to the end of the first bar —that is, as far as "O worship." The first half of the tune

will then go nicely. We call this strict form of counterpoint
" canon," by the way, from the name for the strict law of
the Church.

Free counterpoint means the weaving together of two or
more musical strands, as above, each being different. You
may have heard a music hall pianist playing " The Bluebell
of Scotland " along with Dvořák's best-known " Humoresque." This is counterpoint. Round about 1600 this art
was at its height. Later, its greatest manipulator was
Bach. Perhaps " manipulator " sounds too much like rope-
tricks. In the hands of some well-meaning but not greatly
gifted composers, counterpoint did become little more than
mathematical wangling. Even Bach (rarely, though) nods—
and nodding, continues to spin ropes. When one understands the nature of counterpoint, it is just as interesting
music as block-harmony. Most people find Handel friend-
lier, at first, than Bach just because he mixed his counterpoint with larger doses of harmony. You have dozens of
beautiful examples of his dispensing in his oratorio
" Messiah." The chorus " Glory to God " is a simple
instance, beginning with solid harmony, changing at
" Goodwill towards men " to counterpoint, then back to
harmony at the return of " Glory to God," and so
alternating.

Any of Bach's forty-eight preludes and fugues, his organ
works, his concertos, his cantatas (often broadcast), the
great " Mass " are full of counterpoint of the purest and
most marvellous order. Musicians, most of us know, rave
about Bach : not least because they hail him as a supreme
craftsman ; perhaps nobody knows quite how marvellous
his ease in workmanship is unless he has tried to write
counterpoint himself, but anybody who listens can realise
the skill. Skill alone would not, of course, save music that
had not heart and soul in it. Now and again, as suggested
above, it fails to save even Bach ; but nearly always he
adds the human qualities which the counterpoint glorifies.
There are plenty of gramophone records and radio hearings
of Bach, and of most of the music I shall mention. For one

beautiful feat of contrapuntal writing, hear the finale of the Fourth Brandenburg Concerto. There are many subtleties in the possible uses of counterpoint. The main thing to keep in mind is that all good writing includes a contrapuntal element, though that will mostly be less prominent nowadays than it was in the eighteenth century : the fashion has changed, and Bach did pretty well all that could be done with counterpoint. Still, it has ample resources, and for the attentive ear there is rich pleasure in attending to this woven music, which has to be thought of horizontally, where block harmony is considered vertically. But such attention must be more concentrated, since one may have to follow several lines at once, or at any rate to keep several contrapuntal ideas in the mind, during a composition. It is much easier to follow blocks of chords. Both ways of listening must be cultivated, and each method of writing appreciated on its own terms.

Anyone who can see and hear the Russian Ballet's miming of Tchaikovsky's fifth and Brahms's fourth symphonies (respectively entitled "Les Présages" and "Choreartium") will have a fine demonstration of the meaning of counterpoint, for the movement of the music is interpreted in action. I cannot imagine a more fascinating lesson than the Tchaikovsky work in this new expounding.

## CHAPTER IV

## TIMBRE

Tone quality necessarily colours all our musical enjoyment. The instruments of the orchestra are worth knowing, by sight and sound. An average ear can soon distinguish between any of them. Ears differ a good deal in natural capacity, which is fixed at birth. This fixed power is rarely developed, by most people, to its full extent ; so, although that capacity can never be exceeded, no one need be anxious about his ability to hear sufficiently well to enjoy many of the subtleties of tone-colour. But he must practise so as to get the best out of his aural power. Musicians are very keen that all musical training of children in school should be based on ear-training. Without that, good " appreciation " is impossible. Sadly many people grow up untrained in this way. Some even go to musical colleges, heavily deficient in the power to distinguish between sounds. Training in timbre is best done in the concert room. The other essentials of ear-training are laid down in several good books—Macpherson and Read (Williams, publisher) is one. Mabel Chamberlain's (Novello) is another. The shortest book, but one of the most thorough, and a useful one for the self-helper, for whom there is not a great deal elsewhere, is Annie Lawton's " Foundations of Practical Ear Training " (Oxford U.P.). These are *thorough*. There is no other way to learn to make fine distinctions. The process of gaining such knowledge is very stimulating. But those who just want to sharpen their ear for tone can get most of what they want by listening to all sorts of bands, quartets, brass players, even street singers, most of whom sing out of tune. So should I, maybe, if I had to lead their life. For the musician, singing or whistling out of tune is usually extremely difficult. One who can do it amusingly is Ronald Gourlay, on the radio. For the unmusical, it is easier (and alas, much more common) than falling off a cliff. In my observation, sharp singing is on the increase since the war : perhaps partly as the result of the craze for speed and noise. It is usually the result of " forcing " the voice. All performing that sounds difficult is wrong. However difficult it is, the artist is known by making it sound easy.

Listening to a string quartet for the first time, a friend who had a good ear said : " Why, it sounds out of tune ! " He had been brought up on the piano, which makes concessions, so as to get all its notes tolerably in tune. If it were tuned to the perfect scale (as organs once were) it would sound terrible, in parts. Fiddlers, by themselves, will play in the perfectly tuned scale, for they make their own notes as they go along. My friend's ear, for the time, was rather like the palate accustomed to and with a relish for coarse food, suddenly presented with the most delicate dishes. In listening to orchestras, mark the difference between the oboe (the player puts two thin cane " reeds " into his mouth), and the clarinet (where he puts a wedge-shaped block into his mouth, against which a single reed is held : this point of single or double reed largely affects the timbre ; there are other differences that I need not go into). Apart from the less frequently used instruments, none of those in, say, the normal classical symphony orchestra need cause confusion, except perhaps the violins and violas : the latter are larger than the former, and pitched a little lower. Their contralto tone cannot be missed, when heard alone. The eye can best distinguish them by the angle at which the player's forearm is held out—more nearly straight, because of the viola's extra length, than that of a violinist.

Cornet and trumpet might be confused in a military band (cornets are not found in the orchestra, save in a few special instances). The trumpet is flatter in shape than the cornet, its tone less thick : but much depends on the playing, and the listener's experience. Not all among quite good musicians would infallibly tell the one from the other, by ear. More about the orchestra is told in the fourth Part of this Book. All I want to do here is to make the point that timbre, or tone-characteristic, is a vital element in composition. Since instruments have been so largely perfected, a fine composer thinks his melodies and harmonies right away in terms of the appropriate instruments. He may sketch out a rough " short score," of a few staves only, instead of the dozen to twenty he may ultimately need : but he is not thinking in terms of the piano—simply in terms of the orchestra. A melody comes to him, or he works it out, *as* an oboe theme, or a horn phrase ; a massed effect is born in his mind as lower strings plus bassoons and tenor trombone, or whatever it is. Two very notable composers in this respect are Elgar and Sibelius. The latter in particular has put on paper some of the most astonishing-looking combinations I have ever seen : yet they come off in performance, and the idea, one knows, would not live as it does, or make its proper effect, in any other dress. Indeed, it is not an idea *in* a dress : it is just a whole idea, born complete, with all its elements of rhythm, pitch, timbre, all its harmonic surrounding and its melodic implications (which at the moment we shall not see) : as we say, " inevitable." Only the big man creates his music like that. One of the tests of a composer's greatness is the extent to which he gives us this feeling of inevitability.

The effect of a passage may depend on the register of an instrument. The flute, for instance, is hollow, possibly melancholy, down below : up above he can cavort or be ingenuously sweet. So with most of the instruments. Hence the pitch of a melody may alter its effect. So, obviously, do several other elements, which do not need expansive mention—loudness or softness, pace, emphasis or lack of it, technical management of the instrument—as, for instance, special ways of blowing, muting, playing near the bridge of a stringed instrument, etc. These are all high matters, and none of them must be outside the composer's permanent purview. Thus we see that really to compose for an orchestra is a tremendous business. I was amused on reading what appeared to be full particulars of a new orchestral work that was to be broadcast, and then hearing the composer, who introduced it, add the little remark that the work had been orchestrated by his friend Mr. Y. Z. That note was not deemed worth giving in print : yet such trifle of effect as the music had was almost all the result of the orchestral scoring. One wondered why, if he had thought out particular passages of the work for particular instruments, he had not taken the trouble to learn how to write down the notes. And if he had not thought them out for any particular instruments, why worry an orchestra with his trivialities ?

Examples of the remarkable mental effect of the

composer's clever choice of *timbre* are legion, in " absolute " as well as in " programme " music. One of the keenest pleasures of the listener to orchestras may well lie in noting these happy strokes. Such brilliant use of the brass as Wagner so often makes (take, as a single example among hundreds, the introduction to Act 3 of " Lohengrin ") ; Tchaikovsky's delicious character-scoring in his " Casse Noisette " suite—the Chinese and Arabian Dances, e.g. ; Rimsky-Korsakov's virtuosity in the " Scheherazade " suite ; the appealing slow movement of Dvořák's " New World " symphony with its cor anglais (alto oboe) solo ; the last two minutes of the second movement of Brahms's fourth symphony, where the strings and wood-wind, in heart-easing assurance, reconcile us to the world's devious ways : these and a thousand other memories will be stored up among the rewards of the attentive listener, to whom, it is not too much to claim, a whole new world of interest is opened up as soon as he begins to use the ear for timbre.

About listening to music by an orchestra, by wireless or the gramophone, I may say a word without trespassing on Mr. Blom's Book : much improved as reproduction is, these products are not the real thing ; and sometimes, as when choirs are broadcast with orchestras, they are very far from it, even on the best instruments. Without discussing the many splendid benefits that the media offer, or what is gained or lost by being able to listen thus, I would here only gently insist on the necessity for constantly renewing the impression of reality " at first ear," by taking trouble to hear as much music as possible in the concert room. Only thus can the appreciation of timbre be maintained in the best condition ; but intelligent use of the other aids will quickly and largely widen one's scope in many directions, and no active music-lover can afford to neglect these boons that science now offers.

# C : FORM

## CHAPTER I

# THE ELEMENTS OF FORM

ART OF ANY KIND is inconceivable without form. The beauty of structure can be one of the best of delights to the music-lover, as it is to the biologist, the anatomist, the painter, the sculptor and the architect. Music maybe comes nearest to architecture, in the vital part that form or design plays in its life, though it is really unlike any other art : and analogies are misleading.

The simplest elements count, in form—the building up of a tiny two- or three-note motive against another motive, of phrase against phrase, sentence on sentence, until a series of these constitutes a section of a short piece. This section will be balanced by a contrasting one, similarly built up in general lines, but with subtle variety in detail ; and so a piece grows. The experienced composer can think in long stretches. If we analyse in short ones, we must remember that when he knows his job, much of his building may become *subconscious* work. He knows where he wants to go, and that other mind—call it what you like— having been laboriously instructed in his youth, now knows how to get him there, and does not necessarily worry him often about the road and the vehicle. But he may agonise for days over a transition, or shape and re-shape a phrase. Beethoven was a great re-shaper. His notebooks show his processes, and they should make impatient would-be creators humble. Schubert, on the other hand, scarcely ever sketched or altered. Music just poured out of him. Every man to his type. The one is not necessarily better than the other.

When first man, tired of monotonously repeating a little

figure, varied it, he became a builder of form. Variety in unity is the root of form. There are two such simple roots : one is exemplified in the folk tune that contains two ideas, conveniently labelable A and B, and gives you the two one after the other, as in "Golden Slumbers," and "Billy Boy," where the first two lines are answered by the last two. A neat variant is " The Lincolnshire Poacher," in which the four lines are respectively A, B, B, A—up the hill and down the other side. Still commoner is the other root, found in the song in which A and B are followed by the return of A, to clinch matters. This would take but three lines, and so to make up the four of the verse the first A is almost invariably repeated straight away. This has a little point, in that by hearing it twice one can learn it better, and make a good wind up with it when it comes again at the end. Songs of this A, B, A type are legion—" The Bluebell of Scotland," " The British Grenadiers," " The Minstrel Boy," " The Miller of the Dee," " The Old Folks at Home," and so on. This last shows an artistic difference between the end of the first A, and of its repetition in line 2. Another bit of artistry is in " Robin Adair," where line 4 does not re-produce the whole of A, but only its clinching latter half— the one containing the " Scots snap " (short note followed by longer). A, B, A is a permanent stand-by for all sorts of songs, including those in opera and oratorio.

Composers of music on a larger scale than the song used both the A, B form (known as " Binary ") and the A, B, A (" Ternary "). The majority of the dance pieces of Bach and Handel's suites are in the simple binary form, and so are many of the themes that composers have taken for variations. Nearly all old arias (eighteenth century, e.g.) are in ternary (A, B, A) form.

Before going on to show how these forms became the basis of almost all the great symphonic music, we must see how the early woven music culminated. Vocally, it came to its greatest height around 1600, in masses and madrigals. Then the growth of interest in solo song and opera gradually pushed it out. In instrumental music, counterpoint longer held its own, for there was not a great deal of variety in instruments ; their life seemed to lack the dramatic possibilities that vocal music held. J. S. Bach (born 1685, the same year as Handel) had wrought mightily, and he carried counterpoint to its highest point in the fugue ; so we will briefly consider this before going on to see what happened to A, B and A, B, A in the eighteenth century.

## CHAPTER II

## THE FUGUE

" Fugue " means, literally, " flight." It developed out of early counterpoint, and in Bach's hands came to perfection. To analyse one would be too minute a business ; the chief thing to remember is that the form is so extremely free. Fugue, it has truly been said, is a style rather than a form. Having chosen a subject, and a subsidiary as " counter-subject," you are free to weave with them what you will. As so often in life, when we seem to be most free we have most responsibility, and it takes a fine composer to write a really first-class fugue. (A " double fugue," by the way, is one on two subjects.) Most of the great men tackled it, but Bach specialised in it. The essence of fugue is organic growth out of small material. Often a fugue is grandly filled with elevated emotion, like the " Saints in glory," as S. S. Wesley called the E major one (Bk. 2, No. 9) in Bach's famous set of forty-eight preludes and fugues : or it can be riotously gay, like his " Fugue à la Gigue." (The prelude has usually no organic connection with the fugue, and is not necessary to its well-being. It is more a matter of piquant contrast, as often as not.) Unless a fugue grows it is nothing. Any student can construct one. I have made dozens—and, thank heaven, burnt them. Most people, when they have got the flavour properly, like a good fugue.

Appreciation of its *build* plays perhaps a larger part than in other forms ; and to this, as to all music that has no connection with literary ideas, the remark that " the music itself is the meaning " firmly applies. Try any of Bach's " 48," the " Kyrie " from his Mass, Mendelssohn's piano fugues, and his " Lord, our Creator " from " Elijah," Handel's " He trusted in God," and the " Amen " chorus, both from " Messiah," the wonderful finale from Mozart's " Jupiter " symphony, the one in Franck's " Prelude, Chorale and Fugue," or the last movement of Bloch's (modern) Concerto Grosso. Several of these are recorded.

# CHAPTER III

# "FIRST MOVEMENT" FORM

BACH CARRIED the art of counterpoint, and the forms that had so far been cultivated, as far as they would go. Others were experimenting with the adventures, still contrapuntal, but organically different, of two contrasted themes. One seminal experimenter was C. P. E. Bach, a son of the great J. S. From these experiments came all the Haydn-Mozart-Beethoven symphonic developments. Out of the two ideas, A, B, and A, B, A, grew what we call either " first movement " or " sonata " form. The latter name is misleading, because a whole sonata has (nearly always) three or four movements, and to call one by the name of the whole is unwise. So think of the form I am about to describe as " first movement form," because it almost invariably is used for the opening movement of a large-scale work of the sonata and symphony order.

The sonata's first movement is a growth from two roots—" subjects," as we call them. There is no need for anyone who does not wish it to go closely into the form, but here is an outline of it for those who care to observe the nature of this, one of the greatest of forms, and one of the commonest in a great many kinds of music : for besides making the opening movement of sonatas, quartets, symphonies, and (with modifications) concertos, it is used for overtures and for other single-movement works.

Broadly, it is divisible into three sections : the exposition, development (or "free fantasia") and recapitulation ("reprise"). For anyone wishing to mark the divisions, the end of the first is the easiest to spot. In most older works there is a very strong dividing line, both in ink and in feeling, when the exposition is ended. That is useful for the listener, for a "first movement" may last from say seven to fifteen minutes. In early listening one is inclined, often, to think that the exposition has finished before it has. In this opening section are exhibited the two chief "subjects" (the second of which sometimes proliferates into a little group of ideas), in whose growth and life-story the composer is interested. They are in contrasted keys, and here comes in the value to the hearer of the feeling for key, and, above all, of memory. The old composers gave a double chance of memorising at least the broad shapes of their subjects, for they had the whole of this "Exposition" repeated. Usually conductors and sonata and quartet players miss out the repeat, but you should look out in case they play it.

To connect his subjects and round off their presentation there are several artistic passages and devices of which, as this is not a text-book, I omit mention. I want to give a sketch plan for the newcomer to the form, and detail would only clutter that up.

Next comes the big B section of the first movement—the Development. The name, and the alternative one of "free fantasia," describe it. Here the drama of the two subjects' life begins to unfold. The marvels of composers' insight and creative skill in this section are delightful exceedingly— and awesome, to those who have ever tried to write such a section. After sufficiently playing the god to his creatures, the composer comes to his last section, which is broadly A again (the subjects now in the unity of one key), but (in later music) with much subtle variety. The main idea, however, is to round off the symmetry of the form. Beethoven, not content with mere repetition, sometimes used development copiously even in his last section (the " Recapitulation ")—and, occasionally, in his first. He has well been called " the liberator."

No amount of writing about music is any use unless you hear it. If you can play, or get a friend to play, almost any Haydn, Mozart, or Beethoven first movement, you will not have much difficulty in marking out its form. Probably nearly every pianist will have a book of Beethoven's piano sonatas (he certainly ought to have, even if he can only scramble through them!). As there should be no difficulty in getting hold of someone to play a pretty easy one (I am presuming throughout that readers are non-players— which I hope will not offend those congratulatable people who play), I run through the first movement of Op. 49, No. 2, in G (the twentieth of the great series of thirty-two). In spite of its number, which is misleading (see later, on Opus numbers), it is an early work, and not very meaty. I choose it because the lines of its form are so easy. First subject, bars 1–20. The rippling last five bars (the ripple figure is from bar 1) are the method of leading to the second subject, bars 20–52 (the double bar). Here is illustrated a frequent feature of subjects, notably of second ones —their having more than one limb. This one has three : 20–36 (note the clear key-change at 20 and the change of *mood*) ; 36 (where the music starts to ripple down-scale) to 49 ; and 49–52, a few bars of " little coda " (" codetta "), which introduce a neat little element of unity by using the ripple noted at bar 15. This is the Exposition. The Development of the ideas is very short—bars 53–67. Key management is worth watching in developments. I need not detail the keys touched here, but you will feel the pleasant variety of minor keys, after the major exposition. Even in so short a development, there is a pretty putting together of two rhythms, bar 53 having that of bar 1, and bar 54 that of the second subject (bar 21).

At bar 67 the Recapitulation starts, and the second subject comes at 87 (in key G this time, like the first, which incidentally is shortened).

In any stylish first movement there are numerous little enjoyments for the observant, and one of the legitimate pleasures of the music-lover is in spotting and tasting these ; but of course nobody is obliged to learn to do that if he does not want to. Occasionally people say that such interest spoils the general pleasure in the music. This is twaddle, which I was sorry to find a literary man writing in the "Radio Times" just before I tackled this chapter. Only very simple people would be frightened by that bogey. Why are literary men so often stupid about music ? There are honourable exceptions, like Arnold Bennett, Gordon Bottomley, and Compton Mackenzie, but the level of gumption about our art is low. It is, of course, only an index of the esteem in which it is held by so-called educated people, and an indication of how much music-lovers have to do if we are to become a musically sensitive race.

First movement form can be combined with others, notably with the rondo (described below) or the fugue. These are high matters, which can be found expounded in such books as Macpherson's "Form in Music," a good solid but simple book for those who know their way about just a little. In Beethoven's last days he was working forward to a reshaping of forms, breaking old moulds and imagining new. Few composers since his day have done much for form. Elgar is one of the most remarkable. To attempt to analyse his symphonies on old lines is to find confusion. He works with groups of subjects, and his detail is complex, though the design is clear, as in all great work it must be.

## CHAPTER IV

# THE REST OF THE SONATA

BEFORE saying a word about the other three movements in a sonata or symphony, it may be useful to mention that " sonata " was at first the name of a short piece in a slightly developed A, B form. Domenico Scarlatti is one of the best remembered writers of these. The name (from the Italian word for " sounding ") was given to these early instrumental pieces as distinguishing them from " cantatas "—sung pieces. There is just one by-use of the word " symphony " that is worth noting : the term is loosely used for the instrumental introduction to a song, or the interlude between the verses : but this need never confuse you.

Handel's and Bach's sets of pieces were suites (" Partitas " means the same thing). These, based on dance forms, had as the four pillars (with others added at choice) the Allemande, Courante, Sarabande and Gigue. Bach's " French " and " English " keyboard suites, his orchestral suites, and Handel's harpsichord sets, contain some very attractive short pieces, shapely in their simple form (rooted in the A, B model), sometimes, as in the Sarabande, impressive in their feeling, at others, as in the Gigue, overflowing with effervescent spirits. The suites lack key-variety : that important element was to do its leavening work later, but the variety of time and pace and mood in its movements made the suite an artistic entity.

The simplest demonstration of a small-scale development of the A, B, A form is found both in suites (though not very commonly) and in the later sonata. It is the movement known as the Minuet, which alone of the old suite movements lived on in the sonata, for long unchanged, until Beethoven gave it new life as the Scherzo. You often find it named as " Minuet and Trio," the trio being the middle (B) section—so called because at one time, for contrast, it was played by three instruments instead of the full band. The minuet, then, is usually the third movement of the sonata or symphony or string quartet. To make the minuet movement size up rather better to the others, the A part of it is often a complete little *a, b, a* by itself. An artistic device often employed, also, is to round off the piece, after the repetition of the first section, with a short tailpiece (hence its name, " coda "—" tail "). Codas are common in all kinds of movements.

A fuller development of the A, B, A idea became popular as the last movement of the sonata's four—the Rondo, so called because one subject comes round several times. A, B, A, C, A is the basic plan. Key balance becomes important and effective in a longish movement such as this. Haydn's " Gipsy Rondo " is an old friend of that type. A song often broadcast, Purcell's " I attempt from love's sickness to fly," is a simple example of the charming variety-in-unity that this symmetrical form produces. The form of the finale was not fixed : it could be in " first movement " form, but a change was most often felt to be best, and the rondo nicely provided that.

The second movement is almost always the slow one (rarely, this and the minuet change places, the latter coming second). Here the form is usually some style of A, B, A—often, its simple extension into A, B, A, B, A ; or it might be a set of variations, with which Haydn and Mozart not infrequently delight us. Occasionally we get " first movement " form here, usually somewhat compressed.

A word may be said about " cyclical form." Strictly, this means any form in several movements, such as the symphony or suite ; but the term is also more closely used (particularly by d'Indy) to describe the growth of the material of several different movements from simple germ-matter common to all. Though we find thoughts from one movement being used in a later one of the same work, quite a long way back in " classical " times—by Haydn, Mozart and Beethoven—Franck was the composer who made the most closely-knit and extended use of the idea. His violin sonata and his symphony are beautiful examples.

This is only an outline of a few leading designs, as simple as it can be made. Subtleties and developments have been going on for the last hundred years and more. Beethoven was the greatest experimenter, and no one else brought off so many successes. Towards the end of his life he was breaking the old moulds of form, and if he had lived longer (he died in 1827, at the age of 57) he would have found still greater, significant beauties in musical architecture allied to feeling and philosophy. If Wagner had taken to symphonic writing, he might have carried on Beethoven's torch—or rather, taken a light from it for a great procession of his own. There are hints of this in the way he seemed to be trying in the " Siegfried Idyll." The greatest experimenters since his day are Strauss, Elgar and Sibelius. The Book on orchestral music will take you further on to modern forms and ambitions. The cheapest, most sensible short discussion of modernity that I know is Gerald Abraham's, in " This Modern Stuff " (Archer, 2s. 6d.)[1]

# CHAPTER V

# SOME DEFINITIONS AND TECHNICALITIES

WE MAY as well gather up one or two definitions. When they are so brief, they must necessarily be bald and omit mention of details and exceptions. Sonatas are for one or two players. A symphony is a sonata for the orchestra ; a string quartet, quintet, trio, sextet, octet, and the like is a sonata for string players.

The " Concerto Grosso " (roughly, Handel and Bach period) uses a small body of soloists ("concertante ") over

[1] Since Mr. Anderson wrote the above, we have been given Mr. Constant Lambert's " Music Ho ! " (Faber, 10s. 6d.).—Ed.

against the main body (" ripieno ")—fine counterpointing. A modern work so entitled is usually just a suite, like Bloch's " Concerto Grosso " : the distinction between soloist-body and main-body has disappeared. The later " concerto " (broadly, from Haydn onwards) throws more limelight (too much, sometimes) on one or two soloists (nearly always one), and assumes modified symphonic shape, with three movements instead of the symphony's normal four. The middle movement is the slow one, the Minuet being omitted. Its " first movement " form is modified, to give the soloist-protagonist a dramatic life over against the orchestra's : so that besides the drama in the life of the subjects, we get that of these two protagonists. A double concerto is for two soloists and orchestra. Brahms's, for violin and 'cello, is a noble example.

Beethoven's later Minuet movements became Scherzos, the formal court dance bursting into a wider, more human and lively world.

A few points about the naming and numbering of works may be welcome. " Opus numbers " (meaning the order-number of the work) are the familiar method of identifying compositions : we speak of Beethoven's Op. 12, and so forth. There may be a few people of like mind with the newly-rich engager of a famous orchestra, who pleaded for a programme of " good *pop'lar* stuff : none o' them Ops ! " : but they will not be among the readers of this book. Some works have nicknames, which are handy ; but if they were multiplied, who could remember them all ? We should get confused. Nicknames are pleasant and friendly, so long as we do not imagine they necessarily have anything to do with the music's " meaning." Sometimes (rarely) they were given by the composer : more often, by publishers or music-lovers. The titles of Mendelssohn's " Songs without Words " are, with one or two exceptions, not his. Handel's famous " Harmonious Blacksmith " variations had nothing to do with the toil of the smithy : the piece is simply one movement of a suite, without any special significance (it is not even a particularly interesting set of variations ; Handel never attempted much in that line). The title was stuck on, many years later, by a publisher who wanted to attract buyers. Legends gather round other works, such as his "Water Music," which was *not* written to appease an offended monarch.

Musicians sometimes warn people against titles : that is because they think of instrumental music in terms of its own life, which is not that of words. To think thus is the only real way of " being musical," as we say ; but it may take time, and many people like, at first, to attach imaginative pictures to music to which the composer gave us no verbal clue. There need be no harm in this (modern psychology takes full account of the weaving of fantasies), so long as it is realised that it is, as it were, an elementary way of regarding the music, to be grown out of when we get widening experience of the real nature of the art. The use of attractive titles for children's music, obviously, can be helpful.

As to Op., note that works consecutively numbered were not always written in that order. Part of the numbering was sometimes done after the composer's death, or he was careless. This may be a nuisance, and even at times a snare ; if, for example, one expects an Op. 125 to be an advance in style on an Op. 10. The numeration is more usually that of publication than of composition. Sometimes we find " Op. posth."—a work published after the composer had died.

Several works (and long ones) may be included in one Opus number—as in Beethoven's violin and piano sonatas, Op. 12, Nos. 1, 2 and 3, and his much-played set of six string quartets comprising Op. 18. I know a composer who numbers his works according to the year : all he wrote in 1933, for instance, would be Op. 33, No. 1, 2, or whatever is its order in the year's output. At this rate he will be a long time reaching Op. 100. The numbering system was late in being adopted. For some time systematisation was poor. Handel, to judge by it, would appear to have written only about three works ! In Haydn's and Mozart's time it was getting into shape. Mozart has a special system of enumeration, which is the most authoritative—Köchel's : so his are known as " K. numbers." He wrote, for example, several symphonies in the key of D, but the number " K. 181 " places one of these with certainty, distinguishing it from all the rest.

Music's technical terms are sometimes described by thoughtless people as " repulsive." Of course they are no more repulsive than those of engineering, fencing, architecture, or any other art, craft, science or sport. They are used to save time, just as the chemist, wishing to intimate that one molecule of silver nitrate plus one molecule of sodium chloride equals one molecule of silver chloride plus one molecule of sodium nitrate, writes : " $AgNO_3 + NaCl = AgCl + NaNO_3$," and has done with it. Either statement, the one in words or the one in symbols, will naturally be uninteresting to those who do not care about chemistry. Those who do will learn to use the proper terms. That is why in this Book I have used the ordinary musical terms. If one is interested, beauty wakes in everything. If not, not. Why worry about the if nots ? Musicians naturally hope that everybody will " take to " music, each in his own way ; and according to the measure of his particular kind of interest, he will either get inside it, and like to use its proper terms, or prefer to enjoy it without caring to know how the wheels go round or to criticise. If he wants to discuss it knowledgeably, he will obviously have to learn its terms, but nobody wants to make him do that unless he likes. I have friends of whose talk about radio I cannot understand more than one word in five : but that does not annoy me. My interests happen to lie elsewhere. When I am willing to be instructed, I find them kind to my ignorance. So, I hope, will others find musicians, when the technique of *their* art comes up. Everybody to his liking. It would be a pity if so grand a thing as music were made the means of trying to dragoon people. The only " duty " we have towards it and its reputable practitioners, I take it, is to respect them, as we should respect any other art and those who through it offer us a means of enlarging life.

A general word about all technical difficulties. I have often thought what a pity it is that every layman should not have *some* musician to whom he can go for an explanation of anything that puzzles him. That is one reason why it is so pleasant to keep in touch with musicians, through personal lessons, if possible (occasional " consultation " ones are useful), or through membership of an orchestra or choir. There are now plenty of good musicians who are willing to teach whatever a layman wants, so that he need not necessarily go through any pre-fixed course. All the better if he cares to start at the foundations, but musicians know how to cut coats according to cloth, and can cater for any wants. Even a few lessons can stimulate interest enormously : so can making music in a choir or a band. Often, in that way, one can get lessons free : the observant person can pick up a great deal through mixing with music-lovers ; and professionals are really friendly people, though sometimes shy.

# INTERLUDE:

## PROGRAMME MUSIC

THERE IS one broad classification of music which forms
so pretty a battle-ground that music-lovers still get endless
fun out of it. It is the distinction between what we call
" absolute music " and " programme music " ; that is,
instrumental music (music with words is, broadly speaking,
ruled out here) which on the one hand has no story behind
it, and that which is based on some story or poetic background, or seeks to suggest in any way extra-musical ideas.
Mr. Julius Harrison, in his Book on the orchestra, will
be dealing with this topic, because a great deal of modern
orchestral music is programmatic ; so I will merely put out
the data briefly, and ask you to decide for yourself. The
fullest book on the subject is Niecks's " Programme Music "
(Novello).

First, programme music arises from the natural delight
of man in story-telling. Composers early tried it, long before
their instruments were suited to it. Even William Byrd,
that great master, born nearly four hundred years ago,
wrote " Mr. Byrd's Battell "—for a keyboard instrument
with a tiny tone ! While remembering that programme
music is, strictly, music without words, we may note that
early madrigalists showed the same liking for description :
there is even a vocal Battle (Jannequin's). As you might
expect of British composers, the weather, as a " programme " topic, was not forgotten. Some early programme
music you can try for yourself if you get one of the sets
of Kuhnau's " Bible Pieces " (Novello). They describe
such scenes as David slaying Goliath, and many of their
strokes are clever as well as naïve.

But broadly speaking, there were not sufficient means
for making effective programme music, until the orchestra
grew up. From that time a large proportion of orchestral

music has been programmatic, since romanticism in music became self-conscious, round about the late eighteenth century and the early nineteenth. Think of that period's wonderful efflorescence of romantic poetry and prose, from Percy's " Reliques," through the " shudder " school of " The Castle of Otranto," Mrs. Radcliffe, " Monk " Lewis, up to Scott, Byron, Shelley, Keats, and the rest of the great tribe : with Goethe, Schiller, Rousseau, Hugo, Dumas père : with the painter Delacroix, and a score of others. Musically, you will mark it notably through German romanticism in Weber.

There are all kinds of programme music, from delicate mood-suggestion to frankly imitative music. Broadly speaking, the feeling of music-lovers is that music that is largely imitative is seldom worthy. There are highly descriptive moments in such a masterpiece as Richard Strauss's " Till Eulenspiegel's Merry Pranks," but they matter least : the mastery lies in suggestion, and in the beauties of the music's structure, rather than in the exciting quality of particular strokes. In Beethoven's " Pastoral " symphony, we have both painting (a little), and mood-evocation (much) : and the latter, not the former, is the source of the music's chief delight.

I cannot see why music written with some literary background in mind need be less valuable than that which arises out of " purely musical emotion," if such a thing be possible. (It is arguable that it is not : that all art must well up from *some* human experience, however " purely "— that is, in its own particular terms of shape and form—it seeks expression.) Two things seem worth noting : that it is unfair to expect programme music to be as effective when one does not know its story as when one does ; and that, above all, a good story cannot make up for poor music. If these considerations are held well in mind, we may thoroughly enjoy both programme music and absolute music. The former, indeed, may need more attention, since we have to take in the story as well as the music, and also to decide how far the two hang together.

One thing that musicians think important is that if a composer gives no title to a work, one must, in order to appreciate it fully, learn to think of it in *his* terms, not those of some other art : that is, while many people—probably the majority of us—like at times to day-dream about absolute music, it is only fair to the composer to realise that when he gives no story, he is thinking of his work in terms of its own life : and it takes time for us to understand what those terms are. That, indeed, is a good part of the process of musical education. Whatever the composer may have been moved by, to cause him to compose, he is not bound to communicate that, except so far as the music itself tells us. Nothing is gained by clapping unauthorised titles or stories upon works, and the music is often obscured thereby. Names need do no harm : some people find them useful in remembering works. Musicians, naturally, remember music by its sound.

It is very difficult in a few lines to plead the seminal importance to the serious music-lover of believing what Sir John McEwen has well stated : " Whilst language seeks to express a meaning, *music is itself the meaning*." Whether that meaning can arise without reference to any human feeling, you may doubt ; and it is a matter of experience, for the listener to train himself to hear music without translating it into the terms of other arts. That is why it is a pretty big adventure to take in a symphony that may last forty or fifty minutes, and tells no story but that of the beauty of form and musical emotion. I admit that I have no sure solution of the question " *Is* there such a thing as purely musical emotion ? " Some extremist musicians argue that by keeping " emotion " (undefined) out of their works they have done something particularly meritorious. Yet the great bulk of such music does not seem to be *loved* by anybody, as that of, say, Bach and Beethoven and Brahms and Elgar is loved. And what use is music if it be not loved ?

In musical æsthetics, sharp definitions are often misleading. We find, for instance, the terms " Romantic "

and " Classical " used as dividing music into two categories
—broadly, the modern (say, since round about 1800) is
reckoned " romantic," and the music of Beethoven, Mozart,
Handel, Bach and their predecessors is thought of as
" classical." This is a pity. Romance is the sap that makes
all music live. As in nature, so in music, there are endless
forms and shapes, varying satisfactions and degrees of
emphasis. " Classical " music is not merely that which
places most emphasis on form, and " romantic " that
which stresses feeling more : that definition is too hard-
and-fast. Romance runs through the older music, but it is
mostly more restrained ; though dramatic and romantic
feeling can be readily felt in a great deal of old music—
look at the charming romance of Farnaby's music for
virginals of three centuries ago, the deep sense of musical
drama Bach shows in his great B minor Mass, Handel
in " Messiah," Mozart in the G minor symphony—
magnificent drama, without any programme. You cannot
draw any easy line between " romantic " and " classical."
One thing may be noted : that with the strong infusion of
poetry, romance became self-conscious, towards the late
eighteenth century : and to mark this development of
self-consciousness is about as far as it seems useful to go,
in dividing music into periods. Those who have the best
background of historical understanding will best trace the
reasons for changes in musical outlook. We can gather,
from reading social history, the way in which musicians,
like other artists, were once the servants of princes, and
rarely had great culture, outside their art : note how this
system broke up, and how composers became better
educated, more men of the world, more literary-minded
(hence the development of " programme music "), more
ready explorers of possible new worlds. The older composers
had much to do in foundation-laying and the architectural
planning of the world of composition as they saw it opening
up. The later comers had more leisure to decorate, and
splendidly developing tools and apparatus, in the wealth
of instrumental invention and the possibilities of new

combinations and permutations, alike of forces and of form.

The thought I would like to leave with those who happen not to have heard a great deal of music is just that " classical " composers were as human as the " romantics." It was only their ways of expression that differed. The varying emphasis which they put on this or that means of expression does matter greatly : but it would be a thousand pities if anyone could nowadays grow up with such a fallacious idea in mind as " Classical music is dull : romantic music, exciting." Each has its special beauties, and the complete music-lover enjoys them all.

# D. THE ORCHESTRA AND OTHER INSTRUMENTS

## CHAPTER I

## HOW THE ORCHESTRA BEGAN

"THAT AT WHAT TIME ye hear the sound of the cornet, flute, harp, sackbut, psaltery, dulcimer and all kinds of musick . . ." Thus Nebuchadnezzar commanded the orchestra meet for the worship of his golden image. It sounds rather like the list of instruments with which is worshipped, in these more enlightened days (and nights), the golden calf. Nebuchadnezzar's orchestra was, perhaps, not quite as bad as it sounds ; he suffered at the hands of the translators, and his band probably consisted of the shofar (the ceremonial cow's-horn trumpet), the pan-pipes, familiar to us, not so many years ago, in the hands of the Punch and Judy man or the one-man band, together with a sort of guitar, a harp, a psaltery (a fingered dulcimer : the toy-shop type is much the same, though hammered), and the bagpipe. One would give much to have heard it, or that curious collection in Henry VIII's band—fourteen trumpets, ten trombones, four drums, two viols, three flutes, a bagpipe and four tambourines. Jazz orchestration is not new ! But probably these were not all played at once.

So one might quote many more instances of the heterogeneous collections of instruments that made up the early orchestras. Like a good many other handmaids of art, bands " just growed," and Topsy-growth sometimes produces topsy-turvy proportions.

Though bands of instrumentalists have existed ever since man learned how to make an instrument (getting the hint, likely enough, from the wind in the trees, from twanging a stretched ligament, or from banging upon the skull of a departed enemy) and in due time, with the growth of the social sense, decided it was good fun to twang or blow or scrape or bang with his fellows, we can see at once that instruments were heavily handicapped, in comparison with the voice, from the start of the race. The voice did not need to evolve mechanically ; it was just as ready for its Verdi or Wagner, its Battistini or Caruso, in the year dot as in the nineteenth century : but the music was not there. Instruments have developed—the violin family from the early " fiddles " and later viols : the wind through the inventions of such men as Boehm and Sax, the latter a recent and notable benefactor, even though he *did* give life to the saxophone tribe. Most instruments began by playing music that was written for singing, since this was for generations the dominating form of the art ; and in the period of elaborate vocal writing, much of it was out of the reach of simply constructed instruments.

In all arts invention and æsthetic development have gone hand in hand—or perhaps I should say, pacing : now one, now the other, taking the lead. Someone invents a new stunt in composition, or wants a new timbre, and an inventor produces an instrument to give it. The new capabilities of the instrument inspire another composer to try its player's powers still higher ; and so the mutual encouragement goes on.

Here I can only sketch a few broad lines. In the dimmest days orchestras may be said to have begun at the tail end, with the drum. The fluctuation of the orchestra's constitution has not entirely been due to the varying nature of the material at hand, though that has shaped it a good deal. The bands of some nations have remained almost unchanged through the ages, and we Westerners are as far from understanding their music as ever we were. Anyone who remembers the Chinese orchestra at the Wembley Exhibition will recall the feeling of being desperately at a loss for some thread of connection with our own musical expression. We note. by the way, in the Eastern music the persistence of the affection for the percussion instruments, probably the earliest of all mankind's accompaniments to song and the dance.

Dr. F. H. Wood has happily likened the evolution of the Western orchestra to some Grand Nationals : many the starters, but few the survivors.

What a crowd of instruments has fallen at one time or another ! Those lutes, rebecs, viols, recorders, psalteries, shawms and chalumeaus, bagpipes, portable organs, pipes and tabors, sackbuts, ophicleides, the wooden cornets, the serpent, the hunting-horns—all have gone through the testing fire of time, and either emerged in fuller glory, or been scrapped. Some, like the chalumeaus and shawms, have been refined almost out of knowledge into our present-day wood-wind reed instruments ; others, like the drums, have drubbed their sturdy way, almost unaltered, through the whole great procession. The old viols have become the more subtle instruments of the string quartet (not forgetting the noble double-bass, which, banished from that gentle company, save when a Schubert or a Dvořák reaches out a friendly hand for its help, has its compensation by lording it in the depths of the orchestra). The old limited horn and trumpet have valved their way, in the hands of extra-ordinarily skilful players, into a new lease of life, which promises to be eternal.

# CHAPTER II

# THE STRINGS

OUT OF the score or so of starters in the instrumental Grand National, one family group has curiously outpaced the rest. In the full orchestra of to-day about two-thirds of the instruments are stringed ones, but it has been argued that the proportion is wrong. The strings, in one form or another—lyre, lute, harp, fiddle, guitar—have reigned, singly or in battalions, from the wonderful days five thousand years ago, which Egyptologists are reconstructing for us. Ur of the Chaldees reveals the constructive artistry that links us to the past. They loved beautiful, shapely instruments then, as we do now. But nothing can give us the sound of the Egyptian harp and guitar, the Greek lyre, or the Arabic rebab, the first instrument to be sounded by a bow : for Egypt never heard bowed strings. Chaucer rhymed of the rebec or rubible, and Milton of the " jocund rebecks."

The smaller plucked strings could not hold their own in the orchestra, and only the harp survived. Up from the little rebec, with its pear-shaped body and three noisy strings, grew the viol family, and from them the violins. The viols, from the fifteenth to about the middle sixteenth century, had the mastery, and about the time when the madrigal was going out, the viols, so much cultivated in Tudor and Stuart times, went out too, as far as popular use was concerned. By radio we can still enjoy the gentle beauties of the older strings, at the hands of such people as the Dolmetsch family, the Misses Chaplin, and the French Casadesus combination (Société des Instruments Anciens). British performers and instruments were pre-eminent in the days of the viols. Their music was essentially chamber music. Peacham, in his " Compleat Gentleman," gives a charming picture of the period. In passing, may I smite the ancient lie about the Puritans' hating music ? I have not space to go into this, but Dr. Percy Scholes's book on the subject (Oxford U.P.) disposes of the slander once for all.

The new violin tribe from Cremona came at the right time : thus it is that creations survive—with a bit of luck, and the right constitution. Amati, Gasparo da Salo, Stradivari are names we reverence. (I *must* quote the label inside a violin, about the genuineness of which the opinion of the editor of a musical journal was asked : " My violin says inside, ' Antonius Stradivarius Cremonensis faciebat

1717. Made in Czecho-Slovakia.' Is it a Strad?" Alas, what crimes have been done in that name!)

The strings remain supreme, in their five orchestral types—violins (first and second play the same sort of instrument) ; violas (longer, with thick strings : compass a fifth lower than the violin : that is, to C in the middle of the bass-clef staff) ; violoncellos, going down an octave lower than the violas ; and double-basses, an octave lower still. It is astonishing how much can be got out of a string quartet (two violins, viola, 'cello), and the orchestral strings alone. For a good example of the latters' powers, listen to Elgar's " Introduction and Allegro," or the Scherzo of Tchaikovsky's fourth symphony. For ethereal and mysterious effects, listen to the prelude to " Lohengrin," and the strings' accompaniment to the solo violin's cadenza in the Elgar violin concerto.

# CHAPTER III

# WOOD-WIND, BRASS, AND PERCUSSION

WIND-INSTRUMENTS are classified broadly as wood-wind and brass. The wood includes the flue pipes, simply blown through (flute and piccolo), and the reed pipes, in which the breath sets the reed (a slip of cane) into vibration, and so starts the air-column into life. Of the reeds, there are the single (of which the clarinet is the chief) and the double-reed type, which the oboe most readily represents ; and each type, single and double, has its small family. Family life is the essence of the orchestra's existence, and one has to remember that when writing for it, making each group's harmony complete, as a rule. A beautiful example to mankind is the orchestra—families living in peace and personal dignity, self-contained and working together for good.

We may list the orchestral wind, in the order in which a score presents them, as : *Wood*—piccolo, flutes, oboes, clarinets, bassoons ; *Brass*—horns, trumpets, trombones (these in three sizes) and their bass, the tuba. There are special varieties of most of these, such as the bass flute, the cor anglais (an alto oboe, well named, save that it is not *cor*, a horn, and not English) ; there are alto and bass clarinets, double bassoon, a special trumpet for very high parts, and other wonders, strange to see and hear. In the normal orchestra we get along with two each of the wood-wind (but only one piccolo), four horns, three trumpets and three trombones. As we shall note in a little, Haydn and Mozart managed with a good deal less.

Some of these instruments have their roots in antiquity : who shall say, for instance, when man first blew into a flue pipe ? Others were invented quite recently—the clarinet, for example, unknown before 1690. The flute is of extreme antiquity. The oboe was also known of old. Old English shawms were primitive, coarse-toned oboes. The bassoon is nine feet long, and has to be doubled on itself to be made wieldy. Bassoons can sound either weird (Handel's Witch of Endor, in " Saul," is thus characterised) or comical, as in the " Village Festival " in the " Pastoral " symphony of Beethoven.

The oldest brass instrument had as ancestor a curved animal-horn. Thence the cavalry trumpet, bugle and simple hunting-horn, perfected to a marvel in the modern French horn of the orchestra, perhaps the supremely difficult instrument to play well. Its big-belled, close-curved conical tube looks so simple. With the warm sweetness of its matchless voice, it is born to sing, not bellow, though it can menace magnificently at need. Trumpets anciently denoted high dignity in prince or city. The scale of the simple tube was very incomplete. Slides helped it out. The trumpet of to-day, with its three pistons, masters any scale more nobly than the cornet, its humbler, thicker-toned, perky relation. The alto, tenor and bass trombones (with slides, but no pistons) carry the trumpet tone down to the depths, the bass tuba threatening *de profundis*. Saxophones have their happiest place in the military (brass and wind) band, or, for fun, in a dance combination.

Drums attract us from a very early age. So, probably, did they primitive man. It was so easy for him to make one. The side drum, big drum and tambourine simply mark rhythm. Their note is indeterminate. So ought the triangle's to be, and sometimes it is not. Bells, bars, and other chiming relishes come into modern scores. The best known are Mustel's celeste, harmonium-like, in which steel plates, with resonators below them, are struck by hammers actuated by the keys, and the glockenspiel, a range of steel bars struck with hammers held in the hands. It was the celeste that Tchaikovsky discovered when writing his " Casse Noisette " suite. He had a small triumph in keeping it dark for a while, and so being the first to use it – in the "Sugar-Plum Fairy's Dance." Two kettle drums ("timpani" —with two i's) suffice most composers, but three are not uncommon, and Berlioz, who revelled in masses, asks for four to play awesome chords, in his " Fantastic " symphony. Beethoven was the first to use the timpani with outstanding significance.

# CHAPTER IV

# THE ORCHESTRA GROWS

In orchestral writing, some instruments found their independence slowly. The 'cellos and double-basses, for instance, ran in a restricting handcuffed race, playing mostly from one part, until Beethoven gave them a line apiece. When the variety of instruments was small, and they were, some of them, far from perfect—and often imperfectly played—not much subtlety in their use could be attempted. Wood-wind doubled the strings. The orchestra was then happiest in accompanying opera or oratorio, where the quieter moments had their obvious, suitable instruments, the louder ones coming in for exciting doings. The voices were royal, the instruments merely courtiers, not expecting parts thought out according to their individual characters. Monteverdi made a sensation by seeking effects of tone-colour, to suit the drama, round about 1600. Before this, a small family of lutes (something like a large mandoli.e, with many strings and a long neck), supported by a harpsi-chord (the piano's predecessor), with possibly a viol or two, and a flute on occasion, comprised an average orchestral force. Monteverdi not only added more strings, wood-wind, trumpets and trombones, but experimented to find dramatic life for the band. The keyboard instrument held its place for a good while, but the bowed strings became so much more flexible and expressive that the percussed-string instru-ment dropped out. Oboes and bassoons (developed from the old schalmey and pommer) claimed equality with them in Handel's orchestra, and we cannot imagine this to have been really very nice, because their tone was rather coarse. Now these wood-winds have settled down to the pair system, like the flutes and clarinets. The need for balance, colour and contrast decided that. Rameau, Handel's con-temporary, schemed and experimented, and in the mid-eighteenth century Gossec was a great orchestral preceptor and house-orderer. Haydn's symphonies, demanding finer finish and a higher social sense from the instruments, spring-cleaned all. Even then, first-class skill in fiddling was rare enough. Mozart's exquisite sensibility demanded yet more from his orchestral players, and earlier Gluck had encour-aged subtlety. As the eighteenth century wears out, we find the complete wood-wind used (except for the clarinets, not common yet)—all in pairs ; together with horns and trum-pets and drums, also in pairs ; these being balanced by a small force of strings, about two-thirds of the whole. In Beethoven's time the clarinets had taken their regular place, a third horn (in the " Eroica " symphony), and then a fourth (in the " Choral ") had appeared, and the trombones, used by his opera-writing predecessors, two centuries before (when they were already centuries old), had at last come, towers of strength, into the symphonic orchestra. Their debut, in the finale of the fifth symphony, was grandeur indeed ! Beethoven's horn and trumpet parts were sadly limited by the capacities of the instruments in those days ; and orchestral playing in general was mostly poor, well into his time.

Haydn is called the real " Father " of the orchestra ; Berlioz fathered a new, brilliant generation of orchestrators —Liszt, Strauss, Tchaikovsky, Rimsky-Korsakov, and nearly all who in the last hundred years have written largely for that marvellous medium. The widening of orchestral scope can be marked if we record that Haydn, beginning with strings, drums, and " two up and two down " (four wind, that is), later had six or eight wood-wind, and four brass. The typically developed Beethoven used ten wood and seven brass : Strauss, in the " Domestic " symphony (1904), twenty-two wood and sixteen brass. One or two harps play an important part in many modern scores, and have done so since the days of Berlioz. Add up to half a dozen percussionists, and about twice the wind total, in strings, ponder the rehearsals needed—and you need not wonder why orchestral concerts do not pay. Nowadays the smaller, " chamber," orchestra is cultivated. It fits the need of purse-thin times.

Most of the books on the orchestra are instruction books for those who want to write for it. One or two general ones may be noted : Carse's "History of Orchestration" (Kegan Paul) ; two finely illustrated volumes about instruments, historically considered, are Hipkins's "Musical Instruments" (Black) and Galpin's "Old English Instruments of Music" (Methuen). A splendid book of pictures, with just a short description of each, is "A History of Music in Pictures" (Dent, 30s.). Emanuel Moor, the inventor of a new type of pianoforte mentioned in the next chapter, has written upon the constitution of the orchestra, which not every musician finds ideal ; and there is an American book, by a writer whose name I cannot verify (I believe it is Redfield), which seeks to show that almost all our instruments are defective. A handy pocket-size book giving the compass and qualities of the instruments is Lyon's "Guide to the Modern Orchestra" (Macmillan, or Stainer & Bell, 1s. 6d.).

The Military Band is a reed and brass-wind band, with drums. Its constitution differs a good deal in various countries, but in general it includes the instruments of the orchestra (excepting the strings), with more clarinets, which have to do much of the strings' work in arrangements, and with saxophones (here really at home), both cornets and trumpets, and rather more heavy brass ; with often a single double-bass (stringed) to give a binding bite.

The Brass Band's name defines its nature. I give the make-up of a typical combination, as set out by Mr. Denis Wright, an expert in these matters : 1 E flat soprano cornet, 3 or 4 B flat solo cornets, 1 B flat ripieno cornet, 1 or 2 B flat second cornets, and 1 or 2 B flat third cornets ; 1 B flat flügel horn, 1 E flat solo tenor horn, 1 E flat first tenor horn and 1 E flat second tenor (these are of the saxhorn family, another of the clever Adolph Sax's inventions) ; 1 B flat first baritone, and 1 B flat second ; 1 or 2 B flat euphoniums ; 1 or 2 B flat first trombones, 1 B flat second, and 1 G bass trombone ; 2 E flat basses (or bombardons), and 2 B flat basses.

It may be noted that the "Radio Times" occasionally gives details of its various bands and choirs, with a note of the particular kind of music for which each combination is used.

## CHAPTER V

# KEYBOARD INSTRUMENTS

THERE REMAIN for brief description the keyboard instruments—those which led up to the modern piano, and the organ and its small brethren. The dulcimer is the proto-type—strings stretched over a sound-board, played with hammers. The toy-shop ones have metal bars. A plucked dulcimer came later, the citole. Chaucer mentions it in the " Knight's Tale."

The first of the keyboard instruments was the clavichord : *clavis*, a key, and *chorda*, a string, shows the new principle of control. Keys had earlier been used for the organ. In the clavichord the strings stretch horizontally above the keys, as in our modern grand piano, and are touched by brass " tangents," one upright at the end of each key. You could have keys of different lengths, whose tangents would strike one string in two or three different places. The tangent acts as does the finger on a fiddle string—cuts off a portion of it ; the tiny sound is high or low according to the length cut off. A charming vibrato could be got by wobbling the finger on the key. In no other keyed instrument is this pos-sible. To hear Arnold Dolmetsch play Bach on the clavi-chord is memorable.

The plucked-string keyboard instrument followed on in popularity, but it is difficult to decide which came first. This is the virginal, or virginals. A bird's quill attached to the upright at the far end of the key twanged the string when the key was pressed down. This instrument, with others of Shakespeare's period, can be heard on Columbia records 5712, 3, 4. Very little could be done to vary the sound, and the quill's noise was unsuppressible. Some virginals were made with the strings upright. The name of this variety was clavicytherium. Nearly everybody seems to have had a virginal. Pepys tells of seeing them being carried down to the boats when the folk were fleeing from the Great Fire. Henry VIII had thirty-eight virginals. He was a whole-saler in music, as in other activities. A name often loosely applied is " spinet." It was just a virginal, its case shaped, like a grand piano to-day, to the length of the strings. It therefore looks like a harp, and was sometimes known as the " couched harp." You will see some beautifully decorated instruments of these kinds in the Victoria and Albert Museum.

The harpsichord was a developed form of spinet. Ist strings were longer, and there were several sets, with different pluckers—leather and quills, so that it had more varieties of tone at command. Many harpsichords had two rows of keys, like an organ, with different strings for each. " Stops," also copied from the organ, were used to stop the sound of one of a pair of strings. The harpsichord gave a good deal of tone, but the mechanical noise was tiresome.

To the Italian Cristofori is paid the tribute of chief honour as the inventor of the modern pianoforte, about 1700. Others were early in the field, and men of this country have produced some of the finest work in the elaborate history of the pianoforte (its name means " soft-loud "—we can see where the new boon lay). From wooden to metal frame, from one beautiful subtlety of the action to another, the piano has gone from strength to strength. Indeed, one wonders if the nine-foot concert grand, with its thirty-ton tension, is not too strong. Certainly it cannot very well give us the true impression of, for instance, how Chopin's music sounded when he played it on the gentler piano of his day. To-day the instrument is sometimes treated as a percussion one—e.g., in Bartok's works, and his playing.

Since the full development of the modern piano, one great boon for the home has been invented—the player-piano, in which a wind system, operating through slits cut in a paper roll, each slit representing a note of the music, allows the keys to be depressed and thus the strings to be sounded in the natural way. Reproductions of the actual performances of fine players can also be obtained,[1] and rolls containing letterpress annotations and pictorial and music type illustrations. A good deal of skill can be employed in playing this instrument, and a few lessons are well worth while. The most distinguished British virtuoso is Mr. Reginald Reynolds, whose subtlety in interpreting a

[1] On some players, however, the listener does nothing except start and stop the record of some artist's performance ; there is no scope for personal expression, as in the ordinary player-piano.—Ed .

fugue on the player-piano is the admiration of all musicians.

The best way to realise the beauties of pianoforte construction is to look into typical instruments for oneself, with the co-operation of any musician or dealer one happens to know, who will be delighted to show how they work. The article " Pianoforte," in Grove's Dictionary, gives details fascinating to the mechanically minded, and likely to inspire in anybody admiration for fine craftsmanship.

The problem of the pianist is to get the closest, most subtly sensitive connection between his muscles and the hammer on the string. Variations from the orthodox mechanism have been devised from time to time. Most of them have sought to make playing easier ; some have attempted to provide keys and strings that would offer more finely tuned effects than can the present eighty keys, with the compromise-tuning of their strings. You can read about some typical efforts in the article " Keyboard," in Grove's Dictionary, the standard storehouse of detailed information. Only one device having more than the usual number of keys has made much impression—that of the Hungarian composer Emanuel Moor, whose Duplex-Coupler piano has two keyboards, enabling fuller effects to be obtained, octaves and larger chords to be played with but a small stretch, etc.

Useful books are Hipkins's " The Pianoforte " (Novello), and Bie's " History of the Pianoforte and Pianoforte Players " (Dent). There is a good short account, with pictures, in " The Story of English Music," an excellent survey from 1604–1904 of our achievement. This is one of the " Music Story " series obtainable from W. Reeves, 83, Charing Cross Road, W.C. 1 ; it consists of a dozen or more companionable books, well illustrated, among the subjects dealt with (one in each volume) being oratorio, notation, the organ, organ music, chamber music, the violin, harp, bagpipe, minstrelsy, form, opera, and the carol.

## CHAPTER VI

# THE ORGAN AND SOME OTHERS

I CONCLUDE this Part with a few words about the organ, the " King of Instruments," as it has been proudly called by its devotees. Without troubling about the order of precedence in the instrumental world, the organ may certainly be hailed as the most remarkable effort of mechanical ingenuity in that realm. The principle of putting together a number of pipes to be blown is very ancient : the syrinx or pan-pipes is referred to in the most ancient times. The last generation was familiar, too, with their sound, at the mouth of the " one-man band " or the performing-bear leader. The Romans had their water-organ, in which the hydraulic power compressed the wind. Mediæval organs were portable, for processional use, a hand bellows supplying sufficient air. Imaginative pictures of St. Cecilia will probably have been seen, which show an angel blowing the organ for her in this manner. It is a cause for high pride that English organ makers have always had a great name for their skill and inventive power. Most church organists are glad to exhibit their instrument's mechanism to interested inquirers. It is not necessary to attempt a description of the astonishing skill that has brought forth such instruments as that erected by the B.B.C. at Broadcasting House, the new Albert Hall organ, or the best of the cinema organs. Descriptions of the marvels of organ construction may be found in numerous books, some of them highly technical : Audsley's " Art of Organ Building," Casson's " The Modern Organ " ; and, simpler, Hinton's " Organ Construction," among many. It is impossible to go into details, but the three types of pipes may just be mentioned. The first is the open flue pipe, in which the wind, coming in at the pipe's foot, is partly obstructed by a block of wood, strikes the lip, and then escapes, some through the opening there, and some through the top of the pipe, the nature of the sound being caused by the impact on the lip and the vibration in the pipe being determined by several factors, so that a remarkable variety of tone is obtainable both from wooden and metal pipes. In stopped flue pipes the principle is the same, save that there is a block of wood in the top of the pipe, which makes the air return down it, producing the effect of a longer pipe, and thus an octave deeper pitch. The third type of production is that of the reed pipe, in which the air entering the foot of the pipe (" boot," as it is called) sets vibrating a slip of brass, the vibrations being duly amplified in the metal or wooden pipe : the principle being, as we note, that of the clarinet.

In old organs the means of connection between the player's finger and the valve controlling the entrance of wind to the pipe was a series of wooden " trackers "— simple levers repeated in series, horizontal and vertical, until the distance was covered. I remember venturing, as a young organist, inside the instrument to mend a broken tracker, with a candle to light my labours ; like enough, to burn a few of these thin sticks, and put my master in no small twitter as to the safety of the church. The majority of later organs had pneumatic action : that is, thin metal tubes run from key to pipe, a tiny puff of air being employed to open the pipe's valve, instead of the considerable finger-pressure often needed in a " tracker " organ. Tracker touch could be very heavy, but one had a fine feeling of intimate contact with the pipe which is lacking in the far lighter pneumatic system. One great advantage of the latter is that the " console " or keyboard may be placed wherever, within reason, one desires it, the length of tube connecting it with the pipes having scarcely any effect on the quickness of their " speech." Electrical action has to some extent replaced pneumatic, the use of tiny electro-magnets to make the contact from key to pipe being an obvious application of the resources of electricity. The " extension " system, by which a comparatively small number of pipes is made to give more extensive and varied effects than formerly, has been a good deal used of late. The B.B.C.'s organ is built on this principle.

The chief external difference observable between old and new organs is in the absence, in many new ones, of the familiar stop-knobs. These began by being large and heavy, and pulling out almost a foot, at right angles to the keyboard. Later they became neat little knobs, with a movement of only an inch or two. Now stop-keys or tablets are common, balanced in the middle, the touch of a finger sufficing to put on or off several of them in quick succession. The arrangement of the stops in a semi-circular row in front of the player has also made management more convenient, in the eyes of most players, though some prefer the old banks at each side of the " manuals " (keyboards). In some modern organs the key-weight is specially balanced so that a slight pressure makes certain pipes sound, a heavier pressure bringing on others ; but this " double touch " is not common in church organs.

" The Story of the Organ " is interestingly told by Abdy Williams in the " Music Story " series book of that name (Reeves). The considerable bulk of an organ, and the dispersion of its pipes, make it difficult, obviously, to convey the full tone of all and the ideal balance, so that it is favourably heard by the listener seated in a hall. There are certain factors in the building up of organ tone, also, which make it less easy to grasp than that of the orchestra : the fact that many pipes sound one or more octaves higher or lower than others, and that some stops—" mixtures "— supply not only the melody note played by the organist, but also other notes higher in pitch—these representing the " harmonics " which are present, much more softly, when a fundamental note is sounded. (They may be heard if one puts down the right-hand or " loud " pedal of the piano, and strikes a fairly low note.) Some people are apt to dismiss organ tone as " blurry." Some little patience and experience in appreciating its special nature are well worth while. Much depends on the acoustics of the building, and it must be said that a sadly great percentage of churches and public halls were planned by architects ignorant of the art of building a fit house in which music is to be heard. There is no excuse for such ignorance nowadays, the researches of Professor Sabine and of others having provided ample material for the calculation of the acoustics of any kind of building. Anyone who may have to deal with such a problem can get a clear idea of modern knowledge on the subject in E. G. Richardson's " Introduction to the Acoustics of Buildings " (Arnold, 3s. 6d.), and it is greatly to be hoped (though with some doubt) that in future no building in which music is to play an important part will be so built that sound does not have a fair chance in it. If anyone happens to have to deal with a hall that has too much resonance, it may be noted that stringing wires across it has no effect whatever. Broadly speaking, pillars to break up the sound, which is banging about without interruption from one resonating surface to another, or (usually the most practicable method) cloth hangings to absorb it, are the cure. It will be observed that when an audience fills such a hall, the effect of music is better. Their clothes absorb some of the spare resonance. If the hall is large, however, or of certain shapes, the contrivance of suitable hangings may not be easy or cheap ; and laymen cannot always be sure whether hangings are needed. Reference to an expert may be necessary.

A mere word, for the sake of completeness, may be added about what is sometimes called, with insufficient respect for its best representatives, " the 'moanium tribe "—of which the harmonium and the reed organ called (but not in America) the " American organ " are the most familiar members. In these, as most people are aware, metal " reeds " are set into vibration by wind impelled from the bellows by the player's feet, or occasionally by a small motor. The name " Mustel Organ " commemorates an inventor and his two sons who devised new stops and mechanical improvements for the harmonium, besides a new keyboard instrument using tuning forks, their resonance suitably reinforced.

## CHAPTER VII

# INSTRUMENTS OF THE FUTURE

THE COMING of radio has opened up new possibilities of instruments both with and without keyboards. There was an article by Paul Popper on the chief of these in the " Listener " of September 20, 1933. He gave a photograph of the first " electrical orchestra," presented at the Berlin Radio Exhibition of 1932. Thermionic valve principles were applied to the piano and strings, and various other instruments. With this article may be consulted another (" World Radio," February 9, 1934) from which, with acknowledgments, I extract the names of a number of inventions of this nature. " In U.S.A. we find the ' Emicon ' (designed by Langer and Halmagyi) ; in Germany the ' Spherophone ' (by Mager), the ' Hellertion ' (by Helberger and Lertes), and the ' Trautonium ' (by Trautwein) ; in Russia, Theremin's well-known instrument (to which may be added Maurice Martenot's use of the principle, demonstrated at a London cinema early in 1934) ; and in France, Givelet's organ. The ' Emicon,' ' Spherophone ' and Givelet's organ have regular keyboards, and the ' Hellertion,' ' Spherophone ' and Givelet's organ can play several notes at a time. Lertes, Helberger and Trautwein have now pooled their patents, and the result is the new ' Trautonium.' This instrument plays only one note at a time ; it could, however, be made to play more, but that would increase the price and make it more difficult to play. This new ' Trautonium ' is a simple, cheap and reliable instrument, and it seems likely that all further progress in ' electrical ' music will be based on it." It is said that with it " the typical music of almost every instrument in the modern orchestra can be produced." The varying of the frequency of an oscillator gives the notes, which are " fingered " upon a strip of metal provided with a resistance. When it touches the strip, the note is produced—up or down the " keyboard."

To me, the most striking radio instrument (perhaps because it was the first I saw played) was the Russian, Theremin's. Since then several other types have been produced—that of M. Martenot, another that I saw demonstrated in a music-hall show in 1933, and the " Electronde," of which H.M.V. made some records. I see that an instrument of this type was upon the market at eight guineas in February, 1934. Theremin's performance upon his exiguous apparatus seemed almost magical. All that was noted was a vertical rod rising from a small radio box. By bringing the hand into different positions in relation to the rod, the performer, in effect, makes musical the familiar and normally hideous " howl " of interference—a taming of ugliness somewhat after the manner of beating the sword into a ploughshare ! I have just a little doubt whether, when such instruments become cheap, there will be sufficient people with accurate ear to play them. The degree to which we are able to tune accurately notes not already fixed for us appears to be settled at birth, and it is my experience, from careful observation over many years, that great numbers of the public appear to notice nothing wrong in out-of-tune playing and singing. The difficulty, of course, already exists in fiddling. I hope that if the new radio instruments are taken up, there will be a strong development of aural training, the first necessity for all who hope to perform music.

Apart from this, the chief difficulty in playing the instruments of this type that I have heard seems to be that of avoiding the unpleasant scoop from one note to another. A report upon M. Martenot's instrument, played by M. Cittanova, comforts us by saying that " there was no wobble, except such tremolo as was intended, and no climbing to the note " (portamento). Also, " legato or staccato was equally defined "—that is, smooth or detached playing. Various tone-qualities were produced—those of the violin, 'cello, trumpet, etc. It was remarked that " they had the sound of the organ-stops of those names, rather than of the instruments themselves."

In passing, it may be observed that the wobble has spoilt much popular music-making (especially singing) of late years. It is, of course, regarded by the educated music-lover as a vice; for while the use of vibrant tone, for expressive purposes, is a valuable element in the art of the singer-interpreter (it is one of the rarer condiments), a persistent wobble is simply an admission either of inability to sing properly, or worse, of a mind hopelessly vulgar and unmusical.

The chief instance of new development in an existing keyboard instrument that we here have heard is the Neo-Bechstein piano, of whose performances gramophone records have been made by H.M.V. The tone of shortened strings, struck in the usual way, is amplified through microphones. A pedal controls volume, much as does the swell pedal in an organ, and thus overcomes the greatest weakness of the normal piano—that its tone begins to die away the instant a string is struck. It is of course questionable how far this instrument can be called a piano at all. We may have to invent new categories, definitions, and standards of judgment for such novelties.

It seems likely that the truthful reproduction of instrumental timbre by radio will quickly be achieved. As I write this chapter I hear from an American friend that experiments in " auditory perspective "—reproduction so that the tone of each instrument appears to emanate from a different and definite spot on the stage—have given cause for satisfaction. Frequencies of from 40 to 15,000 were reproduced, and the range of intensity was far greater than that of any orchestra, with " almost perfect " tone qualities. This development, like that of new instruments, may give new scope to composers.

One other curious instrument may be mentioned, though it is not actually a musical one—the colour organ, by playing upon which the performer causes colours to be thrown upon a screen in pleasing patterns. The variation of pace and size, and of the artistic massing of the colours, enables a great diversity of rhythmic effects to be produced;

abstract painting put into motion. The Russian composer Scriabin intended a colour organ to play its part in one of his last works. Even if analogies may readily be drawn between colour and sound and some people associate keys with colours (though few agree on a classification), there is not sufficient scientific or æsthetic basis for regarding such an association as anything more than a pleasing individual fantasy.

# POSTLUDE:

## ON LEARNING AND PERFORMING

THIS WORK is called a "Companion," and so I insert here what I hope will be taken as the most companionable— that is, helpful—statement I can make to those who, being actual or potential music-lovers, want to "get into music." There must be some such among the readers of this book, though of course a good many are likely to be makers of music already. But those who are not, and who honestly would like to regard music as a hobby : who are willing to put into it a little more than is comprised in buying a radio set, or records—how can I best be companionable to them, and help them, in turn, to be good companions of the art of music ? As I was starting to write this, my eye fell on a paragraph written by my friend Dr. Harvey Grace, editor of the "Musical Times" monthly, and as what I want to say could not be put more briefly or surely, I am going to use his words. He is replying to one who says he is "passionately fond of music," but has never been taught to play : knows nothing of rudiments, and so cannot read a score ; but he wants to do something practical. Self-help is his aim. His adviser says : "Well, we suggest for a start that you should begin by taking lessons in the rudiments and pianoforte playing. Go to a good teacher, explain exactly what you want, and leave the rest to him. As soon as you can read and play a bit, ask him to bring you on in mental reading, ear training, etc. It is a long job, calling for money and work, but don't jib at it. If you are 'passionately fond' of anything, be it a person or an art, you'll be prepared for considerable sacrifices. There is really no other way. If we could honestly say, 'Buy such and such a handbook, read it through, and the job's done,' we would. But we can't.

Anything worth having is worth effort. If you follow our
advice you will in a few years' time bless us for helping you
to a world of beauty and pleasure." And that's that. Books
help, and some good ones are mentioned in these pages.
But they will not make anybody learn anything. Only oneself can do that. And the world is different when one
begins to make something. It is not given to many to
create music ; but to re-create it is a stirring thing. After
all, the composer's thought cannot be said really to live for
us until we bring it to life by instrument or voice.

I would emphasise the advice to take the chosen teacher
into your confidence, and tell him your aims. The day is
past when all pupils were put through the same course.
The best teachers never did that. Teaching is like doctoring.
One prescribes for the individual, and we are all different.
In looking out for a teacher, seek individuality, character,
energy : not necessarily the man reputed to be the most
pushing, or the one whose pupils pass most examinations,
but one who brings out their latent musicianship. There is
no room to go fully into this matter, or into that of the many
worthless diplomas that can be tacked to the name of the
less scrupulous, in a profession not yet fully self-governing.
One set of four letters sounds, to the layman, as good as
another ; but there is a terrible amount of adulteration in
our business. One certain way there is of ensuring a
qualified teacher—find out the local secretary of the big
professional society, the Incorporated Society of Musicians
(I.S.M.). Sometimes the local Press will contain an
omnibus advertisement of all the Society's members
practising in the neighbourhood. If not, consult the
Society's annual Handbook, in the local free library. If
there is any difficulty, write to the Secretary, I.S.M., 19
Berners Street, London. There are some four thousand
members up and down the country, so you should not have
much difficulty in finding someone near enough to your
home, who has been admitted to membership only after
proving his qualifications and experience. In Ireland there
is the Ulster Society of Musicians, with like aims. Take

plenty of time about securing a good teacher, and when you have got one, stick to him or her. It is astonishing what a keen music-lover can learn in even six months, if he goes at it with sense and energy. Nothing that is expounded in this work is meant to deter anyone from getting the best tuition he can : rather it is meant to encourage him to do so, if he wants to learn music, or to continue with studies perhaps dropped years ago. That is a common thing. Why should so many grown up people not be able to recreate themselves at an instrument, or with the voice ? How often one hears, " I had lessons for several years, and then somehow I left off, and now I can't play much. Haven't much time, of course. Read ? No—well, scarcely anything." That last remark is the most revealing of all. I am afraid it reflects on a good deal of past teaching : but maybe the fault was not all on one side. There may have been fond parents who wanted examinations to be taken. Examinations are all very well as occasional tests of progress, but too much is often made of them. Like lots of useful things, they become ends instead of means, and that distorts values. Some people work best when they have a test in prospect ; but we do not put as much emphasis on tests nowadays as we used to do ; and the element of fear or anxiety that they not infrequently engender is foreign to all the aims of an art. Besides, examinations very rarely test adequately the most important quality—musicality : many of the deepest things of music are scarcely testable. Don't make music too much a matter of business or hard " duty." By all means stick in at it, as any conscientious person does at whatever he likes doing ; but don't let its hard work be a penance. There is no " easy way," though modern methods avoid some of the drudgery. Also, more scientifically based, the best of them show, from the start, how to avoid inhibitions, muscular or otherwise. For example, ease in playing largely depends on using only the appropriate muscles, at a particular moment, and ceasing to use the opposing ones. Stiff fingers are loosened thus. Then, we learn the *principles* of fingering, and do not need huge scale books, since from a few scales, templates, we can build all the rest. And so on.

A word or two on performing, for those who have heard of " nerves," may be useful. I am not going to say, after a quarter of a century's teaching and observation, and thirteen years of adjudicating on thousands of entrants at competition festivals, that there is no such thing as " nerves." But though the best artists say they are rarely without a certain keyed-up feeling when performing in public, one does not see them wilting and breaking down. Yet once, very likely, they did. So if ever you do break down, forget it, and rise above it. If you take yourself in hand early, you need never fail to do the best you are capable of at the moment—the health, of course, being presumed to be good. The root requisite for success in the art of interpreting music is to know your job thoroughly, and to know that you know it. Don't go on the platform until you do. Hence, tackle small jobs first. Far better to do a tiny thing well than a big one badly. The effect on yourself, rather than on the audience, is important. Every deserved success lifts you up a definite step both in artistry and self-confidence. The only sort of self-confidence that is any good comes through self-knowledge.

In passing, a tiny physiological pointer : a few good deep breaths just before going on the platform are comfortingly steadying.

The second pointer is : think nothing of yourself, all of the music. The question is not " How well am *I* doing ? " but " How finely can the composer's thought be re-created : how greatly can justice be done to him ? " The old injunction to think of the audience as so many heads of cabbage is not psychologically deep enough. You would not seek to convince cabbages of beauty. The audience has rights, but the composer's are infinitely greater. You are the medium bringing the two together. And to be a happy medium you must think as little of yourself as does a medium in a trance—while you must be alive and aware to the tips of every nerve. That does not mean " nerves," but it does explain why real artists are often keyed up when they are going to perform. Without that keying, I doubt if greatness can come out of anyone : but experience helps to cover it, and the old hand never frightens an audience by showing fright. It is a grand thing to feel that an interpreter is raising himself, and us, up to the measure of the stature of great music. You can see, then, why no one, however good he may have been, can play false, dealing out poor music instead of fine, and retain the name of artist. Sometimes you find a difference between musicians' opinions of some performer, and a big public's. That is where the secret lies : it is all a matter of artistry, and nobody can swindle fellow-artists into thinking him a great artist if he performs rubbish. They can see him " putting it over," and every true artist among them despises him : and it isn't " professional jealousy." But the ranks of real artists are thin, always. There are never enough to go round. In England at this moment we lamentably lack great interpreters in singing, and I do not know where they are to come from.

We were thinking not of the greatest, but of our more ordinary, yet aspiring, selves. The third useful word I can give you is " Always think positive thoughts." You will see that I have put that advice in a positive form : I did not say " Never think negative thoughts." People try to inspirit us by saying " Don't be nervous." They should rather say " Be confident ! " Of course, no amount of verbal injunction is any good unless you know your job well ; but when you are sure of that, think all the cheerful thoughts possible ; and put them always in a positive form. Along with this advice goes a last word, that hangs with it : allow no thought of fear ; and above all, never suggest fear to a child. It is simple wickedness to do that. One hears people say " Of course he's such a nervous little chap." I always want to smother such folk. To be harsh with existing fears in children is even worse. If they were brought up properly, they would have very little fear, though the mind of man is an ancient battleground, and we can none of us escape the dead hand of the ages when fear largely ruled primitive man. (Are we so very much better to-day, as nations ?) To my mind there is only one real devil, and his name is Fear. His other name is Selfishness : and you get a glimpse of that other side of the shield whenever you are inclined to think, as a performer, " How am I doing this ? Am I making an impression ? "—that is " Glory for me, me, me " over again.

These thoughts will help anybody who firmly practises in their sense, to give the best that is in him, as an interpreter. There is no secret in that—except the secret of how one and one—interpreter and listener—can make more than two : but they do ; and that is one of the heartening beauties of the arithmetic of artistry.

NOTE.—A Table of Orchestral and Vocal Compasses (Real Sounds) will be found at the end of the volume.

# BOOK II

## THE ORCHESTRA
## AND ORCHESTRAL MUSIC

*By* JULIUS HARRISON

# A: THE RISE OF THE ORCHESTRA

## CHAPTER I

## INTRODUCTION

THE MODERN ORCHESTRA consists, roughly, of four well-defined sections : the stringed instruments, the wood-wind, the brass and the percussion. Through this wonderful " instrument "—an instrument that has taken man thousands of years to perfect in all its branches—the world has been given the greatest masterpieces of music. This Book of THE MUSICAL COMPANION deals, first, with the development of the orchestra from the early days of culture (but not from the time of the savages or early primitives), and then with the music itself. The first part of my subject has been treated in sections more or less corresponding to those given in the opening sentence of this introduction, the various groups of instruments being briefly traced from their Asiatic or European origin, then on through the dark ages and the renascence, to the time when the style of the modern orchestra was definitely fixed by the fusion of its various elements. The remainder of the Book deals with the masterpieces created by man through the extraordinary and uplifting power of this mighty instrument, and also with certain aspects of music that occur to the critical mind in these later and less creative days.

## CHAPTER II

## FIRST BEGINNINGS

Civilisation, spreading westward through the centuries long years ago and bringing in its train much of the culture of the Orient, was the foster-parent of the modern orchestra. But we must not assume too readily, because of this palpable fact, that ancient Greece, land of the classic lyre, the cythara and similar stringed instruments, contributed the major share towards this record of progress. Far from it. Conservatism was the watchword of the Greeks in music as much as in everything else. Eyes and ears rebelled against the importation of alien instruments coming all the way from Arabia, Egypt, Persia, India, and even beyond; instruments that by their very strangeness in both shape and sound constituted a grave menace to the purity of musical style then existing. For the Greeks were not true adventurers in matters of this kind; they had little feeling or use for instruments juxtaposed in brilliant combinations of sounds. And since harmony was then unknown and Greek music only modal and mainly monodic in character, there could have been few chances for varying the tone-colours of whatever was being performed. So the inevitable happened. Just as Euripides, from his "Medea" onwards, introduced a starker realism destined to divide the house of classical drama against itself, so did the barbarian instruments of the mid-Orient sweep across Europe past the waning culture of the Greeks to add to music those new and richer colours so far either undiscovered or rejected by academic prejudice.

We can easily imagine how these primitive orchestras offended the Greek ear. When Aristoxenus of Tartium, in the 4th century B.C., was writing his famous treatise on modes and keys, the foreign invasion had already begun. The orchestra was waging its first war for freedom—freedom from its bondage to the human voice, to which in Grecian lands it had been allowed to play " second fiddlr " only. The fight was bound to come from without; percussion instruments had hardly any place, and wind instruments little more, in the Greek house of music, though to the " Barbarians " of the East and South they meant variety, tone-colours, massed expression, musical vitality unobtainable from a stringed instrument plucked by a gentle hand in support of voices. Although the barbarian instruments must have been raucous in tone and capable of little delicacy of expression—and the music performed scarcely more than improvisations of questionable merit—yet it must be said that all these efforts undoubtedly marked a step in the direction of progress. In these events we discern the woodwind, brass and percussion instruments striving for alliance with the strings. All the same, many centuries of slow progress were necessary before any real consolidation was possible. It was left to other European nations to put their inventive heads together and give us ultimately what the Hellenic peoples in their conservatism could not or would not recognise to be of any value. And so these alleged barbarians, introducing such instruments as harp, guitar, flute, trumpet, bagpipe and tanboura (an oriental lute) into the orchestra, could claim a certain superficial superiority over the cultured race on the other side of the Ægean sea, for such novel combinations must have added many a touch of colour to their primitive music—music performed only in unison or at the octave. Cymbals, drums and other percussive instruments would also act as rhythmical pointers to the melodic phrases, and to produce effects calculated to thrill and to stir the blood of the common people as much as to earn the disdain of the sophists and reactionaries.

Through such developments music of the instrumental kind was beginning to mean a great deal to the life of the people ; it was becoming more democratic, more interesting and much more exciting in its effect. Small wonder then that the Romans, in the heyday of their culture, saw great possibilities in all these newer instruments and bent

Ec

their minds and energies towards improving them. Other types of wind instrument now made their appearance, and it is to the Romans that we actually owe the origins of our modern wood-wind and brass instruments. What the lyre and cythara were to the Greeks so were the tibia, buccina, cornu, lituus and tuba to the Romans. From the tibia family of instruments (tibia=pipe) arose the flute, oboe, clarinet and bassoon, while to the buccina and its relations we owe the trumpet, trombone, horn and other brass instruments.

But although we may say, in general terms, that the Greeks favoured strings and wind, the Asiatic and Egyptian peoples the wind and percussion, and the Romans the wood-wind and brass instruments, yet all these separate or partly combined efforts did not hasten things to their appointed end for many centuries. The world had changed with the coming of the Christian era, and in many ways for the worse. Religious persecution, the fall of the Roman Empire, the devastation of central Europe by Attila and his hordes, all served to retard the progress made in the previous thousand years. And with the rapid growth of Christianity music turned away very definitely from instrumental to vocal expression. The monks of various orders (almost the sole guardians of learning throughout those long dark ages) left unheeded the many invitations and injunctions contained in the 150th Psalm to praise God " with the timbrel and dance," with " stringed instruments and organs," or on the " high sounding cymbals." They preferred the expression of the human voice. Instruments were now looked upon as belonging mainly to the secular side of life and, as such, were left to the minstrels, trouba-dours, jongleurs, minnesingers and others who made so picturesque the centuries immediately preceding the renas-cence of learning among the people at large.

Yet without this lengthy set-back the orchestra might never have come into its own, for during the time when everything instrumental was under many a cloud or even banned by the tyrannical edicts of the Church, the monks were busy working out and recording on their parchments the general theory and practice of music. To such 13th-century pioneers as Walter de Odington of Evesham (who wrote an " Ars Mensurabilis " of music) and John of Fornsete (the reputed composer of " Sumer is icumen in ") we owe more than we can say. Without them music might have remained in a state of unrecorded improvisation for many more years, retarding both its own practical growth and its passage into channels of definite expression.

But although vocal music was being recorded by hand as early as the year 1200 or thereabouts (" Sumer is icumen in "), instrumental music still lagged far behind. Nothing of the latter kind seems to have been written down until early in the 15th century, being even then quite a rarity. And for this we must blame the Church, which, with ruthless power, discouraged or destroyed the cultivation of all instrumental music, leaving to itinerant actors and minstrels the difficult task of preserving what they could from the ruin. Without the enthusiasm of the 9th- to 14th-century minstrels or troubadours as they were called in France—an enthusiasm that eventually won for them the approval not only of the people but also of kings and emperors—all these instruments and the learned skill of the performers thereon would doubtless have perished, to be reborn only after the laborious uphill work of many more centuries. The troubadours, too, began to acquire additional skill in the writing of music. Their efforts, however, were vocal-cum-instrumental rather than instrumental alone, for the chief business of the minstrel's art was the composition and performance of fervent love-songs addressed to ladies of high standing or the creation of romances founded on the " Chanson de Roland " or on the chivalry of Charlemagne.

Even then, there was little done towards the formation of what we would now term an orchestra. Though the jongleur of the 12th and 13th centuries, attached as he was to the troubadour in the rôle of accompanist, was a man of many parts, expected to perform with equal facility on the pipe and tabor, citole, symphony (a precursor of the organ), the mandora (much like the oriental tanboura), the seventeen-stringed rote, the manichord, the harp, gigue (from which the dance of that name was derived), the ten-stringed psaltery and so on, yet he and his fellows of equal talent do not seem to have made any attempt to experiment in concerted instrumental music. Perhaps the nature of their calling, paid servants as they often were in some lordly house—for these were pre-guild days—prevented any social intercourse or prolonged exchange of ideas. Life in those times must have been very scattered indeed : occasions for musical arguments few and far between. Yet there is evidence of a Royal Band in the household of Edward III of England. But what the actual instruments were or what music was performed is a matter for speculative thought alone. The instruments known to western and central Europe had by this time become so numerous and varied, thanks to the activities of the minstrels, that we can hazard the guess that no two bands were ever alike or could perform any piece of music in identical manner. Evidence of a possible band is forthcoming in the Minstrels' Gallery sculptures erected in Exeter Cathedral during the reign of Edward III. These carvings illustrate the cittern, bagpipe, clarion, rebec, psaltery, syrinx, sackbut, regals, gittern (guitar), shalm, timbrel and cymbals.

Mr. Anderson, in Book I, has dwelt with tender care on the names and characters of many of these old instruments, and I, too, could wish to prolong my section with the enumeration and description of countless others. But as time and space both fly, I must content myself with the names of some of those instruments which, for fanciful nomenclature (if for nothing else) are superior to anything found in our 20th-century orchestra. They are given here without any regard for period or chronological order ; nor is it suggested that the instruments could ever combine to produce any " concord of sweet sounds."

Phagotum (bagpipe) ;  Orpharion (cittern)
Saltbox (obviously a kitchen instrument)

Turkish Crescent or Jingling Johnny (19th century)

Wheel Cymbals (lyrichord, an 18th-century keyed yet bowed instrument)

Whittle and dub (18th-century nomenclature for pipe and tabor drum)

Stump, Poliphant (both the same as cittern)

Nakers (drums) ; Trumpet marine (bowed mono-chord !)

Humstrum (a debased rebec) ; Kanoon (a Turkish psaltery)

Chorus (crwth ; also another name for bagpipe)

Bladder-and-string (bumbass, an earlier form of Trumpet marine)

Shagbolt (sackbut or trombone).

Historically there is much to interest the reader in all these many instruments. A dip into Francis W. Galpin's " Old English Instruments of Music " (published by Methuen) will soon convince him that they make a very polyglot collection indeed, and that the multiplicity of their types seriously impeded the evolution of the modern orchestra. For most of these instruments were very limited in the range of pitch; they were non-combinative and dependent entirely on chance improvisation for their musical pabulum. But with the introduction of harmony, matters went a little further. It is to the credit of the instrumentalists of the 10th century that they at once recognised the value of Hucbald's and Otger's system of harmony—the system known as the *Organum* (hence our word Organ) and consisting of the parallel movement of fourths and fifths. On this and on a contemporaneous but more advanced system known as *Discantus* (Descant), a new foundation for instrumental music at last became possible. (See also Book I.)

Things were now beginning to move and music had ceased doubling back on itself. That wonderful feat of technique " Sumer is icumen in " was the early and direct result of the *Discantus* method of harmonisation. Indeed, the three combined themes found in Wagner's Prelude to

" Die Meistersinger," the three simultaneous stage bands in Mozart's " Don Giovanni," each playing in a different time ($\frac{3}{4}$, $\frac{2}{4}$ and $\frac{3}{8}$) ; Bach's " Art of Fugue "—in fact, the sum total of contrapuntal music—can all be traced back to this epoch-making discovery of the 9th and 10th centuries. And what had now been discovered mainly by the monks of England and France might so well have happened 1,500 years previously had not the innate conservatism of the Greeks barred the way to all experiments in descant or harmony, matters already known to them theoretically.

# CHAPTER III

# THE STRINGS

THERE WAS STILL a great distance to go before the practicable orchestra became an accomplished fact. It was now less the fault of the music than of the heterogeneous collection of instruments that were able to express but inadequately the composer's intentions. These instruments were mainly intended for a solo performer and were to be regarded, primarily, only as an accompaniment for voices. The stringed instruments formed a motley collection of all shapes and sizes. Some, such as the rote or crot and the harp, were plucked by the fingers ; others, such as the gittern (guitar) and the citole, needed a plectrum ; while those requiring the bow (which had found its way into Europe from India and Arabia before the 11th century) were the rebec (under its various names of lyra, geige, gigue, rybybe, etc.), the crowd (cruit or crwth), the monochord (manichord), fidula, fithele (fydele, fiddle, or *fithul* as Chaucer has it), all variations of what ultimately became the viol family of instruments.

But drastic elimination of unsuitable and ineffective types was necessary before man's inventive powers could produce a set of stringed instruments capable of expressing the newfangled music now being written with such skill and over wider ranges of pitch. Treble, alto, tenor and bass voices, often singing in four- or five-part harmony, needed some exact counterpart on instruments ; something that would support all voices with a uniform tone and equality of balance. The introduction of the hair bow into Europe gradually solved this problem. But it took a long time to do so, for the majority of the bowed instruments of mediæval times were small in size, indifferent in tone, and usually possessing no more than three or four strings tuned to a treble or middle pitch. In fact it was some time after the renascence that the viol family of instruments displaced the rebec and its variants, and in its turn foreshadowed that now indispensable feature of modern music, the string instruments, known to us all as the violin, viola, violoncello and double-bass.

Quality of tone had been a matter of chance up to the time of the bowed viols, for the best endeavours to sustain the sound at the pleasure of the performer were often nullified by the crude or ineffective instruments themselves. Yet the *ars mensurabilis* of music had been in vogue three or four centuries ; the lozenges and diamonds balanced on little poles or with tails attached (to borrow Mr. Anderson's descriptive phrases) were all crying out for correctness of interpretation as much from instruments as from voices. The viol family—with all its noble members conforming to one pattern yet of several sizes—brought about this much-to-be-desired end, and for the first time placed the quality of instrumental music somewhere within challengeable distance of vocal. The treble or descant viol, the tenor (*Viola da braccio. Braccio*=arm), the viola d'amore (with seven to fourteen strings vibrating sympathetically beneath the seven " played " strings), the bass (*Viola da gamba. Gamba*= leg), and the double-bass viol (*Violone*) now offered to the composer a medium for instrumental expression hitherto denied him. Bows were longer and, in shape and quality, not unlike our modern ones. Instruments were shaped to patterns found to produce rich and resonant tone. By the time of Henry VIII a " Chest of Viols " (as it was called) was the mainstay of the orchestra, and usually consisted of two treble, two tenor and two bass instruments. In the Royal Band of the year 1539 we find " *viij vyalls.*"

The days of the viol family, too, were numbered. Invented in the 15th century and at the height of their popularity in the 16th—Leonardo da Vinci was reputed to be no mean performer on the viol da gamba—these instruments began to wane in public favour from the 17th century onwards. In many ways they had proved cumbersome and not altogether satisfactory, though at the same time we must not forget their good qualities. Their customary six strings were difficult to tune accurately, and the performers themselves were more often than not inferior technicians. Only the viol da gamba seems to have been mastered with anything like ease. From the simple construction of the rebec to the complicated features of the viols was indeed a far cry. The difficulties in the way of satisfactory musical performances on the latter ultimately proved their undoing and so hastened the day when instruments of simpler construction were bound to supplant them, instruments capable of producing all the viols' richness of tone, but by means far less complicated.

Yet it was a long time before the stringed instruments that are in use to-day became consolidated into one homogeneous family. We read of violins being introduced into Henry the Eighth's band in 1547, while the viols were still at the height of their popularity. Many of the older instruments, too, were still very much to the fore, even in the early part of the 17th century. Michael Prætorius, famous composer and theorist at that time, in his " Organographia " describes the String Orchestra known to him as consisting of bandoras, orpharions, citterns, theorboes, lutes, and a bass lyra, to which last-named instrument he recommends the addition of a bass viol for the sake of a stronger foundation. To these instruments were added those precursors of the pianoforte, the clavicymbal (clavicembalo) or spinet. These would help to cover up some of the imperfections of the stringed instruments and would enrich the texture of the music generally by playing the harmonies indicated in what was then known as the *bassus continuus* (figured bass) part.

From the list given above it will be seen that plucked stringed instruments still contended for popular favour with those played by the bow. Not as yet did musicians dare to put aside the seventeen-stringed theorbo-lute (a great favourite with Pepys) or the more plebeian cittern (played with a plectrum) and concentrate on string tone produced by bows alone. Such was the transitional state of music in the 16th and 17th centuries that stringed instruments of a type surviving from the long ago still found themselves cheek by jowl with others that were made but a short time prior to those created by the genius of Antonio Stradivarius.

By the year 1685 the Amatis, Stradivarius, the Guarnerius family and other famous instrument makers living in Cremona had perfected the design and inherent qualities of the violin, viola, and violoncello. And so, at long last, the practical and more easily managed four-stringed instruments known as the violin family took complete possession of the field they were never to leave again, ousting their cousins the six-stringed viols in every department of the String Orchestra. Only the old violone survived for a while as a foundation tone until the double-bass was firmly established at a somewhat later date. The year 1685 witnessed the births of Bach, Handel and Domenico Scarlatti. By that time the String Orchestra so familiar to us 250 years later had come to stay. It had now only to wait for those oncoming geniuses who, with consummate skill, could translate their musical thoughts into the new medium prepared for them. How the composers fared will be told elsewhere. The doom of all plucked stringed instruments, save the harp, had now been sealed (orchestrally), and the violin family was henceforth to reign supreme as the monarch of the modern orchestra.

## CHAPTER IV

# WOOD-WIND

WHEN THE CHURCH, in the Middle Ages, turned against the noisy secular instruments as being obstacles to divine worship, the lyra and cythara alone accompanied the religious service. To these instruments at a later date were added the organistrum and organ, and, strangely enough, small " chime-bells " of the cymbal or gong varieties. But with wind instruments in any shape or form the Church would have nothing to do. These instruments would be kept for public or private merry-makings, royal occasions, fairs, dances, and all those sportive events where the spirit of Pan rather than that of Phœbus Apollo predominated. According to the Church, they were born of " the world, the flesh and the devil " and as such were utterly unworthy of a place in matters spiritual. And so, in a narrow world where the inventive powers of man were crippled by the tyranny of a priesthood continually threatening excommunication and the pains of hell for the smallest deviation from its laws, there was even less chance of progress in this field of music than in that of the stringed instruments.

The ancient Assyrians, the Egyptians, the peoples from Arabia, Phœnicia and further east had known, many centuries before this time, that an orchestra gained greatly in effect if strings and wind were combined judiciously with a discreet admixture of percussive instruments. The Romans knew still more, for their new types of instruments were a great advance on all others previously made. As stated already, they were specialists in the manufacture of many wind instruments, and (like a good north-country-man) loved " a bit of brass " in particular. Yet all these ancient enthusiasms died out in the later centuries, and for many years strings, wood-wind, brass and percussion each ploughed a lonely furrow, caring little whether they acted in any friendly or experimental combinations. We read of Edward the First's Troumpour (trumpeter) Roger, and also of Janino his Nakerer (drummer), but there is no evidence that they belonged to some genuine band containing the flower of all the instruments of their day.

No more than a brief survey of the precursors of the modern wood-wind family is possible in this article. We must pass over the long vertical flutes of ancient Egypt known as *mam* and *náy*, the Greek *aulos*, and the Roman instruments of the *tibia*[1] family and come to the time when European flutes and recorders (pipes with whistle mouthpiece) tried their best to mingle with schalmeys (shawms) and pommers in sounds that must have been even less pleasant than those of the contemporaneous string families. For they were a mixed lot indeed, and, because of their rough designs, incapable of anything like true or tempered intonation. These recorders of the 12th century onwards were actually of the flute family, though played vertically (the German equivalent to recorder is *blockflöte*) and had a compass of some two octaves. Of these instruments there were, according to Prætorius, at least eight varieties extending over a considerable range of pitch. Sometimes as many as twenty-one would be played together, and since their sounds were in agreeable contrast to the crude double-reeded tone of the shawms and pommers, they must assuredly have been the one bright spot in the discordant wood-wind family of the Middle Ages and the Renascence. From them arose the type of flute played crosswise (*flauto traverso*). This instrument made its appearance in France as early as the 14th century (*fleuthe traversaine*) and to this day has retained much of its original character. There were various kinds that corresponded to the treble, alto, tenor and bass recorders, but the lower-pitched instruments soon lost their hold and disappeared from view (the bass-flute excepted), for they were weak in tone and limited in execution.

[1] As the name implies, they were originally made from a leg-bone.

The shawms and pommers (tenor and bass shawms) were played with a double reed like the present-day oboe, cor anglais and bassoon, etc. These instruments, which in all probability found their way across Europe from the East at the time of the early Crusades, were of shrill or raucous quality, almost impossible to combine harmoniously with any other instruments. Their reeds were thick and unskilled in workmanship, as different from those in use today as a piece of cardboard from a wafer, while the instruments themselves, so roughly constructed, must have produced a general out-of-tuneness that would have shocked our ears beyond description could we have heard them. In the 16th century the shawm changed its name to oboe under various spellings worth recording here because of their amusing digression from the original French word meaning "high wood." From haulx-bois or haultbois it became hautbois and was then anglicised to hautboy, hoboy, howeboie, hoeboy, howboy, and, in German, hoboe. The words shawm, shalm, *shalmele* (Gower in his "Confessio Amantis," written in 1393), shalmuse and schalmey, etc., gradually fell into disuse, as well they might in face of this new verbal onslaught. To this interesting family Bach owed the oboe, oboe d'amore and oboe di caccia that so often characterised his orchestration, and from these later types used by him are descended our modern and not dissimilar keyed instruments the oboe, cor anglais, bassoon, contra-bassoon, bass oboe, heckelphone, etc., the first four of which have long since become an integral part of the orchestra. And, in concluding this all too brief survey of the main wood-wind instruments in vogue during the lifetime of Bach and his great contemporaries, it should not be forgotten that the bassoon was actually derived from the bass shawm or pommer, and *not* from the phagotus invented by Afranio of Ferrara about the year 1540. But, alas, the Italians, uncertain about its actual parentage, gave it the name of *fagotto* and the Germans followed suit with *fagott*. Only the French with *basson* (*bas son* = deep sound) and the English with their own variant of this word kept the instrument away from its mistaken origin, though they, too, gave no clear indication that it was descended from the shawm family and that its forbears had rejoiced in such excellent names as the courtal, bumbarde, waighte (hence our Christmas " waits ") and dulcian.

The story of this group of 12th- to 18th-century wind instruments compares unfavourably with that of the strings. Although there was the same constant endeavour to obtain uniformity of tone and to discover a combination of instruments that would prove acceptable to the ear, the results up to 1685 (which year suggests itself as the most acceptable one for my argument) were indeed disappointing. Actually it was the preponderating coarse tone of the thick-reeded oboes that delayed for so long the balance of effects already achieved by the strings. With their many technical imperfections they simply would not combine with the " soft complaining " flutes or with the less strident members of their own class, the bassoons. And if these wind instruments in combination formed nothing better than a house divided against itself, there could be little hope of their assisting concerted music by any unconsidered alliance with the strings. By this time recorders had almost vanished. Whereas in Charles I's reign there were six attached to the King's Music, by 1674 only four remained, for as Evelyn wrote five years later—" the Flute Douce" was now " much in request." So the clear and, at times, brilliant pipe effects of the flutes and the few recorders left were now swamped by these unmanageable reeds; with the result that in 1685 the wood-wind was far behind the strings in general cohesion of tone-colours. Oboes were now rarely heard in indoor music ; their strident tones contended with the trumpets and drums in *al fresco* entertainments, where, in numbers equal to those of the clarinets and cornets found in military bands to-day, they could excite those who, in quantity if not in quality, " wanted their money's worth."

And so for many years bands—for I hesitate to use the word *orchestra*—consisted of two kinds, known as the " whole consort " and the " broken consort." The former contained nothing but instruments of one family : it might be a band of recorders or of viols, or perhaps one of lutes and even of shawms. The broken consort would be, as its name suggests, a combination of instruments of different families. But of any advance towards a real union of all available instruments ranking orchestrally there was as yet, despite these occasional broken consorts, hardly a sign. Strings kept to themselves, no doubt afraid of contamination, and, with these few exceptions, so did the wind and brass. In Mr. Galpin's book there is a most interesting and detailed account of these consorts, with many quotations from Bacon, Shakespeare, Prætorius and others. And from his account we realise what a time it took to place the wood-wind on the solid foundation of the strings.

We of to-day (proud inheritors of all the wonderful music written since 1685) now see what was amiss. Pipe instruments were all too weak, the shawm type far too strong. Whistle mouthpieces could not contend with these thick double reeds ; a compromise was badly needed before ever the wood-wind family could mix together as harmoniously as the strings.

That compromise was found eventually by Christopher Denner of Nuremberg about the year 1690. History relates that it was he who invented the clarinet, an instrument that, because of its brilliant tone, was destined to consolidate the wood-wind family into something like unity. But the clarinet, though a reed instrument, does not come from the shawm family. Its tube is cylindrical, not conical, and, in further contrast to the oboe and bassoon, has only a *single* reed. It was discovered that such an instrument possessed the bright open characteristics of the flute and of the higher-pitched recorders, but with additional power and more roundness of tone that extended over a wide range of pitch. Here at last was an instrument that, for sheer strength, could hold its own against the shawms, and, furthermore, was one whose tone brightened the wood-wind consort to an unbelievable extent. Yet its progress was slow, possibly due to the imperfections of the early types, and

there is no record that it was used orchestrally until after
1750, the year of Bach's death. Although Rameau had made
casual use of clarinets in his "Acante et Céphise" (1751) it
was not until twenty years later that they sprang into
general favour and their special qualities were recognised
by Haydn and, more particularly, by Mozart.

And now the composer, ever striving for an ideal combination of instruments that would express his inmost
thoughts, soon improved the broken consort of bygone days
by reducing the wood-wind to something like proper
proportions. Two each of flutes, oboes (now reinstated in
the concert-room), clarinets and bassoons were found to be
adequate to most requirements. In these limited numbers
they formed not only a satisfactory blend amongst themselves but also added weight and variety to the foundation-
tone strings, and so enabled the composer to think afresh in
terms of the most vivid tone-colours. No longer were the
wood-wind the despised and rejected of men ; they were
admitted to a broken consort that had become whole for
perhaps the first time. Dare we believe that the birth of
the immortal symphonies came to pass through this very
fact ?

## CHAPTER V

## BRASS

But the " broken consort "[1] was not as yet fully
developed, for the call of other instruments seeking
admission to its ranks was even more insistent than that
of the wood-wind. As Mr. Galpin reminds us, the use of
brass and percussion instruments in the middle ages and
for some time afterwards " was restricted to royal and noble

[1] The phrase " broken consort " is so likable as to deserve its repetition here, though it has long since fallen into disuse.

purposes and the panoply of war." Yet a time was bound to come when these two classes of instruments would demand entrance to the consort. The drama of music was slowly unfolding. Composers were throwing off one by one the shackles that had bound their art all too closely to the human voice. They sought the expression of worldly as well as of spiritual matters. They sought to portray the incidents and emotions of everyday life ; the abstract battle between good and evil ; historical scenes ; the strife between Greek and Trojan ; the thunderstorm ; the songs of the birds, and a thousand other phases of life and death that suggested to them many varieties and degrees of sound. All this could not be done with strings and wood-wind alone, and the composers knew it. So they experimented, and by degrees added to the orchestra those heavier instruments that nowadays carry the burden of music's greatest climaxes.

The complete story of the brass instruments cannot be told within the limits of this chapter. Reference has already been made to the Romans and to the interest they displayed in the *buccina* and the other brass instruments of their making. From the *buccina* it is not a far step, etymologically, to the bocine, buysine or buzain of the English and French Middle Ages, nor to the old German word *buzaun* and the modern one *posaune*. These names, severally and collectively, indicate very clearly the ancestry of the trombone. But before this instrument was perfected on modern lines it went through a middle period under the name of sackbut. Actually, the buysine was no better than a long straight trumpet (the trombone in chrysalis form !), while its successor, the sackbut, flaunted its slide action as swaggeringly as do the trombones of the present time.

The Roman cavalry instrument, the *lituus*, was the forerunner of our modern trumpet, which also passed through an intermediate stage in the Middle Ages under the name of claro (clarion). However, the word trumpet, under many spellings, also dates back to the time of Chaucer, and is, in fact, one of few survivors from the old English vocabulary of instrumental names.

In the Latin word *cornu* we recognise the origin of the horn. From the Roman instrument of that name arose eventually those circular instruments—circular for the first time in the 14th century—whose tone, mellower in quality but less bright than that of trombone or trumpet, is one of the most romantic sounds in all music. It can almost be said, *inter alia,* that the great classical and modern composers have been more affected by the tone of the French and German horn than by any other instrument, and, in consequence, have poured some of their finest inspirations into this mould, giving to the world so many passages of such wondrous beauty that we who listen are filled with awe and amazement.

Such, then, were the most important members of the brass family that in company with the drums, cymbals, and, maybe, shawms and cornetts (a curved instrument made of bone, horn or ivory, and known also by the name of *zinke* ; one not to be confused with our modern cornet) formed by far the noisiest broken consort heard by mediæval and post-mediæval ears. To them was allotted all open-air music ; they could scarcely be trusted indoors, for their combined tone and sour intonation must have driven many a good man desperate. And when, as time passed, the serpent and the ophicleide (wooden instruments akin to the cornett or zinke family) helped out the bass of the harmony, the cup of misery must have been full to overflowing. " In the early part of the nineteenth century," comments Mr. Cecil Forsyth on the serpent, in his " Orchestration " (published by Macmillan), " the instrument's tonal inequalities and its deficiencies of intonation had become more than even the men of Waterloo could stand." After this trenchant criticism further comment is unnecessary.

Viewing the consort as a whole, we can realise why the frequent importation of instruments not of the brass family was unavoidable. The trumpet and horn were natural (unvalved) instruments in those days ; that is, unable to produce any but the notes which accorded to the harmonic series of overtones—with certain exceptions on the horn.[1] And the sackbut or trombone also depended on this principle, though, being furnished with a slide, it had greater facility of execution and could therefore modulate from the key during the progress of the music, an advantage not shared by either trumpet or horn. But as the popularity of the French horn increased, so the trombone seems to have gone temporarily out of fashion. In Henry VIII's band we find ten trombones ; in Elizabeth's, four ; and, by Handel's time, there was scarcely a player to be found in all England. Moreover, if the general absence of trombones from composers' scores of the 18th century is anything like a guide, then we may assume that the same dearth of players must have existed on the Continent.

So here was the brass consort, more or less bereft of its heavy bass instruments and dependent on trumpets and horns for a limited supply of notes, and on alien instruments for the remainder.

In the days of Haydn and the first symphonic music the brass usually consisted of two horns and two trumpets, a combination which, when added to the timpani, and two flutes, oboes and bassoons in pairs, balanced to a nicety the strings of the orchestra. In this modest way did the brass consort, consisting of four instruments only, make its first contribution to that now rapidly expanding instrument, the symphonic orchestra.

What they added practically determined the course of all great classical music, for out of the limited number of notes obtainable from the natural (unvalved) horns and trumpets there grew a type of diatonic theme, which, in the best examples, must rank as high as anything ever written. Four of these themes are given below in chronological order, together with a table of the harmonic series of notes on which they are formed, and to which, if necessary, reference can be made by the reader.

When Haydn became the " Father of the Symphony "—

[1] In the brief space at my command a detailed explanation of what is meant is not possible. The article on Harmony in the " Encyclopædia Britannica " covers the whole question.

to give him the title posterity has chosen—he used none of those hybrid instruments of the cornetto or zinke type. His strings, wood-wind and brass were kept free from any such contamination. The serpent survived for some considerable time afterwards, but the higher-pitched zinkes seem to have sung their swan-song at the production of Gluck's "Orpheus" in Vienna (1762). And since Haydn had written his first symphony only five years previously, it is extremely unlikely that he would ever have contemplated the inclusion in his score of any such effete instruments. In other words, with the birth of that symphony came the complete emancipation of the orchestra from the state of indecision that had characterised its best endeavours for so many centuries. And although the brass section was still far from complete, owing to the technical limitations of its members and the absence of trombones from most works then being written (I refrain from mentioning the bass tuba at present), yet a definite " instrument " had at last been evolved on which the composer could play to the top of his bent. The golden age of instrumental composition had arrived simultaneously with the first orchestra worthy of the name. But this was no mere chance. Melody, harmony, the making of instruments, the growth of learning and of general culture, all had progressed side by side until, midway through the 18th century, the long-desired end had come in sight. The future now held a promise of greatness the full measure of which no man could foresee.

## CHAPTER VI

# PERCUSSION. BALANCE. SIX TYPICAL ORCHESTRAS

FROM ALL ACCOUNTS, the desire for sheer noise by congestion of drums, cymbals, tambourine, triangle and other instruments of like character was seldom the way of the ancient peoples of the East, despite their fondness for percussion effects. The Egyptians and early Semites turned these " instruments of war " into something unusually pacific, using them mainly to give definite rhythmical outlines to whatever was being performed on harp, flute or tanboura. And in their reticence and love of quiet effects, obtainable by contrast of one percussion instrument with another, they showed a degree of skill and æsthetic judgment that glorified rather than debased this important feature of the art. That they used them also in martial style goes without saying, for never did a nation exist that found no occasion for the use of clashing cymbals or the " double double double beat of the thundering drum " as thrilling incitements to just or unjust warfare. Yet no one, listening nowadays to any oriental, Moorish or Slavonic music on these or similar instruments, would deny that the subtlety of quiet effects therein must have survived from age-old traditions not born of sheer noise or love of barbarism, and that all other effects have been, in the main, the product of a later European civilization given more to the sounds of war than those of peace.

And in the differences here implied lies the whole unhappy history of the percussion department of the orchestra. Unhappy is the word, for most of these instruments, lending little or nothing to the definite pitch of sounds in either melody or harmony, have indeed been the playthings of chance ever since they were created by primitive man. Deposed from the high position they occupied in their early oriental days, they became synonymous with everything that was noisy and warlike. They could not develop on lines similar to those that led so successfully in the 18th century to the entente between strings, wood-wind and the brass, for their very nature stood in the way. Out of favour with the Church in mediæval times, equally out of favour with all other instrumental combinations save those functioning out of doors, they led a precarious existence solely dependent on noisy brass, pipe and reed instruments for company.

But since the main percussion instruments have come down to us from the long ago merely as improvements on or variants of ancient oriental types there is no need for me to trace their history except in a general way. Drums have existed ever since primitive man beat on the roughest-made membrane stretched across a wooden frame, and to-day much the same sounds are made on them in exactly the same way. The same can be said of the tambourine (O.E. timbrel), which has remained true to its character for 2,000 years or more. On the other hand, the cymbals, with a much more interesting and picturesque history, have varied in size and shape from the small basin and cup-shaped instruments of the Assyrians, Arabs and Indians to the large circular and hard-clashing types for which Turkey has been famous these many years. Except for the last-named, all these have fallen into disuse, though Berlioz in his " Romeo and Juliet " symphony and Debussy in " L'Après-midi d'un Faune " have written parts for the small antique cymbals—parts that are usually transferred, in the absence of the proper instruments, to the glockenspiel (itself, as the name implies, a modern resurrection of the old English " chime-bells " referred to in Chapter IV).

We come to Tudor times and to the introduction into England of the kettledrums, the natural successors to the 14th-century nakers (*nacareh*, in Arabic). These were considered far superior to all other drums yet invented because they could be tuned to a definite pitch. In less than 200 years they were destined to become the most important percussion feature of the orchestra, acceptable to the ear as much in the concert-room as out of doors. Purcell was the first English composer to employ them in concerted instrumental music (" The Fairy Queen ") and by Bach's and Handel's day they were a recognised and most effective method of giving rhythmical point to the loud *tutti* passages. At that time a pair of drums was customary, but, as will be seen later, others were eventually added to the orchestra to meet the growing requirements of modern music. While all other percussion effects were sadly neglected by composers, the timpani (to give the kettle-drums the name in general use to-day) continued to gain in popularity. Comparatively few of the large-scale orchestral works of the 18th century are without a timpani part, though among the exceptions to be found must be mentioned Mozart's famous G minor symphony, written as late as 1791.

Composers now regarded the timpani as the natural reinforcement of the trumpets in all passages requiring sonorous presentation. In Haydn's and Mozart's orchestral works we rarely find them apart, and even Beethoven, to the very end of his life, still made use of much the same traditional scoring. In addition, this happy union of trumpets and drums solved to a large extent the question of balance of tone between the extreme parts of the harmony in all loud passages, for, as we have already seen, the disappearance of the trombones from the brass consort had weakened considerably the effectiveness of that section of the orchestra.

The orchestra now counted among its members representatives from all four families of instruments. True, it was as yet somewhat incomplete in the balance and general blend, but it was indeed an orchestra worthy of the name. It had taken hundreds of years to sort itself out, to get rid of unsuitable instruments of all kinds, to incorporate new types and then to blend them and the old into something like harmonious cohesion. It was a task of great magnitude, bound up inextricably with the progress of music as an art ; made possible only by the ceaseless efforts of the Church and the laity, the monk and minstrel, the theoretician and practician. From the ancient Egyptian rebab to the first Stradivarius violin is a far cry. Yet from the one to the other we can trace the gradual evolution of a type of stringed instrument recognised by musicians of all centuries as the quintessential feature not only of instrumental music itself but also of vocal music requiring instrumental accompaniment. The wood-wind, brass and percussion, less manageable and more assertive than the strings, developed at a slower rate. Not until the days of Monteverdi did it occur to the composer that the general distribution of these instruments, in combination with others less noisy, was palpably wrong.

And now for the first time the balance of the orchestra, inter-sectionally, was *considered* in all seriousness. Strings were augmented and other instruments reduced. Even then it took many years to *achieve* anything like a satisfactory balance. The orchestra of Handel's time—a century later than Monteverdi—is still to be found struggling with a devastating number of oboes and bassoons, horns, trumpets and drums. We can only conjecture the unhappy and drowned condition of the poor strings in such circumstances. But from the days of Haydn all was plain sailing. The orchestra had found not only its feet, but its sea-legs.

It was now fit to weather the many storms that would come its way from the direction of the symphonic and operatic composers. The strings rose from their watery grave to a new and glorious life and became the foundation on which everything else was built. The wind and brass were harnessed at last, mostly in pairs, and took the timpani into their fold. But the degradation of the noisier percussion instruments was now complete. To all intents and purposes they were banished from the new consort. Their eclipse in the classical age of music was to be followed by a vulgar revival early in the 19th century, at which time they became the prey of those operatic composers who are now little remembered by their operas but often indeed by the charming but dreadfully over-percussioned overtures to those forgotten works. And I very much doubt whether these percussion instruments have fully recovered from the degradation to which they were subjected one hundred years ago.

## SIX TYPICAL ORCHESTRAS

(1) ASSYRIA. TIME OF ASSUR-BANI-PAL. (6th century B.C.)
   (a) Harps, trigons (triangular harps), pipes and drums.
   (b) *For the dance.* Lyre, harp, tambourine and cymbals.

(2) TIME OF QUEEN ELIZABETH. (16th century.)
   Viol, flute, cittern, pandora (another form of cittern), lute and viol da gamba.
   *Note.* Only the flute " breaks " the string consort.

(3) TIME OF JAMES I. (Early 17th century.)
   Pipe and tabor, treble violin, 2 bass violins, 2 sackbuts, mandora (lutina or small lute), and tenor cornett (zinke).
   *Note.* The consort is still further broken by the addition of brass instruments.

(4) TIME OF CHARLES II, PEPYS, PURCELL, STRADIVARIUS. (Late 17th century.)

Violins, violas and violoncellos to the number of 39.

3 Bass viols, 2 theorboes, 4 guitars, 4 recorders.

2 Harpsichords, 4 trumpets and kettledrums.

> *Note.* Quite a discreet broken consort that, in an orchestra of 59, would suffer only 8 wind instruments and a pair of drums.

(5) TIME OF BACH, HANDEL, A. SCARLATTI, RAMEAU. (Early 18th century.)

Flutes, oboes, oboe d'amore, oboe di caccia, bassoons.

Horns, trumpets, trombones, drums, bells.

Violins, viols, violino piccolo (small violin), viola d'amore, viola pomposa (large-sized viola), viol da gamba, violoncello, violone (double-bass).

Organ.

Harpsichord or clavichord.

> *Note.* All these instruments were used by Bach, but in various small combinations chosen from the above list. The harpsichord or clavichord helped mainly to supplement the middle harmonies, since many of the instruments could not be trusted to perform their parts adequately if left to themselves.

(6) TIME OF HAYDN AND MOZART. (Late 18th century.)

2 Flutes, 2 oboes; 2 clarinets (on occasions only, and sometimes displacing the oboes), 2 bassoons.

2 Horns, 2 trumpets; 3 trombones (on occasions only, and never in symphonies).

Timpani (one pair only. Other percussion instruments very seldom).

Violins, divided into 1sts and 2nds.

Violas, violoncellos and double-basses.

> *Note.* The personnel of this orchestra was usually about 35 or 40.

# B: THE EXPANSION OF THE ORCHESTRA

## CHAPTER I

## TROMBONES AND HORNS

NOT FOR LONG was the orchestra to remain in the state of calm that had produced the shapely Haydn symphonies, for a great dramatic genius was already finding it insufficient for his musical needs. When Mozart was writing his opera " Don Giovanni " in 1787 the trombones had already returned to some favour with composers. Once the numerical balance between strings, wind instruments and percussion had been settled satisfactorily in the main essentials, there seems to have been little hesitation in accepting the trombones (usually three) as rightful additions to the brass section. Gluck, in particular, used them to fine effect in his operas. But no one at that time seemed to want them in the symphony, not even Mozart. Their subsequent elevation to symphonic rank came from Beethoven some twenty years after " Don Giovanni " was written.

Yet it was actually Mozart who rediscovered the trombones in all their splendour of tone. He it was who in the last act of " Don Giovanni " gave them a new and wonderful significance. He it was who, in " The Magic Flute," four years later, again invested them with an extraordinary duality of character ; first, to illustrate the Temple of Wisdom and Light, wherein Masonic rites were performed by the high priest Sarastro and his brethren ; and, secondly, to depict the final descent of Sarastro's enemy the Queen of Night into her Kingdom of Darkness. If Haydn has been called the " Father of the Symphony," then assuredly we must rank Mozart as the male parent of modern orchestration. And lest the reader think I am overstating matters, let me recall to his mind the scenes in " Don Giovanni," where, in my submission, the three trombones for the first time foreshadow in the most definite terms the birth of the modern orchestra.

In the churchyard stand Don Giovanni and his servant Leporello before the statue of the dead Commandant, who, it will be remembered, had been killed by Giovanni in the first scene of the opera. Suddenly the statue comes to life, warning Giovanni of his impending doom. At this sinister moment, and, be it noted, for the first time in the opera, Mozart introduces his three trombones, and by such means gives to the scene a touch of horror the equal to which can scarcely be found in all music. Nor is that all. When, in the banqueting hall, two scenes later, the statue appears unexpectedly, having accepted Giovanni's mocking invitation to supper, the same type of orchestration recurs and continues throughout the terrifying scene until the unrepentant Giovanni is swallowed up in the flames of Hell.

Beethoven must have known this opera and " The Magic Flute " in his young impressionable days, and could scarcely have remained unaffected by the masterly orchestration at the points I have enumerated. Here indeed was something new. He would have noted the special use to which the trombones were put : how they were introduced at crucial moments in the drama to give the required effect when all other instruments failed to reach the point of intensity demanded by the composer. And, he might have thought, if this could be done in opera, why not in the symphony ? And so it is no mere idle surmise to suggest that the triumphant finale to his immortal Fifth Symphony, in which the three trombones are heard for the first time in *any* symphony, owes its origin to Mozart and his two operas. Since we know of no other music of the period that could have affected Beethoven to a like extent, we must accept this circumstantial evidence and draw the only conclusion possible.

From about this time onwards the orchestra became the centre of feverish activity in all directions. String players were now fairly reliable in technique—witness what Beethoven had the temerity to write—and had greatly increased in numbers. The wood-wind, too, having adopted the clarinet for permanent inclusion, could now produce something like a true blend of tone-colours, while the brass welcomed the trombones when the music was of the kind demanding their presence and their weight. The age of expansion was now drawing near, for instrumental music was making such rapid headway as a powerful and emotional art that the small *poudré* orchestra of the 18th century was proving totally inadequate for the expression of all the thoughts now surging in the composer's mind. Beethoven, as early as his third symphony (the " Eroica ") already felt the need of some such expansion. When he planned this noble masterpiece as a tribute to Napoléon Buonaparte he found that two horns were insufficient to express all that the music contained, and so a third was added. Never was a decision better made, for almost every bar of the music justifies the third instrument. Without it the Symphony could barely exist ; through it we inherited such wonderful passages as those in the trio of the Scherzo— passages at once the pride of all music-lovers and the despair of nervous horn-players. Yet Beethoven, though such an innovator, did not despise the orchestration of his predecessors. He had the supreme virtue of knowing how to vary his instruments according to the requirements of the music, relying on the Mozartian orchestra for many of his finest compositions and departing therefrom only when driven by the dæmonic spirit that created such masterpieces as the Fifth and Choral Symphonies.

The following table shows at a glance where Beethoven added certain instruments to his orchestra for specific purposes. The customary strings and timpani are not included here, being common to all the Symphonies.

The use of the trombones in the symphony was far from regular also among Beethoven's great contemporaries and

| INSTRUMENT | SYMPHO-NIES 1, 2, 4, 7, 8 | 3 (Eroica) | 5 | 6 (Pastoral) | 9 (Choral) |
|---|---|---|---|---|---|
| Flute | 2 | 2 | 2 | 2 | 2 |
| Piccolo | — | — | 1 | 1 | 1 |
| Oboe | 2 | 2 | 2 | 2 | 2 |
| Clarinet | 2 | 2 | 2 | 2 | 2 |
| Bassoon | 2 | 2 | 2 | 2 | 2 |
| Double-Bassoon | — | — | 1 | — | 1 |
| Horn | 2 | 3 | 2 | 2 | 4 |
| Trumpet | 2 | 2 | 2 | 2 | 2 |
| Trombone | — | — | 3 | 2 | 3 |
| Triangle | — | — | — | — | 1 |
| Cymbals | — | — | — | — | 1 |
| Bass Drum | — | — | — | — | 1 |

those romantic composers immediately following him. Schubert omits them in his early symphonies, but makes up gloriously in the " Unfinished " (No. 8 in B minor) and the great C major (No. 7). There is, in fact, no more purposeful or poignant writing for trombones to be found anywhere among the great masters' symphonies than in these two supreme examples. In this connection I would refer the reader more particularly to the slow movements, where there are many quiet passages of surpassing beauty. Schumann included trombones in each of his four symphonies, but, I am afraid, with scant understanding or set musical purpose. But Mendelssohn found them unnecessary in his wholly charming and picturesque Scotch and Italian Symphonies (Nos. 3 and 4). He omitted them purposely, for, of all composers, he knew how to score, using, like Beethoven, no more instruments than seemed necessary to the proper expression of his ideas.

Sufficient has now been written about the trombones to show what an important part they were playing at this period. No less important was the advance of the horns. Between 1841 and 1853 Schumann had used two pairs in each of his four symphonies, an expansion that had already become the vogue in operatic music, noticeably Weber's. All things considered, this expansion was inevitable, and for good reasons. It was still the day of the natural horn and trumpet, when composers had to juggle considerably with their music to make it playable—a difficulty already explained elsewhere. But music, in the hands of romantic composers like Schubert, Schumann, Chopin, Mendelssohn and Weber, had by now travelled far away from the diatonic character that was its chief glory and strength in earlier days. Chromatic harmony was all the rage : quick changes of key the *sine qua non* of this new dramatic art. The old foundations both in instrumental and vocal music were being sapped one by one by a strong undercurrent destined eventually to sweep away the long-established order of things and bring about a complete revolution in every direction. Once more the composer was ahead of the times, caught between the upper millstone of the chromatic harmonies he had discovered and the nether one of those old-fashioned brass instruments unable to give him what he so ardently desired. Again his ingenuity saved him when he installed a second pair of horns in the orchestra, crooked (that is, tuned) in a different key for the purpose of supplementing the other pair that could only play very intermittently when the music had modulated. Even then everything was more or less a makeshift, and, in fact, remained so until the liberation came about the year 1850. At this time valves were added to the horns and trumpets, a revolutionising invention that solved for all time most of the technical difficulties confronting both instrumentalist and composer. Chromatic music could now roam at will over any or all of the brass instruments. Crooks gradually fell into disuse, though hesitatingly ; no longer was the horn-player compelled to carry about with him all those various tube-lengths that have been so often and unkindly compared to sections of gas-piping. The coming of the valved horns and trumpets marked the end of a period.

## CHAPTER II

# THE ORCHESTRAL REVOLUTION

Revolution was now afoot in all directions. Many
of the old classical forms of music were either breaking
down, or, when they did survive, having a bewildering
number of new interpretations put upon them. The prowess
of the composer had advanced with such startling rapidity,
particularly in orchestral music, that instruments could not
keep pace with the general development of the art. From
the moment the nucleus of a real symphonic orchestra was
formed by Haydn and his contemporaries, musical composition of the instrumental kind was continually ahead, out-
stripping its own means of expression and demanding more
and more instruments as each daring composer came along
in all his insurgency.

Naturally it was the group of operatic composers who
showed the first signs of dissatisfaction with their lot. They
ever do, they ever will. Gone were the Mozartian traditions,
lost in an age of vehement romantic music. Now it was well-
nigh impossible for the composer to think in terms of the old
classical orchestra, to write with the same perfect poise and
mastery that had caused Mozart to withhold his trombones
from all but two scenes of " Don Giovanni." To Berlioz,
born ten years before Wagner, the orchestra meant more in
effects of massed sonority and grandeur than it did otherwise, beautiful as some of his more delicately scored compositions may sound to our ears—witness, for instance, the
Queen Mab Scherzo from his " Romeo and Juliet "
Symphony. To Wagner, the orchestra, in all the dazzling
radiance that could be produced by the addition of many
instruments, was the very life-blood of music. In general
terms, it was now an age of musical violence, an age caught
up in the toils of descriptive programme music : one that
demanded much in every direction save the classical. And,

as the old proverb says, much wants more. The great school of classical music, wherein the main object and delight of the composer was the creation of works primarily perfect in design, had now been superseded by that of the romanticists and realists whose chiefest aim was to squeeze the last ounce of sonority from the orchestra.

The orchestra grew apace. New instruments joined forces with those already in use, but not quite so haphazardly as in times past. There was definite order in all the composer put on paper and realised in sound. The age of the old symphonic orchestration had given way to that of the dramatic, and even if this were a musical revolution of the greatest moment, what was done by the composers was done deliberately, with real insight, and yet with respect for the past achievements of the classical masters. Each family of wind instruments was extended, and, to balance this extension, the strings were increased in proportion. The percussion department, too, came back into prominence, for the new music was pricked out with a large array of drums, cymbals and other instruments of no determinate pitch. And again that was done with some discrimination, which was hardly the case with the lighter operatic composers of the period, such as Auber, Suppé, and even Rossini. There was a genuine revival of interest in all those rhythmic instruments that had fascinated the ancient Assyrians and Egyptians but had in subsequent times been so badly mishandled. Nor should it be forgotten, incidentally, that this revival owed its existence to the fact that a single pair of kettledrums was found to be quite insufficient, percussively, to support the massed effects now becoming so frequent in music of a restless fevered age.

And so, with all this added wealth of new orchestral timbres at hand, few composers were now inclined to follow slavishly in the path of tradition, though (as Brahms was soon to prove) music of the classical type was by no means played out.

Berlioz, in many ways more revolutionary than Wagner, though less practical, was the leader of this new movement.

Nothing was too big for him. His conception of the orchestra was on a scale never approached by Wagner, and much of what he advocated in his " Traité de l'instrumentation " (1843) was entirely outside the realms of " practical politics." Here he aimed, theoretically, at the creation of a stupendous orchestra, one that, to perform ideally, must contain no fewer than 242 strings, some 30 grand pianos, an equal number of harps, together with wind and percussion instruments in relatively high proportions. But when it came to scoring his impetuous and intensely vivid music, he was usually contented with a far less lavish display of instruments than his theories demanded. Nor did he altogether prove in practice that he understood intimately the true balance of sounds. In the earlier years of these extravagant theories he soon came to loggerheads with the practical musicians of Paris, and so, for true recognition of his undoubted genius, he was compelled to go abroad : to Germany, Austria, and even to England (1851). In these countries his fecund, semi-crazy ideas, coupled to brilliant orchestration of a kind entirely new, stimulated rather than annoyed his audiences, and he met with much success. " I understand," said the King of Prussia (this I am quoting from Grove's Dictionary), " that you are the composer who writes for five hundred musicians." " Your Majesty has been misinformed," answered Berlioz; " I sometimes write for four hundred and fifty."

On sounder principles was the orchestral art of Richard Wagner founded. Instead of " spreading " his instrumentation in the diffuse, often unpractical and angular manner of a Berlioz, he, in the mature music-dramas of his middle and later periods, sought to concentrate the sounds by a rich and proportioned blending of all sections of the orchestra. That, too, demanded an orchestra of large size. But the one perfected by Wagner in its every blend and balance was in most ways far superior to that of Berlioz because each section was developed *pari passu*. And although it does not always follow that the balance of sounds in an

Fc

orchestra depends on the definite numerical ratio of one section to another, yet, when we listen to the most brilliant pages of Berlioz and Wagner, we realise why the latter's methods are the more satisfactory. Nothing is disproportionate.

In the Overture " Benvenuto Cellini " Berlioz makes brilliant play with his brass and percussion, which sections, in combination, greatly outnumber the wood-wind, as will be seen in the table given below. And, in addition, three notes on the kettledrums are often sounded simultaneously —a device very dear to the heart of Berlioz. Against these weighty effects the pairs of flutes, oboes and clarinets (Haydn used as many), are often quite unable to assist the brilliant top parts of the music to the full extent Berlioz evidently had in mind. Nor are matters helped by the extra sonority of the four bassoons playing well down in the bass. By such errors Berlioz frequently showed lack of judgment. Wagner's instrumental quantities, on the other hand, were in perfect accord with his qualities. Though, in fact, the wood-wind and the brass were so subdivided by him that each type of instrument " grew " a family of its own, yet everything was proportioned most accurately to the whole orchestra, matter and manner of expression being co-ordinated to a degree unsurpassed even to this day.

The table (p. 163), if compared to the list of instruments required for Beethoven's symphonies, makes interesting reading, more especially as the score of " Das Rheingold " (from " The Ring of the Nibelungs ") was completed only thirty-one years after that of the Choral Symphony.

As this chapter concerns the actual growth of the orchestra, consideration of the sounds produced by these new instruments must be deferred until later. But it is well to draw the reader's attention at this point to the enormous expansion of all sections, particularly as required by Wagner. This most practical of all composers, though demanding so much, indulged in none of the freakish tricks that sometimes disfigured the orchestration of Berlioz through miscalculation. True, he more or less

| Instrument | Benvenuto Cellini (Berlioz) | Harold in Italy (Berlioz) | The Nibelungs' Ring (Wagner) |
|---|---|---|---|
| Flute | 2 | 2 | 3 } four players required |
| Piccolo | 1 | 1 | 2 } |
| Oboe | 2 | 2 | 3 |
| Cor Anglais | — | 1 | 1 |
| Clarinet | 2 | 2 | 3 |
| Bass Clarinet | — | — | 1 |
| Bassoon | 4 | 4 | 3 |
| Double-Bassoon | — | — | — |
| Horn | 4 | 4 | 8 |
| Trumpet | 4 | 2 | 3 |
| Cornet (modern) | 2 | 2 | — |
| Bass Trumpet | — | — | 1 |
| Trombone | 3 | 3 | 3 |
| Contra-Bass Trombone | — | — | 1 |
| Tenor Tuba | — | — | 2 |
| Bass Tuba | 1 | 1 ( or Ophicleide) | 2 |
| Contra-Bass Tuba | — | — | 1 |
| Timpani | 3 (two players) | 1 pair | 2 pairs |
| Triangle | 1 | 1 | 1 |
| Side Drum | — | 2 (small) | 1 |
| Cymbals | 1 | 1 | 1 |
| Bass Drum | 1 | — | — |
| Glockenspiel | — | — | 1 |
| Gong (Tamtam) | — | — | 1 |
| Harp | — | 1 | 6 |
| 1st Violin | } Number of players not specified | 15 | 16 |
| 2nd Violin | | 15 | 16 |
| Viola | | 10 ( & solo) | 12 |
| Violoncello | | 12 | 12 |
| Double-Bass | | 9 | 8 |

created that new brass family—a family not always at hand when wanted—the " Wagner Tubas," but that was for specific purposes fully justified in the music. On the other hand, his multiplication of harp parts is now considered fantastic ; somewhat failing in the effect intended, and, in short, impracticable. That apart, in all sections of the orchestra, used either singly or in combination, he set a standard of orchestration that, without doubt, has never since been equalled, though imitated by countless composers of all nationalities. Wagner's 64 string players, when compared to Mozart's full orchestra of 35, are eloquent testimony to the richness of sound desired by the composer. Those readers who have been fortunate enough to hear such numbers in any performance of " The Ring of the Nibelungs " can bear witness to the uncanny accuracy of Wagner's calculations in this respect, for never does any one section of the orchestra obtrude on another. With fewer strings the bloom is no longer on the sound ; everything becomes discoloured and distorted ; the spirit of the composer vanishes into nothingness.

But whether music of the non-operatic kind can live in the luxuriance of all this richly coloured orchestration without palling on the senses sooner or later is a controversial matter into which it would here be unwise to inquire. The post-Wagnerian composers have, on the whole, thought it could ; though, while stating this, we must not forget the heroic lone hand played by Brahms in his masterly endeavour to save the world of classical orchestral music from total extinction—an objective that to his mind could only be reached by curbing all desire for brilliant instrumentation for its own sake.

## CHAPTER III

# THE ORCHESTRA TO-DAY

Remarkable developments have taken place since those days. Such instruments as the piccolo, cor anglais, bass clarinet, double-bassoon, bass tuba, glockenspiel, celeste, harp, and percussion instruments of indeterminate pitch have now taken a regular place in the orchestra ; indeed, an orchestra would be considered unworthy of its name were these instruments not " on the strength." But it is to be feared that many of the composers of this later age, while adopting the Wagner orchestra as a general basis (but employing his methods rather less skilfully), have been far from content to leave it in the state of well-balanced sonority so perfected by their lord and master. The inevitable new instruments had to be added ; though, when listening to some of the best music written since Wagner's day, we often have cause to wonder why. From the time of Richard Strauss onwards the orchestra has become such a complicated piece of machinery that it is an open question whether music has really benefited by it in recent years or progressed in that complete naturalness of style so apparent in the past. And it is equally questionable whether the sheer congestion of sounds so often heard has not nullified the effectiveness of some of those extra instruments found in modern scores—scores which, in their appearance, make Wagner's look almost like a child's copy-book. Yet, whichever way we argue, there has been magnificent music written in this vein, of a kind to set the nerves a-tingle, to make the flesh creep, and to thrill body and soul with its sheer power and genius. Could that have been better done with fewer instruments ? Much of it, undoubtedly ; even by Wagner's most talented successors. At other times, when special effects are intended, there seems to be every justification for an orchestra outsizing even Wagner's. It all resolves itself into a matter of taste. There are many who find music written in pre-Wagner days intolerably dull because of the absence of vivid tone-colours. To them the art of the musical architect falls on deaf ears ; they are unaffected by the beauty of design and cannot appreciate any lightly coloured music : it sounds thin and uninteresting. The more crowded the canvas the happier they are. Dramatic orchestration is their very life-blood ; the classical anæmic and of poor vitality. And if that were the general reaction to music in post-Wagner days, when spiritual values were somewhat at a discount and forceful " Ring " orchestration all the rage, it is hardly a matter for wonder that the new school of composers following in the wake of this movement tried in their enthusiasm to out-Richard Richard, not only in the actual volume of sound but also in inventiveness of new instrumental combinations.

What was done by Wagner for the operatic orchestra soon became the model for many extended works written for the concert-room. And in this direction no one possessed a more virile pen than Richard Strauss. Although his tone-poem " Don Juan " may seem to the more sophisticated to-day little more than the calf-love adventures of an ardent youth fresh from school, yet at its first performance in Berlin in 1888 it caused a great sensation, largely due to its full-blooded Wagnerian scoring. This, however, was only a mild beginning, and Strauss soon followed with other works of a like kind that incorporated more and more of the instrumentation of his great predecessor. While his contemporaries in other lands—Saint-Saëns in France, Rimsky-Korsakov and Glazounov in Russia, casually to name a few—were all content to keep the orchestra within definite numerical bounds, he became more and more venturesome in the use of extra instruments. Yet, in spite of the enormous size of his orchestra, he managed to contrive everything with wonderful skill and knowledge of effects. His scores became bewilderingly elaborate in every detail ; to open at random any one from " Till Eulenspiegel " onwards is indeed like peering into a pavement of mosaic in blinding sunlight.

By the time " Ein Heldenleben " was reached (1898) his orchestra had outgrown even Wagner's.

To extend my argument further would serve no practical purpose, for it is impossible to recount in detail the many wonderful, even fearsome developments undergone by the modern orchestra since " Ein Heldenleben " startled the world anew thirty-six years ago. More has happened in the meantime than could be told in ten volumes of encyclopædic size. The orchestra continued to grow to such proportions that nothing seemed big enough, ten or fifteen years ago, to meet the insatiable desires of certain composers for sound and noise mixed in injudicious quantities. Many instruments, both new and old, were included, often for little apparent reason. The heckelphone (bass oboe), sarrusophone, bass flute, saxophones in all their variety— alack the day when they first saw the light !—small clarinets pitched in D and E flat, large tubular bells, anvil, wind-machine, rattle, xylophone, sheet metal, guitar, mandoline, concertina, grand piano, dulcitone, saxhorn, and even the gramophone have all been pressed into service in modern scores ; and, to the credit of the composer, many of these instruments have justified their appearance. But the clever cheapjack composers, prone to step in where angels fear to tread, have so vulgarised every special effect created by their superiors that the tendency among thoughtful composers of the present time is to return to an orchestra of dimensions no more imposing than those of Wagner's day.

The wave of stark realism that swept over Europe's music in recent years was a natural phenomenon, with an undoubted origin in primitive sounds such as can be found in " The Ring of the Nibelungs " ; and, to illustrate this statement, I would mention in particular the scene in " Götterdämmerung " where the Gibichung vassals assemble for the wedding of Siegfried with Gutrune. Here the din of the cowhorns, interspersed with the fierce shouts of the vassals, belongs to a type of music utterly inhuman and barbaric : savage, lustful, and repellent. From such music to

Stravinsky's "Le Sacre du Printemps" is not a far cry. In this unique work the composer abandons himself to the most amazing concatenation of instrumental forces, all intended to convey the impression of a pagan festival in springtime. Nothing is left to the imagination, for the virtuosity of the orchestral technique is masterly in the extreme. We stand aghast at Stravinsky's expressed abhorrence of everything for which music had stood these many centuries. He makes us feel that the very essence of civilisation, all beauty and romance, all human endeavour and progress are being ruthlessly swept aside to make room for hideous sounds primitive in origin and atavistic expression. At such a pass do we find the world of orchestral music some twenty years ago.

But virtuosity of this kind must come to an end once it has been driven to such extremes. And so it speaks volumes for the common sense of the composer that few have attempted to follow permanently in the footsteps of Stravinsky, despite a certain craze when this composer's popularity was at its height. Had there been any such general desire, music by now might have been in Bedlam. From this fate it was saved by the composer's interest in the living world around him and by that spirit of romance from which there is no escape once he is immersed in the creation of orchestral music. Other Stravinskys may come and go, but the results will always be the same. Stark realism must surrender in the end to rational romanticism. Future composers will, I fancy, emulate those of the present day who are content to write for the medium-sized modern orchestra. Atavism in music has had its fling and been found wanting. Cerebral music, too, is on the wane, for it can only succeed in pleasing its own generation and displeasing the next. But if anything can survive in an age of non-classical music it will be music of the romantic kind, for that comes nearest the hearts of men. It may have its weaknesses, and become, in its worst moments, lush and unbearable. Still, in the hands of men like Strauss, Elgar, Bax, Delius and Debussy, it says something that holds the interest and stirs the

emotions by its oft-expressed beauty. And the further the
noise of the great war of 1914–18 recedes into the distance,
the nearer will the composer approach music in that spirit
of patience without which the great masterpieces of the past
could never have been written. Will he, with all his accumulated knowledge of the beauty of instrumental tones, evoke
in time a new golden age of classical music, in which design
and colour will no longer contend for the mastery ? I
wonder. Limitation of instruments may come before
limitation of armaments.

I cannot conclude this chapter without setting down for
purposes of comparison further examples of modern
orchestral scores. And, in view of what has been written
already, the reader will no doubt take more than a passing
interest in the score of Respighi's " Pine-trees of Rome," in
which the composer, depicting a vivid scene of the old
consular army marching in triumph to the Capitol,
" reinstates " that ancient instrument the *buccina*. But, in
the regrettable absence of the original, he indicates that the
six buccina parts shall be played on *flicorni*, which word,
being itself interpreted, means saxhorns and tubas. In this
interesting work a gramophone record of a nightingale is
also introduced, Philomel in person being beyond the
reach of modern orchestrators, however audacious.

Beyond this point my account of the expansion of the
orchestra need not go. Such scores as Josef Holbrooke's
" Children of Don " are phenomena the like of which we
shall probably never see again. There the oboe d'amore
and corno di bassetto—those links with the days of Bach
and Mozart—strenuously compete with almost every conceivable modern instrument, including a family of five
saxophones. Across a gulf of many years ancient and
modern stare at one another with a gaze none too friendly.
Let me leave it at that for fear I offend.

| INSTRUMENT | HELDENLEBEN (Strauss) (1898) | THE PLANETS (Holst) (1918) | PINE-TREES OF ROME (Respighi) (1924) |
|---|---|---|---|
| Flute | 3 | 4 | 3 |
| Piccolo | 1 | 2 | 1 |
| Bass Flute | — | 1 | — |
| Oboe | 3 | 3 | 2 |
| Cor Anglais | 1 | 1 | 1 |
| Bass Oboe | — | 1 | — |
| E flat Clarinet | 1 | — | — |
| Clarinet | 2 | 3 | 2 |
| Bass Clarinet | 1 | 1 | 1 |
| Bassoon | 3 | 3 | 2 |
| Double-Bassoon | 1 | 1 | 1 |
| Horn | 3 | 6 | 4 |
| Trumpet | 5 | 4 | 3 (also 1 behind the scenes |
| Trombone | 3 | 3 | 4 |
| Tuba | 2 | 2 | — |
| (Buccina) | — | — | 6 (flicorni) |
| Timpani | 3 | 6 (two players) | 3 |
| Side Drum | 1 | 1 | 1 |
| Tenor Drum | 1 | — | — |
| Bass Drum | 1 | 1 | 1 |
| Triangle | — | 1 | 1 |
| Tambourine | — | 1 | — |
| Tambour de Basque | — | — | 1 |
| Cymbals | 1 | 1 | 1 |
| Gong (tamtam) | — | 1 | 1 |
| Glockenspiel | — | 1 | 1 |
| Xylophone | — | 1 | — |
| Celeste | — | 1 | 1 |
| Piano | — | — | 1 |
| Organ | — | 1 | 1 |
| Harp | 2 | 2 | 1 |
| Gramophone | — | — | 1 |
| 1st Violin | 16 | Number of players not specified | ditto |
| 2nd Violin | 16 | | |
| Viola | 12 | | |
| Violoncello | 12 | | |
| Double-Bass | 8 | | |

Chorus of Women's Voices is also to be found in the last movement of " The Planets."

# C: THE ORCHESTRA AS INSTRUMENT

## CHAPTER I

## ARRANGEMENT OF INSTRUMENTS IN A FULL SCORE

IT HAS LONG BEEN the practice of composers to write the string parts almost invariably at the foot of the score, for, since the time when the violin family superseded the viols, these instruments have been rightly regarded as the foundation tone of the whole orchestra to which all else is subservient and purely incidental, however importantly so. It is only natural, therefore, to find the more delicate woodwind instruments at the top of the score, ranged downwards more or less in order of their pitch—the piccolo is the exception—and resting on their own foundation of bassoons and, less frequently, of double-bassoon. Since the woodwind are entrusted with so much music of the *solo* kind, such, for example, as a flute, oboe or clarinet melody against a string accompaniment, it seems but poetic justice that composers should have accorded this group an outstanding position in the score. Besides which, this arrangement enables the conductor better to see at a glance where often the main melodic interest in the music lies. For the same reason the horns, though not so high-pitched as the trumpets, are usually placed at the head of the brass group. Wagner, however, was a notable exception in this respect, preferring to sandwich the horns between clarinets and bassoons because of their accommodating tone-quality. This quality, which, briefly, we can call " round and mellow," permits this instrument to blend as successfully with the

| Group | Instruments in order down each page of the Score |
|-------|--------------------------------------------------|
| WOOD-WIND | 2 Flutes, piccolo |
| | 2 Oboes, cor anglais |
| | 2 Clarinets, bass clarinet |
| | 2 Bassoons, double-bassoon |
| BRASS | 4 French horns (German horns are lately coming into vogue, on account of their broader tone) |
| | 3 Trumpets |
| | 3 Trombones |
| | Bass Tuba |
| PERCUSSION | 3 Timpani ; then smaller instruments such as triangle, tambourine, etc. ; larger instruments such as cymbals, bass drum, etc.; glockenspiel, celeste, bells, etc. |
| HARP | Two are frequently employed, but are less frequently available |
| STRINGS | 1st Violins, 2nd violins, violas, violoncellos, double-basses—all in varying numbers. (14, 12, 10, 8, 8, would fairly indicate the number of strings in a well-equipped modern orchestra.) |

N.B. Miniature pocket-size full scores of most classical and modern works can be bought nowadays ; many of them at trifling cost. See also p. 43.

wood-wind as with the other members of the brass ; in fact with slightly more success, for this very roundness of tone does not always match the open martial ring of trumpets and trombones, yet, in the hands of a skilful orchestrator, can never be said to conflict with the quality of either clarinet or bassoon. This dual nature of the horn —able to take its place with almost equal success in either wood-wind or brass passages—makes the instrument in many ways the most important member of the orchestra after the strings. Listening to a symphony by Brahms, one cannot fail to realise that four horns, shouldering the burden of the middle harmonies in the more sonorous passages, give to the music a sense of cohesion and strength unobtainable otherwise. Whether in combination with woodwind or assisting the brass at moments of climax, they always show up to great advantage ; indeed, without their assistance the modern orchestra would be quite invertebrate.

And since the other brass instruments and the percussion take charge of the heaviest effects, the centre of the page seems a most appropriate position for setting out their share of the music. What is written for them there strikes the eye of the conductor immediately, since in the majority of works there will be found page after page without any reference to these instruments—blank spaces unrelieved by a single note. For it must be remembered that in a wellordered score the heavy brass and percussion instruments have the least to do. They are reserved mainly (but not altogether) for climaxes, adding their weight to the remainder of the orchestra when the music is most insistent in mood. In Brahms's First Symphony the trombones play only 83 bars in a total of 1,262 ; an instance of restraint completely justified by the wonderful effectiveness of the writing when it does occur.

Such admirable restraint is, unfortunately, none too common a virtue amongst the minor composers or even with some more accomplished. A crowded full score is as distressing to the ear as a crowded canvas to the eye : there is nothing to choose between them. But the composer of genius, when writing for the orchestra, gathers to himself what I can best describe as certain instinctive formulæ for group-combinations. Maybe he will use the strings for nine-tenths of the time, or perhaps longer, treating them separately or in combination with wood-wind or horns or both. Then the music may develop in such a way that possibly the strings will be dispensed with for the time being, and wood-wind, brass or even percussion, again used either separately, or in combination, will be left to carry on the burden of the music. In due course the strings will return to emphasize the unapproachable beauty of their tone, justifying their claim to be considered the fount of all orchestral inspiration. Or again, a stupendous climax might arise, one clamouring for every instrument in the orchestra. And the passage involved might even be one where harmony was unwanted, where some theme of irresistible forcefulness called for presentation in stark octaves on strings, wood-wind and brass alike. Imagine what an effect could then be obtained if such a passage, its power all spent, were followed by the quiet murmur of strings in a muted *pianissimo*, or by fragrant harmonies on the wood-wind, perhaps even by chords or arpeggios plucked from a romantic harp. There is no end to the resources of the modern orchestra once the composer's imagination is set in motion, provided that all general rules relating to matters of balance, blend and contrast receive their due observance. Music thus compounded will always look well on paper ; a good musician can tell at a glance what is and what is not true orchestration.

Consideration of some of the more frequently used devices in orchestration will be found in other chapters of this book.

## CHAPTER II

# THE ORCHESTRA ON THE PLATFORM

SINCE EVERY conductor has his own peculiar idiosyncrasies about the placing of his instruments on what is called the " concert platform," the reader is asked to accept the diagram on p. 177 as being but roughly approximate. Moreover, it must be borne in mind that no two concert-halls are alike, and (more's the pity) that few of these are fitted, either constructionally or acoustically, to house an orchestra without a certain disadvantage to the music performed. There seems, in fact, to be some sort of unwritten conspiracy on the part of architects and those advising them to prevent musicians fully qualified giving practical suggestions as to what is actually required.

However, the general placing of instruments on the platform requires little comment here : it is mostly a matter of common sense, a practical setting-out of what is indicated in the full score of the music. In the diagram—which is modelled on the platform conditions existing in the Queen's Hall, London—it will be observed that the strings are nearest the conductor, their primary importance in the orchestra demanding such a position. It must also be remembered that this concert platform, like most others, has a good " rake " or tilt upwards away from the auditorium. The 1st and 2nd violins are usually to the left and right respectively, mainly because the antiphonal effects occurring so frequently between these instruments are the better heard and appreciated this way, both by conductor and audience. The violas also are near at hand, to contribute their warmth of tone to the middle notes of the harmony, for however satisfactory they might and could sound in the auditorium if placed differently, yet it is utterly essential that the conductor shall " feel " them in the total blend of the strings. There is nothing so disturbing to his equanimity (he will tell you) than violas scattered in the distance and half lost behind some barrage of wood-wind or brass instruments heard too strongly. Such a position gravely affects the conductor's control over the strings as a whole ; they seem disunited, lacking " body " in the inner parts. And it is equally essential that the 'cellos and double-basses shall be within friendly hail of one another, for much of the music is shared between these instruments, the double-basses playing many 'cello passages an octave lower.

Cohesion of the string parts is, indeed, the conductor's chiefest care.

What has been stated already about the position of the wood-wind in the full score explains their more elevated position on the platform. The conductor could scarcely deal satisfactorily with the many solo wood-wind passages—passages demanding flexible phrasing, carefully graded expression, and, in addition, some artistic licence on the part of the individual players—were these instruments not immediately facing him. He senses their positions just as keenly as the batsman or bowler is aware of his field. He has to turn his head or stance rapidly from strings, brass or percussion towards wood-wind, there to caress a melodic phrase or to impart a characteristic touch unaccomplishable were the player placed at too great a distance. It must be recorded here that perfect homogeneity *between* these instruments is also often a matter of chance owing to limitations of room (thanks to non-musical architects) ; too frequently it is a case of tempering the wood-wind to the shorn platform.

The brass are, naturally, further away and at a greater elevation. From their imposing position they enter the music with thrilling effect ; there is no mistaking them. But their very position demands great discretion from the conductor. Woe betide the balance of sounds between the various sections of the orchestra if the composer has scored his music too heavily or if the conductor be insensible to the difference between *forte* and *fortissimo* ! The domination of the brass can be made a very unlovely thing ; from their elevation, three trumpets, even when unsupported by trombones and tuba, have been known to obliterate the rest of the orchestra.

Behind the brass are the percussion instruments, with the timpanist in the centre—a veritable monarch of all he surveys, overtopped by the organ alone (when there happens to be one). From this eminence, the timpanist adds, with arresting effect, all those stirring touches without which no orchestral concert would be considered

# GENERAL DIAGRAM

(Subject to much variation in detail)

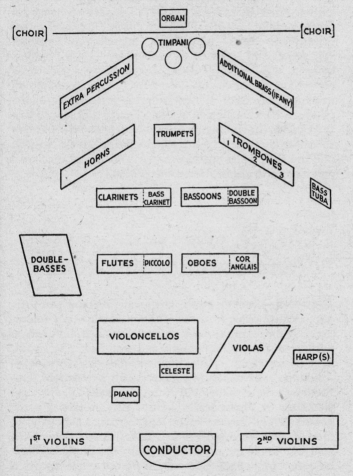

complete. He is looked up to in more senses than one ; he is the apex of the orchestra, able to command immediate attention, either thunderously, or through some remote *pianissimo* as mysterious as it is effective. Near him is gathered that odd collection of the heavier percussion instruments, usually known as " special effects " ; cymbals, bass drum, side drum, tambourine, triangle, glockenspiel, xylophone, and so on. The weaker-toned celeste, which, being a keyboard instrument, is played by a pianist, is always found near the conductor, for its delicate sounds do not carry far. And—to conclude this brief survey of the platform—the harp could scarcely occupy any other place than among the violins. On occasions useful, and at all times the most decorative instrument in the orchestra, its rich and romantic tones combine better with strings than with any other instrument. Hence its position.

# CHAPTER III

# THE CONDUCTOR'S RÔLE

LEGENDS about orchestral conductors are many, for their authoritative (even supreme) position, though fully understood by musicians and the musically-minded, is apt to be misinterpreted by that larger and less discerning world which boasts many millions unversed in the art's intricacies.

For the sake of my argument it can be assumed that Beethoven is a household word : a world-figure, like Napoleon or Shakespeare, Julius Cæsar or even (for the nonce) Primo Carnera—that lately deposed champion of fisticuffs. But whereas there may be millions of the uninitiated who know the pseudo-title if not the music of Beethoven's " Moonlight " Sonata, there are relatively but a few acquainted with his symphonies and still fewer able to appreciate any sustained argument concerning the merits or demerits of a conductor's *interpretation* of those symphonies.

For the word " interpretation," as applied to the conductor of an orchestra, conveys to many folk a meaning so ambiguous as to be almost unintelligible. They find it difficult to appreciate the finer points of an art that, in its technique, is intimately bound up with some kind of mysterious silence, while, on the contrary, the contribution of the players themselves is one of rich and glowing sounds. And so, to them, the conductor is little more than a " time-beater " ; his bâton but a modern development of that roll of parchment which did rough and ready service in those days of long ago when orchestral music was practically unknown.

Yet without the silent gestures, the wave of the arm or the quick exchange of glances between conductor and instrumentalist, the art of interpretation as applied to orchestral music would be in sorry plight. The actual time-beating is nothing more than elementary technique, acquired by instinct or study, incorporated in the course of time as an integral part of the conductor's equipment, and then reproduced by him quite automatically. And until he has mastered the technique of the bâton as a directing agency he will never be able to interpret music with any skill or feeling, for every technical shortcoming is noticed immediately by the instrumentalists supposedly under his control : a feeling of uncertainty will prevail and thereby prevent anything in the nature of stylism or the reproduction of the inner spirit of the music.

The conductor, therefore, learns his technique only to forget it—a palpable truism that applies here as much as it does to all human endeavour. His sole object is to concentrate on the artistic side of the performance and to re-create in living sounds what the composer has put so inspiredly on paper.

Now it can be stated in Malvolio-like language that some are born conductors, some achieve conducting and others have conductorship thrust upon them. No branch of the art of music is so open to misconception and abuse"; charlatanism and insufficiency of knowledge are more in evidence here than anywhere else. Many, indeed, are the conductors who find themselves directing orchestral forces with which they are all too little acquainted. From textbooks they may have picked up a fair amount of theoretical learning, which, a dangerous thing in itself, carries them but a short distance along the road of practicalities. A passing acquaintance with one, or, maybe, two instruments is hardly adequate for dealing with the thousand and one problems that must be faced during the course of rehearsals, problems cropping up from every corner of the orchestra.

For the work of the conductor falls within two distinct categories : rehearsal and performance. Without the ability to rehearse, the conductor can scarcely hope to give a satisfactory performance, however talented his instrumentalists. The composer, who of necessity must be well acquainted with the peculiarities of all instruments, may write the most intricate passages requiring patient, laborious and detailed rehearsal. If on such occasions the conductor is unable to formulate or communicate to his players any definite ideas as to what is required, it is obvious that any meritorious performance is out of the question. In brief, the conductor must be a man of parts, able at all times to explain the music in terms of the instrumentalist he is addressing. It requires, therefore, but a small stretch of imagination for the reader to realise that the perfect conductor, completely equipped, is about as chimerical as the phœnix, since one lifetime is all too brief a span for any man to acquire a full working knowledge of the manifold detail of the orchestra.

Even when a conductor possesses a sound general knowledge of the orchestra—and there are many whose practical experience is quite phenomenal—it does not necessarily follow that his performances will have more than average merit. Other qualities are needed. Magnetism, personality, strong telepathic powers and other marked characteristics are required to set the spirit of the music afire. And this flame of inspiration can only be rekindled through the conductor, whose mind must soar with the composer into the realms of pure fancy. There only can the beauty of the music itself be matched by the beauty of its interpretation. For without the inspiration of the conductor the greatest masterpiece is no better than a heap of dead notes : the composer's temple of sound but a ruin.

And thus it is that the more visible part of the conductor's art can be either eloquent or meaningless. By look and gesture he will convey to the instrumentalists, both individually and collectively, his inner conception of the music. They, on their part, and by some kind of telepathic response, will faithfully reproduce in sound what has been indicated to them in silence.

It follows that the conductor can indulge in many extravagances of style far removed from the original intentions of the composer. By the undiscerning and by the lover of the sensational such extravagances are termed " individual readings," for which the conductor is far too often belauded to the skies when his treasonable betrayal of the composer should earn him universal condemnation. And, unfortunately, such readings are becoming all too fashionable nowadays, the cult of the bizarre having produced that successor to the old-time prima-donna, the " virtuoso " conductor. He, having but an eye to personal advancement and avid for any effect that will keep him prominently before " his " public, upholds with consummate plausibility and with many an extravagant mannerism his own spurious versions of the masterpieces of music.

But the earnest conductor, he who reverences his art, desires no more than the re-creation of the composer in all the expressed detail of the score. He will be sparing of gesture, but such as are used will carry a full significance. Not a single one will occur that is not born of the music itself, for his last thought will be to place himself between the composer and the audience. He will use his right arm, with or without the bâton, mainly to indicate the time of the music ; and, where additional stress or strength is required, will occasionally introduce the left arm as an extra rhythmical pointer. But, generally, the left arm and hand will function independently of the right. " Let not thy left arm know what thy right arm doeth " might well be the motto of many a conductor unskilled in technique. There is nothing so ungainly, so meaningless in interpretation, so irritatingly windmill-like in its movements as the left arm and hand (unconvincingly loose-wristed) of a conductor incessantly reproducing what is being indicated on the right. Such actions but flog the music, bringing to it a sense of monotony, both aural and visual, that renders true interpretation impossible.[1] For the left arm and hand should be the phrase and expression makers : delicately poised " instruments " prompted into action by the conductor's inner feeling for the music and withdrawn when not required. By such means as are here described the heart of the music is sought and found, and, under the spell of inspiration, there is established between conductor and orchestra some altogether inexplicable form of telepathy that galvanises everything into life. The orator's rhetoric is not so remarkable as the conductor's, for the latter, with nothing but silent gestures and facial expression at his command, is able to fashion the sounds of the orchestra according to his every whim and fancy. He is no mere time-beater. His knowledge must cover a wider field than that of any other musician, while his art, viewed as a whole, undoubtedly rises superior to all other forms of musical interpretation.

[1] Nikisch, the great German conductor, is said to have tied a pupil's left arm behind his back for a whole term of lessons—a most convincing preventive.

## CHAPTER IV

# A GLANCE AT ORCHESTRATION

THE ART of orchestration is the blending of instrumental sounds of various timbres and is, indeed, analogous to the art of the painter ; the composer being concerned with tones in characteristic combinations, the painter with colours. And just as the painter can produce an infinite variety of tone-colours in his pictures, so (it is no exaggeration to state) can the imaginative composer with technique at his finger-tips orchestrate the common chord of C major in a hundred thousand different ways and still proceed similarly *ad infinitum*. In this limitless variety lies the greatness of that modern orchestra we have seen grow in the last part of this Book ; from such a combination of instruments have arisen the world's greatest masterpieces in music, master-pieces born of the composer's inspired grasp of the essential qualities of tone-colour. Violin, viola, bassoon, horn, trombone, timpani—to name a few instruments at random —convey the most vivid impressions to the composer's mind and feelings. Maybe he will hear, abstractly, the brilliance, the martial thrill or the solemn pomp of brass instruments, and his inventive power let loose in a flood of inspiration, is then able to create music whose very life-blood springs from combinations such as these. Or again, he hears, similarly, the plaintive quality of the oboe, the rich lyricism of the clarinet or the still richer tones of the violoncello. From his feeling for their special qualities he uses them in solo passages that are set off against a background of accompanying instruments : flowers of melody bejewelled in a meadowland of green. Even the percussion instruments will evoke gems of inspiration, as witness the timpani's glorious share of the rhythm in the Scherzo of Beethoven's " Choral Symphony," or the triangle's bold usurpation of the *shape* of a melodic phrase in Liszt's " Piano Concerto in

E flat." Add to the argument all those important factors in present-day music—(a) a compass of seven octaves over which the composer can roam at will both in melody and harmony ; (b) a range of time-values extending from " square " to " round " and compound times, i.e., two, three, four, six, nine, etc., or even five and seven beats in a bar ; (c) a range of expression extending from the scarcely audible *pianissimo* to the most devastating *fortissimo*—and it requires little stretch of imagination for the reader to realise that the resources of the modern orchestra are inexhaustible.

Yet such progress has taken place only within the last three hundred years, dating from the time when music began to enrobe itself with those richly coloured garments made possible through the gradual improvement of existing instruments, or through the addition or elimination of other types. Before that time orchestration can scarcely be said to have existed, for all " orchestral " music written in pre-Monteverdi days was the chance plaything of any ill-assorted collection of instruments ready to hand. But Monteverdi advanced a stage further when in his opera " Orfeo " he laid the foundations of a definite style in orchestration. True, in his choice of instruments, he still gravitated somewhat towards the past, despite his incorporation of many of the newer instruments coming into vogue. *Gravicembalo* (harpsichord), *violino piccolo* (small violin) *chittarone* (large lute), regal (small reed organ), *cornetto* (zinke), trombone, organ, muted trumpets and so on must have made a strange blend of sounds far removed from what the modern ear now regards as harmonious. Yet what he did must be accounted a beginning, and his use of the harpsichord in particular an early indication of that *continuo* type of orchestration which became the main feature of instrumental music for the next hundred years or more.

*Continuo* orchestration was, in all likelihood, the outcome of imperfect instruments and equally imperfect instrumentalists—a case, no doubt, of *faute de mieux*. Bach and

Handel (both born 118 years after Monteverdi) still had to struggle with many of those problems that had confronted their great predecessor and our own equally great Henry Purcell. And although it was the age of the Amatis, Stradivarius and those other geniuses who perfected the stringed instruments to a degree never since surpassed, yet most wind and brass instruments, untrue in pitch and sour in tone through faulty construction, could scarcely be trusted except in noisy out-of-doors music where their deficiencies would be less noticeable. Indifferent instruments produced indifferent players and so, conjointly, succeeded in frightening away the composer from any serious attempts to use them in company with the strings. And since even the string players were also suspect, the composer could not altogether trust anyone adequately to perform what was written, the magnificent instruments of the period notwithstanding. Thus it was that the *continuo* orchestration became the custom.

This consisted of employing the harpsichord—under its various names or variants such as *gravicembalo*, *clavicembalo*, *cembalo*, *clavecin* (Fr.), *flügel* (Ger.), etc.—to supplement or displace the string players in passages where the sole use of the latter might be considered unwise or even dangerous. The harpsichord was in the hands of a skilful musician who from a figured bass (as shown below) could be trusted to fill in the harmonies with judgment, especially the middle-pitched notes.

Composers of the 17th and early 18th centuries found this *continuo* orchestration not unpleasing to the ear and well suited to their general purposes. Those readers familiar with Mr. Frederic Austin's version of " The Beggar's Opera " will recall the many felicitous combinations of harpsichord and strings that give to the work a special colour linking it to its period. Listening to such music nowadays—in an age when every orchestral device and colour seems to have been explored and, oftentimes, exploded—is, in effect, very like the sound of cool mountain water threading its way through an undergrowth of exotic

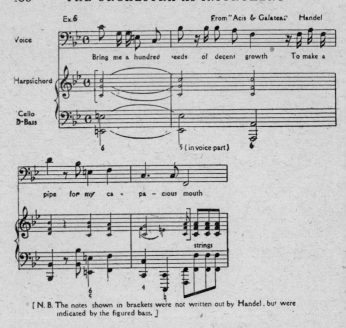

[ N. B. The notes shown in brackets were not written out by Handel, but were indicated by the figured bass. ]

flowers. In fact, it is due to the limitations imposed on composers of this period by the absence of first-rate instrumentalists that we have inherited a school of orchestration unique in certain characteristics. The harpsichord was the universal " stand-by," relied upon as the most satisfactory and convenient accompaniment to vocal recitative both in opera and oratorio. The strings, as a body, but rarely undertook this task, though the violoncello and double-bass did at times supplement the bass of the harmony owing to the weakness of the harpsichord in its lowest notes. In arias, too, the harpsichord had quite a lion's share of the music, for even here the strings could not be trusted with the more intricate detail, however straightforward the time and rhythm. I well remember my surprise at the fragmentariness of Alessandro Scarlatti's string writing in his opera "Il trionfo del onore" when I happened to look through the score at the British Museum some years ago. Nor was that general distrust of all instruments except the harpsichord overcome until the later days of Bach and Handel. These two composers, though failing to grasp the essential features of a full orchestra in the manner achieved by their contemporaries Gluck, Haydn and (in a smaller way) Rameau, yet managed to elevate the stringed instruments to a position of the highest importance. In Bach's six " Brandenburg Concerti " and Handel's many " Concerti Grossi " there is string writing of a contrapuntal kind that has probably never been improved upon to this day.

Bach, more intent (and, I dare say, rightly so) on the substance of his music than on any instrumental problems, contributed little to orchestration as we understand the term to-day. In the "Brandenburg Concerti," composed in 1721, he wrote for diverse combinations ; there was no attempt to blend the sounds in the manner introduced by Haydn with such success in his symphonies less than forty years later. Instead, he strove to invest certain instruments with a definite individuality against a background of strings. And in this he was eminently successful. But beyond that he did not go, preferring to express himself in terms of counterpoint of imperishable worth rather than through lavish tone-colours that might detract from the true essence of the music.

It was much the same with Handel. Few instrumental problems interested him. The original scoring of the " Messiah " would surprise and shock the listener, were it substituted for the usual versions by Mozart, Prout and others less well known. Nor would it be possible, once having heard Sir Hamilton Harty's orchestration of the " Water Music," to endure what was conceived by Handel himself, so meagrely did the composer set it down on paper.

The fact remains that concerted instrumental pieces of extended calibre were as yet purely incidental to the bulk of the music being written. The human voice still enchained the hearts and minds of composers more than all else beside ; operas, oratorios, arias, motets and anthems were their staple products. And whereas voices had long since passed the experimental stage, instruments were still untrustworthy and little understood in combination. Hence the composer's general avoidance of a medium of expression so little mastered ; hence the unconscionable delay before the tone-qualities of instruments were found to be just as amenable to blending as voices. We owe to the efforts of Haydn, Gluck and Mozart this epoch-making discovery. They invested the orchestra with emotion of a new kind. Each instrument now began to speak with a tongue of its own : able to express itself in a thousand different ways, in terms of gaiety, sadness, dignity or impudence according to its kind. The combination of all these qualities brought orchestration at long last to the point when it no longer shambled at the heels of vocal music. It strode abreast and was very soon to forge right ahead.

# CHAPTER V

# SOME STRING DEVICES IN ORCHESTRATION

As no two pieces of music are alike (except those fustian tunes which, to the public amusement, are the subject of copyright actions at law) it follows that in all instrumental music the orchestration, while conforming to certain general principles, will differ in the bulk of the detail. Yet to describe any such detail at length is impossible here, for, were the task attempted, the reader's mind could not fail to become entangled in a mass of abstruse technicalities.

But there are certain devices used so frequently that they have become the general stock-in-trade of every composer : " common denominator " devices on which the main orchestration rests. And of these the majority concern the strings, which, of the several groups of instruments, Rimsky-Korsakov, in his admirable treatise on orchestration (" Principles of Orchestration," published by the Russian Music Agency), has aptly described as "the richest and most expressive of all." For we must remember that, whereas each wood-wind and brass instrument is able to produce only one sound at a time, the strings are capable of playing two, three and sometimes four notes simultaneously, and with a plethora of detail almost endless in scope and variety. Types of bowings, too, are many. The down-bow ( ⊓ ) and the up-bow ( ∨ )—marked in the full score and string parts where necessary by all careful modern composers, though not by the classical masters—give variations of style without which orchestral music would be decidedly less interesting and effective. But since lack of space prevents a lengthy description of the many devices found in string music, I have thought it advisable to tabulate, with explanatory notes, the most important features found in all modern scores. In practice, many of the directions given by a composer, even if he be British, are indicated in Italian (music's common tongue), but as there has been a marked tendency by French and German composers in the past hundred years or so to employ their own language, I have added their lingual equivalents only where commonly used. It should be noted that *pizzicato* is the one Italian word consistently favoured by composers throughout the world ; any other in its place would be almost unrecognisable. Certainly Monteverdi's direction "Qui si lascia l'arco, e si strappano le corde con duoi diti" (Put the bow aside, and pluck the strings with two fingers) would cause most non-Italian musicians some bewilderment.

# TABLE OF DEVICES AND EXPRESSIONS COMMONLY USED IN STRING MUSIC

### (For explanations consult the notes appended)

| Italian | Abbreviated | English | French | German |
|---|---|---|---|---|
| coll' arco[1] | arco | with the bow | (arco) | Bog (arco) |
| pizzicato[2] | pizz. | plucked (pizz.) | (pizz.) | (pizz.) |
| con sordina ⎫[3] | con sord. | with the mute | avec sourdine | mit Dämpfer |
| senza sordina ⎭ | senza sord. | without the mute | sans sourdine | ohne Dämpfer |
| col legno (ligno)[4] | | with the back of bow | (col legno) | (col legno) |
| sul (al) ponticello[5] | pontic. | on (at) the bridge | au chevalet | am Steg |
| sul tasto[6] | | on the fingerboard | sur la touche | |
| punta dell' arco[7] | | point of the bow | | |
| tallone[7] | | heel of the bow | talon | |
| armonici[8] | | harmonics | sons harmoniques: flageolet | Flageolettöne |
| martellato ⎫[9] | | hammered | martelé | |
| spiccato ⎪ | | clearly detached | | |
| saltando ⎬ | | jumping | sautillé, jeté | |
| saltato ⎭ | | ” | | |
| tremolo ⎫[10] | trem. | trembling | (trem.) | (trem.) |
| tremolando ⎭ | ” | ” | ” | ” |
| divisi ⎫[11] | div. | divided | (div.) | geteilt (get.) |
| unisoni ⎭ | unis. | in unison | (unis.) | zusammen (zus.) |
| naturale[12] | nat. | in the natural manner | (nat.) | |
| leggio[13] | | desk | pupitre | Pult |
| corda[14] | | string | corde | Saite |

*Explanatory notes to the above table.*

(1) *Arco* is the word used to indicate the termination of a *pizzicato* passage.

(2) *Pizzicato* effects, in single notes, were used by Monteverdi as early as the 17th century, but did not come into general favour for many years after that. I need scarcely add that the effect is obtained by plucking the strings with the index (usually) and 2nd finger (in certain rapid passages) of the right hand, and, sometimes, as a " trick " effect, with the fingers of the left hand. It is one of the modern orchestral composer's most favoured devices, and, when not used *ad nauseam*, is amazingly effective both in loud and quiet music, in single notes or in spread chords, in dramatic passages or at moments when an atmosphere of mystery and awe prevails.

(3) The mute, clamped on the bridge, deadens the tone, producing effects that can best be described as dreamily romantic. Used with proper discretion, it affords a remarkable and lovely contrast to the natural tone of the strings.

(4) Little more than another trick effect, employed very sparingly, and in characteristic music only. The instrumentalist plays with the wood (legno) of the bow instead of with the hair (which comes from the tails of white horses), producing a tone akin to the xylophone, and sounding something like the rattling of bones. In the course of his symphonic poem " Danse Macabre " Saint-Saëns employs this effect most cleverly to represent a skeleton dancing in a churchyard at midnight.

(5) This expression directs the instrumentalist to play with the bow near the bridge, the effect being employed only in *tremolo* (q.v.) passages. At certain rare moments, when a touch of the sinister is required, a *sul ponticello* effect stands out remarkably. It is not convincing except in quiet passages, for—as Cecil Forsyth states in his most exhaustive treatise on orchestration, published by Macmillan—" a painfully glassy and unpleasant quality is produced." No composer worth his salt would dream of using the effect frequently.

(6) Whereas a brittle hardness of tone is produced by playing *sul ponticello*, here the reverse is the case. With the bow on, or (more exactly) very near to, the finger-board a certain veiled quality is obtainable. This effect is perhaps less noticeable than (5), and, consequently, less frequently felt or desired by composers.

(7) Finesse of bowing is intimately bound up with these indications. Effects of this kind, which are often matters of common sense technique, are, in most instances, left by composers to conductors and instrumentalists to " work out for themselves."

(8) The use of harmonics is an essential part of the string player's technical equipment. They are of two kinds : (a) natural harmonics, where the finger, by lightly touching the string in certain definite places, sets a segment of it vibrating in place of the whole length or " stopped " (i.e. by the finger) length ; (b) artificial harmonics, produced by stopping the string with the 1st finger and touching it lightly with the 4th at the interval of a perfect fourth higher than the stopped note (sometimes at the interval of the perfect fifth above the stopped note). The second kind are unobtainable on the double-bass, because the

size of the instrument prevents the stretch of the hand as indicated above. Since harmonics occur so frequently in string music, examples are given below that will enable the reader to recognise the effect in a full score, should he come across it.

Ex.7 (a) Natural harmonics (indicated by o)

Ex.8 (b) Artificial harmonics (note the method of notation)

(9) Types of bowing detail frequently indicated by composers.

(10) The *tremolo* is an important and largely used device, consisting of two distinct kinds : (a) the *bowed* tremolo which, discovered as a musical effect in Monteverdi's time, was developed by Gluck, to become, eventually, a modern device full of dramatic intensity ; (b) the *fingered* tremolo, which consists of the rapid alternation of two notes, each group of notes being played *without* a change of bow. The effect of either kind, particularly the former, is one of restless vitality. Indeed, it is possible to state that without the *tremolo* such dramatic music as Wagner's " Ring of the Nibelungs " could scarcely exist, so frequently is the device brought into action. The following examples demonstrate both kinds. Once again the double-basses are precluded, by reason of their size, from performing any effective *fingered* tremolo, and, moreover, the *bowed* kind is comparatively infrequent owing to the " grunting " quality of the effect produced.

Ex.9 Bowed tremolo  Finale of 1st Symphony.
Brahms

(1st Violins)

Ex.10 Fingered tremolo (also from the same movement)

(Violas)

(11) *Divisi* is the word employed to indicate a sub-division of parts, each part having different notes. *Divisi* effects are usefully employed in decorative music not requiring emphatic utterance ; in strenuous passages any elaborate sub-division of parts weakens the total effect of the string tone and is therefore accounted poor orchestration. In Strauss's tone-poem " Also sprach Zarathustra " there can be found pages where

the strings are divided into no less than twenty-five parts, the whole being pieced together, jigsaw-puzzle-wise, with infinite care for the smallest details. *Pizzicato* chords and effects with harmonics are here combined with other more normal devices in an array of notes which, dazzling to the eye, fall on the ear in rich profusion and with complete appositeness to the musical context. *Unisoni* is the term employed to denote a cancellation of *divisi*.

(12) After *sul ponticello, sul tasto* and *col legno, naturale* restores the type of tone to the normal.

(13) Where the more complex sub-divisions of string parts take place, *leggio* indicates the number of desks required in performance of special passages—e.g. " *Leggio 1* " or " *Desk 1* " ; " *2 pupitres seulement* " (Fr.) or " *nur erstes Pult* " (Ger.) etc. Here the Italian word is little used ; in most instances the composer's own language conveys the necessary meaning.

(14) Indicates, in special effects, the string on which the music is to be played : e.g. IV corda = 4th string. Sometimes the name of the string is given as an alternative to the foregoing ; *sul G, sul A*, etc. Incidentally, string instruments are tuned as follows :

The five-stringed double-bass with the low C is occasionally found in orchestras.

# CHAPTER VI

# WOOD-WIND DEVICES IN ORCHESTRATION

Of the wood-wind and brass there is less to be said, for these instruments, by their very nature, are unable to produce the great variety of effects possible on strings. Their contribution is consistently the same, save for such brass effects as are obtainable by the use of mutes.[1] They have their own individual qualities, used (a) either in a solo capacity with (more often than not) string accompaniment as a neutral-toned background, or (b) as a reinforcement of string

[1] It is also becoming the custom occasionally to mute the oboe, cor anglais or bassoon by the insertion of a soft pad in the bell of the instrument.

tone in more strenuous built-up music. Beyond that, they can no more change their character than the leopard his spots.

In the capacity of soloist, each wood-wind instrument—flute, piccolo, oboe, cor anglais, clarinet, bass clarinet and bassoon—is able to produce remarkably beautiful effects. Who with any feeling for musical tone-colours can resist the outstanding effect produced by the entry of the flute and bassoon in Beethoven's " Leonora No. 3 " overture ?

Ex. 11

Who the long-drawn-out and lovely oboe melody in Schubert's " Unfinished " Symphony ?

Ex. 12

Or, again, the exquisite touch of Hiawathian romance on the cor anglais in Dvořák's " New World " Symphony, inspired, so it is said, by a reading of Longfellow's poem ?

Ex. 13

And, did space permit further examples, it would be indeed a labour of love to show how the composer—while admitting that the combined blend of the wood-wind lacks something of the homogeneity of the strings—has come to regard these instruments as second to none in their capacity for *individual* expression. Rimsky-Korsakov's descriptions of the wood-wind could not be improved upon. " Artless and gay in the major, pathetic and sad in the minor " is his apt summing up of the oboe. " Suitable, in the major, to melodies of a joyful or contemplative character, or to outbursts of mirth " describes the clarinet equally well ; while, again, no other instrument but the bassoon could possibly suggest " an atmosphere of senile mockery."

And so for varied tonal effects of this kind the composer of genius exploits the wood-wind with rare understanding. If he require a cold effect, he knows that low-pitched notes on the flutes can supply the need ; if a warm and brilliant one, then high-pitched notes on the same instrument can be used to equal advantage. For sinister touches he may explore the low registers of clarinet and bassoon, often superimposing the one instrument on the other in unison passages of eerie character. Of all orchestrators, no one understood the finesse of these instruments better than did Wagner. He, whom we can call the archpriest of the wood-wind, was able by his inspired touches of tone-colour frequently to invest his music with a verisimilitude of greatness completely beguiling the ear of the listener. By such necromantic means, at times little short of black magic (or so it seems to me), he often disguised most success-fully the weak thematic basis of much of his music, deluding us into a false estimation of its actual worth. Yet for sheer coloration he is probably unapproached by any other com-poser. Herein lay his great genius. Listening to the orchestral opening of the second act of " Parsifal," we sense im-mediately the sinister magic wielded by the black knight Klingsor, an atmosphere created mainly by clarinets and bassoons used in the manner I have already described above. Elsewhere in the same work Wagner employs the oboe and clarinet in melodic phrases of real beauty to depict the spiritual feeling we associate with Good Friday morning, while a pulsating background of string tone tells us how the sun itself is pouring down its own benison on the day. Or again, what could be more picturesque than the mocking *staccato* wood-wind passages in the final scene of " Die Meistersinger," that illustrate the crowd's rollicking enjoyment of Beckmesser's discomfiture, hoist, as he is, with the petard of his dishonestly-come-by song ?

For there is a special kind of technique on these instru-ments that gives them their more salient characteristics. And we can say that it is all contained in the wood-wind player's frequent question to the conductor when in doubt about the proper interpretation of a phrase : " Do you want it tongued or slurred ? " The greater part of good wood-wind playing is contained in that simple query. There is no need to delve into the intricacies of a technique which belongs more properly to the text-books, but a brief analysis, by example rather than by precept, should show the reader what is meant.

Such details as are contained in *a* and *b* are the very essence of good wood-wind writing ; long stretches of music such as at *c* are often impracticable, dull in the effect and certainly wearisome to the player, who, deprived of his natural articulation by " longs " and " shorts," can only be compared to a Morse code signaller without dots and dashes. I often think that few composers were better versed in these effects than Schubert. The wood-wind writing in his " Unfinished " and C major symphonies is sheer inspiration fron start to finish, his use of accents to denote a particular type of stressed " tonguing " (especially in the slow movement of the latter symphony) certainly more eloquent than can be found anywhere outside his works.

The following table shows, in actual sounds, the compass

of the better-known wood-wind instruments. But the extreme high notes of all these instruments are rarely used, being squeaky and ineffective, while the lowest notes of the piccolo are too weak to have any value.

## COMPASS OF WOOD-WIND INSTRUMENTS

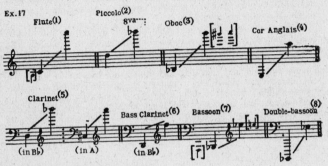

Ex. 17

*Explanatory notes to the above table.*

(1) Some flutes have an extra key giving the low B. The rarely used bass-flute is pitched a fourth lower than the flute. Being what is called a " transposing instrument," music for the bass-flute is written a perfect fourth higher than the actual sounds : *i.e.* the composer will write the middle C when the G below is required to sound.

(2) To avoid too many leger-lines the piccolo part is always written an octave lower than the actual sounds.

(3) The two extreme notes in brackets are for the virtuoso player only.

(4) Another transposing instrument. Cor anglais music is written a perfect fifth higher than it sounds.

(5) Clarinets are of many sizes, ranging from the small E♭—a military band more than an orchestral instrument—to the large bass. With the exception of the C clarinet, now obsolete, all are transposing instruments. The two in constant use are the B♭ and the A. Music for these is written a major second and a minor third, respectively, higher than it sounds.

(6) Music for the bass clarinet is usually written a major ninth (*i.e.* an octave and a major second) above the actual sounds heard, and in the *treble* clef—to conform, no doubt, to the notation of the ordinary clarinets. Wagner's notation is different, however. But I need not confuse the reader's mind by explaining this instance of a composer's waywardness, for the latitude allowed a composer often runs the poet's licence very close.

(7) The bassoon is perhaps the most agile of all the wood-wind instruments. Able to skip about from treble to bass notes in the twinkling

of an eye, it is often looked upon as the low comedian of the orchestra, a reputation not altogether unmerited. Yet it is also capable of depicting tragedy in a manner unequalled by any other instrument in the orchestra. A favourite of Tchaikovsky, it is used to fine effect in this composer's last three symphonies, especially in No. 6 (the " Pathetic "), where its gloomy low notes convey an indelible impression of a man contemplating suicide. The high E♮ at the top of its compass can be found in Wagner's overture to " Tannhäuser," but I should imagine that few players, whatever their golf handicap, have ever holed out in one, so well bunkered is this note. The low A is also used by Wagner, some German instruments having an extra key.

(8) The double-bassoon was greatly admired by Brahms and almost entirely ignored by Wagner, who rarely appreciated its qualities. The former, particularly in his 1st, 3rd and 4th symphonies and in his " St. Anthony Variations," used it to magnificent purpose, its deep booming notes standing out like a 16-foot foundation stop on an organ. To avoid unnecessary leger-lines, music for the double-bassoon is written an octave higher than it sounds, a system of notation shared with the double-bass. It can also be made to sound fatuously amusing, as, for instance, in the opera " Coq d'or," where Rimsky-Korsakov employs its low notes to illustrate king Dodon's scatter-brained imbecilities.

# CHAPTER VII

# BRASS DEVICES IN ORCHESTRATION

THE FUNDAMENTAL difference between the wood-wind and the brass is that between instruments operated by vents and keys and those operated by valves and slides. Compared with the strings and wood-wind the mechanism governing the production of sounds from brass instruments is far less mobile, technically, and far less suited musically to passages of extreme rapidity. For above all else the noble tone of these instruments suggests dignity, and dignity must not be hustled. The actual production of that tone, and, indeed, of the notes themselves, is dependent on the utmost delicacy of lip-adjustment or " embouchure," as it is usually called.

We have already seen in Chapter V of Part A and in

Chapter I of Part B how the clumsy crook mechanism of the horn and trumpet was replaced some eighty years ago by valves (or " pistons "), a modern device that gives to these instruments a *complete* series of notes throughout their compass instead of the very *incomplete* series bounded by the natural laws of sound (see Harmonic Series, Ex. 5). But whatever extra mobility might have accrued to these instruments from this invention, it is and always will be a debatable matter whether brass instruments are really suited by nature to the expression of rapid chromatic music. Not that the old crook system and the restricted use of trombones was always advantageous to the music. Far from it. Many horn and trumpet parts to be found in Haydn, Mozart and Beethoven are utterly unworthy of these instruments, for they contain nothing more than stop-gap notes put in as padding wherever the diatonic sounds admit of it. Yet, on the contrary, many chromatic brass passages heard so frequently in modern works are probably, of all effects, the most wearying that music can produce. They are not a whit better than the sickly chromatic harmonies they are called upon to express, often sounding fussy and even ungainly, the laboured invention of the composer who knows not the virtue of restraint.

No more significant compromise was ever effected than the one to be found in Rimsky-Korsakov's opera " The May Night," where, amid the many chromatic harmonies so characteristic of this brilliant musician, are to be found *natural* (*i.e.* unvalved) horn and trumpet parts. The clarity of the brass writing is, all things considered, quite unique ; the " look " of it on paper little more startling than those older examples quoted on page 147. " This," says Rimsky-Korsakov, referring to his method there, " was purposely done for practice." For, as he tells us so convincingly in another place in his " Principles of Orchestration," " the horn, in spite of valves, has but little mobility and would seem to produce its tone in a languid and lazy manner." Nor is he convinced that the trombones are any better off, since they are " rarely required to perform quick passages "—a statement that the speed-hog composers of these later days might contradict with some show of truth. But the trumpet, we must suppose, will always be favoured with brilliant passages now that the addition of pistons has given it such a turn of speed. And perhaps it deserves many a licence by way of compensation, for never did an instrument suffer so cruelly at the hands of the great masters. Unvalved, untamed, almost unwanted, composers could make little of it in olden days. Music of any distinction would not fit in with its limited number of notes. Its higher notes were of penetrating quality, often obliterating the melodic line of the music through their misapplied power ; its lower notes so few as to be almost unserviceable. The notes that were possible on the unvalved trumpet numbered but fifteen, four of which were untrue in pitch (see Ex. 5, p. 147). " A player on one of these ' natural ' instruments," says Cecil Forsyth in his " Orchestration,"[1] "was like a man continually hopping up and down a ladder, some of whose rungs were so shaky as to be a danger to life and limb." Below is an example of such trumpet writing, taken from Beethoven's third (Eroica) symphony. The unavoidable " hops," as marked by the direction lines, constitute a wicked assault on the ears of the sensitive musician. Modern conductors, however, rescued by the valved instruments, substitute on the 2nd trumpet the notes shown in brackets—a wise proceeding that, in many instances of this kind, somewhat restores the balance of sounds.

Ex. 18

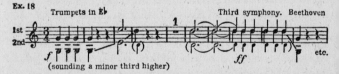

(sounding a minor third higher)

Now that the brass family is modernised it has infused orchestral music with a far greater intensity than was possible heretofore. Though it is, as has been suggested elsewhere, somewhat wearisome in a long succession of

[1] He refers equally to horns and trumpets.

rapid passages wherein the harmonic changes are many, yet, like the wood-wind, it has characteristic devices of tonguing and slurring that are more thrilling in their way than anything else heard in the orchestra. The reader with a flair for analysis will note in the few examples of brass writing quoted below that many of the best effects are obtained (a) by the rapid tonguing of notes that often *remain constant in the pitch* ; (b) by sustained chords; and (c) by those melodic phrases that revolve round the notes belonging to the Harmonic Series in some kind of cousinly way. At the same time he must not assume that I am laying down any dogmatic rules covering the whole range of brass writing. The composer of genius, gifted with real feeling for the orchestra, will always be inventing new devices. In fact, there are so many that to quote them in any detail is not possible. From what has been stated already the reader will understand why the following examples are so effective.

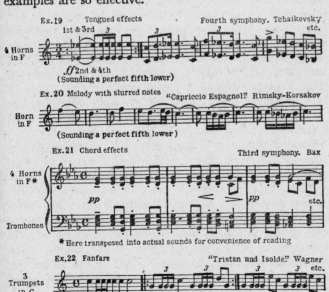

Ex.19    Tongued effects                    Fourth symphony. Tchaikovsky
         1st & 3rd                                              etc.

4 Horns in F

*ff* 2nd & 4th
(Sounding a perfect fifth lower)

Ex.20  Melody with slurred notes   "Capriccio Espagnol." Rimsky-Korsakov

Horn in F

(Sounding a perfect fifth lower )

Ex.21  Chord effects
                                        Third symphony. Bax

4 Horns in F *

*pp*                                         *pp*        etc.

Trombones

* Here transposed into actual sounds for convenience of reading

Ex.22  Fanfare                    "Tristan und Isolde." Wagner
                                                          etc.

3 Trumpets in C

We can pass on without describing the mute, that piece of pear-shaped metal—it was made originally of papier-maché or wood—that from time to time is inserted in the bell of all brass instruments to create a contrast of tone or an effect of distance. Legend states that once upon a time the mute held itself in proud reserve, for it was an effect much esteemed by the great masters and used by them with the utmost discretion. But that was long ago. What, for instance, was used by Beethoven to such fine purpose in his " Rondino " for wind instruments (where muted horns in the concluding bars gently bear the original theme almost out of earshot), or by Wagner in " Die Meister-singer " (where, in the procession of the Trade Guilds, muted trumpets imitate the toy instrument to perfection), has become the prey of those twentieth-century destroyers of music, the jazz vulgarians. And so it is difficult to write with moderation about the mute, for familiarity has nowadays brought it into something of contempt and disrepute. Little employed, in any true music, on the bass tuba, but rather more on the trombones, it has long been used with legitimate effect on the horn and trumpet, especially on the horn. Many beautiful, eerie and amusing passages have been written with it in mind. For sheer loveliness of effect I cannot suggest a better example than the eight bars of muted horn chords immediately preceding the " Liebestod " in Wagner's " Tristan und Isolde," or, if the sinister be wanted, the *leit-motif* in the same composer's " Götterdämmerung " illustrating that mysterious Tarn-helm—which (says Hagen to Siegfried) " serves, when set on thy head, to transform thee e'en as thou wilt."

Again, those readers who are well acquainted with the Strauss tone-poems will recall with delight those extra-ordinary and amusing passages for muted trumpets, horns and violins depicting so vividly the hanging of Till Eulenspiegel, that lovable rogue of the middle ages. Everything sounds so strangulated that we can all but feel the rope round our own necks. And, as an example of muted trombones, there is, perhaps, no more beautiful instance than the chords occurring near the end of the slow movement in Elgar's first symphony.

In concluding my brief survey of these effects I may remind you that the horn player can also mute his instrument by inserting his right hand inside the bell. By this means he stops the free egress of the sound from the instrument, completely altering the tone. The notes so produced are actually called " stopped " notes and play an important part in all modern scores. In fact, some horn players will often manage muted effects by hand-stopping rather than by the use of the metal mute, the effect being practically the same. When blown strongly, these stopped notes are very brassy in quality, or *cuivré* as the French call them—an expression often found in full scores. It is customary to indicate the effect with a small cross (+) over each stopped note. Many examples are to be found in " Tristan und Isolde."

The bass tuba plays something of a lone hand in the brass family, for it is fat in tone, and, owing to its non-combinative quality, scarcely a good bass to the three keen-edged trombones. Yet it justifies its incorporation in the orchestra in many of those more forceful modern works where the bass of the harmony constantly needs replenishing with *forte* or *fortissimo* tone. The instrument frequently reminds us that its most characteristic and, possibly, happiest *métier* is the portrayal of such phenomena as Wagner's dragon Fafner, so somnolent are its rich, slowly uncoiling and deeply-caverned notes. Yet, on occasions, it can skip about " like a two-year old," and amusingly so into the bargain. Its position in the orchestra is somewhat anomalous, for few composers seem to have given it proper consideration. The bass tuba can mean anything from the legitimate orchestral instruments, the F and E♭, to the rich-toned military " double B♭," and even, when all else fails, the euphonium. A strange mixture indeed.

Below will be found the various compasses of the more usual brass instruments, together with certain other sounds possible to virtuoso players only. Explanatory notes are appended.

## COMPASS OF BRASS INSTRUMENTS

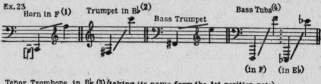

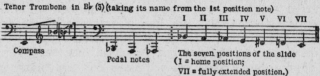

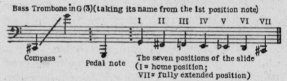

*Explanatory notes to the above table.*

(1) The F horn, by reason of the general excellence of its tone, has become the standard modern instrument. Since all classical and some modern composers have clung to the crook system of notation, despite valves (*e.g.* horns in G, horns in E, etc.), it is here thought desirable, for the sake of those who find it somewhat difficult to "sort out" the conflicting details of a full score, to furnish a table of the more usual transpositions (*see* Exs. 1, 2 and 3, p. 147).

| Horn (crooked in) | Actual pitch of sound below the *written* note |
|---|---|
| Bb alto (rare) | major second |
| A alto | minor third |
| G | perfect fourth |
| F | perfect fifth |
| E | minor sixth |
| Eb | major sixth |
| D | minor seventh |
| C | octave |
| Bb basso | major ninth |

[N.B. The compass of the horn varies, *theoretically*, according to the crook of the instrument. But, for practical purposes, the reader can accept the compass of the F instrument as conforming to the *general* horn range of sounds. To satisfy the curiosity of those interested enough to ask for the exception to the rule, let me cite the low B♭ on the 2nd horn at the opening of Beethoven's fourth symphony—a gloriously rich yet sombrely vibrating sound (when played !) ; also the famous 4th horn passage in the same composer's " Choral " symphony, one demanding an embouchure so flexible that the very mention of it is painful to the player.]

(2) The most favoured trumpets are the B♭, A, F and C. The remaining crooks have fallen into disuse. The size of the mouthpiece, so comfortable to the lips, enables the player to indulge in the most virtuose feats of tonguing. It is interesting to note that double and triple tonguing are controlled technically, as regards articulation, by a recognised system of consonants—*t k* for double, and *t k t* for triple. Hence the amazing brilliance of many trumpet (and cornet) passages on such rhythms as

The cornet—actually a kind of short-length trumpet—is broader in the tone, but with much the same compass. It is a poor substitute for the trumpet, but (it must be deplored) is often used as such. In company with the bright-toned tenor trombones it exposes its own tonal deficiencies to some extent. The bass trumpet is rarely heard outside Wagner's " Der Ring des Nibelungen." In the following table it should be noted that some trumpets transpose upwards and some downwards.

| Trumpet (crooked in) | Pitch of sound in relation to *written* note |
|:---:|:---|
| C | sounds as written |
| B (rare) | ,, minor second lower |
| B♭ | ,, major second ,, |
| A | ,, minor third ,, |
| D | sounds major second higher |
| E♭ | ,, minor third ,, |
| E | ,, major third ,, |
| F | ,, perfect fourth ,, |

(3) In years gone by trombones were more varied in size than they are to-day. For instance, the soprano *discantus* trombone of Bach's time and the alto trombone in E♭ (pitched a perfect fourth higher than the tenor trombone) are now obsolete, though specimens of the latter are still to be seen. Others are the military in E, the D, and the double-bass trombone, the last-named as found in Wagner's scores. It is a thousand

pities that this instrument is not in general use, for it makes a far better bass than the F tuba, and, moreover, can go a semitone lower in pitch. But, as Cecil Forsyth says of it in his " Orchestration " : "The difficulties of adequate tone-production, to say nothing of execution, are terrific." Many classical composers have contributed to the repertoire of the alto trombone in their scores, often employing very high-pitched notes indeed (*e.g.* in the finale of Beethoven's fifth and Brahms's second symphonies). Nowadays the tenor trombone in B♭ and the bass in either G or F are almost the sole survivors of this important family. Two tenor and one bass form the usual orchestral trio. The G trombone, more comfortable to blow than the larger F, is used as the bass instrument in Great Britain, while on the Continent the F is favoured. More often than not French composers write for three tenor and *no* bass trombone.

Although such details belong more properly to the text-books, I have purposely shown in Ex. 23 the seven positions of the trombone from which all the other notes are generated, for there are many misconceptions in regard to this matter. These slide positions act in the same manner as do the three valves (singly or in combination) of the other brass instruments, each position producing a whole series of notes by variation of the lip and breath pressure. Needless to say, each series of notes so produced is but another instance of the functioning of the Harmonic Series. It may surprise some readers to learn that the trombone, unlike the strings or wood-wind, can play many passages without moving the slide. The following, all in the first position, is a phrase of my own invention which illustrates the point.

Ex. 24   Tenor Trombone

1st position only · · · Pedal note

On the other hand, no composer with any knowledge would dream of writing a rapid passage of this kind :

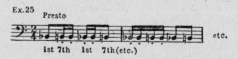

Ex. 25   Presto

1st 7th   1st   7th (etc.)   *etc.*

It would involve the player in a hectic series of travels from one end of the instrument to the other, with no time for anything but a mishit at each note.

The pedal notes are the first notes of the Harmonic Series, obtainable by playing with a very loose lip. They are special effects that do not always materialise. Berlioz was very fond of them : in fact, he overdid them.

The Continental F trombone is pitched one tone lower than the G instrument shown above.

Certain *glissando* (gliding) effects are possible on the trombone on higher notes. Nothing more vulgar has ever desecrated the art of music, unless it be the " wha-wha " of the muted jazz trumpet.

(4) Many modern works have no part for the tuba, for reasons already stated. The double-bassoon has been used extensively to thicken the bass where required. The tuba is most certainly the " odd man out " of the orchestra.

# CHAPTER VIII

# PERCUSSION AND HARP IN ORCHESTRATION

THE PERCUSSION SECTION is the most nondescript in the orchestra : an odd collection of sounds and " noises," some of definite, and many others of indefinite, pitch. Those of definite pitch include the timpani, bells, glocken-spiel—once the equivalent of the old carillon of small bells, now rarely anything but a set of metal strips struck with wooden beaters : the xylophone—usually made of rosewood, walnut or box strips, also struck with wooden beaters : and the celeste—an instrument of the keyboard kind, the sounds of which are produced by the action of hammers on steel plates. Those of indefinite pitch are numerous and can be said to include any effect that happens to take the composer's fancy. For instance, Wagner wrote for eighteen anvils in " Das Rheingold," but as Forsyth says : " In practice the parts are almost invariably 'boiled down.' Few theatres," he adds with sly humour, " can afford eighteen blacksmiths." Mossolov, that modern Russian realist, in his " Music of Machines," finds an appropriate place for the din of metal sheets in a piece representing a factory working at full pressure.

The more usual percussion instruments of no definite pitch are familiar to all and so require little description. However, few modern scores would be considered complete without some reference to the side-, tenor- or bass-drum, the triangle, tambourine, cymbals, and possibly the castanets and gong. With these instruments many a modern composer has oftentimes indulged his noisy fancy, belabouring the rhythmic edge of his sounds with fierce onslaughts from every corner of the percussion. No wonder that the French call these instruments the "batterie," while we, with more humour but with less respect, can find no better designation for them than " kitchen instruments "!

Lest the reader come to the conclusion that I have little sympathy with the percussion, I hasten to reassure him that there are many beautiful and striking effects to be obtained from this section of the orchestra if the composer be discreet. The thrill of the side-drum in martial music— in the roll (a), the flam (b), the drag (c), or the paradiddle (d), heard *pp*, *ff*, *crescendo*, or *diminuendo*,

Ex. 26 (a)   (b)   (c)   (d)
Roll   Flam   Drag   Paradiddle

are effects without which music would indeed be the poorer. But—to quote from Forsyth's masterly " Orchestration " yet once again, in a section where the side-drum is under review—" Like almost all the other Percussion Instruments its principal effect is its entry."

In that phrase lies the secret of any attractiveness possessed by the percussion instruments, particularly those of indefinite pitch, for novelty of effect constitutes their only right of entry into the orchestra. Once they are heard, however arresting the sound, we are twice shy of any further effort they may attempt ; we demand a change of colour, for familiarity with these instruments breeds a certain contempt. The castanets in Carmen's song to Don José in the second act of Bizet's masterpiece is a case in point. When first heard the effect is superb. Yet Bizet, with an unerring instinct for the right touch, knew only too well that the song required something more than castanets as the chief characteristic of the accompaniment. Who, we may inquire, ever spares two thoughts for those castanets once the trumpets (from the barracks outside) intrude upon the song with their dramatic " retreat " ?

The tambourine can be made to sound in three different styles of playing : (a) by shaking the jingles, (b) by striking the stretched parchment with the knuckles, and (c) by rubbing the parchment with the thumb. But of the smaller instruments the triangle is the one most in use. Effective either in single notes or in a roll, it found favour as long ago as the days of Mozart and Beethoven. Thereafter it was subjected to harsh treatment at the hands of those operatic composers who, as stated elsewhere, brought the " batterie " to such a state of degradation.

Many vital effects, too numerous to mention here, are to be heard on the various drums, on cymbals and gong. One reverberating yet *pianissimo* thud on the bass-drum, such as can be heard in the " Credo " sung by Iago in Verdi's " Otello," can suggest to the sensitive mind the most terrifying spectacle of death and decay. Similarly, who can remain unmoved at the dread summons to the unknown contained in that single stroke on the gong near the end of Tchaikovsky's " Pathetic " Symphony ? The cymbals, too, with their various kinds of clashes and that thrilling roll— executed either with timpani sticks or side-drum sticks— have an advanced technique quite their own. The peculiar tone of the side-drum, hard and dry and quite unlike that of the other drums, is the result of the *snares* (lengths of catgut) that are stretched across the lower parchment coming in rapid contact with the parchment itself. This, in its turn, is set in vibration by the action of the drum-sticks on the upper parchment (" batter-head "). By a mechanical device the snares can be loosened so as not to affect the vibrations of the " snare-head." This produces that unique muffled sound usually associated with the solemn pomp of royal and military funerals. Without muffled drums the " Dead March in Saul "—re-orchestrated, of course, from

Handel's poor original—would on such occasions fail completely in its effect.

Of the timpani something has been written already in this volume. In all large orchestras they are found in three sizes, each one capable of being tuned to six or seven different notes by means of the T-headed screws. They, too, can be muffled by placing a cloth over the playing surface (usually made of calf skin). But the effect is comparatively rare, and even then is scarcely worth the trouble involved. In classical scores it is often indicated by the phrase *timpani coperti* (covered).

There remains but the harp, which, in addition to its more normal activities, has two characteristic devices deserving mention here because of their frequency. These are (a) harmonics, and (b) *glissando* passages. The former, of a beautiful evanescent quality, are obtained by lightly touching the string half way down with the part of the hand near the wrist, while the fingers of that hand pluck the string to produce the sound required. In a modern score harp harmonics are indicated by a small circle above or below each note, the sounds heard being an octave higher than those written. The *glissando*, as its name implies, is a very rapid sweep of the fingers over the strings. By various elaborate arrangements of the pedals—a mechanical device far too technical to be explained here—many brilliant effects are obtained. But in recent years the *glissando* has been so overworked that its appeal is no longer what it was. The wise composer avoids it whenever possible, for he knows that one *glissando* in the right place is worth a hundred in the wrong. The harp is a " special " instrument and any misuse of its beautiful tones is perhaps the most cloying effect in all music.

# D: ORCHESTRAL MUSIC: "ABSOLUTE" MUSIC AND THE SYMPHONISTS

## CHAPTER I

## INTRODUCTION

THE READER, of his charity, will not demand of me here to survey completely the whole field of orchestral music, for that is as impossible as would be the inclusion of every poem in a book on poetry. Already it has been shown that the art (if not the science) of music in this, its supreme manifestation, has developed rapidly only within the past two hundred years. To burden ourselves, therefore, with any lengthy historical outlines of the symphony, overture, suite, tone-poem, or other forms of orchestral music could only delay unconscionably the argument now being undertaken, since, in previous chapters, we have already witnessed the centuries-old rivalry between the composer and the maker of instruments.

We are now at the point where the living flesh of all this later music concerns us more than the dry bones of mere research into archaic forms. Those who are interested to go into the subject more deeply can read at length in such works as Grove's "Dictionary of Music and Musicians" how the symphony came into being—and that almost apologetically, so small were its dimensions in the initial stages. There they may read not only of Haydn, the " Father of the Symphony," but of those progenitors before him, such as Abel, Stamitz, Emanuel and John Christian Bach, Wagenseil (not to be confused with that earlier musician of the same name who, in the 17th century, wrote a history of the Mastersingers without which Wagner's opera might never have been composed), Paradisi and that Galuppi whose "Toccata" inspired Robert Browning to such brilliant versification. Yet so absorbingly interesting has this particular form of music become since those early days that many volumes, far too numerous to mention, have been written about and around the symphony. For example, we find the author of the Dictionary just named devoting a whole book to the analysis and appreciation of Beethoven's nine symphonies ; or, again, some other author supplementing a concert-programme with a dozen or more pages of explanatory notes in order that the beauty of thought or the structural outlines of some particular piece shall be fully realised.

For obvious reasons such a task cannot be mine here. Rather, in the space at my command, let me follow the advice of the author of " Religio Medici " when he wrote : " Capital truths are to be narrowly eyed ; collateral lapses and circumstantial deliveries not to be too strictly sifted." The following chapters, therefore, endeavour to show the general structure and internal characteristics of the various forms of orchestral music, beginning with the symphony (as the most important type of orchestral composition), continuing with the suite, the overture and other works of similar kind, and concluding with an account of programme music.

Music is of two kinds : " absolute " and programmatic. The former, with which we are immediately concerned in the ensuing chapters, speaks solely a tongue of its own, voicing nothing but abstract thoughts and expressing the intangible in moods of gaiety, sadness, comedy or tragedy that cannot be linked with anything more definite. Such music, to the listener, can well bear a thousand different interpretations, their contradictory nature inevitably going to prove the enduring " absolute " quality of the music itself. Programmatic music, analysed in a later chapter, is equally interesting, even if not on such a high plane as absolute music. But where absolute music ends and the other kind begins, or where the classical loses itself in the

non-classical, are matters that have not so far been decided
very definitely. We need not worry overmuch on this
ccount as long as we have the music itself.

## CHAPTER II

# THE SYMPHONY

IT IS A STRANGE FACT that the germ of the symphony
originated in Italian opera and was actually the direct
offspring of the 17th century " Sinfonia avanti l'opera "
that, in overture style, preceded the opera itself. And it is
equally strange that fifty years later the sinfonia detached
itself from opera because theatre audiences of those days
were as unconcerned with purely instrumental music as
was that audience which, at Covent Garden in 1934, provoked the just anger of Sir Thomas Beecham. For those
18th century operatic composers who were endowed with
a higher gift than their fellows were often at pains to provide an engaging piece of music that should stimulate the
listener into a receptive frame of mind before ever the
opera started. But then (as now) he sowed his good seed on
stony ground, despite the novel instrumentation of an
inventive age that was exploiting the orchestra as never
before. The composer, with a pride in his work and encouraged by that minority who took an æsthetic delight in
the newly-born orchestra, soon began to transfer some of
his interest from the theatre to the concert-room and to
those royal and ducal *salons* where instrumental music was
almost a daily necessity. And since on these occasions the
supply of suitable operatic sinfonias—detached from their
surroundings—would be strictly limited, while such important orchestral and string pieces as Bach's " Brandenburg Concerti," overtures and suites, and Handel's " Concerti Grossi " were scarcely yet in circulation, composers

soon fell to writing other sinfonias that were entirely independent of stage music and less liable to be victimised by the ill-mannered.

The impetus thus given to orchestral music of the absolute kind brought about a definite cleavage in the styles of composers, some favouring the opera, others the symphony. Thereafter the true development of music on symphonic lines was only a matter of time. Whereas the " Sinfonia avanti l'opera " consisted of one movement only (though it usually included three distinct sections of slow and quick music), the newer sinfonias were soon expanded into three and four separate movements, each movement being of distinct type but bearing some relationship to the others.

Yet for many years the symphony (as I shall now call it) remained in a certain unprogressive state, once its three and four movements were firmly established. For to a great extent it was " period " music. One can imagine that the peruked patrons of the symphony would not willingly forgo the stately and popular minuet, which, coming after a long *adagio-allegro* first movement and an equally long *andante* movement of sleep-inducing character (the port having done its work !), would rekindle the interest and so enliven the mind still further for that final sportive *presto* wherein the quips and pleasantries of the composer made all hearts young again. Therefore it must be presumed that as long as royal and lordly patronage was forthcoming the composer would hardly dare to vary the form of music so acceptable to the age. Instead, he would utilise his genius towards the invention of new themes and instrumental combinations and leave the general form of the symphony more or less where it was. Further, the style of music was often dictated by the exigencies of the moment, for amateur string and wind players flourished in those days. More than that, an amateur of sufficient social importance was able to cajole the composer into writing passages suitable to his (the amateur's) skill. Haydn was a past-master at this game of *oblige*. For instance, in the slow movement of his " La

Reine de France " Symphony, written for the ill-fated Marie Antoinette, there are extended variations for the flute that continually decorate the main theme. These, it is said, were specially composed for an accomplished amateur flautist in the royal band.

But from this time onwards Europe was plunged into more than a quarter of a century of bloodshed. In the general welter all these pleasant *poudré* vanities disappeared and with them that fashion for the minuet set by Louis XIV more than a hundred years previously. In place of the symphony's minuet (third movement) so favoured by Haydn and Mozart—a minuet which, it should be added, had become considerably " speeded up " since its stately dance origin—Beethoven introduced a quick one-in-a-bar *scherzo* that in every respect but the 3–4 time-signature was entirely different from its predecessor.

This was a momentous event. The symphony had now arrived at the point where it had loosed itself from alliance with characteristic dance-music. It was free to express itself in terms born of its own innate power. No longer would it incorporate movements that, however acceptable in themselves, were but alien to its true nature, concessions to an age given over to artificial pleasures. Henceforth it would stand on its own feet with no custom to stale its infinite variety. For in that time of revolution in Europe Beethoven made of the symphony a rebel. It no longer stood for kings and emperors, attired in court dress, the servant of the age, charming, polite, amusing and well-groomed. From his time onwards it was to be nothing less than the expression of mankind in nature and nature in mankind ; a flood of sound picturing good and evil, life and death, and, in its supremest moments, even affording us a glimpse of some spiritual kingdom beyond the limits of time and space.

The symphony has never since then been able to conform to one strict pattern, though, in most instances, it has kept within the well-defined limits of four separate movements. Its character can be such that almost every academic law may be broken with impunity and still it will retain the elements of greatness. Even when its movements are reduced in number, it can, in the hands of a master, yet be made to sound as satisfying as a full-length work. And, when its themes are of great intrinsic worth and their development on an equally high plane, the absence of rich orchestral colouring seems rather to aid than hamper the total effect.

For (to borrow an analogy) it can be said that the symphony, of all forms, is the great river of music. The very name itself, because of its recognised worth and meaning, has become a household one, with connotations often far removed from its original Greek. Ever increasing in volume from some gushing mountain torrent or tiny spring of sound, the main stream of the symphony goes on its way oceanwards, receiving its tributaries one by one, which, in their turn, have been swelled by the brooks and rivulets of the composer's passing fancies.

The following diagram—for practical purposes resolved into straight lines—will serve to illustrate my analogy, and at the same time act as a general guide to much of the argument that will follow. It should be understood, however, that this diagram can only *approximate* to the structure of a symphony, for, as has been inferred above, each individual work develops its own architectural points according to the inner life or substance of the music. Many symphonies by Haydn, Mozart and Beethoven have a *rondo* for last movement. But since the creation of those symphonies wherein Beethoven showed that such smaller forms as the minuet and rondo were quite inadequate to express all he felt, it has become almost customary for composers to write their final movement in a form more or less corresponding to that of the first. And rightly so. The symphony with a first movement conceived in the grand manner demands a fourth of equal importance.

For the reason named I have therefore omitted from the diagram the rondo form as not being truly characteristic of the fully developed modern symphony.

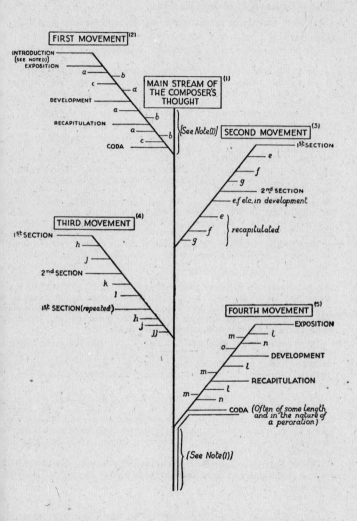

FIRST MOVEMENT (2)

INTRODUCTION (SEE NOTE(1))
EXPOSITION
a
b
c
a
DEVELOPMENT
a
b
RECAPITULATION
a
c
b
CODA

MAIN STREAM OF THE COMPOSER'S THOUGHT (1)

[See Note(1)]

SECOND MOVEMENT (3)
1st SECTION
e
f
g
2nd SECTION
e.f. etc. in development
e
f } recapitulated
g

THIRD MOVEMENT (4)
1st SECTION
h
J
2nd SECTION
k
l
1st SECTION (repeated)
h
j
JJ

FOURTH MOVEMENT (5)
EXPOSITION
m
l
n
o
DEVELOPMENT
m
l
RECAPITULATION
m
l
n
CODA (Often of some length and in the nature of a peroration)

[See Note(1)]

*Explanatory notes to the foregoing diagram.*

(1) The underlying mood subsisting throughout the symphony. This can be :

> a central idea such as a " motto " phrase common to some or (occasionally) all movements ;
>
> a closely connected scheme of keys governing the four movements ;
>
> a cousinly relationship between the main and/or secondary themes of the first movement and other themes heard subsequently ;
>
> a scheme of instrumentation which, though containing vivid contrasts, can be said to be always in keeping with the music ;
>
> a combination or part combination of the foregoing.

(2) Extended sonata form is the basis of most first movements. The Introduction, usually consisting of music in slow time, is frequently omitted. The main theme (*a*) is, in the longer symphonies, followed by other secondary themes (*b*). These act as a bridge passage to the second main theme (*c*), which latter is rounded off with a *codetta* (*d*) that precedes the Development section. It is rare indeed to find any reference to the *second* main theme (*c*) in the Development section, but notable exceptions can be found in Beethoven's Second and Brahms's Third Symphonies. I fancy that composers unconsciously regard this " second subject " (to give it its book name) as some kind of feminine counterpart to the masculinity of the opening theme. And since more often than not the music, in the Development section, goes in search of thrilling adventure, there is no place there for anything suggestive of tender romance (which is undoubtedly the characteristic note of most second subjects). So, as the diagram shows, themes of the (*a*) and (*b*) types constitute the main part of the development section. The Recapitulation naturally reasserts much of what has been heard in the Exposition, followed by a coda, frequently of big dimensions, to give to the movement a balance of structure and a sense of thematic consolidation.

(3) A movement in binary form is shown here with themes and their development indicated by (*e*), (*f*) and (*g*). But, of all the movements in a symphony, this is the one that is most subject to variation and free rhapsodical treatment—a river with many other streams flowing into it from directions most unsuspected.

(4) A scherzo or minuet in ternary form is shown here. The first section is divided into two sub-sections (*h*) and (*j*), the latter being usually a lengthy development of the opening theme (*h*). Exactly the same plan is followed in the case of (*k*) and (*l*) in the middle, or " trio," section. A return is then made to the opening music, with occasionally an elaborate coda (*jj*) to finish.

(5) The plan of this movement is, in most modern symphonies, similar to that of the first, and therefore requires no further explanation as to its structure.

Enough has now been written to indicate the general structure of the symphony. Let us now proceed to the music itself and see what composers did within the form.

## CHAPTER III

# HAYDN AND MOZART

AT THIS POINT in the argument there is no need to take into account the early pioneer work done by such symphonists as Stamitz, Emanuel and Christian Bach, nor yet the work of Gossec, a contemporary of Haydn. Fine as was their contribution to the symphony, the works of these composers have more historical than musical signi-ficance, and, being now but infrequently performed, scarcely call for extended comment here.

Haydn stands out above them all like some great patri-arch. Arriving on the scene of his labours while yet the symphony was in the overture stage—some of his own early examples were of this type—he, in the course of his long life, wrote over a hundred works in this form. And however fine many of his symphonies may be as music, yet much of their significance lies in the fact that Haydn was the first real experimentalist in orchestration ; the first great composer who could be called a definite colourist in music. Legend states that his patron, Prince Nicolaus Esterhazy, gave him *carte blanche* to experiment on the court orchestra whenever a new combination of instruments occurred to him. A bell would be rung to summon the players ; Haydn (happy mortal !) would then appear, try over the passage, make adjustments where necessary, and in such a way would bequeath to the world yet another of those orchestral sallies of wit and good humour that make his symphonies such a perpetual joy.

Of all musicians he was the happiest, and nowhere gayer than in his symphonies. Rarely permitting himself any great depths of sentiment,[1] for he lived mostly on the

---

[1] I am reminded here of a lovely wood-wind passage in the slow movement of what is called the " London " Symphony that is an exception to this.

surface in conditions eminently suited to his nature and work, he composed his symphonies one after another, turning them out with machine-like regularity, yet with a spontaneity and freshness of thematic interest that increased with each new work. The slow introduction to a first movement, that relic of his early days when the " Sinfonia avanti l'opera " was the fashion, he could rarely forget ; with him it never lost its appeal. Often it would be in the minor key, solemn and mock-portentous. Hearing it, one could scarcely imagine that it was nothing more than the preludial strains to some gay symphony most decidedly in the major key.

The " Clock " Symphony in D major is a good example of this. After an introduction such as has been described,

Ex. 27 Adagio

String parts only shown here.

which, it will be noticed, includes expression marks very dramatic for the age, we are, twenty-four bars later, introduced to a most cheerful *presto* in 6–8 time,

Ex. 28

with impish little accents that sound like Haydn chuckling with glee over the deceit he has practised on us.

And, for humorous treatment, what could be scored with more effect than the second (*andante*) movement—that movement which gave the symphony its name of the " Clock." Bassoons join with *pizzicato* 2nd violins, 'cellos and basses (the last-named, an octave below the 'cellos, sounding just like the rusty creak of a pendulum) to give a "tick-tock" accompaniment to an engaging theme heard on the 1st violins.

Ex. 29

Space does not permit a complete analysis of the many felicitous touches to be found here. Haydn exploits each instrument in turn with masterly knowledge of effect. At the return of the *maggiore* (major key) section, there is a solo quartet section scored for flute, oboe, bassoon and 1st violins that is as novel as it is amusing. Even the horns take charge of the "tick-tock" later on and at a disconcerting altitude; another example of Haydn's humorous appreciation of the lighter points of orchestration.

Again, in the *menuetto*, we are shown how the timpani can take the bass of the harmony without assistance elsewhere—a touch of resourcefulness that is fascinating in the effect. Here, too, the trumpets are called upon to play the 11th and 13th notes of the Harmonic Series (see Ex. 5), which on a D instrument, be it said, is one of Haydn's jokes in the higher regions of pitch that some trumpeters might not appreciate.

In his finales Haydn again shows a *penchant* for irresponsible humour of a type that only a confirmed pessimist could withstand, for the music is fun at its best. Not only do we hear contrapuntal music of the highest order with individual parts scampering about in some kind of mad frolic, as well as themes so tuneful that they linger in the memory long after we have heard them, but, once again, orchestral humour that seems to "cap" everything else heard in previous movements. I know of no more laughable effect in the whole range of symphonic music than the simple passage

Ex.30 Presto

that the 2nd horn is required to execute three times at top speed in the finale of the " Oxford " Symphony as an accompaniment to this light-hearted tune.

Ex. 31

The rapid pursing and " unpursing " of the horn-player's lips on alternate notes is a sight not to be missed. That Haydn often had an *inverted* sense of humour must be the verdict of many an unfortunate orchestral musician.

But while such humorous effects in his symphonies are almost as common as blackberries in September, we must not forget that Haydn also possessed a gift for melody and harmony that, in his more serious moments, was of a rare order. He would take a simple theme and embroider it, often as a set of variations, till the whole movement took on something of the character of an old tapestry. His perfect adjustment of detail is constantly a matter to marvel at ; we find no loose threads anywhere, for everything fits into place with the precision born of genius.

Nevertheless, the sheer jollity of Haydn is his chief charm. Inevitably we must think of him cracking jokes with childlike relish ; writing a " Farewell " Symphony that ends in darkness with no other performer left but the conductor ; and, best of all, perpetrating that deafening bang in the slow movement of the " Surprise " Symphony to wake up a slumbering audience that had dined not wisely but too well.

Mozart was of different calibre. Many of his symphonies written in early " prodigy " days, show much of the same style as his great contemporary, but the fun is, perhaps, less infectious ; there is not the desire to joke with the orchestra.[1] Yet the absence of that devil-may-care spirit unquestionably made of him in maturity a composer of even greater genius than Haydn. While Haydn rode on the surface, he plumbed the depths, showing a gift for emotional expression that, it can be stated without exaggeration, was more than anything else the foundation of the modern symphony in all its glory. Beethoven was his lineal descendant, learning most things from him and adding to the symphony that immeasurable degree of inspiration never equalled since. Had Mozart lived to Haydn's great age the history of the symphony would undoubtedly have been very different. In all probability his output would have been no less, and the symphony would then have been developed on lines far in advance of Beethoven's starting-point.

Passing over the earlier works we come to that amazing period of productiveness that was the culmination of his life's work. From 1786 to 1791 his most famous operas and symphonies almost fought with one another in their efforts to be born, as if afraid that death would claim him before they could be created. The year 1788 witnessed the creation of his three famous and most developed symphonies, Nos. 39 in E flat, 40 in G minor and 41 (the " Jupiter ") in C major, all completed within the incredibly brief space of six weeks. A trilogy of happiness, melancholy and strength, they seem to contain between them the quintessential features of symphonic art ; perfect models for all time, both architecturally and emotionally.

Mozart largely discarded the slow introduction so beloved by Haydn. His ideas came " straight from the shoulder " ; he would plunge into the main subject of a symphony without preamble or ado (No. 39 is an exception), and, once started, the symphony never flagged. For perfect melody, developed contrapuntally with deepest feeling and skill and with the loveliest instrumentation imaginable, let me recommend the reader to a close study of the slow

[1] The nomadic circumstances of his early life undoubtedly told on him in every way, making him serious long before his time.

movement of this 39th Symphony, with particular regard to the section commencing

[Strings & Horns not shown here]

Again, as an example of bold modulation, it is hardly possible to imagine anything more spontaneous or convincing than the following quotation from the first movement of the G minor Symphony,

where the composer, concluding the first section in the key of B flat, harks back to G minor for one chord only and then plunges into F sharp minor. It is difficult to explain on paper the actual effect such a quick transition to a remote key has on the mind, for inspiration of this kind defies cold analysis. But we who have known the symphony most of our lives hear in this and similar passages an intensity of expression hitherto unknown : something foreshadowing the music of Beethoven in all its immensity of thought. And, what is indeed extraordinary in this symphony, Mozart was able to achieve this with a small orchestra that consisted of one flute, two oboes (two clarinets were added by him in a later version), two bassoons, two horns and strings.

As a concluding example of Mozart's style, a quotation from the finale of the " Jupiter " Symphony can scarcely be omitted here, for the movement is one of the most wonderful pieces of music ever written.

Ex. 34

[ Complete instrumentation not shown here ]

Practically the whole movement consists of the fugal and imitative treatment of the themes I have numbered in the above quotation. These are treated separately, sometimes by inversion, and then, after the most extraordinary development, are subjected to the ingenious combinations shown above, continuing as shown at the end of the quotation. I can only compare this amazing movement to a game of chess in which Mozart saw from the very first every possible move on the board, no matter what combination of pieces might occur.

Of such material many symphonies are not made. Yet each instrument should, as in the " Jupiter," contribute its logical quota of sound ; not in disconnected fragments but in an organised sequence as important to the whole symphony as is the proper flow of words to a language.

After the " Jupiter " Mozart wrote no other symphony.

Hc

But his mighty achievement there must stand for all time as a model for those composers who know that a great symphony cannot be written without a mastery over counterpoint. " The period of Haydn and Mozart," wrote Sir Hubert Parry, " is in every respect the principal crisis in the history of the symphony."

## CHAPTER IV

## BEETHOVEN

OUT OF THAT CRISIS Beethoven emerged, a giant figure, sublime and aloof, with an entirely new conception of the symphony. From his first essay in this direction written in 1799 during that stormy period in history that was destined to change the whole face of Europe, he demonstrated his unique powers. The old-time Minuet, dear to his heart in other directions, was banished, but for one exception. In its place there was substituted that scherzo, with the invention of which he is often credited, quite erroneously. For the name means a *jest*, and jesting under the name of scherzo was indulged in by J. S. Bach, Telemann, Haydn and others long before Beethoven's time, though it did not appear in the symphony until Beethoven himself introduced it. From that time onwards it has survived. Few symphonies are found without it, for it seems the very embodiment of that kind of musical jesting that can yet hold its head high in the company of still greater music. From the outset Beethoven must have felt the urgent need of this type of music for third movements. Even in his First Symphony (which is somewhat over-credited with the Mozartian manner), the mood of the *first* movement shows unmistakable signs of the power to come. After the significant introduction, in which there is actually not a trace of Mozart, we are soon taken to a full passage that

foreshadows in remarkable style the Fifth Symphony in its
most triumphant moments. For the sake of comparison the
two themes are quoted here. That from the First Symphony
corresponds to theme *b* indicated in the diagram of the
symphony given on p. 217.

Ex. 35

Ex. 36

Such passages considered, it would be difficult to imagine
Beethoven, for third movement, complacently surrendering
to the constrained elegance of the Minuet and Trio. The
(symphonic) fate of such old-fashioned forms was sealed
from the very opening of this symphony, where even the
first chord is in the nature of a revolt. In fact, the whole
*adagio* introduction is a remarkable piece of music, far in
advance of anything similar written up to that time.
Beginning with a dissonant chord that most surprisingly
favours the key of F, it contrives to delay any full close into
the C major key of the symphony until the *allegro* arrives.
If, then, in his very first symphony, Beethoven could hear so
far ahead that he was able to postpone the actual determination of the key for no less than twelve long bars, we can
realise to some extent what developments were in store
before the end of his life was reached.

Now such developments imply an all-round expansion of
the symphony. Beethoven, before long, found that the usual
25 minutes taken up in the performance of such symphonies as the " Jupiter " were quite insufficient fully to
express the logical development of all those magnificent
themes and auxiliary themes that made up his great movements. The 50 minutes of the Third (Eroica) and the 70 of
the Ninth (Choral) are indeed expansions of musical
thought of the utmost significance if compared with the

normal length of the First. We can trace this expansion
from the introduction of the First Symphony, through the
lovely slow movement of the Second, up to that epoch-
making masterpiece, the "Eroica." Here we find music
outpoured from a mind so great that there is not a single
movement or theme but would have suffered in beauty of
utterance had less time been given to the task. The noble
grandeur of the opening movement, with its Napoleonic
background (the first instance of that "personal note" in
the symphony, soon to become such an important factor),
the unparalleled poignancy of the funeral march, the
scherzo that is something more than mere boisterous
jesting, and that wonderful finale the profound qualities
of which no man has ever fully grasped, make of it a work
truly immortal.

There is by no means such expansion in that strange
mixture of seriousness and irresponsible gaiety, the Fourth
Symphony, except in the slow movement. Here there is a
romantic mood coupled to an especial loveliness of theme
that, at the time, might well have represented all that Beethoven felt for the beautiful Theresa von Brunswick. The
scherzo was also lengthened by having its trio section
repeated, an innovation that Beethoven re-introduced in the
Seventh Symphony. But in spite of its tremendous fun, as
enjoyable as any he ever wrote, more than all else I hear
deep down in this great symphony that underlying mood
of seriousness characterising the first and second movements. The low B flat on the 2nd horn in the opening bars
of the lengthy introduction seems like some black shadow
thrown across music that should be nothing but sunny,
the depth of which shadow is intensified by those mysterious rolls on the timpani (also on a B flat) darkening the
development section of the *Allegro* so ominously.

In the entire output of symphonies up to this point,
whether by Haydn, Mozart, or Beethoven, there was little
adventure in the choice of keys for the two middle movements. Something of a convention seems to have been
established that disallowed any other keys than those most

nearly related to the actual key of the symphony. The following table, compiled from symphonies mentioned in the last chapters, shows this absence of adventure.

| Symphony | Composer | Key of Each Movement | | | |
|---|---|---|---|---|---|
| | | 1st | 2nd | 3rd | 4th |
| La Reine de France | Haydn | B♭ | E♭ | B♭ | B♭ |
| The Clock | ,, | D | G | D | D |
| No. 40 | Mozart | G minor | E♭ | G minor G major | G minor |
| The Jupiter | ,, | C | F | C | C |
| No. 1 | Beethoven | C | F | C | C |
| No. 2 | ,, | D | A | D | D |
| No. 3 (Eroica) | ,, | E♭ | C minor C major | E♭ | E♭ |
| No. 4 | ,, | B♭ | E♭ | B♭ | B♭ |

Now this restricted choice of keys had long stood the classical symphony in good stead, mainly, I should imagine, because the music was always moderate in length and contained rhythmical schemes of great variety to counterbalance any monotony of key that might otherwise be felt. But in the long " Eroica " Symphony we get a foretaste of what was bound to come. Here, although the actual choice of key for each movement shows no more adventure than is found in No. 40 of Mozart, yet there are many lengthy passages within these movements that explore very remote keys indeed.

In such manner Beethoven's glorious Fifth Symphony in C minor was a new departure in more ways than one. Not only do we hear the music turning from its long and fateful turmoil in the minor key to its eventual apotheosis in the major, but, in addition, we recognise those first definite thematic links between movements that have since consolidated the symphonic form more than all else besides.

The first movement, with its powerful suggestion of " Fate knocking at the door," is nothing short of amazing in its concentrated purpose. Everything grows from its first four notes ; even the second theme (Ex. 38), which, in this instance, concedes little or nothing to a softer mood.

Ex. 37

Ex. 38

It all sounds like the breaking loose of elemental forces that have with difficulty lain dormant beneath the surface of the previous symphonies : restless pent-up energy now finding release.

From that relentless mood, " rugged, terrible in force " (Sir Hubert Parry), to the exquisite beauty of the slow movement is a contrast too well known to need description here. What is more interesting, as the following quotations suggest, is that the first three notes (a) seem to have unconsciously prompted Beethoven to the opening phrase of the scherzo (b) ; the marked relationship is felt most strongly.

Ex. 39

And then, after the tentative start (b), we are soon left in little doubt as to the origin of the main theme of the scherzo (c). That it sprang from the opening bars of the symphony itself is indisputable, even though it may have come to Beethoven only through some unconscious functioning of the mind and not by deliberate metamorphosis of idea.

No less remarkable is the triumphant finale of the symphony, for it is the most noble culmination possible to all
the many moods and thoughts that, one by one, have
advanced unfalteringly towards the appointed goal. The
scherzo, in its later stages, becomes but a prelude to it—a
prelude fraught with such power and mystery that we
almost dread what will befall. Yet from its final bars,
compounded of music so hushed and awesome that we
instinctively think of the sun's eclipse and of vast penumbral
shadows, there arises a mighty song of gladness in the *major*
key, one banishing the spectres of darkness. Even if those
spectres, in shape of the scherzo's warning notes (*c*), make a
brief return half-way through the finale, do they not merely
remind us that the victory has been hardly won ? And, what
is again wonderful, the great theme of this finale (see Ex. 36)
is undoubtedly derived from the three notes of the scherzo
here shown in brackets.

Ex. 40

Beethoven, in his Sixth Symphony (the "Pastoral"),
went to the countryside for inspiration, giving to each
movement a sub-title. These are :

1. Awakening of joyful feelings on arrival in the country.
2. By the brook.
3. Village Festival.
4. Thunderstorm.
5. Shepherd's Song. Thanksgiving after the storm.
(The last three movements are written to be played without
a break.)

Here again there is an entirely new technique, largely prophetic of that programme-music which was soon to flood all
Europe. The whole symphony is one of rare beauty, with
effects such as the imitations of nightingale, quail and
cuckoo, so naïve that no one but a great genius would have
dared to write them. The timpani are reserved for the

thunderstorm only—a master-stroke ; while the thunder-storm itself—with the raindrops, the uneasy stir of the leaves, the forked lightning, the crashing thunder and, finally, the gradual disappearance of the storm—has never been equalled for sheer and convincing pictorialism. Beside it Wagner's fulminations in " Die Walküre," though having the advantage of richer orchestration, seem less and less real as the years roll by. In the Pastoral Symphony the " speck of blue sky " on the flute that ushers in the Shepherd's Song is inspiration at its finest.

And the older Beethoven grew, the more joy, *mirabile dictu*, crept into his symphonies. The Seventh in A and the Eighth in F are outstanding in this quality, though we must not, at the same time, forget to pay tribute to the noble seriousness of the Seventh's slow movement. The Eighth—with Beethoven's one concession to the older type of symphonic thought, a *tempo di menuetto* movement in place of the usual scherzo—contains the composer's most boisterous fun, not only in conception but in the highly imaginative and amusing orchestration. The principal theme of the *allegretto* second movement is said to have resulted from a farewell supper given to Maelzel, the inventor of the metronome, at which Beethoven extemporised the melody to the words " Ta ta ta, lieber Maelzel, lebewohl." There seems some truth in this story, for the music is most amusingly metronomic.

The Ninth (Choral) Symphony was outlined by Wagner in very eloquent terms. He compared the first movement to " a conflict of the soul striving after joy against the weight of that inimical power which places itself between us and happiness," while " a mad delight takes possession of us with the first rhythm of this second movement ; it is a new world into which we enter—a world in which we are carried off in a dizzying and confusing whirl ; it is as though, driven by desperation, we were flying before it in order to capture . . . a new and unknown happiness." The third movement moved him deeply. " How differently these tones appeal to our hearts. How purely, how soothingly do they resolve the defiance, the wild impulse of the soul . . . into tender and melancholy feelings." And, to conclude these references to his analysis, he finally wrote : " With the beginning of the last movement Beethoven's music takes a decided declamatory character. . . . The progress of the musical poem urges a decision—such a decision as can be pronounced only by human speech. Let us admire the manner in which the master prepares the way for the introduction of speech and voice . . . in this thrilling recitative of the bass instruments, which . . . address themselves to the other instruments, urging them to a decision, and finally themselves intone a song-theme which sweeps the other instruments along in its current so full of simple but solemn joy, and thus swells to a mighty intensity. . . . Shouting and exultation fill the air . . ."

Such was the last symphony Beethoven wrote, a work that ended with an " Ode to Joy," set to words by Schiller. So far had the master travelled along the road of the symphony that now voices must needs be incorporated to express all he felt with such transcendent power. The Choral Symphony is the truest musical conception of humanity ever penned : its message, the triumph of man over every obstacle. It was written in circumstances that beggar description. In 1822 Benedict visited Beethoven at Baden where found him composing in a room " in the most appalling disorder—music, money, clothing on the floor, the bed unmade, broken coffee-cups upon the table, the open pianoforte with scarcely any strings left and thickly covered with dust, while he himself was wrapped in a shabby old dressing-gown."

And about this time there was being written that " Ode to Joy " in completion of a supreme masterpiece, not a note of which the composer would ever hear (though he was actually present at its first performance), so terrible was his infirmity. How Beethoven turned from the orchestra back to chamber music and found escape from his suffering in those superhuman posthumous string quartets is told elsewhere in this volume.

CHAPTER V

# THE ROMANTICISTS AND AFTER

AFTER BEETHOVEN the symphony lived more adventurously, if less nobly. Classical music came almost to a halt. It was now the age of romantic music ; the age of acute personal expression, wherein manner far often outweighed matter and sheer orchestral pictorialism was of more importance than robust contrapuntal patterns in sound. Still, it was Beethoven himself who showed the way to these new developments. In several instances, as we have seen, his symphonies met the romantic style more than half-way. This far-reaching change was bound to come, especially as the orchestra was now so much better equipped with instruments. In brief, the symphony, parted from its own classical traditions, was soon to be the veritable prey of those composers who desired to use its general form as a means to romantic ends. The day of the symphony "with a story" was now not long in coming ; developments on a grandiose scale were close at hand.

But criticism of this newer school need not be unduly derogatory, for it is not given to every symphonic composer to scale the full heights of Parnassus with Beethoven and Mozart. These romanticists, whose divagations from the classical style are actually linked with Beethoven's lifetime, have given us many a masterpiece without which the world of the symphony would be far from complete.[1]

Schumann, though in some ways failing to survive the adverse judgment of posterity, contributed four symphonies of pictorial interest. While the actual material used by him was largely derived from those fussy short-length figurations characteristic of his piano music, yet with such slight means he did manage to sound a new note, and that in spite of

[1] Schubert and Dvořák are left to another chapter for reasons there stated.

orchestration usually poor in blend and technique. For
whatever may be urged against his music, he had vitality,
restless and disordered though it was. By rhythmic variation he frequently made a theme serve various purposes.
For instance, the dignified introductory theme of the First
Symphony in B flat is soon metamorphosed into a sturdy
*Allegro*,

Ex. 41

while in the Fourth in D minor, we hear a similar linking
up of themes with the finale. In such a way Schumann was
largely prophetic of those extended modern symphonies
written in cyclic form, where by the use of recurrent themes
the composer consolidates his entire subject-matter.
Schumann's symphonies can be listened to with genuine
pleasure if we accept their limitations as being but
characteristic of their romantic origin.

On the other hand, Mendelssohn was a most accomplished symphonist of the quasi-romantic order, though, it
must be stated, he contributed nothing to the actual development of the form. In fact, his five examples, perfect
in workmanship, with many a beautiful theme, can be
judged almost as classical specimens, albeit they are
adorned with such titles as " Reformation," " Lobgesang "
(Hymn of Praise), " Scotch " and " Italian." Exquisitely
scored—save for an over-indulged passion for the timpani
—the two last-named have by sheer merit survived the
hurly-burly of modern times, finding a frequent place in
programmes all the world over. Their sentimental slow
movements, particularly that in the " Scotch," tend to pall

after frequent hearing, while the absence of trombones from the orchestration somewhat impairs the vitality of the sound at certain climaxes in the *Allegro* movements. An undoubted complacency of musical thought excludes these symphonies from the highest class ; they are deficient in fundamental strength but have much individual charm.

Passing the work of Spohr, whose *nine* symphonies posterity has rejected as of no material account—some were labelled with such ornate titles as " The Consecration of Sound," " The Earthly and Divine in the Life of Man " (the latter a symphony for double orchestra)—we come to the starker realism of Liszt and Berlioz.

Here sheer pictorialism raised its head in no uncertain manner, often with dramatic effect. In such works as the " Harold in Italy," " Romeo and Juliet " and " Fantastique " Symphonies Berlioz revealed an uncanny power for effect that stamped him as a great inventive genius. In the last-named work particularly, which he sub-titled " Episode in the Life of an Artist," he rose to real heights of imaginative expression, making of the symphony a drama in sound with an *idée fixe* running throughout. In all these symphonies there is a newness of thought and treatment that singles Berlioz out as one of the most vital, if unstable, forces in music. His orchestration, usually superb and coruscatingly brilliant, is sometimes harsh and uncouth by accident. His ideas, vital and at times even terrifying in their descriptive power, will verge on the commonplace and even on the ludicrous when least expected. For a thorough analysis of Berlioz I cannot do better than recommend the reader to Sir Henry Hadow's " Studies in Modern Music " (Oxford University Press) wherein all the composer's many-sided characteristics are examined in masterly style. And, for a general summing up, the same author's criticism in Grove's Dictionary is most precise : " time after time he ruins his cause by subordinating beauty to emphasis, and is so anxious to impress that he forgets how to charm."

Liszt had not the originality of Berlioz. Again, with him, there was the same desire to expound a story or some personal mood attached to definite pictorialism in the orchestration, but the substance of the music itself was of far less value than that of his co-revolutionary. In fact, in such over-developed symphonies as the "Dante" and "Faust"—it is strange that Berlioz, Liszt and Wagner all succumbed to the influence of Goethe—there is a certain empty pretentiousness that often makes these works unbearable to the discerning mind. But the Liszt idiom has survived considerably and has attracted such composers as Richard Strauss, often doing a kind of tongue-in-the-cheek service when reality of utterance proved elusive.

Tracing some other modern developments of the symphony that have followed in the wake of the earlier romantic composers, mention must be made of Raff's facile and pleasantly attractive "Lenore" and "Im Walde" Symphonies and Rubinstein's "Ocean" and "Dramatic" Symphonies. All are works of programmatic type, of distinct merit but little played nowadays. And much about this time Bruckner was busy with his *nine* symphonies. Leaning heavily on his Wagnerian prop, he was at one time—and, in certain parts of Austria and Germany, still is—spoken of in the same breath as Brahms. But the æsthetic judgment of most serious musicians has since decided that his symphonies, replete as they are with pedantic technicalities and self-conscious mannerisms, are in no wise worthy to rank with those of the great masters. Much the same can be said of the *nine* composed by Mahler: works of enormous size, interesting at times but laboriously put together and lacking that vital spark of inspiration that made Beethoven's nine the only nine springing direct from the nine Muses.

Wagner, too, wrote a symphony—an early indiscretion in C. Undernourished from birth, having no real symphonic ideas to feed upon, it soon died of infantile paralysis and returned to the dust from which it sprang. For Wagner's music never tended the symphonic way. The piecemeal end-to-end joining up and repetition of phrases, however cleverly done, is many times removed from true symphonic art—a matter about which Wagner was singularly obtuse all his life. The early Symphony in F by Richard Strauss has also failed to survive, while the same can be said of his later " Domestic " and " Alpine " Symphonies. But these last two belong more properly to the domains of the symphonic poem.

French and Belgian composers of more modern times, such as Saint-Saëns, Lalo, d'Indy and César Franck have also been attracted towards the symphony. Nevertheless, it must be admitted that outside their own countries little permanent success has attended their efforts. It would seem that the Gallic nature is too volatile for the composition of great symphonies. Certainly none has been written that can compare with those of Germany, Austria, Russia, Finland and England. The three by Saint-Saëns have remarkable command over the actual technique of composition, yet they fail to contribute to music anything of a deep and lasting character. Those by Lalo and Chausson are quite undistinguished. Vincent d'Indy, on the other hand, showed something of a mistaken interest in the *structure* of the symphony, and, in two examples, put certain highly ingenious theories into practice. The cyclic principle of recurrent themes was used by him with great deliberation. Yet, despite the cleverness of these cerebral methods, he scarcely infused his symphonies with a master's inspiration.

Of all these symphonies César Franck's in D minor has alone attained a world-wide popularity. Once again moulded in the cyclic form, its three movements have for many an extraordinary appeal. The so-called mysticism of its character, together with a very individual type of chromatic harmonisation, has gained for it many ardent admirers. Its popularity may wane eventually, for it has faults and miscalculations that take it right out of the highest class of symphony. The cyclic principle is somewhat arbitrarily employed ; nor is true development of its themes a marked feature. Yet in the second movement there is a beauty of utterance and a sincerity of purpose that capture the feelings in unmistakable fashion, while the first movement at its moments of climax assumes a stern grandeur not often found in music of French origin. Unfortunately, the finale is less attractive because of its unconvincing references to themes from the first movement. The orchestration of the symphony shows the skilled hand of a musician whose natural home was the organ-loft.

# CHAPTER VI

# SCHUBERT AND DVOŘÁK

Two outstanding symphonists, Schubert and Dvořák, deserve our special attention, for although their lifetimes were separated by many years they have much in common. On Dvořák's shoulders there fell the mantle of a certain type of spontaneous lyrical melody that was also the very essence of Schubert. Not that Dvořák displayed quite that measure of greatness possessed by the other. But both were musicians of the people, turning out melody after melody inspired by contact with everyday scenes and emotions. Therein lay their genius.

Now although it is true that an unchecked flow of melody, however beautiful, will not produce a well-designed symphony, yet there is not a musician alive who would exchange such a symphony for one bristling with superb feats of technique but less inspired in ideas. For, as stated elsewhere, a symphony's character can be such that " almost every academic law may be broken with impunity and still it will retain the elements of greatness."

Such were the representative symphonies of Schubert and Dvořák. They made their own laws. If an extra melody suddenly flashed through the mind of the composer—one that by another composer might be deemed superfluous to requirements—then that melody would be included, even if it meant six or more themes to each movement. Somehow or other Schubert and Dvořák always managed to do the " wrong " thing in the right way. Once started they never flagged ; each new melody was the natural outcome of the one preceding it.

Their orchestration was superb in colour and rarely at fault in the main essentials. Here and there there might be an ill-judged effect of balance, but that very seldom.

Schubert wrote ten symphonies, of which the earlier ones, written in boyhood or youthful days, scarcely fore-shadowed the greatness to come. They are little more than modest offerings at the shrine of Haydn and Mozart, immature work, profuse in surface ideas of somewhat platitudinous quality, and often expressed in poor orches-tral terms. Of these No. 4 in C minor (the " Tragic ") and No. 5 in B flat are the best examples. The latter in its first and last movements is buoyantly light-hearted, but, for such a modest Haydnesque work, contains a slow movement inordinately long and sentimental.

But in the Seventh Symphony in C—which, owing to its great length, is known in Germany as the " himmlische lange " (heavenly long)—and in the Eighth in B minor (the " Unfinished "), Schubert reveals himself as a noble symphonist indeed, one worthy to stand in company with Beethoven. In these two works this composer of 600 songs, most of them priceless jewels of melody, let loose a stream of inspiration so extraordinary that criticism is silenced. We can only marvel at the wealth of ideas displayed and at the manner of their expression. Pretending to no pro-gramme, these two symphonies yet contain the very heart and soul of the composer. The orchestration (save for a few miscalculations) is of a kind quite new to the age, rich in colour, daring in its effects and individual in every way. The mood that the " Unfinished " Symphony expresses is so poignant, its themes so ravishingly beautiful, that the very incompleteness of the work seems to suggest that Schubert was urgently needed in Elysium to entertain the spirits of the departed with melodies such as these.

In this symphony and in the Seventh Schubert became
the master of a new expressiveness in the orchestra. Not
only were his melodies scattered about the instruments with
deep feeling for their characteristic tone-colours, but the
actual range of dynamics was considerably enlarged. He
was the musician *par excellence* of the hushed effect. What
could be lovelier than the *pianissimo* of the 'cellos in the
melody of the " Unfinished " ?

Ex. 43

What more desecrating to its intimate spirit than the
frequent full-blooded version accorded it by disregard of the
*pianissimo* ?

Lack of space permits little further allusion to his work.
But were I asked what I considered to be the most com-
pellingly beautiful slow movement in all symphonies I
should unhesitatingly point to that of Schubert's Seventh,
and perhaps, for a really supreme moment, indicate that
wonderful passage for strings and horns that is quoted
below. (The horns reiterate the crotchet G while the
strings play the harmonies.)

Ex. 44 Andante con moto

And, in conclusion, there is nowhere to be found a more concentrated movement than the magnificent finale to this symphony. Here there is let loose a veritable torrent of dæmonic energy that, originating in the simplest of rhythms, surges along to a most stupendous climax. Genius at white heat.

" Dvořák," comments Dr. Ottokar Šourek in his article on the composer in Grove's Dictionary, "is akin to Franz Schubert in his natural gift of spontaneity, which permits him to evolve works on a grand scale from flashes of passing fancy, apparently without much intellectual and creative effort." Possibly no more capricious genius than the Bohemian master ever existed, unless we except Berlioz. But, unlike Berlioz, Dvořák was simple by nature and also possessed the inestimable quality of bonhomie, which permitted him to exercise his great gifts in a direction highly acceptable to the musical public at large. His fiery Czech temperament found its outlet in many of the dance forms of his country ; in the Polka, the Polonaise and the wilder Furiant. And so it is not surprising that such a vehement nature as this could not refrain from investing his symphonies with many characteristic rhythms closely allied to these dances.

He wrote five symphonies, one of which, No. 5 in E minor (" From the New World "), has attained a popularity equalled by few works of its kind. The other four are less appreciated, though all contain music of rare individuality and charm. For, like Schubert, his melodies were poured out in an endless stream, regardless of context and equally regardless of form. His Symphony in D, No. 1, is an unjustly neglected work. Sounding at times like a Bohemianised version of the D major Symphony by Brahms, it rises to superb climaxes and contains melodies of a type worthy to rank with those of Schubert. The Furiant that acts as Scherzo is a wild and explosive affair, with, by contrast, a Trio of delicious charm containing one of the best melodic phrases for the piccolo ever written. The same praise can be bestowed on No. 4 in G, which is in every respect a masterpiece.

In his symphonies Dvořák never concerned himself with undercurrents definitely programmatic, being content to write just what his vivid imagination dictated on the spur of the moment. The happy result was to give us symphonies that can always be enjoyed for their own sake ; we are never called upon to translate his sounds into extra-musical terms. Only in the " New World " Symphony can there be found traces of any foreign matter—in the shape of distinct allusions to American Negro melodies. But even then the lovely transmutations of these themes only speak Dvořák's native tongue in their every accent. It has been said that Dvořák wrote the beautiful *Largo* (with its cor anglais solo) after reading Longfellow, the movement being supposed to illustrate the courtship of Hiawatha and Minnehaha. Be that as it may, the movement requires no picture to make its meaning clear ; its own loveliness is enough. The close of the finale is remarkable for the striking concatenation of themes gathered from the various move-ments—Dvořák in festive cyclic mood ! I, personally, most remember in this symphony that inspired moment in the finale, where, underneath a theme heard previously, Dvořák introduces a new counter-melody on the bassoon.

In a few bars of exquisite tenderness we can here visualise the sun going down over the vast prairies of the middle west.

Dvořák's orchestration is always superb, rich in coloration and glowing with a thousand points of light. And in the music itself melodies jostle one another in play-ful rivalry, particularly in the " New World " Symphony.

It would be a clever man indeed who could recall to mind every melody that lurks beneath the surface of this truly great work.

## CHAPTER VII

# BRAHMS

Brahms, almost a unique musical figure of the 19th century, is often alluded to as the last of the classical masters. To that proud title he has many claims. Born in Hamburg in 1833, he was brought up on the strictest counterpoint by a famous teacher Marxsen, and, never able to forget his tutelage, continued those contrapuntal exercises to the end of his days. For no composer ever reverenced his art and the great masters more than Johannes Brahms ; no composer ever realised as much as he that the creation of true music depended on craftsmanship acquired by years of patient study, study never to be relaxed.

As a young man he fell under the influence of that great romanticist Schumann, and but for his own strict musical upbringing might easily have become such another. But common sense prevailed. Before he had reached the age of twenty-five he, with an artistic courage remarkable for one of his years, chose the older forms of music as his means of expression, withstanding every temptation to copy the new school of romantic and realistic composition practised so successfully by Schumann, Liszt, Chopin, Berlioz and Wagner. And into those forms he poured his musical soul and gave us many a masterpiece of great individuality and beauty. Once out of his nonage, he spurned the pictorial and the sensational just like so much poison, his one desire being to create absolute music beautiful for its own sake. And in this he succeeded mightily.

For more than twenty years he pondered over his first symphony. Sketches of the great C minor existed in 1856,

et the work was not completed until 1876. But when it did
appear its effect was such that Brahms was immediately
hailed as the legitimate successor to Beethoven. Thereafter
each new work of his was eagerly awaited by an admiring
and impatient world of music.

Brahms's art, as exemplified in his four symphonies, is one
of the most remarkable manifestations of created music that
the world has ever seen. In an age when the orchestra had
swollen to an enormous size he wrote for one no larger than
that used by Beethoven in his Ninth Symphony. In an age
when harmony was running riot with chromaticism he
rejected such effects as being a sign of weakness and chose
instead the plainer diatonic chords of the classical masters.
He would hold no candle to the devil : he remained aloof,
untouched by every decadent influence that in the nineteenth century had afflicted music like a plague. He was, in
truth, a great all-seeing genius who pandered to no fashion
and stooped to no trickery of orchestral effects. His powers
of invention and his orchestration went hand in hand in
perfect companionship. But while it cannot be said that he
touched the profoundest depths of inspiration as did Beethoven in his finest symphonies, yet he brought to his own a
degree of craftsmanship that is unequalled anywhere. His
themes have that uplifting quality that links them with
Beethoven's. His developments and climaxes are always of
immense power, vitally interesting and full of inspired
individual touches quite unlike those of every other
symphonist.

To him every note mattered. Each instrument had its
appointed task. Each key-relationship, either within or
between movements, was in perfect accord with an organised scheme. Each theme, too, was related to its
context in either a primary or secondary capacity till,
finally, the whole symphony resolved itself into a work
complete in form and detail.

Now such methods might argue dry cerebration and
nothing more. But with Brahms that was not so. His intellectual grasp of music was such that he could harness this

gift to his inspiration and create symphonies having th
fundamental quality of greatness. Beauty and strength o
theme were his in noble measure; the architecture of hi
movements, with few exceptions, perfect models of sym
phonic structure.

By making a wider choice of keys for his movements h
enlarged the general scope of the symphony; the forn
became more plastic. We have already seen how th
classical masters were insensitive to any such variety, bein
usually content to pitch three movements out of the four i
the same key. But Brahms's method was very different, a
the following table will show.

| Symphony | 1st movement | 2nd movement | 3rd movement | 4th movement |
|---|---|---|---|---|
| No. 1 | C Minor | E major | A flat major | C minor, then major |
| No. 2 | D | B | G | D |
| No. 3 | F | C | C minor | F minor, then major |
| No. 4 | E minor | E major | C | E minor |

In this short article I cannot pretend to analyse th
æsthetic reasons for these far-reaching changes. Yet th
whole question is a fascinating one, especially if the themati
content of each symphony be considered in relation to th
keys chosen. I can only instance the case of the Firs
Symphony and that of the Third. In the former each move
ment is pitched a major third higher than the one precedin
it till the " wheel comes full circle " and the grim minor-ke
conflict of the first movement is resolved into the triun
phant C major conclusion of the finale. Absolute music
may be, yet the imaginative listener must surely feel tha
this noble work somehow represents the struggle of abstrac
forces contending for the mastery. It may appeal to him a

the triumph of good over evil or of the sun over the dark forces of the night. Whichever way, there is no doubt that Brahms's First Symphony is one of the greatest masterpieces of intellectual thought and beauty ever conceived in symphonic form.

The Third Symphony in F major is quite exceptional in the choice of keys. Founded on the motto-phrase F, A, F,[1] (in this instance, F, A *flat*, F), it opens in heroic manner with a magnificent sweep of theme. Yet by the time the third movement is reached the music has become sadly retrospective, even gloomy. And, to follow it, the finale is in the unexpected key of F *minor*, with dark themes of strange character that recall the austere mood of the First Symphony. This stern mood is retained until near the end, where the motto F A F returns with the major key and the music sinks to a close so beautiful that we are left spellbound.

Brahms planned his material with the utmost care. For instance, in the opening of the first movement of the Second Symphony there are three main themes, used not only separately but in combination.

Ex. 46

It will be noticed that the first note of each theme combines to produce the triad of D major. Of this Brahms was undoubtedly aware, for each melody is interlaced from time to time with the happiest results and with never a suggestion of artificiality or cleverness for its own sake. This is true symphonic art. Everything is utilised to secure a maximum of effect both contrapuntally and harmonically. In fact, so masterly is the workmanship that it is difficult to say where counterpoint ends and harmony begins. Brahms's intellectual grasp of each detail is so secure that not a point escapes his notice. We are not surprised, therefore, to find

[1] A device frequently used by this composer.

that at the very conclusion of this Symphony, when our
engrossment in the climax has temporarily swept away all
recollection of the first movement, a loudly-proclaimed triad
of D major is heard on the three trombones.

Ex. 47

In this epitome, simple as it is, Brahms consolidates the
whole symphony. What could be more logical or more
symphonic than this ultimate fusion of the thematic
material (quoted above in Ex. 46) into this final triad of
D major ? Knowing Brahms's methods, it is impossible to
believe that all this was merely a matter of chance.

Those who take an especial delight in the structural
points of a symphony should study the opening of the
Third. After the motto-phrase has been stated in the
opening bars it is employed as the basis of the main theme of
the movement, cropping up in many unexpected places
with a show of technique as natural as it is ingenious.

The Fourth Symphony is perhaps Brahms's finest inspiration. Not even a whole book, let alone an article, could
do anything like justice to its remarkable beauty. The
general austerity of its mood (save for its ebullient third
movement), its other-worldliness and the perfect balance of
its orchestration make of it a work before which we can
only bow the head in homage. To some musicians it is a
closed book, but that is not the fault of the symphony.
Others find in it a musical solace scarcely to be found
elsewhere ; a link with the spirit world, a vision " seen
through a glass darkly," sustaining the soul with the
grandeur of its conception. The slow movement, with its

solemn opening on the horns and the eerie *pizzicati* that are
founded on that phrase,

Ex. 48    Andante moderato

takes us into realms where material things exist no more.
The third movement, hardly a Scherzo, displays tremendous power in rhythms of great vitality ; while the *Passacaglia* that forms the finale, based on a chromatic version of
a ground-bass borrowed from Bach's 150th Church
Cantata " Nach dir, Herr, verlanget mich," is overwhelming not only in its technical achievement but in the
music itself. In the E major section the entry of the trombones on those awesome chords quoted below is one of the
most inspired moments in all music.

Ex. 49    (Slowly)

[ String arpeggios not shown here ]

The symphonic Scherzo form did not appeal to Brahms, and
he discarded it in all his symphonies. In the first three, a
gentle type of *allegretto* movement took its place, acting as
a quiet interlude before the powerful finale. In the Fourth
Symphony he roused himself to some purpose, but this
wonderful third movement has nothing in common with the
Scherzo, either in form or feeling.[1]

[1] Those who wish to study further the intimate details of Brahms's
methods could not do better than consult Mr. Harrison's own mono-
graph—" Brahms and his Four Symphonies " ; Chapman & Hall ; in
the press.—Ed.

## CHAPTER VIII

# RUSSIA, SCANDINAVIA, AND FINLAND

WITH THE RISE TO POPULARITY of the Russian composers and a national style based largely on folk-melody, the symphony underwent further drastic changes, diverging more and more from the ideals set by Beethoven and cherished by Brahms in his own individual way.

Foremost of all was Tchaikovsky. He wrote six symphonies, the fourth, fifth and sixth of which have achieved an almost notorious popularity. For they contain music of a type that, in its day, was entirely new ; music that expressed itself in paroxysms of emotion wrung from the very depths of the composer's being.

Now such music, while of definitely less value than that of the great masters, has given to the symphony a new outlet that is, in its way, quite remarkable and acceptable. It arouses the physical emotions rather than stimulates the mind. Tchaikovsky wore his feelings on his coat sleeve and was not ashamed of it. In his later symphonies he exhibited a sincerity of manner and an aptitude for luscious melody and highly imaginative orchestration that have given to these works a definite place in the affections of the musical public. For he did not mind " going the whole hog."

His Fourth Symphony in F minor is quite a *tour de force*. The counterpoint may be a little manufactured, with an insistence on symmetrical patterns that becomes extremely wearisome after a while, yet the total effect is extraordinary. Taking, at the beginning, a kind of " Fate knocking at the door " motif,

Ex. 50   Andante sostenuto

he hammers at it in the first and last movements with a vehemence that is quite overwhelming and immensely effective, while, for middle movements he gives us contrasts of mood that show real genius for the symphonic form. A lovely *canzone* for the oboe and other instruments, in the slow movement, and a most original *pizzicato* (with alternating wood-wind and brass sections) for third movement are possibly the best balanced music he ever wrote.

Much the same plan is adopted in the Fifth Symphony in E minor, the cyclic form being used again to thrilling effect. But this time the motto *theme* (for it has now become more than a *phrase*) is introduced in all four movements. Its character and rhythm undergo various changes. Appearing in the slow introduction of the first movement as a solemn theme in the minor key foreshadowing a great drama to come (and it certainly does), it is, in the slow movement, charged with a sinister intensity that shatters in brutal fashion all the exotic passionate melodies of which this extraordinary and beautiful movement is composed. In the third movement—a waltz that soon loses its identity—the motto theme again assumes a sinister aspect. This time, with its rhythm greatly altered, it seems like a spectre at the feast—Banquo's ghost breaking in on the banquet at Macbeth's castle. But in the finale it is resuscitated as a great triumphant theme in the major key, sweeping the symphony along to a climax of phrenetic power, one that excites the listener to the highest degree.

The last of his symphonies, No. 6 in B minor (the " Pathetic "), is a remarkable human document. Written shortly before his death, it is charged with a morbidity of feeling quite unique in all music. " Much," says Mr. Edwin Evans in his volume on the composer (published by Dent), " has been made of his pessimism, but it is at least open to doubt whether this was personal or racial. In every Slav there lies hidden a fatalist, and, combined with a certain fluidity of emotion, running rapidly over the whole gamut of human joy and sorrow, this fatalism engenders in every true Russian moments of gloom and depression such as we

Westerners can little appreciate." Whichever view we take, there is no doubt that Tchaikovsky produced a masterpiece in his own peculiar idiom, one that voices the very depths of tragic personal expression as no other symphony before or since. Each movement, save the brilliant and exciting third that has something of the invigorating rhythm of a march, is given over to a mood harrowing in the extreme, while in its concluding bars we are led to the very brink of a grave that is the end of all. The music is so powerful in its expression that, despite its materialistic background, it has stirred the musical public into a profound admiration for its morbid strains. For the public dearly loves the sensational. Tchaikovsky's death from cholera ten days after the symphony's first performance gave to the work a notoriety that might not have arisen had fate dealt more kindly with the unfortunate composer. Nevertheless, the " Pathetic " Symphony is a work of great genius, a phase in music that was bound to happen sooner or later. Tchaikovsky's " Manfred " Symphony is programme music of another kind, written in the descriptive vein characteristic of those works by Liszt and Berlioz mentioned in Chapter V of this Part.

By comparison with Tchaikovsky, the symphonies of other Russian composers are much less known. Yet there are many of great merit indeed, full of national characteristics and supremely good orchestration. Of these perhaps the most decidedly Russian are those by Borodin, whose three symphonies, in E flat, B minor (the popular one) and A minor (left unfinished at his death and afterwards orchestrated by Glazounov) have many points of interest, though they are poorly developed thematically. Glazounov himself has been the most prolific of the Russian symphonists, writing no less than eight, of which No. 6 in C minor is indeed a fine and unjustly neglected work. At times he is less typically Russian than some others, his style leaning towards the German school. His orchestral technique is superb and the development of his material masterly. Other outstanding symphonists of this school

are Rachmaninov, Kalinnikov, Rimsky-Korsakov (his
" Antar " Symphony is frequently performed), Miaskovsky,
Stravinsky, Scriabin and Prokofiev.

Scandinavia, rich in colourful music of another kind, has
produced no outstanding symphonies. Niels Gade, the
forerunner of Grieg, wrote eight, but beyond a certain
picturesque quality combined with an excellent technique,
they strike no deep note. The two by Svendsen have also
failed to equal the popularity attained by his " Carnival in
Paris " and his two Norwegian Rhapsodies. Atterberg is a
contemporary Swedish musician who has also written
symphonies that have little vogue outside his own country.

But further east, in Finland, there has arisen a symphonic giant who bids fair to go down to posterity in
company with the great masters. Jean Sibelius wrote his
first symphony as long ago as 1898 and for many years this
masterpiece went unrecognised. He has since followed it
with six others. An eighth, which is alternatively rumoured
to be either sketched or merely in the composer's head,
is eagerly awaited by rival concert promoters in this
country clamouring for its first performance.

Sibelius's symphonies are very wayward at times, not too
easy to grasp. Their style is so individual and so characteristic of the composer's remote Northern land that the
somewhat severe outlines and quickly changing moods of
the music cannot always be taken in at a first hearing. They
are never à la mode and thus command the admiration and
respect of those who are best able to assess their qualities.
Of all the great writers since the last of the classical composers Sibelius is the one recognised by cultured musicians
as the most fitting successor to the immortal Brahms. He is
in the royal line of succession because he makes no concession
whatsoever to the cheap and tawdry tastes of the moment,
his music being singularly free from sentimental harmony
and from artificially clever and complex orchestration.

On the other hand, it must not be assumed, because of
Sibelius's individual methods, that his music is so far removed from everyday speech that the listener cannot get the

" hang of things." There are few experiments with the harsher dissonances ; there is hardly an effect that could not have been written many years ago. Sibelius is a remarkably quick thinker, and, we must assume, an equally rapid composer (that is, in the actual putting down of notes on paper), and it is this rapid way of getting at things more than any out-of-the-way combinations of sounds that sometimes baffles the listener. Herein lies the chief difficulty in the way of a full understanding of his music, for his method of working is more concise and very much outside the influence of the symmetrical classical form perfected by Beethoven and Brahms. Sibelius bounds from rock to rock with the inconsequence of a Dvořák, caring little how he moves along, contemptuous of the pleasant valleys of lyrical melody (here so unlike Dvořák) and moving only with the relentless strides of some Titan.

Those listeners, therefore, who look for lyrical melody as the first essential in music, will of necessity be disappointed on a first hearing of these symphonies ; those who can be carried along by the spontaneous utterance of prodigiously strong ideas must experience the sensation of being uplifted to the mountain-peaks of sound.

Again it must not be assumed that Sibelius is an unmelodious composer. It would be a false conjecture to imagine that in the great bulk of his music his total melodic output was restricted to a few popular orchestral works of non-symphonic kind and a few songs and piano pieces. His symphonic melodies at times border on the obvious, though it would be a very wise man indeed who could always discriminate between the commonplace and the inevitable in their character. His finest climaxes are sensational in the extreme. In his earlier symphonies, particularly No. 1 in E minor, he has been likened to Tchaikovsky. There is certainly the same broad sweep of melodic outline and the same galvanic force that drives everything home with hammered emphasis. Yet the similarity is only superficial. There is as much difference between the two composers as between the steppes of Russia and the vast forests of Finland. Tchaikovsky never approached the elemental power exhibited by Sibelius in his symphonic music ; his was a personal idiom, while that of Sibelius is one circumscribed by no such inhibitions. Though we may often be reminded of the gloom of the long bleak Finnish winters, yet the sheer strength of Sibelius's best work is something that we recognise as belonging to that type of music we call imperishable.

## CHAPTER IX

# THE BRITISH SYMPHONISTS

THE SYMPHONIC FORM was introduced by English composers somewhat apologetically. Wagner, writing in his autobiography "Mein Leben" (published by Constable), makes the following interesting observations in connection with his visit to London in 1855.

" I made the acquaintance, too, of a curious man, an old-fashioned but very friendly composer named Potter. I had to play a symphony of his, which entertained me by its modest dimensions and its neat development of counterpoint, the more so as the composer, a friendly, elderly recluse, clung to me with almost distressing humility. I had positively to force him into accepting the right *tempo* for the *Andante* in his symphony, thus proving to him that it was really pretty and interesting. He had so little faith in his work, that he considered the only way to avoid the danger of boring people with it was to rattle through it at a disgraceful speed."

Cipriani Potter was from 1832 to 1859 the Principal of the Royal Academy of Music, an industrious composer who knew Beethoven and from whose pen there flowed yet another *nine* symphonies. But, like that by Sterndale Bennett and those by G. A. Macfarren and others of that period, they have long since been relegated to oblivion. For it cannot be said that the British school of composition was as yet fully alive to continental developments, since the smug Victorianism then existing nearly killed an art that could have done with a few rogues and vagabonds to give it courage and vitality.

Later on matters improved greatly and those important native contributions to the history of the symphony that were to follow in the 20th century owe their existence largely to the splendid pioneer work done by such composers as Parry (five symphonies), Cowen (six) and Stanford (seven). Two of these symphonies, Cowen's " Scandinavian " and Stanford's " Irish," at one time enjoyed a great popularity. Of late years, however, they have given place to the newer 20th century school that includes such fine composers as Elgar, Bax, Vaughan Williams and Holst.

The later Victorians, Cowen, Parry and Stanford, scarcely showed the originality of thought that has characterised the work of their successors. Stanford was a whole-hearted admirer of Brahms and rightly so. It is therefore not surprising that beneath his delightful Irish veneer there peeps out the technique of the great Hamburg master. Even Sullivan wrote a Symphony in E, but in spite of its many excellent points, particularly in the orchestration, it has failed to achieve the popularity of, say, "The Mikado."

Since those times Granville Bantock has used Hebridean melodies as the basis of a virile symphony; McEwen has written one entitled the " Solway "; while the " Irish " by Hamilton Harty is full of splendid tunes and rhythms. To these must be added two by Edward German, the second of which, the " Norwich," has recently been revived with some success.

But it is in other directions that we must look for the real development of the symphony in Britain. In 1908, Elgar, at the mature age of fifty-one, introduced his First Symphony. It represented something entirely new in British symphonic art. It was conceived on a grand scale in cyclic form (taking 50 minutes in performance), having a motto-theme of real beauty and nobility that framed the whole work in the key of A flat. But, strange to relate, the main movements were pitched in the remote keys (from A flat) of D minor and major and F sharp minor—a development of Brahms's methods of key variation that is indeed remarkable. In this symphony, which has many moments of sheer loveliness, Elgar has made use of heroic and romantic melodies in his own very individual way, consolidating his thematic material with the utmost skill into contrapuntal patterns of great interest. The very elaborate orchestration also shows the hand of a real master of the symphony. Yet to my mind nothing in the whole work is finer than the ingenious way in which he turns the opening semiquavers of the second movement (scherzo) into the lovely melody that forms the chief subject of the slow movement. For the sake of comparison the two themes are quoted here.

Ex. 51 Allegro molto ( 2nd movement)

*pp* 1st Vns.

Ex. 52 Adagio (slow movement)

*pp* cantabile

There is the same elaboration of technical points in his Second Symphony in E flat, to the score of which is attached a line from Shelley : " Rarely, rarely comest thou, spirit of delight." Whatever the programme may be, the music is by turns ecstatic, dignified, vivacious, austere and, in the slow movement (a funeral march), deeply moving. In fact, this movement has frequently been compared to the "Marcia funebre" in Beethoven's "Eroica" Symphony. Written in the same key, it certainly evokes a similar mood, though the themes and their treatment are entirely

I c

different. This symphony is generally considered to be a more mature work than the First. A third symphony was in sketch form at the time of the composer's death.

Other English symphonists are Holst, Bliss, Vaughan Williams and Bax. Holst's contributions to the form are an early symphony, the " Cotswolds " and a later choral one to words by Keats. Bliss startled the world of music in 1922 with his " Colour " Symphony, a fantastic work that has its four movements labelled purple, red, blue and green—an experiment in tones that has scarcely justified itself. Vaughan Williams has contributed three symphonies of great merit. The first, a " Sea " Symphony to words by Walt Whitman, employs soprano and baritone soloists and a chorus in addition to the orchestra. It is a work nobly conceived, highly imaginative in its every aspect ; one that illumines the best traditions of that type of music we regard as essentially English—music descended from the great Elizabethan composers and from Purcell. His other two symphonies, the " London " and the " Pastoral," are equally English. " The ' London ' Symphony," comments Richard Aldrich in Grove's Dictionary, " undertaking to suggest various aspects of the great capital, sombre in spirit, is a remarkable achievement in the embodiment of the moods with which it deals." The " Pastoral " is perhaps less appealing because of its somewhat remote quality. It depends for the most part on the placid enunciation of melodies of folk-song type, and, in this way, seems to be a work more for the connoisseur than for the general musical public.

Arnold Bax is possibly one of the most original composers the world has ever seen. With a perfect command over resources of every description, he exhibits characteristics that can be likened to those of no other composer. If in his closely knit harmonies and his deep sense of the poetry of sound we momentarily imagine his music to be like that of Delius or other similar composers, further acquaintance with it causes us to reject the comparison as of no value. If in his orchestration, such as that in "Tintagel," we hear traces of Wagner, again the comparison will prove to be but superficial. He seems to have absorbed into his being the very quintessence of all possible combinations of musical sounds and to have an equal facility for reproducing their beauty or their strength in his own individual way at almost any given moment.

It is therefore not surprising that in recent years the symphony has made a great appeal to his creative sense and that through it he has found a most happy release for all those sounds that must assuredly be part and parcel of himself.

Since 1921 he has written five symphonies which are now acknowledged the world over as extremely important contributions in the history of the symphony. Romantic in origin, yet never unduly sentimental, they avow no programme. But at the same time there is in them some definite conflict or outpouring of the emotions in certain well-defined channels that stamps them with the hall-mark of greatness. The majority of modern symphonies are concerned with some such emotional phases, and those by Bax are no exception to this rule. The music itself is usually of ornate character, the orchestration equally so. There are climaxes of immense power sometimes coupled to a certain type of cacophony that, however, does not fall on the ear with that sense of grating so nerve-racking in other modern works. Bax's methods of composition are indeed very logical in every respect. Like all great symphonists, he is a master of form. His melodies are very individual—no one can mistake a Bax melody—in which it often happens that reiterated notes of diatonic character are made eloquently moving against a shifting background of chromatic harmonies. There is a strange, distant atmosphere about these symphonies ; they part company with the world of realities from the very first note. Indeed they are very beautiful, full of lovely themes and touches that cannot possibly be appreciated in full measure at one hearing. It has taken thirty years for the symphonies of Sibelius to percolate through into the affections of the musical public in this conservative country of ours. Those by Bax are much more ornate and, in their way, more subtle in character and technique. While it must be admitted that their fine qualities are being appreciated to a great extent at the present time, yet I fear that it will take many years before they arrive at that happy stage when the " man in the street " is able to dissect their many beautiful points with the understanding he brings to bear on Beethoven, Brahms, Tchaikovsky and possibly Sibelius. Symphonies have one thing in common with trees ; they are planted for future generations.

# E: ORCHESTRAL MUSIC OF MANY KINDS

## CHAPTER I

## MAINLY OF SUITES

I HAVE ANALYSED the symphony at some length, for it is by far the most important branch of orchestral music, a subject not to be dismissed in a few generalisations. By comparison with it the many other forms, though of immense interest in themselves, are less significant. Since the days of the " Sinfonia avanti l'opera," suites, overtures, rhapsodies, variations, divertimentos, serenades, tone-poems, symphonic poems, dances, impressions, ballets, preludes, fantasias, capriccios, marches, scherzos, idylls, scenes, romances, music for string and wind combinations and many other examples of orchestral art have multiplied to a bewildering extent. To classify them all here would give my narrative the appearance of a telephone directory —which would be fair neither on the reader nor on myself.

In pre-symphonic days the orchestral repertoire was very limited indeed. There were a few suites, overtures, fantasias, ballets, concertos for strings by Purcell, Lully, Corelli, Bach, Handel and others, and little else. Music for strings largely occupied the attention of these composers, and much of what was written still graces the programmes of the 20th century. The " Concerti Grossi " by Handel and Corelli are masterpieces of classical design and beauty ; their frequent performance testifies to their worth. Nor must we forget those many beautiful string pieces by Purcell. Of Bach's " Brandenburg " concertos and of Handel's " Water Music " mention has already been made.

Bach, in company with Corelli, Handel and others of

his time, can be said to have perfected the older suite form. But, if we except those by Bach, the true *orchestral* suite as we now know it was the product of a later age. There was too, an intermediate post-symphonic stage of the suite when Mozart wrote many under the titles of Divertimento, Serenade, Cassation and the like. These, usually composed for small combinations of instruments or for wind or strings alone, mark an epoch where an old dance form like the minuet was introduced between *allegro* and *andante* movements that began to reflect the prevailing influence of the sonata and symphonic forms. In other words, they were almost symphonies in miniature, with movements certainly less developed yet planned similarly. And in these " suites " Mozart gave us some of his most inspired music.

But in more modern days the suite became quite another affair. Gone were all the corantos, jigs, minuets, sarabands and gavottes that made the 18th century harpsichord suites so fresh and entertaining in their dance rhythms. Commanding the full resources of the orchestra, the modern suite deserted from the classical style just as the symphony had done before it. Actually its more novel developments are of comparatively recent growth ; we need scarcely go further back than the days of Bizet and Tchaikovsky to discover the first examples of any importance. Strangely enough, the eminent German and Austrian composers of more recent times have made few important contributions to the form. The finest and most pictorial suites emanate from Russia, France, England, Spain, Norway and Hungary. Brilliant orchestration and sharp contrasts between movements are the main characteristics of these suites. Their movements, being of much shorter duration than those of a symphony, submit themselves more readily to a type of pictorial orchestration that might be considered extravagant in symphonies. And so the many novel effects to be found in the suite have made it an extremely popular form of orchestral music. Often it is nothing more than an effective concert version of incidental music to a theatrical production or of operatic numbers strung together in somewhat loose fashion. But whether written originally for concert purposes only or garnered from the theatre, there is no doubt that the form has stimulated composers of many nationalities to some of their most picturesque efforts.

Among the Russians Tchaikovsky takes a leading place. In addition to his well-known " Casse-Noisette " Suite, arranged from the ballet of that name, he wrote four other suites, the third of which (in G) has for finale a set of variations that have achieved great popularity. The fourth is called " Mozartiana," a title that speaks for itself. Tchaikovsky's ballets " The Sleeping Beauty " and " The Swan Lake " can almost be included among his popular suites. Rimsky-Korsakov in his brilliantly scored " Scheherazade " went to " The Thousand and One Nights " for inspiration, while his equally brilliant " Capriccio Espagnol " is also in reality a suite. Others are Stravinsky's vivid " L'Oiseau de Feu " (arranged from the ballet), and Prokofiev's " Scythian " Suite. Glazounov has written a number of which the best known are " Raymonda " (ballet), " Chopiniana " and a *concert* suite " Scènes de Ballet," that, curiously enough, did not originate in the Terpsichorean art.

Sibelius's " Karelia " is a highly imaginative suite frequently performed. His other suites, such as " King Christian II," have not experienced the same public favour.

Grieg's orchestral suites were derived from incidental music to plays or were coloured versions of piano pieces. Whichever method he adopted, he managed to enrich the orchestral repertoire with some very pictorial and acceptable examples. The two suites from his incidental music to Ibsen's " Peer Gynt," his " Sigurd Jorsalfar," " Lyric," and " Holberg " suites (the last for strings alone) are all of great value, full of Scandinavian touches in their melodies and having harmonies that, as Debussy once wrote, reminded him of " bonbons stuffed with snow." Grieg is a far greater composer than his *salon* piano pieces often suggest ; his descriptive powers are of a very high order indeed.

The French and Spanish composers show themselves equally at home in the suite form. As long ago as the 'seventies Bizet gave us his " Roma," the two " L'Arlésienne " (after Daudet's play), his " Jeux d'Enfants " and his " Carmen " suites, all of which bear the stamp of his great genius. The " Arlésienne " suites, with their drama and warm southern colouring—for Bizet's music nearly always touched latitudes far south of his native Paris— are so popular as to be nowadays somewhat hackneyed and maltreated by small *café* bands. Of the two by Saint-Saëns the " Suite Algérienne " is frequently performed, while Charpentier's " Impressions d'Italie " has somewhat fallen away from the success attending its early performances. The more modern French and Spanish composers, such as Debussy, Ravel, Milhaud and De Falla, have given us some very interesting suites indeed. Debussy's " Printemps," " La Mer " (three symphonic sketches), Ravel's " Rhapsodie Espagnole " (a suite in all but name), the ballet-suite " Ma Mère l'Oye," " Le Tombeau de Couperin" and De Falla's "El Amor Brujo" (adapted from the ballet) are all works of much individuality. Their chief charm lies in the fertility of their orchestral devices ; they create an exotic atmosphere that links them with some of the best impressionistic music written in modern times. For delicacy and whimsicality of mood Ravel's " Ma Mère l'Oye " (" Mother Goose ") is altogether fascinating.

Of lighter texture are the many earlier suites by Massenet, Delibes, Messager, Lacombe and other kindred composers. Massenet's " Scènes Pittoresques " and " Scènes Alsaciennes " and the " Sylvia " and " Coppélia " ballet-suites by Delibes are of particularly striking character, enjoying a great popularity. The same can be said of Luigini, whose Italian name somewhat belies his French birth. His light suites have been literally hacked to death by over-performance on every conceivable and inconceivable combination of instruments.

Modern Hungarian composers are also paying attention to the suite form. Dohnányi, Bartók (three suites), and

Kodály have produced excellent examples. Of these Kodály's " Hary Janos " has met with great success whenever performed.

With the renascence of British music in late Victorian and early Edwardian days the orchestral suite greatly interested such composers as Parry, Mackenzie, Cowen and German, notable examples coming from their pens. Parry's " Lady Radnor's Suite " (for strings), his Suite in G, Mackenzie's " London Day by Day," a number by Cowen, and three by German foreshadowed by their many excellent points the school of a later day. Others by Bantock, Holbrooke and other British composers followed at a later date.

But it is within more recent times that the finest British suites have made their appearance. Elgar's two " Wand of Youth " suites—orchestrated in maturity from ideas of youthful origin—are wholly delightful, while his " Nursery Suite," written but a few years before his death, is equally happy in conception, though perhaps lacking the complete spontaneity of the earlier suites. Amongst others, Holst has given us his picturesque ' Beni-Mora ' Suite (the outcome of a holiday in Algeria), his ' St. Paul's ' Suite for strings and that notable work ' The Planets.' The last-named has indeed achieved a popularity almost unprecedented for modern British music. Frank Bridge's suite " The Sea " has much fine music therein, and among those by Vaughan Williams " Flos campi " has many points of interest. Bax, on the other hand, has as yet shown no desire to write a suite.

Mention should also be made of the many light "popular" suites written by other British composers. Examples by Foulds, Eric Coats, Haydn Wood, Ketelbey and Fletcher have certain qualities that make them very acceptable to that section of the musical public desiring straightforward tunes coupled with picturesque orchestration. While not for the æsthete, they should not be despised.

## CHAPTER II

# OVERTURES, VARIATIONS AND RHAPSODIES

IN ITS STRUCTURE the overture is very like the first movement of a symphony, but less elaborate. It usually consists of two or three well-defined themes that undergo a restricted amount of development and are then recapitulated in brief before a coda that (in most cases) brings the music to a brilliant conclusion. In the 17th and 18th centuries, disguised under the name of " sinfonia " or " toccata," the overture was, as we have seen earlier, the actual precursor of the symphony. But since the structure of the symphony has already been analysed in detail in this Book, there is perhaps no need further to examine that of the overture.

The overture has had many ups and downs. Originally conceived as an instrumental prelude to an opera, it has now, in the hands of modern composers, entirely lost its old identity. Its frequent transference to the concert-room a century and a half ago gave it a new lease of life dependent in no way on any alliance with the opera for which it was written. Being a prime favourite with audiences it soon multiplied exceedingly, and at a later date even developed in non-operatic style into an extended form called the " concert overture." This term, being interpreted, means that overtures were written just for their own sake, acting in a preludial or even postludial capacity in programmes including other music.

But the real operatic overture did not die out until the later days of Wagner and Verdi, and so, by comparison, concert overtures are fewer in number and by no means as popular as those many operatic examples written since the days of Gluck and Mozart.

Almost every composer of note, old and new, has written overtures. So formidable is the list that I cannot pretend to enumerate the countless examples by Gluck, Mozart, Beethoven, Schubert, Weber, Mendelssohn, Wagner, Gounod, Smetana, Dvořák, Brahms, Borodin, Auber, Berlioz, Hérold, Bizet, Nicolai, Rossini, Humperdinck, Sullivan, Stanford, Tchaikovsky, Rimsky-Korsakov, Glinka, Suppé, Elgar, Mackenzie, Hindemith and many others. It is far more interesting to note that all these overtures fall into four distinct categories. They are :

(a) Operatic overtures whose music is not found in the opera itself. Such are Rossini's " Barber of Seville," Suppé's " Pique Dame," Mozart's " Così fan tutte."

(b) Operatic overtures whose music is a *précis* or part *précis* of the main themes in the opera itself. Such are Mozart's " Don Giovanni," Weber's " Oberon," Wagner's " Flying Dutchman," Beethoven's three " Leonora " overtures written for his opera " Fidelio," Humperdinck's " Hänsel and Gretel," Berlioz's " Le Carnaval Romain."

(c) Overtures that form part of the incidental music to a play. Such are Beethoven's " Egmont," Mendelssohn's " Midsummer Night's Dream," Vaughan Williams's " The Wasps."

(d) Concert overtures of non-operatic type having a pictorial or sometimes a literary basis. Such are Dvořák's " Carnival," Elgar's " Froissart " and " Cockaigne," Mackenzie's " Britannia," Walton's " Portsmouth Point," Wagner's " Eine Faust Ouvertüre."

There is little doubt that the finest examples come from the second category, for the composer builds up the most significant themes of his opera in a style that is quite symphonic and highly acceptable to the musical sense of the listener.

Since many operas are of a light character composers have frequently written overtures to them in which the note of high comedy is uppermost. These overtures are most refreshing. Smetana's " Bartered Bride," with its *presto* quavers chasing one another like rats in the " Pied Piper," is one of the most exhilarating overtures ever written.

Going to the other extreme, what overture has a greater nobility than Beethoven's " Leonora No. 3 " ? His masterly use of themes from " Fidelio," especially of the dramatic trumpet call that heralds the timely arrival of Don Fernando, surely makes of it the finest overture ever written. Times have changed. I have in my possession an English edition of this opera published in 1851 from which the " Leonora No. 3 " is omitted, because, says the supremely confident editor (a certain J. Wrey Mould), in a footnote to Overture No. 2, it (No. 3) is " very inferior to the Composition here presented " !

Because of the opportunities it affords for real inventiveness, skill in counterpoint and pictorial orchestration, the variation form (as a separate composition) has made quite an appeal to certain modern composers. Although used extensively by the classical masters from the time of Bach onwards in non-orchestral guise, it was not taken up by orchestral composers until more recent times. The number of orchestral sets of real importance is therefore small.

Brahms's " Variations on a Theme by Haydn " (Chorale St. Antoni) undoubtedly take pride of place. On a melody of great dignity and beauty, taken from an unpublished divertimento for wind instruments, he has constructed variations that can be said to be the acme of perfection both in classical design and in musical content. The whole work unfolds like an opening flower ; there is not an effect, not a note but what seems the logical outcome of all that has gone before, while the unswerving loyalty of the composer throughout the whole work to the five-bar phraseology that characterises the theme is an example of intellectual mastery almost without parallel. Strauss's " Don Quixote " variations, of immense cleverness, belong more properly to programme music. Dvořák's " Symphonic Variations," Tchaikovsky's from his Suite in G, Reger's on a theme by Mozart and German's " Theme and Six Diversions " are other sets that command much attention.

But among those by British composers the finest are unquestionably Elgar's " Variations on an Original Theme," the " Enigma." Dedicated by the composer " to my friends pictured within," each of the fourteen variations is intended as a musical portrait, the identity of the friends being but half concealed under initials or a pseudonym heading each variation. Since the first performance of the work under Richter in 1899, it has been hailed everywhere as a great masterpiece. Elgar's happy display of ideas, the inspired treatment and really beautiful orchestration have given the " Enigma " variations a permanent place in the world's repertoire.

Of the making of Rhapsodies there is no end, for the composer can " gang his ain gait " without much regard for formal design. Surely every modern composer, no matter what his nationality, has some time or other either written or contemplated writing a rhapsody ? While some works of this type, such as the " Slavonic " by Dvořák, are thematically original or nearly so, the majority are founded on folkmusic. There are Hungarian rhapsodies ; Roumanian, Spanish, English, Scotch, Welsh, Norwegian—there is no need to extend the list—and, in the case of English composers, one for almost every *county* !

In form they are very free. Often beginning with a slow section that contains a quiet type of theme or folk-melody, they wander about at will (yet in most instances quite effectively) until a brilliant section of *vivace* character is reached for finale. Sometimes, as in Vaughan Williams's " Norfolk " or Holst's " Somerset " rhapsodies—both of which are based on local folk-songs—the placid mood of the start is recaptured in the concluding bars. This device seems admirably to preserve the bucolic atmosphere of the music : what comes to us in the mist of a May morning disappears in the mellow sunshine of an autumn evening. Delius's " Brigg Fair "—a Lincolnshire rhapsody—answers this description in much the same way. Of all the English rhapsodies it is perhaps the most beautiful. " Mai-dun," a symphonic rhapsody by John Ireland, deals with the Wessex of Thomas Hardy, while Butterworth's " A Shropshire Lad " is based on melodies from his song-settings of Housman's poems. The latter is a remarkably beautiful work, one that makes us lament the untimely loss of a great English genius in the war of 1914–18.

Other rhapsodies are less mindful of such niceties and often end in a blare of brass purposely designed by the composer to " bring the house down."

# CHAPTER III

# MISCELLANEOUS MUSIC

WITH THE EXCEPTION of the more important examples of programme music that come under consideration in the next chapter I have now dealt with the chief forms that have occupied the attention of most orchestral composers. To attempt here anything like a complete survey of the many miscellaneous works of smaller calibre (often of a programmatic nature) is as impossible as it seems unnecessary. For these smaller works are mostly *pièces de genre* : inspirations that have flashed like lightning through the composers' minds, and which, set down in the ecstasy of the moment, have enriched the goodly store of orchestral music to an untold extent. The idyllic loveliness of Delius's " On Hearing the First Cuckoo in Spring," the inspired tone-colours of Debussy's " L'Après-midi d'un Faune," the macabre atmosphere of Sibelius's " Valse Triste " or the stirring patriotism of his " Finlandia," the brilliance of Svendsen's " Carnival in Paris," the barbaric splendour of Borodin's " Polovetz " dances from " Prince Igor," the infectious humour and gaiety of Grainger's " Shepherd's Hey," all and many other pieces like them are needed to give buoyancy, colour and variety to orchestral programmes that might otherwise tend to monotony.

Each nation has contributed something. We may hold diverse opinions on the value of French symphonies ; nevertheless, France has given us many smaller works of great originality and charm. In addition to works by those French composers mentioned in the last chapter but one, there are many pieces by Gounod, Chabrier—his " España " is a *tour de force*—Roussel, Rabaud and others—works that are constantly performed with success. Harking back to pre-impressionistic days, there are the inimitable Hungarian dances arranged by Brahms (orchestrated by another hand) ; Dvořák's Slavonic dances ; Grieg's Norwegian ; Spanish dances by Moszkowski and Granados ; Piedmontese dances by Sinigaglia ; English by Quilter. Nor must we forget the many contributions to the stringed orchestra. Serenades by Tchaikovsky and Dvořák ; many charming arrangements from the classics by Charles Woodhouse, and as a final example Elgar's very beautiful " Introduction and Allegro " for string quartet and string orchestra. Hugo Wolf's " Italian Serenade " (orchestrated from his string quartet) is a delightful work, most unjustly neglected.

Many admirable shorter pieces have been written by British composers. Of these Bax's " Happy Forest," Delius's recently published " Fantastic Dance " and Howells's " Puck's Minuet " must be mentioned here. For many years, too, incidental music and entr'actes, transferred from the theatre, have brightened programmes with many delightful tunes. Schubert's " Rosamunde " and Mendelssohn's " Midsummer Night's Dream " excerpts spring to the mind as perhaps the best examples of this type of music. Then, too, we must not forget Beethoven's classic " Rondino " for wind instruments ; nor yet Wagner's " Siegfried Idyll " and the many extracts from his operas that still cast their sonorous spell over thousands of music-lovers.

To omit any reference to either Johann Strauss (father and son), Waldteufel, Gung'l, Lanner, Lehar and many other Viennese waltz composers would be doing a grave injustice to a form of light music that has conquered the world by its inspired melodies. Brahms, the great philosopher of music, melted to them. Who of us, too, does not listen entranced to a fine performance of such waltzes as Johann Strauss's " Tales of the Vienna Forest " or Lehar's " Gold and Silver " ?

Modern Italian composers are now concentrating their attention on orchestral music. Pizzetti, Malipiero, Respighi and a number of others have since the war produced many works showing great fertility of orchestral devices. It may be that they are a little too ornate in that respect at the expense of a definite creative urge, for their works have not as yet secured universal recognition. But, on the other hand, Respighi's orchestral arrangements of ancient lute dances and other music of the Rameau school are perfect models of discretion and good taste.

# CHAPTER IV

# PROGRAMME MUSIC

WHEN DR. JOHN BLOW, organist of Westminster Abbey and teacher of the great Henry Purcell, wrote his Masque " Venus and Adonis," he showed a gift for dramatic expression that was very remarkable for the age. Not content with illustrating such scenes as the death of Adonis in musical terms deeply affecting, he also contrived to be really pictorial. In an earlier scene of this Masque we hear on violins a reiterated figure meant to illustrate the baying of the hounds when Adonis goes a-hunting.

Ex. 53 Allegro

Now despite its naïve instrumentation this simple effect has the ring of truth about it—I have conducted the Masque and so can speak from experience—and it can be said to be one of the earliest known orchestral examples of genuine programme music.

But the uncertain state of the orchestra for fifty or more years after that time delayed the development of this type of music. True, Bach did give us in his " Phœbus and Pan " a musical illustration of the braying of the ass whose ears were inflicted on Midas to punish him for his tactless choice of Pan as winner of the song contest. Gluck also, in his " Orpheus," gave us a very good example of " hot " music when he so vividly pictured the flames of hell, while Beethoven, in one of his very few musical indiscretions, " The Battle of Vittoria," attempted a realism that, popular as it was in a time of national stress, was unworthy of his greatness in every way. For orchestral technique was as yet hardly ready for anything of the kind, though in stating this we must at the same time not forget the wonderful pictorialism of Beethoven's Pastoral Symphony.

The first big impetus given to programme music was in the days of Liszt and Berlioz, as has already been noticed in Chapter V of Part D. Liszt invented a new form called the *Symphonic Poem*, writing thirteen examples in all, eight of which are orchestral illustrations of actual poems. " His intention," says Dr. Colles in Grove's Dictionary, "was to produce a musical paraphrase of the thought, feeling and colour of the poem, to say in the language of music what the poet says in that of words." Some of these symphonic poems enjoyed (and still enjoy) a great popularity, especially " Les Préludes," which is founded on a poem by Lamartine. This romantic idea soon " caught on," and in a few years Smetana, the Czech composer, followed with other symphonic poems that depicted scenes and incidents of his native country. But whereas Liszt and Berlioz were more intimately concerned with securing a musical parallel to the *emotional* content of a poem, writing what can be called " subjective " music, Smetana on the other hand, with an art more alert, discarded poetry as the basis for his music and strove instead to obtain a real objective *pictorialism*, one that could reflect in music the very sounds of nature he heard around him. In the six symphonic poems linked by him under the name of "My Fatherland," Smetana was at times very successful in this, as witness his "Vltava" (Moldau). Assisted by most eloquent orchestration, this work traces in sound the course of the river from its twin mountain streams to its junction with the Elbe.

From that time onwards the symphonic poem, like some hydra, grew a new head the moment fashion decreed the decapitation of the old. And in that process it often lost its symphonic designation, becoming a " tone-poem " instead, or even concealing its identity further under such names as " ballad " or " sketch." By whatever name it has gone it has proved to be one of the most attractive forms of modern romantic music ever invented. Even if the original examples by Liszt have now paled in the fierce light of modern criticism, we do, indeed, owe something to this composer for starting a fashion that has afforded us so much interesting music.

The Russian composers have given us many fine examples, such as Balakirev's "Thamar," Tchaikovsky's "Romeo and Juliet" (fantasie-overture), and "Francesca da Rimini." The last-named is tone-painting of extraordinary power. Here in our mind's eye we are literally made to see the descent of Dante and Virgil into that grim second circle of the Inferno, where, for their sin, the unfortunate Francesca and her lover Paolo Malatesta are condemned to be whirled about everlastingly in a wind of scorching intensity. Equally picturesque are Borodin's sketch " In the Steppes of Central Asia," which most effectively illustrates the approach and disappearance of a Kurdish caravan procession, and Rimsky-Korsakov's " Sadko," that takes us so fancifully to the bed of the ocean, there to join in aquatic revels performed by all sorts of queer fish.

Saint-Saëns's symphonic poems are among his most

effective works. " Le Rouet d'Omphale," " Phaëton,"
" La Jeunesse d'Hercule " display his appreciation of
classical mythology ; his " Danse Macabre " illustrates a
gruesome graveyard subject so effectively that, at the end,
we are quite loth to lose the ghoulish fiddler. Other French
composers have also contributed important symphonic
poems. Scarcely more than bare mention can be made of
César Franck's " Le Chasseur Maudit," d'Indy's sadly
neglected trilogy " Wallenstein " (founded on Schiller's
drama of the great soldier-statesman) and " L'Apprenti
Sorcier " by Dukas, a work that deals so entertainingly with
the ballad of Goethe in which the magician's apprentice,
by the misuse of his master's arts, finds himself engulfed in
a devastating flood of water he cannot stay.

Modern British composers have given us a number of
notable examples of programme music. Even as long ago
as in Victorian days Hamish MacCunn with a flash of
genius demonstrated in his illustration of an old Scotch
ballad, " The Ship o' th' Fiend," what could be done in
this direction by native composers. Later on, William
Wallace gave us his very poetical " Villon," while Bax,
later still, in " November Woods," " Tintagel " and " The
Garden of Fand," has exercised his genius in this field to
the great gain of music. Bax, with an uncanny instinct for
true proportions, has wisely kept to a somewhat general
programme in these works, one that greatly assists the true
development of the music itself. By such simple means he
has written music of great beauty that has convincingly
avoided the many unnecessary distractions marring so
much programme music. The most interesting of Holbrooke's symphonic poems is " The Raven " (based on
Poe's poem) in which there are moments of inspiration and
power. Harty's " With the Wild Geese " is also a very
imaginative work, written with real fluency and a dexterous
technique round a stirring episode in Irish history. And to
all these must be added Elgar's masterly symphonic study
" Falstaff," which, like the rascally old Sir John himself,
is English to the very core.

Of the German composers, Richard Strauss stands pre-eminent in this type of music. His " Don Juan," written at the age of 24, has long since been accepted as a work of great genius. With a licence natural to his subject the composer has caught in fullest measure the atmosphere of eroticism characterising Lenau's poem. The appeal of the music itself is such that most people do not bother overmuch about following any line-by-line illustration of the programme during the progress of the work. I doubt whether it ever crosses the mind of the listener that he ought to catalogue Don Juan's conquests like some Leporello in Mozart's opera.

Programme music of the over-illustrative kind is apt to fall between two stools. Many composers less distinguished than Strauss have often laid too great a stress on the literary side of their tone-poems. Intense subjectivism or pictorialism that is not pleasing in itself wearies the mind and the ear alike and gives the listener little chance to appreciate the music at its true *musical* worth. While there is much to interest us and " thrill to " in Strauss's " Tod und Verklärung," his Nietzschean " Also sprach Zarathustra " and his introspective self-admiring " Ein Heldenleben," even then we are apt to find the attention wandering at times because the music is too much concerned with a detailed illustration of its literary subject-matter, and too little with its symphonic development. Strauss always shows up to great advantage when he is frankly and amusingly pictorial. Here, divested of everything in the nature of " soul problems," he gives rein to a fancy that is vastly entertaining and clever in the extreme, even if some of the effects be open to question. The hanging of that merry rogue Till in " Till Eulenspiegel " and the bleating of the sheep in " Don Quixote " are two instances of his genius in purely pictorial music.

With other composers this kind of pictorialism has often been driven to extremes, for it requires a well-balanced creative mind to adjust the pictorial and emotional elements in a tone-poem to the point where æsthetic criticism approves of all. Indeed, opinions on the value of programme music, both of the objective and subjective order, are about as divided as those held by the League of Nations on Disarmament. Tastes differ. Few people hear, let alone think, alike. The problem of the real value of programme music has not yet been solved satisfactorily. The effects suitable to the taste of one generation become anathema to another. " The songs of the birds, the clang of bells, the roll of thunder, the swirl of the wind or the crackling of fire," writes Dr. Buck in Grove's Dictionary, " are capable of an imitation so exact as to be scarcely distinguishable from the genuine original." True as all this is, yet we cannot help looking upon programme music as belonging, primarily, to the flotsam and jetsam of the art ; floating about on troubled waters, with but casual harbourage, glittering in the sun with many a bright spot of colour, striking the fancy and then disappearing behind us, perhaps to be soon forgotten. On much programme music there lies the stigma of illegitimacy and we are often led to wonder how much of it has been really worth while.

## CHAPTER V

# WHAT OF THE FUTURE?

IN AN AGE that delights in the invention of a sonorous word-phrase for every world-phase, music has not avoided the fashion. To-day it has acquired a new vocabulary of explanatory terms all its own, and from the frequent recourse that is made to these terms it can almost be assumed by the satirically-minded that the art only now rejoices in a freedom denied it ever since its birth. But in all this there is what is commonly called a " snag." Music, although speaking a language most eloquent and persuasive, has never yet been able to converse with us or explain itself in terms of our own speech. And so, when requiring explanation, it has had no alternative but to place itself unreservedly in the hands of those members of the human race considered intelligent enough to bestow praise or blame whenever due.

That plan worked very well for many centuries and the art was truly grateful to mankind for the simple and direct explanations accorded to it. But a day came, in an age of speed and noise, when a section of musical mankind lost touch with the hidden beauties of the art and was driven to many a subterfuge to cloak the unhappy fact. And so in this way music had a new and dangerously plausible interpretation put upon it, one that trampled on it without any regard for the past.

Now this new interpretation (which has happened in our day) is unlike any other revolution that has ever come the way of music. In other times the revolutionary composer would tell the world quite simply that " from the old springeth the new " and would act accordingly. Conforming to this creed, he would in due course evolve a new type of musical thought that was gradually acknowledged to be but a legitimate development of the old order of things. Then the historian, at a still later date, was able to compare the results of each revolution, piece everything together, and prove beyond all shadow of doubt that what had seemed so destructive in one generation was actually the further constructive development of the art based on fundamental principles as old as the hills. And so, to sum up, man was still able to explain *seriatim* all the new revolutionary ideas and composers in terms as acceptable to music as they were in the long ago. For it was seen that Haydn begat Mozart and Mozart begat Beethoven ; Beethoven begat Schubert and Schubert begat Dvořák, and Dvořák begat that present-day Weinberger (of " Schwanda the Bagpiper " fame) whose begettings, if any, are a matter into which we cannot at present inquire.

To-day the recognition of the genealogical tree of the art is almost totally ignored by a certain type of composer whose sense of musical sounds has been subverted by the unhappy exigent conditions of modern life. And nowhere have his iconoclastic practices been more in evidence than in the orchestra. Hence my long general preamble to this chapter. The orchestra, in all its variety, lends itself more readily to malpractices than any other " instrument." It is capable of harsher and more ear-splitting noises than anything save the pneumatic road-drill, the circular saw of a timber-yard and the low gears of a London omnibus. " But," says this certain type of modern orchestral composer, " these are the very things we are trying to illustrate in sound, for they represent Life as we know it ; they excite and stimulate us and through them we put ourselves into our art, reproducing in sound everything that is around and within us."

And so, to justify their attitude towards music, they have found themselves under the necessity of coining all these new and—dare I say it ?—plausible word-phrases to explain an " art " that has cut from under itself almost every ladder by which the truly great revolutionists of the past have mounted to their immortality. If they be realists and try to put into top gear what the London omnibus says in bottom, they give a verisimilitude to their work by referring to the " counterpoint of sonorities," whatever that may mean. If, on the other hand, they belong to the group not attracted towards programme music, they indulge in " neo-classicism "—a term that, good as it is, is strained to the utmost to include all such ambiguous distinctions as " atonality," " polytonality," and all the other " alities " and " ophonies " found in an art now distracted to the point of a nervous breakdown. If they be stylists, they may possibly adopt Schönberg's twelve-tone scale through which they can write either " horizontally " or " vertically." If they be more sensuously inclined (but this is rather old-fashioned), they may even employ Scriabin's " synthetic chord " and dabble in a musical theosophy that includes perfumes and perhaps a " colour-organ."

All these things have happened in our time, and in nearly

every manifestation they have amounted to but one thing—the worship of the dissonance. I am not taking sides ; I am merely stating facts on which you, as reader and musical enthusiast, must pass judgment according to your inner convictions. Every week on the wireless you will hear somewhere works by Bartók, Alban Berg, Schönberg, Hindemith, Honegger—his " Pacific 231 " is a splendid *jeu d'esprit*—Mossolov in his factory sounds, possibly Scriabin in ecstatic tone-poems such as " Prometheus " or Stravinsky in some of the multi-styled exhibitions of his strangely varying music. Then you can sum up for yourself and form a considered judgment of modern music in general.

Of one thing I myself am certain. Orchestral music has somehow lost a real grip on itself. Gone from it seem to be most of the old beliefs on which it has been founded since the days of Pythagoras and before him : beliefs which in their practice by the great masters gave us that golden age of classical compositions that has never been surpassed. Music to-day has become involved in those " world-phases " that seem to represent nothing of endurable quality ; its ephemeral character excites us at the moment and then, more often than not, is discovered to be so much sham and make-believe. There is no true relationship between concords and discords. In the eyes of most modern composers there appears to be no glory in writing the common chord of C major, a chord that in its tens of thousands of examples in the field of orchestral music continues to thrill us whenever we listen to all the great masters from Handel to Wagner. To the composer nowadays all such things are too plain and too unsophisticated in an age where sincerity is preached and insincerity practised and where the banishment of all repression has only resulted in new doctrines that scoff at the old and well-proven beliefs. Most of the orchestral music of to-day sounds alike, for all those dissonances that played such a magnificent part in the works of the great masters have had their strength sapped by constant misuse and abuse, bringing us to the point where we, with brains too saturated to take in any more, argue resignedly that a few million more " wrong notes " do not matter much. A sad state of affairs, but only too true.

The belated recognition of Sibelius is perhaps the best augury for the future. His whole style depends on a subtle yet straightforward admixture of the concordant and discordant elements in music, with the concord triumphant in the end. These were the methods of Bach, Beethoven and Brahms. Throughout the work of Sibelius we feel the same strength of design and theme and the same implicit trust in the old beliefs. He adapts the sonata form to his larger movements (though, of course, with some modern differences) and carries it off with a success that belies the misguided criticism of those who would have us believe that this form is dead and buried. Whenever I hear his symphonies, or, as a matter of fact, any great symphony, I feel instinctively that music cannot do without this form. It is the most satisfactory mould into which the orchestral composer can pour his best work. Even the finest symphonic poems, tone-poems or what you will in this direction, owe their success more to their adherence to form than to any spectacular display of programme effects.

All great music is compounded of themes and sections that are complementary one to the other. As Shelley wrote :

> *The fountains mingle with the river*
> *And the rivers with the ocean,*
> *The winds of heaven mix for ever*
> *With a sweet emotion ;*
> *Nothing in the world is single,*
> *All things by a law divine*
> *In one another's being mingle—*
> *Why not I with thine ?*

Than this you will not find a better definition of symphonic form, even by searching all the text-books of music ever written.

If composers of the future will found their art more on new expressions of the old principles (like Sibelius) and less on fancifully-named experiments which they themselves do not wholly trust, then, in my own opinion (and I have heard both sides of the argument for many years), orchestral music, however new in its outlook and methods of expression, will continue to flourish as in those days when the writing of a concord was not considered a crime.

# BOOK III

## OPERA

*By* EDWARD J. DENT

# A: HOW OPERA AROSE

## CHAPTER I

# THE OPERATIC CONVENTION

THE SIMPLEST WAY of describing what an Opera is, is to say that it is a play set to music. In some operas, such as those of Wagner, the music is continuous from the beginning of an act to the end of it ; in others, such as the earlier operas of Verdi, the music is continuous, but it is broken up into pieces that we can recognise as songs, and in many theatres the audience applauds them and even encores them. If we listen to an opera by Mozart, we may find that the songs, duets, etc., are separated by what is called *recitative*, a sort of mongrel thing that is neither plain talking nor real singing, accompanied by uninteresting chords on a pianoforte. Readers of Dickens will remember that Mr. Skimpole in " Bleak House " had a curious habit (being a gentleman of dangerously artistic tastes) of conducting ordinary domestic conversation in recitative, playing his own pianoforte accompaniment. And there are other operas, generally of a comic type, in which the business of the play is carried on in ordinary speech, but every now and then the characters burst into song.

Children and uneducated people who see an ordinary play for the first time in their lives often suppose that what happens on the stage is " real " and not pretence. It may take them some little time, perhaps indeed several visits to the theatre, before they can adjust their minds to the convention by which we receive some emotional excitement, whether tragic or comic, from what we are watching on the stage, while the whole time we know perfectly well that it all mere pretending. Persons who have had a little more experience of theatre-going soon begin to discover that even in an ordinary play of modern life things do not happen exactly as they do in the world of reality ; but there is at any rate some illusion of reality, and certain authors, actors and producers take endless pains to be as realistic as they possibly can, just as certain portrait painters try to paint as much like a coloured photograph as possible. Some clients prefer it.

The person who demands strict realism in a play or a portrait will be bewildered, annoyed, or possibly amused at what he sees on his first visit to an opera. He is accustomed to the methods of modern comedy, let us suppose ; he will find it absurd that people should sing everything that they have to say. People do not sing in ordinary life except in the bathroom. Let us assume a play-goer who has arrived at enjoying Shakespeare. We can get him to admit that though people do not habitually talk in poetry, they may do so in a play the scene of which is remote from our own times ; and if he will admit that, it is no great step to admitting that they may sing. Some of Shakespeare's characters do in fact sing, and they are generally those still further removed from our own human environment, a little mad, it may be, or spirits from another world such as Ariel. But in Shakespeare, even at his most fantastic moments the characters behave with some semblance of human reason, whereas in an opera they just stand about waving their arms, singing long soliloquies at the tops of their voices and sometimes, just when something " dramatic " ought to happen, standing all together in a row at the footlights and holding up the action by an interminable joint performance. Opera plots are so fatuous ; besides, most of them are in Italian. Opera singers never act ; if they are not ludicrously corpulent they at any rate never look in the least like the sort of people they are pretending to be. The whole of opera, be it Mozart, Verdi or Wagner, is a mass of absurd conventions, and there can be only one motive that leads people to pretend that they enjoy it—pure snobbery.

Here the serious musician, the frequenter of classical concerts, joins hands with the play-goer and man of letters ; for the one the opera spoils the play, for the other it ruins the music. What can be said in its defence ?

It is perfectly true that opera is a mass of conventions, but the same is really true of every form of art, musical or visual. The difficulty of understanding and accepting the operatic conventions arises chiefly from the fact that whereas the plays which the average man in this country is likely to see fall roughly into two classes, modern plays and Shakespearean plays, the ordinary operatic repertory (as for example that of the Vic.-Wells or the Carl Rosa Company) includes operas belonging to many more different periods. The play-goer who enjoys Shakespeare and Shaw may well be a little out of his depth when he goes to see a tragedy, or even a comedy, of Dryden ; he may easily find Goldoni foolish, and the drama of a hundred years ago ludicrous. There is hardly a play between those of Shakespeare and those of the present century that has not become at the best a " museum piece " ; but in the operatic world a repertory company—and all opera companies work on the repertory system—will be quite normally presenting musical drama of any period from 1762 to the present day, and indeed it is more likely to present what musicians would call " museum pieces," such as Purcell's operas, than works of the last twenty years.

The hardened opera-goer has in fact accustomed himself, probably without being aware of it, to what would make almost a complete series of illustrations for a lecture on the history of musical drama, and the result is that those readers who are only just beginning their operatic experience must here be treated to the lecture without the illustrations.

## CHAPTER II

# ORIGINS

THE ASSOCIATION of music with drama goes back far
beyond the beginnings of what we can call the history of
music. It is well known that drama originated in the ceremonial dances of primitive peoples, and these dances were
naturally accompanied by music—by singing and by such
instruments as those peoples possessed. The tragedies of
ancient Greece were largely dependent on music for their
original presentation, and the theatrical shows of imperial
Rome employed musicians in large numbers. In the Middle
Ages the drama passed largely into the hands of the Church,
and it is at this point that we may begin to watch the growth
of a type of spectacle that contained the principle of Opera,
although it was not yet known by that name.

For the last three hundred years we have drawn a sharp
distinction between Opera and Drama, between plays that
are sung and plays that are spoken ; but as we know ourselves, there is even now a border region between the two,
and in the Middle Ages it was hardly necessary to make
the distinction, because practically no play was ever performed without some kind of music. In the liturgical drama
the words were sung, or at least intoned, throughout. Some
very interesting sacred dramas with music were composed
by a woman, St. Hildegard, abbess of a German nunnery,
about 1150–60. A drama in plainsong may not sound very
operatic to us at the present day ; but it must be always
borne in mind that throughout the centuries the musical
drama has of natural necessity always had to employ whatever kind of music was in use at the time. If we consider
the ordinary repertory of to-day we may find that some
operas strike us as more " dramatic " than others ; in some
the words seem to be more important than the music, while
in others the reverse is the case. But our judgment may

very easily be at fault owing to a lack of the historical sense. Two centuries ago, in the days of Handel, operas consisted of a string of songs separated by stretches of recitative ; many modern listeners find such operas unbearable when they are revived as " museum pieces," and complain all the more because the songs themselves involve a great deal of repetition, both of music and of words. But to our ancestors who heard those operas for the first time this was not in the least unnatural, at any rate for those who were musical and understood the language in which the operas were performed. The music was in that particular style and shape because all music of that period was in that style and shape ; no other style was conceivable. The same thing applies to the words ; sometimes they were written by poets of high distinction. If a modern audience does not understand their merits it is not altogether the fault of the original writers.

If we study the early history of drama we shall notice that changes in dramatic method are paralleled by changes in general social life. Mediæval drama was religious and popular ; it was religious because the Church was the home of all literary and artistic culture, and popular because the Church wanted to use drama as a means of religious instruction for those who could not read or write. It was only comparatively late in the Middle Ages that literary and artistic culture spread from the Church to the upper ranks of society. For many centuries after the fall of Rome the main function of a nobleman was fighting ; those of noble birth who had no taste for it took refuge in the monasteries. It was considered disgraceful for a nobleman to be able to read and write, or to take pleasure in things intellectual, unless he was in holy orders ; we have the positive testimony of mediæval writers to this effect. And even as late as about 1500 we can still see traces of this attitude towards the arts ; Castiglione, in his famous " Book of the Courtier," which describes the court of the Duke of Urbino, at that time the most cultivated society of Europe, tells how a certain noble warrior refused to dance or to listen to music

Kc

and was very properly reproved by his hostess, who told him
that he ought to be well oiled and put away in a cupboard
along with his own armour until the next war, in order to
prevent him from becoming more rusty than he was already

It is only in the sixteenth century that any form of
cultured drama begins to emerge. The religious drama was
in many places organised on a very elaborate scale, and
it certainly involved a great deal of music ; but the musical
records are scanty, and it is clear that the organisers of it
had no idea of creating something that should be musically an organic whole, composed by one single musician,
like the operas of Verdi or Wagner. Some of the music may
have been composed for the occasion, some of it may have
been put together from whatever sources were handy ;
plays with music are still often produced in this country
on similar principles.

# CHAPTER III

# THE RENAISSANCE

It WAS OBVIOUSLY a moment of the greatest importance
in the history of drama when permanent theatres began to
be built and companies of actors performed in them with
some degree of regularity, if not every day. In the Middle
Ages all actors, singers, dancers, acrobats and minstrels had
been regarded as rogues and vagabonds, unless they were
in the regular employ of some prince or nobleman and were
classed as his servants. The Church had its Mystery Plays,
but they were got up only for certain festivals, and the
humbler drama, performed in inn yards or in the open
street, was even more irregular in its appearance. It was
not until after the beginning of the great social and intellectual change to which we give the general name of
the " Renaissance " that drama and music, separately or

together, could be organised on something like a regular system.

The Renaissance began in Italy, and for the rest of the world it may be said that the Renaissance meant the discovery of Italy as the source of all intellectual and artistic inspiration. It is only natural, therefore, that Italy should have been the original home of Opera. Italy created Opera, because Italy had no drama, at least, no drama comparable to that of England and Spain. There is nothing in Italian literature corresponding to the plays of our Elizabethan poets or to those of Lope de Vega and Calderon, unless we go back to the " Sacred Representations," as they were called, which in Spain at any rate had a longer life than in other countries and developed more continuously into normal drama. The Italian religious plays were often of high literary value, but just at the moment when they might have followed the example of their Spanish relatives, they were forbidden to be acted. The only drama that the Italians possessed in the sixteenth century was either the old Latin drama of Plautus and Terence, translated into Italian, and certain imitations of Latin drama written by court poets, such as Ariosto, for occasional court performances, or else the Comedy of Masks, which was acted by strolling players, wherever they could find a " pitch," for the amusement of the common people.

The various Italian courts set the example to the rest of Europe in the extravagance of their pageants and masques, as we may call them. There is no need to describe them here, for most readers will have some idea of the masques and other entertainments which were provided on various occasions for our own Queen Elizabeth and for James I, and it has recently been shown that practically all of these were modelled as closely as possible on the entertainments of the courts of Florence and Mantua in the preceding generation. Music played a large part in them, but it had not yet reached the point of becoming a complete musical setting of a play. None the less, the materials of opera were all ready to hand ; the madrigal, which was the main musical form of the century, was gradually leading the way towards musical drama.

It may be well to warn the reader that madrigals (see also Book IV, Part C, *et seq.*) in the sixteenth century were not invariably sung by a chorus without accompaniment. There is abundant evidence to show that they were very often accompanied by instruments, and that they were also sung as solos for a single voice, the other parts being played by instruments. At court festivities they were often performed by singers and players in some sort of theatrical costume, with the adjunct of scenery. Another thing to note is that even as early as in the days of Castiglione (about 1520) people used to recite poetry to the accompaniment of a viol, though we have no very definite record of how this was done.

In considering the history of opera we can observe three different ways in which music is employed. First, it is the direct expression of emotion. The ordinary man expresses himself in prose ; in a more exalted form of drama the characters speak in verse, because poetry is a vehicle of intensified self-expression ; and singing is a still further intensification of poetry. The singer in an opera appears in fact to create out of his own emotions the music that he sings, and even to-day an opera singer cannot really convince his audience unless he acts in such a way as to make them believe that it is his emotions, and not the conductor's beat, that cause the orchestra to play the music written by the composer to express them.

The second use of music in opera is for the purposes of dancing, and under that head we must include not merely set dances, but all movements such as processions, marches, battles, and in fact any kind of dumb show action. Thirdly, music can be used for what we may call " background " purposes ; music that describes natural phenomena such as storms, or that fulfils any other function which might perhaps equally well be performed by visible scenery. We shall see that these three functions of music have been treated in different ways by different composers at different periods.

## CHAPTER IV

# EARLY ITALIAN OPERA: MONTEVERDI

The first attempt at what we can really call an opera was made at Florence in 1597 by a group of musicians and men of letters who were in the habit of meeting to discuss artistic matters at the house of Count Bardi. Their idea was to revive the methods that they believed characteristic of classical Greek tragedy, and their first experiment was a drama on the legend of Apollo and Daphne, written by the poet Ottavio Rinuccini and set to music mainly by Jacopo Peri. The words have survived, but none of the music, except two small fragments composed by Jacopo Corsi. " Dafne " was repeated in 1598 and 1599 ; in 1600 Rinuccini and Peri produced " Euridice," an opera on the story of Orpheus and Eurydice. The music of this was printed at the time and has been reprinted in modern form ; it is the first opera that has survived complete.

To the same year 1600 belongs what has generally been called the first oratorio, "La Rappresentazione dell' Anima e del Corpo " (The story of the Body and the Soul) ; the words were put together from older religious plays and the music was by Emilio de' Cavalieri. The work, however, is not an oratorio as we now understand the term, but an opera, although on a religious subject ; it is set to music all the way through, and it was intended to be acted in costume. The " Anima e Corpo " was produced at Rome, but the idea of it was no independent discovery of Cavalieri's ; he had been working at Florence for some fifteen years as director of the court entertainments and he was a regular member of the Bardi circle.

Another work that ought to be mentioned here is " L' Amfiparnaso " (1597), composed by Orazio Vecchi, a canon of the cathedral of Modena. It is a series of fourteen madrigals in five parts set to words representing scenes of the comedy of masks. As the printed part-books have little woodcuts representing the characters, many historians have supposed that this work was intended to be acted, perhaps in dumb show, or by puppets, while a chorus sang the madrigals. This is quite erroneous ; the poet (most probably Giulio Cesare Croce of Bologna) says clearly in the pro- logue that this comedy is to enter by the ear and not by the eye. The " Amfiparnaso " is in no sense an opera ; it is merely a musical presentation of the typical comedy of masks, and as such it is both brilliantly amusing and at the same time a most valuable document for the history of the mask plays. It is no more an opera than were the madrigals on street cries written by contemporary English composers.

The creators of these first operas were for the most part men of noble birth. Peri was rather amateurish as a musician ; Rinuccini was a poet of real distinction. " Dafne " and " Euridice " were not written for popular audiences, but for the exclusive society of a highly culti- vated court. It was only audiences of that calibre who would appreciate the literary quality of these dramas of classical mythology. The next step in the history of opera is the performance of Monteverdi's " Arianna " at Mantua (1607), followed by his " Orfeo " in 1608. Most of the music to " Arianna " has been lost, and the reader must not judge of its quality by the fragment which has been much dressed up for modern concert purposes. " Orfeo " was performed a few years ago at Oxford, and no more appropriate place could have been found for a revival of it, since it was originally written for a society of ardent young intellectuals. To us it is inevitably a " museum piece," but for all that it is a great masterpiece of musical drama, and it ought to be staged periodically in order that all musicians may see it and hear it and learn from it the fundamental principles of dramatic composition. Monteverdi was a much more pro- fessional composer than Peri ; he had already had con- siderable experience as a writer of madrigals and of church

music. He saw how to utilise simultaneously all the resources available in his day. He collected a large orchestra,
and had the imagination to employ different instruments to
suit different situations. He has been described as the
inventor of very daring harmonies ; as a matter of fact most
of his devices had been used before, either by himself or by
others, but in " Orfeo " he saw how to turn them to account
at the appropriate dramatic moments and to do so without
destroying the general sense of musical design running all
through the opera. " Orfeo " is a great opera, not so much
on account of the striking and ingenious effects of detail, as
because of its broad sense of musical continuity ; considering the date at which it was written, it is a wonderful
organic whole, whereas many operas of later times that
present singular moments of dramatic power have suffered
from the defect of patchiness.


# CHAPTER V

# STANDARDISATION

An opera in those days was a large undertaking, such
as could only be organised by some great prince for some
special festivity ; architects of the period who write about
the building of theatres take it for granted that a theatre
was a purely temporary structure put up for a single
occasion. The Barberini family at Rome were great patrons
of opera, and it is interesting to note that quite soon after
the success of " Orfeo " a comic element began to make its
appearance in opera. In 1637 the first public opera-house
was opened at Venice by the composer Cavalli, and Venice
developed such a passion for opera that within the next half
century there was not merely one opera-house but half a
dozen or more in that city.

As soon as opera was thrown open to the general public

on payment it necessarily became standardised. The orchestra was standardised, and it is at this date that the quartet of strings becomes its regular normal basis. Plots were standardised too ; Venetian audiences did not want stories from ancient mythology, in which the main interest lay in the beauty of the poetry, but stories about human beings, though they did at least want their human beings to be heroes. The history of ancient Rome, and still more of the later Roman Empire, was the favourite material of the operatic poets ; but a love interest was required too, and gradually a sort of standard form was evolved in which we generally find four princes and three princesses whose love affairs resemble more or less a game of musical chairs. The comic element became more and more prominent ; here we see the influence of the comedy of masks. Still more important was the scenery ; it was a great age of engineering, and the transformations and other spectacular effects, if they really answered to the stage directions and the designs that have come down to us, must have been far beyond anything that our most ingenious and ostentatious producers can show us to-day.

Venice was a city of great wealth and a great international centre of trade ; the only places which could attempt to follow its example were Hamburg and London. But the Opera spread from Venice to various other cities in Italy and also to Vienna and other German courts. We must cast a brief glance at the beginnings of opera outside Italy.

## CHAPTER VI

## VIENNA AND PARIS: LULLI

THE IMPERIAL COURT at Vienna was in those days the most magnificent in Europe, and it was always closely in touch with Italy, especially with Venice. Italian operas, chiefly by Cavalli and another Venetian, Cesti, were produced at Vienna on the most sumptuous scale ; the designs for scenery by Burnacini, who worked chiefly at Vienna, are among the most beautiful that have ever been made for the stage. Munich, Stuttgart and other small German courts followed the example of Vienna as lavishly as they were able.

In Paris there had been various performances of a spectacular kind, and some of them served as models for the English masques ; the most famous was the " Ballet comique de la Reine," organised by Balthazar de Beaujoyeulx (who was really an Italian) in 1581. It was more like a masque than an opera, and the music was put together by various composers. From 1643 onwards Cardinal Mazarin made continuous attempts to establish Italian opera in Paris, perhaps more from political than from artistic motives, but it was a long time before he had any success. Madame de Motteville was on duty as a lady in waiting at an Italian opera in February 1644, and wrote in her memoirs that there were only about twenty people in the room, " and we all thought we should have died of cold and boredom." In 1655 Michel de la Guerre produced an opera to French words, but the French composers achieved nothing of real importance. Cavalli himself was brought over by Mazarin in 1660 and his "Serse" (Xerxes) was given with magnificent scenery by the great Italian engineer Torelli, but there were endless intrigues among the Italians themselves as well as the intrigues of the French musicians, who were always bitterly jealous of the Italians, and Cavalli finally left Paris in disgust. French audiences did not really care for Italian music ; they found it too noisy and violent. It is difficult for us who are accustomed to Verdi and Puccini to find passion and violence in the Italian operas of the seventeenth century, but there is definite evidence to prove that the French regarded them as almost an outrage on good taste.

Giovanni Battista Lulli, born of humble parents at Florence in 1639, was discovered by the Chevalier de Guise on his way from Malta to Paris in 1646 and taken by him to France, where he was soon handed over to Mademoiselle de Montpensier as a sort of page boy. His natural gift for singing and dancing attracted attention to him, and so did his talent for making scurrilous songs. He eventually became a sort of companion to the boy King Louis XIV and danced with the King himself in the court ballets. After various collaborations with Molière in plays with ballets, he astutely managed to secure a patent from the King giving him the sole right to produce operas in Paris, and produced the first really notable French opera, " Les Fêtes de l'Amour et de Bacchus," in 1672.

If ever opera was a court function, it was in the days of Louis XIV. Every opera of Lulli had to begin with a prologue of gods and goddesses in praise of the King, and the whole opera was carried out in a style that reflected the stiffness of court etiquette. To our ears Lulli's music sounds dry and conventional ; how much of it was actually Lulli's is very uncertain, for he employed several assistants. But the conception of the whole was his, as was the characteristic style of the recitative, entirely different from that of the Italians, although as a matter of fact Lulli never learned to speak French correctly himself. The declamation is said to have been modelled on the great French actors of the day. To French ears the declamation of verse was more interesting than the singing of airs, and both ballet and chorus played a much larger part than in the Italian operas. Lulli's music has little of the inward beauty that we find in his contemporaries Purcell and Scarlatti, but he had a genius for construction on the grand scale, and there are few to equal him for grandeur and stateliness.

# CHAPTER VII

# ENGLAND: PURCELL. GERMANY

ENGLAND, as one might expect, treated opera as a field for amateurish experiments. Just at the moment when opera might have had a chance of establishing itself, the Civil War put an end to theatrical enterprise. But the Puritans were at any rate lovers of music, and Sir William D'Avenant, who had been the last writer of masques under Charles I, saw that it might be possible to get opera accepted when plays were forbidden. What he really wanted to do was to produce his own heroic dramas in verse ; in 1656 he got his play " The Siege of Rhodes " set to music by various composers in collaboration, and produced it on a diminutive stage such as one might find in a village hall of to-day. But it excited interest, and more operas were given, the music of which was chiefly by Matthew Locke. These English operas were quite unlike the Italian or French ones in subject and style, for they were conceived as plays with incidental music. After the Restoration the theatres were re-opened, and D'Avenant's operas were succeeded by adaptations of Shakespeare, such as " The Tempest," in which large quantities of music to words by D'Avenant were introduced. The best of these so-called operas on a large scale was " King Arthur " (1691), by Dryden and Purcell ; but it is not an opera in the modern understanding of the term, for most of the principal characters do not sing at all.

The music of " The Siege of Rhodes " is lost, but we possess that of " Psyche " (1674), a very curious opera by Shadwell and Matthew Locke, imitated (but not adapted) from the French " Psyché " of Molière and Lulli. It could only be revived now as a " museum piece," if at all, but it is interesting as showing the English feeling for picturesqueness in preference to formality. Blow's " Venus and

Adonis " (1685), though called a masque, probably because it was performed quite privately at court, is a true opera, for it is set to music all through ; it was revived a few years ago by Mr. Rutland Boughton at Glastonbury. " Venus and Adonis " served as the model for Purcell's " Dido and Æneas," the earliest opera that, in this country at any rate, we can call almost a repertory work and not a mere museum piece.

" Dido and Æneas " was composed in 1689 for performance at a school for young ladies in Chelsea. The reader will note that neither of these two genuine English operas was intended for the public stage ; the English public of those days would probably have refused to tolerate them. Both of them are isolated and exceptional works ; one may say that they had neither ancestors nor progeny. They are both of them chamber works ; they stand to the public theatre as a string quartet of Mozart does to the great symphonies, and are too delicate and intimate for anything but a small theatre. But " Dido and Æneas " is none the less one of the great masterpieces of early opera. " It lasted only an hour," said a modern opera-goer once, " but I felt as if I had been through all the emotions of ' Götterdämmerung ' ! " It is fairly often performed by schools nowadays, but if we possessed a national opera house in London, it ought to be one of the standard works in the professional repertory.

In Germany native opera took much longer to establish than in England and France. The first attempt was made by Heinrich Schütz, a famous composer of Protestant church music. Schütz had been a pupil of Gabrieli at Venice, and in 1627 he got Rinuccini's " Dafne " translated into German by Martin Opitz, a poet of some distinction. It was performed at Torgau, a small town in Saxony, to celebrate the marriage of a princess of the Electoral house. The music is lost, and we cannot even be certain whether Schütz composed new music to the play himself, or whether, as is more probable, he arranged the original music of Peri. But the Thirty Years' War (1618–1648) was as disastrous to

German opera as the Civil War was to English opera. The great German music of the seventeenth century is mostly sacred, and such attempts at German opera as were made in Nuremberg, Leipzig and Hamburg were mainly on Biblical subjects. The first permanent opera in Germany was started at Hamburg in 1678.

Hamburg was the Venice of the north in those days, and in some ways the life of Hamburg was very like that of Restoration London. Jeremy Collier's denunciations of the London stage were a mere trifle compared to those of the Hamburg clergy, and although Hamburg had begun with a sort of religious opera in 1678, the public soon preferred those of Reinhold Keiser, whose first opera at Hamburg in 1701 dealt with the crimes of a notorious local highwayman. The Hamburg opera must have been a very rough-and-tumble affair, depending largely on amateur performers. Keiser was a man of wildly dissipated life, but there was a spark of genius in him, and he exercised a powerful influence on the young Handel, who came to Hamburg in 1703.

## CHAPTER VIII

# SURVEY OF THE 17TH CENTURY

IF WE TAKE a general survey of operatic history in the 17th century we see at once that the main line of its development lay in Italy, though we must not neglect the very important branch of French opera. French opera was the creation of an Italian, but we shall see that France in the following century had very notable contributions to make to the musical drama. In Italy we see opera initiated by a small coterie of aristocratic intellectuals at Florence. It gradually becomes more professional in style, but for a long time it remains associated with the courts of princes, except at Venice. Even at Venice it can hardly have been a popular entertainment ; it must always have been supported by the wealthy classes, and we know that .the Venetian theatres were built mostly by the great noble families such as the Grimani. At Bologna it was the Formagliari family who did most to establish opera ; at Naples, where opera began with the visit of a Venetian company in 1671, it was dependent on the court of the Spanish viceroys, or of the Austrian viceroys during the years in which Naples belonged to Austria.

Looking at the music of the operas by itself, we see a gradual transformation of style and method. At all periods composers of opera have had to employ the musical language and the musical forms of their own day. (For the history of those forms the reader must be referred to other parts of this volume.) We have at all times to take into account the interaction between the theatre and the concert-room. The concert-room standardises the regular forms of song, dance, fugue, etc., because they are in constant demand there. We ought perhaps to warn the reader that we are using the word " concert-room " not in its modern sense, but simply as a collective term for all the occasions, not being church or stage, where music is performed and listened to for its own sake.

But the theatre, as soon as it was definitely established, gradually became the supply centre of musical expression, as opposed to musical formalism. Musical form is not the contradiction of musical expression, as some amateurs imagine ; it is the shaping of a series of sounds in order to make them expressive. Take any simple piece of music that you feel to be expressive, an ordinary hymn tune or even a chant ; the expressiveness is due not merely to the particular note that excites emotion, but to the particular place in which it occurs ; if it was put in a different place, it would lose its significance. But expression becomes conventionalised with repetition and loses its emotional force, and it is then that we need the influence of the theatre to stimulate a keener expression of emotion, which in its turn gets transferred to the concert-room and again becomes standardised.

And it often becomes standardised in the theatre too ; when that happens we have a period of operatic decadence. But in listening to old operas, and especially to museum pieces, we must try to put ourselves back into their own period, and learn to adjust our minds to their methods of expression ; and it is in these cases that the value of emotional expression is settled not by its violence, but by its being placed exactly in the right situation.

The whole tendency of opera in the seventeenth century was to become more musical and less like an ordinary play in verse ; that means that the emotion, instead of being distributed more or less evenly throughout the opera (and therefore never covering a very wide range) became concentrated in the songs, while the recitative (which was necessary to carry on the story) became more and more conventional and dull. We notice this all the more in the Italian operas, because the Italian theatre made hardly any use of " background music." A palace may fall to ruins, or a dragon rise from the sea, but the music takes no notice of it whatever. Music had not yet discovered the technique for that sort of thing, and if it had, it would probably have been impossible to synchronise it with the stage effects— we know how difficult it is to achieve this even nowadays in an opera of Wagner.

We notice more and more the over-elaboration of scenic effects and spectacle ; if it were possible to carry out an exact reproduction of an opera by Cavalli to-day, we should probably think that the music was negligible in relation to the scenery. This passion for " machines " was characteristic of the age ; it affected the French and English theatres no less than the Italian. It was a worship of mechanism at which we moderns have no right to scoff, for we moderns are at this moment worshipping mechanism just as foolishly, and with considerably less sense of beauty.

The seventeenth century at any rate realised that opera

must deal with subjects remote from common life. Shakespeare, though he never adopted an operatic attitude to music itself on the stage, had something of the Italian operatic view of drama, in that he separated the lofty style of his tragic and serious parts from the low comedy of his clowns. The opera never attempted comedy of manners, and such a thing did not exist in Italy, even in the spoken drama. An Italian opera by the end of the century bore a considerable resemblance to a Victorian melodrama, with its chivalrous hero, its villain, its persecuted heroine, often in disguise, and its comic servants, male and female. The reason is that our English melodramas are actually descended from the opera, just as our Victorian pantomimes were descended from the so-called operas of Purcell. The word melodrama means music-drama, and *melodramma* was for most of the seventeenth century the regular name for an opera ; we meet it constantly in the word-books, though sometimes the work is called *dramma per musica*. The name *opera* appears to have been a colloquial expression, and it penetrated to French and English fairly early in the century. Evelyn's diary speaks of an " Opera (for so they call shews of that kind) " at Rome in 1644 ; D'Avenant uses the word in 1656. The word *opera*, it need hardly be said, simply means " a work."

# B : THE 18TH CENTURY

## CHAPTER I

# ITALIAN INFLUENCE: SCARLATTI

Purcell died in 1695 and it so happened that there was no English composer living who was equal to carrying on his work for the theatre. Early in the following century an attempt was made to introduce Italian opera in London, and though the first efforts were not in themselves very successful, Italian opera soon became so firmly established that it is with us still. There was nothing surprising about this. Paris was the only great city which supported an opera of its own in its own language. The German courts all had their Italian operas, and Hamburg was becoming gradually Italianised ; Keiser's operas were often sung in a mixture of Italian and German. Madrid and Lisbon set up their Italian operas in the course of the century ; Copenhagen and St. Petersburg did the same. All over Europe Italian was the language of music, except in France, and even France had eventually to yield to the Italian invasion, though it did so by the process of swallowing the Italian composers, as it did Lulli, and doing its best to make Frenchmen of them.

When we say that Italian was the language of music, we do not mean that all musicians habitually talked Italian, or even that they always set Italian words to music ; though even in the matter of spoken language Italian was certainly the one in which musicians of different nationalities would most probably converse with each other. When Dr. Burney travelled over most of Europe in 1770–72 in search of materials for his " History of Music," he seems to have found Italian the most useful language, as he had very little knowledge of German. Germany was overrun with

Italian musicians, and German musicians had to Italianise their musical style if they wanted to be anything more distinguished than mere church organists. Ever since about 1600 German musicians, if they could possibly manage it, had gone to Italy to learn composition, and even German church music in the seventeenth century shows the ever increasing influence of Italy. Most of the great palaces and churches of the period were not only designed by Italian architects (or at least by pupils of Italians) but actually built by Italian stonemasons, who travelled everywhere, for no country could produce their equals in skill. Readers who have been to Dresden may remember a restaurant on the river near the opera-house, called the *Italienisches Dörfchen* (Italian village) ; it derives its name from the fact that there actually was an Italian village there in the eighteenth century, inhabited by the descendants of the masons who came to build the court church.

When Handel went to Italy in 1706 as a young man of twenty-one, the greatest composer living was Alessandro Scarlatti, who divided his career between Rome and Naples. Most of his operas were written for Naples, and he is the creator of what was then the standard Italian opera form and style. To-day his operas are not even museum pieces, and the only songs from them that are familiar to the ordinary concert-goer, such as " O cessate di piagarmi," belong to his very early works and are not typical of his maturity. The favourite opera songs of Handel will give the general reader a sufficiently adequate idea of his riper style.

Scarlatti's operas show a gradual reform of operatic method, though those reforms led to conventions that a modern musician finds very hard to appreciate. In the first place, the chaotic libretti of the Venetians were simplified and made more dignified in style ; the poets were in all probability influenced by the plays of Racine. We see the comic characters being kept in order and put in their proper place ; they gradually sink like a sediment to the ends of the acts—in the third act entering just before the final *dénouement*, which is really an untying of knots. A little later on the two comic characters drop out of the opera altogether, and their scenes become *intermezzi* which could without trouble be transferred from one opera to another.

In the second place, Scarlatti is responsible for the standardisation of the *aria* in the *da capo* form that is the horror of musicians nowadays. His own audiences would never have felt that there was anything odd about it ; it was much clearer and more concise, capable too of more intense expression, than the forms it superseded. It could be adapted to any emotion—joy, sorrow, rage, despair. Scarlatti also invented the accompanied recitative, as it is called. Most recitative, the dull parts which had to get on with the story of the play, were accompanied only by the harpsichord in what is called *recitativo secco*, dry recitative, as many writers have with obvious facetiousness observed. To bring in the stringed instruments to accompany recitative created a new emotional atmosphere. Most readers will remember the way in which Bach, in the " St. Matthew Passion," always brings in the string quartet to accompany the words of Jesus. We have been taught to notice this effect in Bach, but we are apt to neglect it in the oratorios of Handel, for few singers and conductors realise that the entry of the strings means a change of mood and a new emotional atmosphere in the character who is singing.

A third and a very important invention of Scarlatti was the " ensemble of perplexity " which is still characteristic of opera and a valuable means of effect that cannot be obtained in a spoken play. A situation arises, affecting perhaps four characters on the stage, each in a different way ; they express their feelings simultaneously in a quartet. Sullivan parodied the device in " The Mikado " —" Here's a how-de-do ! " Old Scarlatti had parodied himself nearly two centuries before.

## CHAPTER II

# MORE ABOUT CONVENTIONS

IT IS APPROPRIATE at this point to discuss some of the conventions of opera which are apt to irritate unmusical people and those who expect absolute realism in opera. Even in the eighteenth century, as we shall see, some people objected to the action being held up in order that a singer might show off his voice. But the cause for objection lay not in the musical form but in the music with which second-rate composers filled it. Nobody ever complained of the ensembles in " Carmen " or "Meistersinger " for holding up the action, simply because the music is so enthralling that we only wish it would go on longer.

Supposing that in some play a messenger comes on and says " The queen is dead." This is a mere piece of information ; it must be made as clear as possible, so that nobody can miss it. In an opera, therefore, it must be stated in recitative. But the queen's death will certainly produce various emotional states in the characters on the stage, possibly in the messenger himself. Any actor knows how difficult it is to express these emotions if he has no words to say. A poet can give him words, though they are not the words he would use in private life ; the musician must give him music to sing, and the shape of that music will depend partly on the quality of the emotion and partly on the normal musical style of the period. Handel will have to do it one way, Wagner another ; their styles will differ just as Shakespeare's will from a modern poet's. The musician, especially in Handel's day, will hold up the action longer than the poet ; but it is a curious property of music that it can destroy our sense of time, as long as it really holds our interest. An " ensemble of perplexity," if it were spoken, would probably be unimpressive and possibly ridiculous ; even if a great poet achieved it, the actors would find it

curiously difficult to speak, for it would have to be timed
accurately and very carefully rehearsed, so that the different
speeches dovetailed into one another like a piece of music.
Like a piece of music—music does this for the singers
without their having to think about the technique of it.

## CHAPTER III

# THE MALE SOPRANO

Handel's operas are mentioned here in preference
to Scarlatti's because most English readers are more or less
familiar with the Handelian style of music ; moreover since
1920 there has been a great revival of Handel's operas in
Germany, although their vogue is now already over, and
they have returned once more to our category of museum
pieces. Between 1711 and 1741 Handel produced nearly
forty operas on the London stage. Scarlatti's last opera came
out in 1721 and Handel, whose real genius belonged to the
theatre, carried the Scarlattian type of opera to its climax ;
but by force of external circumstances Handel's operatic
career was on the whole a failure.

Italian opera now began to be a profitable business, and
Italy's chief export. What made the success of Italian
opera was not so much the music as the singers, and here
we must speak of that curious phenomenon, the Italian
artificial soprano. It had been discovered more than a
hundred years before that a boy's treble voice could be
preserved by a barbarous surgical operation, and it was
further discovered that in favourable cases such voices
could be immensely strengthened in the course of years.
This horrible practice did not begin in the theatre, but in
the church, owing to the difficulty of obtaining good
choirboys in Italy ; it was officially condemned but con-
nived at in practice, and singers of this type were singing

in the Papal choir at Rome almost up to the end of the nineteenth century. As far as can be ascertained, the practice was confined exclusively to Italy, with the exception of a small number of Germans ; male sopranos dominated the operatic stage in all countries except France, but the singers themselves were Italian. Dr. Burney made great efforts to find out where the operation was generally performed, but there was not unnaturally some mystery about it ; he came however to the conclusion that Naples, as one might expect, was the chief source of supply.

The first Italian male soprano heard in England was Siface, who came over at the desire of Mary of Modena, wife of James II, about 1687 ; he had previously been a member of the Pope's chapel. The last who appeared on the English stage was Velluti, who sang in London in 1825 ; he died in 1861. For practically two centuries all the hero parts in Italian opera were sung by sopranos (or sometimes contraltos) of this kind ; at certain periods women were forbidden altogether to sing on the stage in Rome, and male sopranos had to take female parts as well. In the early days of Italian opera in London, on the other hand, the male soprano parts were sometimes sung by women. Nicolini, whose acting was highly praised by Addison, was the first to make a success on the London stage. Out of the thousands who submitted to the operation, only comparatively few attained eminence, but the most famous of them obtained gigantic salaries, especially in London.

The great difficulty of reviving Handelian or even later Italian opera nowadays lies in the fact that the chief male parts were always written for sopranos. If they are sung by women, they lose their dramatic character ; we find it difficult to-day to tolerate even a female Siebel in Gounod's "Faust," though we still accept Mozart's Cherubino. (The reason is that Siebel is a serious character and Cherubino a comic one.) If we transpose the music for tenors, the music suffers, especially as hardly any modern tenors can sing the florid passages. The singers of the eighteenth century, and especially the male sopranos, cultivated an extraordinary agility in florid passages ; audiences of those days delighted in a type of *coloratura* that would have horrified even the age of Patti. The only opera songs approaching that style which are heard now are those of Mozart, and even the songs of Costanza in "Seraglio" and of the Queen of Night in "The Magic Flute" are simple compared with the flourishes every singer was expected to throw off in the days of Handel.

## CHAPTER IV

# METASTASIO.
## THE FRENCH SCHOOL:
## RAMEAU

OPERA HAD INDEED BECOME no more than a concert in costume, though there were a few composers who maintained a fairly high standard. The curious thing is that just at this very moment there arose the strange case of a librettist who was a real poet—Metastasio. His first drama for music was "Didone," set to music by Vinci in 1724. Metastasio devoted his life to writing libretti for operas ; they have great dramatic force, within their peculiar convention, and they belong to the great things of Italian literature—on this point all Italian critics are agreed. The result was that every composer in Italy, and many outside, set Metastasio's dramas to music over and over again; there are even cases of composers setting the same play twice, to entirely different music. Audiences of those days must have known the plays by heart, and this tended even more to turn operas into a sort of singing competition.

All this time France remained severely apart. Lulli died in 1681 and his tradition was continued by Campra and

Destouches ; in 1739 Rameau, then no longer a young man, started on his career as an opera composer. Rameau's operas, for some of which Voltaire furnished the words, have all the stiff ceremonial of Lulli's, but Rameau was a really great musician and his operas have fairly recently been revived in Paris with no less success than those of Handel in Germany. Rameau's music is little known in England, except a few of his harpsichord pieces ; unfortunately the performance of one of his operas would entail enormous labour and expense if it was to be at all adequate. His subjects, like those of Lulli, are chiefly classical, but treated in the manner of Racine, one may say ; the declamatory recitative, of which Rameau was a consummate master, was a great attraction for his own audiences. The songs, exquisite as they are, seldom have the passion or grandeur of Handel's ; on the other hand, the choruses and ballets are magnificent. The art of Rameau was essentially French, and intimately associated with the French language. To most English people, even to those who know French pretty well, French poetry is singularly difficult to appreciate ; but if our ears are open to music, Rameau's operas will do much to explain to us its beauty.

## CHAPTER V

# COMIC OPERA IN ITALY AND FRANCE

PRACTICALLY ALL THE OPERAS we have so far considered were composed for court theatres and for audiences of highly cultivated people with a dignified taste both in literature and in music. The modern reader may think it shocking that in those days culture was the privilege of an aristocracy, but it was culture carried to a very high degree, and we shall see later on how the destruction of that aristocratic culture has imperilled the future of opera.

We must now turn to an altogether different type of musical drama, which from the eighteenth century onwards has acquired increasing importance—Comic Opera.

Quite early in the seventeenth century there had been attempts at comic opera, especially at Rome, and one or two composers produced some very amusing scenes of popular life, but there was no continuous tradition of comic opera as a *genre* by itself until 1709, when a little theatre at Naples was opened for operas in the local dialect dealing with everyday characters instead of classical heroes. Even the great Scarlatti himself wrote a comic opera for this theatre in 1718, when he was nearly sixty, and seems to have thoroughly enjoyed making fun of his own grand manner. Pergolesi's " La Serva Padrona " (1733) gives some idea of their musical style, but this charming little work is not a real comic opera of its period ; it is only a set of comic *intermezzi* intended for performance between the acts of a serious opera. The comic operas were generally in three acts, and sometimes even had their own comic *intermezzi*. They were generally performed by people who regarded themselves as actors ; the artificial sopranos never sang in them, although the custom was kept up of giving the chief male parts to high voices, sung by women in male costume. We see here the origin of the " principal boy " of a Victorian pantomime or musical comedy.

A Neapolitan comic opera company came to London in 1740 and performed " La Serva Padrona " with fair success, but its great reputation was made in 1752, when an Italian company acted it in Paris. The visit of this company was the cause of the famous *guerre des bouffons*, the war of the musicians (and still more of the journalists) over the relative merits of French and Italian music. The ultimate victory was with Italy ; French audiences were becoming tired of the grand academic manner of Rameau, and could hardly resist the natural spontaneous humour of the Italians and their lively tunefulness. Here it may be mentioned that in those days French opera was unbearable to anyone who was not a Frenchman ; both English and Italian travellers give the most ludicrous accounts of it—to their ears it simply was not music at all.

Pergolesi was by no means a great composer ; his grand operas are often dull and carelessly written, and Martini, the learned theorist who taught Mozart as a boy, quite rightly said that his famous " Stabat Mater " was in the style of a musical comedy. But he is a historic figure, and he had a certain sentimental charm so attractive that it conquered the whole of musical Europe. In another section of this work there is an account of the complete change of musical language that took place at this time in German instrumental music, the change from the suites and concertos of J. S. Bach to the sonatas of his son Emmanuel and the symphonies of the men who just preceded Haydn and Mozart. The new style of melody was not their invention ; it came from Naples, from the trivial comic operas which everybody wanted to hear. People in provincial towns north of the Alps, who could not go to see an Italian opera, wanted to play the music at home on their own violins and harpsichords ; the composers provided them with suitable sonatas. Electors and Prince-Bishops wanted Italian musical comedy tunes played during dinner ; as their chapel-masters could not obtain the originals (for they were never printed), they composed something that sounded much the same. And they wrote sonatas and symphonies, not because they thought there was anything particularly noble or uplifting about that particular form, but simply because it was the ordinary musical form of the opera songs, whether serious or frivolous.

More Italian comic operas came to Paris ; Naples was always the chief source of supply, but Venice contributed a good many. A composer from Parma, Egidio Romualdo Duni, settled in Paris, followed the example of Lulli in writing his name as Duny, and created a prolific school of French comic opera, in which he was followed by Monsigny, Dalayrac and others. The main difference between the French and Italian comic operas was that the French preferred the connecting dialogue spoken, whereas the Italians always stuck to recitative.

## CHAPTER VI

# ENGLISH COMIC OPERA.
# THE EUROPEAN POSITION

In England there was a similar wave of comic opera ; but it had begun much earlier, with a more or less native product. In 1728 there came out " The Beggar's Opera," a brilliant social and political satire by John Gay ; it also satirised the Italian opera in its form, as it contained a large number of amusing songs which Dr. Pepusch, a learned German musical antiquary, adapted to the popular tunes of the day. People sometimes talk of " The Beggar's Opera " as if it was all made up of English folk-songs, but many of them were of French or Italian origin, and there were bits of Purcell and Handel as well. Gay's amusing sequel to this opera, " Polly," was forbidden performance by the censorship of the government ; the enormous crop of English " ballad operas " which delighted popular audiences up to the end of the century gradually drifted more and more into mere namby-pamby sentimentality. Italian influence made itself felt in London, as in Paris ; Galuppi of Venice enjoyed an enormous vogue, and his comic operas contributed a good deal towards the formation of the characteristic English style.

England being always closely in touch with Hamburg, the first English ballad operas made their way to Germany, and just as the German theatre owed its rise to the visit of the English actors in the days of Shakespeare, so German comic opera derived its origin from English music. J. A. Hiller and Dittersdorf were the most successful composers in this line. German comic opera, however, was also influenced by the Italians ; Galuppi had been fortunate enough to have librettos written for him by the famous playwright Goldoni, and Goldoni's librettos were often adapted by the German composers.

Let us pause for a moment and review the general operatic situation of Europe as it was about 1760. We saw opera start in Florence as the experiment of a few intellectuals. It is taken up as a diversion for princes. Venice commercialises it and to some extent vulgarises it, but at the same time gives it an impetus that causes it to spread beyond the Alps. Wherever it goes, it requires the patronage of a cultivated court ; if it fails to find that soil, it degenerates either artistically, as at Hamburg, or financially, as in London. The small Italian courts lose their political importance, and in the eighteenth century their place (as far as opera is concerned) is taken by Paris and the German courts that are trying to follow the model set up by Louis XIV. In Paris opera is French, but everywhere else it is Italian. Italy makes the operas and exports them, along with composers, singers, players and scene-painters. For Italy, at any rate, it is a huge commercial business, and as soon as opera becomes commercial, it becomes degraded. French grand opera only survived up to the end of Rameau's days because it was purely French.

Comic opera, as a work of art (for we can regard the Neapolitan comedies as artistic), could only come into being after serious opera had established a routine technique of composition. It was a welcome reaction against the over-conventionalised form of the grand opera which it often satirised ; but comic opera became commercialised even faster than serious opera, because it was cheaper to produce and more lucrative to undertake. When the last performance of Rameau's " Dardanus " took place in 1760 there was not a single composer in Europe whose operas had the least claim to distinction, except Hasse at Dresden and Jommelli at Stuttgart, the last survivors of the dignified old Italian style.

## CHAPTER VII

# GLUCK

THE MOMENT was right for the historic reforms of Gluck. Gluck was born on the borders of Germany and Bohemia ; he had been sent to Italy to learn composition and had written several operas of a conventional Italian type. In 1745 he was in London, where his opera " La Caduta dei Giganti " (The Fall of the Giants) composed to celebrate the battle of Culloden was a complete failure. But he met Handel in London, and is pretty certain to have heard some of Handel's oratorios ; he went on to Paris, where he heard operas by Rameau and met some of the leaders of French musical criticism. For some years he continued writing Italian operas, and French comic operas too, for Vienna, until in 1762 he produced his " Orfeo " in Italian. How far Gluck himself was the originator of the theories attributed to him is a matter of some uncertainty ; it is probable that he was a good deal directed by his librettist, Calzabigi, and by the influence of Algarotti, a diplomatist and man of letters, who had written a severe criticism of Italian opera in general a few years before.

" Orfeo " is still in the European repertory and is the oldest opera that is not revived merely as a museum piece. The version now generally performed is not that of 1762, nor even the revised French version of 1774, but a re-arrangement of the latter made by Berlioz in 1859 for Madame Viardot-Garcia, the great contralto, and it is mainly due to her superb interpretation that the opera has remained as a classical display-piece for contraltos.

" Orfeo " in its Italian shape is quite unlike any Italian opera of the period. It could only have been produced at the court of Vienna, where the imperial family were all accomplished musicians and sometimes themselves performed musical entertainments for which Gluck composed music. It is almost a chamber opera in style, and its libretto suggests a deliberate reversion to the ideals of Rinuccini's " Euridice." It is French in its use of the chorus, French in its ballet-music and its little instrumental interludes for stage ceremony, French in its systematic use of accompanied recitative to the total exclusion of *recitativo secco*, although vocally its musical style is Italian. The fact that it has only three characters, instead of the six or seven princes, princesses, confidants and confidantes traditionally required in Handelian opera, suggests that it was composed for an intimate audience of connoisseurs. The same applies even more to Gluck's later and less known opera " Paride ed Elena " .(1770), which also has three characters only, and a large quantity of ballet. Both these operas are far more lyrical than dramatic in the ordinary sense of the word ; very little happens on the stage, and all along we know exactly what is going to happen. The interest lies in the beauty of the treatment and in the subtle presentation of delicate grades of emotion. Much of " Orfeo " is terribly dull unless one understands the words and can follow every sentence ; they do not give us much positive information of importance, but they take us through a series of emotional experiences.

The audience thought " Orfeo " depressing, for it began with a funeral, and there were no showy florid songs. There is one in the modern version, but it was put in for the French performance of 1774 ; it is taken from one of Gluck's earlier Italian operas. " Alceste " (1767) was considered to be a funeral from beginning to end. It is more dramatic than " Orfeo," and is notable for the overture, which was deliberately designed to prepare the audience for the tragic atmosphere of the opera and leads into it in a strikingly effective way.

Gluck enjoyed the favour of the court, but the public was decidedly hostile to his reforms, as may be imagined. In 1774 he succeeded in getting his " Iphigenie en Aulide " produced in Paris, mainly through the patronage of Marie Antoinette, who had been his pupil in Vienna. " Orphée " (the French version) followed in the same year, and a

French version of " Alceste " in 1776. In 1777 he composed " Armide " ; although it is the most beautiful of his
operas and technically the most finished, it has had few
revivals. His last work was " Iphigenie en Tauride " (1779).

The war of words over the *bouffons* was nothing to the
war of the Gluckists and Piccinists. Gluck was a German
and under the protection of Marie Antoinette ; that set
both the old French party—the admirers of Rameau—and
the pro-Italian party against him. Piccini, a Neapolitan
composer who had written some very successful comic
operas, was brought into the field against him, very much
against his own wish, it is said. Piccini was defeated, and no
wonder, for he was not very much at home in grand opera ;
but the Italians really won the battle, for after Gluck went
back to Vienna to die, Paris once more capitulated to the
fascinations of Sacchini, Paesiello and Paër, writers chiefly
of sentimental opera, a new type that had come into being
in response to the general craze for sentimental novels and
*comédie larmoyante.*

Handel said of Gluck that he knew no more of counterpoint than his own cook did ; and the weakness of Gluck lay
in his clumsiness of musical technique. The ordinary listener
perhaps does not notice this ; one certainly hopes that he
does not, but the conductor and the other people who have
to study the operas and prepare them for performance soon
discover those awkward places that it requires so much
forethought and ingenuity to cover up. What charms a
modern audience in Gluck is the illusion of classical dignity ; they are ideal museum pieces, for they give the
modern listener the impression of a purely imaginary
ancient Greece populated not by human beings but by
statues of white marble. We enjoy a strange and wonderful
sense of calm beauty remote from all human passion, like
the happy spirits in Gluck's Elysian fields ; but it may be
doubted whether that was altogether what Gluck intended.

## CHAPTER VIII

# MOZART

WE REACH the moment at which Vienna becomes the centre of the musical world—the age of Haydn and Mozart. A new factor has arisen in musical life, the classical orchestra, with its concertos, its *divertimenti* and its symphonies ; it has learned its new skill because the players, both strings and wind, have been trying for a generation to imitate the airs and graces of the Italian opera singers. They have acquired a new elegance of phrasing, a new tenderness of expression ; the orchestra is the new toy of the moment, and enterprising music-publishers in Vienna and Paris are turning out sets of symphony parts by the hundred. The classical orchestra has become standardised, and so has the symphony. This is the background of Mozart's youth ; circumstances, if not natural inclination, made him a symphonist, an instrumental composer, before he had the chance of writing an opera, apart from his efforts as a child prodigy.

But it was the opera that had created the symphony and the opera created the concerto too, for it was a deliberate adaptation of the grand operatic *aria*. Mozart's greatest works, the works in which he is most intensely himself, are his operas, and also his concertos. He could never have composed those concertos unless he had had a genius for opera, and one of his great achievements in opera was the utilisation of the symphonic technique—not just what people call orchestration, but the building up of a stage scene on the lines of an orchestral work.

In the whole history of music there are few operas that achieve the incomparable grandeur of the one with which Mozart opened his real dramatic career at the age of twenty-five—" Idomeneo." It is so rarely performed nowadays—its first production in this country was that of the

Glasgow amateur operatic society in March 1934—that it must be classed in our category of museum pieces. It belongs to the age of Gluck and Jommelli with its classical story and its soprano hero, but it achieves their ideals with a far higher mastery of craftsmanship, for it has all the Italian serenity of Jommelli and all the dramatic sincerity of Gluck, together with a new sensitiveness to the expressive power not only of the orchestra but also of what was at that time modern harmony. To present "Idomeneo" adequately it ought to be given with a superb cast of singers and on a vast stage with every magnificence of spectacle, for it belongs to an age when time, labour or expense did not enter into the considerations of the illustrious patrons of the musical drama.

Mozart's next opera, written in 1782, was a comic opera in German, " Die Entführung aus dem Serail," generally known in England as " The Seraglio." Only a few years earlier he had scorned the idea of writing a German opera ; German opera in those days meant a trivial affair for the common herd. " The Seraglio " is the first German comic opera by a great composer and for that reason it is historically epoch-making. It is full of delightful things, but in style it is a jumble ; Costanza's famous song might have come out of " Idomeneo," Pedrillo's " Im Mohrenland " is Neapolitan comic opera, some of the other airs are purely German, and the finale is in the French style. The opera holds the stage now by the irresistible charm of the music, whatever its style may be, and by the humorous characterisation of the comic bass, Osmin.

" The Seraglio," for all its success, could not keep the German company alive, and the court preferred its comic opera in Italian. For his next three operas, all in Italian, and all comic, " Le Nozze di Figaro " (1786), " Don Giovanni " (1788) and " Così fan Tutte " (1790), Mozart had the inestimable advantage of collaborating with Lorenzo da Ponte, one of the wittiest and most skilful librettists in operatic history. It is no wonder that two such accomplished technicians produced undying masterpieces. Owing

Lc

to the stupidity of nineteenth-century audiences and critics, especially in Germany, " Così fan Tutte " remained for about a hundred years under a cloud ; we owe it to Richard Strauss that it was interpreted afresh in its true character, and it at present enjoys an extraordinary popularity, especially in England.

" Figaro " and " Don Giovanni " are the foundations of all subsequent comic opera, Italian, French, German or English. But we must not forget that Mozart had his predecessors too, and that much of what people now think characteristically Mozartian is merely the conventional small-talk of dozens of minor Italian opera-manufacturers. The chief technical achievement in operatic construction that Mozart found ready to his hand was the comic *ensemble* and the comic *finale*. In the Scarlattian opera all interest was centred on the *aria* for a single character ; it summed up the emotion of its particular scene, and after singing an *aria* that character invariably left the stage. Duets were rare, and any larger *ensemble* most exceptional. When Scarlatti first introduced a formal *ensemble* he called it an *aria a quattro*, a song for four people, and it conformed exactly to the conventional shape of an *aria*, including the *da capo*. It was only the comic characters who could be allowed to sing bustling duets, generally expressing some sort of altercation. Out of these there gradually grew up the bustling *finale*, which became bigger and longer as years went on. The *finales* of Leo and Pergolesi suggest that no curtain fell at the end of an act, for the characters come on gradually, and go off gradually too. (In the English Restoration theatre the curtain never fell till the end of the play, and it was not until about 1760 that it was let down after each act. Opera had its own habits in stage practice, and not much is known about its details, but Rameau's method of ending an act with a short recitative after a long ballet and chorus suggests that the Paris opera followed the same rule.[1]) Later Italian comic operas developed the well-known comic device, a scene of confusion in which all the

[1]See Montague Summers, *The Restoration Theatre* London, 1934.

characters are singing at once and no one in the audience can realise exactly what is happening ; on a scene of this kind it is evident that the curtain must fall in order to bring it to an end.

It is probably to the operatic *finale* that the symphonists owed their conventional habit of ending a movement or a section of a movement with a good deal of empty repetition of the dominant and tonic chords ; it always sounds as if the composer and orchestra were applauding their own music, and in Mozart's case we gladly grant him the right to do so. In the theatre it is obvious that applause was wanted, and the example of the orchestra might well stimulate the audience. Mozart and Da Ponte accepted the convention ; we have Da Ponte's very amusing corroboration of this in his autobiography. Mozart, with his long experience of symphonic writing, built up his *finales* on a larger scale than his predecessors, with the result that in each of them there are several pages in which all are singing together at the top of their voices and it is a matter of complete indifference what the words are ; the singers for the moment have become an orchestra. We accept this in Mozart ; he compels us to believe that whatever he does is always right. But in the course of later generations we shall begin to find this symphonic *finale* something of a nuisance.

Mozart's operas bring the eighteenth century to an end. Beaumarchais's " Mariage de Figaro " was the prologue to the French Revolution, and one can imagine how Mozart remembered the days when he too was a mere servant and was kicked out of the presence of his archbishop. Don Giovanni, last remnant of the old nobility, is taken down to Hell, and his servant and peasants only laugh at his disappearance. In " Così fan Tutte " Comedy in the person of Despina the chambermaid makes fun of everybody and everything.

" The Magic Flute " (1791) opens the mysterious door to a new age. It is the first great work of music—perhaps it was the only one—that was composed for the humbler classes of society.

# C: FROM MOZART TO WAGNER

## CHAPTER I

## CHERUBINI. BEETHOVEN

THE FRENCH REVOLUTION and the Napoleonic Empire affected the course of opera no less than that of European life in general. The spirit of the Revolution gave a serious and ethical turn to what was officially called comic opera. What the French designated as *opéra comique* was opera with spoken dialogue, and the adjective lost its original meaning so completely that in later years the French had to invent a new category, *opéra bouffe* (from the Italian word *buffo*, comic) to signify operas the main function of which was to stimulate laughter.

We find this serious turn in the operas of Méhul, whose "Joseph," composed during the Revolution, is still performed in France and Germany; it deals in a style of great dignity with the Biblical story of Joseph and his brethren. The most important composer of this period is Cherubini, an Italian who spent most of his life in Paris. Cherubini was associated with the musicians of the Conservatoire founded by the Republic in 1795, and was never on good terms with Napoleon, who disliked his independence of spirit and preferred Paesiello. Cherubini is remembered now only by "Les Deux Journées" (1800—known in England as "The Water-Carrier") for which Beethoven had a profound admiration. Another Italian composer favoured by Napoleon was Spontini, whose "La Vestale" came out in Paris in 1807. "La Vestale" is thoroughly typical of the Empire; it has all the frigid stateliness of Empire architecture and furniture. Like Mozart's "Idomeneo," it achieves with greater technical skill what Gluck set out to do, but it lacks Mozart's warmth and sensuous beauty; its dignity is too deliberately " antique," at any rate to modern audiences. It is still revived occasionally in France and Italy, and it deserves revival, as a museum piece on the grand scale.

The one opera of this period that still remains intensely alive for all of us is Beethoven's " Fidelio " (1805). It has often been said that Beethoven had no understanding of the stage, but he undoubtedly had a keen ambition towards it ; at the same time, his ethical idealism made him unwilling to write what was merely attractive and amusing, and even led him so far as to condemn the subjects of " Figaro " and " Don Giovanni " for their immorality. His models in opera were " The Magic Flute " and " The Water-Carrier."

Schikaneder, the theatrical manager who commissioned Mozart to write " The Magic Flute," was a character who might have been invented, name and all, by some German Dickens as a German equivalent of Mr. Crummles. Giesecke, who actually wrote most of the libretto, was a young intellectual passing through a momentary phase of Bohemianism at the time. The opera was intended to be no more than a fairy pantomime, but in the course of composition it became a Masonic allegory with a profound mystical symbolism. Beethoven was not himself a Freemason, but he had associated with those who were. German Freemasonry in the eighteenth century had stood for the principles of English libertarianism, which were naturally regarded with horror by continental autocrats and by the Catholic Church. Masonry had done much to bring about the French Revolution, and " The Magic Flute " is full of the spirit of enlightenment.

It was for this reason that the opera sank so deeply into Beethoven's creative mind. But he did not wish to write another fairy pantomime ; for the libretto of his opera he turned to a French model. Serious *opéra comique*, like Cherubini's, appealed to the new revolutionary public, whereas spectacular grand opera on the lines of " La Vestale " was the glorification of the autocratic state.

Beethoven has been so much monumentalised in the

course of a century's reverence that his modern devotees fail to understand the true significance of " Fidelio." In Germany, after the Revolution of 1918, " Fidelio " was often played as a drama of revolution ; the characters, described in the libretto as being of the sixteenth century, were transferred to the end of the eighteenth, and the final release of the prisoners was supposed to be brought about not by royal clemency but by a rising of the people. Such treatment of the opera did less injustice to Beethoven than the attempt to exaggerate the moral grandeur of the music itself. The monumental treatment is futile, for the only characters that can be monumentalised are Leonora and the chorus, so that the net result is for " Fidelio " to become a *prima donna's* opera, a producer's opera, and what is worst of all, a conductor's opera. The other character simply will not stand exaggeration, as experience has shown over and over again. The only way to interpret " Fidelio " is to accept the limitations of its form and style. It requires an intimate theatre, and an intimate style of singing, and the conductor must realise that his function is to accompany an *opéra comique* and not to turn it into a symphony concert. " Fidelio " begins quite naturally as a comic opera ; it passes gradually through a phase of sentiment to a climax of anxiety. Like " Don Giovanni," it reaches, as if accidentally, a moment in which anxiety is deepened into tragic terror ; it is a " rescue opera," like " The Water-Carrier," in which a poor peasant risks his own life to save that of a political prisoner, and, as in " The Water-Carrier," its dramatic form is balanced by a happy end. The secret truth is that the happy end has to be monumentalised in order to disguise the conventionality of it ; Mozart's use of the symphonic *finale* tempted Beethoven, the greatest of symphonists, to forget the exigencies of the theatre and to prolong his ending to an inordinate length.

Operas of a later period have caused audiences to find " Fidelio " conventional, because it is written in the musical language of a long past age. It is not " realistic," but it is intensely real and human ; Florestan and Leonora are not intended to be eternal symbols, like Wagner's gods and goddesses, nor even heroes of antiquity like Gluck's and Spontini's ; they are human beings, and (allowing for the necessary artificialities of all stage plays) they go through experiences such as might perfectly well have happened to real people during the French Revolution.

## CHAPTER II

## CIMAROSA. ROSSINI

"FIDELIO" stands isolated in the history of opera ; it represents a " dead end," for it has no musical descendants. The main line of operatic history still derives its inspiration from Italy. In the days of Mozart one of the most popular Italian composers had been Domenico Cimarosa ; some of his contemporaries thought him to be the greatest living master of serious opera, but his serious operas are utterly forgotten and he is remembered now only by a single comic opera, " Il Matrimonio Segreto " (1792), first produced at Vienna, where the Emperor was so delighted with it that after the curtain fell on the first performance he commanded supper for the whole company and then ordered them to perform the whole opera again. " Giannina e Bernardone " (Venice, 1781) was revived in Florence in 1870, and might well be put on the stage again ; it seems to have influenced Mozart in " Così fan Tutte."

" Il Matrimonio Segreto " has often been revived in England and elsewhere and is a good example of the comic operas which Vienna preferred to those of Mozart. Cimarosa's music has an irresistible verve and sparkle, though looked at closely it is seen to be very thin stuff. Mozart took over all his conventions—his breathless back-chat in recitative, his charming tunes, his patter songs for the comic bass, his chattering *ensembles*—and added to them his own

warmth of harmony and ingenuity of orchestration.
Mozart's audiences thought that he had given them too
much ; they were quite content with Cimarosa's elementary
accompaniments, and probably they talked freely during
the long and rather vapid instrumental introductions to his
songs.

Cimarosa belongs musically to the eighteenth century—
to a century when an Emperor could encore a whole opera ;
but humanly he belonged to the new age, for in 1799 he
took the side of the French republican army which marched
into Naples and was imprisoned and condemned to death.
His sentence was eventually commuted into one of banishment, but before he could take refuge in Russia he died
from the effects of his imprisonment.

The operas of Cimarosa served as the chief models for
those of Gioacchino Rossini. Many people would share
Beethoven's opinion that comic opera was the form in
which Rossini was supreme, and at the present day " The
Barber of Seville " (Rome, 1816) is the only one of his
operas which is familiar to the general public. But the work
which made Rossini famous throughout Europe was the
serious opera " Tancredi " (1813). In 1822 Rossini visited
Vienna, where his operas had the most extravagant success.
The German musicians were naturally infuriated, but not
even they could resist the extraordinary vitality and
excitement of his music. They may have hated Rossini for
his success, but his melodies went to their heads and stuck
there ; Weber and Schubert show the influence of Rossini
very conspicuously, and even Beethoven, deaf as he was,
managed to pick up something from him and use it in the
most unexpected situation.

Rossini learned a good deal from Germany too. He had
long ago earned the nickname of " the little German "
because of his devotion to Haydn and Mozart, and in
Vienna he heard Beethoven's " Eroica " symphony and
Weber's " Freischütz." But German music taught him
nothing new in the way of melody, for he must have known
better than anyone how much the great German composers

owed to Italy; what he learned from Germany was the use of the orchestra and probably the art of building up movements in the symphonic style. "The Barber" may owe something to Mozart, but it owes far more to Cimarosa, and so does "Cenerentola"[1] (1817); and it is interesting to note that in a letter of about this date he speaks of the German composers, Beethoven especially, as having brought the art of music to utter ruin. He probably changed his mind after his visit to Vienna in 1822.

Rossini's latest operas were produced in Paris; "Semiramide" (Venice, 1823) was the last that came out in Italy. "Semiramide" and "Moïse" (Paris, 1827) show great dignity and solidity of style, but they could hardly be revived now. "William Tell" (Paris, 1829), on the other hand, still remains in the repertory of the greater operahouses, though its appearances are not frequent, as it demands singers of exceptional powers. After "William Tell," Rossini, mainly for reasons of ill-health, retired into private life and wrote no more for the stage.

## CHAPTER III

# BELLINI. DONIZETTI. AUBER

AFTER THE NAPOLEONIC PERIOD Paris became the centre of musical life; the hegemony of Vienna ended with the death of Schubert in 1828. Opera had by now become part of the normal routine of life, one may say, but it had always to be subsidised by princes if it was to have any solid foundation. Paris passed through various revolutions, but it did not matter whether France had a republic, an emperor, or a king; the government supported the opera as a national duty. Paris was not only the centre of musical life, but of all artistic and intellectual activities; it was an

[1] Revived in Berlin in 1932 and at Covent Garden in 1934.

international city and it supported an Italian opera as well as a French one. Italian opera still went on in Italy itself, but even at Milan and Naples performances were often very rough, except from individual singers of outstanding merit. In London also the opera band was regarded by contemporary critics as " a torture to the ear." In Germany there was a perpetual struggle between the Germans and the Italians, and it was a long time before the Italians were finally turned out.

The history of opera at this point becomes complicated, because Italy, France and Germany develop on distinct lines of their own which are constantly crossing. The Italian line is the clearest, and shall therefore be treated first. Rossini at the end of his operatic career deserted the Italian theatre for the French, but the Italian line was still continued by a number of composers now forgotten, and also by three who are remembered—Bellini, Donizetti and Verdi.

Bellini has little in common with Rossini ; he was gifted neither with comedy nor with the grand manner. But he had a vein of pure and rather elegiac melody which can still appeal to us, though most musicians of to-day are acquainted with it only at second-hand ; Bellini's operas are the source from which Chopin drew many of his most moving themes, and there are constant reminiscences of them in Liszt, quite apart from the actual transcriptions that he made from the operas. Bellini's influence extends even to the days of Tchaikovsky, who had a great affection for his music. Whether modern audiences would tolerate a revival of Bellini's operas may be doubted, for his orchestration is " like a big guitar," as it used to be said ; the entire interest of his operas has to be carried by the singers, and there are few singers now who have the purity of style needful for a convincing interpretation. " Norma " is occasionally performed in Italy, and so are " Sonnambula " and even " I Puritani," for Italian audiences have never broken with their old traditions. " Norma " has dignity and beauty when it is sung with conviction as well as with adequate skill, but a mediocre performance makes it painfully ridiculous.

Donizetti's tragic operas have moments of Bellinian beauty, but for the most part they are flashy and empty in style ; they belong to a period when the only object of an opera was to show off the voices of singers. His comic operas " Don Pasquale," " L'Elisir d'Amore " and " The Daughter of the Regiment "—this last once enormously popular in England—have much the same object, but achieve it in a charming and amusing way. Apart from these, comic opera almost ceased to exist in Italy ; it degenerated into utter triviality, and a later generation preferred to import its trivialities from France and England.

Italian opera had again become commercialised. Italy itself could hardly be said to support opera ; it produced it, and the verdict of an audience that was growing steadily more and more democratic decided its success or failure. If an opera made a success in Italy, the composer might hope to make more money out of his work in Paris or London. Italian audiences were supposed to be critical, and they are even said to be so now, but their criticism of music is that of complete ignorance. They can enjoy an obvious tune, and they are accustomed to a high standard of vocalisation ; the gallery speaks its mind without hesitation or restraint—that is all that their critical faculty amounts to.

Verdi accepted the situation and wrote frankly for commercial purposes, at any rate for the earlier part of his career. He achieved popularity all over the world by his extraordinary concentration on *l'effetto*, a word that constantly recurs in his letters ; but instead of resting content with popular success he managed to go on educating himself—stimulated in later life by the influence of his intimate friend and librettist Arrigo Boito, a poet of profound intellectual culture, and something of a composer himself. The result was that he ended his long career not as a tired survivor from the past but as a pioneer and prophet of the future.

In France the early nineteenth century gave birth to what we might call " political opera," as the natural outcome of the grand manner of Spontini. Rossini's " Moïse " was followed at once by Auber's " La Muette de Portici " (1828), better known in England under its Italian title of " Masaniello." There were many reasons for the immense popularity of " Masaniello "—its catchy tunes, its Neapolitan atmosphere, and the curious vagary which made the heroine congenitally dumb (though not deaf !), so that the part was acted not by a singer but by a star of the ballet ; the plot deals with the rising of the Neapolitan people against the Spanish rulers in 1647, and it was a performance of the opera at Brussels in 1830 that started the rising of the Belgians against the Dutch King. Rossini's " William Tell " (1829) was another opera glorifying the revolt of an oppressed people against a foreign tyrant.

Auber's slender talent was not equal to opera on the grand scale, and " political opera " was carried on by Meyerbeer and Halévy. French grand opera of this period is a plutocratic modernisation of the grand operas of Lulli and Rameau. Every resource was utilised, chorus, ballet, machinery and orchestra, on the largest scale and on a standard conventional design. The opera-house at Paris (erected 1861–75) might have been designed as a monument to Meyerbeer, for it shows the same mastery of construction and the same oppressive wealth of ornament.

The French genius for neat craftsmanship saved comic opera from the decay into which it fell in Italy. Here again Auber took Rossini as his model ; " Fra Diavolo " (1830) is an admirable example of French comic opera. But, like the grand opera, it became stereotyped and commercialised, and out of the hundreds that were produced in the course of the century, hardly one is remembered now, though a few may still be seen in France, especially in the provinces.

## CHAPTER IV

# ROMANTICISM AND WEBER

NEITHER FRENCH NOR ITALIAN OPERA was seriously affected by the Romantic movement, in spite of the fact that Paris was one of its leading centres in literature and the other arts. In Germany romanticism expressed itself more characteristically in music than in any other form, and most intensely in the opera. Romanticism, in the exploitation of the supernatural and the macabre, had indeed made a momentary appearance in Mozart's " Don Giovanni," though ghost scenes had been a common feature of opera as far back as the seventeenth century. The distinguishing feature of the romantic treatment of the supernatural, however, is the prominence of the satanic element, the heroic treatment of the power of evil. Meyerbeer's " Robert the Devil " (1831) is the last word in neo-Gothic romanticism as far as subject is concerned, but in his musical technique Meyerbeer remains for the most part classical. It was only in Germany that romanticism changed the whole outlook of composers on musical form.

The great pioneer of romanticism in German opera was Carl Maria von Weber, whose " Der Freischütz " (1821) is a landmark in the history of German music. Weber's musical style is found to be a mixture of very heterogeneous elements, if we take the trouble to analyse it. A great deal comes from Rossini, and sounds like scraps remembered and played on the pianoforte by ear after coming home from the opera-house ; much is derived from the popular German music of the day, the triviality of which many writers seek to excuse or glorify by calling it " folk music." And there is too the whole background of German symphonic music, including the works of Beethoven's middle period. Weber's works for the concert room show that he was no great symphonist ; they are showy and rhetorical rather than intellectual or deeply emotional. Brought up in the theatre, he had a vivid sense of stage effect, but his operas, and his choice of librettos, show that he had very little sense of drama as a whole. His opera songs start often with a fascinating melodic phrase, generally more instrumental than vocal, and curiously difficult to sing owing to the awkwardness of the words ; after that the music only too often collapses and is bolstered up by symphonic conventionalities that again are instrumental in style and utterly unvocal. As to his " unfailing sense of the stage," those who have to work out the details of stage management know that Weber presents the most uncomfortable problems in every one of his operas ; his greatest opera, " Euryanthe " (1823), is by common consent practically impossible to put on the stage.

Despite all these things Weber—especially in " Der Freischütz "—has an extraordinary power of thrilling an audience, even to-day. His music has a rapturous impetus that carries us off our feet ; in the middle of some movement that may by now have become commonplace and tedious we are suddenly struck by some masterstroke of emotional expression, and behind everything there is the picturesqueness of what we recognise as the modern orchestra. Weber had a marvellous genius for " background music," as we have called it. Previous centuries had hardly attempted it, though we may find something of it even in Lulli, and more in Rameau and Gluck, but the scene of the Wolf's Glen in " Der Freischütz " was something entirely new, and it is the foundation of all the descriptive music, operatic or otherwise, of the nineteenth century.

" Euryanthe," a story of mediæval chivalry, contains much beautiful music, but it is so badly constructed that it has always been a failure. In 1826 Weber was invited to compose an opera for London, and Planché, a hack playwright with a great knowledge of heraldry and other antiquarian lore, provided him with a libretto planned on the lines of Purcell's " King Arthur " and borrowing copiously from "A Midsummer Night's Dream" and "The Tempest."

Absurd as it was, it provided Weber with exactly the right opportunities for his genius, and " Oberon " ought certainly to be revived in England, for it exhibits Weber's characteristic style at its very best.

The Romantic movement, in which the revival of Shakespeare played a notable part, broke down the exact distinction between grand opera and comic opera. " Der Freischütz " is technically a comic opera with spoken dialogue, and the romantic operas of Marschner, once enormously popular in London, continue the mixture of the comic and the macabre. Pure comic opera in Germany is represented by Lortzing, who is still popular in his own country, but there, as in France and Italy, comic opera soon became commercialised and degenerated into operetta.

From the days of Weber onwards the orchestra plays an increasingly important part in German opera. The late Dr. Adolf Weissmann pointed out that the orchestra was the only medium for representing these supernatural powers with which the romantic heroes and heroines found themselves in conflict. The singers of these parts soon became acutely conscious of the conflict. Mozart was accused in his day of making the orchestra more important than the singers, and the same accusation has been brought against practically every German composer up to the present day, though history shows us that whatever the balance of power between singers and orchestra may be, audiences gradually accustom themselves to the standard of the generation before their own, and regard that as right and proper. The Germans have always been more interested in instrumental music than in singing, and the development of the orchestra, and consequently of pure orchestral music, has been mainly a German achievement.

The danger of this to opera has lain not so much in the amount of noise that the orchestra produces (for in these days we all know that the largest orchestra can be kept under adequate control if the composer has written for it with proper skill) as in the tendency of German composers to regard the orchestra as the chief medium for the expression of their thought. Many operas of recent times, not only by German composers, have failed to convince an audience simply because the main interest of the music was in the orchestra and not on the stage. The only thing that a character in an opera can do to convince the audience that he is a real person in whom they are compelled to take an interest is to sing, and the amount of interest they take in him (as a character in a drama, be it understood, not as Mr. So-and-so, the famous tenor) will be proportionate to the interest of the music the composer has put into his mouth. He may drop into recitative when it is necessary to give us some definite information about facts in order to carry on the play, but otherwise the moment he ceases to hold our emotions by music he fades out of existence. We may easily cease to be conscious of his bodily presence on the stage altogether. The Italians have never lost sight of this fundamental principle of opera. One could listen to an opera of Verdi, such as " Il Trovatore," sung without any accompaniment at all, and still obtain some dramatic satisfaction from it, but an opera of Wagner would be meaningless without the orchestra, and indeed we could get a considerable idea of it from that alone without the singers.

## CHAPTER V

# WAGNER

THE WARS of the *Bouffons* and of the *Gluckists* were insignificant as compared to the perpetual war of controversy that surrounded Wagner. The Wagnerian war was a war of journalists too, with Wagner himself as journalist in chief, but it was a war of musicians as well, to a greater extent than the operatic wars of Paris a century before. At the present day, when Wagner sits safely enshrined among the classics of the past, there is little need for any except historical researchers to trouble their heads much about Wagner's theoretical writings. Wagner's position in the history of music is due simply to his genius as a musician. His constructive theories about opera as a *Gesamtkunstwerk*, a joint work of art produced by the union of poetry, drama, music and all the subsidiary arts of the theatre, were nothing in the least original ; their fundamental principles were laid down by the early Florentine group and were reaffirmed in the eighteenth century by Algarotti and Gluck. Wagner felt compelled to assert them once more, because in his day, as in Algarotti's, commercial opera had become standardised and the average opera, now utterly forgotten, was of negligible musical value. Wagner stood for " music-drama " as against " opera," and many of his later admirers have clung to this distinction as if it were a dogma of religious faith, but it really means nothing. The old Italians called their operas *dramma per musica* too ; if " Idomeneo " is an " opera " rather than a " music-drama " it is only because its convention belongs to its own age. We must not forget, however, that Wagner has taught us moderns to try to produce all operas, however " operatic," in a Wagnerian spirit, that is, with proper attention to the interaction of all artistic factors, and to listen to them in a Wagnerian spirit, that is, without interrupting the course of an act by applause after each song. The question whether the music of an opera should be continuous or divided into separate movements is purely a question of musical technique, which varies according to the general musical style of the age. It is true that most operas have been saddled with bad librettos, but with the examples of Rinuccini, Metastasio and Da Ponte before us, we cannot lay the blame on the operatic form itself. Wagner probably judged opera librettos by the current German translations of Mozart's and by the standard of Weber's collaboratress Helmine von Chezy, whose nonsense has made her immortal ; some critics have even dared to suggest that Wagner himself was more of a musician than a poet.

Wagner's first important opera, " Rienzi " (1842), continues the style of Meyerbeer ; " The Flying Dutchman " (1843), reverts to Weber and Marschner. " Tannhäuser " (1845), combines Weber with the construction of Meyerbeer, while " Lohengrin " (1850) derives so much from " Euryanthe " as to make it fortunate that Weber's opera is hardly ever performed. But with all their faults (and the present age is beginning to be uncomfortably conscious of them) these romantic operas of Wagner have a strength that Weber could never achieve. Wagner in his own day was abused by the adherents of " absolute music," but although he wrote next to nothing in that line he was himself a genuine symphonist ; he could conceive of a whole act, indeed of a whole opera, as one organic piece of music. The second act of " Freischütz " (the Wolf's Glen) attempts that, and Mozart certainly visualised his operas as organic wholes, although the technique of his day did not permit of their being continuous and unbroken.

Wagner had the benefit of coming after Beethoven ; he assimilated the constructive technique of his latest symphonies and the " Missa Solemnis," and he gradually absorbed that of Liszt and Berlioz too. The Wagnerian method of composing is based on the development sections of Beethoven's symphonies, and this was further assisted by Wagner's employment of the *leit-motiv* (guiding theme) that is of musical themes associated with particular characters or ideas. Later composers sometimes tried to imitate this practice, about which Wagner's enemies said that each of his characters presented his visiting-card ; and in the music of later composers the " guiding-themes " are indeed no more than labels. The value of Wagner's themes lay not so much in their repetition and development as in the fact that they were singularly arresting and musically significant in themselves. Whether they " represent " or " depict " the ideas associated with them is a matter of opinion, but they serve their purpose ; the entry of an important theme at a critical moment always impresses us by its musical value, even if we have forgotten its particular name in the directory.

The *leit-motiv* occurs in the early operas, but it does not become a systematic method until after Wagner's flight from Dresden in 1849, followed by his close association with Liszt and his careful study of Liszt's symphonic poems. If the early operas seem now to be a little old-fashioned—and considering that they were composed nearly a hundred years ago it is not surprising—this is due mainly to their rhythmical monotony. We are not much troubled by the fact that " Lohengrin " is almost entirely in common time, and most of it *andante*, but we do become wearied of the perpetual alternation of feminine and masculine verse-endings, and the favourite metre of Wagner's verses —11, 10, 11, 10—as well as of his characteristic Meyerbeerian way of accenting it.

The complete change of literary style and metrical method which Wagner adopted for " The Ring " and " Tristan " contributed very greatly to the formation of his new personal style in the music itself.

With these operas we are in an entirely new world. Removed by the circumstances of banishment from Germany from the daily contact with standardised opera inevitable to a working conductor, Wagner had the leisure and the mental freedom to construct for himself an ideal opera and to plan the construction of an ideal theatre to house it. It is advisable here to give the dates of composition of Wagner's later works : the libretto of " The Ring " was not written in the order of the operas, but in the reverse order, beginning with " Götterdämmerung " and ending with " Rheingold " (1852). The music of " Rheingold " was composed 1853-4 and " Die Walküre " in 1854-6. " Siegfried " was begun in 1857, but laid aside for " Tristan und Isolde " (1857-9) and " Meistersinger,"[1] begun 1862 ;

---

[1] Generally so-called, or " The Mastersingers." Correct full title is " Die Meistersinger von Nürnberg."—Ed.

" Meistersinger " was interrupted by the resumption of
" Siegfried " in 1865, and finished in 1867, " Siegfried "
not reaching completion till 1871. " Götterdämmerung "
was partly sketched in 1848, then left until 1870 and finished
in 1874. The complete " Ring " was first performed at
Bayreuth in 1876 ; " Parsifal " was first sketched in 1857,
but mainly composed between 1877 and 1882, in which
year it was first performed.

## CHAPTER VI

# WAGNERIANISM

A GREAT DEAL of nonsense has been written—some indeed by Wagner himself—about the philosophical and
moral significance of his operas. To us at the present day
they are simply masterpieces of what has now become
classical music ; we see them and listen to them in the same
spirit as we do those of Gluck or Mozart. Wagner's ideas of
" redemption through love " and so forth could be applied
to any opera or any play that was ever written ; it is
obviously quite impossible to translate philosophical ideas
of this sort into musical notes, and those who try to translate
musical notes into words are by no means certain to agree
in their interpretations. All that is now necessary to the
enjoyment of a Wagner opera is an unprejudiced mind, and,
if possible, a previous reading of the libretto.

There is, however, one aspect of Wagner's philosophy
which we must take seriously. His ideal of creating a truly
German art is a matter of purely local interest, and it may
be observed that Wagner was extremely pleased to find
his works appreciated in other countries, just as our English
patriots would be, if any other countries (or even their own)
were to put their operas on the stage. But Wagner's view of
opera as a festival drama, to be approached in what for

want of a better word we must call a religious spirit, was fundamental to his philosophy. Here again the idea was not Wagner's own, as he knew perfectly well ; all he wished to do was to insist on its importance at a period when it had been forgotten. Wagner's own age was already tending to approach music—such music as the Ninth Symphony of Beethoven—in this spirit, and English audiences of to-day are quite ready to hope that attendance at the Albert Hall on Sunday afternoon will be reckoned up by the recording angel as equivalent to attendance at church. But except at Bayreuth and on a few other occasions when a Bayreuth atmosphere is carefully staged, few people even now can bring themselves to regard an opera as an opportunity for mystical experience.

It is difficult to write of these things, for as soon as we begin to think about them we are confronted with ultimate problems of life, art and religion, which everyone has to work out for himself as best he may. Mozart offered us initiation into these mysteries in " The Magic Flute " ; Beethoven exalted our conception of humanity in " Fidelio." But if we have in these days learned to approach opera, or even to wish to approach such operas as are worthy of it, in the spirit of " Fidelio " and " The Magic Flute," it is Wagner, more than any other musician of the theatre, who has pointed our minds in that direction.

## CHAPTER VII

## OPERETTA

It has been said that the real history of music is not the lives of the great masters but the history of bad music—the history of the kind of commercial popular music, secular or sacred, that at all periods has formed the general background against which the men of genius

stand out. They do not always stand out from it very
clearly ; they too were influenced to some extent by the
popular music of their day, and it is often impossible to
arrive at an intimate understanding of the great men
without some knowledge of the ephemeral music that they
could never escape hearing. For this reason it is necessary to
say a few words here about the more trivial forms of dramatic music, more especially as they were a very characteristic product of the second half of the nineteenth century.

All music tends to become classical as time goes on, and
we have witnessed in recent years a great revival of what we
may call classical rubbish. This has been due partly to
modern movements in music, which have apparently
widened the gulf that always existed between serious music
and that of the less educated classes. Operas or operettas that in their own day would never have been allowed
mention within the walls of a state-supported theatre are
now revived there as classical works ; age has conferred
respectability on them, but managers hope that it has not
lessened their powers of attraction.

Many of the comic operas of the eighteenth century must
in their own day have appealed mainly to what we should
now call a " musical comedy audience " ; that type of
audience became much more numerous in the days of
Louis Philippe and young Queen Victoria. The title
*opérette* was first used by the French composer Florimond
Roger, known as Hervé, and the music he wrote in these
little works was appropriately described as *musiquette.*
Hervé's career began in 1848, but it was in the 1860's that
he achieved his greatest popularity, both in Paris and in
London, with " Chilpéric " and " Le petit Faust." He
became naturalised as an Englishman in 1874.

Hervé's successes, however, were eclipsed (at any rate
until 1880) by those of Jacques Offenbach, whose real name
was Juda Ebersct, born at Cologne. He came to Paris as
an eccentric violoncellist, but in 1855 he began producing
operettas at a small theatre which from that time came to
be known as the Bouffes-Parisiens. Before his death in 188

he had composed some ninety operettas, as well as the
unfinished score of " Tales of Hoffmann " which was
completed by Guiraud and produced in 1881. Offenbach's
operettas, of which the best known are " Orphée aux
Enfers " (1858), " La Belle Hélène " (1864), " La Vie
Parisienne " (1866), " La Grande Duchesse de Gérolstein "
(1867), and " Madame Favart " (1879), enjoyed an enormous popularity all over Europe, and indeed they deserved
it for the inimitable gaiety and spirit of their music, which
has hardly even yet lost its exhilarating vitality, although
the topical wit of their librettos has to a large extent
evaporated.

Needless to say, Offenbach during his lifetime found
imitators in other countries. Vienna has always copied the
fashions of Paris, and Johann Strauss, the composer of the
" Blue Danube " waltz, supplied Vienna with a succession
of operettas, beginning with " Indigo " in 1871. Several of
these are still popular in Germany—" Die Fledermaus "
(1874), " Eine Nacht in Venedig " (1883), and " Der
Zigeunerbaron " (1885), but their eternal waltz tunes are
often cloying, and Strauss's sentimental Austrian temperament could never quite achieve the reckless drollery of
Offenbach. A little later England produced a native
rival to Offenbach in Arthur Sullivan, who in the earlier
part of his career had made his name as a composer
of oratorios and church music. " Onward, Christian
Soldiers " dates from 1872, and " The Lost Chord " from
1877. But as early as 1867 he had written music for " Cox
and Box," adapted by F. C. Burnand from Maddison
Morton's well-known farce, and in 1871 he collaborated
for the first time with W. S. Gilbert in " Thespis, or The
Gods Grown Old." During the 1870's Offenbach's operettas
were very popular in London, and in 1875 Sullivan and
Gilbert produced, for an Offenbach season, a so-called
" dramatic cantata," " Trial by Jury," the success of which
led to a long collaboration between librettist and composer. The first of their operettas was " The Sorcerer "
1877) ; it was followed by " H.M.S. Pinafore " (1878),

" The Pirates of Penzance " (1880), and many others, the names of which it is not necessary to set out here in full.

The aim of the collaborators was to create a type of entertainment that should compete successfully with those of Offenbach and also attract a class of theatre-goer who regarded Offenbach as " rather too French." Gilbert's librettos were considered exceedingly witty in their day, but for the present generation they must contain many allusions now quite incomprehensible without historical foot-notes. These operettas were enormously successful in America, and " The Mikado," a satire on the Japanese Village exhibited in 1885 at Knightsbridge, had some success in Germany, but otherwise they never achieved the international fame of those by Offenbach. Probably Gilbert's librettos were too local, and often too much concerned with purely English political satire, for foreigners to understand ; Sullivan's music, despite its charm, had not quite the lightfootedness of Offenbach or Strauss. Sullivan could never completely shake off the character of the church organist, and it is perhaps that very quality of respectability which has endeared him to generations of English listeners.

To chronicle the lesser lights of operetta is impossible. The French composers have always kept up the highest standards of elegance and finish, as exemplified by the operettas of Audran and Messager. Vienna had Suppé and Millöcker in the days of Strauss ; their operettas are occasionally revived, but they are held to be unpresentable without considerable modernisation. This rewriting of old operettas is a convenient way of securing a new copyright in a work that has long been public property. The later Viennese school has exploited the waltz for all it is worth, and apparently the public are not yet tired of it. Towards the end of the last century England produced a yet more trivial type of operetta which was given the name of " musical comedy " ; some of these even enjoyed a certain popularity abroad, notably " The Geisha " (1892) by Sidney Jones. Their foreign popularity was due not so much to stage performances as to the fact that the favourite tunes were much played by bands in places of entertainment. " The Geisha " has a certain historic importance owing to its obvious influence on Puccini's " Madame Butterfly."

# D: FROM VERDI TO THE PRESENT DAY

## CHAPTER I

## VERDI

TIME TENDS to make all music " classical," and the early operas of Verdi, which contemporary criticism found tawdry and brutal, have in recent years been revived in a Wagnerian spirit of devotion as a reaction against those of Wagner himself. The passage of years, assisted by the ingenuity of modern conductors, has reduced their " brutality " to " dramatic intensity," and the barrel-organ tunes that excited our ancestors to disgust or laughter have acquired the sentimental associations of a picturesque period. All the same, " Nabucco " (1842) and " Macbeth " (1847) can hardly become anything more than museum pieces; but "Rigoletto" (1851), "Il Trovatore" (1853) and " La Traviata " (1853) have held the stage continuously since their first appearance, although " La Traviata " was a complete failure at first. Popular audiences have always adored them ; serious musicians detested them for many years, and are now coming round to an appreciation of their merits.

Verdi in his youth was a frankly commercial composer, but his inborn musicianship was too strong for him. This is clear from the way in which he continuously educated himself up to the end of his life, and even in these earlier works what marks him off from Bellini and Donizetti is the thoroughness of his workmanship, his firm yet daring sense of harmony and his sensitive and ingenious orchestration. " Rigoletto " is remarkable for a new kind of music that hovers between recitative and *aria* ; the character of the title-part is a marvellous psychological study, and this new medium was evolved from the necessity of this characterisation. " Il Trovatore," the plot of which has become the classical example of unintelligibility, lives by virtue of its intense dramatic concentration ; most people in the audience have not the remotest idea what is happening, but the relentless *crescendo* of emotional excitement carries them along with the force of a torrent. To old-fashioned opera-goers " La Traviata " was no more than a display-piece for a prima donna's voice, Paris gowns and diamonds, while the rest of the cast appeared in costumes of the seventeenth or eighteenth century, because no audience could stand opera in the dresses of its own period. That period has now passed into the era of the picturesque, and recent productions have made " La Traviata " into a chamber opera of singularly touching delicacy.

" Aïda " (1871) marks a new stage in Verdi's development. As it was composed to celebrate the opening of the Suez Canal at Cairo, the subject was taken from ancient Egypt, and the opera was made as spectacular as possible ; it is still the best spectacular opera in the repertory, both as opera and as spectacle. After " Aïda " Verdi's operas appeared at longer intervals ; he had ceased to be a commercial composer and was beginning to write for himself, now that his position was assured. In those days Verdi and Wagner were continually placed in opposition by journalists who wanted to enjoy a controversy, and Verdi was sometimes accused of having submitted to Wagner's influence, but he always indignantly repudiated the charge. After Wagner's death in 1883 Verdi was the only great opera composer living, so that his " Otello," produced in 1887, was awaited with considerable excitement. Verdi's technique had by now matured beyond all expectations, and " Otello " was found to be considerably in advance of its time, at any rate for Italy. A still more astonishing achievement was " Falstaff " (1893), especially as Verdi was then in his eightieth year. For many years neither of these operas obtained real popularity in Italy ; they were more appreciated in Germany, but even there their progress was slow.

Needless to say Verdi was still further accused of imitating Wagner ; but his attitude to opera remained fundamentally different. The change of style represented by " Otello " and " Falstaff " was due in large part to the new type of libretto provided for him by Boito, whose adaptations of Shakespeare are the work of a real poet, and partly to the gradual change that was going on in all musical technique, which made it possible for Verdi to acquire a looser and more supple texture than he had been able to employ in " Aïda." The example of Wagner no doubt stimulated him, or rather encouraged him, for he did not need the stimulus, to take opera seriously as a work of art rather than as mere commercial entertainment. But for Wagnerian ideas of " music-drama " Verdi had not the slightest sympathy. In Wagner's later works the characters recede further and further away from us ; we see them only through the haze of the orchestra. It is the orchestra, with its perpetual development of *leit-motiv*—a development that only the orchestra could carry out—that expresses the inward mind of the composer. With Verdi the orchestra, however exquisitely treated, is no more than an accompaniment to the voices ; the characters seem to stand in front of it, and Verdi's aim is not to use them as the vehicles for his philosophy but to make them intensely real and alive. German conductors, accustomed to regard the orchestra as the most important thing, often misunderstand " Falstaff " completely ; its vocal line is complex and broken up, at least on paper, but it is the vocal *ensemble* that carries the real thought of the composer, and the voices must always bear that burden and consciously take the lead.

Arrigo Boito was not only a poet, but a composer as well. His opera " Mefistofele " (produced 1868, revised 1875) was the attempt of a pure idealist to summarise in one musical drama the whole of Goethe's two Faust dramas. His technique is in many respects amateurish, but his work is profoundly thoughtful with a singular beauty of its own ;

during the last thirty years it has almost achieved popularity in Italy. "Nerone" (1924), on which Boito worked for forty years, was not brought out until after his death ; it is distinguished in style, but too much overloaded with archæological learning to be effective on the stage.

## CHAPTER II

## FRENCH OPERA

F RANCE during the latter half of the nineteenth century contributed little to the history of opera, but it produced a small number of works destined to attain popularity all over the world. The first of these is Gounod's " Faust " (1859). Gounod's other operas, fairly often performed up to the end of the century, seem now to have lost their attraction, though " Philemon et Baucis " (1860), " Mireille " (1864) and " Roméo et Juliette " (1867) contain many delightful numbers. The charm of Gounod's music lay in its delicate sensuousness ; the colossal manner of Meyerbeer was unsuited to him, and he professed to take Mozart as his model. Ambroise Thomas survives only by " Mignon " (1866). We see in both " Faust " and " Mignon " a type intermediate between grand opera and *opéra comique* ; its emergence is due to the gradual change taking place in opera audiences. Opera was no longer the exclusive property of a highly cultured aristocracy ; it had (especially in France) to make its appeal to a *bourgeoisie* whose culture was steadily improving, but had not yet reached a very elevated standard.

That public could hardly be expected to enter into the spirit of Berlioz's few attempts at opera. " Benvenuto Cellini " (1838) has been revived recently, but with little success ; " Béatrice et Bénédict " (1862) receives occasional performances as a respected classic. " Les Troyens,"

Berlioz's double masterpiece (it consists of two operas, "La prise de Troie" and "Les Troyens à Carthage") completed in 1858, was never performed in its entirety until Mottl, the great Wagnerian conductor, produced it at Karlsruhe in 1897. It still waits, like some vast imperial city of antiquity, to be restored to light in all its austere stateliness.

Bizet's "Carmen" (1875) took some years to become popular ; it is now perhaps the most popular of all operas in the repertory of the world. The most unsophisticated listener who walks into an opera-house for the first time in his life is fascinated by it, and the most jaded of learned musicians is never tired of it. It owes its obvious attraction to its powerful story and to the opportunities it gives to the singer of the title-part, especially if she considers herself to be a highly temperamental actress and a woman of irresistible charm. More educated listeners will appreciate the picturesque Spanish colour of the music, and the way in which Bizet combines a wealth of ravishing melody with harmonic devices of great ingenuity and originality.

"Carmen" is also of historical importance, for it is the foundation of what in later years was called *verismo*, the operatic treatment of sordid and brutal subjects with every emphasis on these characteristics. We shall revert to this later on.

The voluptuous manner of Gounod was further developed by Massenet, whose "Hérodiade" (1881) attempted to combine it with something of the Wagnerian method. "Hérodiade" (on the story of St. John the Baptist and Salome) is still popular in France, especially in the provinces, but its allurement has now become decidedly elderly. "Manon" (1884) retains a certain "Dresden china" charm, and "Werther" (1892) is a really masterly study in sentimentality. Massenet had a truly French standard of delicate craftsmanship, and it was this that made "Le Jongleur de Nôtre-Dame" (1902) an exquisite musical illustration of the well-known story by Anatole France.

Of the various operas by Saint-Saëns, only " Samson et Dalila " (1877) has remained in the repertory ; it is strange to think that its merits were first recognised by Liszt, who brought it out at Weimar, and that its first French production took place at Rouen in 1890. It has often been described as being more of an oratorio than an opera ; perhaps that is why (ever since the Lord Chamberlain was persuaded— it is said by a very illustrious personage—to license it) it has become a great favourite in England. Its solidity of workmanship commands the respect of all musicians.

Two more French composers must be mentioned here, though their operas have almost disappeared from the stage. Alfred Bruneau created some stir with a series of operas for which he utilised librettos in prose, taken from the works of Emile Zola. At first Zola's stories were adapted for Bruneau by Louis Gallet, but the later librettos were written for Bruneau by the great novelist himself. Unfortunately the last of them, " Messidor," was brought out at the time of the notorious Dreyfus case, when Zola's courageous intervention had made him thoroughly unpopular in Paris, and Bruneau's career as a composer of operas came to a premature end. " L'Attaque du Moulin " (1891) had a great success in England ; it was a story of the Franco-Prussian war. Bruneau was in those days considered very Wagnerian, but to a modern audience his music would sound completely French. Bruneau's chief claim to originality was his serious attempt to treat contemporary (or almost contemporary) life in terms of opera. He cannot be classed among the *veristi*, for his moral attitude to his subjects, like that of Zola, is one of pity and not that of the police reports ; it was probably this that made his works rather too melancholy for the majority of opera-goers. But Bruneau, with his prose librettos, had an influence on Gustave Charpentier, who created a new type of opera with " Louise " (1900), the story of a humble dressmaker and her artist lover in the slums of Paris. Charpentier was seriously interested in the musical education of the working classes, and " Louise " had a genuine social idealism behind it. Musically it is not very original, but it is well put together and attractive, so that it enjoyed great popularity for many years : not so its sequel " Julien."


## CHAPTER III

## MASCAGNI. LEONCAVALLO. PUCCINI

IN 1890 THE MUSICAL WORLD was startled by the sudden appearance of " Cavalleria Rusticana," an opera that had won a prize offered by a publisher, and the composer, Pietro Mascagni, leapt into a fame that he has never since been able to sustain. The success of " Cavalleria " was due to its crude realism and brutality, enhanced by melodies of no great distinction that immediately fixed themselves in the ear of the public. It was followed at once by Leoncavallo's " Pagliacci," an obvious imitation of " Cavalleria," and though the subsequent imitations by Giordano and others had only a short-lived success, " Cavalleria " and " Pagliacci " have become inseparable twins indispensable to the repertory of every opera-house in the world. The realistic opera of low life is derived, as has already been said, from " Carmen " ; it made its appearance at a time when opera was becoming still more democratised. It was easy to write, for it needed only a sordid libretto and a rough-and-ready acquaintance with the coarser aspects of Verdi's technique ; but the public has gradually become tired of *verismo*, although its evil example still affects certain types of opera, both in Italy and outside.

Mascagni's later operas have never had any real success, but he deserves credit for honesty and sincerity in his " Iris " (1898). " Iris " must have been written to satisfy some inner craving of the composer, for it makes not the slightest effort to please the average audience ; it is a grim story of Japanese

life, treated in a quasi-mystical manner, with obvious
reminiscences of Wagner. It was the first opera in which
a Japanese subject had been employed and treated with
ruthless seriousness ; this ought to be remembered in view
of subsequent (and earlier) operas and operettas in Japanese
costume.

· " Real and permanent success," wrote Hugo von Hoffmannsthal to Richard Strauss in 1909, " depends on a
combined appeal to both the coarser and the more refined
sections of the public, for the latter create the prestige without which one is lost just as much as one is without popular
appeal." This was thoroughly well realised by Giacomo
Puccini, the most uniformly and universally successful
composer of operas since Verdi. All Verdi's operas except
one had dealt with what one may class as heroic subjects,
for " Falstaff " is heroic comedy ; " La Traviata " is the
only one treating of emotions that any ordinary person
might experience. Verdi's heroine is the ancestress of the
various misguided females whom we meet in the operas of
Puccini—Manon, Mimi, Tosca, Butterfly and Liù. It is
significant that when Puccini planned his last opera
" Turandot," an entirely new character, Liù, had to be
added to the original play ; and Liù became Puccini's real
heroine.

Puccini's technical craftsmanship was in every way far
ahead of that of Mascagni ; whether one likes his music or
not, one is forced to admire its skilful orchestration, and the
supple way in which it adapts itself to the exigencies of the
stage. His languishing melodies are admirably suited to the
voice, especially to the voices of those Italian singers who
have no shame about exploiting an erotic appeal that would
have horrified the audiences of Handel and Rossini, probably those of Verdi too ; lest the humblest member of the
audience should fail to catch them, they are generally
played by the bass of the supporting harmony, as well as
by the treble. Any demarcation between grand opera and
*péra comique* of the sentimental order has entirely disappeared ; with one exception Puccini's operas are all

Mc

" tragic," in that they come to an unhappy end, but of
tragedy in the classical sense there is not the slightest trace
—they are all *comédies larmoyantes* in everything but the concluding death-scene. Puccini seems to have taken a curious
delight in the musical representation of physical torture.

Apart from certain conspicuous mannerisms, which make
the music of Puccini recognisable to everyone, his musical
texture is always eclectic ; he owed much to his contemporaries in France and even in England, though his English
borrowings came from the lower grades of theatrical entertainment. It was only natural, as we shall shortly see, that
his world-wide popularity should cause composers in other
countries to borrow from him, and his very eclecticism
made this all the easier, for reminiscences of Puccini could
be made to fit into any style, French or German.

Since the death of Puccini, Italy has produced no operas
of equal popularity ; those that attempt to continue his
manner need not be mentioned here.

## CHAPTER IV

# FROM WAGNER TO STRAUSS

LET US now pick up the thread of German opera after
the death of Wagner. Even during his lifetime German
opera has little to interest us ; along with Lortzing's there
are the equally provincial comic operas of Flotow and
Nicolai. A little later there appeared three comic operas
that have never attained popularity despite frequent
revivals, although they have always commanded the
respect of serious musicians—Cornelius's " Barber of
Baghdad " (1858), Goetz's " Taming of the Shrew " (1874)
and Hugo Wolf's " Der Corregidor " (1896). None of these
can be called Wagnerian in manner, although Cornelius in
many ways anticipated the style of " Meistersinger."

The only outstanding opera of the generation which followed Wagner is " Hänsel and Gretel " (1893), by Humperdinck, who was one of Wagner's most intimate assistants during the preparation of "Parsifal" in 1880–81. " Hänsel and Gretel," which ever since its first production has been the delight of all opera-goers from the youngest to the oldest, may be described as Wagner for the nursery. " Königskinder " (produced as a play with music 1896, revised as a complete opera 1910), by the same composer, treated fairy-tale in a more tragic form, and never became popular ; but it has certainly exercised a strong influence on Hans Pfitzner.

Various attempts were made to imitate the grandiose heroic manner of Wagner, but all of them have disappeared into oblivion, even in the country of their origin. The only hope lay in comic opera. Humperdinck's success led to a small output of one-act comic operas, of which D'Albert's " Die Abreise " (1898) was about the best. Unfortunately D'Albert turned his attention to melodramatic opera in the " veristic " style, and after his " Tiefland " (1903) had achieved unparalleled popularity in Germany, owing to its adroit combination of " Carmen," Puccini and Wagner, he pursued a very successful financial career with works over which it is better to draw a veil. " Die Abreise," however, which is fresh, witty and clever, would be well worth reviving.

Richard Strauss was already famous as a composer of symphonic poems for the concert-room before he made his first operatic hit with " Feuersnot " (1901), a comic opera in which his librettist more or less openly proclaimed him the successor of Wagner. " Feuersnot," despite all its cleverness, has not yet become a serious rival to " Meistersinger." In " Salome " (1906) and " Elektra " (1909) Strauss laid the foundations of modern German music, but after shocking public opinion both morally and musically with these two operas (which still remain his greatest works for the stage) he reverted to a more popular style in " Der Rosenkavalier " (1911). At the present day Strauss at the age of seventy is regarded by many musicians as the last great survivor of a remote epoch, and indeed we are obliged, in this rapid survey of operatic history, to class him among the post-Wagnerians rather than among the pioneers of modern opera.

Strauss belongs in fundamental principle to the devotees of " music-drama " in the Wagnerian sense. Every one of his operas has a libretto of high literary quality, and the basis of his system has always been that the orchestra should carry on the main fabric of the opera while the characters on the stage declaimed, as forcibly as possible, the words of the play. From the earliest beginnings of opera musical drama has hovered between recitative and *aria*, between talking and singing ; and the rare experiments that have been made at utilising exclusively either the one or the other have always proved failures. Strauss has always been far too clever, and indeed far too much of a natural instinctive musician, to fall into this trap. As his single songs clearly show, he has an unconcealed delight in the sensuous sound of the singing voice, and in his later operas this joy in pure singing is exploited into a virtuosity recalling the age of Donizetti.

From " Elektra " onwards (with the exception of " Intermezzo," for which he wrote the words himself) Strauss has collaborated with Hugo von Hoffmannsthal. Some of their correspondence on the subject has been published, and it seems that Hoffmannsthal, who was a poet and a scholar of aristocratic breeding, must have had need of all his Austrian courtesy in order to cope with the robust practicality of the musician, as the extract quoted a few pages back will have suggested. Strauss has always shown an astonishing subtlety and ingenuity in the handling of the orchestra, but his vocal invention, fluent and full-blooded as it is, is far from subtle, and at times approaches perilously near to vulgarity. It may be doubted whether Hoffmannsthal was the right librettist for him. In his dramas on classical subjects—" Elektra," " Ariadne auf Naxos " and " Die Ægyptische Helena," he was too much of a scholar for the composer, and in his Viennese conversation-pieces " Rosenkavalier " and " Arabella " too much of an aristocrat, one may say, for his dialogue is often too delicate in its inflexion to stand the inevitable exaggeration of a grand-operatic musical setting. Strauss has been a dangerous example to the younger German composers who had neither a Hoffmannsthal to write for them nor the riotous physical energy of Strauss's own inspiration. The post-Wagnerians, like Wotan's offspring, may be classed in various families, and Strauss belongs to that of the " Rheingold."

## CHAPTER V

# THE RUSSIANS

THERE IS YET ANOTHER ASPECT of nineteenth-century opera that must be considered before we pass to the moderns. One result of the Napoleonic upheaval was the emergence of nationalism, and opera was an obvious field for its expression. We have already noted this in Weber's " Freischütz " ; a still more aggressive example is Glinka's " A Life for the Tsar " (1836). We are told that the Russian aristocracy of the time called it " the music of coachmen " and that Glinka replied " What does it matter since the men are better than their masters ? " The answer was equally characteristic of its age. The libretto belongs to the category of " rescue operas," like Cherubini's " Water-Carrier," but the historic enmity of the Russians and the Poles forms a strongly nationalistic background to it. The music makes copious use of folk-tunes, both Russian and Polish, and to Western ears this exotic colouring may well be singularly attractive. It may be observed here that, since German folk-song was absorbed into German artistic music at a very early date, musicians outside Germany have hardly ever discovered in it the peculiar fascination they have derived from the folk-music of remoter nations. For some three centuries Germany's chief contribution to music in general has been the intellectualisation of the art, and consequently we who have learned to revere and love German music for the spirit that created Bach's Mass in B Minor and Beethoven's Mass in D are inclined not unnaturally to regard the romantic reversion to simple folk-song (except perhaps in the case of so childlike a composer as Humperdinck) as a descent into trivial commonplace.

Glinka's opera is picturesque, but his dramatic technique was feeble, and his music collapses into conventionalities just where it needs to be most forcible. Much the same might be said of the Polish national opera, Moniuszko's " Halka " (1850), though the dramatic parts are certainly better managed than in Glinka's work. The most successful specimen of folk-song opera of this generation was Smetana's " The Bartered Bride " (1870), in which the peasant comedy of the libretto provides the folk-song of the music with its natural happy environment, with the result that this opera has not only become the national opera of the Czechs, but has won unstinted popularity in other countries.

Folk-song has been prominent in most of the operas of the later Russian composers. Tchaikovsky's " Eugen Oniegin " (1879) uses it merely as a background to the main drama, which is based on a story by Pushkin of the Byronic period. " Eugen Oniegin " belongs to the same category as " La Traviata " ; it is intimate opera and requires a theatre small enough to secure this character in its interpretation. It has the lyric charm of Tchaikovsky's songs rather than the vehemence of his orchestral works, and its sensitive handling of intense feeling, always restrained within the limits of a high-bred delicacy, makes it one of the most touching operas ever put on the stage.

Nationalism elevated to an almost epic grandeur is to be seen in Moussorgsky's " Boris Godounov " (1874) and " Khovanstchina " (left unfinished at the composer's death in 1881, completed by Rimsky-Korsakov and first performed in 1886). Both of these works have a religious background difficult for the Western listener to enter into, but they have a singular impressiveness that lifts them into a plane far above the usual type of opera, even of heroic opera.

Rimsky-Korsakov, whose editing of Moussorgsky's operas has been the subject of much controversy, into which it is not possible to enter here, is a link between the music of the nineteenth century and that of our own day. He was at his best in legend and fairy-tale, as " The Snow-Maiden " (1882), recently produced at Sadler's Wells in London, admirably shows. Others of the same type were " Tsar Saltan " (1900), " Kitesh " (1910) and " The Golden Cockerel " (1910). After the " battle, murder and sudden death " of the majority of nineteenth-century operas, these provide a contrast that at first is enthrallingly attractive, especially as the composer had an unfailing vein of characteristic Russian melody and a masterly command of the orchestra ; but after frequent hearing they become monotonous and cloying, for there is a certain sameness about their music and one soon foresees what is coming. " Kitesh " has a religious background which, as in " Khovanstchina," is difficult for Western hearers to appreciate. " The Golden Cockerel " is satirical, and perhaps for that reason has made a peculiar appeal to English audiences.

## CHAPTER VI

# A NOTE ON
# SOME ENGLISH OPERAS

A FOREIGN HISTORIAN of opera might very possibly include under the heading of " national " operas our old friends Balfe's " Bohemian Girl " (1843) and Wallace's " Maritana " (1845) ; to English audiences they are out of the reach of analysis or criticism, and if we ever came to possess a state-supported national opera-house, they would certainly have to be permanent items of the nation's classic repertory. Heroic efforts in the cause of national opera were made by Stanford, and if our operatic managers had the courage (and the capital) to offer British opera to British audiences with systematic perseverance, they might find that some of Stanford's operas would win genuine popularity, notably " Shamus O'Brien " (1896), " Much Ado about Nothing " (1901) and " The Travelling Companion " (1926). At present it is significant that the only British operas that show any signs of holding the stage are those which have a pronounced folk-song colouring, such as Rutland Boughton's " The Immortal Hour " (1914) and Ethel Smyth's amusing comedy " The Boatswain's Mate " (1916), to which we hope we may add Vaughan Williams's two operas " Hugh the Drover " (1924) and " Sir John in Love " (1928), although at the time of writing neither of these has been given much chance to establish itself in the affections of the British public.

## CHAPTER VII

# "THE MODERNS" IN FRANCE AND SPAIN

From the first beginnings of opera in Florence about 1600 up to the death of Puccini (1924) the main stream of opera has been Italian, though we have traced in the foregoing pages the gradual emergence of other national schools of musical drama. At the present moment there is considerable activity in the operatic world, but since Puccini no composer of any nationality has been able to claim outstanding leadership either artistic or commercial, with the possible exception of Richard Strauss, and it is still unclear whether his more popular operas will retain their position or whether his later ones will eventually establish themselves firmly in the repertory. In considering the operas of the last thirty years or so it is therefore useless to group them according to nationality ; we shall do no more than pick out individual works on their own merits and point out their characteristic features.

What is at this moment called " modern music " begins with Claude Debussy, and his " Pelléas et Mélisande " (1902) made a complete break with all the operatic traditions of the past. It represents a deliberate reaction against Wagnerian opera, but at the same time it could hardly have been written unless Wagner had put forward the doctrines of " music-drama." Debussy's opera sets Maeterlinck's drama almost as a spoken play ; it hardly ever leaves the level of recitative, and the recitative itself is reduced almost to a monotone, partly because it follows the natural intonations of spoken French, and not the theatrical intonations on which the recitative of Lulli and Rameau was based, partly in order to reproduce the shadowy and ethereal quality of Maeterlinck's prose. The orchestra is treated in the thinnest and most subdued colours ; it is never more than a background, suggested rather than heard ; in fact the whole opera is conducted in a mysterious whisper. Many people have found " Pelléas et Mélisande " tedious, at any rate on a first hearing ; but closer acquaintance reveals gradually the consummate art with which Debussy has constructed his drama, and the gradual *crescendo* of rhythm that proceeds by imperceptible stages up to the overwhelming moment of Melisande's death.

" Pelléas et Mélisande " was an opera that could never be imitated, even by its own composer ; it had to remain unique. But for all that it has had a certain influence on other composers ; we can observe this in Bela Bartók's " Duke Bluebeard's Castle " (1918). Bartók's music is not in the least French, and has in fact a definitely Hungarian character, but the spirit of Debussy is apparent in the mysterious symbolism of the work and in its aloofness from all conventional operatic practice. Debussy's influence is more directly apparent in Willem Pijper's Dutch opera " Sieur Halewyn " (1933), which has the same sense of aloofness and the same use of symbolism. None of these operas is likely to become popular in a wide sense, but those who are prepared to approach opera in a spirit of idealism will find in them an experience of rare beauty.

The Spanish composer Manuel de Falla has written two operas in which vivid Spanish local colour is combined with a certain sense of symbolism, " L'Amor Brujo " (The Ghost Lover) and " El Retablo de Maese Pedro " (Master Peter's Puppet-Show), an episode from " Don Quixote " treated as a puppet-play with a second puppet-play within it. Along with these we may class Darius Milhaud's " Le Pauvre Matelot," a *Grand Guignol* story set to Breton folk-songs of the sea treated with very daring harmonic technique, and his " Christophe Colomb " (1931), a strange and decidedly impressive combination of opera, oratorio and film, for which Paul Claudel provided a libretto with a markedly religious background.

## CHAPTER VIII

## "THE MODERNS" IN GERMANY

THE OPERAS of Ferruccio Busoni are among the most remarkable of modern times. " Die Brautwahl " (1912), on a libretto taken from E. T. A. Hoffmann, was not very successful, but " Arlecchino " (1917), a brilliant satire on various aspects of human nature, especially on militarism, is gradually gaining ground. Busoni's last and greatest work, left unfinished at his death and completed by Philip Jarnach, is " Doctor Faust " (1925), on a deeply poetical libretto by Busoni himself (in German). It treats the Faust legend in a way that is entirely different from the "Faust" of Goethe. Busoni in his later years was a violent anti-Wagnerian, and his own style was developed mainly from Verdi's " Falstaff " ; his extreme intellectualism was the product of his German training at an earlier period of his life, but his attitude to opera and to the human voice remained consistently Italian. " Doctor Faust " is no opera for the ordinary public, but its grave dignity and tragic intensity make it a work for occasional performance before an initiated audience.

Hans Pfitzner is another composer who stands somewhat aloof from his public. By date he belongs to the generation of Richard Strauss, and in some ways to an earlier one, for his musical style, consciously and intensely German, traces its origins to the late works of Schumann and to " Parsifal." He also owes a good deal to the example of Humperdinck's " Königskinder." His early operas, unknown outside Germany, deal with romantic subjects with a painful insistence on emotions of moral anguish ; his Wagnerian ancestor is Amfortas. For nationalist reasons he has recently come into considerable prominence in Germany, although his intense Germanism is purely poetical and in no sense political. His " Palestrina " (1917) is a very free treatment of the legend that grew up around the famous sixteenth-century composer of Roman church music, but Pfitzner's hero is really a portrait of himself. It is a long and on the whole tedious opera, but commands sincere respec for its lofty idealism and also for moments of striking beauty. Pfitzner's last opera, " Das Herz " (1931), owes a great deal to Busoni's " Doctor Faust," although Pfitzner attacked Busoni very acrimoniously in his critical writings during Busoni's lifetime. " Das Herz " has a symbolical and rather incomprehensible story ; painful emotions are again prominent, but it must be admitted that Pfitnzer never leaves a certain high plane of spiritual fervour.

Spiritual fervour was the last thing that the newer composers of Germany during the years of the Weimar Republic (1918–33) desired to attain. The reaction against the old régime produced an intellectual and moral liberation that encouraged all artists to break new ground, sometimes with more haste than discretion. The operas of Franz Schreker deserve a passing mention here, even if they seem at present to have been consigned to utter oblivion, for they were a strange example of unbridled eroticism and sensationalism, although Schreker, to do him justice, was inwardly far more of an idealist than a commercial composer. He voraciously absorbed every modern technique of his day, but he was not gifted with genuine musical invention, and it was the fundamental musical weakness of his work, even more than the schoolboy crudity of the librettos which he wrote for himself, that prevented his operas from maintaining their momentary popularity.

Far more real invention was shown by the younger men, although the social environment of their age led them into some exaggerations. Just as the French Revolution produced the " rescue opera " of Cherubini's day, so the German Revolution produced a type of " proletarian opera " which emphasised the socialist and communist tendencies of the moment, although the audiences that went to see it were unmistakably *bourgeois*. Kurt Weill, a pupil of Busoni, achieved immense popularity with " Die Dreigroschen-Oper " (The Threepenny Opera—1921), based on a curious perversion and modernisation of Gay's original book of " The Beggar's Opera," the scene being laid in a very imaginary modern London. The music employed a jazz-band as orchestra and for the vocal numbers the English term *song* was adopted as an up-to-date substitute for *lied* or *aria*. The opera outraged most English people who saw it, but it was extremely amusing and original, while at the same time the venomous bitterness of its satire was the sincere expression of a deeply felt sympathy for the sufferings of the starving and destitute. The same sense of a horror too grim for pity was apparent in Weill's " Die Bürgschaft " (The Surety—1931), a serious allegory of modern social and economic conditions, which in its stage technique derived much from Milhaud's " Christophe Colomb " ; an oratorio chorus seated above the orchestra by the proscenium commented on the moral significance of the action. " Die Bürgschaft " contains much genuinely fine music, and the teaching of Busoni bore evident fruit, both in technical detail and in moral idealism.

Proletarian opera, however, reached its highest point in Alban Berg's " Wozzeck " (1922), based on a play by Georg Büchner, a forgotten dramatist of a century ago. Arnold Schönberg, of whom Berg was a pupil, had already made some very curious experiments in opera, notably in " Erwartung " (composed 1909, first performed 1924), a one-act opera with only one character, a woman who walks through a wood to meet her lover and at the end finds his corpse. The technical system of Schönberg's music and that of his disciples is mentioned elsewhere in this volume. Berg's music to "Wozzeck" is in theory based on various conventional forms—fugue, variations, passacaglia, etc.—but in the theatre one is not conscious of this. The play, a peculiarly grim and sordid story of humble life, is acted in recitative that rarely gives way to lyrical song, while the orchestra underlines every emotion with a poignancy that is almost unbearable. The music of " Wozzeck," considered by itself, is to most concert-goers completely incomprehensible ; in the theatre its emotional force is so intense that few people can hear it for the first time without being profoundly overcome by it. " Wozzeck " is the only opera of the ultra-modern type which has definitely established itself in the repertory. Before 1933 it had been performed at a large number of German theatres, including many quite small ones ; since the National-Socialist revolution of that year it has been under a cloud, but it has already won appreciation outside Germany and its return to the stage is probably a mere matter of time.

# E: A RETROSPECT AND
# A PROSPECT

In these pages we have not been able to offer more than the merest outline of operatic history, and many works of interest have of necessity been omitted altogether. Our aim has been not to compile a work of reference, but rather to suggest to ordinary opera-goers points of interest in the operas they are reasonably likely to have some chance of seeing on the stage, and to show how in the course of centuries opera has developed into an art-form with conventions of its own that are constantly changing as time goes on, in accordance with the changes that have affected all music.

We have drawn attention systematically to the social history of opera, because the social background has always had a very noticeable influence on operatic development. The social aspect of opera is at this moment of urgent importance, for recent political and economic changes have practically destroyed the social class that for some three centuries was the chief mainstay of the musical drama. Opera, if it is to live, has now got to pay its own way. The history of music, however, shows us that most of the music now acknowledged to have been of epoch-making importance was in fact originally composed for a small and exclusive circle of initiates—it matters not whether at various times they were princes and dukes, cardinals and bishops, or poets and intellectuals. The great masterpieces of music do not reach a popular audience until they have attained a respectable age. But however profoundly we may venerate the great masterpieces we cannot, if we are artistically alive, rest content with the art of the past alone. The artist must still create and it is our duty to find him an audience.

Under modern conditions of life the appreciation of serious opera (to consider only this branch of music) has spread to wide circles ; but music-lovers of limited education require, generally speaking, the operas of fifty or a hundred years ago, rather than those of to-day. It so happens that most of the operas of that period were written for social conditions very different from our own and demand for their adequate performance a financial outlay that the present generation is utterly unable to face. They could be made economically practicable by performances in vast auditoriums, as has been shown by recent performances of Meyerbeer's operas in the Roman amphitheatre at Verona, which holds some 30,000 spectators ; but even for Italy the amphitheatre of Verona is an exceptional building, and we are not likely to erect opera-houses on that scale in England while we cannot make opera pay in the theatres we already possess.

The intolerable expense of opera-production is due not so much to scenic requirements, as many people might imagine, but to the cost of large orchestras and the necessary rehearsals ; we cannot lower this cost without sacrificing artistic efficiency and the players' right to an honourable wage. The reader of these pages will already have learned who were to blame for the fact that modern audiences, especially the more sophisticated ones, have come to regard a large orchestra as an indispensable requirement of opera. Modern composers may have reacted against Wagner's theories and against his musical technique, but for the most part they have been even more extravagant in their orchestral demands.

Musicians of to-day often express grave concern at the gulf that is alleged to have divided modern artistic music from the understanding of " the people." History shows us that this gulf has always existed, and that it has always been gradually bridged. Whether we are more conscious of it now than our ancestors were it is impossible to estimate, but if we assume, as many people do, that the gulf is at this moment far wider than it ever was before, it may be accounted for by the enormous growth of a partially educated musical public. The only solution for this difficulty is to educate that public still more ; it is fatal for composers to write down to it.

Opera in the future ought to be one of the most effective means of educating this public, for opera by its very nature makes an appeal through various channels. The case of " Wozzeck " is a conspicuous and timely example ; if the music is hard to understand, the drama is a helpful guide. There are certainly many people who derive more pleasure from an opera than from a concert, or who would at any rate admit to doing so if our musical educators had not, from a deplorable sort of puritanism, suggested to them that opera was both artistically and morally an inferior form of art.

We have seen how at the end of the eighteenth century, when opera had reached a low general level, Germany saved it and restored it to higher standards—to higher ideal standards indeed than it had ever attained before. Germany owed this standard of opera to the idealism of her princes, who for the most part took the view that it was their duty to maintain opera, not so much for their personal amusement or for the gratification of their vanity, as for the artistic education of their subjects. We English people are inclined to smile at the uplifting inscriptions they placed over their imposing façades, such as the " To the True, to the Good, to the Beautiful " on that of the Frankfurt opera-house, and to say that we will not have our theatres turned into lecture-rooms. The composers of " Figaro," "William Tell " and "Falstaff" would probably have agreed with us. And if amateur societies in this country can produce such operas as Monteverdi's " Orfeo," " King Arthur," " Iphigenia in Tauris " and " Idomeneo," we need have no fears for the cause of operatic idealism.

# BOOK IV

## THE HUMAN VOICE

*By* FRANCIS TOYE AND
DYNELEY HUSSEY

# A: BY WAY OF INTRODUCTION

## CHAPTER I

## MODES AND PLAINSONG

THE HUMAN VOICE, though it may not have been the first, remains potentially the most expressive of all musical instruments. Primitive man may have thumped some kind of drum before he sang, but he must have sung before he fashioned any kind of pipe. A complete history of vocal music should doubtless chronicle the most rudimentary attempts at song by human beings, just as it should certainly include an account of the vocal music of Oriental, and other, races outside the European orbit. These races have, in fact pushed vocal expression very far ; indeed their art of vocalisation is at least as expressive and as complex as our own. For the present purposes, however, all this must be neglected. Even the vocal art of the Egyptians, the Greeks and the Romans, though the direct ancestor of our own, remains too remote to justify consideration in the scheme of this Book. We are concerned only with European vocal music in the sense meant by the ordinary person to-day, and the origins of it need only be considered in so far as they have any direct bearing on the subject.

All of our music may be said to have developed from the Gregorian Chant. The kind of music indissolubly linked with the name of the great Pope Gregory was not an invention ; it was rather a compilation, a standardisation of current tunes that existed for centuries before Gregory. They were used in churches ; St. Ambrose of Milan had even made a hymn book of them. Nobody knows very much about their origin. To some extent they may have been a direct legacy from the music of Greece and Rome ; they were almost certainly influenced by the old Jewish ritual music practised in the synagogues. What Gregory did was to eliminate the tunes he thought unsuitable for ecclesiastical purposes and to codify the rest, as well as the various liturgies to which they were sung in different European centres. This happened about the year six hundred, and, thanks largely to the devotion and enthusiasm of the Benedictine order, his standardisation gradually became accepted by all civilised Europe.

The fundamental characteristics of the Gregorian Chant will be familiar to those who have attended a Catholic Church, though the embellishments were far more ornate and the rhythm far freer than what we usually hear to-day. During the sixteenth and seventeenth centuries under the guise of "reform" new editions of Plainsong, as it is called, were issued which did violence to its very nature but made it easier to accompany on the organ. Thanks mainly to the scholarship of the Benedictines of Solesmes the genuine characteristics of the Gregorian Music are now once more known and accepted, but they are by no means universally practised.

Plainsong was written in what are known as modes. As explained in Book I (Part A, Chapter III) the modes can be understood if the reader will imagine the scale of C major and then build scales on each of the notes without any accidentals. Thus, the mode which we suppose built on the note D would have semitonal intervals between the second and third, and the sixth and seventh, notes; the mode supposedly built on F would have a semitonal interval between the 4th and 5th and between the 7th and 8th notes; and so on. These modes had Greek names, Dorian, Phrygian, Lydian, Mixo-lydian, presumably because they came to the Roman via the Byzantine Church, which in its turn inherited both them and their names from the Ancient Greeks. The old names, in fact, were quite wrongly used, but the principles underlying both the Greek and the mediæval modes were the same, especially the very important principle that each mode had a definite æsthetic, even a moral, character of its own. Except to point out that this may have been the reason underlying during many centuries the Church's severe attitude towards tampering with the modes, and to remind the reader that from them eventually sprang our minor and major scales, nothing more need be said about modes, though this does not imply that they are not of the greatest importance. Apart from the fact that they are in current ecclesiastical use to-day, contemporary composers like Vaughan Williams have made great use of them in their music. Nobody can truly understand vocal music without knowing at least what they were.

By about the end of the tenth century the characteristics of Plainsong may be said to have been definitely fixed. To this music were sung not only the various parts of the Mass but various Latin hymns. The reader must imagine them usually sung unaccompanied, one group of monks answering another antiphonally, which is indeed the origin of the chanting of the verses of the psalms in Anglican churches, first by one half of the choir and then by the other. At the culmination of its development, when its characteristics had been standardised, the use of Plainsong was extended to other purposes than the Mass and hymns ; apparently whole Mystery- and Passion-Dramas were sung to it. Thus Plainsong remains a link between the past and the present civilisation of Europe. To anyone initiated in the convention, it remains even to-day highly expressive, a form which, when practised by singers of talent and imagination, covers a considerable range and is capable of much variety.

## CHAPTER II

# MINSTRELS AND TROUBADOURS

THE ORIGIN of what may be termed secular music is considerably more obscure. It seems to have been practised mainly, if not exclusively, by jongleurs, vagrant minstrels who provided the music at fairs and popular festivals. Probably most of the songs of these minstrels were in fact allied with some kind of dance, rather like our own Helston Furry Dance or the familiar children's singing games. Some of the songs were rather coarse, and perhaps on this account, or from a dislike of seeing its prerogatives invaded, the Church viewed the jongleurs with a by no means favourable eye, treating them as the rogues and vagabonds which no doubt they often were. Anybody who reads Anatole France's short story, " Le Jongleur de Notre Dame," subsequently made into a particularly charming opera by Massenet, wherein is depicted the scandalised attitude of the clergy at one such minstrel's effrontery in daring to offer his songs and dances as a tribute to the Virgin, will understand exactly both the social position and the kind of art associated with the jongleur. It is not till we come to the Troubadours that secular song can be said to have risen to any important position in the world. For the Troubadours were noblemen who seem to have originated in France, south of the Loire. We even know the name of the first of them, who was Count of Poitiers and Duke of Aquitaine, and lived between 1071 and 1127. Up to that time practically all the education of the nobility had been military ; this practice of the art of music was something quite new. In the first instance the Troubadours do not seem to have sung or played themselves, but to have handed over their compositions to some attendant minstrel. It was not for some time that the Troubadour of the popular song, touching his guitar and singing to his lady-love, became an actual fact. From the outset, however, their style of composition was of this nature. The popular music which they took as a basis of their activities was often gross, not to say downright coarse. They idealised it, particularly where love was concerned. Indeed love as depicted in the songs of the Troubadours was of a very rarefied and ideal kind, for, as often as not, the Troubadour considered himself to be in love with a lady he did not even want to know !

After a time, however, the Troubadours ceased to be exclusively noble and by the fourteenth century were to be found also in the ranks of what we now call the middle classes. It was these middle-class Troubadours, with their greater sense of practical values, who gradually abandoned the pure idealism of chivalry for what may be called songs of personal gallantry. In practice the old chivalric songs seem to have become the prerogative of definitely aristocratic gatherings, while the others acquired a wider popularity, perhaps competing with, if not supplanting, the songs of the minstrels on their own ground.

Probably this Troubadour music, in its eventual evolution, should be regarded as the basis of all modern European secular song. In that the modes were used, it remained definitely akin to that of ecclesiastical hymns, though, in the end, there is to be found an undoubted feeling for our modern major scale in some of the songs. The reader should realise that at this time practically no distinction was made between words and music. Indeed, the words were often regarded as the more important, though sometimes fitted to famous tunes already in existence. Most of the subjects were conventional, the usual kind of themes associated with the Pastourelles, Rondels and Ballads we still know. There were, however, narrative and dramatic subjects, such as that of lovers like Tristan and Yseult surprised by King Mark. There were also curious debating songs where the singers would improvise a discussion as to whether it were better for a lover to be blind or deaf ; whether it would be preferable to deceive one's mistress or to feign ignorance that one is oneself being deceived, and so on. Generally speaking, however, it is the simpler songs of nature or love that have a real interest for us to-day. Thus, we can still appreciate the beauties of the "May Song" by Moniot d'Arras. Here we have what appears to us a real tune, still so fresh and charming that it has been found worthy of a gramophone record.

It will be noticed that France can claim the honour of being the cradle of the Troubadours. Their influence spread gradually to Italy, Spain and Portugal, but it may be doubted whether the Troubadours of those countries ever attained to the level of skill and taste to be found in France. The Minnesingers in Germany, taking over the French ideas lock, stock and barrel, adapted them to their own uses, and the famous Walter von der Vogelweide, who flourished in the fourteenth century, may be defined as the link between them and the Mastersingers who eventually supplanted them. Incidentally, it is by no means certain that the Mastersingers, who, as everybody familiar with Wagner's great opera knows, were artisans, registered an improvement. It has been said that their style was definitely less refined, and it seems certain that the influence of their rigid principles, which lasted till the seventeenth century, retarded the development of vocal music in Germany compared with other European countries.

# CHAPTER III

# DIAPHONY AND DISCANT

Exactly how or why men developed the desire to sing in two parts instead of one, we do not know. Anybody who listens to a modern crowd singing knows that there are certain individuals who seem naturally inclined to sing below the tune, usually at the interval of a fifth. This, however, may be an inherited habit rather than a primitive instinct. In the first instance, as we have seen, Gregorian music consisted of only one vocal line, but by the tenth century, if not the ninth, we find the practice established of placing a note at the interval of a fourth or a fifth above or below each original note of the Plainsong. This particular technique was known as the art of Organum or organising. It was extremely simple. As the Plainsong moved in one direction or another the second part slavishly followed it, note by note, the mediæval theorists regarding these intervals of a fourth or a fifth as the normal concord corresponding, let us say, to our major third. Gradually, however, musicians began to discover that it was at least as agreeable, if not more so, to have the two parts moving in contrary, instead of similar, motion. This extremely important discovery once made, the way was open for further and comparatively rapid progress. Some time in the twelfth century there appears what is known as Discant, which consisted of a vocal line, in definitely measured rhythm, above the Plainsong. In the first instance this rhythm was always in triple time, apparently for the typically mediæval reason that the personages of the Holy Trinity numbered three, and that, therefore, anything in threes was preferable to anything else. Duple time did not make its appearance till more than a hundred years later.

Discant is especially interesting to us English because an English theorist called Walter Odington was one of its foremost champions. Indeed, England seems to have played a leading part in the evolution of music about this time. It has even been claimed that the singing of popular music in Wales and the north of England was largely responsible for the introduction of the revolutionary intervals of thirds and sixths into the Church Discant, though he would be a bold man who asserted this with any certainty. In any case, the reader should be warned here and now against any attempt to view mediæval music in terms of national-ism. Anything and everything that we understand by that term would have been incomprehensible to the mediæval mind, to which countries were only so many geographical expressions. This was particularly the case with France and England, with their inextricably linked traditions of culture and feudatory allegiances. Therefore, to attach any nationalistic importance to works like "Sumer is icumen in," as is sometimes done in histories of music, is, unfortunately, mistaken pride.

This famous composition, probably written by a monk of Reading, called John of Fornsete, in the first half of the thirteenth century, is one of the wonders of musical history. The Troubadours, in their Rondels, may already have achieved something approximating to what we now call rounds or catches ; the Church, in its motets, may have experimented with a third part added to the Plainsong and the Discant ; but the fact remains that "Sumer is icumen in" appears to us like a work that has taken wings and, soaring above all the limitations and prohibitions of mediæval musical theory, come to earth again a couple of centuries before its time. It may, of course, be the sole surviving specimen of a school of composition of which we otherwise know nothing ; it may be a freak of genius. The astounding fact remains that the smoothness of the counterpoint of this Rondel remains acceptable even to modern ears. (See also frontispiece, and Book I, Part A, Chapter II, p. 30.)

In practice "Sumer is icumen in" must be regarded as the culminating point of all the music written before those great, if shadowy, figures of the fifteenth century, like John Dunstable, Guillaume Dufay and Josquin des Près, whom we are accustomed to regard as the first true ancestors of composition in the modern sense of the term. Chronologically, however, nearly two centuries were still to pass. In general, it may be said that these centuries were characterised by every kind of complex experiment that mediæval ingenuity could possibly reconcile with mediæval theory. An authority has described Church music at that time as being very much like a modern composer "taking for his bass an Anglican chant and spreading it

out so that each note occupied three or four bars ; then
for his treble using ' Take a pair of sparkling eyes '
(*allegro molto*) ; and for his alto part fitting in as much
as he could of ' Tipperary ' or ' Onward, Christian soldiers,'
or both." This strange state of things was finally checked
by a Papal Decree of 1322, which insisted on the original
Plainsong not being unduly obscured, though a school of
theorists soon successfully reconciled the delightful novelty
of thirds and sixths with the new ordinance. And thus the
ground was prepared for planting the seed of Polyphony.

F. T.

# B: THE POLYPHONIC PERIOD

## CHAPTER I

## ENGLAND AND FLANDERS:
## DUNSTABLE AND DUFAY

As THE EXISTENCE of " Sumer is icumen in " proves, there must have been as early as the 13th century a knowledge of the principles of counterpoint and a considerable skill in its use within restricted limits. It is not, however, until early in the 15th century that we find the beginnings of a true polyphonic style. All the music that has come down to us from the Middle Ages is, with the exception of the Reading Rota or Rondel, Church music, and the Church was, as it ever has been, conservative. The ecclesiastical authorities frowned upon innovations and especially upon those derived from secular sources, such as the canonic devices of the Rota. They could, however, do no more than retard the development of a new style of Church music, which was bound to take place in an eager and inquiring age. It would have been as impossible for them to stop their architects from building Gothic cathedrals instead of adhering to the old Norman style. It needed only a great composer to give impetus to the new methods of composition by introducing some measure of system into its hitherto crude and haphazard manner. That composer was found in England, where the great period of polyphonic music began with John Dunstable even as it ended there with William Byrd and Orlando Gibbons.

Dunstable was the most important of a group of English composers who seem to have spent the greater part of their working life on the Continent. Their music shows a very distinct advance upon anything that had so far been achieved. Dunstable himself was, indeed, the first composer in the modern sense, in that he created something like a personal style. His music, archaic though it may sound to modern ears, has a suavity and a regard for euphony hitherto unknown. The voices move with a new freedom, not being perpetually tied to one another in the note-against-note manner of what we may call the true English School of this period, that group of composers, possibly members of the Royal Chapel at Windsor, whose work is represented in the MS. at St. Edmund's Catholic College at Old Hall, Hertfordshire. The most enterprising of these composers ventured no further than to make a rare and very rudimentary use of canon. We have only to compare with such timid efforts Dunstable's motet, " Quam pulchra es," which is printed in Grove's Dictionary, to see what an enormous advance he made both towards a more melodic and independent treatment of the individual parts and towards an avoidance of irrational dissonances. The wreathed figures of the " Alleluia " at the end of this motet produce a most charming effect, as if the pomegranates mentioned in the concluding lines of the text had indeed burst suddenly into flower.

Dunstable made little or no use of canon in his Church music, probably on account of its secular associations—a supposition that is confirmed by his use of the device in his secular compositions. It may, indeed, be said that this is the only feature that distinguishes such things as the *chanson*, " Puisque m'amour," from his settings of sacred texts. This is a suitable place at which to mention two famous English songs of the first half of the 15th century. One is the patriotic " Agincourt Song," which has been attributed to Dunstable, and the other, rather later in date, " Alas, departing is ground of woe," which in a simple way achieves a considerable degree of emotional expression.

In addition to his contribution to the formation of a true polyphonic style, Dunstable must be credited with great learning and ingenuity. He is described in a contemporary epitaph as " an astrologian, a mathematician, a musitian and what not." The mathematical side of his mind is shown in his musical puzzles, which, though of no intrinsic interest, exhibit a command of theoretical resources that is astonishing at so early a date. The construction of these ingenious compositions, which were carried to absurd extremes by the Flemish composers of the next generation, is to be regarded as the whetstone of his technique.

Among Dunstable's English contemporaries the only one who calls for mention is Lionel Power, whose music is found both in the Old Hall MS. and in the foreign libraries along with that of Dunstable. Power shows himself an accomplished practitioner in the suave style of his master, but there is no evidence in his music of any individual contribution towards the development of the polyphonic style. He deserves to be remembered, however, as the author of a treatise in which for the first time the use of consecutive unisons, octaves and fifths is forbidden. Like most theorists, Power was merely formulating a law that was already being generally observed. The prohibition is not an arbitrary one, like the superstitious avoidance of thirds which was only now beginning to be set aside by advanced composers. The new musical law is based upon the fact that these intervals—and especially consecutive fifths—tend to confuse the tonality of the music. The appreciation, intuitive rather than conscious, of this fact is an indication of a growing feeling for tonality, and it is the first step towards the replacement of the old modes by the major- and minor-key system, which was to serve as the basis of European music from about 1600 until the beginning of the present century. Viewed from one point of view the musical history of the two centuries between Lionel Power and Orlando Gibbons is that of the gradual crystallisation of the major and minor keys, which were precipitated, as it were, by the action of polyphony upon the modes.

The epitaph preserved by Stow and recently restored in St. Stephen's Church, Walbrook, proves that Dunstable was not without honour in his own country, but it was on the Continent that he was held in the greatest esteem and it was there that his influence was most deeply felt. The leadership in music passes now to the Flemish School, whose first masters were Guillaume Dufay and Gilles Binchois. Even if we had not the authority of the contemporary French poet, who praises the Englishmen for their " mélodie si belle," which aroused the envy of Binchois and Dufay, their own music is sufficient evidence of the effect of English example. The earlier compositions of Dufay, written before 1436, when he was appointed Canon of Cambrai, are dry and discordant. After his appointment to Cambrai there is a complete change in his style, which happens to synchronise with the poem just mentioned. As Mr. Woolridge says, " no more dryness in the melody nor intolerable harshness of arbitrary discord are to be heard, but we perceive a new conception of music altogether, similar to that with which we have become acquainted already in the works of Dunstable." In one technical feature Dufay's music differs strikingly from that of the Englishman. He makes frequent use, even in his Masses, of the canon, and even combines it with the older devices of augmentation and diminution (the statement of a theme in longer or shorter notes). Many of his Masses, too, are composed upon melodies derived from popular songs and bear their names, " Rosa bella," " Douce mémoire," " L'Homme armé." The ecclesiastical authorities seem to have been less austere in Flanders than in England and allowed Church music to be enriched by devices and melodies borrowed from secular art.

The music of Dufay is occasionally to be heard in performance, and there are even one or two gramophone records of it. It is characterised by a charming mellifluousness almost bordering on prettiness. There is a setting of the "Gloria" recorded in the Parlophone " Two Thousand Years of Music," for two treble voices, with a ground-bass for trumpets, which is altogether delightful. The voices tumble over one another in a succession of canonic imitations while the trumpets keep up a steady figure below them. In listening to it one seems to hear the music that Memlinc's angels sang, it is so pure and sweet. But it moves not at all. There is, indeed, an effective climax arbitrarily imposed upon the static figurations, repeated over and over. It does not grow naturally out of what has gone before, like the final "Alleluia" in Dunstable's "Quam pulchra es." As a composition this "Gloria" is technically less distinguished than "Sumer is icumen in," which it somewhat resembles in both its use of canon and its fresh spring-like feeling.

Nothing could be in more striking contrast with the wayward, almost feminine, charm of Dufay's music than the severely intellectual and learned works of Jean de Okeghem, who is the most important figure in the next generation. Okeghem seems to have studied with Binchois at Antwerp, and at the time of Dufay's death in 1474 he was at the head of the Royal Chapel in Paris, where for forty years he served the Kings of France. His contribution to music was technical rather than artistic. He was, above all, an experimenter, and delighted in the solution of complex problems. Like so many pioneers, whether in the arts or in science, he achieved, as a by-product of his experiments, results that were far more important than those he was definitely aiming at. In his relentless pursuit of technical difficulties for their own sake, he has been likened to Arnold Schönberg, but what he unconsciously accomplished for choral music in his day may be compared with Haydn's creation of the String Quartet. Up to this time the melodic material of a composition was always provided by the tenor, around which the other parts were woven, but the very complexity of the problems in fugue and canon which Okeghem set himself forced the tenor voice out of its dominating position and established equality between the several parts. Just as Haydn in his Quartets turned the first violin from a soloist with accompaniment into a sharer of the musical interest, equal with his colleagues, so Okeghem, with very different ends in view, deprived the tenor of its real, though often unobtrusive, domination. He added, therefore, not only a greater complexity but also a new freedom of movement, without which polyphonic music could not have attained perfection.

It is seldom that pioneers reap the advantage of their experiments, and it was left to Okeghem's pupil, Josquin des Près, to make full artistic use of this new technical mastery. Josquin combined the learning of his master with an artistic genius that turns even his most recondite exercises into beautiful music. Not only is his music incomparably richer in texture than that of the older masters, but it is capable of reflecting the character of the words in a way that was inconceivable in the days of Dunstable and Dufay. The change that had come over music might be compared with that which the researches of the Florentine painters into the problems of perspective and of pigments wrought during this same century upon their art. There is a new depth, a richer colour, a greater mastery of form and a more subtle expressiveness. Josquin is the earliest composer of whom it can be said without reserve that his music will appeal to an uninstructed audience on its own merits. Sometimes, indeed, his melody seems extraordinarily modern. We even find him anticipating in his 4-part motet, " Ave Cœlorum Domina," the first strain of Schubert's " Du bist die Ruh'." This coincidence, in itself of no importance, shows how far music had by this time gone along the road towards diatonic harmony.

Josquin's music is more varied than that of any of the composers we have so far mentioned. It ranges from a light and satirical humour, which is not always excluded from his sacred works, to the most profoundly moving expression of grief. Nothing could be more poignant than his famous setting of David's Lament for Absalom or the elegy which he composed on the death of Okeghem. In the expression of devout religious feeling he could rise to the level of the great masters of the later Roman School. Josquin usually lavished upon the Mass the whole resources of his technical skill, and his recondite artifices have sometimes been criticised. He was, however, only glorifying the central rite of the Church, after the manner of the architects who

Nc

adorned the choir more elaborately than the rest of a cathedral. As he developed, he did, indeed, simplify his style in the direction of a purer musical expressiveness, and in his later Masses and the motets this side of his great genius is most clearly displayed. To sum up, Josquin is the first composer to base his music fully upon the principle of harmonic propriety, so that his phrases become intelligible musical sentences, quite apart from their expressiveness as renderings of the text.

It is not surprising that we cannot find among the immediate followers of Josquin any composer worthy to be placed beside him, but there now comes on the scene an embarrassing galaxy of talent, to whom it is impossible to do justice within the space at our disposal. Reference must be made to Clément Jannequin, a French composer whose fame rests mainly upon his secular music. He specialised in the composition of four-part *chansons*, in which the songs of birds, the sounds of hunting, the street-cries of Paris, and the noise of battle are imitated. These descriptive pieces, whose titles remind us of the instrumental music of his 17th century compatriot, Couperin, are full of a naïve charm which has ensured their revival in recent years by such bodies as the Oriana Madrigal Society. Among his other songs is the famous " Ce moy de May," in which we find persisting the tradition of the Troubadours.

## CHAPTER II

# FLANDERS AND ITALY: PALESTRINA

FOR A HUNDRED YEARS the Flemish composers had dominated European music. Their influence spread through Germany, where Heinrich Finck and Heinrich Isaac established a solid and powerful tradition. Of this Hans

Leo Hassler, organist to the great Augsburg merchant, Octavian Fugger, is the chief ornament a century later. From Germany it passed to Poland, the native country of Finck, where the Royal Chapel of Sigismund the First formed a compact body of composers in remote Cracow. But the main tide flowed southwards through France towards Italy in the full glory of the Renaissance. Dufay had been a member of the Papal Choir in Rome before he returned to his native Cambrai and fell under the influence of Dunstable. Josquin likewise served in the Papal Chapel as well as at the ducal courts of Florence, Milan and Ferrara, which was one of the most important musical centres in Italy, before he entered the service of King Louis XII of France.

In the next generation, that is to say in the first half of the 16th century, we find Flemish composers permanently settled in Italy, chief among them Adrian Willaert, a Netherlander, in Venice, and Jacob Arcadelt, a native of Roulers in Flanders, at Florence. Italy now begins to take the leading position in European music, which she was to occupy for more than two centuries, and it was in Italy that polyphonic music reached its highest point of development. One of the first signs of Italian influence at this time is the rapid growth of secular music, which soon becomes an independent form of art equal in importance to the music of the Church. This was a natural enough development, since in every other art the adventurous minds of the Renaissance were turning more and more from an exclusive preoccupation with sacred subjects.

The chief form taken by secular music in Italy was that of the madrigal, in style far more complex and subtle than the French and Flemish *chansons*. The term had been applied centuries before to songs of a pastoral nature, but for our purposes the history of the madrigal begins about 1530. Most of the early madrigals are homophonic, that is to say, the melodic interest is concentrated in one of the four parts in which they were usually written, and it appears likely that they were sung as solos with instrumental accompaniments as well as by voices with or without accompaniment. The madrigal was in fact a wedding of Flemish contrapuntal technique with the Italian *frottola*, which was a form of song popular in Northern Italy. The words of the *frottole* were either comic or sentimental, though they were not without wit in the one direction or poetry in the other. It was the sentimental element in these songs that the madrigal composers developed most freely, though there are also many examples of madrigals that are frivolous and gross. The Italian madrigal is a typical product of aristocratic culture, and its chief characteristic is a refined voluptuousness, the erotic double meanings of the poems being delicately underlined by the music.

At first the chief exponents of the madrigal were the Italianised Flemings, Arcadelt and Willaert being the chief among them. Arcadelt, whose name was until lately familiar only through a spurious " Ave Maria " transcribed by Liszt for the pianoforte, was a composer of considerable distinction and charm. The revival of interest in these old composers has familiarised us with some of Arcadelt's madrigals, notably the beautiful " Il bianco e dolce cigno " on the favourite theme of the swan's last song. Willaert adopted a more massive style, which, though stiff, has a certain grandeur, and he is the first of these composers to give us the impression of thinking vertically in chords, rather than horizontally in separate parts whose harmonic effect is fortuitous and subsidiary to the interweaving of the voices. His chief pupil, Ciprian van Rore, another Fleming who came to Venice at an early age and succeeded his master as organist of St. Mark's, followed his example, and by his experiments in chromaticism carried a stage further the trend towards a more harmonic conception of music. His own efforts do not seem to have been very successful, but he was taking one more step towards the disintegration of the modal system, for in them the chromatic notes are not introduced merely as a means of avoiding a discordant clash between the several voices, but are a part of the scale in which they occur. He did not always write in this novel style, and his considerable fame as a composer rests upon his more conservative compositions, but these chromatic madrigals opened the way for the more daring experiments of Gesualdo, Prince of Venosa, and of Luca Marenzio at the end of the century, and we soon begin to find madrigals written frankly in the diatonic keys.

All the composers we have just mentioned also wrote Church music, in which as yet the effect of the new madrigal style hardly appears, and in the next generation we come to the great triumvirate who brought the music of the Roman Church to the highest point of perfection. Orlande de Lassus or Orlando di Lasso, to give his name its more common Italianised form, was the last and greatest of the Flemish School, but like his contemporaries, Giovanni Pierluigi da Palestrina, the Roman, and Tomás Luis da Victoria, the Spaniard, he transcends the boundaries of school and nationality. Of the three Lassus was the most versatile, the most profound. There is no form of vocal composition, sacred or profane, no depth of emotion, grave or gay, that he did not touch. We find him at one moment setting the words " rore tegens " to chromatic harmonies by way of punning reference to Ciprian, at another creating in his setting of the Penitential Psalms a profoundly moving masterpiece. Of these psalms Mr. van den Borren has written : " It is marvellous that, having to treat a subject relatively monotonous, Orlando remained throughout equal to his task. Without any failure of inspiration he makes to pass before us all the states of soul which the Psalmist describes, ranging from the profoundest grief to the brightest hope. All this he has depicted in a musical language ideally concise, in which the madrigalesque element intervenes largely, but with the utmost discretion and with the most exquisite sense of proportion." It is significant that in spite of his love of puns and other frivolities, Lassus's finest achievements should be in this tragic vein, for at Munich, where he spent the greater part of his life in the service of the Duke of Bavaria, he died insane of melancholia.

Palestrina's is a name universally familiar, and popular opinion is right in regarding him as the embodiment of all that is best in the music of the Catholic Church. His position in that hierarchy is that of Beethoven in symphonic music, with this difference, that Palestrina summed up once and for all the glories of the Italian polyphonic style, whereas Beethoven, looking forward, trod out new paths along which future composers were to follow him. The essential quality of Palestrina's music is its absolute purity. It seems almost to come from another world, divorced from the common emotions of humanity. In their place is a religious devotion whose intensity saves it from any feeling of frigidity. Such perfection could only be achieved within a narrow scope, and Palestrina had none of the versatility of Lassus. His madrigals, lovely though they are, show hardly any marks of a secular style to differentiate them from his sacred music. But it is sufficient that in his Masses, notably the famous Mass of Pope Marcellus and the not less beautiful " Assumption " Mass, he should have set up once and for all a pattern for the Roman Liturgy. The legends surrounding the Marcellus Mass may be false in fact, but in spirit they are true enough, and his example saved the choral music of his Church from abuses and from possible extinction. Perhaps the most striking quality of his best music, from the modern point of view, is its agelessness. So great was his mastery of his material that he avoided the commonplaces of idiom that stamp the music of lesser men and fix for the listener its date in time.

Palestrina's music has not the sumptuousness that marks the more worldly school of Venice, best represented in the works of the Gabrieli family, and comparable with the rich compositions of their fellow-citizens, Veronese and Tintoretto. He has often been likened to Raphael, and his music has the same kind of spiritual beauty free from insipidity as that painter's best work ; on the technical side his complete mastery produces an effect of shapeliness and balance, of depth and roundness, that accords with Raphael's complete solution of the problem of representing a solid body upon a flat surface. The aloofness of his Masses is in the very spirit of the Catholic Church, whose central rite is regarded as a sacred mystery not to be approached too closely by the uninitiated. But in his motets he comes nearer to the common mind of humanity, without tainting the purity of his style, and it is probably in such things as the Good Friday Antiphon, " Popule meus, quid feci tibi," that the lay listener will find the greatest musical pleasure.

If Palestrina sums up the past, Victoria, his Spanish contemporary, looks towards the future. He is the true representative of the Counter-Reformation, which had its centre in Spain and the Inquisition as its instrument. Although trained in the Roman School he remained a true Spaniard, and his music breathes the exalted mysticism of his race, which in painting finds its extreme expression through the work of El Greco. His mastery of the resources of his time is equal to that of his great contemporaries, and, though his mysticism leads him sometimes into an almost morbid sensualism, and even into sensational effects of ecstasy, at their best his raptures are constrained by a noble and dignified bearing. If there were any doubt of Victoria's claim to stand as a master in his own right and not, like Anerio and others with whom he used to be classed, as a mere satellite of Palestrina, it is only necessary to set beside the Roman master's Good Friday Antiphon, to which reference has already been made, Victoria's " Tenebræ factæ sunt." In the one the emotions of the text are fused into a single, sublime musical idea, perfect in its shapeliness and tranquil beauty ; in the other there is an exaltation and a dramatic force undreamt of by Palestrina. Each emotion—the gloom of the darkened skies, the despairing cry of Jesus in the hour of death and the tender sorrowfulness of His last emission of breath—passes in turn across the texture of this magnificently tragic piece.

Palestrina's death in 1594 marked the end of a musical era. Already Luca Marenzio had brought the Italian madrigal to its highest point of development, and the next decade was to see the revolution destined, under the leadership of Monteverdi, to alter the whole course of musical history. The immediate cause of this revolution was the desire to find a more dramatic means of expression in music than was possible within the smooth texture of polyphony. The madrigal had never been a really satisfactory musical form for the expression of Renaissance ideas, based as they were upon a revival of interest in classical art and literature. That 16th century notions of Greek and Roman art were fallacious is beside the point. The experiments of Gesualdo and his kind were attempts to create an essentially Gothic form more consonant with the greater violence of contemporary thought. Technically these experiments resulted in a further dethronement of the modes in favour of the key-system, or rather of a concentration upon the two modes which we know as the major and minor keys, to the exclusion of the rest. A deeper cause was the unconscious feeling that the rich mine of polyphony had been worked out, that all that could be said in that way had been said, and that new country must be explored. That the path actually taken was that of diatonic harmony may have been natural, but it was not inevitable. Nor did it bring progress in the sense of immediate improvement. Music, having sacrificed the technical resources accumulated during two centuries of effort in favour of a more naturalistic and forceful dramatic expression, had to go to school again. It is more than a century before we find composers worthy to rank with Lassus, Victoria and Palestrina.

## CHAPTER III

# TUDOR TIMES:
# MORLEY AND GIBBONS

We have seen how the tide of polyphony flowed southward from England through Flanders and France to Italy. It ebbed again towards the north, passing by the French, who have always been more impervious to foreign artistic influences than any other nation. The final triumphs of polyphonic music were achieved in England. Ever since the time of Dunstable an unbroken musical tradition had persisted here, submerged at times by the dynastic wars that preceded the establishment of the Tudors. It was a sturdy, individual tradition, little affected by the developments taking place on the Continent. During the more settled time of Henry VII's reign there is a prolific school of composers, the chief among them being Robert Fayrfax and William Cornysch. It is not, however, until the following century that we find, under the favourable influence of Henry VIII (himself an amateur composer)' any English composers of a distinction comparable with those of Flanders and Italy. The leading composers of this reign are John Taverner, Christopher Tye, Robert Whyte and Thomas Tallis, who, surviving into his eightieth year, became with William Byrd one of the founders of post-Reformation Church music.

The influence of the Flemish composers begins to appear in the music of Taverner and Tye, not only in matters of polyphonic technique, but in the use of popular melodies as the basis of sacred compositions. As Josquin des Près wrote Masses on "L'homme armé" and "Una masque de Biscaia," so Taverner and Tye each composed one upon the folk-song "Western Wind." Neither Taverner, in spite of his bold rhythms and the grand scale of his work, nor

Tye broke entirely free from the rigidity of the conservative English style. Even Tye's six-part Mass " Euge bone," usually considered his masterpiece, is not free from dryness, in spite of its fresh melodiousness and masterly construction. Indeed, Dr. Walker advances the opinion that Tye " (like other English composers of a later date) was artistically more inspired by words that gave some opportunity for emotional feeling than by the purely impersonal words of the Mass."

The music of Whyte and Tallis is free from the antique stiffness of the older men. In sheer technical facility Tallis is the equal of the greatest composers of his age, but even the famous forty-part motet for eight choirs of five parts each is something more than a *tour de force*, while his volume of " Cantiones Sacræ" contains masterpieces of a grandeur that makes them comparable with the finest compositions of the great Continentals. His majestic style is seen at its best in " O Sacrum Convivium," the most familiar of his motets, and " Audivi media nocte," while the noble expressiveness of his " Lamentations " makes them worthy of comparison with the Penitential Psalms of Lassus.

During the life-time of these composers there occurred an event that was to have a profound influence upon music in England, namely, the Reformation of the Church. In so far as music was concerned, the most important feature of the Reformation was the substitution of the vernacular for the Latin Liturgy. The simplification of Church music, decreed by the Reformers and summed up in Archbishop Cranmer's *dictum* " One syllable, one note," was incidental and was not, in fact, carried out to the letter. With characteristic complacency English composers quietly worked out a compromise that satisfied both the ecclesiastical authorities and their own artistic consciences. In fact Cranmer's ideal was precisely the same as that of the Council of Trent, which was simultaneously engaged in an investigation of the abuses in Roman Church music and ended likewise in compromise by accepting Palestrina. It is interesting to compare with events in England what happened north of the border, where John Knox ruthlessly swept away everything except psalm-singing in unison. From that day to this, apart from the settings of the metrical Psalms, there has been no Scottish Church music.

One rather surprising fact is the tolerance that was shown to heretical composers on both sides during the Reformation and the Counter-Reformation in the reign of Mary. John Merbecke, who hastily provided an admirable setting for the English services in the First Prayer Book of Edward VI, was permitted to retain his post at St. George's Chapel, Windsor, through the Marian reaction, while William Byrd, steadfast Catholic to the end, remained unmolested through Elizabeth's reign. Taverner seems to have been the only composer who lost his artistic soul as the result of these events. Repenting of his " Popish ditties," he sought in a fanatical Protestantism his possibly less important personal salvation.

This tolerance was fortunate for English music, since Byrd, one of its greatest ornaments, was born too late to have achieved his masterpieces under the Catholic régime. Tolerance, indeed, is too negative a word to describe the attitude of the Elizabethan authorities, since Byrd and Tallis were granted a patent, amounting to a monopoly, for the printing and selling of music and music-paper, English and foreign. In his turn Byrd showed compliance with the conditions of his time by supplying the English Church with the first great settings of its Services. But it is in his Masses and Latin motets that his genius is not unnaturally seen at its finest. He himself indicates the mystical attitude of his approach to the Roman rite in the preface to the "Gradualia" (1605), where he speaks of " a certain hidden power in the words themselves, so that as one meditates upon the sacred words and constantly and seriously considers them, the right notes, in some inexplicable fashion, suggest themselves quite spontaneously." It is hardly surprising that a temperament so essentially religious should have found difficulty in adjusting itself to the lighter style of the madrigal. Like Palestrina's, Byrd's secular music has a gravity not always wholly consonant with the texts. There are, indeed, one or two madrigals, of which " Though Amaryllis dance in green " is the most familiar, wherein he exhibits a gayer manner, but these are rare exceptions to the rule.

The introduction of the vernacular in the Church Service turned the attention of English musicians to their own language, and the importation from Italy of madrigals by Luca Marenzio and others gave them an example of the way to put the rich resources of our literary genius to musical use. England is the only country in which the madrigal became entirely naturalised and took on a distinctive character of its own. Compared with the hot-house sensuality of the Italian madrigals, the English have a fresh and vigorous air. Whether they were celebrating, in " The Triumphs of Oriana," the glories of Elizabeth or writing light love-songs or setting graver semi-philosophical poems, the composers were able to draw upon an inexhaustible fund of melody, and, while not lacking in science, their music is, at its best, spontaneous and free from artificiality. There is no pedantry in Byrd's elaborate cross-rhythms and his bold harmonic style, which led him to warn singers against the hasty emendation of supposed misprints, is as striking as the consistent tunefulness of all the parts in his music.

Thomas Morley is the most characteristically English of the madrigal-composers. His taste lay in the direction of cheerful subjects, which he treated with an exquisitely light touch. He was especially happy in using the ballet-form, which he himself describes as " a slight kind of music and as I take it devised to be danced to music." The ballet was of Italian origin and is distinguished from the madrigal by its quick dancing rhythm and fa-la-la refrain. Morley completely anglicised the form, and his ballets are among the most delightful things in the music of this period. His madrigals and canzonets, with their more elaborately contrapuntal style, however, contain Morley's finest music, and it should not be forgotten that he also composed some Church music, including the noble anthem, " Out of the deep," and a Burial Service, which Dr. Walker describes as "wonderfully serene, tender and strong." Altogether Morley, with his variety of achievement, his great rhythmical invention and his almost complete emancipation from modal influences, must be reckoned as one of the greatest composers of his time.

Out of the multitude of Elizabethan composers, to whom individual justice cannot here be done, two stand out as men of exceptional genius. Thomas Weelkes presents a contrast to Morley. His music is far closer to the Italian models, and his fondness for bold contrasts of mood expressed by means of chromatic progressions gives his music the same kind of passionate expressiveness that characterises the madrigals of Marenzio and Gesualdo. At the same time there is a certain antique quaintness in his style and, in spite of his harmonic inventiveness, he adheres more closely than most of his contemporaries to the modes. Like Morley, Weelkes wrote ballets, but his essays in this form are comparatively heavy-footed. John Wilbye is generally accorded the first place of all among the English madrigal-composers. He certainly combines the expressiveness of Weelkes with a smoother workmanship. He is equally successful in the light vein of such things as " Flora gave me fairest flowers " and " Lady, when I behold," in which he rivals the delicacy of Morley, and in the tender gravity of his more serious pieces, which need not fear comparison with the madrigals of Byrd himself.

We must pass by Bennet, Bateson, Tomkins and a dozen more, each of whom in an age less prolific of talent would have merited discussion. There remains one great figure, belonging to the next century and to the reign of James I, Orlando Gibbons, whose genius brings the long line of polyphonic composers to a glorious close. For, although of course polyphonic music continued to be written, the main stream of music began to flow into a different channel at the beginning of the 17th century. Even in the music of Gibbons himself there is already a change, not of method but of underlying mood. Dr. Colles acutely assimilates the distinction between Gibbons and the Elizabethans to that which we commonly make between the classical and romantic composers. "While Byrd, Morley and Weelkes can find their musical inspiration anywhere, Gibbons searches out words which reflect his own temperament." In a word, his attitude is subjective. The best of his Church music is contained in the anthems, where there is more scope for personal expression than in the setting of the ritual words of the Services. "Hosanna to the Son of David," "O clap your hands," and "Lift up your heads," to name three of the most famous examples, are texts suggestive both of physical movement and strong human emotion, and Gibbons set them to music that is essentially direct. These joyful anthems are not, however, as characteristic of the composer as "Behold, thou hast made my days as it were a span," for he was of a melancholy, introspective temperament. The poems he chose for his madrigals—Raleigh's "What is our life?" is typical—are without exception pessimistic, and the only humour that relieves them is the bitter one of satire. It is only necessary to compare with Arcadelt's most famous madrigal, "Il bianco e dolce cigno," with Gibbons's "The Silver Swan," likewise the most familiar of his compositions, to see how far he had moved both in words and music away from the voluptuousness of the Italian madrigal and towards a more philosophical standpoint. This poem ends with the couplet :

> *Farewell all joys, O death come close mine eyes*
> *More geese than swans now live, more fools than wise.*

It is in a double sense the swan-song of the polyphonists.

D. H.

# C: ENGLISH SONG

## CHAPTER I

# JOHN DOWLAND AND THE ELIZABETHANS

IT WAS POINTED OUT in the last part of this book that a cause of the sudden decline of polyphonic music in Italy was the search for a more dramatic mode of expression, which was discovered in the declamatory style of Monteverdi, and we have traced the gradual crystallisation of diatonic harmony, which gave to Monteverdi's declamation its distinctive character, in spite of lingering traces of the modes. Yet another influence towards the change that occurred at the beginning of the 17th century was the improvement of musical instruments. Although it is quite clear that both sacred and secular music had for a long time been accompanied by instruments of various kinds, these accompaniments were in no way independent. They merely supported the voices and may be described, in modern terminology, as being *ad libitum*. Towards the end of the 16th century we find an increasing tendency to use viols to support the voices in madrigal-singing, and it is quite clear that madrigals were sometimes sung by a solo voice accompanied by viols, which played the remaining parts. Byrd's third set of madrigals, published in 1611, is described on the title-page as being " fit for voyces or viols," from which one may infer that they could be treated as instrumental pieces.

It is not surprising, therefore, to find developing concurrently with the madrigal in England what we must call, in default of a better name, the art-song. Solo songs—folk-songs, ballads and so on—had, of course, been in existence all along, and had, as we have had occasion to observe, supplied composers with material for Masses as well as for madrigals. Indeed, if the latest researches of Mr. Arnold Dolmetsch are to be credited, we must antedate the conscious composition—as opposed to the traditional art of folk-music—of solo vocal music with instrumental accompaniment by many centuries. For Mr. Dolmetsch has at last succeeded in deciphering the early Welsh bardic music in the British Museum and shows that it consisted of a kind of rhapsodic recitative with a highly organised harmonic accompaniment for the harp. This discovery is in itself a warning against dogmatism about musical practice in the Dark Ages, for it was until now generally supposed that such an elaborate art could not then have existed. It is, however, too early even to speculate upon any possible connection between the bardic music of Wales (and Ireland ?) and the songs of the Elizabethan lutanists, the chief of whom may have been an Irishman.

John Dowland, " whose heavenly touch upon the lute doth ravish human sense," was one of the great virtuosos. He travelled about Europe singing his songs at the courts of kings and princes. In England he seems to have been without fame or honour, for he himself contrasts his " kingly entertainment in a forraine climate " with his inability to " attaine to any place at home." Indeed it was not until the present century that the music of this great song-writer became generally known through the researches of Barclay Squire, the Reverend E. H. Fellowes and Philip Heseltine. Dowland had been anticipated by Byrd in the composition of solo songs with instrumental accompaniment, such as the well known " My sweet little darling " for voice and viols, but he was the first composer to specialise in this form ; as Barclay Squire says, " the *Lieder* of Schubert are the lineal descendants of Dowland's Ayres with lute accompaniments."

Dowland's best songs—his early ones are somewhat square-cut in spite of their melodic charm—set at once the standard of agreement between " music and sweet poetry " (to quote once more from Barnfield's famous sonnet), which has been one of the chief virtues of English vocal music ever since. When Milton wrote of Henry Lawes :

> *Harry, whose tuneful and well-measured song*
> *First taught our English music how to span*
> *Words with just note and accent . . .*

he grossly abused the poet's licence to a measure of historical inaccuracy. The Elizabethans knew as much as and more than Lawes about the fitting of words to music. Dowland and his fellows—Morley, for example, in his settings of Shakespeare's songs—were solving in a characteristically English way the very problems which in Italy were consciously exercising the minds of Monteverdi and the other theorists. Dowland's songs have this in common with the madrigal, that they are free in rhythm. To cut his phrases up with regular bar-lines, as was done in some of the earlier modern editions, is to destroy their musical and poetic sense alike, while the transcription of the lute-part for the pianoforte—though some adjustment is necessary for technical reasons—has too often resulted in the substitution of commonplace for his original harmonic invention. Nothing is more remarkable than the ingenuity with which, like all great artists, he surmounts the limitations of his medium and indeed turns them to account. His songs are for the most part love-songs and his mood is usually sad. Indeed his music hardly bears out Fuller's description of him as " a cheerful person, passing his days in lawful merriment," and if we cannot accept as a description of his songs the " doleful ballad made to his mistress' eyebrow," there seems more truth in the punning reference, which heads one of his " Lachrymæ Pavans," *Semper Dowland, Semper Dolens.*

Dowland's melodies are always extraordinarily beautiful and often are derived from known folk-songs. There is, however, nothing consciously artificial in this connection between his songs and the music of the people, for that music was then a living thing, not an almost lost art, revived just before it was too late by enthusiastic collectors. There is, therefore, much difference between the modern, conscious use of folk-material and Dowland's natural and spontaneous resort to that inexhaustible source of melodic inspiration. As a recent writer has put it, one would not hear a London bus-conductor whistling the melodies of Vaughan Williams's "Hugh the Drover," but it is certain that Dowland did hear from some comparable source the melody of "Now, O now I needs must part." It is sometimes possible to hear one or two of his songs in the concert-hall—"Flow not so fast, you fountains" and "Dear, if you change" are usually chosen and are beautiful examples of his art—but, in spite of their publication, they remain neglected. Indeed there are lamentably few singers with sufficient sensitiveness to their literary and musical qualities to do them justice.

Dowland's example was copied by other composers, among whom Thomas Campian, the poet, was the most prolific. His songs are simpler than Dowland's and less elaborate in their accompaniments. Yet the best of his songs, among which "Follow your Saint" is one of the most familiar, are marked by the aptness of their settings and their poetic imagination. Philip Rosseter, Robert Jones, William Corkine and Thomas Ford, whose "Since first I saw your face" is among the most familiar of Elizabethan songs, are other composers who can here have no more notice than mention of their names.

## CHAPTER II

## STUART TIMES

UNHAPPILY neither Henry Lawes, the subject of Milton's eulogy, nor his contemporaries maintained the standard of excellence achieved by the song-writers of the previous generation. There was as serious a falling-off in the

quality of English music during the reign of Charles I
and the Commonwealth as there was in contemporary
Italy, where none of the followers of Monteverdi was able
to achieve in the new *stile rappresentativo* anything of lasting
merit. In England much the same process was taking place
as in Italy, though the actual change was more gradual
and its causes different. Whereas in Italy the new music
was the outcome of a theory put into practice, an intellectual movement, in England it was the natural result of
musical conditions. The most fashionable form of musical
entertainment was the Masque, which had already taken its
place, in a small way, in the last of Shakespeare's plays, "The
Tempest." The Jacobean and Caroline masques involved
a large number of singers, dancers and instrumentalists,
most of whom were amateurs. It will be readily understood
that, in order to keep the singing and dancing in time with
the orchestra, which was apparently not so closely in touch
with the performers on the stage as it is in a modern
theatre, a more regularly rhythmic music than the free
madrigalian style, where accents fell at uneven intervals
according to the sense of the words, was absolutely necessary. It was inevitable, therefore, that the music of the
masques should be in square-cut rhythms derived largely
from dance-music, which is by nature regularly accented.
The bar-line, hitherto used in vocal music only to aid the
eye of the performer, becomes henceforth an important
factor in the structure of all music. Added to this influence of
practical conditions is the fact that diatonic melodies,
which had by now almost completely supplanted the
modes, seem to predicate a regular rhythmic pulse.

The fact that Henry Lawes is the most distinguished
composer of the Caroline and Cromwellian periods is,
despite Milton's eulogy, a measure rather of the decline
in musical standards than of his greatness. His music is
dullest when he is most concerned with the fitting of "just
note and accent," which meant that he was attempting
to translate into music the rhythm of a poet's reading
of his verse. When he forgets about the problems of

declamation, his music is often charming. These two aspects
are exemplified in the music for Milton's "Comus,"
which is the most familiar of his compositions.

The rule of the Puritans had important reactions upon
music. In the churches the organs were silenced and the
choirs banished. Yet in spite of this severity and the dis-
approval of dancing, music was given an unexpected
stimulus under the Commonwealth. Cromwell and some
of the other leading men were fond of music, and when
the theatres were closed an exception was made in favour of
performances with music. In consequence of this dispens-
ation, the enterprising Poet Laureate, William D'Avenant,
offered to the public, starved of recreation, an "Entertainment by Declamations and Musick," which was introduced by a prologue beginning :

> *Think this your passage, and the narrow way*
> *To our Elysian field, the Opera.*

From this cautious beginning of "declamations and music,"
D'Avenant succeeded in developing a genuine English
opera.

With the restoration of the monarchy, music returned
to the Church. Old part-books were brought out and
new choristers were trained. But the tradition of Church
music had been broken, and, though it might have been
restored, tastes had changed. King Charles II set the fashion
for the new French style of music, in which violins,
hitherto unknown in England and, in the opinion of John
Evelyn, more suited to the tavern than the church, played
an important part. What Charles liked was a good jigging
rhythm to which he could beat time, and this was provided
in the instrumental *ritornelli* that were introduced between
the sections of the anthems. These passages were completely
secular in style and rarely bore any relation to the musical
or to the literary material of the composition as a whole.
They may be likened to the cherubs, growing every year
more and more like Cupids, with which the interiors of
churches were being decorated at this time. After the

anxieties of the Civil War and the repression of the Commonwealth, England wanted to be amused, not edified, and
readily fell in with the tastes of the " merry " King.

## CHAPTER III

## PURCELL

THE NATURE OF THE WORLD into which he was born
and the conditions under which he had to work explain
how it is that Henry Purcell, who had as much natural
genius as any composer of any other period, failed to attain
a place among the great classics alongside Bach and
Handel, Haydn and Mozart. In instinctive musicianship
and fertility of invention, as well as in the brevity of his
career, it is with Mozart that Purcell is most nearly comparable. Had he lived in the later age, when the opera,
the oratorio and the symphony were in process of formation
or already established, there is little doubt that Purcell
would have added to the common musical wealth masterpieces to become as familiar as " Messiah," " Figaro "
or the " Jupiter " Symphony. As it is, his music is for the
most part buried in forms that are difficult (and some of
them impossible) to rehabilitate under modern conditions.
With one or two exceptions—for example the magnificent
Coronation Anthem, " My Heart is inditing," in which is
embodied all the dignity of a great ceremonial occasion—
his choral works are hardly suitable for the large choirs
of to-day, though that is no reason why they should be
unaccountably neglected by smaller bodies. The B.B.C.
might well devote to the resuscitation of Purcell's choral
music the same energy that it has so rightly directed to the
cantatas of J. S. Bach. His dramatic music, which is
dealt with in another part of this volume, is for the most
part embedded in plays that an ordinary audience would

find insufferably dull, or in recensions of Shakespeare
that would offend the pedantic purism of modern taste
with its exaggerated respect for the antique. His songs,
again, demand for their adequate performance great technical skill and intelligence, and yet a lack of sophistication
and all those professional artifices of singing rightly applied
to the interpretation of the later classics. So, like Dowland,
Purcell is discreetly omitted from the programmes of most
song recitals.

Of Purcell's sacred music, the most famous examples,
beside the Coronation Anthem already mentioned, are
" Rejoice in the Lord " (the so-called Bell Anthem), the
setting of the Psalm, " Jehovah, quam multi sunt hostes,"
and the " Te Deum and Jubilate " in D, which are of
Festival dimensions and were, indeed, performed at the early
meetings of the Three Choirs until they were ousted by
" Handel's superior knowledge and use of instruments."
In addition to these we must mention the " Evening Hymn "
for treble voice, whose sheer beauty has ensured its popularity, along with " Dido's Lament," among such singers as
pay any attention to Purcell at all, and the dramatic setting
of the scene between Saul and the Witch of Endor, which
is a miniature oratorio. His secular choral works include
a number of " Welcome Odes," which celebrate the return
to Town of the several sovereigns whom he served. The
sycophantic words of these odes would arouse amusement
in a modern audience, and it is hardly surprising that sometimes the music is perfunctory. Far more distinguished are the
" Odes for St. Cecilia's Day " and, although the baroque
adornments of the poems might likewise raise a smile,
the sincerity and beauty of these hymns in praise of his
art lift them above such incidentals. Of these the finest is
" Hail bright Cecilia," written in 1692. The songs for one
or more voices, which range from dramatic scenas, like
" Mad Bess," to rounds and catches, are innumerable
and testify to Purcell's unlimited fund of melodic invention
in which he is rivalled only by Schubert, and his exact
sense of the setting to music of English words, which has

served as a model to our composers, with one or two notable exceptions, ever since.

If the claim for Purcell's potential greatness in a later age seems exaggerated, let it be remembered that he, almost first of composers, shows an instinctive sense of key-relationship, which is the basis of sonata-form, that his feeling for dramatic expression in music was equal to that of the greatest operatic composers, and that his fertility and variety of invention were unfailing. It may be that he was too ready to fall in with the conditions of his time, but, even had he been less complacent, it is difficult to see how he could have created music that would take its place in our theatres and concert-halls to-day, without the instruments, the artists or the forms ready to hand. To have created the forms would alone have been a stupendous task, unparalleled in the history of art, and to have done so would have been to write music which could not have been performed in his own age. It is not until modern times that composers have claimed to compose for the benefit of posterity.

## CHAPTER IV

# FROM PURCELL TO WESLEY

Among Purcell's contemporaries the outstanding composers were John Blow and Matthew Locke, both older men, from whom he learnt his art. Blow preceded Purcell as organist of Westminster Abbey and resumed the post when his great pupil died in 1795. He deserves to be ranked among the great English Church-composers, for his music, though not free from the mannerisms of the period, has real nobility and power. His best-known anthems are " I beheld and lo " and " I was in the spirit," but, as Dr. Walker says, they are " far from representing him at his best, clean and stately though they are." At his best he was capable of a striking originality and of real expressiveness. Locke is known to modern audiences through the noble " Music for the King's Sackbuts and Cornets " (performed nowadays by trombones and trumpets), which was written for the progress of Charles II through London for his coronation. His vocal music includes a setting of Shirley's " Masque of Cupid and Death," a pretty work that has been successfully revived in recent years, and the fine anthem, " Lord let me know mine end."

Of the younger men, William Croft, who succeeded Blow at Westminster Abbey, has rightly retained his place in our cathedrals, while his Burial Service has become an integral part of the Anglican ritual on almost all great occasions of mourning. It has the directness, the severity and the complete freedom from any sentimentality which make it ideal for its purpose.

In the next generation English music was dominated by the figure of Handel, his Italian operas and his English oratorios. So powerful a personality coupled with a dearth of native genius makes the history of English music in the 18th century comparatively insignificant. Only in the Church was a steady tradition maintained by men like Maurice Greene and William Boyce, who between them incidentally saved from oblivion a great quantity of the older music, though not without a certain amount of damaging editorial emendation, in the three-volume publication, " Cathedral Music," which contains examples of all the chief English composers from Tallis to Blow.

Among the secular composers of the Handelian era, the most popular and famous was Thomas Augustine Arne, who composed chiefly for the theatre, his most notable achievements being the classic settings of the songs in " The Tempest " and "As you like it," some of which, in particular "Where the Bee sucks," have never been surpassed. Apart from these occasional gems, however, Arne produced nothing but a vast quantity of ephemeral music that won him great favour with the public.

The most important musical event of this period was the establishment in 1724 of the Three Choirs Festival, to raise funds for educating the children of the poorer clergy in the dioceses of Gloucester, Worcester and Hereford. Apart from its charitable object, this Festival, which became the precursor of many others in various provincial centres, has had an influence that can hardly be overestimated upon the development of choral music in England during the past two hundred years. Among the conductors at the early meetings was Boyce, who composed various works for performance on these occasions. But the Festival soon came to be dominated, like all other musical activities in England, by the works of Handel. It was not until the latter part of the 19th century that the opportunities provided by the Festival were turned to good account in the service of English music. Then the names of Parry, Sullivan and Elgar appeared in turn to prove the utility for artistic purposes of a regular and established organisation for music-making on a large scale.

These days were, however, far ahead, and, in view of the desert which confronts the musical historian during the reigns of the later Georges, it is hardly surprising that the public should have maintained their devotion to the palpably great music of Handel. It was for the Church still that the best music was being written. Jonathan Battishill worthily bridges the gap between Boyce and the next composer with pretensions to greatness, Samuel Wesley. The son of the hymn-writer and nephew of the founder of Methodism, Wesley was the foremost English organist of his day. In spite of his antecedents he seems to have had leanings towards Rome, even if he did not join that Church, for his works include several Masses and services from the Roman liturgy, as well as anthems and services for the English Church. Although his setting of the Psalm, " In exitu Israel," is still sometimes to be heard in our cathedrals, Wesley's fame has been eclipsed by that of his natural son, Samuel Sebastian, organist in turn of Winchester and Gloucester Cathedrals, and the greatest Church-musician of the 19th century. His anthems—"Ascribe unto the Lord" is a familiar example—surpass anything achieved by men like Thomas Attwood and William Walmisley, who had made distinguished contributions to Church music in the preceding generation. If the later Georgian era was barren, producing nothing (apart from dull imitations of Handel) better than the once popular ballads of Charles Dibdin and Thomas Shields, which were supplanted in the public favour by the pretty songs of Sir Henry Bishop, the first half of Victoria's reign presents a hardly less depressing spectacle of subservience to the worst in Mendelssohn. William Sterndale Bennett had, indeed, talent, but it failed to mature. Among the rest—men like Henry Smart, John Goss, John Stainer and Joseph Barnby—S. S. Wesley stands like a solid rock, the only firm thing amid the gushing waters of a debased sentimentality.

D. H.

# D: FOLK-SONG

## CHAPTER I

## THE BRITISH ISLES

THE TERM "FOLK-SONG" connotes the melodies sung by the peasant class in any country. These melodies are a spontaneous expression of the musical feeling of the people. The tunes are anonymous and traditional, and in any region there will be found groups of songs conforming to a pattern as well as variants of individual melodies, since the songs have been preserved by oral tradition, not fixed by publication. Yet such is the strength of oral tradition among an illiterate people and a naturally conservative class that Cecil Sharp found songs and dances in the Appalachian Mountains of America differing hardly at all from those persisting in England, despite the lapse of several centuries since the ancestors of the present inhabitants left England. Indeed, according to Sharp, the traditions have been preserved more strictly in those remote places than in their native land, where contacts with modern developments are more easy. Although it is still possible to find in England villages where some of the inhabitants have never been in a train nor gone further afield than their own feet or a horse could take them, the motor-omnibus is rapidly abolishing such isolation, and the ubiquitous wireless and gramophone are bringing symphony and fox-trot without discrimination into every cottage. Folk-music, spontaneously created, is, at any rate in England, a thing of the past, superseded by the popular music of the cinema and the dance-hall written according to stereotyped patterns, just as smock and kerchief have been superseded by town-made shirt and

trousers. Even its spontaneous performance is rare. It belongs
now to the antiquities—a thing to be revived, to be preserved
by societies, to be discussed at meetings of connoisseurs.

Some of the songs that have survived are of great anti
quity, as is evident both from the modal character of the
music and from the words, which have often become so
corrupt as to lose their meaning. The numerical songs
constructed on the " House that Jack built " principle
seem to have been educational, designed to inculcate the
elements of theology and so on. " I will sing you one, oh ! "
and " The partridge in a pear-tree " are familiar example
of these cumulative songs, in which the words have so far
been corrupted by oral transmission, the child imitating
incorrectly the sounds made by his father, that only expert
philologists can hope to unravel their meaning with the
aid of versions existing in other countries.

English folk-song generally is characterised by directness
and simplicity, healthy jollity and contented humour. The
music is free from excessive ornament and eccentricities of
rhythm. The subjects of the songs are usually the homely
ones of the countryside—hunting, poaching, the employ
ments of agriculture and, of course, love-making, which is
expressed with tenderness rather than passion. Other
songs deal with the pathetic subjects of youth cut off in its
flower and of maidens deserted by false lovers. In these songs
there is often a peculiar eeriness that may be accounted
among the most remarkable characteristics of English
folk-song. Events of national or local importance are also
commemorated in ballads (e.g. " Lord Rendal," which
seems to refer to the belief that the " Young King,"
Henry II's son, was poisoned, and " The Wraggle Taggle
Gypsies," which records the elopement of Lady Cassilis)
and the frequent references to murders and hangings show
that the popular Press of to-day caters for a long-ingrained
interest in such matters. In form the majority of these songs
conform to the A–A–B–A design—a statement repeated
twice, a contrasting phrase and a return to the original
theme. Even before the revival of interest in folk-song

created by the enthusiasm of the Rev. John Broadwood
and his niece Miss Lucy Broadwood, the Rev. S. Baring-
Gould, Dr. Fuller-Maitland and, more recently and most
thoroughly by Cecil Sharp, a great many traditional
melodies had been preserved in collections like the " Fitzwilliam Virginal Book," and Playford's "Dancing Master"
and in " The Beggar's Opera."

The folk-songs of Scotland, Ireland and Wales have each
a distinctive character, though they are related to one
another by their common Celtic origin. In contrast with
the songs of England, those of the Scottish Highlands are
wild and irregular in rhythm. The older specimens are
rhapsodical recitatives rather than songs and show little
or no attempt at rhythm or formal shape. Of the Lowland
music there is no record before the 17th century, though it
is probable that some of the melodies then written down
are of a much earlier date. A few of them are written in
a scale of five notes such as is used by the bagpipes. It may
be mentioned that the " Scotch Snap," which consists of a
semiquaver followed by a dotted quaver, is not a general
characteristic of Scottish music, but is confined to certain
dance-rhythms, such as the Strathspey Reel, though it
appears occasionally in songs based upon these dance-tunes,
e.g. " Green grow the rashes." The snap was incorporated
in the common musical language of Europe by Italian
composers of the 18th century, and was much used both
by Beethoven, who seems to have regarded it as the
characteristic of all Scottish music, and by Mendelssohn.

The music of Ireland is more melodious than that of
Scotland and either more plaintive or more light-hearted
than that of England. Few countries can boast anything more
beautiful than the long melody known as "The Londonderry
Air " and sometimes called " Emer's Farewell to Cuchul-
ain." For the preservation of a vast quantity of Irish
music we have to thank Thomas Moore, who collaborated
in the publication of seven volumes of songs for which he
wrote the words, as Robert Burns did for many melodies
of Scotland.

In view of the long tradition of music in Wales and the natural beauty of Welsh voices, we should expect to find there an exceptionally rich treasure of folk-music. But Welsh music is on the whole disappointing. There are a few fine melodies, but they are exceptions, and artistically the Welsh songs are less interesting than those of other parts of the British Isles. The popular "March of the Men of Harlech" is quite characteristic of Welsh melody, both in its lack of subtlety and in the stirring effect of the tune as a whole. This tune contains in its final phrase an example of the "Scotch snap," to which reference has been made above.

## CHAPTER II

# EUROPE

WHEN WE CROSS the Channel to France we find a folk music with more artifice in it. It seems almost as if the pastorals of Watteau were true representations of French peasantry and not mere courtly affectations, even if they have not the authenticity of Morland's English scenes. The graceful and charming *chansons* have wit and polish. There are, of course, other styles, as is only to be expected of a nation containing peoples so diverse as the Provençals the Bretons[1] and the Gascons. There are serene songs like the beautiful "Angelus" collected by M. Bourgault-Ducoudray in Brittany, which might be the musical counterpart of Millet's famous picture—a work quite wrongly despised by certain connoisseurs on account of its popularity. There are, too, simple, unaffected songs from Normandy

---

[1] I remember once being struck "all of a heap" on hearing Paul Ladmirault's arrangements of some "Chansons de Haut-Bretagne. In modality, as well as in atmosphere, they were of the closest kinship with some Welsh folk-songs I had heard shortly before. The common origin parallels interestingly the facts about the Appalachian melodies mentioned in the last chapter.—Ed.

and delightful children's songs and lullabies from the South.

The Italians, too, show much variety in their folk-songs, ranging from the barcarolles of the Venetian gondoliers, and the street-songs of Naples, which have furnished the models for a hundred popular operatic airs, to the music of Sicily, where there are still to be found traces of the old Hellenic civilisation, besides the influences of other races that have from time to time established themselves in that much occupied island. The folk-songs of modern Greece seem to have no connection with the ancient culture, but are of Byzantine and liturgical origin.

In Spain the influence of foreign culture is even more obvious. The *Cante hondo* of Andalusia, with its narrow compass and reiterations of short phrases, is clearly a relic of the Moorish occupation, though its Oriental character lies rather in the manner of its performance than in the melodic material. As a whole the folk-music of Spain, in contradistinction to that of Italy, is instrumental and rhythmical rather than vocal. It is essentially music to be danced to, and singing plays a subsidiary part. A false notion of Spanish music has been widely disseminated through the use of a few well-worn *clichés* by European composers in search of exotic ornaments with which to deck out their trite ideas. But in recent years this notion has been corrected by the music of men like de Falla, Granados and Albeniz, who have shown, especially the first-named, that Spanish music is not a pretty affair of a high comb and a shawl to be donned at will, but something harsh, cruel and passionate.

Apart from their fondness for reiterated phrases, there is little in common between the Spaniards and the Russians. Yet Russian composers have been, after the French, the most prolific writers of " Spanish " rhapsodies, possibly owing to a nostalgia for a warmer climate. Russia is enormously rich in folk-music, and, owing to the peculiarly backward condition of her musical culture in the 19th century, her composers were able to turn that wealth to good account in a way that could not be achieved (though

it has been attempted) in a more advanced country like
our own. One characteristic of Russian folk-song is its
frequent use of uneven measures (five beats in the bar), a
feature conditioned by the peculiarities of the language,
which inevitably has an enormous influence upon the folk-
songs of any country. The popular vogue of Russian music
twenty years ago was due, like the similar vogue of Spanish
music, to its strange and exotic character, but it was not
long before the short phrases repeated again and again,
and the halting rhythms, at first so exciting, began to pall
upon our ears and made us once more realise that there
was, after all, some merit in continuity and shapeliness.

The music of Czecho-Slovakia and of Hungary has
attractions and limitations similar to that of Russia, though
each, and especially the Hungarian, has a very distinctive
character of its own. Hungarian music, which is not to be
confused with the Gypsy-music that has so often passed
for it, is, indeed, as distinct from other European music as
the Magyar language is philologically unrelated to any
others except those of Finland and Turkey. It may be worth
recording that before I was aware of this fact I was struck
by a resemblance between Kodály's " Psalmus Hungaricus "
and the music of Sibelius—a resemblance which certainly
could not be defined on paper but which seemed none the
less striking. True Hungarian music is so much conditioned
by the language that it is exceedingly difficult, even with
the help of Bela Bartok's elaborate treatise, for one who
does not understand the language to grasp its significance.
It is strongly rhythmical and, like the Spanish, essentially
dance-music. For the characteristics of Czech folk-music the
reader may be referred to the familiar works of Dvořák
and to Smetana's opera, " The Bartered Bride."

There remain the Germanic peoples, whose folk-songs
are of an intimate and homely kind. They are sentimental
but vigorous, and, in spite of their simplicity, highly
organised and compact. It is, indeed, but a step from the
folk-song to the art-song or *lied* of the great composers. It
is quite impossible, for instance, to detect, except by

external evidence, which of Brahms's strophic songs are based upon traditional melodies and which are entirely his own invention. Indeed, the whole of German music from Bach down to Mahler is intimately based upon the idioms of national melody. The reader need, perhaps, hardly be reminded that Haydn, consciously or not, made frequent use of Croatian folk-melodies in his compositions.

## CHAPTER III

## CAROLS

AKIN TO FOLK-SONGS are the carols, which are religious folk-songs celebrating the chief festivals of the Church, but especially connected with the season of Christmas. Many of the finest English examples, however, are not Christmas carols, even though some of them have in recent times become associated with that season. The commonplace words of " Good King Wenceslas " were fitted by a worthy clergyman of the last century to the beautiful melody of the spring carol, " Adest tempus floridum " (" Now the time of flowers is here "), which is at least 350 years old. And among the finest is the lovely " Corpus Christi Carol," which attains a mystical beauty and an eeriness unsurpassed in any other music. Another carol connected with the same festival is the "Coventry Carol," which was sung at the Coventry Nativity Play on Corpus Christi Day. Many of the Christmas carols celebrate the secular side of the festival. Such are " The Boar's Head Carol," which is still sung annually at Queen's College, Oxford, as the boar's head is carried in solemn procession into Hall on Christmas Day, and the Wassail-songs, which date from pre-Norman and very possibly from pre-Christian days.

Among other nations the French are most rich in carols

Oc

or " Noels," and one of the earliest is the Norman melody, which survives in " Hymns Ancient and Modern " with the words " Soldiers, who are Christ's below." Many of the " Noels " have what were originally secular melodies, and we need not be shocked at the discovery that the tune of the rollicking Drinking Song in "The Beggar's Opera" belongs to a "Noel," for Pepusch was only putting the tune to its original purpose. A far less suitable adaptation is that of the joyous Christmas hymn " Freuet euch ihr Christen alle " to the doleful Lenten " Forty days and forty nights." English hymnody has, indeed, borrowed freely from the carols and Christmas chorals of Germany, whose Church music is rich in noble melodies suitable for congregational singing.

D. H.

# E: ORATORIO AND OTHER CHORAL MUSIC

## CHAPTER I

## ORIGINS

THE VERY NAME OF ORATORIO commemorates the popularisation rather than the invention of a form. Throughout the fourteenth and fifteenth centuries there were frequently performed musical settings of incidents from the Old and New Testaments, deriving in all probability from the old mystery plays. But it was St. Philip Neri, the founder of the congregation of Oratorians, who first laid special stress on the advantages of such pieces for instructional and devotional purposes, introducing them before or after the sermon in the Oratory of his own church in Rome. Hence the title that became attached to them. These performances proved so popular that they were not discontinued after his death in 1595. On the contrary, his successor, Emilio del Cavalieri, developed them with enthusiasm, for his performances seem to have been more elaborate in every way than St. Philip's. We know that in the most famous of his works, an allegorical piece called " The Representatives of the Soul and the Body," there were not only soloists, a chorus and an orchestra hidden in the manner subsequently practised at Bayreuth, but elaborate dresses and a ballet.

Perhaps it is not mere coincidence that this definitely dramatic form of Oratorio, as distinct from the hortatory kind, coincided almost exactly with the invention of Opera in Florence. As a matter of fact the Oratorio form, so far as Italy was concerned, must, generally speaking, be considered to possess a dramatic rather than a reflective nature. When the subject had no dramatic character, or at any rate was entirely unsuited to performance in action, it was called a Cantata. Composers like Carissimi, and his even greater successor Alessandro Scarlatti, practised both forms with equal success. Scarlatti, indeed, one of the greatest composers in the whole history of music, wrote oratorios that are practically indistinguishable from operas ; and this is true of Italian Oratorio as a whole up to comparatively modern times, till, when we come to a work like Rossini's " Mosè in Egitto " (1818), it is difficult to say which label should more appropriately be attached. Midway, so to say, between the Oratorio and the sacred Cantata came the Passions, which represented, without action but with definite dramatic feeling, the final scenes in the life of Our Lord. The Cantatas, written in the first instance for a solo voice, could of course equally well be secular or sacred in character. Indeed, it was Carissimi who first perceived the possibility of adapting the form to church requirements. Later, Scarlatti wrote no less than five hundred chamber cantatas of various kinds, and they represent, if not better work than is to be found in his operas, work superior to anything that he wrote for the church or for instruments alone.

Such were the pillars on which the great vocal edifices of Bach, Handel and their successors were to be raised during the eighteenth century. Inevitably there were also subsidiary pillars, such as the music of Schutz in Germany, but the foundations of Oratorio and Cantata alike were laid in Italy. The Passions on the other hand cannot claim an exclusively Italian origin, for they seem to have been more or less the legitimate descendants of the mystery plays, which were, of course, found all over Europe in mediæval times.

## CHAPTER II

# JOHANN SEBASTIAN BACH

IT IS IMPOSSIBLE, in the space at our disposal, to do much more than indicate the characteristics and the range of J. S. Bach's achievements in the domain of vocal music. Generally speaking he may be defined as the great, the greatest, exponent of the reflective forms, just as Handel was *par excellence* the exponent of the dramatic. A tendency to institute comparisons between Bach and Handel is perhaps inevitable owing to the accident that they lived at the same time. It is none the less regrettable, because, alike in their music and their lives, no two men could have been more dissimilar. Religion was the mainspring of Bach's every important musical activity ; Handel, pious and upright though he was, was essentially a man of the world. Bach approached music via the organ-loft, Handel, generally speaking, via the theatre. Bach, despite an undoubted interest in certain works by his foreign contemporaries, remained in essence wholly German ; Handel was the very embodiment of cosmopolitanism. The only real connection between the two lies in the fact that they were both supreme masters of two different facets of the art of music. The assignment of superiority to one rather than the other is probably more a matter of musical fashion and the idiosyncrasies of personal taste than anything else.

Bach, like Handel, wrote oratorios, it is true, but they were always oratorios of a reflective, not of a dramatic, nature. The best known of these is the " Christmas " Oratorio, in reality rather a collection of cantata-numbers than an oratorio in the narrow sense of the word. Indeed, Bach here definitely made use of four numbers of an early cantata called " A Musical Drama in Honour of the Queen," and six others from another cantata called " The Choice of Hercules." This fact is of importance and interest because it illustrates to perfection, first, the essentially craftsmanlike attitude of the early eighteenth-century composer, who would never willingly sacrifice any material that could usefully be saved ; second, the then shadowy line of that distinction between sacred and profane music which used, at any rate, to be so popular in England. How many music-lovers would have known that some of this apparently devout music was originally written to illustrate the dilemma of a Greek demi-god or to celebrate the glories of a queen of a German kingdom? In this case, as in so many others, the matter is merely one of verbal association, the character of the music itself being hardly, if at all, affected. On the other hand it is only fair to state that Spitta, Bach's great biographer, is of opinion that all Bach's music, however secular the words it sets, remains essentially religious, partly owing to the nature of the man himself, partly owing to the fact that, fundamentally, he always thought in terms of the organ.

The majority of Bach's vocal output consists, in fact, of Church Cantatas, though in this form, too, in addition to the two already indicated, he wrote several secular works such as the " Peasant " Cantata and the " Coffee " Cantata, agreeable but comparatively unimportant compositions. In the Church Cantatas, on the other hand, we find the very life-blood of Bach's especial genius. He probably wrote some two hundred and ninety of these, though only a little more than two hundred now survive, one for every appropriate occasion in the ecclesiastical year.

The principal difference between Bach's Church Cantatas and their Italian prototypes, apart from any question of personal characteristics, is in the important part played by the Chorales, which were, of course, typically German and Protestant institutions, and of which some of the best, such as " Nun danket alle Gott " and " O Haupt voll Blut und Wunden," have passed into our own hymn-book.

Though, however, what may perhaps be defined as a typical cantata consisted of recitatives, arias, duets and choruses, some of them are written on a different plan, occasionally even for solo voice only. Inevitably, in such a mass of material, some of the cantatas are not so interesting as others, but it may be doubted whether any musician has ever produced anything more remarkable than the collection as a whole.

Generally speaking, the best cantatas belong to the last twenty years of Bach's life, though he wrote some beautiful specimens during, and even before, the Leipzig Period. But it is among the later cantatas, when he had perfected his consummate technique and had entirely assimilated in his own personality all the traditions of his predecessors, that we find most of the works that remain household words to-day. For instance, the splendid " Wachet auf " and " Ein' feste Burg " belong to this period. It is not a mere matter of coincidence, perhaps, that of all the cantatas, they are, in their earnestness and solidity, two of the most thoroughly Teutonic in style and feeling.

Though the cantatas represent the bulk of Bach's vocal output, and though it is impossible, without some knowledge of them, truly to appreciate his characteristics as a composer, what are usually admitted to be his two supreme masterpieces stand outside them. These are the " Passion according to St. Matthew " and the " Mass in B Minor."

Bach had written Passion music before, notably the " St. John Passion" which still survives, but the " St. Matthew Passion," beyond question the greatest of them, consisting, as it does, of twenty-four scenes, with double choruses, choruses, chorales, recitatives, arias and concerted numbers, will be seen to be planned on an exceptionally grand scale. Yet the main outline of the structure is exceedingly simple, and the composer has contrived with complete success to achieve that balance between the reflective and the dramatic indispensable in this kind of form. Though the definitely dramatic stress is more pronounced here than is customary in Bach's music, the general effect of the whole is unquestionably devotional. Sir Hubert Parry has indeed rightly described it as " the richest and noblest example of devotional music in existence." Possibly, from another point of view, its comparative romanticism should be emphasised ; nowhere are the personal piety of the composer or his pictorial sense so obvious as in this stupendous masterpiece.

There are many musicians who regard the B Minor Mass not only as the greatest of Bach's compositions but actually as the greatest of all compositions. If an attempt to classify music in this matter is ever permissible the Mass would certainly seem to be one of the few possible candidates. Though in a sense hardly so personal, perhaps, as the " St. Matthew Passion," it represents to perfection, as music pure and simple, Bach's peculiar attributes in their most striking form. It may seem curious to the reader that so convinced a Protestant as Bach should have set the Catholic Mass to music at all. Doubtless, in the first instance, the composition and the despatch of the original two numbers, the *Kyrie* and *Gloria*, to the Roman Catholic Elector of Saxony were due to strictly practical motives. Doubtless the Mass was never even intended to be performed as a whole in a Catholic church, as were some of the small previous Masses written by the composer. But the fact remains that in the gradual completion of the work, whether by fresh composition or by the adaptation of numbers already written, Bach achieved a universality of outlook rare, if not unique. The actual setting of Latin and not German words may have had something to do with this, for it has been pointed out with justice that his previous setting of the Latin *Magnificat* is the least Teutonic of all his works. Possibly, however, the cause lies deeper. Bach, we know, took a definite interest in theology, and he may well have desired to emphasise his claim to be regarded as a Christian belonging to the Church Catholic in the widest sense of the term. To this he devoted all his unparalleled resources of polyphony and expressiveness, so that the Mass, alike in its choruses and its solos, remains perhaps the most impressive statement of religious faith in existence. The best possible tribute to its universal appeal may be found in the fact that both Roman Catholics and Protestants have found in it an ideal interpretation of their particular attitude towards the mysteries of the universe.

A few words may usefully be written here about Bach's technical treatment of the human voice. It must be remembered that he never at any time wrote for skilled singers in the professional sense, because such singers at that time in Germany were only to be found in the opera-houses. Moreover, to be frank, his writing for the voice nearly always betrays an instrumental bias, the influence of the organ remaining paramount. For this reason the ornamentation of his vocal parts, of which there is a great deal, often seems tortuous and awkward, the reverse of grateful to a singer. Any student of Bach will have noticed that a line or even a word in his text often suggests a particular musical idea. The vocal patterns and the ornamentation grafted upon them always reflect Bach's striving for this kind of expressiveness, and must be treated accordingly. The singer whether as soloist or member of the chorus, should never regard his *fioritura* as essays in vocalisation in the manner of Handel or Purcell. Little of it, perhaps, is to be commended as a model of writing for the human voice, but, performed with conviction and skill, it achieves exceptionally moving effects of musical expression.

## CHAPTER III

# HANDEL

THOUGH the fundamental divergences between Bach and Handel have already been noted, they can hardly be too frequently stressed. For the purposes of this Book we are not concerned with Handel as a composer of opera, the capacity in which he was best known to the world at large and which, indeed, must be regarded as the very foundation of his musical activities. Nor are we concerned with his concertos and other instrumental compositions, though here, as a matter of fact, a certain comparison between him and Bach is perhaps legitimate. But in the domain of vocal music nothing could well have been more dissimilar than the work of the two great musical giants of the early eighteenth century. This is shown even in the forms that each respectively favoured, for whereas the oratorios of Bach must be regarded as by-products, Handel's sum up (operas apart) practically the whole of his most important contribution to vocal music. Though he wrote two Passions, some Italian cantatas, a little Latin and much English Church music, mostly anthems, the English oratorios of Handel remain imperishable monuments to the greatest exponent of the art of writing for the human voice who ever lived.

Handel's preoccupation with this particular form may be said to have been due to sheer accident. His career was full of such accidents. When he first came from Italy to England he came as a composer of Italian Opera. And it was as a composer of Italian Opera that he was known for many years. When, living in the service of the Duke of Chandos at Cannons, he wrote the music to a masque by Pope entitled " Haman and Mordecai " he never dreamed that twelve years later, under the title of " Esther," this would become the first English oratorio, owing to the refusal of the Bishop of London to allow a biblical subject to be produced on the stage with scenery, costumes and action. Yet so it was, and nothing could better illustrate the dramatic origin of a style of composition that was to prove itself particularly dear to the English temperament.

Even in Handel's lifetime the oratorios had such a success that one or more of them became a regular feature at his theatre during Lent, when operatic performances were forbidden. For practical purposes we can include the purely secular works, such as " Acis and Galatea," " Alexander's

Feast " and " Semele " under the general heading of Oratorio, though it is, of course, actually inaccurate so to do.

It will be seen from this brief recapitulation that in essence Handel's English oratorios were direct descendants from the original Italian model, though with considerable adaptations to suit the changed environment, especially in respect of the greater importance attached to the chorus. Indeed, one of the first of them, the Serenata " Acis and Galatea," originally written about the same time as " Haman and Mordecai " for the Duke of Chandos, was a new treatment of a subject that he had already handled in his Italian days. Moreover, what may be called the epic tradition, characteristic of Carissimi's oratorios, rather than the purely dramatic tradition, was perpetuated in Handel. The fact that in recent years " Messiah " has become much the best known and is the most frequently performed of all his works has tended to make people forget that it is unique among his oratorios in being of a specifically reflective nature.

The range covered by Handel's oratorios is so immense that little more can be done than give a general indication of them. " Messiah " is so familiar that it is perhaps unnecessary to write anything about it. A word of warning, however, may not be amiss. Owing to an unfortunate tradition grown up in this country this great work, one of the masterpieces of the world, has come to be regarded as what may be termed an edifying Christmas digestive. Owing to the sublimity of the conception it is undoubtedly edifying, but only incidentally. " Messiah " is first and foremost a work of art, characterised by all the poetry and vivid imagination of a work of art. It has little or nothing in common with the Lutheran piety of Bach's religious music ; it is full of colour and studies in intentional contrasts ranging round the central mystery of Redemption. It is neither Catholic nor Protestant, but very definitely Christian.

When we come to the other oratorios, it is very difficult

to know where to begin, a selection from their many-faceted beauties being so much a matter of individual taste. The supreme merit of Handel, in what still remains, perhaps, the ordinary view, is well exemplified in the massive choruses and above all the unparalleled finale of " Israel in Egypt." There are, of course, many examples of choral effects of this nature elsewhere, notably the great double chorus at the end of " Solomon," " Then round about the starry throne " in " Samson," or in a slightly different vein, " How dark, O Lord, are Thy decrees " in " Jephtha," not to mention the overwhelming effect of works like the " Coronation Anthem." It was of music such as this that Mozart was thinking when he wrote of Handel, " When he so wills, he strikes like a thunderbolt."

Though no composer has ever known so well how to achieve the irresistible effect of that choral sonority which his name conveys to most people, it must not be imagined for one moment that his genius was not equally remarkable in other directions, even in choral writing. The reader need only be reminded of the graphic quality of " He saw the lovely youth " in " Theodora," which Handel himself thought the best of all his choruses, the voluptuous quality of the bridal choruses in " Solomon," or the sheer rusticity depicted in " Mirth, admit me to thy crew " in " L'Allegro."

Perhaps it is not wholly true to say that most people would think of Handel primarily as a writer of choruses, but too many people think something of the kind. Yet no man ever wrote more exquisite or more diverse music for the solo voice. Indeed, it is extraordinary that one mind should have evolved conceptions so utterly varied yet all so perfect as " As when the Dove " (" Acis,"), " He shall feed his flock," " The people that walked in darkness " (" Messiah "), " Oh Sleep why dost thou leave me " (" Semele "), " With thee, the unsheltered moor I'd tread " (" Solomon "), " Deeper and deeper still " (" Jephtha "), to mention only a few of the most familiar. In all these and many more again the voice is written for with a plasticity, an expressiveness and an imagination such as no composer has ever surpassed and indeed, in my opinion, never equalled. Above all the mood and particular psychology of the situation are established immediately, almost in the first phrase, showing that in dramatic insight Handel was no whit inferior to the great masters of opera, Mozart, Wagner and Verdi.

Even at the risk of becoming wearisome, I must stress anew the altogether exceptional range of Handel's versatility. There are far too many people who think of Handel as a man of genius, it is true, but exclusively pompous and rhetorical. He could be pompous, as in the " Te Deum " ; he could be rhetorical as in " Alexander's Feast." But there is real pomp in the pompousness, and the rhetoric is of as splendid a quality as that of Dryden's words to which the music is set. Let the reader, however, bethink himself of the outstanding characteristics of other works : the perfection of conventional pastoralism in "Acis and Galatea"; the love of and feeling for nature in " L'Allegro " ; the splendour and lusciousness of " Solomon," which is like a series of great frescoes by Michael Angelo ; the psychological subtlety of " Hercules " ; the tragedy and despair of " Samson " and " Jephtha." It is an extraordinary catalogue of variety, which we who love Handel claim to be unmatchable in all the annals of music.

Doubtless Handel's extraordinary versatility was due in part to his cosmopolitanism. Not even Mozart, who possessed two musical nationalities, was so cosmopolitan as Handel, who possessed three. To view him as a German composer pure and simple is, despite the efforts of certain German scholars, quite absurd. Needless to say, he owed much to Germany : his original bent of mind and the solidity of his workmanship. But he owed almost if not quite as much to Italy, where he learned the value of clarity and the secret of writing mellifluously for the human voice. In all probability he owed more to our own despised England than is usually supposed. He certainly must have heard Purcell's music at the very outset of his English career;

there is a typical English freshness about " L'Allegro,"
while the oratorios he wrote towards the end of his life show
that his long practice at setting English words to music
was beginning to have its effect.

It would be futile to deny that some of Handel's writing
was at times conventional, not to say mechanical ; like all
composers of his time his output was so large that inevitably
music of secondary importance is by no means rare—
though one is unable to see that the more fastidious composers of the later twentieth century are in fact free from a
similar defect. Further, he undoubtedly borrowed exces-
sively, not only from himself but also from other composers.
This proceeding, too, was characteristic of the time, and
its legitimacy can only be judged by its results. In Handel's
case there can scarcely be two opinions as to those results.
What does it matter if " For unto us a child is born " was
originally a duet of his written in Italian for two sopranos ?
What does it matter if many of the numbers in " Israel
in Egypt " are based on the ideas of other men ? The
fact remains that the genius of Handel's treatment has
invested them with the immortality to which, in their
original form, they could never have aspired.

The exceptional psychological subtlety shown in Handel's
music has already been mentioned. It may largely be traced
to the composer's vivid visual imagination. We know that
this trait was especially strong in him, and it was this,
perhaps, rather than a definite religious exaltation that is
indicated by his well-known remark that when writing the
Hallelujah Chorus he seemed to see the heavens opened.
Incidentally this same Hallelujah Chorus well exemplifies
how mistaken are those who view Handel as worthy and
rather stodgy ; to his contemporaries, as still to those of us
who understand him aright, he was the most exciting of
composers. For it was, be it remembered, the excitement
provoked by this chorus that caused King George to rise to
his feet and thus unwittingly start a tradition that still
persists after nearly two hundred years.

## CHAPTER IV

# CHORAL MUSIC AFTER HANDEL

HANDEL'S GENIUS in oratorio was such that it almost may be said to have paralysed the world in general for the best part of a century, as it notoriously paralysed England in particular. At any rate most people will agree that during the remainder of the eighteenth century only one oratorio of first class importance was produced, for Beethoven's " The Mount of Olives " is decidedly a work of the second order and Mozart never wrote an oratorio at all. It was Haydn in " The Creation " who can claim the honour of providing the exception that proves the rule. " The Creation " is not dramatic as are Handel's oratorios ; it is essentially pictorial. The naïve realism with which Haydn paints the various natural phenomena depicted in the Book of Genesis will be familiar to almost everybody, but the naïveté (which, be it remembered, seemed very daring and original to Haydn's contemporaries) should never blind us to the extraordinary musicality of Haydn's various conceptions, while the massive grandeur of a chorus like " The Heavens are telling " is worthy to stand beside Handel's best pages. Parenthetically a tribute should be paid to another choral work by Haydn, " The Seasons," which, as an idealisation of simple rusticity, is in a way unique in musical literature. But this setting of Thomson's famous poem must be classed as a cantata rather than as an oratorio.

It was not till the third decade of the nineteenth century that oratorio, properly speaking, can be said to have come into its own again. For at this time Mendelssohn wrote " St. Paul," the first of his oratorios, which eventually established him, in England in particular, as the legitimate successor of Handel.

It has sometimes been claimed that Mendelssohn turned

his attention to the oratorio form as a result of his well-known enthusiasm and propaganda work for Bach's music. This, however, is not wholly true because, during his lifetime, Mendelssohn not only continually performed Handel's oratorios but actually rescored certain works. Moreover, the dramatic effects in the first part of " St. Paul," the " Watchman Scene " in " The Hymn of Praise," the conflict between the priests of Baal and the Prophet, and the coming of the rain in " Elijah " remind one more of Handel than of Bach, though it is scarcely necessary to add that none of Mendelssohn's oratorios can be classed with the works of those two supreme masters.

Nobody is less inclined than the writer to belittle Mendelssohn's genius, but it is scarcely to be found at its best in the oratorios. The charm of Mendelssohn is to be sought mainly in his lyricism, his admirable sense of orchestral colour. Traces of these qualities, of course, can be found in the oratorios, especially in " Elijah," wherein, further, many of the choruses are admirably and most expressively written. But Mendelssohn did not possess either the religious depth of Bach or the dramatic sense of Handel. His piety, entirely genuine though it was, was too apt to degenerate into a kind of smugness, and the dramatic qualities of " Elijah," about which we have heard so much recently, consist in reality of the picturesque and the effective rather than of the genuinely dramatic. There is no denying, however, their complete success.

England especially took them immediately to her Victorian heart, and within a very short time " Elijah " ranked with " Messiah " as the most popular of all musical compositions—a pre-eminence that it has by no means wholly lost even to-day. In view of the many merits of the work itself, this would not have been a matter of great importance but for the fact that Mendelssohn's influence, as distinct from the excellence of his own accomplishments, was thoroughly bad. It encouraged a kind of religiosity, which led to any and every composer who visited England writing " sacred music " often entirely unsuited to his real characteristics. Leaving out of account altogether the smaller fry, one has only to think of composers of the calibre of Gounod and Dvořák to realise the harm done. Even outside England Mendelssohn's influence on Oratorio must be accounted sterile, for, with the exception of César Franck's " Les Béatitudes," a work which truly reflected the glowing mysticism of the composer, oratorio in Europe during the second half of the nineteenth century cannot be regarded as of any great importance. A partial exception must be made for certain works by Parry and Stanford, who should have the credit not only for having broken the Mendelssohnian tradition in England but for having made possible the remarkable achievements of Elgar. Moreover the works themselves possess merit as such. Stanford's admirable Church music and vigorous cantatas like " The Revenge," Parry's " Job," and, better still, " Blest Pair of Sirens," a model of massive choral writing, deserve a high place in the esteem of their fellow-countrymen and more respect than they have in fact met with in the world at large.

The interest, then, of choral music since the days of Handel is to be sought in directions other than the Oratorio, primarily, perhaps in the settings of the Catholic Mass. It is impossible to do more than mention the school of ecclesiastical composition usually associated with the name of Vienna. But it comprises several Masses by Mozart and Haydn of great beauty and importance. This particular school of church music is sadly out of fashion nowadays, contemporary taste in this matter having definitely returned to the ideals of Palestrina. Beyond question the most important work which may, generally speaking, be regarded as a product of this school is Beethoven's great Mass in D. This, a product of Beethoven's complete maturity, is one of the great choral masterpieces of the world, containing as it does some of the most expressive and intensely felt music, for soloists and chorus alike, ever written in the history of music. As a work of art it seems to me the superior in every way of the choral movement of the " Ninth Symphony," which may have attempted more but scarcely can be said to have achieved as much in the way of expression.

The very essence of Beethoven's music is an expression of personality, and it is from this essentially personal expression that most of the great choral works of the nineteenth century derived. Apart from Cherubini's Masses, which retain a certain classical objectivity, very attractive in its way, all the great choral music of the nineteenth century was definitely subjective. Brahms's " Requiem " and Verdi's " Requiem," probably the greatest works of their kind, are typical instances of this. Brahms's " Requiem " is not really a requiem at all, but a setting of certain passages from the Bible. Though he himself held agnostic views, it represents with as great sincerity as success the fundamental characteristics of his mentality. And the same may be said of Verdi's " Requiem," which is not really an ecclesiastical composition at all but a utilisation by a master of drama of the words of the liturgy to express the most profound emotions of the composer. The result is essentially what appears to Anglo-Saxons to be a theatrical work, but the theatricalism is not evidence of its insincerity, rather the opposite. It would have been as unnatural and as insincere for Verdi in his Mass or, for the matter of that, for Rossini in his " Stabat Mater " or his " Petite Messe " to write in the style of the early Italian church composers, as it would have been for Brahms to write the " German Requiem " in the manner of Bach or Handel.

F. T.

# F: EUROPEAN SONG IN THE 19TH CENTURY

## CHAPTER I

## INTRODUCTION

ANY STUDY of European vocal music during the last century demands in reality a preparatory essay on a scale impossible within the limits of this chapter. A few general facts, however, may usefully be summarised.

On a broad view it may be said that the songs of all countries already show during the eighteenth, if not the seventeenth, century the main outlines of the characteristics that were subsequently to distinguish them. Mainly, of course, the basis of Song in all nations is folk-music. The extent of the influence of the folk-music, however, varies in each country. It was very strong in Germany and Russia ; less strong in France and Italy, and comparatively slight in England. In England, for instance, there has on various occasions been a struggle between the vocal models imported from abroad (in the main from Italy and Germany) and the Folk or National songs. The success of the Ballad Operas in general, and of " The Beggar's Opera " in particular, was perhaps the most noteworthy instance of a reaction against vocal forms of an origin foreign to England. Eighteenth-century composers, such as Dibdin and Arne, not to mention many of those who provided songs for the entertainments at the famous Vauxhall Gardens, may at least claim credit for having preserved in their music a genuine English flavour, subsequently lost in the perhaps more scholarly but less attractive vocal compositions of the latter part of the nineteenth century.

In Italy folk-song has always been kept alive in the

various provinces but with little effect, so far as one can see, on what would nowadays be termed Art Music. Indeed, the history of Italian Song, glorious as it is, is identified in practice with the history of the Opera, so that it mostly lies outside the scope of this Book of THE MUSICAL COMPANION.

The characteristics of French Song in the seventeenth and eighteenth century up to the time of the Revolution are well known. The French have always had an especia. gift and affection for the art of the *chansonnier*, apparent at the very outset. Weckerlin's famous collection of songs of this period, familiar alike in our concert halls and drawing-rooms, show all the typical characteristics of French *chansons*. They are malicious, tender, usually gallant, some-times definitely lascivious, always elegant. The artificial but delicious pastoral setting of many of these will be familiar to nearly everybody, and need not be further stressed. With the advent of the Revolution these attributes vanished, giving place to political songs that emphasised the civic virtues and the glories of democracy. Nevertheless, in their very reaction, these revolutionary *chansons* were the lineal descendants of the songs of the monarchical age, serving, together with them, to fix the characteristics of French Song as a whole.

Though the outstanding features of French Song pre-served many of the typical features of French folk-music, the two were rarely so inextricably intertwined as in Germany. At the beginning of the seventeenth century, when solo songs first seem to have made their appearance there, it is often difficult to tell exactly where the Folk Song ends and the Art Song begins. Italian operatic influences may at times have made themselves felt but the exceptionally intimate connection between the *Lied* and the folk-song persisted, not only in the compositions of rather shadowy figures such as Kirnberger and Sperontes (who have been hailed as the real begetters of the *Lied* in that they first set different verses differently and varied the accompaniments), but in the songs of the comparatively late eighteenth-century composers, of whom Hiller and Schulz may be regarded as the patriarchs. As a matter of fact the influence of folk-song remained exceptionally strong in all the masters of the German *Lied* up to, and including, Brahms ; apart from any question of general feeling and sentiment, this is shown by the diatonic character of much of the music and the almost aggressive prevalence of four-square rhythm.

# CHAPTER II

# SCHUBERT

FOR MOST PEOPLE the German *Lied* begins with Schubert. There were, however, songs of the first importance written before his day. As song-writers pure and simple, Handel and Bach may be passed over, and it can scarcely be maintained that either Haydn or Gluck were conspicuously successful. Weber's songs possess both individuality and distinction, but Weber was practically a contemporary of Schubert. Among the earlier songs, then, only those of Beethoven and Mozart need even be considered. Mozart wrote at least two masterpieces in pure song form, " Abendempfindung " and " Das Veilchen " ; Beethoven wrote one or two very fine songs, notably " Die Ehre Gottes aus der Natur " and " Vom Tode," apart from that song cycle in embryo, " An die ferne Geliebte." Still, the fact remains that both these composers rose to far greater heights in other fields, whereas Schubert, though he wrote plenty of lovely music in other, and, incidentally, in choral, forms, remains first and foremost a song composer.

Of all the musicians who ever lived Schubert excelled the most in grasping, as it were, in the twinkling of an eye, the salient characteristics of a poem and wedding them, almost as he read, to music ideally adapted to the human voice. As a rule the fundamental impulse was lyrical; but by no means always. There are songs that are definitely dramatic, even to the extent of employing recitative; there are songs that are pictorial, descriptive, even philosophical. But in all of them, whatever their character, it is generally true to say that the process of manufacture was not so much intellectual as instinctive, almost unconscious, if you will. Doubtless Schubert's lack of purely technical training has been exaggerated. Professor Tovey's fine essay on Schubert in " The Heritage of Music " makes that abundantly clear. But two things about him cannot be exaggerated; his natural facility and his inaptitude for what, for lack of a better term, may be defined as self-criticism. In their combination these characteristics sum up his countless merits and few defects as a song-composer.

Examples that prove his facility and instinctiveness are so numerous that we cannot even begin to cite them. The mere number of his songs (of which he wrote in his short life nearly 600, representative of every kind of mood, grave, gay, passionate, tender, simple and complicated) provides the most striking evidence of them. He could and did write songs as easily as the average person writes a letter, and, like Rossini, he would have found no difficulty in setting anything, even a laundry bill, to music.

The song, " Gretchen am Spinnrade," alone suffices to illustrate to perfection Schubert's extraordinary natural gifts. It is difficult to understand how any boy of seventeen, even a Mendelssohn or a Mozart, could have written such a song, but it is impossible to offer any rational explanation as to how a raw, inexperienced youth like Schubert produced a masterpiece of this kind. Nor does this particular song stand alone, for in the following year, when he was only eighteen, he wrote no less than a hundred songs of which such masterpieces as " Erlkönig," " Rastlose Liebe," " Meeresstille," and " Wanderers Nachtlied " remain the outstanding examples. Still, " Gretchen am Spinnrade " came first in point of date and may usefully be employed as the type-song of Schubert's earlier production. To begin with, by his accompaniment to this song Schubert may be said to have revolutionised the whole of German *Lied*. Never before had a German song-writer achieved such expressive and, it may be added, such difficult writing for the piano. That in itself is remarkable enough, but in reality, perhaps, the capacity shown to enter into the subtle feelings of Goethe's heroine was more remarkable still. Indeed, it may be doubted whether such an emotional achievement on the part of a youth in his 'teens can be paralleled in the whole history of music.

Now there can be no question that this miracle—for a miracle it remains—was a miracle of instinct. During the subsequent years Schubert somewhat developed his technical resources, but he can scarcely be said ever to have produced a song more satisfactory as an entity. Or, if this statement be considered too strong, let us say that he never produced a song that was better except in degree—" Der Atlas," for instance, or " Der Leiermann " or " Der Doppelgänger."

Another point also is worth noting. It was in his earliest years that Schubert chiefly set to music the words of Goethe, needless to say by far the best words that ever came his way. In later life his choice of words became less, not more, satisfactory, which would appear to dispose once and for all of any evidence of intellectual development. Apart from isolated instances too numerous to mention, take his two famous song-cycles, " Die Schöne Müllerin " and " Winterreise," both collections of poems by one Müller. If these words are examined with an unprejudiced eye they will be seen as what they are : the sentimental nonsense of a third-rate poet. " Die Schöne Müllerin " possesses the advantage of a certain naïve charm, but " Winterreise," full of a whining self-pity, is one of the very worst products of romanticism. One of the most learned French historians, who does not approach his subject with that snobbery of sentiment that characterises the approach of most English and German writers, has well defined it as a "long elegiac monologue of intolerable garrulity."

Yet, in fact, the inferior quality of these words seems to have made little difference to Schubert's inspiration, for some of his greatest masterpieces are to be found precisely in these two song-cycles. Words as words must have meant very little to Schubert; he often set them with a callous disregard of stress and accent. All that he demanded was that a poet should provide, as it were, the spark to light his musical imagination. Whether that spark was a Müller or a Goethe remained practically immaterial; we cannot even be certain that he was conscious of any qualitative difference between the two. The unerring instinct of his genius, however, was such that he in fact interpreted the general sense of a poem with an insight difficult to parallel among song-writers. Sometimes, as for instance in "An Schwager Kronos" and "Geheimes," he achieved almost by accident a perfect unison between the music and the individual words as such. Generally speaking, however, it is as the interpreter of a mood, an emotion or a situation that Schubert remains the supreme master.

With the reservations indicated above Schubert is undoubtedly the greatest of song-writers. To those who regard melody pure and simple as the most important factor, outweighing all others, he is undoubtedly the greatest song-writer without any reservation whatever. The spontaneity, the variety and the originality of Schubert's melodic gift cannot be exaggerated. Nor must it be imagined for one moment that his inspiration was exclusively confined to the vocal line. The importance of the piano part in "Gretchen am Spinnrade" has already been emphasised, but only because it provided the first outstanding example of his methods in this respect. There are countless other instances. Let the reader but think for one moment of how the accompaniment in "Die Forelle" typifies the play of a fish in a brook, how the triplets in "Erlkönig" convey the breathless horror of the poem's atmosphere. His harmony, too, is as happy as are his figures, being almost always perfectly adapted to the mood and the sentiment he wishes to convey. Small wonder, then, that Schubert's influence can be traced in the works of every song-writer who came after him. Sometimes it is more, sometimes less, marked ; but it is always there. He set in fact a standard. He is the very foundation and embodiment of the German *Lied* as we know it.

## CHAPTER III

# SCHUMANN AND SOME OTHERS

Before passing to the other major exponents of the German *Lied* there are four figures of interest who must be considered for a moment. The best known is Mendelssohn, whose songs as a collection are marred by a certain weakness that has been, not unjustly, dubbed effeminacy. Nevertheless, some half dozen of them are wholly charming : the graceful " Der Blumenkranz," for instance, and " Suleika," not to mention the familiar " Auf Flügeln des Gesanges." But to me, at any rate, the duets for female voices, despite their hackneyed associations, show Mendelssohn at his best as a vocal writer. " Gruss " and " Ich wollt' Meine Liebe " may be sentimental, but they are very pretty ; " Abschiedslied der Zugvögel " is a model of delicacy, and the once so familiar " Maiglöckchen und die Blümelein " is almost worthy to rank with the " Midsummer Night's Dream " music.

Franz is a composer of lighter calibre, almost entirely neglected nowadays, but the sincerity and the lyrical charm of his simple songs, which are largely in strophic form, deserve a better fate. So do the songs of Jensen, very fresh and attractive in their way. In a sense Loewe is the most important of all the minor song-writers, owing to the fact that he may be said definitely to have created the German dramatic ballad. Even now his setting of " Erlkönig " has not been entirely swamped by Schubert's, and in the opinion of some competent judges his interpretation of the text is more conscientious if not more effective.

It is Robert Schumann who must be regarded as the next legitimate successor to the great achievements of Schubert. His career as a song-writer was very curious in that it was practically confined to the year 1840, when he suddenly wrote more than a hundred and thirty vocal pieces, having up to that time, as he himself admitted, rather despised song-writing than otherwise. Schumann's admirers claim for his lyrical compositions in song form a spontaneity equal to that of Schubert. In my view this claim cannot be maintained. There is an intimate charm, an elegiac tenderness about Schumann's best songs that cannot be surpassed even in the glorious annals of the *Lied*. One has only to think of the most familiar numbers of the song-cycle, " Dichterliebe," the exquisite " Frühlingsnacht," " Mondnacht," and " Schöne Fremde " from the " Liederkreis." Nevertheless it is fair to describe even these as the product of an artist who is less spontaneous than conscientious, though in no derogatory sense. Perhaps this attribute becomes more easily distinguishable when we consider Schumann's least, rather than his most, successful songs. There is something, for instance, very self-conscious in his deliberate essays in the folk-song manner, which sometimes seem almost a parody of themselves ; the settings of Burns appear to an Englishman, at any rate, very artificial, and some of the " Frauen-Liebe und Leben " cycle is rather fussy. Nevertheless there are one or two things that Schumann achieved as a song-writer more successfully than any of his predecessors or contemporaries. His sense of literary values, to begin with, is decidedly more intimate. More striking still, perhaps, is his capacity to intertwine the vocal line and its accompaniment on the piano so as to construct a perfect unity of expression. Two songs, very different from one another, both show this characteristic to perfection : " Der Nussbaum," which everybody knows, and another, " Hidalgo," which is not so well known as it should be. Altogether Schumann's handling of his accompaniments must be regarded, perhaps, as even more successful than his handling of melody. This is scarcely a matter of surprise in a composer who wrote so much and so successfully for the pianoforte. The paradox remains that a little gem like the piano-epilogue to the " Dichterliebe," so satisfying, so exactly right, remains, perhaps, the most striking attribute of Schumann's as a song-writer !

## CHAPTER IV

## BRAHMS

BRAHMS, the next great exponent of the German *Lied*, must in a sense be considered more akin to Schubert than to Schumann. First, on account of the fact, often forgotten, that his vocal compositions in lyrical form, not counting his arrangements of folk-songs, constitute approximately one-third of his total output. True, his contemporary admirers professed to regard them as of secondary importance in comparison with the works of larger calibre, which they hailed as the legitimate offspring of Beethoven. But the modern view is rather different. There is a tendency to-day to value Brahms primarily for his qualities as a miniaturist, and it is in his songs and his piano-pieces that these qualities are most consistently shown. It is legitimate, then, to view Brahms, unlike Schumann, as fundamentally a song-writer. Moreover Brahms's music, like that of Schubert, possesses a natural affinity with German folk-song. There is nothing self-conscious in his approach to it ; it was a part of his being. Even when, as in " Vergebliches Ständchen," the piano accompaniment to a folk-song theme is comparatively elaborate, it is just the right kind of elaboration ; the spirit remains exactly akin to the original. As for that gem " Wiegenlied," one of the most popular as well as one of the best examples of Brahms's essays in simplicity, it could not be bettered ; the accompaniment suggests to perfection both the mood and the picture of a mother rocking her child to sleep. It was doubtless this love of folk-song that prompted Brahms, despite the elaboration of most of his songs, to declare that in his heart he preferred the simplicity of the strophic form. Lastly, he shared with Schubert a tendency to look at words primarily from the musical point of view, rather than with any great appreciation of their literary value as such. His superior education saved him from Schubert's worst lapses in this respect, but his treatment of stress and accent is sometimes equally cavalier. However, in what may be called the alliance of literature and music, Brahms is at a disadvantage compared with Schumann.

One of the outstanding characteristics of Brahms's vocal output is its wide range. But the range is one, as has been well said, rather of musical than of emotional material. Many people must have felt conscious of the fact that Brahms's music reflects the limited emotional experience of his life, so that passion seems almost a closed book to him, though he comes near to it in some of the " Magelonelieder." Generally speaking, however, the theme of his best love-songs may be defined as being rather placid or introspective ; " Nicht mehr zu dir zu gehen " and " Sapphische Ode " are examples of such songs at their best.

In the very large number of Brahms's songs there are many in which we feel that the workmanship comes first and the inspiration second, which is scarcely strange in a composer who avowedly attached a secondary value to inspiration as such. The occasions, however, where the workmanship leaves anything to be desired are exceedingly rare, for Brahms possessed in a high degree the faculty for self-criticism that Schubert lacked. This excellence of workmanship explains the consistent interest of Brahms's songs to musicians. In a very great number of instances, however, the addition of melodic inspiration to this work-manship has endeared the songs to professionals and amateurs alike. " Wie bist du, meine Königin," " Feldein-samkeit," "Ständchen," "Immer leiser wird mein Schlum-mer," " Botschaft," are instances selected at random that will occur to everybody, apart from songs already mentioned in other connections. The fact is that nowhere, perhaps, more strikingly than in his best songs did Brahms display his very personal melodic gift to greater advantage.

Space forbids any examination of the different types of subject treated by Brahms, but mention at least must be made of the " Vier Ernste Gesänge," four beautiful songs that constitute an essay in philosophic resignation akin to the mood of the " Requiem." Lastly, there are the " Liebes-lieder " and " Zigeunerlieder " written for four solo voices and piano duet accompaniment. It is difficult to say which is the more successful of these two compositions. The " Liebeslieder " are a wholly admirable embodiment of the Viennese waltz that sprang from the Ländler of Schubert and his contemporaries ; the " Zigeunerlieder " reproduce to perfection the ardour and the flaunting colours of "Hungarian" gypsy music. It may be doubted, indeed, whether any other composer has achieved equal success in this particular form, which has come in practice to be exclusively identified with Brahms.

## CHAPTER V

# HUGO WOLF

OWING TO THE PITCH of development to which Hugo Wolf brought the German *Lied*, one is always inclined to view his songs as the culmination of the whole school. So in fact they are, æsthetically ; for the songs of Richard Strauss cannot be compared with them intellectually, despite their undoubted charm. In time, however, it should be remembered that Wolf was practically contemporary with Brahms, a composer whom he, as an ardent disciple of Wagner, cordially disliked. Of all his predecessors Wolf, perhaps, owes most to Schumann, though it would be unwise to exclude altogether the influence of Liszt, who is of far greater importance as a song-writer than is usually realised in this country, having in fact achieved half a dozen first-rate compositions in the form.

In a sense, however, Wolf is akin to no other German writer of *lieder*, even his purely musical treatment being often associated with the new *leit-motiv* procedure of Wagner's music-dramas and Liszt's symphonic poems. Indeed Wolf's treatment of the piano in relationship to the voice has been compared with Wagner's treatment of the orchestra—not always to Wagner's advantage. For whereas Wagner's vocal line is often subordinate in interest, Wolf's admirers claim for him, with reason, a contrapuntal sense so admirable that he succeeded in attaining a perfect parity of interest between the vocal and the instrumental parts of his songs. As we have seen, many of the German song-writers, notably Schumann, attached great importance to the piano, but none of them carried the principle so far as Wolf. The piano parts of his songs are not only as important as the vocal parts, but often seem to be almost complete in themselves. At the same time the vocal parts, though rarely lyrical in the Brahms-Schubert manner, are delightful to sing for anyone able to grasp the principles of their wonderfully plastic line.

In a necessarily brief summing up of Wolf's attributes as a song-writer, stress must be laid first and foremost on the care he showed in choosing poems to set to music, and the skill, unrivalled before or since, with which he handled words. There is no question here of a worthless poem being chosen as a kind of peg on which to hang the music. As Mr. Newman has rightly pointed out, it is the poem itself that fixes the style and the contours

of the music. No composer has ever equalled Wolf in his
psychological penetration of literary meaning. Alike
in the fifty-three songs by Morïke, the forty-seven by
Goethe and the twenty by Eichendorff that he set to music,
his grasp of the implications of a poem is almost uncanny ; just
as in the thirty-four songs of the " Spanisches Liederbuch "
and, even more, in the forty-four songs of the " Italienisches
Liederbuch " his grasp of the fleeting colours and moods
of the words is almost uncanny. No kind of style or subject
seems alien to him. Moreover, he is able to suggest an
atmosphere or depict a situation with that economy of
means that comes from the highest possible degree of
concentration. In short it may be doubted whether music
as a whole can show any art-products more beautifully
finished than the songs of Hugo Wolf.

As we might expect in a musician of such literary per-
spicacity, his actual handling of the words was invariably
conscientious in the highest degree. It is difficult to find
in any of his songs a stress that is unjustified or an accent
that is misplaced. Of none of his predecessors, not even of
Schumann, can this be said, so that this new respect for
words as such may perhaps be singled out as Wolf's most
important contribution to musical development. Since his
day it has been impossible for any serious song-composer
to take the liberties associated even with a Brahms, and
to this extent the whole of contemporary art-song may be
said to derive from Wolf.

From the technical point of view so many of Wolf's
songs are perfect that it seems futile to single out even
half a dozen of them as masterpieces. In the case of such a
composer, so skilled, so completely a master of his medium,
the final appraisement of the song depends on the extent to
which the musical ideas themselves seem more or less
felicitous, because, in every analysable attribute, Wolf's
work is almost invariably beyond criticism. The musical
value of a phrase, however, remains in the last resort,
unanalysable. In the hands of Wolf's successors and imitators his methods have often been successfully copied,

but their ultimate musical value has very rarely been the same. Those who love and admire Wolf's songs claim that at their best they are the greatest of all. Inevitably among his output there are inequalities ; sometimes the treatment is laboured ; sometimes the means seem disproportionate to the end. As a collection, however, Wolf's songs strike a balance between idea and treatment more perfect than that achieved by any other master.

## CHAPTER VI

## FRENCH SONG

THERE CAN BE LITTLE DOUBT that after the German the school of French Song was the most important in Europe during the latter half of the nineteenth century. Up till that time the French had largely gone to the theatre for their songs, but with the new orientation in French music based on Saint-Saëns and César Franck there grew up a form of song modelled very much on the lines of German *leider*, though wholly different in feeling. Practically all composers have at one time or another written songs, and the French are no exception. Berlioz, for instance, produced some uncommonly interesting songs ; Franck and Saint-Saëns did not neglect the form. Indeed Franck's " La Procession " is one of the most beautiful of French songs.

Still it is fair, perhaps, to say that the edifice of modern French Song is founded on Gounod and Massenet, whom it is the fashion to despise in this country. Nevertheless, the fact remains that Gounod wrote a number of very charming songs and at least one masterpiece, " Venise " ; while those who would belittle Massenet should bethink them of the grace and clarity of songs like " Crépuscule," " Les Oiselets," and, best of all, " Si tu veux, mignonne."

Needless to say, the songs of both these composers are comparatively simple, being, often, especially in the case of Gounod, in pure strophic form, and delving but little into the more subtle implications of the poetry. They remain, in fact, exclusively lyrical.

Even, however, had Gounod and Massenet been in themselves of less importance than they were, they would be noteworthy for the influence they exercised on their successors. The most original of French composers, Debussy, never attempted to conceal his early debt to Massenet, while the earliest songs of Gabriel Fauré, in my opinion not only the greatest of French song-writers, but also one of the truly great song-writers of the world, bear evident traces of the influence of Gounod.

Fauré's claim to greatness is not usually conceded outside France, in the main because few of his songs except two or three, comparatively elementary, are sung elsewhere. As a collection, however, the three volumes that contain his sixty separate songs, and the nine settings from Verlaine's poems grouped together under the title of " La Bonne Chanson," stand head and shoulders above the vocal achievements of any other French song-writer. This may seem a bold statement in view of the pre-eminence rightly accorded to Debussy as a composer, but Debussy's songs are, perhaps, the least important feature of his work. He showed in them, as ever, an amazing sense of colour and great imagination in setting words to music, but, generally speaking, the vocal line seems definitely subordinate in interest to the piano part, remaining more or less a study in free declamation. This is not true of his best songs such as " Mandoline," " Fantoches," " La Chevelure " or " Green," this last, incidentally, providing almost the only example among the many settings made by Debussy and Fauré of the same poems where the superiority may indubitably be assigned to Debussy. Nevertheless, his songs as a whole must be adjudged, despite their admirable and highly poetical qualities, somewhat deficient in true melodic inspiration.

Pc

Two other French composers, also, must be mentioned in this connection, though the first of these, Reynaldo Hahn, scarcely falls within the limits of this Part of Book IV. As a song-writer pure and simple he possesses great merit. Indeed, he has achieved the distinction, in his setting of Verlaine's beautiful poem, "D'une Prison," of having produced a song more satisfactory than that written by Fauré to the same words. Still, his output as a whole is of too slight a calibre, too facile, if you will, despite its elegance and charm, to be compared with Fauré's achievement. The other, Henri Duparc, is a composer of far more serious import. Many people consider that his best songs, "L'Invitation au Voyage," "Phidylé" and half a dozen others, register the high watermark of French vocal composition. The faultless quality of their workmanship has certainly not been surpassed, while their strength of utterance and intensity have, perhaps, not been equalled, by any other French song-writer. Duparc, it is well known, himself destroyed most of his compositions, leaving only the sixteen songs by which the world now knows him. He may have acted wisely, but the result seems too meagre a basis for the setting up of any claim to pre-eminence.

Fauré, in his songs, can be said to have explored the whole avenue of intimate emotions, and to this extent the designation of him as the "French Schumann" is not inapt He resembled Schumann, moreover, in his "sweetest melancholy," though the care and discrimination with which he handled words was more akin to that of Wolf. Further, though Fauré's songs are full of sentiment, they are rarely sentimental, much less naïve. Nothing could be more French, alike in their grace, their clarity or their delicious sensibility.

From the purely musical point of view Fauré is remarkable for two things, notably the continuous evolution of his style. It is not till one becomes impregnated with the flavour of his musical personality that one can trace any connection between the first volume of his songs and the last collection called "La Chanson d'Eve"; his output between these two reflects the whole development of French music. Then there is the amazing suppleness of his modulation. It would be impossible to take any particular chord and say " This is typical Fauré," but the manner in which he treats the sequence of harmonies remains entirely his own. It will not be necessary to remind those acquainted with the familiar songs, " Après un Rêve," " Nell," " Claire de Lune " and so on, of the beauty of his melodic line, but there are less known examples such as " C'est l'Extase " and " En Sourdine " which, when their comparative complication has been mastered, can be seen to be equally remarkable, alike for their beauty of melody and for the subtle suggestion in the piano accompaniment. There can be no doubt, however, that Fauré's masterpiece is " La Bonne Chanson," wherein he showed an insight into the mind of Verlaine equal to Wolf's penetration into the meaning of Goethe and Mörike. These songs, too, apart from their exquisite workmanship, show a vitality, and what can only be described as a luminous quality, rarely met with in the rest of his vocal compositions. Compared with the great German masters, Fauré's characteristics remain essentially feminine ; one is almost tempted to describe his Muse, so distinguished, so refined, so subtly perfumed, as " The Great Lady of European Song."

## CHAPTER VII

## OTHER NATIONS

THOUGH, needless to say, the composers of all nations wrote songs, it hardly seems necessary to isolate, so to say, any other national school, except the Russian. For instance, very little, except the charming "Stornelli" of Gordigiani, came out of Italy ; while most English nineteenth-century songs, apart from a few by Stanford and Parry, are best forgotten. The Russian School, however, is remarkable not only for quantity but also for quality, and deserves, in fact, more attention than can be given to it. Thus, Rimsky-Korsakov left about eighty and Tchaikovsky more than a hundred songs, those of the former being in the main lyrical; those of the latter, elegiac. "Nur wer die Sehnsucht kennt" and "Don Juan's Serenade" are perhaps two of the best examples of Tchaikovsky's great, if unequal, talent.

A little more detailed consideration is imperative for Moussorgsky, because his songs are in their way unique in the literature of vocal music. Though he did, in fact, write some songs in purely lyrical form, his vocal art as a whole is characterised by a declamatory setting of words, the music serving primarily to throw the various points of the poem into the strongest possible relief. In this respect Moussorgsky showed genius of the highest order. Whether he is dealing with scenes from peasant life, as in so many of his songs, or with children, as in " The Nursery," or indulging in pure satire as in " The Seminarist," he succeeds in painting a musical picture that for sheer vividness of colour and directness of expression can scarcely be matched in the whole range of vocal writing. Moussorgsky's songs possess a flavour all their own, and it has been claimed with some justice that in them may be found his most valuable attributes as a composer, in that it was in the imaginative setting of words that he particularly excelled. Certainly nowhere else, not even in " Boris Godounov," does his music interpret with such uncanny genius the various characteristics of the Russian people that he delighted to portray. From the purely musical point of view, moreover, his very fidelity to the text served to correct a shapelessness often noticeable in his instrumental compositions.

Finally, mention must be made of Grieg, whose songs appear to have been relegated by the caprice of fashion to comparative obscurity. Yet they form a very remarkable collection. It may be doubted, indeed, whether for spontaneity and simplicity more charming songs have been written since the death of Schubert. Like Schubert, Grieg suffered from the defects of his qualities, and it would be idle to deny that in far too many of his songs there is an abuse of the strophic form. Those, however, who think of him only as the composer of the popular " I love thee," or "Solvejg's Song," will be surprised at the variety and the range of his vocal compositions as a whole. Even if we discount the more exclusively Norwegian songs, which are not often met with in this country, but in fact contain some of the finest examples of his talent, there remain in the five volumes of his collected songs more than sufficient to attest his great gifts as a song-writer. A few of them, such, for instance, as " From Monte Pincio," are masterpieces, but many are wholly charming. The fact is that the best of Grieg, even more than the best of Moussorgsky, is to be found in his songs ; for here are seen to the greatest advantage the national flavour of his idiom, the piquant colouring of his harmony and the freshness of his melodic inspiration. The very simplicity by which he achieves his effects has perhaps tended to lead many people to overlook their originality.

F. T.

# G: VOCAL MUSIC IN THE 20TH CENTURY

## CHAPTER I

## DEBUSSY. STRAUSS. MAHLER

AT THE TURN of the century there were four composers in Europe, each about forty years of age, whose music may be regarded as typical of the first decade after 1900—Richard Strauss (the youngest and already the most famous—or notorious!) in Germany, Claude Debussy in France, Gustav Mahler in Austria, and in England Edward Elgar, the senior in age.

Debussy stands apart from his contemporaries in all except his orchestral virtuosity, and even in that sphere his reticence is in striking contrast to the opulent display of the others. Debussy's songs, the most important of his vocal compositions except the opera, " Pelléas et Mélisande," have already been noted, and there remain to be considered here only the early cantatas, " L'Enfant Prodigue " and " La Demoiselle Élue." It was with the first of these that Debussy won the Prix de Rome at the Paris Conservatoire. As might be expected of a student work, it is derivative, and the " Air de Lia," which has kept a place in concert-programmes, is a fair sample of its indebtedness to Massenet. " La Demoiselle Élue," a setting of Rossetti's " Blessed Damozel " for female voices and orchestra, is more important, though slight. The music reflects the spirit of Rossetti's poem more accurately than the French translation of the words. It may be added that in " Sirènes," the third of the orchestral " Nocturnes " produced in 1899, Debussy uses a small chorus of female voices as part of his orchestra, following the example set by Verdi in the storm-music in the last act of "Rigoletto," and that the incidental music to d'Annunzio's " Le Martyre de Saint Sébastian " contains some choral numbers. But by 1911 Debussy's peculiar vein of inventiveness seems to have been worked out and his mind exhausted.

Strauss's contribution to vocal music is likewise, in comparison with his work in other spheres, of secondary importance. In spite of the very high quality of his craftsmanship in setting words to music, his writing for the voice, as whole pages of " Der Rosenkavalier " will bear witness, is often intrinsically uninteresting, besides being awkward to sing. One has the impression that in these passages the voice-part has been imposed upon a pre-conceived and in itself complete orchestral work. On the other hand he is capable of writing such beautiful passages for the voice as the final trio and duet in " Rosenkavalier," the recognition-scene in " Elektra," and, perhaps most enchanting of all, the Trio of Nymphs in " Ariadne auf Naxos." Even in these we are sometimes conscious of a certain awkwardness in the vocal line. In his songs Strauss shows the same craftsmanship and insight into the poems he has set, though the quality of his songs varies with that of his texts. For, as in his operas, he has often chosen ugly subjects and set them to music of which one may doubt the æsthetic value, even though marvelling at its skill. On the other hand no one can deny the sensuous beauty of such songs as " Traum durch die Dämmerung," " Morgen " and " Ich schwebe." The charm of their melodies and the picturesque aptness of their accompaniments make them a valuable addition to the corpus of German lyrics. But Strauss has also shown that he can out-ballad the ballad-mongers with " Zueignung," which is everything that a popular sentimental song should be.

It is not improbable that, of Mahler's music, posterity will cling to the songs and let the rest go. Mahler's talent was essentially literary, but, since it was also profuse, his music is at its best when restricted by the limits of a poetic form.

After the long orchestral magniloquence upon some trivial texts of the fourth symphony, what a relief it is to come to the amusing song from " Des Knaben Wunderhorn " in the *finale*. These children's songs appealed especially to Mahler's naïve temperament, and his numerous settings of them are among the most delightful things in music. The charm of his melodic gift is evident, too, in the setting of five poems by Rückert, of which " Ich atmet' einen Linden Duft " is the best known, while the " Kindertoten-lieder," with words by the same poet, reveal his tenderness towards childhood in another, more gloomy, aspect. The most important of Mahler's later works on a large scale is " Das Lied von der Erde." One says " on a large scale " because, although these are only six songs from Hans Bethge's " Chinese Flute," Mahler has transformed them from miniatures into a work of symphonic proportions. Indeed there is something rather ridiculous in his solemn and literal-minded treatment of the word " ewig " (" eternal ") at the end. But these songs, which include the airy-light " Von der Jugend," are far preferable to the imposing *finale* of the eighth symphony, where the Latin hymn " Veni, Creator Spiritus" as well as some of the more metaphysical passages from the second part of Goethe's "Faust" are allotted to eight solo voices, a double chorus and a boys' choir, the performers numbering, together with the vast orchestra, about 1,000. In this work and in Schönberg's "Gurrelieder," written about the same time under Mahler's influence, the megalomania of Central Europe reached its apex.

## CHAPTER II

## ELGAR

OF THE FOUR COMPOSERS mentioned at the beginning of the last chapter, Edward Elgar is, from the standpoint of vocal music, the most important. Nothing is more

typical of the English genius and consequently of the
character of English music and musical institutions than
the career of this composer. A Roman Catholic, he achieved
fame in the Anglican cathedrals of the Three Choirs
Festivals without abating his own Faith, though not always
without offence to stricter Protestant susceptibilities.
Having no professional training of any kind, he developed
a technical craftsmanship that has hardly been equalled,
and, despite his lack of connection with the official conservatoires, he became the acknowledged leader of music in
England and reaped every official honour open to his
profession. Aloof and touchy in his personal relationships,
he was a good courtier. Profoundly religious, a cultivated
reader of poetry and a lover of country quiet, he had all
the Edwardian liking for pomp and circumstance, and he
followed his royal namesake's taste for horse-racing, music-
halls and other worldly amusements. He was, indeed, a
combination of opposites, and in nothing more paradoxical than in the reticence that went hand in hand with
effusive sentiment in his music.

Of Elgar's early vocal works little need be said, for their
good qualities are those that are also to be found in his
mature work, while the obvious weaknesses are the faults
of a mind finding its own way slowly towards the technical
means and methods of expression best suited to it. There is,
indeed, all too little of the later mastery, except in one or
two individual movements, in such works as " King Olaf,"
and " The Banner of St. George." Yet, when mastery came,
it appeared with startling suddenness in the " Enigma "
Variations. In the same year (1899) Elgar produced the
" Sea Pictures." In these songs, written for Clara Butt to
sing at the Norwich Festival, the qualities and defects of
his vocal writing are clearly displayed. Like Strauss, Elgar
could go straight to the heart of his text and produce music
expressive of all that is essential to it. Yet for an assiduous
reader of poetry and for an English composer, he was
curiously insensitive to the niceties of poetic rhythm and
even to the more simple problems of accentuation. One has

the impression that, even though the melodies have grown out of the spirit of the text, they have not sprung from the rhythm and sound of the words, which have subsequently been fitted to the notes. This is a perfectly legitimate method of setting words to music and may be defended on the ground that, if the letter is sometimes ignored, the spirit is preserved. But it is not the best way nor the one characteristic of the greatest English composers.

No such reservations need be made about Elgar's choral works, in which, whether he is writing a part-song or a large-scale oratorio, his technical mastery is absolute. This is not, of course, to say that his musical inspiration was always on the same high level. Even in " The Dream of Gerontius," which is the most consistent of his oratorios, there are lapses of imagination, especially in the second part. The first part of this work, which portrays the death of Gerontius and the setting-forth of his soul into eternity, is of so fine a character, of so great an originality, that it never fails to entrance the ear and astonish the mind of the hearer. That the composer should not have risen so success-fully to the ineffable heights of the angelic choruses in the second part, is perhaps only to say that he did not achieve the impossible. " Gerontius," as a whole, is the product of native genius coupled with a depth of learning for which Elgar has not always been given credit. Yet it is only necessary to listen to the " Kyrie," the prayers for the dying Gerontius and the bass solo and chorus with which the first part ends, to perceive, without biographical evi-dence, that Elgar knew a great deal about " Palestrina and all that." The surprising thing is that he should have turned his knowledge to so little account. Apart from the early " Ave Verum," his published music includes no specifically liturgical music, and it has been left to an Anglican composer to add a great modern example to the English settings of the Mass.

" Gerontius " was followed by an even more ambitious project, a trilogy of oratorios, of which the first part, " The Apostles," was produced at Birmingham in 1903 and the second, "The Kingdom," in 1906. The third part was never completed, and thereafter Elgar concentrated on symphonic works, producing no choral work on a large scale nor indeed anything of importance in that medium, with the exception of the setting of Binyon's poem, "For the Fallen," a poignant elegy for those who fell in the War of 1914–18. Neither "The Apostles" nor "The Kingdom" has achieved the popularity of "The Dream of Gerontius," and, although both the later works contain noble music and at times show an even greater mastery in the handling of the material and a more subtle expressiveness, popular opinion is probably, as it usually is in the long run, right.

## CHAPTER III

# THE ENGLISH RENAISSANCE

Elgar's most important contemporary in England was Frederick Delius, whose main contributions to music were, however, orchestral. Even the treatment of the voices in his choral works is often deliberately instrumental, and his imagination is displayed at its finest in such things as the wordless chorus which enters to form the climax of "The Song of the High Hills." Delius had even less than Elgar's regard for the niceties of accentuation in the setting of English poetry, a failing that was as much due to his own temperament as to his foreign parentage and domicile. A dreamer of dreams, he cared as little for the rules of prosody as for the technique of fugue and symphonic form. They were things inessential to the expression of his musical ideas. His songs are, therefore, not to be accounted among his successes. The best of his vocal music is contained in the profoundly expressive "Sea-Drift" for baritone, chorus and orchestra, in such miniatures as the wordless "Songs to be sung on a summer night on the water," and in the more tranquil passages of his uneven masterpiece, " A Mass of Life."

Among other composers of the older generation mention must be made of Granville Bantock, whose prolific output of large-scale choral works presents an accurate reflection of the passing fashions in European music during the first fifteen years of the century, and of Ethel Smyth, whose combination of masculine vigour and feminine charm has secured for herself a position unique in musical history. Ethel Smyth has, however, never quite fulfilled the promise of the finest parts of the early and unequal Mass produced in 1893.

In the next generation the outstanding figures in England are Ralph Vaughan Williams and the late Gustav Holst, both, like Elgar, natives of the Western Midlands. Both came under the influence of the folk-song revival, but neither remained enslaved by it. Vaughan Williams, in particular, has so absorbed the spirit of English folk-music into his system that it seems to have become an integral part of his own intellectual process. He no longer presents us with " Rhapsodies," literal stitchings-together of collected tunes. An even more important influence on these composers has been the revival of interest in the Tudor composers, for here they were able to find a way out of the *impasse* reached when it seemed as if, for the time being at any rate, music had exhausted the possibilities of diatonic harmony. In the music of Byrd and Tallis, of Weelkes and Morley, Holst and Vaughan Williams have found not models for slavish imitation in " ye olde " style, but a starting-point for explorations into a new harmonic world. Their progress has not always been certain. The adoption of modes in place of the major and minor keys has sometimes led to the repetition of cadences that pall on the ear far more quickly than the old tonic-and-dominant. Both composers, too—and particularly Vaughan Williams—have shown a bewildering diversity of styles which almost seems to argue a lack of direction.

Holst, intellectually the more simple, expressed himself with a directness that left no doubt about his absolute sincerity, even though one might suspect that, especially in his later music, he had not really put down all he meant to say. In the " Choral Symphony" he seems to play upon his hearers the trick practised on the Wizard in " The Perfect Fool," substituting clear spring water for the magic potion. His finest choral works are " The Ode to Death " and " The Hymn of Jesus," in which his peculiar susceptibility to *nuances* of timbre, his exact knowledge of the effect produced by any given combination of voices and instruments, and his bold, yet never perverse, handling of the modal material are fully exploited. The curious combination of ecstasy and austerity, of ice and fire in this work is characteristic of Holst's best music, and goes hand in hand with the compound of simplicity and recondite mysticism in the texts he usually chose.

Vaughan Williams, technically less proficient than Holst, has a more profound mind. If Holst is apt to be so elliptical in his directness of statement that he omits to give us the essential information, Vaughan Williams sometimes obscures his meaning by a stumbling and clumsy delivery. His uncertainty in handling his material is naturally most obvious in his earlier works, and his constant remodelling of them is evidence of the weakness as well as of his artistic conscientiousness. The vigorous choral " Sea Symphony," the best of his early works, exemplifies both his strength—the bold, swinging melodies, the delight in the picturesque details of the sea and ships and the characteristic and essential transformation of the sea-faring into a mystical adventure of the human soul—and his inability to make smooth and convincing transitions or to work his material into a really coherent form, independent of conventional formulas.

From the " Sea Symphony " to the " Mass in G minor," " Sancta Civitas " and " Flos Campi " is an enormous step, the measure of the composer's advance in mastery. The gap is bridged by numerous smaller works as well as by two symphonies and an opera, which do not come under discussion here, and the war accounts both for blank years and a perceptible deepening of his spiritual nature. In the Mass the composer takes up the traditions of the great Tudor polyphonists, and yet it is in no sense a pastiche or a false antique. While conforming to the conventions of a different age, it bears indelibly the stamp of the composer's personality. In " Flos Campi," a work based upon texts from the Song of Solomon, the chorus is used orchestrally, as Holst had used it in " Neptune " and Delius in " The Song of the High Hills." No work of Vaughan Williams's is so bewildering as this mixture of naïve exoticism and native mysticism. The only thing to do is to forget about the texts, which should never have been attached to the music, since the composer admits that they are not illustrated in it, and enjoy its strange attractiveness. " Sancta Civitas," a cantata with a text drawn mainly from the Apocalypse, presents no problems to the intelligent listener. This is undoubtedly Vaughan Williams's masterpiece, and it is astonishing that a work so consistently beautiful should have fallen into neglect since its first performances. Of his smaller vocal works, the justly popular " Songs of Travel " and " On Wenlock Edge " represent Vaughan Williams's early and middle periods. His numerous choral arrangements of folk-songs and carols, all treated with mastery and understanding, are a valuable addition to the repertory of choral societies.

Arnold Bax, though mainly an orchestral composer, has written also a large number of songs, in which his Celtic predilections are usually apparent along with his taste for elaborate arabesques in the accompaniments. In spite of this baroque adornment, the songs are essentially simple, melodious and attractive. Bax has also composed a number of choral works, of which the two unaccompanied motets, " This Worlde's Joie " and " Mater, ora Filium " are the most distinguished examples. Here Bax rather surprisingly resorts to a purely polyphonic style, not entirely free from conscious archaism, which is even more evident in the carols " Now is the tyme of Christymas " and " Of a Rose I sing," beautiful though these are as settings of the old words. Of other English song-writers, Walford Davies, who has also produced choral works of genuine distinction, John Ireland, a little hampered by an over-rich harmonic idiom, Philip Heseltine, who based his art upon a scholarly knowledge of Dowland and an admiration for Delius, Arthur Bliss, whose " Pastoral " has an individual lyric charm, E. J. Moeran and Patrick Hadley exemplify the diversity and accomplishment of the contemporary English School, without exhausting the list of names that might be given. The songs of Bernard van Dieren are highly esteemed by a small circle of musicians, but their learned obscurantism has not commended them to a wider public.

Two of the younger men must have individual mention on account of their rapid rise to fame. Constant Lambert has not yet followed up the success of his clever and effective " Rio Grande," perhaps on account of his pre-occupation with conducting and musical criticism. William Walton, on the other hand, after an even earlier revelation of cleverness and wit, has consolidated the ground and proved himself a composer endowed with more solid gifts. Having displayed in some instrumental works a delicate lyricism as well as a brilliant incisiveness, he startled the musical world, in 1931, with one of the most powerful choral works ever written. " Belshazzar's Feast," though based upon a biblical text, is entirely secular in spirit, expressing in an astonishing degree (especially as the composer appears to be of irreproachably Aryan origin) the fanaticism of the Jewish race and their hatred of the Gentile oppressors. Nothing could exemplify the difference in spirit between this work and a " sacred " oratorio than a comparison of the bloodthirsty exultation of Walton's setting of the words " Babylon is fallen," and the music provided for the same words in Vaughan Williams's " Sancta Civitas." Amid this atmosphere of hatred and pagan splendour, there shine out several passages of remarkable beauty, such as the setting of " By the Waters of Babylon " and the unaccompanied chorus, " The trumpeters and pipers are silent." Throughout the work from the grinding dissonances of the mournful opening to the ecstatic Alleluias of the close, Walton shows a complete mastery of his material and of every device of choral effect.

# CHAPTER IV

# THE EUROPEAN FRONT

CONTEMPORARY MUSIC in other countries must be cursorily treated, and if it seems that a disproportionate space has been given to English music here, it may be asked what other country can boast an output of vocal works comparable in quality, number and diversity with that represented by the names of Elgar, Delius, Holst, Vaughan Williams and William Walton ? It is time, too, for us to realise that, in choral music at least, England has once more regained the leadership of Europe.

In France after the wit and polish of Ravel, often whetting his jaded appetite upon exotic tit-bits from Spain or Greece, there is nothing but the Parisian smartness of such ephemeridæ as Poulenc and Auric. Further south, in Switzerland, the art is represented by Arthur Honegger and the exiled Igor Stravinsky, both of whom find Paris their spiritual home. Honegger's most important work, " Le Roi David," in its original form a play with incidental music, is practically an oratorio with the narrative portions spoken instead of sung. The choral movements are impressive in their austerity and exhibit a real dramatic power. As for Stravinsky, what can we say of a composer who, after writing for years in the manner of Handel or Bach or Tchaikovsky, according to the latest vogue, has settled down to the supreme task of transcribing his early works as duets for pianoforte and violin, except that he must be placed among Professor Tovey's Waxworks, " The Interesting Historical

Figures " ? Of other Russian exiles Rachmaninov and Medtner, representing an older tradition, have written some fine songs, those of Medtner being practically duets for voice and pianoforte, so important has the " accompaniment " become.

In Italy composers like Ildebrando Pizzetti, whose early setting of d'Annunzio's " I Pastori " is among the best modern songs, and Mario Castelnuovo-Tedesco have been influenced by the revival of interest in folk-music, but it would seem that Italian composers as a body have sold their birthright of vocal melody for a mess of cosmopolitan instrumentation. Spain, on the other hand, has refused to level her music down to a common European standard and discard the comb and mantilla for a felt hat that might be bought in any store in any continent. Manuel de Falla, the chief composer, has however published no vocal music, except arrangements of folk-songs and the exiguous and charming puppet-opera upon an episode in " Don Quixote," though he has for some time been engaged on a large sacred choral work.

Even in Austria and Germany we find plenty of candidates for entry into Professor Tovey's Museum, but no likely claimants to the heritage of Bach and Beethoven, of Mozart, Haydn and Brahms. The megalomania of Strauss and Mahler has dwindled to the dry, unpalatable essence of counterpoint distilled by Schönberg, who, seeking to jump off his own romantic shadow, invented the kind of declamation called " Speech-song," which has neither the force of speech nor the beauty of song. It is true that his pupil, Alban Berg, has been able to turn Schönberg's principles to good account in his opera " Wozzeck," but it is to be noted that the passages which most strike the hearer in that work are those in which the composer has forgotten about the theories of atonality. The mechanical counterpoint of Paul Hindemith, whose chief quality is his almost Rossinian facility, is even less interesting. Like Stravinsky in his " Bach period," Hindemith is applying the contrapuntal conventions, which belong to a particular harmonic system, to an entirely different style of harmony, without regard to the incongruity. It is worth noting, too, that the music of Schönberg, Berg and Hindemith is most effective when it is portraying a drab, an ugly, a perverse, a satirical or a morbid idea. It is the music of pessimism and decadence, incapable of positive affirmation.

It is pleasant to end this section upon a less damnatory note, and fortunately we can find, beyond Germany, in Hungary, a choral work that can be hailed as a masterpiece, even though it is an isolated one and on a small scale. No one who heard the performances of Zoltán Kodály's "Psalmus Hungaricus" given in London and elsewhere a few years ago can have failed to recognise the difference between the impression made upon audiences, sophisticated or amateur, by this work and by the average new work. The passionate intensity of expression achieved by the composer transcended all differences of national idiom and the disadvantages of a translation that almost inevitably destroyed the true accentuation and rhythm of the music at many points. Taken from the Psalms of David, the text has been converted by the composer into a true Hungarian Psalm, an expression of national aspiration and of that Protestantism which has survived all efforts to stamp it out. Kodály's rhythm is conditioned by that of the Hungarian language, and his main material is a simple chant. He makes little or no use of contrapuntal devices. Yet there is no monotony in the rhythm, such as we often find in Russian music, and out of the simple material the composer has fashioned a work whose fierceness and poignancy are unforgettable. Although Kodály's harmony might shock a 19th-century professor, there is here nothing perverse or wilful or obscure. His music has the simplicity, the directness and the supreme quality of sounding "right" (whatever theoretical justification for it there may or may not be), which we admire in all good music, whether it be by Palestrina or by Mozart or by the Unknown Master of 1934.

D. H.

# BOOK V

## CHAMBER MUSIC

*By* EDWIN EVANS

# A : BEFORE BEETHOVEN

## CHAPTER I

## EARLY BEGINNINGS IN ENGLAND AND ABROAD

THE MOST ADMIRABLE recent definition of the term " chamber music " is that which describes it as the music of friends. Though much of it is now performed in public, it is essentially the music of those who come together to make music for themselves, as distinct from those who gather at concerts to have music made for them. Soloists rarely play or sing to themselves, except for study or practice, and even an amateur orchestra comes together with the view of eventually performing to an audience, but the true devotees of chamber music have no need of an audience for the enjoyment of their pursuit. They find it in the interplay of individualities, in the dovetailing of their individual contributions to the whole. They meet as friends and admit a few friends to their intimacy. That is the real spirit of chamber music, by this it was animated during a great part of its history, and this still inspires countless private societies in which it is cultivated for the sheer joy of performing it.

The public concert is a comparatively modern institution. In Italy, where the term " musica da camera " originated at the time of the Renaissance, it was used to indicate the music provided at princely houses, as distinct from that intended for the Church, or, in later times, for the stage. Though the hospitality of such houses might extend to a multitude of guests, the performances were, in their essence, private, as distinct from public performances given elsewhere. When the practice extended to Germany the distinction was further narrowed. A reigning house—and they were many in those days—might distinguish between *Hofmusik* (Court-music) and *Kammermusik* (chamber-music), the latter being for the delectation of the princely household, the former for the enlivening of Court functions. Germany becoming eventually the scene of the greatest expansion of chamber music, it is from this, rather than from the Italian precedent, that the term acquired its present connotation. During the later part of the eighteenth century and nearly the whole of the nineteenth the cultivation of chamber music in this modern sense spread quickly among the middle classes, and as the German classics began to become known in other countries, so did the cultivation of chamber music.

It would, however, be a mistake to begin our survey of chamber music from the rise of the German classics, for, although it took a new form then, it really had a much longer history, and existed for generations before the term came into general use. Chamber music is in fact as old as concerted vocal music. As has been pointed out elsewhere in this volume already, it is quite wrong to imagine the music of the polyphonic period as consisting entirely of unaccompanied motets and madrigals. Instruments were in use for purposes of accompaniment and for entertainment, and as the resources of vocal counterpoint were developed it was natural for instrumental performers to avail themselves of them. But vocal music had a long start, and instrumental music was at first slow to follow. It should, however, be borne in mind that the madrigal enshrined the same ideal as chamber music in being the music of friends. The part-books would be handed round in the same spirit, and no doubt if any present could play an instrument he was invited to join in. Thus originated in Italy " madrigali per sonare e cantare," and in England madrigals " apt for voices and instruments." It is even possible that the almost incredible wealth of compositions for any number of voices from three to six was one of the influences retarding the growth of instrumental chamber music. When such beautiful music abounded, why seek elsewhere ?

Thus the early records of concerted instrumental music are scant, but there can be no doubt of its antiquity. At Florence there is a manuscript containing a piece for four viols by Philippe Caron, who was a pupil of Binchois and Dufay, the founders of Franco-Flemish polyphony, besides others by Anthoine Busnois and Alexander Agricola, both of whom were pupils of Okeghem, one of its earliest masters. This places the beginning of chamber music back in the fifteenth century. The English claim the invention of instrumental music for Hugh Aston, who appeared a little later, but the evidence is somewhat scanty. What is, however, incontestable is that concerted instrumental music in the form of pieces for a " consort of viols " took a tremendous leap forward in this country. King Henry VIII composed numerous pieces for three and four viols and extended his patronage to William Cornyshe. In 1599 Thomas Morley published his " First Book of Consort Lessons, made by divers exquisite Authors for six Instruments." By then the " Fancy " or " Fantasy " had established itself as the most popular form of consorted piece. Both William Byrd and Orlando Gibbons wrote Fantasies for viols. Another noted composer of concerted music of that period was John Cooper, known by his Italianised name as Coprario. From their day to that of Henry Purcell appeared a constant flow of such pieces by, among others, Martin Peerson, Michael East, Thomas Tomkins, William Lawes (pupil of Coprario), Simon Ives, Christopher Simpson, John Jenkins, and Matthew Locke. Finally in Henry Purcell's string Fantasies of 1680 the story of this early English chamber music reaches a brilliant culmination, after which, however, the curtain falls for many a long year.

Developments in France do not offer the same interest. In fact André Maugars, an eminent French viol-player of the early seventeenth century, who visited the Court of James I, has left on record his opinion that the English school of his day far surpassed that of any other nation, including his own. To judge by the publications of Pierre Attaignant, the famous French music printer of the mid-sixteenth century, the instrumental music most in demand consisted of dances, of which he issued several sets for viols. Of these the most attractive are the " Six Livres de Danceries à quatre et cinq parties " by Claude Gervaise. Greater importance is, however, attributed to the " Fantasies à trois, quatre, cinq et six parties " of Eustache du Caurroy, Sieur de St. Frémin, which, no fewer than 42 in number, were published in 1610, the year after his death. Later in the seventeenth century French taste favoured larger combinations, equivalent to what we should nowadays call a chamber orchestra.

Considering the long period during which English music succumbed to German influences there is a certain satisfaction in knowing that, in the period when chamber music was represented by the consort of viols, German aspirants came to England to study these instruments, and English musicians found a profitable field of employment in Germany. John Dowland, the lutanist, was their forerunner. He was followed by William Brade ; John Price, who formed a *Kleine Kammermusik* at Dresden for the Elector of Saxony ; Walter Rowe, who occupied a position of similar eminence at Berlin ; and Thomas Simpson. Many of their works were published in Germany, together with others by English composers. Their greater German contemporaries were occupied with Lutheran song and with that noble school of organ playing to culminate later in Johann Sebastian Bach. But numerous societies existed for the cultivation of instrumental music in private and drew upon the works of such composers as Johann Schein, whose " Banchetto musicale," dedicated to Duke Johann Ernst of Weimar, contains twenty suites of pieces, Johann Rosenmüller, and at a later date Heinrich Biber, the violinist. But the great days of German chamber music were yet to come.

In Italy the favourite instrumental form was the canzone, at first adapted from its vocal counterpart, but then developed for instrumental performance. Thus Florenzio Maschera published a book of instrumental " Canzoni a quattro voci " at Brescia in 1584, and Floriano Canali one of " Canzoni da sonare a quattro et otto voci " at Venice in 1600. Like Maschera, and Merula before them, he had been organist at Brescia, which seems to have been an important centre for instrumental music. It was also the birthplace of Biagio Marini, who was to effect a revolution in this early chamber music and virtually to place it on its modern footing. He wrote a large number of compositions, many of which are definitely described as *per musica di camera*. Brescia also preceded Cremona as the home of great makers of the new instruments, the violin family. The two Magginis, the two Pastas, Bente, Rodiani and Zanetto flourished there. Thus in both senses it is at Brescia that the new era in chamber music was inaugurated.

## CHAPTER II

# THE COMING OF THE VIOLIN

NEARLY ALL the music so far mentioned was composed for viols. Some of it has appeared in modern garb for the instruments of the violin family, but it must not be assumed that the effect is that intended by the composer. The violin has superseded the viol by virtue of its greater brilliance. A cynic has said somewhere that in the evolution of musical instruments the law is the survival of the loudest. The tone of the viols, played as they were with the bow over the hand, was far more delicate, as anyone will know who has attended a Dolmetsch concert. Adaptation is bound to involve a certain amount of sound distortion. Therefore, apart from concerts given by those who specialise in the old instruments, authentic chamber music begins for us with the rise to power of the violin with its companions the viola, 'cello and bass. Once these instruments came into general use, the development of chamber music as we understand it to-day set in at a rapid rate.

The first stage was represented by the succession of Italian violinist-composers who developed the manner of writing for the instrument. The outstanding names are those of Maurizio Cazzati and his pupil Giovanni Battista Vitali, Giovanni Legrenzi, Giuseppe Torelli, Giovanni Battista Bassani, and finally Arcangelo Corelli. They were not specialists in chamber music. In fact their greatest achievement, the Concerto grosso, created by Corelli, lies outside the scope of this Book as it represents an early stage of orchestral music. But all of them wrote works that come under the description of chamber music. This phase reached its culmination in the four sets of sonatas by Corelli, two of which consist of *Sonate da chiesa* and two of *Sonate da camera*. Not only are they of great musical interest in themselves, but they represent the standard form taken by a vast quantity of early chamber music, that of the sonata for two violins and a figured bass which was played plainly on the double-bass (violone) or with the figuration on a keyboard instrument, organ or cembalo according to circumstances. The annals of the period show a superabundance of such sonatas in all European countries. Such were for instance the sonatas of Henry Purcell. The type continued long afterwards. William Boyce published a set of twelve in 1747. A set by Pergolesi was published in England about 1780, almost a generation after Haydn had written his first string quartets.

This figured bass, or continuo accompaniment, is in fact the hall-mark of an entire classical epoch of chamber music which Professor Tovey describes as characterised by " a scheme of instrumental music in which the main parts are left completely free to execute polyphonic designs, while the task of supporting these designs with a coherent mass of harmony is relegated to a continuo player extemporising on a suitable keyboard instrument from a figured bass.' The continuo thus represented a kind of impersonal background before which the real characters of the tone-play disported themselves. It was essential to the whole, for composers made no attempt to make the parts cohere or themselves as the voices do in choral music. But it was not supposed to intrude itself. Philipp Emanuel Bach declares it to be necessary even when not distinctly heard, as in larger instrumental bodies. When no keyboard instrument was available, the playing of the bare notes of the continuo on a 'cello or bass was considered a mere makeshift. In some scores provision was made for both being available, in which case the 'cello would be provided with an ornate version of the bass part whilst the continuo player would improvise on its bare notes. It is of importance to understand the actual function of the continuo, for its passing out of current usage marks two revolutionary changes in the essential character of chamber music. The first consists in the tendency to make the instrumental parts cohere without its support—an ideal that was to be realised in the string quartet. The second consists in the promotion of the keyboard instrument, when included in the combination, from the mere ancillary position of a harmonic background to a valued and sometimes even predominant collaborator.

## CHAPTER III

# THE PARENTS OF CHAMBER MUSIC

To WHAT EXTENT those early Italian composers anticipated the coming of the form that was to represent the ideal in chamber music—that of the string quartet—will always be a matter of dispute among the erudite, for it is not easy to discern the intention of the scoring. A plausible case has been made out for a piece by Gregorio Allegri, the composer of the famous " Miserere " which Mozart wrote down from memory when in Rome in 1770. The piece in question, dating from about 1630, is certainly written in four parts, but so are some of his concertos. A much stronger claim is put forward by Professor Dent on behalf of the elder Scarlatti. He writes : " The first real string quartets were written within a few years of Corelli's death (certainly under his influence), by a composer who was traditionally his personal friend—Alessandro Scarlatti." Certainly the form was not unknown to the Italians, whether Scarlatti or another was the first to use it. But the point is not of great importance since the credit for having developed it must be given to the German-speaking countries. Meanwhile the Italians divided their attention between the solo sonata, which does not come within the purview of this Book, and the concerto, which very soon became incontestably orchestral music. Thus Tartini, although he wrote quartets that dispensed with a continuo, still has access to our concert-rooms solely with his sonatas, as Geminiani, Locatelli and others have with their concertos. Of those who concerned themselves mainly with chamber music the most prolific was a comparative late-comer, Felice de Giardini, composer of eighteen string quartets, but as he outlived Mozart he clearly belongs to a later phase of our subject.

The influence of the Italian violinists was widespread. They travelled to all musical countries and set a fashion, not only in playing, but in composition. In each country they had their imitators. In Germany there were many, few of whom achieved any noteworthy success. Although Bach himself was attracted, as is evidenced by the many Italian works he arranged, the robust art of North Germany was too firmly entrenched to " go down " before the invader. To that art is sometimes ascribed the first music for string quartet composed in Germany. The reference is to the " Hortus Musicus " of Johann Adam Reinken, the Hamburg organist whom Bach as a young man tramped many miles afoot to hear. It would, however, be stretching a point to regard this work, published in 1704 and consisting of six suites, as a prototype of the string quartet. It is laid out for two violins, viola da gamba, and figured bass, and is rarely in more than three independent parts. The position of Bach is better defined. A considerable portion of his music comes under the wider application of the term " chamber music," but the circumstance that it consists largely of solo and duo-sonatas excludes most of it from our purview here. In the narrower sense his chamber music consists of a trio for two violins and continuo, and two for violin flute and continuo, the second of which forms part of the " Musikalisches Opfer " that he wrote for Frederick the Great in 1747. This was the second of two works based on a theme supplied by the King himself, the first being the " Art of Fugue." It exploits some of the theme's yet remaining possibilities. As the continuo part has been worked out by Bach's pupil, Kirnberger, his version presents the nearest approach to chamber music in the modern sense to be found in his works. His contemporary, Telemann, is another German composer credited with having forestalled the coming of the string quartet. His Tafelmusik is certainly an anticipation of the spirit of chamber music, but as to the form the evidence is contradictory. Finally Evaristo dall' Abaco, musical director to Max Emanuel of Bavaria, another claimant, and an interesting composer to boot, can be left out of account as he did not dispense with the continuo. The birth of the new art must be dated after his time.

## CHAPTER IV

# THE NEW ART IS BORN

ITS BIRTHPLACE can almost definitely be stated to have been Mannheim, where Johann Wenzel Stamitz, the founder of the Mannheim school of violinists, began giving chamber concerts in 1743. Among his pupils were his two sons, Carl, who remained at Mannheim, and Anton, who went to Paris, as well as Cannabich who succeeded him as conductor. Others associated with the Mannheim group were Franz Xavier Richter, Anton Filtz, and Carlo

Toeschi. Meanwhile Jan Zach, a Czech like Stamitz, Georg Matthias Monn, and Georg Christoph Wagenseil were producing chamber music in Vienna, and Placidus von Camerloher was doing the same at Munich. Most of these wrote quartets and more than one of them has been put forward as having done so before Haydn, but a whole army of precursors in the form would not detract from his merit in having endowed it with substance as none did before him. There is therefore no interest in investigating the claims of composers none of whom, save Stamitz, who seems to have the best title, produced music of sufficiently outstanding merit to endure.

Curiously enough Haydn himself would almost appear to have unconsciously stumbled upon the form. In his young days he acquired a reputation for writing cassations, divertimenti, serenades and the like for any instruments that happened to be available, often to be played in the open air. On the strength of that reputation he was invited in 1755 to a country house at Weinzirl, near Melk, whose owner, von Fürnberg, was accustomed to have such music played. Haydn wrote a number of these compositions and at first made so little distinction between them that what was undoubtedly his first symphony has somehow got among his quartets, where it figures as Op. 1, no. 5 ! Others appear to have been played at first indiscriminately by string quartet or string orchestra. The idea of the string quartet as a form seems to have emerged gradually at some stage of the writing of the first two sets of six, which have five movements apiece, except the one that is a symphony in disguise. But he came away from Weinzirl with eighteen of these compositions in his portfolio, and it seems beyond doubt that the third set of six, apart from their having the four movements that were to establish the tradition, can only have been intended as quartets.

Hitherto, on the authority of the Paris edition begun in 1764, the quartet in B flat which opens the first set has been accepted as Haydn's first string quartet, but recently Miss

Marion Scott made the discovery that the Hummel edition published in Amsterdam opened with a different quartet altogether, in E flat; this is plainly inscribed Op.1, no.1, but disappeared from later editions. It is of course just possible that Haydn himself arranged its withdrawal, as composers will, deeming their early works no longer worthy of them, but that seems both unlike him and unlike the age in which he lived. In any case it appears that we must accept this E-flat quartet as the starting-point of modern chamber music ; if we have any sentimental regard for 83 as the long-established number of Haydn's progeny in this form, we can retain it by discarding the symphony in E flat which figures as no. 5. This first quartet may have been one of the works Haydn took with him to Weinzirl, in which case the traditional date of 1750 may be vindicated, or it may have been composed there, in which case Pohl's date of 1755 for this historic event stands proven. The former date has a fascination for historians. In that year Bach died, and his death is the landmark dividing his era from that of modern music, of which " Papa " Haydn is acclaimed the father.

## CHAPTER V

# A PAUSE FOR DEFINITION

HAVING NOW REACHED the threshold of chamber music as it is understood by the modern world, it behoves us per- haps to pause and take stock of what it comprises. Strictly speaking it includes all concerted music for any number of performers from two upwards to the point at which the orchestra begins. That point is commonly understood to be the one at which individual instrumental parts are dupli- cated, as is the practice in orchestral music. But there is an intermediate point at which a combination, without duplicated parts, is called a chamber orchestra, and that really transcends the ordinary limits of chamber music. Although, for instance, Schönberg's Chamber Symphony really conforms to the definition, few people would be disposed to regard it as chamber music, because the number of players is too large for the intimacy that is the true characteristic of the " music of friends." At the other end of the scale it is not customary to include music for voice and piano, or even pianoforte duets, the former constituting the domain of the *Lied*, and the latter being essentially piano music, though shared between partners. For the purposes of this Book all duet-sonatas have been similarly excluded, being discussed by Mr. Bonavia in Book VI, and chamber music is taken as beginning with works for three performers. Although the pleasure of duet-playing is essentially that derived from chamber music, there is a certain logic in this, for the same reasons which elsewhere ordain that two are company and three none would operate here in the opposite direction, two being somewhat exclusive, and real company commencing with three. We will therefore begin by defining chamber music as consisting, for our purposes, of works performed by not fewer than three players and, except in very rare cases, not more than nine.

The majority of this music is for strings. Long experience has established the string quartet as the most perfect, concise, and self-contained combination in all music, consisting as it does of four instruments of similar hue, whose collective range is comprehensive in the sense that they can reach every part of the scale except the extreme bass, which is not required with so small a volume of tone, and that they are sufficient for four-part harmony. Almost all composers—even opera-writers like Rossini, Auber, or Verdi—have experienced the desire at some time to write for this ideal combination. But it is a treacherous field. Precisely because it is so self-contained it demands scrupulous musicianship. In the turmoil of the orchestra a composer can " get away " with workmanship that would be mercilessly exposed in a string quartet. That is why so many composers have either preferred to keep out of this field until comparatively late in life, or have abandoned it, temporarily or permanently, after an early venture that brought them little satisfaction. If a composer is honest with himself, the writing of a string quartet is a searching test.

Works for fewer of strings than four are not common. Most of those for two violins and 'cello are a legacy of the continuo period, but from Mozart and Beethoven to modern writers, such as Hindemith, composers have gradually furnished an attractive selection of trios for violin, viola and 'cello, to which others, such as Kodaly, have added trios for two violins and 'cello. In fact one might say that if any member of a quartet party disappoints there is no reason why, with an adequate library at hand, the other three should not console themselves for his absence. For upwards of four players there exists ample material : quintets, some with two violas, some with two 'cellos, sextets, and octets, which are double quartets. Some combinations include a double bass, but the unwieldiness of that instrument makes it really unsuitable for chamber use, and the depths to which its range extends belong more properly to the orchestra.

The instrument most frequently associated with the strings in chamber music is of course the piano. We have seen how the keyboard instrument entrusted with the continuo performed purely ancillary functions, but, with the advent of chamber music as we understand it, it was not long before the keyboard was reinstated in a more honourable position. The process was begun by Haydn in his Trios, but more than any one work it was Mozart's G Minor quartet that established the piano in its new functions as a partner, later to become sometimes a predominant partner. Musical purists occasionally demur at the blend of piano and strings as not perfectly harmonious. It is a fact that whereas string players use natural intonation in enharmonics, the " well-tempered " piano substitutes a compromise, but only the most sensitive ear

Qc

can be incommoded by the difference. On the other hand it may be admitted that the percussive quality of the piano gives it an advantage which is foreign to the real free-masonry of chamber music and that, especially in late romantic works, the pianist is readily tempted to regard himself as playing a concerto with stringed accompaniment. There are, in fact, many modern chamber works weighted with piano parts that make as heavy demands on virtuosity as any concerto. On the whole the combinations with piano have not the same purity as those of strings only, but in practice that has not deterred the greatest composers from writing splendid chamber music in which the piano is prominent. It consists in the main of trios for piano, violin and 'cello, quartets for piano, violin, viola and 'cello, and quintets for piano and string quartet. For convenience these are commonly referred to as piano trios, piano quartets and piano quintets. Piano sextets are relatively uncommon.

The association of one wind instrument with strings is usually successful, the piquancy of contrast compensating for the disturbed balance of tone. Such works are numerous, the wind instrument being the flute, oboe, clarinet or horn. One calls to mind Brahms's horn trio, the clarinet quintets of Mozart and Brahms, the recent oboe quintets of Bax and Bliss, and many other charming compositions of this class. A larger admixture of wind instruments produces good effects but of a more orchestral timbre, and as the wind element increases in importance we seem, illogically but instinctively, to be moving away from the essential quality of chamber music. When we reach combinations for wind instruments alone—generally wind quintets for flute, oboe, clarinet, bassoon and horn—the quality of tone produced demands a greater space than a private room, in which it is apt to prove overpowering, and, since it sounds far more satisfactory in a concert hall, it partakes more of the nature of concert music than of chamber music. There is a large literature of such music, but for this reason we propose to touch upon it more sparingly.

There is one other combination that has contact with chamber music. It is that of one or more voices with a small combination of instruments. It ranges from songs with string quartet accompaniment to chamber operas, such as Holst's memorably beautiful " Savitri." But for practical reasons we prefer to regard the former as belonging more properly to the domain of song, and the latter to that of opera.

## CHAPTER VI

# CHAMBER MUSIC AND SONATA FORM

BY FAR THE GREATEST bulk of chamber music, particularly in classical and romantic times, is composed in sonata-form. At the end of the eighteenth century there were divertimenti, and occasionally in the nineteenth some composer would venture to write a suite, but for practically the whole of that century the string quartet was so closely associated with sonata-form that to mention one was to imply the other. The devotees of chamber music were so imbued with this tradition that it was difficult for them to take seriously any work not in sonata-form. Friedrich Kiel must have been a very venturesome fellow indeed to write two sets of waltzes for string quartet, and when, later, the Russians began to write agreeable sets of pieces for that sacrosanct combination, it was taken almost as a mark of self-confessed inferiority to German standards. This priggish attitude has done chamber music an incredible amount of harm. It was peculiar to the nineteenth century. The eighteenth liked its music crisp, clear and on occasion gay, the twentieth likes it pungent, concise, and on occasion ironic. But it is the nineteenth that has contributed the bulk of the repertoire, and that is the reason why to the man in the street—or, let us say, the wireless listener—the term chamber music is commonly accepted as indicating lengthy, erudite works for the consumption of the few. It is a misconception that time alone can eradicate by enriching the repertoire with works of lighter calibre to restore the balance. Meanwhile, if chamber music is to regain the hold it had on the musical public in the days of the Saturday and Monday Pops, it behoves the organisers to leaven their programmes in accordance with modern taste, and flank the greater classics with music affording relaxation by contrast.

If the Mannheim school is most probably to be given the credit for launching upon the world in its definitive form the institution we know as the string quartet, the shape of the music written for it was determined by the new symphonic form the introduction of which is generally attributed to Carl Philipp Emanuel Bach. He it was who gave sonata-form its new direction, and though Haydn does not appear to have been associated with him at any time, there can be little doubt that in his search for the ideal form he was influenced by the elder master. C. P. E. Bach wrote a quantity of chamber music as did also two of Johann Sebastian's younger sons, Johann Christoph and Johann Christian, the latter known as the English Bach, from his long residence in this country. These younger Bachs were, however, Haydn's contemporaries, not his precursors.

## CHAPTER VII

## HAYDN: FIRST PERIOD

HAYDN'S LARGE OUTPUT of chamber music is conveniently divided into two periods by an interval of ten years between two consecutive sets of quartets, Op. 20, composed in 1771, and Op. 33, composed in 1781. Of the latter he has himself said, in a letter, that they are in an

" entirely new style." This interval also corresponds with a period of great activity in Mozart's career, from his fifteenth to his twenty-fifth year. Haydn was destined to outlive Mozart by many years, and if the younger composer benefited at first from the elder's example, there can be no doubt that the debt was amply repaid in the end, Haydn's later works, such as the well-known Salomon Symphonies, being distinctly influenced by Mozart. Although this influence is not conspicuous in the first quartets that followed the ten-years' interval, it asserted itself also in these before the last of them were penned. This gives an added significance to the subdivision of Haydn's chamber music. The earlier period was one not so much of experiment, for which Haydn had little need after the experience gained in the first dozen quartets, as of quest—search for the most congenial mode of expression. As Professor Tovey has said : " If Haydn's career had ended there (after Op. 20) nobody would have guessed which of some half-dozen different lines he would have followed up," and he proceeds to enumerate them, but begins the next paragraph with : " Something different happened."

This first period of Haydn's chamber music itself permits of subdivision into two groups, each comprising three sets of six quartets each. The first eighteen quartets were composed, as we have seen, consecutively, though possibly incorporating some earlier material. Of these the first twelve could equally well be described as consisting of eleven divertimenti and a symphony. Yet they contain some highly characteristic and even prophetic movements, such as, for instance, the Andante of the F minor quartet, Op. 2, no. 4, and some of those that are in variation form. The third set, however, shows such progress as to make it appear probable that the two earlier sets represent the accumulated material he had by him at the time, and the third the outcome of his experience at Weinzirl. One of this set, Op. 3, no. 5, in F major, with a serenade for its slow movement, ranks with his most popular quartets and the minuet from Op. 3, no. 3, nicknamed the *Dudelsack* or Bagpipes Minuet, is a universal favourite. In these three sets Haydn has definitely found the solution of the problems that confronted him at the outset. The first of these, the distribution of the functions formerly filled by the continuo, was very early disposed of, and the others, mainly formal, were brought to the stage where principles were established and only amplification remained for the future. In fact, in these three sets the modern string quartet was not only born, but reached adolescence.

An interval divides them from the next three sets. Haydn had meanwhile entered the service of Prince Esterhazy, written a large quantity of music for his band, and generally broadened his experience. This shows in the next set, Op. 9, one of which, no. 4, in D minor, is fairly well known. The six comprised in Op. 17 are more important. It is here that we begin to encounter the regular concert repertoire, which may be said to include most of the six quartets comprised in Op. 20, the first to be known in the literature of chamber music as " great " quartets. They bore another description, being known as the " Sun " quartets, though one of them, the fifth, in F minor, is anything but sunny. With this set Haydn's development period is completed. Not only had he, so to speak, put the string quartet on its feet, but in certain movements he had attained to a height not often surpassed in his later works. It is the sustained quality of these and their maturity of thought that constitute their superiority.

Whilst Haydn gave the continuo its quietus so far as the quartet was concerned, he was at the same time paving the way for the modern use of the keyboard instrument in chamber music. The majority of his numerous piano trios belong to this early period and though few of them approach the quartets in musical value, there is a special interest in the manner of their progress. At first the 'cello part is almost limited to duplicating the essential notes of the bass already present in the piano part. Such trios form the connecting link with the continuo period. Nor can it be said that subsequent emancipation proceeds very far, but it proceeds far enough to afford an inkling of the role the keyboard is to fill in later chamber music. It was left for Mozart to give a clearer indication, but not until he had won his spurs in quartet writing.

## CHAPTER VIII

# MOZART

THIS WAS IN 1770. His first quartet, in G major, made its appearance at Lodi on March 15th, and is plainly inspired by Italian influences. Two years later he wrote three more at Salzburg in which these influences are blended with that of Haydn. These, however, he described as divertimenti. Before the end of 1773 he had added a round dozen more (K. 155–160 and 168–173) in which the Haydn influence is powerful, but not enough to stem the assertion of the growing Mozartian idiom. To these he added the first of his string quintets (K. 174). Then ensued, as with Haydn, a break that lasted nine years, towards the end of which appeared Haydn's Op. 33, the six " Russian " quartets. In fact at this stage the most objective way of dealing with the works of the two composers would be to follow them chronologically, year by year, but to avoid confusion it will be more practical to complete our survey of those by Mozart.

During the respite from quartet-writing he wrote his first piano trio, two flute quartets and one oboe quartet, this last being frequently heard in our concert-rooms. Then followed the six quartets composed in 1782–5 which, col-lectively, he dedicated to his " dear friend Haydn." Never-theless, though this may be regarded as an acknowledg-ment of what he had learned from the elder composer's example, these quartets are far more definitely Mozartian than any of their predecessors. The second of them, in D minor, reveals Mozart in tragic mood, and the last, in C major, is preceded by an introduction with " false relations " that set contemporary teeth on edge and have been a subject of controversy ever since.

During the same four years he wrote also a piano trio, a quintet for piano and wind instruments, and the first of his piano quartets, in G minor, from which may be said to date the rehabilitation of the keyboard instrument in chamber music. There are many who regard this work as the direct ancestor of the great piano quintets of Schumann and Brahms. The second, in E flat, followed in 1786, with two more trios, and the isolated string quartet in D (K. 499). The most popular work of the following year lies really beyond the domain of chamber music, but it is difficult to resist mentioning the Serenade, " Eine kleine Nachtmusik," which, though orchestral, can be played as a quintet and even as a quartet. It is by far the most popular concerted work of 1787-8, the others being mainly trios, apart from the noble string quintet in G minor (K. 516) ; the most famous work of 1789 is just as certainly the clarinet quintet to which that of Brahms has so often formed a pendant, with some other work to furnish an intermediate contrast of sonority. In that and the following year Mozart wrote his last three quartets, the so-called " Berlin " set, commissioned for King Frederick William II of Prussia (K. 575, 589, 590). These are fine works, but not more so than their predecessors. Most chamber music enthusiasts turn even more eagerly to Mozart's quintets, especially the one in G minor already mentioned, and the two in D and E flat which now followed (K. 593 and 614) and complete the list of Mozart's more important chamber works.

# CHAPTER IX

# HAYDN: SECOND PERIOD

HAYDN'S OP. 33, which seems to have had such a stimulating effect on Mozart, and with which he resumed the series of his quartets, consists of six of them, variously known as the "Russian," from their dedication to the Grand Duke Paul of Russia, "Gli Scherzi," from the fact that its minuets are thus designated by Haydn, and "Jungfernquartette." Their central point is the well-known quartet in C, nick-named the "Bird," from the duet which serves as trio to its scherzo. The whole set stands very high among Haydn's works, both for the rich quality of the first movements and for the lightheartedness of the finales, which breathe the spirit of serene comedy. They are followed by an isolated and somewhat short quartet in D minor, Op. 42. The next set of six, Op. 50, was, like the last three of Mozart, dedicated to King Frederick William II of Prussia. The best known of them are the last three, respectively in F sharp minor, F and D. The two last are of those known among enthusiasts by their nicknames. The one in F, a particularly lovely one, is called "le Rêve," from its slow movement, and the one in D is known as "The Frog," from the leaping character of its finale. This brings the number of quartets to 49, comprised in eight sets of six each and one isolated one. From this point the numbering is apt to cause confusion. In 1785 Haydn composed "The Seven Last Words" in response to a request received from the chapter of the Cathedral of Cadiz for instrumental music appropriate for performance on Good Friday. It was also produced in London as a "Passion instrumentale" and afterwards enlarged by the addition of vocal parts. From this music seven movements were arranged as string quartets under the same title. They have, of course, nothing to do with Haydn's other works in this form, but in some editions they are inserted here, on chronological grounds, as nos. 50–56, whilst in others they are added as a kind of supplement to the 76 quartets proper, numbered 77–83. The next two sets, Op. 54 and 55, comprise only three quartets each, in which are included some of the finest examples. Those in C, E and A (Op. 54, nos. 2 and 3, Op. 55, no. 1), are universal favourites among quartet players, public or private. Op. 55, no. 2, is known as " The Razor." The story is that in 1787 Bland, the English music publisher, visited Haydn at the request of Salomon, to commission some music from him. He came at an awkward moment, for the great man was shaving, and in difficulties. Hearing him exclaim : " I would give my best quartet for a good razor," Bland is said to have rushed back to his inn and fetched his own pair, which he presented to the composer.

Of the next set, Op. 64, the fifth, in D, is the best known by the entry of the first violin, from which it derives its nickname of " The Lark," and the short rapid movement with which it concludes, but the sixth runs it close in popularity, and the third and fourth are often played. The neglected ones are the first and second, the former perhaps with reason, the latter undeservedly. Then follow once more two sets of three each, Op. 71 and 74, the latter including another famous one in G minor, known as " The Rider " from the jog-trot rhythm of its opening movement, but specially admired for its Largo. Then follow the six quartets, Op. 76, of which the third contains the famous " Variations on the Emperor's Hymn " from which it takes its name, and the fourth is known as " The Sunrise." With the two quartets, Op. 77, Haydn's last completed works in this form, and in the opinion of many his greatest, and an unfinished fragment in B flat which brings the number to 76 (or 83 if the " Seven Words " are included), we reach the end of our survey.

## CHAPTER X

# SOME CONTEMPORARIES OF HAYDN

HAYDN'S REMAINING CHAMBER WORKS are so completely overshadowed by the greatness of his later quartets that there is no point in dwelling on them here, especially as they are rarely played except in private. It is more profitable to turn to some of his less known contemporaries, whose works are a happy hunting-ground for the curious. A few of them have already been mentioned, such as Franz Xavier Richter, whose best quartets coincide in time roughly with Haydn's Op. 9, 17 and 20, and Johann Christian Bach, who began publishing his chamber music in London soon afterwards. Some mystery surrounds the story of Franz Beck, a Mannheimer who became involved in a duel and had to escape to France, where his symphonies met with success. He is not credited with any chamber music, but Dr. Sondheimer, a scholar of repute, is of opinion that he influenced Boccherini, and it is also possible that Gossec was indebted to him. He was preceded in France by Johann Schobert, an Alsatian harpsichordist who was one of the pioneers in the use of his instrument in chamber music otherwise than as continuo. Gossec is referred to by Mozart, in a letter dated April 5th, 1778, as his very good friend and a very dry man. Besides being a successful composer of operas, he is described in Grove's Dictionary as the "founder of symphonic music in France" and has an almost equally good title to be called the founder of French chamber music. His works include eighteen string quartets which had a spell of popularity. Boccherini was the greatest Italian composer of instrumental music of his day, and Haydn's most serious rival. One has to be wary nowadays in the use of the epithet "feminine," but it is permissible to quote a violinist of the period, Giuseppe

Puppo, who, comparing the two styles, declared that "Boccherini is the wife of Haydn." Certain it is that, but for Haydn, Boccherini would be ranked to-day with the great classics. Like Mozart, he owed something at the outset to the influence of Sammartini, possibly also to that of Pugnani. In 1768 he came to Paris, where he was extra-ordinarily successful and where his first chamber works were published. Yet he left very soon for Spain, where he spent much of the rest of his life, though he was for a few years in Germany as chamber-composer to King Frederick William II of Prussia, whose name recurs frequently in the annals of chamber music. Boccherini wrote an enormous amount of music, including 113 string quintets and 102 string quartets. Yet to the average man, and even to many music lovers, he is represented only by a certain charming but hackneyed minuet, which is a sample of many. One would have thought that its popularity would have stimu-lated interest in the others.

Another prolific composer was Karl Ditters von Ditters-dorf, at once a friend and a rival of Haydn, whose junior he was by seven years. His principal output was, however, in opera, and though he also wrote chamber music, to-day he is remembered only by six string quartets which were reprinted in 1866. Emanuel Aloys Foerster, composer of a large quantity of chamber music, was probably among the first to hear a Beethoven quartet, for the younger composer was a constant visitor at his house and so were Schup-panzigh and his companions, who were his favourite performers. Koželuch, who succeeded Mozart as Court Composer to Leopold II in Prague, wrote a vast amount of chamber music which is remembered only because Schubert professed to admire it. Ignaz Pleyel was a pupil of Haydn ; he eventually settled in Paris as a music publisher and founded the firm of piano-makers that still bears his name. He wrote a considerable amount of chamber music, of very unequal value, among which, however, are a few quartets that have been deemed worthy of revival. Dussek, who lent Haydn his favourite piano while they were both in London, was a celebrated performer on that instrument, and, as might be expected, it plays an important part in his chamber music, which includes only three string quartets. Though his works for piano and strings are marred by a tendency to the abuse of virtuosity, they are the most important of their kind between Mozart and Beethoven, whose immediate predecessor he was.

# B : FROM BEETHOVEN TO BRAHMS

## CHAPTER I

## BEETHOVEN: FIRST PERIOD

MUCH HAS BEEN SAID of the division of Beethoven's creative career into three periods, which was first suggested by Fétis, then worked out by Wilhelm von Lenz, and has since been adopted by practically every writer on music. For the major works it is a well-proved classification. Beethoven's masterpieces do indicate three distinct styles or modes of expression, which Vincent d'Indy has defined as periods of imitation, of externalisation and of reflection. The first is that in which the young artist continues the art-production of his time after the manner of his predecessors, or of his favourites among his contemporaries. The second is that in which he begins to walk alone and to reach self-expression. The third is that in which he retires within himself to create in pure joy and sorrow, without external preoccupation. Obviously that is also the period in which from the ripeness of his experience he enlarges the confines of his art. But if this classification can safely be followed, for instance, with Beethoven's string quartets, it is unwise to trust it implicitly. Such phases of a composer's work are not sharply marked off one from another. There is no ascertainable date at which they move forward from one to the next. If, therefore, we adopt this classification here, it is with the reservation that it is to be regarded simply as a matter of convenience and not as dogma.

Beethoven's earliest chamber music consists of three piano quartets composed in 1785, when he was fifteen, but not published until 1832, five years after his death, a sure guide to his opinion of them. His practice with the works of his youth appears to have been to revise such as he thought to have been of any value and to ignore the others. His next chamber work, a piano trio in E flat, composed in 1787, also remained unpublished until after his death. In 1791-2, however, he began to compose music for which he subsequently had a higher regard. He then wrote an octet for wind instruments, of which the original version did not appear until 1834, though he made an arrangement of it for piano quintet, which he published in 1797 as Op. 4 and in later years another for piano trio, Op. 63. It was about the same time that he wrote the Rondino for wind instruments, frequently heard at the Queen's Hall Promenade Concerts, and the first version of the trio for violin, viola and 'cello which was eventually published as Op. 3. With two other works mentioned below, this completes what has survived from the Bonn period. Late in 1792 the composer settled in Vienna and was for a time immersed in study. The earliest chamber work of this period is a trio for two oboes and cor anglais, said to have been composed in 1794 but not published until 1806 when it appeared as Op. 87. We now reach the stage at which the composer felt himself ripe to produce his Op. 1. This consists of three piano trios composed early in 1795 and published by subscription. The following year produced the quintet for piano and wind instruments, Op. 16, and two revisions of early works, one a serenade trio for violin, viola and 'cello, Op. 8, and the other a sextet for string quartet with two horns, which was to reach its final form in 1809 as Op. 81b. The three string trios, Op. 9, were probably also begun that year and completed in 1797. They were published July 21st, 1798. To that year belongs the trio for piano, clarinet and 'cello, Op. 11, the variations in which are on a theme taken from an opera by Joseph Weigl, " L'Amor marinaro," produced on October 18th, 1797. This finale was the occasion of the encounter with Steibelt that caused Beethoven to dislike it ever afterwards.

Many of the above works still hold their own in the chamber repertoire, but they pale in significance beside the two with which Beethoven's first period reaches its conclusion : the six first string quartets, Op. 18, and the septet, Op. 20. Both were completed in 1800, but there is evidence that some of the quartets had been begun some years earlier and probably the septet had been in preparation at least a year. Beethoven was now thirty. He had produced many well-known works, such as the " Sonate Pathétique " for piano. As long ago as 1795 Count Apponyi had commissioned a string quartet from him. That he delayed so long may perhaps be taken as an indication of how acutely he felt the responsibility. Be that as it may, it was only now that he embarked upon the series of quartets which, to chamber music enthusiasts, are the most important works ever conceived in this form. Here, however, he is still within the period of indebtedness to his predecessors, notably C. P. E. Bach and Haydn, but perhaps also F. W. Rust, whose influence can be traced in Beethoven's development of sonata-form. The first of the six quartets to be composed was the one which, in order of publication, appears as no. 3 in D. It was followed by that in F which now opens the series. The next were the second, in G, and the fifth in A, the fourth and sixth being the last completed. These six quartets belong clearly to the aftermath of Haydn and Mozart and do not show as much advance upon these as is revealed in the contemporary piano sonatas. It was scarcely to be expected. But if perhaps there is less to be discerned in them than generations of enthusiasts have claimed to discover, the fact remains that they are fine works, fully justifying the affection in which they are held.

The septet for violin, viola, 'cello, double bass, clarinet, bassoon and horn is one of Beethoven's most popular works. It was first heard at a private party given by Prince Schwarzenberg, and then performed in public at the Court Theatre on April 2nd, 1800. The theme of the variations forming the fourth of its six movements is a folk-song from the lower Rhine, which Beethoven probably heard as a boy at Bonn, and the Minuet is a different version of that belonging to the little piano sonata in G, Op. 49, no. 2, composed in 1796. The septet was an immediate success, and soon appeared in numerous arrangements, which caused Beethoven afterwards to hold it in light esteem, although one of them, for piano, clarinet (or violin) and 'cello, was from his own pen and published as Op. 38.

## CHAPTER II

# BEETHOVEN : SECOND PERIOD

As if to show how arbitrary are the limits held to divide one period from the next, Beethoven's second period opens with two works of practically the same date as the septet : the string quintet in C, Op. 29, and the Serenade for flute, violin and 'cello, Op. 25, of which the former was published in December 1801, and the latter at the beginning of 1802. It is only on looking at the contemporary piano sonatas, which include the " Moonlight " and the " Pastoral," that one realises why these two works are included in the second period and not the first. But a very different story has to be told concerning the three string quartets, Op. 59, begun on May 26th, 1806, and dedicated to Count Rasoumovsky, by whose name they are familiarly known in musical circles. Count Rasoumovsky probably became acquainted with Beethoven through his brother-in-law, Prince Lichnovsky, who was one of the composer's patrons. He was a highly cultured man and a good musician, playing the second violin in a quartet party comprising Schuppanzigh, leader, Weiss, viola, and Lincke, 'cello. Presumably out of compliment to his nationality Beethoven included two Russian folk-tunes in the quartets. The first is a simple little song which furnishes the theme of the finale of the quartet in F, Op. 59, no. 1, and the second is the well-known " Slava " which Moussorgsky has used as the Coronation Chorus in " Boris Godounov." Here it forms the trio in the Scherzo of the quartet in E minor, Op. 59, no. 2.

Though the severest critics deny to these quartets the formal perfection of those still to follow, their judgment savours of the academic and does not reflect the attitude of those whose knowledge of them is derived from the intimacy of performance. Among devotees of chamber music the Rasoumovsky quartets rank with the best appreciated works of their kind and not a few prefer them to the posthumous quartets as being more accessible and less of a tax upon musical understanding. They were followed, before the end of 1808, by the two piano trios, Op. 70, respectively in D and E flat, the first Beethoven wrote in this form since his Op. 1, which naturally show a tremendous advance, but are in turn so completely overshadowed by one that was to follow, that they have perhaps met with less than their due appreciation. Then followed another string quartet, the tenth, in E flat, Op. 74, composed in 1809 and published the following year with a dedication to Prince Lobkowitz. It is famous for its beautiful slow movement in A flat, one of those which foreshadow the Beethoven of the third period. Yet another quartet, the Eleventh, in F minor, Op. 95, was composed in 1810. It has two features calling for special notice. The first is the remote key, D major, chosen for the second movement. The second is the evidence afforded in the finale of the composer's desire, as in the sonatas, to emancipate himself from the convention of the final rondo, to which he returns only once in the later quartets, in the fifteenth. It was followed in 1811 by another of those works that have been held in general affection by generations of players for upwards of a century without showing any signs of becoming staled by familiarity. This is the " Archduke " Trio in B flat, Op. 97, so called because it is dedicated to the composer's great friend, pupil and patron, the Archduke Rudolph of Austria. The Variations and Finale of this work belong to the greatest movements to be found in Beethoven's chamber music. A short posthumous trio in one movement

written in 1812 " for his little friend, Maximiliana Brentano,
to encourage her in playing the piano," falls within this
period, but is otherwise scarcely worth mentioning.

## CHAPTER III

# BEETHOVEN: THIRD PERIOD

THE THIRD PERIOD opens with two string quintets of
which the first, Op. 104, is merely an adaptation to this form
of an early piano trio, Op. 1, no. 3, to which the composer
was provoked in 1815 by someone else having undertaken
this task and performed it badly. The second is a Fugue in
D, composed in 1817 for a collection projected by Tobias
Haslinger, the publisher, but not published until 1827. We
now reach the last of Beethoven's string quartets to be published during his life-time, the twelfth, in E flat, Op. 127,
composed in 1824, performed for the first time on March
6th, 1825, and issued in parts in March, 1826. It had been
commissioned by Prince Galitzin in 1822, but Beethoven
was then deeply immersed in his ninth (Choral) symphony.
D'Indy calls this quartet the last of his pastoral symphonies,
for it was written in the country and breathes the love of
nature that was so characteristic of the composer. It contains yet another great slow movement, an adagio with
variations.

The posthumous quartets stand alone. They were not
composed in the order in which they are numbered, the
first being the fifteenth, in A minor, Op. 132, which dates
from the illness the composer suffered in the summer of
1825, to which he refers in the inscription that heads the
third of its five movements : " Song of Thanksgiving in the
Lydian mode, offered to the Divinity by a Convalescent."
Then followed the thirteenth, in B flat, Op. 130 in six
movements, which was begun in 1825 and finished in the

summer of 1826, the finale then consisting of a " Grande Fugue tantôt libre, tantôt recherchée," but the composer's friends were so intimidated by its vast dimensions that they prevailed upon him to substitute the present finale, which was composed in November 1826. It is in this, the substituted finale, that will be found the theme which instigated, rather than inspired, Borodin's quartet in A major. The Fugue, one of Beethoven's most colossal conceptions, is now known as a separate work, Op. 133. The fourteenth quartet, Op. 131, in C sharp minor, and the sixteenth, Op. 135, in F major, were both composed in 1826, the latter being dated October 26th. Another fragment that dates from November of that year is the Andante maestoso in C major from the sketches of a projected string quintet commissioned by Diabelli, and published by them about 1840 in arrangements for piano solo and piano duet under the title " Beethoven's Last Musical Thought." He died on March 26th, 1827.

The comments to which the posthumous quartets have given rise would fill volumes. They made their way in the world but slowly. For many years after Beethoven's death they were regarded as, to say the least, enigmatic. Even to-day, when their glorious achievement has long been acknowledged and understood, there are still some who pause before them as before some temple to which initiation is necessary. This is the less surprising in that Beethoven's immediate successors for the most part misunderstood his teaching, both as regards cyclic form, and as revealed in the Beethoven variation. When Liszt and Wagner initiated so-called metamorphosis of themes they were thought to have diverged from the classic line, represented by Brahms, whereas in reality they were carrying out the indications of the Beethoven variation. As for cyclic form—the development of a cyclic sonata from thematic cells—there exists scarcely a sign of it between Beethoven's posthumous quartets and the mature works of César Franck. But the subject of Beethoven's last quartets is too vast for treatment here. One can only refer the reader to Vincent d'Indy's wonderful analysis in Cobbett's

Cyclopedia, and to Joseph de Marliave's volume, of which an English translation by Hilda Andrews was issued in 1928 by the Oxford University Press.

## CHAPTER IV

# THE ROMANTIC DAWN

BEFORE PROCEEDING with Beethoven's contemporaries in his own part of Europe it is appropriate that we should turn aside in favour of one who was not only his senior by ten years, but with whom there was an exchange of influences recalling that between Haydn and Mozart. Beethoven had the highest regard for Cherubini, whom he esteemed above all living writers for the stage. He even declared that if ever he wrote a Requiem, he would borrow from Cherubini's. On the other hand Cherubini was profoundly impressed with Beethoven's quartets, of which eleven had appeared before he, the older man, wrote his first, in E flat. This was in 1814. Cherubini's second quartet, in G, is merely an adaptation of the Symphony composed in 1815 for the Philharmonic Society of London, with a new Adagio added in 1829. His best quartets were yet to come. The third, in D minor, was completed on July 31st, 1834, the fourth February 12th, 1835, the fifth June 28th, 1835, and the sixth July 22nd, 1837, after which he wrote a string quintet which was completed on October 28th, 1837. Beethoven had then been dead ten years, and Cherubini was advanced in his seventies. He had absorbed all that Beethoven had written, and, like him, had reached a stage of inward reflection, composing without external preoccupation. A further analogy is that Cherubini's last three quartets were published posthumously. He was a great musician. He could scarcely have been otherwise and earned Beethoven's warmly expressed admiration. The worst that can be said of him is that his great skill is sometimes too apparent. But by the eighteen-thirties the Romantic Movement had set in and he was too austerely classical to find favour at such a time. Nevertheless, his quartets held their place in the repertoire until comparatively recent times. The only other composers in France who were writing chamber music of note at this time were Baillot, Onslow and Urhan.

Returning to the German-speaking countries, a passing mention is all that is due to Gyrowetz, Steibelt, Romberg or Reicha, prolific as they all were, but in the compositions of Hummel there is much that is still of interest to-day. His best-known work is the septet for piano, flute, oboe, viola, 'cello, double bass and horn, Op. 74, which is still occasionally heard, but there is greater merit in the piano quintet, Op. 87 (with double bass), which is his best chamber work. He also wrote seven piano trios, three string quartets, and a " Military " septet, Op. 114, so called because of the inclusion of the trumpet, the other instruments being piano, flute, violin, clarinet, 'cello and double bass.

Weber is the first of the great Romantics we encounter in the field of chamber music, but it was not congenial to his flamboyant temperament and his contribution amounts to no more than three works, the composition of which was spread over many years. Thus the adagio of the piano quartet, Op. 18, was composed at Karlsruhe, on October 15th, 1806, but the work was not completed until September 25th, 1809. This is the best known of the three. The clarinet quintet was begun in 1811, on the composer becoming acquainted with Heinrich Joseph Baermann, a virtuoso of that instrument, with whom he travelled, but it was not completed until August 24th, 1815. Strictly speaking, it is a solo work for clarinet with string accompaniment, and in no way to be compared with that of Mozart. The slow movement, bearing the title " Shepherd's Lament," of the trio for piano, flute and 'cello, Op. 63, originated in October 1813, the rest of the work in 1818 and 1819. It was not so much a case of sketching and revising as of piecing together movements that were not part of a self-contained musical conception.

## CHAPTER V

## SCHUBERT

IT IS RATHER TO SCHUBERT that we turn as the pioneer of the Romantic Movement in chamber music, to which he was inured from boyhood. His was a musical family, and quartet meetings were frequent ; at them two of his elder brothers played violin, he the viola, and his father the 'cello. When he grew older the meetings took place elsewhere, but all his life he was an active participant in chamber music, and it is therefore not remarkable that it should represent a substantial proportion of his creative output. It was many years, however, before any of this music became known beyond the circle of his friends, and it took even longer to persuade publishers that it had any value. In all probability what has survived is only a part, for Schubert wrote with such ease that he often forgot all about his compositions and many of them went astray. He wrote fifteen string quartets, besides one for flute, guitar, viola and 'cello. Although even the earliest of them, dating from 1812, show individual movements in which the essentials of his style are present, it is not surprising that this boy of fourteen, gifted as he was, took a little longer to gain complete technical clarity and assurance. The eleventh quartet, composed in 1817, is in this respect a landmark. Other works belonging to this early period are, in order of composition, a sonata-movement for piano trio (1812), " Eine kleine Trauermusik " and the minuet and finale of an octet, both for wind instruments (1813), the guitar quartet (1814), an Adagio and Rondo for piano quartet and string trio in one movement (1816), and a string trio in B flat (1817). Although Schubert was not yet twenty, such was the experience gained that this may be said to close the youthful period of his productivity.

The next phase opens with " The Trout " quintet, Op. 114, for piano, violin, viola, 'cello and double bass, so called because it includes variations on the composer's song of that name, composed at the request of Paumgartner, a friend of Vogl the singer, with whom he was travelling at the time in Upper Austria. It dates from 1819, a period when otherwise Schubert was not much concerned with chamber music, his " home team " having meanwhile grown into a small orchestra requiring symphonies for its provender. It was in 1820 that he returned to the string quartet and wrote the single movement in C minor which ranks as twelfth in the series. This remarkable movement, in no way comparable to the youthful quartets, shows Schubert in his early maturity. It is followed by a break lasting four years.

In 1824 Schubert wrote the octet, Op. 166, for strings and wind instruments, and two string quartets in A minor, and D minor respectively, thirteenth and fourteenth in the series, the latter known as " Death and the Maiden," from the variations on the song of that name. These, however, were not composed to comply with any suggestion from without. The spirit of the song, composed seven years earlier, permeates the greater part of the whole work, which is one of Schubert's most moving compositions. Another string quartet, the fifteenth and last, in G major, followed in 1826, a work which seems to indicate a new departure in method, of which, alas, we were not destined to see the further outcome. Then, in 1827, he wrote his two finest piano trios, Op. 99 and 100, respectively in B flat and E flat. These are the two works which Schumann described as one " passive, feminine, lyrical," the other " active, masculine, dramatic." Not only did Schubert hear these performed in public, but the second of them was actually bought by a publisher for the munificent sum of 20 florins, 60 kronen, equivalent to something less than a pound English money ! Another publisher was found to pay him 30 florins for the great C major string quintet, Op. 163, which he composed in 1828, within a few months of his death. In the opinion of many, it ranks among the finest of all chamber music works.

In his concerted chamber music, Schubert, whilst producing half a dozen works that retain their hold upon our affections, did not develop to any extent the forms used by his contemporaries. On the contrary, as the first of the Romantics in this field, he may be said to have sown the seed which, many generations later, was to lead to formal disintegration. The looseness of his form, and the fluid, freely modulating tonality, which is so characteristic of him and in which he had such remarkable skill, were the first signs of that general departure from classic coherence and conciseness destined to mark the last stages of the Romantic Movement.

## CHAPTER VI

# THE ROMANTIC LEADERS

LIMITATIONS OF SPACE forbid that we should embark upon a detailed consideration of the chamber works of Ludwig Spohr. Excluding duets they number nearly sixty, of which no fewer than thirty-three are string quartets. Probably the only one that concert-goers have heard is the E minor octet for strings, which has been played occasionally in recent years. It is possible that here and there may be found works that would bear reviving, but Spohr never forgot that he was, first and foremost, a violinist, and generally gave himself " le beau rôle," which is not in keeping with the freemasonry of chamber music, and the somewhat sickly sentiment of his slow movements would meet with little response from a twentieth-century audience.

Another prolific composer, who was born the same year as Schubert, but lived nearly twice as long, was Carl Gottlieb Reissiger, some of whose twenty-seven piano trios may still be heard in private, but they would be bold players who would include such innocent music in a public programme to-day. It is, however, curious how faithful amateurs have been to his work in this form. He wrote eight string quartets and about a dozen other concerted works, but of these one never hears a note, even in private, although critics speak well of, among others, a string quartet in F minor, Op. 155.

With Mendelssohn we approach the main phase of the Romantic Movement. It will therefore be expedient if we digress to explain that Movement in relation to chamber music. An important school of æsthetics describes the history of any art movement as divisible into three chapters, primitive, classic, and decadent. In the first the artist fashions the idiom, in the second he finds it ready to his hand and exploits it, and in the third he is driven to expedients to eke it out, which he does either by emotional exhibitionism or by calling to his aid elements with which it is not immediately concerned. From that point of view romanticism (as distinct from romance, which exists always) indicates the phase which, after the classics, heralds the decadence, and its hall-marks are the free rein given to subjective emotion, and the tendency to choose themes from outside the art—in the case of music, literary or pictorial themes. Though the term " programme music " is usually applied to that originating from the latter procedure, in reality it applies to both, for subjective emotion is itself a " programme." Chamber music is, however, by its very nature, not well suited to excesses in either direction. The outpouring of great passion demands more violent means, and the representation of literary or pictorial themes more colour, than lie within its scope. Hence, when we speak of the Romantic Movement in chamber music, we are speaking of its mildest manifestation. There has been scarcely any avowed " programme " chamber music, nor has there been much that was highly charged with emotion except in a purely lyrical sense. Thus during the later decades of the nineteenth century chamber music was mercifully preserved from the Byzantinism that overtook the orchestra. The string quartet was never acutely threatened with the excesses that at one time appeared likely to bring the symphony to destruction.

Mendelssohn was a romantic, but his aristocratic fastidiousness made him averse from excesses, even when writing for the orchestra. For a time it became the fashion to decry him on account of the gentle romanticism that to later generations appeared as mere sentimentality, but in the revaluation of the past that has resulted from the reaction against later excesses, he is gradually becoming rehabilitated on the ground, not of his romanticism, but of his almost classic formal elegance. It is now realised, probably more vividly than when he was at the height of his fame, that, whatever may have been his weaknesses, his sense of form was well-nigh impeccable. His initiation into chamber music took the form of three piano quartets, Op. 1, 2, and 3, composed 1822–5, the first in his fourteenth year. Of these the third is the most interesting, albeit the piano part is made more prominent than accords with the nature of chamber music. About the same time, he also wrote a piano sextet in D, posthumously published as Op. 110. But the most important work of this early period is the famous octet, which is an astonishing composition to have been produced by a lad of sixteen. It is still delightful to hear, and the scherzo, said to have been suggested by a passage from the Walpurgis-Nacht of Goethe's " Faust," is the equal of any that he wrote in adult years. It is sometimes heard in an orchestral arrangement. The six string quartets were not composed in their numerical sequence, the order being, 2, 1, 4, 5, 3, 6. The one in E flat, Op. 12, contains a charming Canzonetta, which is one of Mendelssohn's " best-sellers " ; but the best of them are the three comprised in Op. 44, and composed in 1837–8. The sixth, in F minor, Op. 80, is generally believed to have been inspired by the death of his beloved sister Fanny, which would explain its elegiac feeling. He contemplated writing another quartet, but only the two middle movements came into existence and these were posthumously published with a Capriccio and Fugue of earlier date. Mendelssohn also wrote two string quintets, in 1826 and 1845. But next to the octet the works most frequently heard are the two piano trios in D minor and C minor, Op. 49 and 66, composed respectively in 1839 and 1845. Of the first Schumann wrote : "This is the master-trio of our time," but the second, which he had not then heard, has a more profound significance. Its mysteriously dramatic opening is typical of the early maturity of the Romantic Movement.

Though Schumann outlived Mendelssohn by nine years, he was only one year that composer's junior. It is mainly Mendelssohn's precociousness and Schumann's tardiness to approach any form of composition except that for piano which makes them appear as if separated by a longer interval of time. As is well known, having kept to piano music for nearly ten years, he plunged headlong into other kinds of music in turn. Thus 1840 is commonly called the "song year" and 1841 the "symphony year," there being in both cases ample reason. Then, at the beginning of 1842, he took a headlong plunge into chamber music. In the spring of that year he and Clara had been studying together the Haydn and Mozart quartets. By the end of June he had composed the three string quartets, Op. 41. In September and October he added to them the magnificent piano quintet Op. 44, at the first performance of which Mendelssohn played the piano part at sight. In November and December he wrote the piano quartet, Op. 47, and the three Phantasies for piano trio, Op. 88. Well may 1842 be known as Schumann's "chamber music year." He did not return to this field until five years later, when he wrote the two piano trios, Op. 63 and 80, in D minor and F major. A third trio followed in 1851, Op. 110 in G and a set of "Märchenerzählungen" for piano, clarinet and viola in 1853, the last year of Schumann's creative life. Despite the excellent and strikingly personal quality of the string quartets, Schumann's triumph in this sphere is represented by the two great piano works, the quintet, which held the field unchallenged as the finest work of its kind until Brahms supplied a worthy pendant to it in 1864, and the quartet, which may perhaps be a little less effective in the spectacular sense, but is almost equally full of musical interest. The best of the piano trios is the first in D minor. The string quartets are attractive as exhibiting the many facets of Schumann's musical imagination, but on a lower plane of achievement. Even so, the feat he performed in that one year has not ceased to impress lovers of chamber music.

## CHAPTER VII

## MINOR ROMANTICS

It was in England that Mendelssohn became acquainted with Moscheles, whom he invited to join him at Leipzig when founding the Conservatorium there. Moscheles wrote some chamber music, among which a trio won Schumann's approval, but he was mainly a writer for the piano. Soon afterwards there came to live in England Bernhard Molique, a violinist-composer, pupil of Spohr, whose quartets had a spell of popularity during the time when Mendelssohn was the height of musical fashion.

In Germany the contemporaries of Mendelssohn and Schumann included the three brothers Lachner, who wrote pleasing chamber music of a not very exciting kind ; Ferdinand Hiller, an earnest and accomplished musician, some of whose works are still admired ; and Robert Volkmann, whose chamber works began to be favourably known in the fifties.

Meanwhile Chopin, who shares with Mendelssohn and Schumann the glories of the Romantic Movement, had given to chamber music nothing more important than a very youthful trio which scarcely deserves attention, but

Félicien David, the composer of " Le Désert," and, after
Berlioz, the most prominent French composer of the
Romantic Movement, wrote " Les Quatre Saisons,"
consisting of 24 string quintets in four sets. In Italy the
corresponding phase was represented by Bazzini, who lives
in the " Ronde des lutins " for violin, but whose chamber
music was curiously eclectic, sometimes showy, but generally facile.

Of the composers who preceded Brahms in the wake of
Schumann, the most important is Raff, the former's senior
by eleven years, who, after writing five string quartets in
the accepted form, added to them three more of a special
character, the first a Suite in the Olden Style, the second a
romantic cycle, entitled " Die schöne Müllerin," and the
third a Suite in canon-form. Of these the second is the most
attractive, but in any case Raff deserves praise for breaking
away from the despotism of sonata-form. Raff wrote many
other chamber works, and so did Friedrich Kiel, who also
deserves to be remembered for having had the courage to
write waltzes for string quartet. Others are Kirchner,
Reinecke, Goldmark, and Hans von Bronsart, whose
piano trio is still remembered. But we have now reached
a period which might almost be described as one of mass-
production in German chamber music—a period when
every German city had its group of highly respected composers, each one of whom considered himself more or less
under a moral obligation to supply the countless chamber
music organisations, amateur and professional, with a
succession of works. Curiously enough, these rarely fell
below a certain acceptable level of competence. Though not
epoch-making, they were pleasant to play ; they overtaxed
neither the executive proficiency nor the musical understanding, as may hardly be said of much music composed
to-day. But the bulk of this music is as dead to-day as any
music can be. It would be far easier in the present state of
musical taste to revive Boccherini than Raff. Whether the
reason is the same as that which makes the feminine fashions
of a few years back appear frumpish, whereas those of half

a century ago have become picturesque, is difficult to say. It may be that in the twenty-first century musicians will delve as industriously among neglected music of the nineteenth as those of the twentieth delve in the eighteenth. But it would serve no useful purpose to crowd this survey with such annals, and until modern times are reached it will be well to be more sparing in the citing of names.

## CHAPTER VIII

## BRAHMS

Thus we reach Brahms, the outstanding figure in nineteenth-century chamber music, to whom is due, more than to any other composer of his time, the extraordinary cult of which that music became the object in its later decades. Excluding duet-sonatas his contribution is represented by seventeen works ; among them there is not one in which it could be said that " Homer nodded." There was one—the first piano trio, Op. 8—but the composer substituted an entirely new version. That was his first surviving chamber work, composed originally in 1854, the first version of which was certainly somewhat undisciplined, but so attractive that habitual players were, for a time, reluctant to transfer their allegiance to the 1891 edition. The next work, the string sextet in B flat, Op. 18, shows a pronounced reaction towards classical form, as if already he were conscious of the imperfection of Op. 8. The slow movement comprises a splendid set of variations. Next followed the two vast piano quartets, Op. 25 in G minor and Op. 26, in A major, in which the form attains to that personal compromise between classical and romantic which is Brahms's characteristic achievement. Of this we see the immediate effect in the magnificent piano quintet in F minor, Op. 34, which had been a string quintet and a two-piano sonata before reaching its final form. It has often been said that Brahms's works followed each other in pairs which were not similar but contrasted. This is commonly applied to the symphonies, but in the chamber music there are similar instances. Thus the G minor piano quartet, the piano quintet, and the G major string sextet which followed as Op. 36, have for their pendants in the other mood, the A major piano quartet and the two string quartets, in A minor and C minor, which appeared in 1873 as Op. 51. These were his first published string quartets, but he had discarded many earlier works before producing one to his satisfaction. He was to write only one more, in B flat, Op. 67, and this, the lightest-hearted of the three, followed as a complete contrast to the piano quartet in C minor, Op. 60, which had meanwhile appeared, and which opens with one of his most tragic movements. An interval of six years separates Op. 67 from the next concerted chamber work, which is the piano trio in C, Op. 87. Neither this, nor the work immediately following, the string quintet in F, Op. 88, can be reckoned among general favourites. Once again, they form a contrasted pair, the former being introspective, whilst Specht compares the latter to " the meadows at Ischl in the sunshine." Its first movement is said to have been a message of congratulation to Ignaz Brüll on his betrothal. Yet another dissimilar pair of works followed : the piano trio in C minor, Op. 101, and the second string quintet, in G, Op. 111, the former passionately tragic though with moments of tenderness, the latter irrepressibly high-spirited. The playing of Richard Mühlfeld, the great clarinettist, furnished the incentive to the two works which conclude the list, the clarinet trio, Op. 114, and the clarinet quintet, Op. 115, both published in 1892. Both are fine works but the quintet has so completely put the trio in the shade that one seldom hears the latter, the presence of a clarinettist usually prompting that of a string quartet, and this leading insensibly to the inclusion of Mozart's clarinet quintet in the proceedings.

With so much ground to cover it is impossible to give these seventeen works individually the consideration they deserve. Whilst nobody nowadays contests the greatness of Brahms, not all are agreed as to its nature. In the first place he added little or nothing to the wealth of musical resources that came to him from the classics. Almost alone among the great masters, he was not an inventor, he did not expand the means of his art. Then there are still many who regard him as at his best in the art of the miniature, who extol the best of his songs and look upon the last twenty piano pieces, Op. 116-119, as the most ideally perfect addition to the literature of the instrument between Chopin and Debussy. His own greatest admirers unconsciously did him a disservice in fostering the legend that comprehension of his works was the mark of a superior musical intelligence, or of high caste, whereas in reality any difficulty of apprehension there may have been was due, not to the profundity of his thought, but to one of his weaknesses which can be colloquially described as the urge to pour a quart into a pint-pot. It is because of that urge that his best chamber works are those which include the piano and those which employ a large number of strings, such as the sextet in G. That is also probably the reason why he wrote only three string quartets. Good as these are, the effort to subdue his luxuriance to the sonorous possibilities of four stringed instruments would not seem to have been congenial to him. He needed more elbow room. He was the exact opposite of a Latin artist on whom limitation of means acts as a tonic. He was essentially a great German lyricist who served and enriched his art with deep devotion.

## CHAPTER IX

# GERMANY AFTER BRAHMS

As ALREADY STATED, the impetus given to chamber music by the works of the early Romanticists precipitated such a plethora of works that it would be hopeless to attempt

Rc

to deal systematically with them. For those whose curiosity is not satisfied we append a few names of composers they might follow up with advantage. They are, in order of birth-dates: Draeseke, Bruch, Rheinberger, Goetz, Herzogenberg, Klughardt, Fuchs, Philipp and Xaver Scharwenka, Huber, Wolfrum, Röntgen, Woyrsch, Thuille, Rezniček, Weingartner, Beer-Walbrunn, D'Albert, Robert Kahn.

Meanwhile, the opposite wing of German music, the antithesis of which had been the subject of much controversy, had mostly held aloof from this sphere. Wagner wrote in his youth an adagio for clarinet and string quintet, but it would be stretching a point to call the Siegfried-Idyll chamber music. Bruckner wrote a string quintet and left a posthumous Intermezzo also for string quintet, but neither is representative. Mahler is unknown in this field, and Strauss forsook it from his early twenties, after having written a string quartet, a piano quartet and a Serenade for thirteen wind instruments.

The most important post-Brahmsian writer of chamber music is clearly Max Reger, who had much in common with him. He, too, was a lyricist of a rather more sentimental type, as shown in his songs, but against this he was keener than Brahms on counterpoint for its own sake—in fact almost a forerunner of the modern " back to Bach " movement, with the result that there is in the majority of his works a perceptible conflict between the eruditely constructive musician and his simplicity of soul. Generally it is the former that gains the ascendant, and then one needs a thoroughly Teutonic brand of earnestness to derive much pleasure from his music. But occasionally the poet gains the day and then one catches a glimpse of real beauty. By a striking coincidence his concerted works reach exactly the same number as those of Brahms, seventeen, but as he has never attained to any popularity in England, it is unnecessary to describe them in detail. Among many other writers of the post-Brahmsian epoch may be mentioned Hans Pfitzner, composer of a piano trio, a string quartet, and a piano quintet, a typical German, though, as it happens, born in Moscow. And this, finally, may serve to remind us of another composer, also born in Moscow, Paul Juon, a Russian whose entire professional life has been spent in Berlin. His chamber works are numerous and well worth study. Many of them reveal a piquant and purely personal contrast between a Slavonic mode of thought in the melodic line and a wholly Teutonic method of treatment and construction.

# C : NATIONAL SCHOOLS

## CHAPTER I

## NATIONALISM AND CHAMBER MUSIC

THE GRADUAL ASSERTION of musical nationality in the course of the nineteenth century is due to two causes. One is the subjective tendency inherent in the Romantic Movement. Once the composer stood committed to the subjective expression of things not necessarily connected with music—literary themes, pictorial impressions, his own emotions and so on—it was only to be expected that he would take themes from the literature with which he was most familiar, record impressions of the scenery of his native country, employ a national melodic idiom and, consciously or unconsciously, express that side of himself characteristic of the nationality to which he belonged. The other incentive to nationalism was the stifling effect of the German predominance. The influence of the German classics had become so universal that practically all music except that of French and Italian opera was perforce conceived in a German melodic idiom ; as Germans naturally handled that idiom better than all others, it was almost impossible for a non-German composer to excel in his art. This seems a strong assertion, but subsequent history justifies it. Take our own country as an example. Our musical renascence dates from the time when we ceased to take our musical instruction from Leipzig.

As we observed when dealing with the Romantic Movement, the nature of chamber music rendered it all but immune from the excesses of programme music, and as nationalism in music has in itself something of the nature of programme, it follows that chamber music was correspondingly slower to show the outward symptoms of nationalism, whatever changes might be taking place in its inner substance. There is very little in chamber music corresponding to Smetana's " Vltava," Glazounov's " Stenka Razin " or Vaughan Williams's " Norfolk Rhapsody," and what little there is is mostly of quite recent date. In chamber music nationalism began quietly, almost surreptitiously. There is no sign of it in the chamber works of Sterndale Bennett—English nationalism was as yet unborn—and there is but the faintest suggestion of it in those of his Danish contemporary, Niels W. Gade. The former's sextet, and trio, both with piano, are practically forgotten, but Gade still has some popularity with amateur devotees of chamber music, the favourite work being his Novelettes for piano, violin and 'cello. His string octet is also occasionally heard.

## CHAPTER II

## BOHEMIA

Apart from the rather mild suggestions of Gade, the first country to raise the flag of musical independence was Bohemia, where a national school was created by Smetana, followed by Dvořák and Fibich. Smetana wrote chiefly operas and orchestral music, the latter of " programme " type. His chamber music also is definitely programme music and autobiographical at that. The trio (1855) records the death of his eldest daughter, who at the tender age of four had shown signs of musical talent, and concludes with a funeral march. The two string quartets (1876 and 1882) are aptly described as " Aus meinem Leben." The first depicts in turn his early romanticism, the days of his youth when he wrote dance music (in this case a Polka), his love and marriage, and his discovery "how to treat the national material in music." The second, an incoherent work with moments of beauty, takes up the story after the catastrophe of the composer's deafness. "It expresses the whirlwind of music in the head of one who has lost his hearing. Nobody has a notion how musical ideas fly about in the brain of a deaf man." Of the three works the first quartet is the only one that maintains itself in the international repertoire, but the trio is frequently played in the country of its origin.[1]

Antonin Dvořák, the second of the pioneers of Czech music, was a copious contributor to all forms. Apart from seven unpublished works of his youth (five string quartets, a string and a piano quintet) he has bequeathed to us twenty-one concerted works for more than two instruments, thirteen for strings alone, and eight with piano. Taking them in chronological order, the first, consisting of ten Love Songs for string quartet (1865), need not detain us. Nine important works were composed during the five years 1874–8. Some of them bear misleading opus numbers owing to belated publication. To 1874 belongs the string quartet in A minor, Op. 16; to 1875 the string quintet in G, Op. 77, the piano trio in B flat, Op. 21, and the piano quartet in D, Op. 23; to 1876 the piano trio in C minor, Op. 26, and the string quartet in E, Op. 80; to 1877 the string quartet in D minor, Op. 34; to 1878 the string sextet, Op. 48, and the string quartet in E flat, Op. 51. To these may be added the Bagatelles for two violins, 'cello and harmonium (or piano), Op. 47, composed the same year. The interest in these works seems to grow in the degree in which the national character asserts itself, culminating in the fine quartet in E flat. This work was commissioned by the Florentine Quartet with the condition that it should be in the composer's "Slavonic" style. It is amusing to note that the writer of a work on chamber music published in 1904 still finds it necessary to say of Dvořák:

[1] It has been given at least twice on the platform of the Sunday Chamber Music Society.—Ed.

" True, the Slav idiom pervades a number of his works, but this is, as it were, a mere accident of his nationality and in no way detracts from the splendour of his achievements." The implication that it might have been expected to do so is evidence of the pertinacity of the general belief that music, to be good, must sound German. Of the E flat quartet in particular the same writer says :

" The melodic substance of the work is chiefly Slavonic in character, but the genius of the composer has transformed and ennobled that which otherwise would have remained as the rough material of a mere musical dialect," as if that were not precisely what the German classics did in their day with the rough material of the German musical dialect ! The national feeling also pervades the charming little pieces grouped as the Bagatelles.

The next string quartet, in C major, Op. 61, composed in 1881, is less characteristic of its composer. It is as if, having begun to write under the influence of Schubert's romanticism and passed thence to nationalism, he now felt the need of Beethovenish classicism. It was followed in 1883 by the fine trio in F minor, Op. 65, a work of sombre splendour. Three years passed without producing any more chamber music and then, in 1887, two works made their appearance. The first was a miniature, a trifle, written for three amateur friends for two violins and viola, a charming intimate composition, which, out of place in the concert-room, has endeared itself to many for enjoyment in private. The other was the great piano quintet in A major, Op. 81, which was for many years considered to be the third panel in the triptych of which the two first were represented by the piano quintets of Schumann and Brahms. Almost of equal rank is the piano quartet in E flat, Op. 87, which followed in 1889. A highly characteristic work is the Dumky Trio, Op. 99, for piano, violin and 'cello, composed in 1891. The word " Dumka," which has been freely translated as " Elegy," describes a movement of which the chief feature is an alternation of yearning melancholy with unrestrained gaiety. Dvořák frequently uses the form for slow movements, or scherzi, sometimes making the rapid section, usually a " Furiant," into a separate movement. Here he has taken six Dumky, of which, however, the first three are linked together, whilst the others correspond to slow movement, scherzo and finale. Of course the style does not make for the coherence of a cyclic work in sonata form, but its folk-tune character and charming simplicity have long since established the Dumky Trio as a firm favourite.

The following year Dvořák accepted the American engagement, the memory of which was to be perpetuated in the symphony " From the New World," and in the so-called, or miscalled, " Nigger " quartet in F major, Op. 96, of 1893. The composer had paid a visit to a colony of his countrymen who had emigrated and settled at Spillville. He was charmed with his surroundings and pleased to find such peace after his hectic experience of New York. Though the " negro " melodies have attracted more attention there is very nearly as much of lyrical, nostalgic feeling expressed in the work. In the middle of the finale there is even a suggestion of the organ in the Spillville Church, upon which Dvořák was invited to play during his visit. The same year also produced a string quintet in E flat, Op. 97, in which American suggestions are equally plentiful. Its scherzo is said to have been prompted by an Indian dance. But even in this work the Slavonic Dvořák is not long silent. On his return he wrote the string quartets in G major, Op. 106, and A flat, Op. 105, in that order. Apart from a glimpse of America in the former, these two fine works reveal the composer back in his own country. The rest of his life was spent upon operas, and upon symphonic poems on subjects derived from the national folk-lore. In these two quartets, among the most beautiful he wrote, he bade a last farewell to chamber music.

Zdenko Fibich, the third of this trio of pioneers, was not the equal of the other two, but an active participant in the rise of Czech music. Moreover it was he who, in an unpublished quartet, composed in 1874, introduced for the first time into a chamber work the national dance of Bohemia, the Polka, said to have been invented by a country waitress in 1830, and brought to Prague by some students. Smetana introduced one two years later in his first quartet. Fibich's published works comprise a string quartet, and a trio, quartet and quintet, each with piano.

## CHAPTER III

# SCANDINAVIA

MEANWHILE THE EXAMPLE of Gade in Denmark remained for a time without a follower, but a great nationalist arose in Norway in the person of Edvard Grieg. Not only did he employ the folk-songs and dances of his native country, but he caught in his harmony a certain Northern quality which his studies at Leipzig failed to eradicate. Though mainly a miniaturist, he was one of the most original composers of the later nineteenth century. Had he worked on a larger scale he would be regarded to-day as a great innovator, but it is an obstinate trait of musical criticism to take dimensions into consideration when estimating quality, and Grieg is accordingly undervalued. Apart from his sonatas, which do not come under our purview, he wrote a string quartet and left another unfinished. But sonata-form did not suit his temperament, and the episodic beauties of the quartet are not displayed to advantage. Yet Grieg, like Smetana and Dvořák, is an outstanding figure in the early history of musical nationalism. His contemporary, Johan Svendsen, wrote a string octet which has proved more tenacious of its place in the repertoire than either his string quartet or string quintet.

The succeeding generation of these early nationalists is represented in Denmark by Asger Hamerik and Carl Nielsen, in Norway by Christian Sinding and Johan Halvorsen, in Sweden by Emil Sjögren and Wilhelm Stenhammer, and in Czecho-Slovakia by Josef Bohuslav

Foerster. But although in all of these composers, and in their minor contemporaries, the influence of nationality can be felt, that of Germany retained its ascendancy. Even to-day, in these countries complete emancipation is shown only by musicians belonging to the " left wing "—that is to say, those classed as " modern." Conservatives everywhere still cling to the German models. But we have yet to consider one nationalist movement which rapidly became the most remarkable of them all : the Russian.

## CHAPTER IV

# RUSSIA: TCHAIKOVSKY

IN THE FIELDS of the opera and of symphonic music Russia has furnished the classic example of the rise and full fruition of a nationalist movement followed by a return to eclecticism, once its object of emancipation had been attained. From our specific standpoint, however, the example is less complete, because chamber music does not provide any early illustrations of it and because, even in its prime, chamber music remained the section least affected by it. The founder of Russian musical nationalism was Glinka, whose operas " A Life for the Tsar " and " Russlan and Ludmilla " inaugurated the movement. But his chamber works, comprising a Trio Pathétique, a string quartet and a string sextet, are of earlier date and reflect his striving for technical mastery of form rather than any desire to be Russian. In texture they show a grounding in the German classics, in style a leaning towards Latin elegance and refinement, but they do not aspire to any great achievement in either direction, and even in Russia they are seldom played. His immediate successors, such as Dargomijsky and Serov, did not write chamber music, and contemporary eclectics like Afanassiev, Bachmetiev or Asantschevsky, who did, produced works worthy of respect, but little more.

It was Anton Rubinstein who added most to the repertoire
of Russian chamber music, and though he occasionally
made use of a Russian theme, as Beethoven had done before
him, his whole musical personality was so saturated with
German tradition, German ideals, and German methods
that there remains little ground for regarding him as a
Russian composer. His output of chamber music was,
however, extraordinarily copious. Excluding half a dozen
sonatas, it comprises twenty-one works, among which are
no fewer than ten string quartets. Considering the time he
spent as a travelling virtuoso of international celebrity
and as the founder and head of the St. Petersburg Conservatoire, he must be considered among the most prolific of all
composers. But of all this chamber music there is little that
lives to-day. Among the quartets one may find here and
there an attractive movement, and the five piano trios
are still played in private, but Rubinstein appears, by tacit
agreement, to be banished from the repertoire of chamber
concerts.

It is characteristic of Tchaikovsky's position in musical
history that, whilst non-Russians are almost unanimous
in regarding him as eclectic, with or without Teutonic
bias, Russians have become almost equally unanimous
in regarding him as a national hero, now that the bitter
controversies concerning nationalism are forgotten. And
it is of interest to note that, whereas the avowed nationalists
were less uncompromising in their chamber music than
in opera or symphony, Tchaikovsky allows more of the
Russian idiom to come to the surface in his chamber music
than in his dramatic or symphonic works. He wrote three
string quartets, in D, F, and E flat minor, completed
respectively in 1871, 1874, and 1875, a piano trio in memory
of Nicholas Rubinstein (1882), and a string sextet, " Sou-
venir de Florence " (1890). The first string quartet is
famous for an andante cantabile based on a folk-tune
communicated to the composer by a carpenter of the
government of Kaluga in Great Russia. It is an exquisite movement and deservedly ranks with the most

popular of Tchaikovsky's many "household words." There is also a typically Russian movement in the second quartet, but this time it is the scherzo, which is in a characteristic septuple rhythm. The third quartet is dedicated to the memory of Laub, the violinist who had led the Moscow String Quartet in performances of its two predecessors and was a close friend of the composer. It includes what has been described as the saddest movement in all chamber music, a very beautiful *Andante funebre e doloroso*, after which the brisk little Russian tunes of the finale come as a welcome relief. The trio, consisting of an Elegy in sonata-form followed by a monumental set of variations, is one of Tchaikovsky's greatest works. The theme of the second part is one that Tchaikovsky, Nicholas Rubinstein, and some of their colleagues from the Moscow Conservatoire had had performed to them by some peasants during a country walk. It appealed to the composer as peculiarly suited to enshrine the memory of his friend. The trio is a profoundly impressive work. There is little to be said in favour of the sextet, which is well written but scarcely worthy of Tchaikovsky.

## CHAPTER V

# RUSSIA: THE KOUCHKA

Meanwhile the banner of nationalism had been raised at St. Petersburg by the "Kouchka" or Big Five: Balakirev, Cui, Borodin, Moussorgsky and Rimsky-Korsakov. Of these Balakirev left only an unpublished octet of his nonage, and Cui, whose inclusion in the group was due more to his ardent championship as a publicist than to the intrinsic merit of his compositions, need not detain us. His three string quartets do not rise to any distinction. Moussorgsky, the composer of "Boris Godounov," wrote no chamber music. It was Borodin, the composer of "Prince Igor," who not only made Russia prominent in this field, but also exercised considerable influence in other countries, notably in France. He remains the arch-type of the amateur possessed of genius, for he never abandoned his original scientific profession, but his fame lives on as one of the most important of modern composers. He was devoted to chamber music and played the 'cello in a quartet of friends. His youthful works have remained unpublished, and at least one, a string sextet, is irretrievably lost. His reputation as a writer of chamber music rests thus mainly upon two very beautiful string quartets completed respectively in 1878 and 1880. The first of these is described as prompted by a theme of Beethoven from the finale of the B flat quartet, Op. 130, but this relates specifically to the first subject of Borodin's first movement. No other use is made of the theme, and both quartets are written in a manner that diverges completely from the German tradition. The themes have a more sensuous and plastic quality and the treatment of the instruments is of the kind which, whatever may be the case now, a conscientious German critic of the time would have condemned as too orchestral for chamber music. Its brilliance is now universally recognised and players of chamber music have long since accustomed themselves to a certain measure of quasi-orchestral effect in quartet-writing. The prejudice against such alluring thematic material took longer to die. In my younger days I introduced Borodin's second string quartet to a team of players that used to meet at my house, and one of them dismissed it very contemptuously as a "mere bunch of tunes," so deep-rooted was the antipathy, inherited from Germany, to any music pleasing to the senses. One of the said tunes has become widely known. It is the second movement, a Nocturne, which has been arranged for many combinations of instruments and, like the andante cantabile of Tchaikovsky's first quartet, has even penetrated to the cinema. The two Borodin quartets rapidly made their way to Paris, where they so charmed the musical world that two of the best known French quartets, those of Debussy and Ravel, are said to owe their incentive to a desire to emulate Borodin's example.

Of Rimsky-Korsakov, the master of picturesque orchestration, there is less to relate. His only complete chamber works, a string quartet, a string sextet, and a wind quintet, belong to his formative period, when, in the laudable desire to improve upon the defective technique of his early works, he plunged with such ardour into technical studies as to become, for the time being, a typical school composer. His quartet, in particular, resembles a set of contrapuntal exercises. In later years he contributed a few movements to the Belaiev *cénacle* (see below), but made no further attempt at a complete chamber work in cyclic form.

Before continuing, in the second generation, the story of the St. Peterburg nationalists, it will be expedient to return to Moscow for the sake of a composer who, to a greater extent than any of his Russian confrères, specialised in chamber music. This is Sergei Ivanovitch Taneiev, a pupil of Tchaikovsky, and author of what is probably the most practical manual of orthodox counterpoint in existence, which so facilitated the progress of Russian students in this direction that a whole generation of them appeared to the outsider to be concerned with little else. As might be expected, the interest in his own works, and particularly in his six string quartets, is largely contrapuntal, but he never allowed this propensity to trap him into dry writing. There is always a lyrical vein near at hand and in those works in which the piano appears—a quintet, a quartet and a trio—even a tendency to " mass effects " such as he, a master pianist, knew how to contrive. Yet on the whole his works address themselves to trained musicians rather than amateur players who are liable to overlook their subtlety as, in fact, the general musical public has done.

## CHAPTER VI

# RUSSIA: GLAZOUNOV

RETURNING TO ST. PETERSBURG we meet one of the greatest composers of chamber music Russia has produced : Alexander Glazounov. He is, so to speak, a discovery of the " Kutchka." Balakirev christened him " the little Glinka," and conducted his first symphony in March 1882, when the budding composer was only seventeen. Before the year was out, his first string quartet had also passed the test of a public performance. The story of Glazounov's career embraces the heyday and the decline of nationalism. His early works were imbued with it, but with the passing of time he became more and more eclectic. In this he may be regarded as almost a symbol for Russian music in general, which was nationalist only so long as was necessary to secure rights of citizenship for the Russian idiom, and gradually ceased to be so when there was no longer any dominant influence to keep it in subjection. In this, as in many things, Russian experience furnishes a precedent for what has happened in our own country, where Norfolk and Shropshire Rhapsodies came opportunely to help in the problem of emancipation, but are no longer being composed to-day, having served their purpose. Thus all we shall find of nationalism in Glazounov's chamber music will be in the earliest works.

The first two quartets, Op. 1 and 10, have Russian finales and other movements of distinctly Slavonic colouring. They were followed by the five Novelettes, Op. 15, Glazounov being one of the courageous pioneers who broke down the tradition that quartets must be in sonata-form. This one, delightfully and picturesquely scored, comprises Spanish, Oriental, Viennese and Hungarian genre pictures with an old-world Interlude as the central number. Scarcely anything so bright as this had ever been written for string quartet, and for some years afterwards it was customary in chamber music circles to look upon it as a strange escapade on the part of a distinguished musician who, fortunately for himself, had meanwhile furnished other proofs of his artistic integrity. Old prejudices die hard, and the ones harboured in these circles were no exception. Moreover, Glazounov's next work, the third quartet, Op. 26, described as " Slavonic," not only contained a mazurka in lieu of scherzo but actually concluded with a brilliant fantasy entitled " A Slavonic Festival," a dazzling feat of quartet-writing, but somewhat loose of shape. And this, again, was followed by a suite for string quartet, Op. 35, which presented its credentials in an opening fugue, but included an Orientale suggested to the composer by the music of a Tartar band heard in the Crimea, and ended with a buoyant waltz. This was throwing down the gauntlet with a vengeance. Only the dazzling technical finish of this music could condone its affront to the solemn earnestness regarded as essential to chamber music. But almost immediately Glazounov wrote a string quintet, which, apart from the Russian character of its finale, shows a return to classic sobriety. It was, however, the next two quartets, the fourth, Op. 64, and the fifth, Op. 70, that marked the return of the prodigal. These two fine works, composed in the dying years of the nineteenth century, are models of the musicianship of their day, beautifully constructed, full of interest, and imbued with the genuine classical spirit. Even in their own day they represented the conservative wing of the musical community, but they represented it beyond all question at its best. Germany, the home of the classics, had nothing finer to offer, for the dry rot of pedantry was invading the conservative wing of her music, and the radical wing was absorbed in orchestral programme music with Strauss as leader. Glazounov's fifth quartet, published in 1899, may be regarded as the swan-song of the kind of chamber music with which Beethoven had ushered in the century. Since then Glazounov has written a sixth and a seventh quartet, but in these post-war days the spirit has changed and such works are in some danger of being considered anachronistic.

## CHAPTER VII

# RUSSIA: BELAIEV'S INFLUENCE

WHEN GLAZOUNOV burst upon the Russian musical world as an astonishingly precocious boy, among those who applauded his first symphony was a wealthy amateur, a timber merchant and banker who determined on entirely altruistic grounds to become his publisher. This was M. P. Belaiev, who three years later established the famous publishing house that bears his name. He used his wealth judiciously yet unsparingly for the furtherance of Russian music, and there is scarcely a Russian composer of his day who was not indebted to him, for his Mæcenas-like activities were by no means limited to publication. Naturally his house became an important musical centre whose Friday gatherings, at which generally string quartets were performed, were attended by all the leading composers and performers of the time. The composers delighted to do him honour with works specially written, often in collaboration, for his birthdays and other special occasions. Thus originated the B-la-F Quartet, consisting of four movements founded on the musical notes of his name : B flat (in German, B), A (la) and F. The opening allegro by Rimsky-Korsakov is followed by a scherzo contributed by Liadov, a charming Spanish serenade by Borodin, and a finale by Glazounov. Another quartet, entitled "Le Jour de Fête," dedicated to Belaiev on his name-day, consists of a Russian carol by Glazounov, a liturgical " Glorification " by Liadov, and a Horovod, or Russian choral dance, by Rimsky-Korsakov. Another work in this category consists of variations on a Russian theme by a number of Russian composers. The smaller pieces are collected into two sets entitled " Les Vendredis " (Fridays). Among them are a polka contributed by Sokolov, Glazounov and Liadov in collaboration, and a scherzo by Borodin that he afterwards amplified as that of his unfinished Third Symphony. These pieces are evidence of the feeling that pervaded the Friday gatherings, which, although their object was personal, was the true spirit of chamber music as the " music of friends." One can imagine the curiosity of Belaiev himself and of his quartet-players as a composer would mysteriously extract from his pocket something for them to " try over." They are well known to amateurs, who recapture some of that spirit in playing them.

Three of Rimsky-Korsakov's older pupils deserve mention : Kopylov, Sokolov, and Ippolitov-Ivanov, the last-named the composer of familiar " Caucasian Sketches." So far as chamber music was concerned the paradoxical antithesis between the cosmopolitan St. Petersburg, the stronghold of nationalism, and Slavonic Moscow, the home of Western eclecticism, soon ceased to exist. Anton Arensky, another pupil of Rimsky-Korsakov, early transferred his allegiance to Moscow and Tchaikovsky. He wrote two string quartets of which the second, for the unusual combination of violin, viola and two 'cellos, is dedicated to the memory of Tchaikovsky and includes a fine set of variations on the theme of one of the latter's " Children's Songs " ; he also wrote two piano trios, one of which, in D minor, had a spell of quite outstanding popularity with chamber music enthusiasts, and a piano quintet. Another work commemorates the passing of Tchaikovsky. Not only is Rachmaninov's early piano trio dedicated to his memory, but in form it follows the precedent of that which Tchaikovsky inscribed to the memory of Nicholas Rubinstein, consisting of two sections of which the second is a set of variations. Rachmaninov made no other contribution to chamber music as defined in this Book, but wrote one 'cello sonata.

From the eighties to the eve of war Russia, and particularly St. Petersburg, has been a copious contributor to the chamber music repertoire. Almost every composer belonging to the Belaiev group felt under an obligation to write at least one string quartet. Even Felix Blumenfeld, who otherwise wrote mainly for piano, composed one. It is impossible to do more than enumerate a few names : Grechaninov, Malichevsky, Gliere—a prolific writer of highly polished but not very adventurous chamber works— Zolatariev, Persiani, and Rimsky-Korsakov's son-in-law, Maximilian Steinberg. Of composers whose associations were not with these should be mentioned Balakirev's friend and pupil, Liapunov, who towards the end of his life wrote an excellent piano sextet ; Catoire, a pupil of Liadov, who migrated to Moscow and showed in his early works the influence of Tchaikovsky, but afterwards came to be regarded as, relatively speaking, a "modernist"; and Goedicke, whose style is sometimes compared with that of Medtner, and whose string quartet, Op. 33, may be regarded as representative.

# CHAPTER VIII

# FRANCE: BEFORE FRANCK

THE RENASCENCE of "absolute music"—symphonic and chamber music—in France, is, despite its strong national character, not comparable to the nationalist movements we have hitherto described. France did not need to emancipate her music from foreign influences or to re-discover in the domain of folk-lore the sources of a national idiom. At most did she need a renewal of contact with her musical past. But in France music had become consistently an art of the theatre. No composer could hope to win fame except by writing for the stage, and, in the striving for popular success which is the incentive in the theatre, French music had lost sight of its ideals. It is the recovery of these, rather than any assertion of nationality, that is the achievement of the French renascence, and it is significant that, although it had set in earlier in the century, it began to gather momentum after the chastening experiences of 1870. It would seem as if these had induced a mood of *recueillement*, and that, precisely, is the mood in which the noblest music thrives.

Although Gossec, one of the earliest writers of string quartets, outlived the French Revolution and the First Empire, and Grétry had somehow found time, between his innumerable operas, to write half a dozen of them, one does not imagine those disturbed times to have been conducive to indulgence in chamber music. Nor are the serious works of Cherubini, who was both a predecessor and a successor of Beethoven, likely to have found much favour in the Philistine days of the Restoration. The nineteenth century was well on its way to middle age before signs of a revival of interest became apparent. If then performers sought a repertoire abroad, it is no occasion for surprise, as the native repertoire was at its lowest. The older generation was represented by Boëly, the younger by Reber, and although both had musicianly qualities, neither was of absorbing interest. Yet they were superior to those who actually set the ball rolling again : Gastinel, alleged to be the first French musician of his time to give his attention to music other than opera ; Vaucorbeil, an undistinguished pupil of Cherubini ; and Georges Mathias, a specialist of the piano, who studied with Chopin and taught Raoul Pugno. Add the name of Henri Bertini, composer of piano studies, but also of some chamber works, and the national resources in chamber music are wellnigh exhausted. Small wonder that typical programmes displayed an anti-national bias resembling that of our own, then and later.

The first outstanding figure in French music to occupy himself with chamber music was Ambroise Thomas, when he was in residence at the Villa Medici with a Prix de Rome. One of his works is the subject of a nicely balanced criticism by Schumann. At an earlier date Hérold, under the same conditions, had sent home three string quartets, but they remained unpublished. These works are intrinsically not of great importance, but they indicate that the period of apathy towards chamber music was approaching an end. Presently there appeared upon the scene a succession of composers destined to quicken the interest, but when in 1840 César Franck, then a student at the Paris Conservatoire, wrote his three trios for piano, violin and 'cello, followed two years later by a fourth, few can have had any conception either of the status the young composer was to attain in the musical world or of the influence he was to exert on others. Long before Franck came to write the later works on which his fame now rests, and before his pupils began to make their way in the world, two other composers simultaneously entered the field of chamber music, Edouard Lalo and Saint-Saëns. The former, whose Symphonie Espagnole is so well known, wrote three piano trios and a string quartet which, although not ranked with his best works, are characterised by the sense of colour and rhythm one associates with him. Saint-Saëns's output in this sphere was more copious and more important. It began in 1855 with a piano quintet, Op. 14, and continued almost to the end of his life. The general favourite among his works is the piano quartet, Op. 41, but that may be because the interest in his music had begun to wane before the two string quartets made their appearance. He suffered the fate of conservative composers. He was a superb craftsman and a master of the classic style, but whilst producing brilliantly polished work, he contributed to it little that was new, and to-day he lives more securely in the Concertos, which serve for the display of virtuosity, than in his more solid work.

The next composer to claim attention was one of the earliest pupils of César Franck, Alexis de Castillon, one of the most gifted musicians of his generation, who in three years produced a piano quintet, a string quartet, a piano quartet, and two trios, besides a violin sonata, and died the following year in 1873 at the early age of 35. He it was who,

inspired by his revered teacher, led the van in that remarkable renascence of French music which set in on the morrow
of Sedan. But if the hopes to which he had given rise were
doomed to disappointment it was not long before another
musician appeared who was destined for a long and fruitful
career. This was Gabriel Fauré, whose first violin sonata
was composed in 1876. His concerted works include two
piano quartets in C minor and G minor, composed respectively in 1879 and 1886, which made rapid headway in the
world of chamber music and are still frequently heard ;
two piano quintets, a piano trio and a string quartet.
Towards the end of his career Fauré carried the refinement
which was his cardinal virtue almost to a fault, and it is
much to be doubted whether his later works can ever share
the popularity of their predecessors. They have been
unkindly described as the music of a retired ambassador,
but for those who have remained susceptible to a reticent
delicacy they have an attractive charm and much distinction.

Before we pass on to other serious composers, a word may
suitably be interpolated here in favour of a composer who
had no pretensions, but wrote to please, in which he succeeded admirably. This is Benjamin Godard, whose
Berceuse (" Angels guard Thee ") enjoyed for a time a
devastating popularity and is still remembered. It is not
so well known that he wrote three string quartets and two
piano trios which give unfailing pleasure to such amateurs
as do not consider the furrowed brow an indispensable
adjunct to music.

## CHAPTER IX

# FRANCE : FRANCK, DEBUSSY AND AFTER

In 1878 César Franck began the composition of his piano quintet, his first chamber work after an interval of thirty-six years, during which he had attained to mature mastery. It is scarcely necessary to dilate upon the quality of this work which has long since taken its place beside the great quintets of Schumann, Brahms and Dvořák. In a truer sense than any of these, Franck shows himself in this work, and perhaps even more in the string quartet of 1889, a close follower of Beethoven, carrying out what might be termed the latter's testamentary dispositions as indicated in the posthumous quartets. In recent years there have been signs of a reaction against César Franck, and perhaps his Symphony in D is not quite so great as was once thought, but the shapeliness of the string quartet is incontestable. It is not, however, only in his works that César Franck lives, but in his disciples. Among these the foremost place must be conceded to Vincent d'Indy, the founder of the *Schola Cantorum*, whose long career was devoted to the highest musical ideals. In his application of the principles of cyclic form, he was perhaps even more intransigent than his teacher, and there are not a few who see in this an indication of pedantry, but there was in him an equally strong vein of romanticism, and to those who know his music well there is a peculiar attractiveness in the process by which he was constantly striving to reconcile his poetical instincts with the austerity of his musicianship. His first chamber work, a piano quartet, coincides in date with his master's quintet. It was followed by a piano trio, two string quartets, a piano quartet and a string sextet, of which the last-named was composed when he was seventy-six. Perhaps this is the place to mention the eldest of d'Indy's pupils, Albéric Magnard, who was, if anything, more austere than his master. He wrote a quartet for piano and wind instruments, a string quartet and a piano trio, and was shot down by the Germans in 1914 when unwisely defending his home against the invaders. Of César Franck's other pupils the most distinguished was Ernest Chausson, who died in 1899 at the age of forty-four and bequeathed a concerto for piano and violin soli with string quartet, an excellent piano quartet in A, an unfinished string quartet and a posthumous piano trio. Another whose career was tragically short was the Belgian, Guillaume Lekeu, whose best work is a violin sonata, but who also wrote a piano trio and left a string quartet unfinished at his death, which took place in 1894 when he was only twenty-four.

It seems strange that only four years should separate the string quartets of César Franck and Debussy, but one was the fruit of a mature mind of classical build, the other the utterance of a young composer whose entrance into the musical world had about it something of the dramatic. Scarcely known at first beyond the limits of a small coterie, Debussy created on the general public the impression of being that rare phenomenon, a genius without precursors. We know now where his antecedents were to be found. As for his string quartet, two influences presided at its birth. Debussy had attended Franck's organ class at the Conservatoire, and although he never studied composition with him, it is unlikely that he left without knowing something of cyclic form as understood by the master who was so devoted to it. The concerts of Russian music organised by M. Belaiev in connection with the Paris Exhibition of 1889 had precipitated a great vogue in Paris musical circles for the members of the " Kutchka." Borodin's string quartets suddenly became famous. They had the qualities of formal elegance that appeal to Latin taste, and more than one French composer found in them an ideal to emulate. Thus Debussy's quartet recalls in its substance Borodin and in its form César Franck. It is not strictly cyclic, but one theme is common to three of its four movements and the other has a remote affinity to certain movements of Borodin. At the same time its harmonic texture is intensely characteristic of Debussy himself, of the course his development was to take. He did not write another piece of concerted chamber music until within two years of his death, when, in 1916, he composed a sonata for flute, viola and harp, a work of concentrated delicacy that seemed to open new vistas, unfortunately fated to remain unrealised. A decade separates Debussy's quartet from that of Maurice Ravel, a pupil of Fauré, who was beginning to attract attention by the originality of his harmonic ideas. He, too, is said to have been prompted by the example of Borodin. He is also said to have been influenced by Debussy, but that is scarcely borne out by a comparison of contemporary works by each. Ravel's whole outlook was more formal, more precise, and more pointed than Debussy's. He had an eighteenth-century passion for clarity, and was temperamentally averse from the " atmospheric " effects that played so important a part in the art of Debussy. His string quartet, which is dedicated to his master, Fauré, is transparently clear, despite an apparent complexity of construction. Ravel's next chamber work was an Introduction and Allegro for harp, flute, clarinet, and string quartet, commonly described as his septet, which made its appearance three years after the quartet. Ten years later he set three poems of Mallarmé for voice, piano, string quartet, two flutes and two clarinets. But the most important of his chamber works is undoubtedly the piano trio, completed in 1915, which is one of the finest chamber works of modern times. Since then he has written a sonata for violin and 'cello unaccompanied which is of great technical interest by virtue of innovations in the direction of bitonality. Another Fauré pupil is Florent Schmitt, who produced in 1908 a monumental piano quintet, with an extraordinary wealth of ideas brilliantly treated, but so overgrown that the composer himself has admitted the need of pruning.

It was scarcely to be expected that these developments should remain without effect upon the younger composers of the César Franck clan, but this is not shown as freely in their chamber music as elsewhere. On the whole it must be admitted that the most interesting works were not forthcoming from those who were most faithful to their inherited doctrine. The most distinguished graduate of the *Schola Cantorum*, Albert Roussel, soon gave evidence of emancipation. His most important chamber works are a piano trio, a Divertissement for piano and wind instruments, and a Serenade for harp, flute, violin, viola, and 'cello. A somewhat isolated figure is that of Jean Huré, represented chiefly by two string quartets and a piano quintet. Another, even more so, is Charles Koechlin, whose chamber works are full of interest, but little known.

The story of " Les Six " has been told so often that there is no particular point in repeating it here, but it so happens that without exception the members of that long-since dissolved association are all keenly interested in chamber music. Louis Durey, the eldest of them, has written two string quartets of which the first is another attempt to emulate the virtues of those of Borodin. Darius Milhaud has composed six symphonies for various combinations ranging from seven to ten instruments, but these are not usually included with his chamber music, the list of which is headed with seven string quartets. He employs mostly simple diatonic tunes, and is not even afraid of occasional banality, but his use of polytonality makes some of his works fall harshly on the ear. The works of Arthur Honegger are more orthodox, and perhaps for that reason have made more headway in this country. They include two string quartets. Germaine Tailleferre has also written one. Poulenc made his début as a composer with a Rhapsodie Nègre for piano, flute, clarinet, string quartet and voice *ad lib.*, and has shown a special predilection for wind instruments, for which he has written several sonatas. His outstanding chamber work is a trio for piano, oboe and bassoon. Auric has published no chamber music in the ordinary sense of the word, but, commissioned to compose incidental music for a play produced at the Comédie des Champs-Élysées in 1925, he wrote it for a septet of piano, clarinet, bassoon, trumpet, violin, viola and 'cello, and it has had many performances as chamber music.

The story of French chamber music abounds in names that have scarcely travelled beyond the borders of the country. There was, for instance, Théodore Gouvy, an Alsatian composer of French descent, whose reputation fell between two stools, his musical sympathies being German, so that he was acclaimed in neither country, but, being of independent means, he did not allow this to deter him from writing many chamber works of somewhat academic quality. There was Louis Lacombe, who wrote three piano trios and a piano quartet which showed remarkable merit in their day, but failed to make their way before the turn of the modern tide. There was Théodore Dubois, a musician of the academic or mandarin class, who reached the age of sixty without writing any chamber music, and then produced eight works, some of which possess the kind of merit one expects to meet in the circumstances.

These belong definitely to the past. In recent times there has arisen one composer the failure of whose music to reach England occasions some surprise, for it is both original and attractive, albeit somewhat difficult of execution. This is Georges Migot, whose chamber compositions include trios for piano, violin and 'cello, and for flute, clarinet and harp, besides other works bearing " programme " titles, such as " Cinq Mouvements d'Eau " for string quartet.

## CHAPTER X

## ITALY

THE PROBLEM of the modern Italians resembled that of the French, but took a more acute form. From the third quarter of the eighteenth century, apart from the Church, music and the opera had become almost interchangeable terms. It is true that both Rossini and Donizetti wrote in their nonage string quartets that are negligible, and Verdi one in his maturity that is not, but their countrymen must have regarded these as curious eccentricities on the part of operatic masters. Yet Verdi's string quartet was in reality the harbinger of a new attitude towards instrumental music in general and chamber music in particular. It was composed in 1873, and only three years later Giovanni Sgambati, to whom belongs the glory of having written the first modern Italian symphony, produced the first of his two piano quintets, the second following a year later. For their day these are fine works, but they are eclipsed in musical interest by the string quartet of 1884. Meanwhile Martucci had written in 1883 the first of his two piano trios, the second following in 1888, and the piano quintet in 1893. Marco Enrico Bossi followed in 1896, with a piano trio, and another in 1901. Alessandro Longo, the editor of the complete Scarlatti, produced a piano quintet in 1897, and about the same time the Sicilian, Antonio Scontrino, began to be known for the excellence of his string quartets, of which he wrote four, besides a Prelude and Fugue for the same combination.

Ermanno Wolf-Ferrari, better known as a composer of operas, has testified to the efficacy of his German training with a couple of piano trios in 1901 and 1902, followed by a chamber symphony in 1903. This last work is for eleven instruments, piano with five wind and five strings, which brings it to the very verge of the orchestral domain, but it is conceived in the spirit of chamber music and not too overwhelming to be enjoyed in intimacy. These collectively represent the precursors of modern Italian chamber music corresponding, let us say, to the stage of Parry and Stanford in England.

The next stage is of to-day, for it is ushered in by Pizzetti and Respighi with their string quartets respectively of 1906 and 1907. Since then, apart from his well-known sonatas, Pizzetti has more recently composed a piano trio and Respighi has given his string quartet a successor in the Dorian mode. Among their contemporaries may be mentioned Carlo Perinello, a Triestine composer, with a piano quartet and a string quartet composed respectively in 1911 and 1913; and Vincenzo Tommasini, the clever adapter of Scarlatti's music for "The Good-Humoured Ladies," with a string quartet composed in 1912. These composers might be said to represent the right wing of modern Italian music. Respighi's talent inclines more to the orchestra, as becomes a one-time pupil of Rimsky-Korsakov, but Pizzetti, who has an almost Hellenic appreciation of line, writes with an intimate sense of beauty and restraint that belongs essentially to chamber music.

We now reach those who are commonly described as "moderns," if not "ultra-moderns." They are headed by Casella and Malipiero. Although the younger of the two, Casella has acquired more prominence—some might say notoriety—in the musical world outside of Italy, where his position as leader of the modern legions is unchallenged. He is one of the most proficient of living musicians, a fine pianist and a capable conductor, and his general knowledge of music extends far and wide. As a composer he leaves one with the impression that there is nothing he could not do if he chose. Yet somehow the output of this extraordinarily equipped musical organism is for the most part curiously unsatisfying. It may be that such virtuosity as his is itself a danger. Often it lures him to parody, as, for instance, in the "Valse Ridicule" of his Five Pieces for string quartet. His best chamber works are a concerto for string quartet and a serenade for strings and wind, both of which post-date the spell of neo-classicism through which he passed like so many others, and represent his present mature style. He has derived considerable benefit from his migrations among Italian classics, and his championship of Rossini corresponds to something in his musical temperament which, long overweighted by his modern exuberance, has now found free expression. Though still underrated by the more severe of critics, Casella has given the world of chamber music some exhilarating moments which call for gratitude. Gian Francesco Malipiero, the Venetian, the hermit of Asolo, is the very opposite of Casella. The latter is a musical man-of-the-world, familiar with every fashion that has had a vogue in his day, and frequently suspected of a desire to " go one better " than most of them, not turning inwards upon himself until he had reached the prime of life. Malipiero has worked out his salvation in comparative solitude, commencing with the Italian classics, drawing such stimulus as he needed from the tradition created by them, and almost indifferent to currents and tendencies. His two string quartets " Rispetti e Strambotti " and " Stornelli e Ballate " are among the most characteristic products of modern Italy. Both are episodic, consisting of a succession of short sections held together by a kind of organic affinity difficult to explain, but so real that they sound quite concise when by all precedent they ought to sound diffuse and disjointed. Since these two works he has written a piano trio, or rather *Sonata a tre*, of which one movement is for piano and violin, one for piano and 'cello, and only the third for the three instruments. The best known of their contemporaries is Riccardo Pick-Mangiagalli whose early string quartet is, however, not representative except in the sense that its pictorial quality foreshadows his later preoccupation with the symbolism of the ballet.

The younger Italian composers are for the most part neo-classicists at heart, animated by a desire to recapture the lyrical qualities and also the light-heartedness of an earlier age. Mario Labroca's string quartet is a good example of his work, which is concise, rhythmic, and objective. Vittorio Rieti's is a comparatively early work, and the sonata for piano, flute, oboe, and bassoon is more representative. In him the lyrical vein is combined with a lively sense of humour. This is not at all uncommon among the young men of Italy, who have come to no harm through the " back to Rossini " movement which counterbalanced the " back to Bach " phase of neighbouring countries. The genius of Rossini, before he took to " grand " opera, was racy of the Italian soil, and others than Italians have experienced delight in renewing contact with it. Occasionally one hears Italian chamber music of another kind, approximating more to preconceived notions of what chamber music would be if leavened with the national operatic idiom, but such works suffer by the inevitable comparison with other countries where the art of chamber music has had more recent development, whereas Italian neo-classicism seems to have struck a vein that one is prepared to accept at its face-value, without *arrière-pensée*.

# D: BRITAIN AND AMERICA

## CHAPTER I

# PIONEERS: ELGAR AND VAUGHAN WILLIAMS

THE BRITISH RENASCENCE stands on a different footing from that of any other of the nationalist movements that originated in the nineteenth century. Its task was the heaviest, for surely never was any musical nation so completely subject to alien influences as England a century ago, never did a musical nation break so completely with its own past tradition as England did with that bequeathed by the Tudor classics, and never did a group of composers have to face so stubborn an anti-national prejudice as that which confronted the pioneers of that movement. If the battle has been won, credit must be given not only to these pioneers, but even to those precursors who, though they did not yet produce music that we recognise as English, did at least show such audiences as were prepared to listen to them that English birth was no insuperable impediment to the writing of music on classical models. And in each generation there has been some one composer who did this with so much credit as to pave the way for the renascence that was to set in later. In that sense the story goes back to Mendelssohn's contemporary, Sterndale Bennett. His piano trio is a rather frail plant, and even his piano sextet is not very sturdy, but how pleasant both are in comparison with the works of his contemporary G. A. Macfarren! Again, the piano trio of Francis E. Bache, who died in 1858 aged only twenty-five, may not be a work of great genius, but compare it with the compositions of Charles E. Stephens, or even of that erudite musician Ebenezer Prout, and it is impossible to avoid the conviction that somehow, somewhere, in this allegedly barren soil seed was germinating. Then came the age of the great precursors Parry, Stanford and Mackenzie. Of these the last-named produced a piano quartet in 1874, Parry wrote several concerted works between 1879 and 1884, and Stanford, in the face of lack of encouragement, continued writing them most of his life. Despite the Scottish strain in Mackenzie, and the Irish in Stanford, the influence of early German studies weighs so heavily upon all this music that it is difficult to realise its bearing upon later developments ; but one must admire the persistent hammering upon the door of British prejudice, against which was being waged a war of attrition the results of which were to show later. Moreover, Stanford exercised a wholesome influence upon two generations of his successors, who owe to him the sense of form inculcated at the Royal College of Music.

Elgar, who was the first British composer to make a definite breach in the wall of prejudice that surrounded them all, did not turn his attention to chamber music until he was over sixty. His battle against the national apathy had then been long since won, and he was already a little inclined to rest upon his laurels. Despite the manifold beauties of his string quartet and piano quintet, one does not meet in them the strong impulses of his earlier works. This was not to be expected. But though sedate, they are in no sense academic. If they have scarcely met with as much appreciation as they deserved, the reason is that they appeared a little late for that particular style of music. The temper of the audience was no longer that of Edwardian days, and though it continued to treasure the music inherited from them, its sensibilities were dulled for additions to it. Dame Ethel Smyth's Op. 1, is a string quintet, published in 1884. Her string quartet, which dates from 1902, has two fine movements and two others that exhibit the angularity so frequently met with in her compositions, the appreciation of which is a matter of individual temperament. Delius wrote two string quartets of which, however,

Sc

only the second has been published. It is a comparatively late work and very characteristic, both in the beauty of its texture and in the looseness of its form. To this group belongs, at least chronologically, the indefatigable Algernon Ashton, the list of whose compositions can only be described as formidable. He was a pupil of Raff and his early works promised well for his future as a good follower of the German romantics, but as the years went on his industry defeated itself by becoming a habit.

Next in order of date should be mentioned four contemporary composers whose chamber music deserves attention. They are Sir John McEwen, Sir H. Walford Davies, Dr. Ernest Walker and the late Dr. Charles Wood. McEwen, in particular, is associated with a date that is almost a historical landmark. During the whole of the nineteenth century, as far as can be ascertained, not a single string quartet by a British composer had been published in England. The very few that had found their way into print appeared in foreign catalogues. When in 1903 Novello's published his fourth string quartet, they took a step which augured well for the twentieth century, in the course of which this reproach has been completely removed. McEwen has now written fifteen quartets, not all of which are published. Some of them bear sub-titles, such as " Nugae " the 7th, " Biscay " the 8th, " Threnody " the 9th, and " Jocund Dance " the 11th. There is in his music a strong tinge of Scottish nationalism, subtle rather than aggressive, and a vein of somewhat wistful lyricism which frequently expresses itself with much charm. Walford Davies is better known as the highly popular broadcasting authority on all branches of music than as the author of the " Peter Pan " suite for string quartet (Op. 30, 1909). Dr. Wood's string quartets are, despite an occasional reminder of his Irish birth, of more scholastic type, and most of Dr. Walker's chamber music, though frequently performed, has remained unpublished.

At the head of our next group stands Dr. Vaughan Williams. The twelve years from 1872 to 1883 saw the birth of a group of composers who, by brilliant and constant effort forced their way into the breach created by Elgar, and compelled the recalcitrant English public to give them a fair hearing. Those of them who have enriched the world of chamber music are chiefly : Vaughan Williams, Waldo Warner, Donald Francis Tovey, Dunhill, Holbrooke, Cyril Scott, Frank Bridge, John Ireland and Arnold Bax. Vaughan Williams is mainly a composer of symphonic and choral music. Compared with these, chamber music is to him a less congenial medium, but possibly for that very reason his approach to it is more personal than that of many who have, so to speak, grown up in it. He is less affected than they by the inhibitions that cluster round firmly established art. Apart from unpublished works, he is represented by two song-cycles, a string quartet, and a Phantasy string quintet. Song-cycles do not come strictly within the purview of this section, but there is inherent justification for including " On Wenlock Edge " for voice, piano, and string quartet, and " Merciless Beauty " for voice, violin, viola, and 'cello, because their texture is essentially that of chamber music, and their remarkable beauty owes no less to it than to their vocal line. The string quartet, which was revised many years after composition, is a close-knit work whose movements are held together by a certain affinity, not amounting to identity, of thematic material. The Phantasy quintet is one of the many works due to the initiative of Mr. W. W. Cobbett, and may therefore serve as motive for a digression with the object of describing how these works came into existence.

## CHAPTER II

# W. W. COBBETT AND LIONEL TERTIS

WALTER WILLSON COBBETT is, at the moment of writing, in his eighty-eighth year and still one of the keenest amateurs of chamber music in the country. Nearly thirty years ago, in 1905, he instituted a series of competitions for works in a form which was intended to be a modern equivalent of the "Fancy"—short instrumental compositions that were common in the Golden Age of English music from Tudor times to the Restoration. It then enjoyed comparative freedom from formal rules, but modern practice, with its devotion to sonata form, interpreted the Phantasy as a kind of condensation of the usual three or four movements, in which sections equivalent to a slow movement and scherzo were interpolated between exposition and recapitulation. Even so, considerable freedom remained in the choice of thematic material, which might be related or contrasted, and in the general method of construction. The first competition was for a string quartet and the prize went to W. Y. Hurlstone, a young composer of great promise whose career was unfortunately cut short at thirty years of age. A second competition followed, for a Phantasy trio, in which the three prizes went to Frank Bridge, John Ireland and James Friskin. Yet others followed, and by 1915 the repertoire had been enriched by no fewer than twenty-four works in this form. Mr. Cobbett did not weary of well-doing. A few more competitions were held, in addition to which numerous works were commissioned from composers of established repute. Nor does this exhaust the list of Mr. Cobbett's benefactions, for he has instituted free libraries, prizes at the Royal College of Music, and a Cobbett medal for services to Chamber Music. He has also compiled and published a monumental Cyclopedic Survey of Chamber Music. But from our point of view the salient fact is that there are very few English composers of chamber music whose works do not include at least one due to his initiative, and this applies to many whom we shall not have space to mention.

Whilst discussing influences that have proved incentives to our composers it would be ungracious to omit a reference to Lionel Tertis, whose wonderful playing of the viola has inspired a large number of chamber works in which that instrument is prominent. If England now possesses a viola literature that is second to none, it is almost entirely due to the joy composers experienced in writing for so fine an interpreter. Incidentally, Tertis is not a composer. The circumstance is worth mentioning, as it is a remarkable fact that in many string quartets, in this country and elsewhere, the viola player is a composer. In England Frank Bridge was long a noted player of that instrument, and Waldo Warner, the viola of the original London String Quartet is a composer, as is also Rebecca Clarke. To mention only a few others, in Germany Paul Hindemith, in Bohemia Oskaz Nedbal, in Spain Conrado del Campo, in Brazil Villa-Lobos, have played the viola in various teams, and, to go further back, in France Benjamin Godard was first drawn to chamber music through playing the viola in a quartet. There are many other instances, but we must not be led away from our subject.

## CHAPTER III

# THE ENGLISH TREASURY: BRIDGE, IRELAND AND BAX

As it happens, Waldo Warner is the next composer on our list. His contribution includes three Phantasy string quartets, the third of which is based on a folk-song, a string quartet in C minor, and another on a descriptive theme, "The Pixy Ring," and a piano trio. He has been remarkably successful in winning prizes with his works, both here and in America. In fact, nearly all his outstanding works were originally written for some competition or other, but they are none the worse for that. His music is spontaneous and personal, and if it does not soar to greatness it is always grateful. Donald Francis Tovey is one of the most erudite of musical scholars. It is in fact not impossible that his great and well-earned reputation for theoretical and historical knowledge may have handicapped his works by predisposing his audiences to regard them as emanating from academic lore. A Professor is in this respect always at a certain disadvantage. Tovey's chamber music has the profound esteem of a large circle of admirers, but has never captured the affection of the greater public. Nor has that of Dunhill, although his services to chamber music have endeared him to its devotees, and certain of his works, such as the Phantasy string quartet and the "Pleasantries" for two violins and viola are popular for private performance, being more accessible to players of moderate ability than the majority of contemporary chamber works, the difficulty of which is so great as to be a contributory cause of the decline in amateur playing of chamber music. Holbrooke's predilection is for orchestral colouring, and this shows in his copious output of chamber music by the frequent use of wind instruments no less than by a tendency to massiveness in his string writing. His fluency occasionally tempts him to non-critical composition, and there are many of his works which might have been better than they actually are if only he had exercised more self-discipline. But in spite of their defects one is conscious, especially in the earlier works, of a vigorous and inventive musical organism and of an exuberant phantasy. Among his best works are a string sextet, Op. 43, a Phantasy string quartet, and a trio for piano, violin and horn. A remarkable incursion into the field of programme music is his third string quartet, entitled "The

Pickwick Club," and described as a humoresque. It comprises thirteen sections, all dealing with some episode or personality from Dickens's masterpiece. Holbrooke's career began so brilliantly, at a time when English music was struggling to emerge from Victorian dullness, that the most extravagant hopes were built upon it, and it is impossible to avoid the feeling that the inevitable reaction has led to his receiving less than justice in later years. The same applies to some extent also to Cyril Scott, whose beginnings were even more startling, since the idiom he employed was then more novel. His published chamber music, consisting of a piano quartet, a piano quintet, a string quartet and a piano trio, besides a charming Idyllic Phantasy for voice, oboe and 'cello, has much to commend it. He now disavows the piano quartet as well as most of his manuscript chamber works, but the quintet, of which the original version was written when he was twenty-five, still stands to show that the welcome extended to his early works was not greater than they deserved. Unfortunately his later development has not proved commensurate.

We now reach three composers who have done more than any others of their generation to raise the standard of English chamber music. The first to win the suffrages of its devotees was Frank Bridge. As far back as 1906 he was awarded a " mention d'honneur " in an international competition held at Bologna, for the first of his three string quartets. At the same time he had already to his credit several minor works for the same combination : Novelettes, Idylls, a Phantasy quartet, to which he has since added some clever adaptations of folk-songs. His other works include Phantasies for piano trio and quartet, a piano quintet, and a piano trio. His style has undergone considerable change. Always resourceful, he was at first somewhat conservative in method, and it is only in his later works that his harmonic evolution has taken an emancipated personal direction. Apart from sonatas, he is now best represented by his third string quartet and the recent piano trio. Sonatas form the greater part of John Ireland's chamber music and the remarkable success of one of them, the A minor violin sonata, in 1917, helped much to draw wider attention to the progress made in this field by English composers. Of concerted works he has written only two piano trios, both in one movement, the first being a phantasy, the second, and more remarkable of the two, a very free adaptation of variation form. The third and youngest of our three composers is Arnold Bax. A trio for piano, violin and viola dating from 1906 may be disregarded as immature, but, apart from several sonatas, he has from 1915 onwards enriched the repertoire with a succession of works of great beauty. The first was a piano quintet of vast dimensions which justifies its unusual length by the nobility and richness of its material. Then followed two string quartets, a quintet for harp and strings and another for oboe and strings ; a short piano quartet and various minor works. In some, but not all, of these the Irish strain is prominent, but it is not actually based on folk-song. A striking instance occurs in the last section of the first string quartet in which there is a tune which has often been mistaken for an Irish folk-song, but is actually an original melody.

## CHAPTER IV

## LATER DEVELOPMENTS

CHIEF AMONG the next chronological group are Arthur Bliss, Eugene Goossens and Herbert Howells. Bliss's first works, a string quartet and a piano quartet, have been withdrawn from circulation. Their immediate successors comprised " Madame Noy," a song with six instruments ; a rhapsody for two wordless voices, and seven instruments ; and " Conversations " for five instruments—three works of remarkable individual character, which established his reputation as a writer of buoyant, often exuberant, music somewhat unjustly attributed to recent French influences. There is a tendency to-day, equally unjust, to regard this phase as one of " wild oats," probably because his present style, represented by an oboe quintet, and a more recent clarinet quintet, is in comparison more sedate, though technically more polished and perhaps more durable. Goossens's activities as conductor have latterly tended to reduce his output, which however includes a Phantasy string quartet, a piano quintet in one movement, a string sextet, and a wind nonet, sufficient to rank him as an important contributor to our chamber repertoire. Howells, one of many composers hailing from the West Country, is represented by a piano quartet, a Phantasy string quartet, and a clarinet quartet, but one of his best works, a string quartet, bearing the title " In Gloucestershire," has remained unpublished. His style is quietly lyrical and poetically fanciful. To this group may be added on chronological grounds a pupil of John Ireland, E. J. Moeran, who has written a string quartet and a piano trio, of which the former, an excellent work, is the more interesting.

Of our younger composers, the most prominent is William Walton, but his chamber works are of early date and scarcely representative. Other writers, whose names alone can be mentioned from considerations of space, are : James Friskin, Gerard Williams, Armstrong Gibbs, Edric Cundell and Eric Fogg. At the moment much is expected of a very young composer, Benjamin Britten, whose quartet for oboe and strings was performed at the last festival of the International Society for Contemporary Music. A noteworthy feature of the times is the number of young women composers who have entered the field of chamber music, to which they are contributing works of much interest. Among them should be mentioned Helen Perkin and Elisabeth Maconchy.

Though Bernard van Dieren is not of English birth, his long residence in this country indicates this as the place to refer to his chamber music, which is of considerable importance, chiefly represented by string quartets, of which seven have appeared. Like all his works they vary considerably in style, the first being, curiously enough, the most intricate, whilst his later tendency is markedly in the direction of simplification and conciseness.

Even then, the subtlety and occasional tortuousness of his musical thought rarely make him easy of access and his progress in public estimation has been, for these days, singularly slow considering the intrinsic worth of his music. At present, however, he is generally recognised as one of the most distinct musical individualities of our time.


# CHAPTER V

# THE UNITED STATES

IT BEHOVES AN ENGLISHMAN to write with sympathy of American musical endeavour, for the American composer has still to contend with, in an aggravated form, the disadvantages that his English colleague has overcome with great difficulty and only within recent years. Chief among these is the apathy, not to say direct hostility, of those to whom he was entitled to look for encouragement, his own countrymen. In addition, he was confronted with the ethnical difficulty of finding a national alternative to the idiomatic and stylistic factors derived from Europe, and, as in other countries, chiefly from Germany. The history of American music may be said to comprise two distinct phases that are more sharply divided than anywhere in Europe, the earlier, conservative, based upon European tradition, and the later, energetically, sometimes even violently, seeking an outlet from the trammels, real or imaginary, of that tradition. At the head of the first chapter stands the name of George Whitefield Chadwick, German-trained, moderately influenced by the example of Dvořák, the composer of numerous works of sterling merit but naturally conservative. With him may be classed Arthur Foote, Edgar Stillman-Kelley, Mrs. H. H. A. Beach, Henry Hadley, F. S. Converse, Rubin Goldmark, and Daniel Gregory Mason, all composers of marked attainments, having to their credit works that are still assured of appreciation in circles where good workmanship and sound musical ideals are given their due.

A kind of intermediate position is occupied by two American composers whose style is affected, not by German, but by French influences. The elder is Charles Martin Loeffler, an Alsatian by birth, naturalised since 1887 and the composer of several works reflecting a delicate impressionism which has been compared to that of Debussy. The younger, Blair Fairchild, found a more congenial atmosphere in Paris and might almost be classed as a French composer. He was a prolific writer, among whose recent works may be mentioned a piano quintet as representative. An earlier work takes the form of a chamber Concerto for piano, violin, and string quartet (with double bass *ad lib.*) on the precedent of that of Chausson, which however it does not otherwise resemble.

Chamber music does not so far appear to have attracted the attention of the " wild men " referred to above. Allowing for the fact that the " centre " has itself moved a little to the left in recent years, the younger writers of chamber music belong to the " right wing " of American music. The most noteworthy of them are Arthur Shepherd, Louis Gruenberg, Emerson Whithorne, Frederick Jacobi, and Leo Sowerby. Of these the one who has attracted most attention in Europe is Gruenberg, mainly through performances of " The Daniel Jazz " for tenor voice with piano, clarinet, trumpet, and string quartet, but he is also the composer of duet-sonatas, and of " Four Indiscretions " for string quartet. Whithorne was for a time resident in England, where his " Greek Impressions " for string quartet have been performed.

Consideration of American music is apt to be complicated by the tendency to include, as American, composers of repute who settle in the States. Thus Ernst Bloch, who has now returned to Europe, is still classed as American. His chamber music consists mainly of two remarkably fine works, a string quartet and a piano quintet, the latter of which may be classed with the best of its kind produced in recent decades, a worthy successor to those that established the form. He has also written some interesting " programme " pieces for string quartet.

It would be ungracious to leave the subject of American music without paying tribute to Mrs. Elizabeth Sprague Coolidge, who by means of competitions and direct commissions has done in America what Mr. W. W. Cobbett has done in England, but on a larger and more international scale. The number of important compositions that owed their incentive to her munificence forms a catalogue of absorbing interest, in which many famous names are represented.

# E : MODERNISM

## CHAPTER I

## SOME NATIONAL SCHOOLS

THERE ARE STILL a few nationalist movements of more recent growth, which claim attention. Of the three founders of modern Spanish music, Pedrell, Albeniz and Granados, only the last-named wrote any chamber music, and that of little importance. The first to turn his attention to this field was Joaquin Turina, probably through having been a pupil of the *Schola Cantorum* in Paris, where chamber music was assiduously fostered. He has written a string quartet, a piano quintet and a piano trio, besides several works bearing " programme " titles, such as " Escena Andaluza " for piano, viola and string quartet, " La Annunciacion " for piano sextet, and " La Oracion del Torero " for string quartet. Then there is Conrado del Campo, the viola player, composer of numerous quartets, of which few are published. Of these, " Caprichos Romanticos " is the best known. Oscar Espla and Adolfo Salazar have also written chamber music, but the most important of living Spanish composers, Manuel de Falla, is represented only by his concerto for harpsichord accompanied by six instruments, a work of profound interest, and by a song accompanied by five. His pupil, Ernesto Halffter, has published a string quartet.

There is a more fertile activity in modern Hungarian music. Some years ago Hans Koessler, a German musician, pupil of Rheinberger, with some excellent chamber music to his credit, became the director of the Royal Hungarian Academy of Music at Budapest. Like Dvořák, in similar circumstances, he paid his hosts the compliment of introducing the Hungarian idiom into his works, where it is scarcely more prominent than in those of Brahms, on whom he modelled himself. He derives, however, some historical importance from the circumstance that Hungarian music to-day is completely dominated by his three most gifted pupils : Dohnanyi, who, like himself, is of a conservative turn of mind ; Bela Bartok, who, on the contrary, sides with the left ; and Zoltán Kodály, who, after also showing signs of an inclination to the left, has gradually settled down to a middle course. Dohnanyi's works include several string quartets, two piano quintets and a Serenade for violin, viola and 'cello, all highly polished and technically interesting but showing relatively little individuality. Bartok is the composer of four very remarkable string quartets, of which two belong to early periods of his evolution and two to his maturity. Those most representative are the second and fourth. Both the earlier quartets reflect his deep and prolonged study of Magyar folk-song, but in the second the assimilation of the idiom is less self-conscious and more complete. The fourth has a brilliance amounting to virtuosity and requires a quartet of virtuosi to play it, but when well played it is one of the most effective of modern quartets. Kodály is more romantic—one might say a kind of Hungarian Schubert, with something of that composer's melodic instinct and also some of his diffuseness. He has written two string quartets and a Serenade for two violins and viola. Among other Hungarian composers should be mentioned Alexander Jemnitz and Tibor Harsanyi, the latter a pupil of Kodály, who now lives in Paris and has published several concerted works of great interest.

Polish music is dominated in the land of its birth by Karol Szymanovski, but as with many countries of Eastern Europe it also includes a contingent domiciled in Paris, among whom Alexander Tansman is eminent. The former has composed a string quartet, Op. 37, with a scherzando finale that is a remarkable instance of polytonality, the four parts being written in different keys. Tansman has given more attention to chamber music, his contributions to which include several quartets and a sinfonietta for ten instruments. A promising young composer is Jerzy Fitelberg, son of the Warsaw conductor. Prior to these Polish music was mostly influenced by the German tradition. There is little to differentiate such composers as Noszkovski, Stojovski or Statkovski from the army of composers of Central Europe.

Georges Enesco, the foremost Roumanian musician of the day, is Paris-trained, and so is Stan Golestan, but the former went to the Conservatoire, the latter to the *Schola Cantorum*, at a time when the difference between their teaching was marked. Both have written chamber music. A younger Roumanian composer, Fonel Perlea, approaches more to modern Germany. Of Roumanian nationalism the signs are not conspicuous.

Nor does one speak of nationalism in referring to Willem Pijper, the most interesting of contemporary Dutch composers, and still less in connection with such Swiss composers as Andreae or Schoeck, both of whom have written excellent chamber music of a less controversial order. One should not forget that both Arthur Honegger, who was associated with " Les Six," and Conrad Beck, who, like Honegger, has made his home in France, are by birth Swiss composers.

It only remains to bring up to date some of our earlier references to nationalism. Scandinavia has produced in modern times but one outstanding figure, that of Sibelius, the Finn. He is, however, little drawn to chamber music, in which he is represented solely by the string quartet " Voces Intimae," Op. 56, and a " Suite Mignonne " for seven instruments. The quartet departs considerably from traditional form and its harmonic idiom is very personal, but it is full of interest and charm.

The post-revolution chamber music of Russia is as yet little known in Western Europe. Roslavetz was beginning to be heard of as a composer of subversive ideas before the great interruption. Alexander Mossolov, of " Steel Foundry" fame, has sent us a string quartet. One has heard the names of Evseiev, Alexandrov, Shebalin, Shirinsky and others, but so far they remain only names to us. A recent performance in London of a few quartets recommended by the Soviet musical authorities gave a general impression that political radicalism is not incompatible with bourgeois sentiments in music, the general tone being more conservative than it would have been at a corresponding concert of music from any Western European country. That, however, proves nothing. The selection was more or less official and officials have their own standards. There may be music in Soviet Russia that will completely change our views when it meets a Western audience. Meanwhile modern Russian music, for us Westerners, still means that of the Russian *émigrés*.

Czecho-Slovakia is one of the most active musical countries in Europe. It teems with composers to such an extent that, even in Brno, a provincial capital, they have their own club. That, however, was due to the magnetic personality of Janacek, Moravia's leading composer, who, after labouring a lifetime in obscurity, suddenly became world-famous at seventy with his opera " Jenufa." He is the composer of a remarkable string quartet, a suite for wind instruments, and a concertino for piano, two violins, viola, clarinet, horn and bassoon. In Prague, Novak and Suk represent the older post-romantic generation of Czech composers, whilst the newer blood is represented by such writers as the two Habas (of whom Alois, the elder, is the well-known specialist in quarter-tones), Jirak, and in the German-Czech group, Ervin Schulhoff. One of the most promising of Czech composers, Bohuslav Martinu, composer of two string quartets and a string quintet, migrated to Paris where, like Conrad Beck, he became a pupil of Albert Roussel. Paris has, in fact, become the home of a large number of composers, some of whom have found a refuge there from political conditions in Russia or, more recently, Germany, whilst others have been drawn by the cosmopolitan atmosphere that has reigned there since Belaiev brought Russian music to the first Paris Exhibition (1889), but which is perhaps a little less liberal to-day, its hospitality having become attenuated through economic conditions.

## CHAPTER II

# ANTI-ROMANTICISM

THE OUTSTANDING FEATURE of the last two decades has been the reaction against romanticism. Many are inclined to attribute this to the psychological effect of the war and its shattering of ideals, but it had set in before then, and was even then overdue, for the phase of which the Romantic Movement was the opening had run its full course and we had reached one of those climacterics that seem to recur in musical history at intervals of about a century and a half. The last can be dated by the death of Bach in 1750 and the one before that by the appearance of the *nuove musiche* about 1600. It produced a general feeling of dissatisfaction, which expressed itself in the feverish invention and exploitation of new technical devices, but a dominant factor in this unrest was the reaction against excesses such as had brought about the disintegration of the classic forms. This reaction reveals many different aspects of which we can only examine three.

Schönberg is typical of the first. He began as a convinced post-Wagnerian, as will be recognised from his string sextet, " Verklärte Nacht," composed in 1899 and symptomatic of the times. Two string quartets followed, in D minor and F sharp minor, Op. 7 and 10, the second of which includes two movements with voice. Then, with almost dramatic suddenness, Schönberg appears to have realised that romanticism was on a dangerous slope, for he made a *volte-face* and began a searching analysis of his material, from which new methods have resulted. " Pierrot Lunaire " for reciter with piano, flute, clarinet, violin and 'cello, composed in 1912, is one of the landmarks of twentieth century musical progress. But it also revealed the immense difficulty that confronts a composer desiring to extricate himself from Teutonic romanticism, for, with all its apparent modernity, its emotional quality is distinctly of the 'nineties. From this Schönberg turned to a doctrinaire conception of music as founded upon a system of twelve notes possessing equal importance (atonality). That is to say, he passed through doctrinaire stages, during which he was dominated by his new-found dogma. Of this a good example is the wind quintet, Op. 26, composed in 1924. But there came a time when the positions were reversed, when he had mastered the implications of his new dogma so completely as to recover his freedom within it. This is exemplified in his third string quintet, Op. 30, composed in 1927, a thoroughly representative work. His other chamber compositions are a Serenade in seven movements, Op. 24, for clarinet, bass clarinet, mandoline, guitar, violin, viola, 'cello, and in one movement a tenor voice ; and a suite for piano and wind instruments, Op. 29. Of Schönberg's many pupils the most important are Anton Webern and Alban Berg. Webern is one of the most elusive and " difficult " of present-day composers. He writes short movements that rarely rise above a whisper—he is known as the master of the *pianissimo*—and require the most delicate execution. His works include " Five Pieces " and " Six Baga-telles " for string quartet and a string trio. The latter was one of the works performed at the Siena Festival of 1928, where the Italians hissed it, as might have been expected, for one cannot imagine anything more antagonistic to Italian musical ideals than these strange spasmodic utterances. One of the Germans present retaliated by shouting " Mandolinists ! " And they call music an international language !

Berg, the composer of " Wozzeck," has proved himself in that work to have assimilated Schönberg's idiom so com-pletely that he is able to forget all about it and employ it as his natural musical speech, a stage reached by Schönberg himself only after long struggles. In his early days Berg wrote a string quartet, Op. 3, but his most representative work is the "Lyric Suite" for string quartet, composed in 1927, which is one of the outstanding examples of modern chamber music. This movement towards complete atonality has thus proved its worth. Whether it has also provided a means of escape from late-romantic excesses is more doubtful. Beneath all these works there still flows a romantic under-current that seems to be almost ineradicable.

The second form of reaction is that known as neo-classicism, which consists in a deliberate return to severe classic forms and to contrapuntal construction, whilst retaining the modern idiom and texture. The forms are thus dynamic and the counterpoint dissonant, in some cases polytonal. Though few recall the fact to-day, neo-classicism really began with Busoni. It would, however, be absurd, in his case, to speak of a " back to Bach " movement, since Busoni had never lost sight of that master. He brought a modern musical mind to bear upon him, and from this originated the neo-classic vein in his own works and in those of his pupils, chief among whom is Philipp Jarnach. It is more as influence than as personal teaching that this tendency to neo-classicism seems to have radiated from Busoni in Germany, but among German neo-classicists to-day one is frequently conscious of a mode of thought that could be traced back to Busoni's æsthetic. His own chamber music is, however, of too early date to reflect this. Meanwhile two distinct neo-classic movements have set in elsewhere. In 1919 Stravinsky was commissioned to adapt, for a ballet entitled " Pulcinella," some music by Pergo-lesi. At that time his only chamber music consisted of three pieces for string quartet and some vocal pieces, the most important of which was " Trois poésies de la lyrique japonaise " for voice, piano, flute, clarinet, and string quartet. The quartet pieces composed in August 1914 belong to the aftermath of " Le Sacre du Printemps." Contact with Pergolesi seems to have directed Stravinsky's attention to a whole mass of problems of form and, since he is temperamentally attracted by problems, from that moment he became absorbed in that of recapturing the

logic of the past that had become submerged by the intervention of romanticism. So far as chamber music is concerned the outcome was shown in the concertino for string
quartet of 1920, and the wind octet of 1923, but these represent an early stage of a process that has produced many neo-
classic works. The last so far is a Duo Concertante for violin
and piano. Though there is otherwise little in common
between them, Stravinsky's fellow-countryman Prokofiev
also follows a pronouncedly neo-classic path. His best known
chamber works are an Overture on Jewish Themes for
piano, clarinet and string quartet ; a quintet for oboe,
clarinet, violin, viola and double bass ; and a string quartet.
Meanwhile in France a number of young composers, from
totally different causes, were striking out in a parallel direction. They were reacting not so much against romanticism,
which had already waned in France before they set to work,
as against the impressionism of Debussy. Satie was their
" elder statesman " and Jean Cocteau their hierophant.
We have already had occasion to refer to " Les Six " as
followers of this tendency, which is now so general that it
affects even alien composers who have found a domicile in
Paris. In fact, neo-classicism of one brand or another is one
of the most powerful currents of the moment, though one
feels that the time is not far distant, when, having accomplished its mission, it will fade out. Even then, however, its
effect will on the whole have been beneficial.

The third form of reaction against romanticism belongs
to the order of ideas known in Germany as the *Neue Sach-
lichkeit*. Its chief representative is Paul Hindemith, whose
objectivity has reached the stage when he declares that no
music should be written that does not serve some practical
purpose. His own evolution followed a course that took him
by well-defined stages from Brahms through atonality and
neo-classicism to " Gebrauchsmusik," which may be
translated as work-a-day music. Each stage is copiously
represented by chamber music in many different forms,
and of late years he has also written ensemble music
specially suited for schools and for amateurs. He has written

some fine works, but his very facility is his undoing, not so much because of any falling off in style as because he tends to satiate his public, which in the end accepts a new Hindemith work every year without much distinguishing one from another. The most recent, however, a second trio for violin, viola and 'cello, proved on the whole more ingratiating than its more matter-of-fact predecessors. For those to whom Hindemith is new, the best approach is through his early string quartets, and particularly the third. Of other German composers who have consciously turned away from Teutonic romanticism may be mentioned Ernst Krenek, Ernst Toch, Max Butting and Kurt Weill, all of whom have written chamber music ; but it must be confessed that, just as cynicism is often inverted sentimentality, their objectivity is often itself a kind of inverted romanticism.

## CHAPTER III

# MUSIC AND MECHANISM

IT IS DIFFICULT TO ESTIMATE the effect of mechanical devices on chamber music. The world of amateur players was already crumbling before they became dangerous, and even to-day the cheap motor-car is a worse peril than either gramophone or wireless. The latter has made both friends and enemies for chamber music, friends whom it has converted to the charm of intimacy, and enemies whom it has enraged by too heavy programmes—for which, of course, the nineteenth-century despotism of sonata-form is chiefly to blame. The gramophone has proved a boon to those who were already addicts, if one may use the word, for of all recordings the most sensitive, the most accurately reproducible, are normally those of a string quartet. The records made for the Haydn Society by the Pro Arte Quartet should become the foundation of numerous libraries of recorded chamber works, but the difficulty is in persuading the potential convert to take the first step. It is singularly unfortunate that chamber music has become associated in the mind of the " man in the street " with a kind of " highbrow " atmosphere that acts as a deterrent. Once disabuse him of that, and his conversion is only a matter of easily acquired experience.

But whether the amateur performer of chamber music will ever play as active and prominent a part in its life as he did in the nineteenth century is much more problematical. For one thing a higher standard of proficiency is postulated to-day, not because modern music is so difficult, but because people who have heard, on the radio or on the gramophone, a first-rate performance of even an easy Haydn quartet are not going to be so readily satisfied with their own efforts as they were when a visit to St. James's Hall was a red-letter day for all except those who lived within easy reach. And since the ideal conception of chamber music is " the music of friends," this dwindling of the actual friendly circles is a serious matter. For chamber music the effect of the mechanical appliances is to make us, if we listen in the right spirit, eavesdroppers, overhearing the music of friends, in happy oblivion of the fact that the friends in question are playing, not for our enjoyment, but for their living.

# BOOK VI

## THE SOLO INSTRUMENT

### *By* F. BONAVIA

# A : KEYBOARD INSTRUMENTS

## CHAPTER I

## COMPOSER AND INSTRUMENT

THE HISTORY of musical art, as exemplified by the solo instrument, is germane to the history of the development and growth of the instruments themselves. As composers grew more exacting in their demands, devoted craftsmen sought to meet their requirements during the centuries that preceded the modern era (which, for our present purpose, may be taken to begin with Beethoven), when all essential progress in the development of the two chief musical instruments, the violin and the pianoforte, was an accomplished fact. No better violins have been made than those built by Stradivari and although the pianoforte of to-day is a better instrument than that which served Beethoven, the music Beethoven wrote for his instrument makes full use of every improvement the ingenuity of present-day makers has been able to devise.

The demand of the composer came first ; technical developments followed. When the maker attempted to anticipate the composer, his experiments were not so successful ; take, for instance, the saxophone which, in spite of Berlioz's eulogy, is an instrument fit only for the jazz bands that employ it. The great period of violin making, remarks Parry, nearly coincides with the early period of music for string instruments and he goes on to say that the highest point in violin making was reached when string music took definite and permanent shape in the works of the great school of Italian violinists and composers. This statement is perfectly accurate historically ; but it ignores the force of the impulse given to instrumental as well as to vocal music by the *musiche nuove* of the Florentine school. Monteverdi's "Orfeo" was performed and published before Stradivari was born and the violinists who took part in those performances must have been acutely conscious of the poverty of their instruments. The dashing passages typical of the true instrumental style, the *tremolando* that Monteverdi was the first to use, must have lost much of their effect when played on the instruments of the period and thus called the makers' attention to the possibility of improvement.

For the pianoforte the evidence proving how the maker followed the composer is more definite still. The earliest example of a "sonata" we possess is that of Giovanni Gabrieli, which was published in 1597, the year when Dr. John Bull delivered his inaugural address as first Gresham professor of music at Oxford. Gabrieli calls his first sonata "Pian e Forte" the name which, slightly modified, the instrument still bears. It is true that the Gabrieli Pian e Forte sonata was not written for a solo instrument but for cornet, violin and trombones. It must be remembered, however, that vocal and not instrumental music was then the main concern of the composer and that any new departure in the instrumental field would at once attract the attention of all instrumental musicians. Like Monteverdi, if in a lesser degree, Gabrieli had the genius of the instrumental composer. That is to say he realised that if in dissociating instrumental from vocal music, in setting the Sonata ("a piece played") against the Cantata ("a piece sung") there was bound to be a loss, there could also be some compensations and he found them in the contrast between extreme loudness and extreme softness, a sharper contrast on instruments than in voices.

The invention of the piano is attributed to Cristofori who in 1711 made the first instrument known to us and called not by its present modified name but, as in Gabrieli's sonata, Pian e Forte. But there is reliable evidence to show that instruments known as Pian e Forte were being made only a very short time after the publication of Gabrieli's sonata.

It is then not improbable that Gabrieli's venture started the quest for dynamic contrast, especially in the case of the only instrument that could reproduce the full harmonic range of Gabrieli's chamber orchestra.

The pianoforte is the first instrument to claim our attention. It is the most unsightly, most unpoetic of all musical instruments. Unfortunately it is also the most useful since, apart from the organ, it alone reproduces a harmonic and melodic whole. It has inherited the literature of clavichord and harpsichord. It can and does absorb, with slight alteration, the greater part of the organ repertory. It could, but wisely does not, absorb the repertory of the violin. As a substitute for the full orchestra it is invaluable. It is also the cause of much imperfect musicianship in some modern composers and conductors who, having never been trained to seek the finer shades of tone and colour in sustained harmonic sound, have lost the power to appreciate them.

The attitude of mind created by the pianoforte has left its mark on the course of musical art. The pianist as composer often missed his objective because he could not completely adapt himself to the new medium. The scores of the early nineteenth century abound in designs and figures of accompaniment which, devised to overcome the pianoforte's congenital inability to sustain sound, are artificial and utterly pointless in an orchestra. Not until the coming of the true orchestral composers—men such as Berlioz and Wagner—were these swept aside.

It is true that the pianoforte ranks amongst its prophets such men as Beethoven, Schumann and Chopin. But Beethoven's noblest creations are reserved for the string quartet and the orchestra. In the concertos of Chopin, the orchestra is so badly used that the solo is more effective when accompanied by a second piano. Yet in his pianoforte writing Chopin was often trying to enlarge the range of colour and harmony. There is no other composer who so often arouses hopes of a willing orchestral adapter only to disappoint him ; the funeral march has two parts of which one is easily translated into orchestral idiom, while the other is never as satisfactory in the orchestra as on the piano. The weakness of Schumann's music can be traced directly to his keyboard outlook ; his symphonies sound like an orchestral arrangement ; in his pianoforte quintet the strings often do no more than double the piano part ; the solid, four-part harmony betrays the long familiarity with an instrument where one hand hits four notes naturally and with ease.

## CHAPTER II

# VIRGINAL AND HARPSICHORD

### (a) THE ENGLISH SCHOOL

THE FOUNDATIONS of an instrumental style were well and truly laid by the English composers of the Tudor era. It is poetic justice that the glory of opening up the path which led to the music of the nineteenth century should belong to an age that, more than any other, honoured and understood the art. There was then no misconception ; the Tudor age did not believe in the Greek fallacy of music as a science—the fallacy which, inherited by later generations, caused music to be linked, in the Quadrivium, with astronomy, arithmetic and geography. But it was given an honourable place by the side of science and philosophy.

Just as it was customary for philosophers to meet at the University or in the house of a great nobleman and dispute on a given theme, so musicians gathered together to play and sing. There is a vivid account of the journey through Elizabethan London by an Italian philosopher on his way to the house of Fulke Greville where a debate was held. We know in the same way of the " vertuous contention in love " between William Byrd and Ferrabosco when they improvised forty ways " showing most rare and intricate skill . . . upon the playne songe ' Miserere.' "

The final achievements of the Tudor composers in vocal art has led the historian to give less attention than is due to their instrumental compositions. String music was, at first, intended as a support for the voices and was certainly not practised to the same extent as in the later Jacobean times. But the virginal—a much more modest and attractive-looking instrument than the modern " concert grand "—was in favour with old and young. Both Elizabeth and her sister were able musicians, and the " prodigy " was also known, for it is said that the daughter of Castlenau, Maria, aged six, could handle musical instruments so well " that you cannot tell if she is of bodily or incorporeal substance."

The greatest collection of instrumental music of the time is Queen Elizabeth's Virginal book in the Fitzwilliam Museum at Cambridge. Other valuable collections are the virginal books of Benjamin Cosyn and Will Forster ; Lady Neville's book, which contains forty-five pieces by William Byrd, and " Parthenia," the first book of music to be printed in England ; it appeared in 1611 and contained twenty-one pieces by Byrd, John Bull and Orlando Gibbons.

A glance at the titles of their pieces is sufficient to show how wide the sources were from which the Elizabethan composer drew his inspiration. William Byrd's battle piece (" Mr. Bird's battaile " of Lady Neville's collection) may not stand higher amongst his compositions than the Battle of Vittoria does in Beethoven's ; it provides a link in the chain of not particularly successful battle pictures in music, extending from the early fifteenth century examples to the modern essays of Tchaikovsky, Strauss and Bantock.

The Elizabethan composer, however, addressed himself to all sorts and conditions of men and provided music for every occasion. He wrote dances for the nobleman's palace and, for the village green, corrantos and jigs ; he paid tribute to the church with psalm-tunes and compositions which, written upon a plainsong melody, were entitled " In Nomine " ; the songs of the common people with their attractive names—" John come kiss me now," and " Bonny sweet Robin "—inspired him ; merrymaking at the tavern was celebrated in "Watkin's Ale" and "Malt's come down."

These songs provided the theme of elaborate variations wherein the skill of the musician could shine. A florid style, the natural outcome, penetrated even religious music and led to a protest by Cranmer who objected to music " full of notes." What was ill-becoming to religious music was eminently adapted to the instrument. Trills and ornaments were of practical value to the player on the virginal, for he had no other means of sustaining sound. Moreover while the bulk of the music remained rare and unpublished it was impossible to think even of altering a theme. The notion of modifying a set melody could never occur to the Tudor composer, since in improvising it was obviously important that the subject of the improvisation should remain untouched, the solid basis on which graceful fantasies and embellishments could be elaborated. It is difficult for us to realise exactly how far the musicianship of the Elizabethans went, for, like the Italians, they placed highest the art of improvisation which leaves nothing behind but a tradition when the improviser dies. It is said of one so well remembered as Frescobaldi that the full extent of his abilities could only be grasped by those who heard his improvisations. But we know that they were executants of consummate skill, for only an exceptionally gifted performer on the harpsichord could undertake to play elaborate passages with ease so long before it occurred to anyone to make use of the thumb. We have it on the authority of Daniel Speer that in the seventeenth century the scale was played with two fingers—3, 4, 3, 4, 3, 4, 3.

Evidence of an instinct for form and novelty is not lacking. In his admirable study of Byrd, Dr. Fellowes comments upon the way in which in the variations on " O Mistress mine " Byrd quite simply re-states the theme in the last variation and notes that the device has since been employed with great effect by other composers, including Schubert, who made use of it in the " Death and the maiden " variations of the string quartet in D minor. Another historian is struck by the way in which in " The Carman's Whistle " Byrd dallies for a short while in the key of D minor before returning to the tonic, C major, and sees in this a promise of a wider harmonic scope. John Bull's " The King's Hunting Jigg " appears even more significant when looked at from a purely æsthetic point of view. This remarkable composition conveys an excellent idea of the excitement and the joy of pursuit ; but it has also an imaginative quality not often found in the music of the period ; it does not only imitate, but also gives the impression of one who knew what magic there is in the sound of hunting horns in the woodland.

After the Elizabethans, the greatest figure in the world of music in England is Purcell, whose genius cannot fully be appraised from those of his instrumental works falling within the limits of this chapter. These, however, are by no means negligible. The minuet which takes the place of the traditional jig in the G major suite, the gavotte of the suite in C major, have some of the freshness and charm that endear his more important compositions. If his harmonic range is not here particularly daring and striking, there is no error of taste. He indulges the fashion of the time for elaborate ornamentation, but not to excess. He is at once grave and care-free ; some pieces are slight ; the Chaconne of the G minor suite is serious, sterling, sincere.

Purcell's teacher, John Blow, also wrote a set of " Lessons " for the harpsichord. It is, however, as a composer of vocal music that he is remembered.

### (b) THE FRENCH SCHOOL

Amongst the French, the most remarkable contributor to instrumental music is François Couperin, descendant of a long line of musicians. We are indebted to him on many counts. He reduced harmony to a system ; he taught performers to use their thumbs on the keyboard ; he was the first, in the compositions for two violins and bass, to write chamber music for three players ; he made of the

" suite " something more than a collection of oddly assorted fantasias. These very valuable contributions to the art of the time do not fall, however, within our scope ; our concern is with his music for the harpsicord.

Couperin left a good number of compositions for harpsicord ; the most important are the four sets of Pièces de Clavecin, divided into " Ordres," and " L'Art de Toucher le Clavecin." Some of these bear bold, provoking titles—La Dangereuse, Les Baccanales. He is, however, no revolutionary. Even Les Baccanales falls very far short of one's conception of a bacchanalian orgy. He is the courtly composer *par excellence*, who found court atmosphere as congenial as the convent is to the mystic and the ascetic. His gentle melodies are his own ; the heavy ornamentations with which they are overlaid are of his time. He held an appointment at the court of Louis XIV and dedicated to him " L'Art de Toucher le Clavecin." It is all very remote from life as we understand it, rather precious and artificial. The little pictures, whether inspired by the pseudo-pastoralism which celebrated Phyllis and Corydon, or by types of womanhood—La Manon, La Diane, La Diligente, La Voluptueuse—are sometimes beautiful, often vague, always fictitious. They represent not so much the music of a people as of a class which exercised a very powerful influence on the military history of the world, and one in which the musician was of value only in so far as he could add to its splendour ; a class with an etiquette, a mode of life and an art all of its own, as far removed from the world of men and lively passions as a company of Trappists.

### (c) THE ITALIAN SCHOOL

In Italy the most notable personality in keyboard music was Domenico Scarlatti, son of the more profound and thoughtful Alessandro Scarlatti, who created the Italian overture in contradistinction to the French overture of Lully. Domenico Scarlatti, an original composer of a genial and sunny temper set aside the " agréments pincés " and

" flattés " which benumb the music of Couperin. A lively fancy and very exceptional technical skill enabled him to invent a number of new and charming melodic designs. Hans von Bülow sees in his sparkling, witty numbers the germs of the future Scherzo of Beethoven. Czerny found Scarlatti's keyboard compositions worthy of remembrance on account of their originality, and because of their " fresh and manly vitality." A collection of his works edited by Czerny contains no less than 200 pieces. His best known work is, perhaps, " The Cat's Fugue," the theme of which represents a series of notes sounded by a cat treading on the keyboard. It hardly does justice to his genius. His most representative works are in the collections of Peters (Alte Klaviermusik) and Ricordi.

Charming things are to be found in the works of three other Italians, Francesco Durante, Benedetto Marcello and Domenico Zipoli. The Divertimenti of the former are exquisite miniatures ; Marcello's and Zipoli's sonatas may yet attract, as they deserve, the attention of modern players.

### (d) BACH AND HANDEL

The early instrumental music of Germany is, of course, dominated by the genius of J. S. Bach. If nothing of his had come down to us beyond the compositions for organ, clavier and violin his fame would stand no less high than it does. We should indeed be poorer without the Passions and the B minor Mass ; but the concertos, the figures, the suites, would still entitle him to a place amongst the greatest prophets of music.

Two impulses have been noted in him—the emotional and the practical. No doubt, his work derives its monumental qualities from the technical, practical mastery of the medium that he uses with such consummate ease. But even more striking is his combination of gentleness and strength, which is, in my view, the hall-mark of the great composer. Not a few minor composers have excelled in one character or the other, as lyrical or dramatic, as singers of

Tc

tender romances or as designers of bolder musical structures. Bach reaches both poles and his lyrical melodies are all the more moving because they are the expression of an essentially manly, robust nature.

Bach came at the end of a period ; he did not set out to modify the art of his time but to enrich it. He did not avoid ornamentation as Marcello did ; he controlled it and used it for a more correct purpose. The slender French Courante would seem overweighted by ornament that the more solid structure of a Bach prelude can carry with ease. He did not invent the fugue ; he carried it to its highest peak of perfection. The greater bulk of his output is choral, yet he understood perfectly the genius of instrumental music and was one of the first to see how the well-tempered clavier (*see* Book I, Glossary) opened up a store of rich harmonies undreamt of in the days when instrumental music still bore the signs of its vocal origin.

It is not too much to say that while his predecessors wrote preludes and fugues, it was Bach who breathed the spirit of life into them. Couperin looked upon preludes as a poet, if he is not himself a prose writer, may look upon prose. He wrote them for an eminently practical purpose, to help— as he said—players who had not the gift for improvisation, and he warned them not to obey strictly indications of time, so as to be able to give the impression of a free, fanciful excursus—a preparation for the real piece, which was to follow. In Bach's hands, the prelude makes as great a demand on our faculties as the following fugue. It does not predicate an audience that has to be conjured into a state of alertness, but one already alert. " There is not one prelude in the collection," says Parry, " which does not appeal to the hearer's feelings as much as, if not more than, to his intelligence, and with infinite variety." Parry also remarks upon the unity of the E flat minor prelude of the " 48," the underlying basis of whose harmony is not presented in figurate form but in chords. " The effect of coherence," says Parry, " is attained by these chords being systematically grouped in threes . . . which serves as the unifying principle throughout the long rhapsodical melody." This is but one example of that spiritual unity, against the unity of balanced formulæ, found also in the concertos and suites.

This spiritual unity, frequently met in other works of Bach, the outcome of intellectual discipline as well as of a sure instinct, is entirely at the mercy of the interpreter. The last movement of the B minor suite for flute and strings, for instance, consists of a set of dances of different cast and measure. Rightly interpreted they appear as a chain every link of which, outwardly varied, is of equal strength. When their pace and proportions are not accurately gauged they seem unequal, unrelated, and we resent the disproportion between them. The relation between some of the preludes and fugues is of a similar character. The apparent link is that of tonality and nothing more ; yet we cannot but feel that they complete each other in an organic whole. The truth is that the real unity of any great work of art is not given by adherence to a pre-conceived, infallible plan. A true sense of measure and unity is as much part of that elusive faculty called genius as is the ability to write lyrical or dramatic music. No one can ever sound the depth of the problems connected with the construction of a shapely piece of music, any more than account for its beauty.

In the space at our disposal it is impracticable to enumerate and utterly impossible to examine Bach's output. The works of Parry and Schweitzer are recommended to those who wish to study his music. His life has been told admirably in the biography of Dr. Sanford Terry. The most reliable guide to the organ works is Harvey Grace's " The Organ Works of Bach." Spitta's three tomes are invaluable, but not so easily handled.

A few facts about Bach may be usefully recalled here. Bach never knew the nationalism of a later day. His music, thoroughly German, owed a good deal to Italian influence. The sonatas and concertos of Italian composers he heard at Weimar opened his eyes to the superiority of the Italian models over those of Buxtehude and he attained perfection, says Schweitzer, by the devoted study of Vivaldi, Albinoni, Legrenzi and Corelli. All he did was touched by the same modesty. He had written a good deal before he published his first composition—a partita—at the age of forty-one, feeling, no doubt, that the work he was to do was " not to be raised from the heat of youth or the vapours of wine." He certainly never thought the day would come when his " Art of the Fugue " was somehow to be orchestrated and performed before an admiring audience. Present day technique and tastes alike have brought about a marvellous revival. Enthusiasm, however, can be carried too far. The organ was Bach's instrument and a Bach fugue well performed is to us what it was to him and to his contemporaries. The high standard of modern technique has brought even the variations written for his pupil, Goldberg, within reach of any average solo pianist. But the works written for harpsichord lose as much of their true character when played on the modern piano as "Die Kunst der Fuge" loses in the solemn performance by a modern orchestra. Of all composers he stands to gain most by close, intimate study. His instrumental music is all chamber music in the most literal sense. One learns to love it by trying to play oneself— not by listening to performances in which players are multiplied so as to fill with sound a vast hall.

The death of Bach passed almost unnoticed and the very place of his burial was soon forgotten. When his great contemporary, George Frederic Handel, died in London, he was carried to a grave in Westminster Abbey by a mourning nation. As a composer of keyboard music, however, Handel can never be compared with Bach. Possibly he himself did not attach great importance to the compositions for the organ and the harpsichord. The organ concertos, whose vigour and freshness delight us, are said to have been written solely in order to fill in the intervals of performances of oratorio with pieces that could give the organist the opportunity to display his dexterity.

It is also said that Handel kept a number of fugues and

arias always ready at hand to be incorporated and adapted to the requirements of a new opera or oratorio. The first collection of concertos of 1738 described as "for the harpsichord or organ" seems to point to a singular disinterestedness about the medium. With the possible exception of the once famous variations known as "The Harmonious Blacksmith"—more honoured in the classroom than in the concert-hall—his harpsichord music is as completely forgotten as the concertos of Hasse and Graun or the partitas of Muffat. It deserves a better fate, for it is always clear and fluent, never dry or purely didactic.

With his immediate successors, Haydn and Mozart, the pianoforte, as we know it, comes into its own. Haydn wrote sonatas, divertimenti and no less than twenty concertos for the clavier. These have been ruthlessly and thoughtlessly swept aside by new fashions. It is inconceivable that of all this vast output nothing should be worth saving. But modern pianists are a singularly incurious race. Fortunately the works of Mozart survive.

## CHAPTER III

## PIANOFORTE SONATAS

### (a) MOZART

THE SONATAS of Mozart, however, are not to be ranked amongst his finest work. They include much that is good and something that is very good ; but those excellences scattered in such profusion in the quartets, the symphonies, and even in the sonatas for pianoforte and violin, are met more rarely. There is no poverty of ideas—rather the contrary. But the thought, never very deep, retains a certain formality of design (including the so-called Alberti bass) bearing witness to swift composition and to the character of work undertaken sometimes merely in order to point the lesson for an interesting pupil. Had Mozart left nothing else he would still take precedence of Clementi, who also wrote limpid, formal piano music ; but he would stand below rather than above Haydn. The piano sonatas are like the diary of a man of genius, setting down every day events in a tasteful and spirited but not necessarily inspired manner, without any thought of fame and posterity. They possess stylistic distinction ; there is a sense of freedom in the treatment of the form and his easy mastery of every device known to the technicians of the time gives him a grace of movement of surpassing charm. But one looks in vain for the typical Mozartian miracle such as, say, the finale of the G major quartet where he goes from a severe fugal subject to an impish popular tune, joining at one stroke the twofold sources of all music, the art of the learned and the art of the people.

The approach of the romantic era led some commentators, determined to find them, to discover romantic elements in Mozart's sonatas. The discovery need not cause surprise, since literary circles found romantic elements in Homer. But there is nothing to connect Mozart with the romantic movement and its prophets. Here and there we find a more passionate utterance than that of Haydn. Dramatic touches are unmistakable in the A minor sonata (K. 310), in the Fantasia in C minor (K. 396) and, less marked, elsewhere. The slow movement as the centre piece of the sonata, in place of the minuet, opens up new possibilities and the purging of plethoric ornamentation points to a more earnest and thoughtful attitude of mind.

All this does not make Mozart into a romantic composer. He is, indeed, the last and choicest flower of the classical order. He never gave in to the possibilities of the time ; he had not the childish delight of Haydn in pointless, too innocent jesting ; there is nothing in his work to match the " Clock " and the " Farewell " symphonies ; he did not compose music, like Pepusch, to imitate the grunting of pigs. These things delighted courtiers too gross to see how

nobly Mozart represented all that was good in their civilisation. He was a courtly composer, not because he once consorted with kings and princes, but because he had in himself all the refinement the age had acquired. He did not
revolutionise music ; he purified it from within. His sympathies were with the old order that had cast him ruthlessly
aside, and nothing was further from his thought than the
possibility of destroying or subverting it. His touch is as
gentle as that of a child and has the magic power that the
touch of the innocent was supposed to have in the middle
ages.

When Mozart left the household of the un-gentle bishop
Hieronymus, the event really marked the end of the era of
patronage in music. No one would have been more surprised
than Mozart if he had been told that artists were to be free
from the caprice of patrons. He saw himself, as he was, the
upholder of a tradition, strict and orthodox when imparting
knowledge to pupils. But he knew he could add to it, though
it may be doubted whether he realised exactly how deeply
the world was to love his contribution.

Music and musical instruments were, however, evolving
towards a new order. When he began to write, a pianoforte
was something of a rarity. When he played in London in
1765, the instrument used was a harpsichord. A portrait
painter five years later shows him in the act of playing on
a clavecin. In 1777 he tried and expressed his delight in the
pianoforte of the Augsburg maker, Stein. It was, then, with
the characteristics of more than one instrument in mind
that he wrote the earlier sonatas.

As regards form, the thematic material of Mozart has
greater character than that of his predecessors and the proportions of his movements are generally more ample. He
used grace notes mainly for the purposes of variation where
their use was most rational. Even here, however, he is more
sparing than other composers. Couperin has twelve
" Agreemens " in the first eight bars of the sarabande
" Les Sentiments " ; Mozart has but seven in the same
number of bars in the XIth variation of the D major sonata.

## (b) A DIGRESSION ON ROMANTICISM

With the death of Mozart in 1791 we find ourselves on the threshold of the romantic era. But before considering the contributions of the romantic composers it will be useful to glance briefly at the main characteristics of the romantic movement in so far as they affected the art of music, for the terms " classical " and " romantic " are often loosely and illogically used.

Romanticism is an essentially literary and philosophic movement, which had its roots in the transcendental movement of German philosophy from Kant to Hegel. It affected, in time, literature, politics and even religion, acquiring different features and characteristics according to the nature of the soil on which the fruitful seed was carried. No single definition of Romanticism can embrace all its achievements. What is true of the English romanticism of Coleridge and Wordsworth need not necessarily apply to Rousseau, to Kant or to Manzoni.

Such a movement, which in its far-reaching effects can be compared to the First Crusade or to the Renaissance, could not leave the arts untouched. But of all the arts, music is the least able to reflect clearly and sharply the current thought of the time. It is detached from logic and reasoning. There exist didactic poems ; there is no didactic music. Pope's " Essay on Man " was once thought to embody a philosophical system ; no symphony or opera could be supposed to do as much. The emotion from which music springs may be much the same as that which inspires the poet ; but the musician can make its thought clear and definite only by the addition of words. An obvious piece of romantic music is Schubert's " Der Doppelgänger," for the music is joined indissolubly to a romantic poem and would have no meaning apart from it. We may even suggest that Schumann's "Kinderscenen" owe something to an interest in childhood kindled by romantic writers such as Rousseau, Blake and Wordsworth, and that Beethoven's Pastoral symphony reflects somehow that ideal relation between man and nature first revealed by Rousseau. But we are on debatable ground if we identify Beethoven's C minor symphony with the French revolution rather than with any other stirring event. All that can safely be said is that its new and magnificent energies harmonise with a period of history in which men strove mightily for the achievement of an ideal.

### (c) BEETHOVEN AND THE EARLY ROMANTICS

The romantic composers moreover were not consciously working for a revolution in art. Beethoven, who meant to dedicate the " Eroica " to Napoleon, never considered his method revolutionary. The classical model that had been evolved from Corelli and Domenico Scarlatti to Emanuel Bach, Haydn and Mozart served him well. He did not revolutionise it, but he enlarged and modified it so as to make it bear the weight of more pregnant ideas. His pianoforte sonatas begin where Mozart's ended ; they later develop into something more individual, more important and more complex, following the natural development of mind and sensibility. There was no thought of winning a fancied freedom at a single stroke. Freedom, said Goethe, is fully enjoyed when it is daily won ; Beethoven's spiritual freedom was a new and a daily conquest which yet recognised and enlarged the conception of music's laws. He did not make a vast plan and then set about filling it to the best of his ability ; he enlarged the plan to fit the thought.

No formula exists that will cover Beethoven's innovations. As to his form, Sir John McEwen remarks in " An Introduction to an Unpublished Edition of the pianoforte sonatas of Beethoven " that " the problem of composition . . . must be solved anew with every fresh work." One may note in a general way that with Beethoven the second subject is more important, that the " development section " has great range and importance, that he is less bound by keyrelationship. Form, remarked Wagner, was for Beethoven " the transparent veil through which he looked at music." In the sonata Op. 26 (in A flat major) he substituted an *andante con variazioni* for the common first movement ; he substituted the scherzo for the minuet (more frequently in the quartets and symphonies than in the sonatas) and made it into a mould fit for giants or elves. Fugal elements are employed with great freedom and efficacy, although here, too, Beethoven's respect for the law is evident and an examination of the great fugue that concludes the Hammerklavier sonata shows that his qualification *con alcune licenze* is only the easing of a too-scrupulous conscience. We are authoritatively assured that Beethoven's form is found to be most strict just when it is " popularly supposed to be broken down."

But whether dealing with new or old forms, the old minuet or the new scherzo, with melody conventionally sustained or with fugal designs, Beethoven is always himself and instills new life into the driest academic devices. Professor Tovey rightly remarks apropos of the " cancrizan " canon in B minor of the Hammerklavier fugue, that it is unique in being not only a thing for the eye but interesting to the ear. And Professor Tovey's " Companion to Beethoven's pianoforte sonatas " is the guide they must follow who wish to study closely Beethoven's form as applied to the sonatas.

Beethoven had no direct successor. Czerny, his pupil, wrote much, but only his didactic work is now available. Hummel, once considered Beethoven's rival, has been rather drastically dismissed by modern taste ; he remains, however, the most attractive of the minor pianoforte composers of his time. The friendly, graceful pianoforte music of Weber does not claim a place by the side of Beethoven's. He wrote a good deal ; yet the performer of to-day hardly ever thinks it worth his while to apply to him. He is, however, well remembered by the amateur to whom his easy charm and vivacity must appeal, by the teacher who finds him an invaluable aid and by the historian.

The pianoforte sonatas of Mendelssohn are likewise—and with better reason—forgotten. Schumann's are remembered, though rather as a diversion from more popular works not in sonata form, such as " Carnaval " and " Kreisleriana."

Mention must be made of a pianoforte composer and performer of whom Beethoven thought highly, Muzio Clementi, and his two pupils, J. B. Cramer and John Field. Clementi was a neat worker, clear and concise in expression, scholarly in respect of form. Once a competition was held before Joseph II between him and Mozart. The result of the contest is, apparently, unknown. Clementi, however, praised his rival afterwards, while Mozart described Clementi as a " mere mechanician." The verdict cannot be accepted without qualifications for there is evidence to show that as a pianist Clementi was in the front rank. His sonatas are now used mainly for tuition purposes. J. B. Cramer, born in Germany, lived the greater part of his life in London where he established the firm of J. B. Cramer & Co. John Field, said to have been Clementi's best pupil, had a varied career, leaving behind at his death a number of compositions, amongst them the delicate Nocturnes that may still be heard and undoubtedly had their influence on Chopin.

Nearest to Beethoven, as regards genius and originality, is Franz Schubert. But those of his compositions that fall to this chapter are not adequate samples of his work. He wrote ten sonatas for the piano of which but three are considered worthy to bear his name.

### (d) LISZT, CHOPIN AND BRAHMS

Characteristic of its composer and characteristic of the new spirit is the sonata of Liszt. It has some of the strength of Beethoven without Beethoven's austerity. Liszt is ever reaching out for new sensations, new emotions and is sometimes not too fastidious in the choice. He is unquestionably rhetorical and repels those who dislike emphatic utterance. The sonata, like all his work, has been often attacked on these grounds. But it is impossible to deny that real gold is mixed with baser metals or that it is originally conceived and brilliantly written.

For Liszt, however, the sonata is no longer the favourite medium it was for Mozart and Beethoven, and the same is true of Chopin. Chopin wrote two sonatas and Liszt but one against Beethoven's thirty-two. But Chopin's two sonatas are more important than is the single example of Liszt as creations of a mind exceptionally responsive to the stimulus of certain romantic ideas. With Liszt one feels that sometimes the hands take control and the pianoforte virtuoso comes to the fore, while the original composer retires in the background. In Chopin's music, on the other hand, its virtuosity, its new, enlarged technique, represent an absolute, imperative need of the composer. Not by any other means could his thought have found true expression.

The funeral march of the first Chopin sonata (in B flat minor), one of the most popular pieces in the whole of pianoforte literature, gives us the measure of the change that has occurred in the general outlook. Individual feeling now takes the place of abstract emotion ; musicians celebrate no longer heroism but one particular hero ; they no longer hail " divinest Melancholy " or " The mountain nymph, sweet Liberty " but sing of this man's melancholy and that nation's hopes of liberty. Beethoven's funeral march (in the A flat major sonata) is impersonal, a tribute to any life spent in high achievement, which might have been inspired by a hero of antiquity, Hector or Scipio ; Chopin's motif is entirely personal ; his is the grief occasioned by the breaking of all earthly ties in death, a tribute of sorrow paid to one near and much loved. The epic has become lyric ; it has lost some of its grandeur and acquired a wider range. There is nothing to connect the funeral march with the other three movements of Beethoven's sonata ; in Chopin, the whole sonata is permeated through and through by the poignant, heart-stricken sense of tragedy for which the funeral march provides the climax. Beethoven's scherzo and last movement might have fitted equally well any other sonata. Chopin's grim scherzo is of a piece with the rest. The last movement, a-rhythmic, shorn of all harmony, of dynamic effects, gives an eerie feeling of unreality, of pursuit in utter darkness—a magnificent piece of daring fully justified by its effect and a worthy conclusion to the sonata.

The second sonata in B minor comes a little nearer to the bulk of Chopin's work—to be considered later—and shows well the peculiarities of an idiom that can be as distinctly chevaleresque and gallant as it is passionate and picturesque. A posthumous sonata in C minor (a very early work) does not equal the other two and is now forgotten.

Not long before his death Schumann discovered a successor in Johannes Brahms, whose early pianoforte sonatas were amongst the compositions Schumann read and praised very highly. Brahms justified Schumann's hopes and, indeed, surpassed them in his orchestral and chamber compositions. The pianoforte sonatas cannot be compared with these or even with the pianoforte concertos. Like Mozart, Brahms was a pianist of great ability who never did his best when composing for his own instrument. Like Schumann, he was too deeply pledged to the tradition to discard lightly whatever of it as was less suited to his genius. There is a curious mixture of heroic and romantic elements in most of his works which, in the sonatas, results in elaboration and inordinate length.

It is easy to see, however, the reason why the sonatas impressed Schumann. In spite of a certain divergence of style they are essentially Schumannesque in method and often in effect—obviously the work of a young composer determined to make the most of his feelings, inclined to overstress emotions understood rather than experienced, not the less sincere for being a little pompous and self-conscious. The effect is not always commensurate with the effort it demands.

## (e) AFTER BRAHMS

Modern composers have paid tribute to the sonata, if with considerably less zeal and eagerness than was shown by their predecessors. It would be unjust to suppose that no composer will ever add to the great pianoforte sonatas we possess ; but it is true enough that, so far, no one has seriously attempted it.

Good organ sonatas have been written in comparatively recent times by Rheinberger and Max Reger—the former a scholarly and genial romantic composer of conspicuous talent ; the latter more academic and less genial ; both masters of their medium. Russia gave us the sonatas of Alexander Scriabin whose work is most attractive when it is least original ; France the very charming sonatina of Ravel ; Italy the austere sonatinas of Ferruccio Busoni ; Hungary the highly sophisticated sonatina of Béla Bartók.

All these are valuable and attractive in their different ways, but they cannot be classed together with the sonatas of Chopin or Brahms. And it is significant that Bartók, Sibelius, Ravel and Busoni prefer, apparently, sonatinas to sonatas. Evidently the special opportunities offered by the sonata were not found as attractive as they were wont to be. Yet Busoni, at least, did attempt in other compositions to restore music to its classical dignity and he gives the impression of a composer who might have found the pianoforte sonata more tempting than the sonata for violin and piano. The long catalogue of his works records two sonatas for piano and violin but only one for piano—in F minor, composed in 1883 and never published.

There is more freshness and more vigour in the works of English composers than in Continental productions, in the supple sonatina of John Ireland and the four sonatas which bear witness to the conspicuous gifts of Arnold Bax for characteristic, flexible melody and unusual design. In the early sonata of Benjamin Dale a natural, unforced idiom compensates us for excessive length. Length and matter are evenly balanced in the sonata of Constant Lambert, which is modern in outlook and stimulating without being provocative. There are also two wholly admirable and characteristic sonatas for organ by Edward Elgar.

# CHAPTER IV

# THE CONCERTOS

## (a) BACH AND MOZART

THE WORD " concerto " dates from the early seventeenth century, when it seems to have been applied to church music in which an organ supported the voice parts. Later on other instruments were added, constituting the formal " concerto di chiesa." On the other hand, the " concerto da camera," the secular form, only dates from 1686. It appears to have resembled the sonata very closely in its construction. Corelli, Geminiani and Vivaldi were exponents of the embryo concerto as we know it, and they first developed it and gave it artistic value. When Bach wrote his Italian Concerto, it was held in Germany to create an important precedent " which should provoke the envy and emulation of all our own great composers and be vainly imitated by foreigners," as a German critic said. As a matter of fact, only the minor composers of Germany followed Bach's plan at the time. But Bach anticipated the classical form in having in his harpsichord and violin concertos three distinct movements : the first of an animated character, the second thoughtful and the third brilliant. " In the first movement," wrote an English critic, " Bach takes us as it were to church, composing our minds as we go with strong and able talk about subjects appropriate to the religious season . . . the second movement is the service and the Finale is the afternoon walk or dance."

If the three-movement concerto originated with Bach, the cadenza appears to be the invention of Handel, who in his organ concerto in D minor gives the soloist repeated occasions for improvisation.

The pianoforte concertos of the modern repertory begin with J. S. Bach, who arranged sixteen violin concertos of

Vivaldi for the clavier and three for organ. In listening to them, we are never conscious that they are adaptations. He gives the bass hitherto unknown freedom and range ; he enriches the inner parts and provides counterpoints to support the solo. Spitta does not overstate the case when he concludes that, in most cases, Bach has added to the musical value of the piece and at the same time produced genuine works for the clavier.

The classical concerto begins with Mozart. He wrote twenty-five, and modern pianists are only now discovering them. They are much more important than the sonatas. Here and there the limitation of the harmonic scheme makes itself felt. But there is a freshness and spontaneity that rises above the boundaries of time and taste. Amongst the slow movements of the concertos are to be found some of the finest imperishable gems of musical art.

The effect a Mozart or a Bach concerto produces on the listener sometimes falls short of our expectations, on account of modern conductors' partiality for large orchestras. It is true that a large but well-drilled orchestra is capable of producing tone as soft as that of a small orchestra. But the quality is different ; the tone of a large orchestra when thoroughly subdued is apt to lose vitality as well as weight. Moreover when, in the *tutti*, the tension is relaxed and the full force of the orchestra makes itself felt, a disproportion between soloist and orchestra is immediately apparent. The modern pianoforte is a match for the modern orchestra in power whenever the texture of the music provides an excuse for sonority. The texture of Mozart is so slender that no responsible interpreter of the solo part ever uses the full power of the piano, while Bach's concertos are still chamber concertos. Mozart's are not chamber concertos in the literal sense ; but both their texture and their sentiment are those of chamber music. In an ideal performance of Bach or Mozart the soloist should be accompanied by a small orchestra and might even dispense with the conductor. For modern orchestral players know the requirements of chamber music ; they even play better when additional responsibilities call for a special effort. In such music no tricky rhythm or entry demands the conductor ; all that is required is a sign (which the soloist can give) to mark the beginning.

## (b) BEETHOVEN

Such niceties of adjustment and balance do not arise in connection with the bolder style of Beethoven who demands the utmost power as well as the utmost gentleness from both soloist and orchestra. It has been said that his first and second concertos are nearer in spirit to Haydn and Mozart than to the characteristic Beethoven. This is true of the second concerto ; it is but partly true of the first. Some sections in the second and third movement might have come from the pen of either Haydn or Mozart ; the first movement is early Beethoven, unmistakably. The surprises he provides for us are infinitely more unexpected than those of Haydn. The very quiet opening with its short, staccato chords, leading to the loud statement of the theme, is one of Beethoven's typical jests. It is like a gentle tap at the door and a soft voice asking permission to enter ; then suddenly the door is thrown open wide and the visitor boldly announces himself and his mission. Such touches, mingling fine delicacy with boisterous good humour, abound, and the whole movement has a freshness and vigour that even the modern craze for speed cannot completely obliterate. Excessive speed, on the other hand, is fatal to the concluding *rondo*, the effect of which depends almost entirely on clearness of rhythm and of melodic design.

The second concerto is less characteristic, but the third, written in the same year, and probably after the first symphony, marks a long step towards greater intensity of expression. No first movement written before it spoke in such bold, imperious tones ; no *adagio* commanded so vast a range of delicate, thoughtful lyrical phrases. The final *rondo*, less striking on the whole, has, nevertheless, many points of special interest, amongst them not least the very happy change of a theme originally heard in the minor key and 2–4 time into a 6–8 theme in a major key, with all its sting and strenuousness turned to gentleness and good humour.

The first movement of the fourth concerto is cast in a pleasing, happy mood. It opens not with the usual orchestral *tutti*, but with a plain statement of the chief subject by the soloist. The re-entry of the piano (after the *tutti*) is one of those flashes of genius found only in the works of great composers. It partakes of the nature of the cadenza and arrests the listener's attention, not because of its special importance but because of the manner in which the material is presented ; it seems to challenge the orchestra to compete less in force than in persuasiveness. The orchestra answers with a matter-of-fact statement of elements derived from the first theme, bluntly refusing to take up the challenge and inviting the pianist to " stick to business." It is well that the challenge is ignored. Beethoven and Chopin give the piano an eloquence that even the orchestra, with its wealth of colour and resource, finds it hard to match.

The second movement provides a perfect instance of dialogue between soloist and orchestra. It reminded Schumann of Orpheus's victory over the powers of darkness, and the comparison would be fitting but for the essentially feminine character of the pleading piano part, pitted against the hectoring tones of the orchestra. The contest, whether representing Orpheus and the dark spirits, Saul and David, or Lear and Cordelia, shows as well as anything the working of Beethoven's mind. For it is not force that wins, but tenderness. The growing harshness of one questioner is met by the more and more poignant expression of the other. When the victory is assured and anger silenced, there is no exultation, no joy in the triumph, but continued, softly eloquent pleading ending in a " suspension " that comes as near to a sigh as music ever can be.

The third and last section abounds in original, Beethovenish touches that give it a distinction seldom found in last movements. Opportunity is also provided for a cadenza. Beethoven added the warning : " Let the cadenza be short," not because of any misgiving as to the uses of cadenzas but because a long cadenza here would completely alter the proportions of the movement.

The " Emperor " concerto, fifth and last of the series, opens, like the fourth, with the solo instrument. But its more elaborate, improvisation-like character recalls not the first but the second piano entry of the concerto in G. The whole work is conceived on a grand scale, and reminds us, in the first and third movements, of the heroic periods of the third and fifth symphonies. The virility of these movements finds perfect contrast in the exquisite tenderness of the second ; somewhat sombre in colour when first heard in the orchestra, it acquires a new and delicate graciousness when, with the addition of a few grace notes, it is played by the soloist. We may search long for such another example of a magical change secured by such economical means.

### (c) SCHUMANN, CHOPIN, AND LISZT

With Beethoven the great era of concerto composers comes to an end. Of his great successors, none wrote more than two for the pianoforte, Schumann only one, which owes little to the classical composers he worshipped. He is cut off from them by the new romanticism which insisted on personal feeling and personal experience. He left us no symphonic poems ; nothing that could be said to have been " fertilised by poetry." Yet the literary influence is clearly felt in the outlook of this musician who communed constantly with Jean Paul and who, surely, must have delighted in " Die Leiden des Jungen Werther." Like that romance, his music gives the impression of having been written by candlelight. Quiet intimacy, and delicate sentimentality give its appeal to the concerto—a work that is not and does not mean to be " great " in any sense, but the musings of a fine spirit intensely egotistic, yet most lovable. The concerto is one of Schumann's ablest creations and quite free from the striving after heroic expression, from the cheapness of, say, the last movement of the pianoforte quintet and from the too, too solid blocks of chords in the Études symphoniques. Schumann has written nothing else quite as graceful or light-hearted as the playful last movement, which has also the advantage of an adequate orchestral setting.

If in Chopin's concertos the solo parts were supported by an orchestra as responsive and as efficient as Schumann's, they would be found in the repertory of every pianist. But Chopin, who, in his Études and Preludes, often made the piano into a perfect substitute for the richest orchestral texture, could never make the orchestra an adequate substitute for the piano. This past master of every shade of pianistic tone and colour was devoid of all sense of orchestral colour. Nor does he seem to have been aware of the thousand and one ways in which orchestral scores are made more interesting and substantial by tactful doubling or the insertion of contrapuntal detail. His writing for the piano is frequently more orchestral and his orchestral writing always more " pianistic " than that of any other composer.

The piano part of a Chopin concerto is irresistible to the pianist ; there have been and there will be revivals. But the listener whose interest is aroused by some charming idea is bound to be disappointed when the same idea appears again, lifeless and conventional, in the orchestra. Unsuccessful attempts have been made at re-scoring the concertos by Klindworth and Tausig ; they can only be re-scored effectively by some one endowed with original genius as well as skill ; Tausig, no doubt, knew his Chopin well and Klindworth was equal to any average work of translation from piano to orchestra and vice versa. But only a Wagner could re-touch the work of a Gluck or a Beethoven.

The pianoforte concertos of Liszt are under a cloud at present—for a very different reason. They are too much of their own time. It is difficult for us to realise, now that what was then the new technique has been placed within reach of everybody, what those new acquisitions in every field of music meant to men dazzled by the new brilliance of the orchestra of Mendelssohn and Berlioz, by the heady tones of

Paganini's fiddle, by the dexterities of an infallible player like Tausig. It was inevitable that every creative artist should desire to surpass his rivals in sensational brilliance, as he now vies in cacophony ; and Liszt, alive to every new movement and to every opportunity, succeeded too well. He enlarged pianoforte technique—at a price ; and deliberate sensationalism resulted in artificiality and in cheapening music which has yet some of the characteristics of genius. Paganini enhanced the effect of the " Clochette " concerto by having a bell tinkled at the appropriate moment. In the E flat concerto Liszt substitutes a triangle for the bell (the concerto has been nick-named " the triangle concerto ") much for the same purpose. But " La Clochette " can be played without the bell while the concerto cannot be performed without its triangle. Those who wish to know the best of Liszt may ignore the concertos, too brilliant and too facile to represent the more notable and serious aspects of his mind.

### (d) MENDELSSOHN, BRAHMS, TCHAIKOVSKY, AND SOME OTHERS. THE PERCUSSIVE SCHOOL

A certain superficial brilliance is to be found also in the concertos of Mendelssohn, but it is allied with craftsmanship that, within its limitations, is faultless. Of all composers Mendelssohn is the one who won most completely the heart of his contemporaries. One can imagine his winning every prize schools and academies could offer, for he did with ease what most mediocre musicians labour vainly to achieve. There is no flaw in his technique ; his invention is happy and original. One feels sure he never hammered away at a theme until it became the perfect symbol of his thought, as Beethoven did. In the slow movement of the G minor concerto there is found a touch of solemn sentimentality, too rich and luscious not to surfeit the appetite. But for all that, the concertos are good music which please us the more because nowadays they are not often played. " Elijah " and the violin concerto will stand many performances. The piano concertos are not comparable to those masterpieces.

Of the minor composers of pianoforte concertos—Hummel, Tausig, Moscheles, Henselt—hardly a trace remains. The past generation still paid rare tribute to Hummel (who well deserves it), and to Anton Rubinstein, whose concerto in D minor is far from negligible. But these works are not likely to get justice from a generation that, after recovering from the after-effects of a belated and exaggerated romanticism, is now inclined to look very closely into the claims of all romantic composers. Undoubtedly Rubinstein's concerto sounds a little rhetorical and artificial. But it is extremely well written for the piano, it is plausible and effective. Rubinstein was not the only composer who mistook the glimmer of the glow-worm for the ray of a star.

There are far greater depths in the two piano concertos of Brahms ; they aroused controversies when they were first performed and still find critical opinion far from unanimous. And, paradoxical as it may sound, upholders and opponents each have some reason on their side. There are passages in the first concerto which show a giant's strength and in the slow movement of the second a loveliness which has a child's gentleness and grace. Not since Beethoven had German music spoken so nobly or so sweetly. But both concertos are long and the heavy burden they put on the interpreter can only be borne without obvious labour by a pianist of very exceptional talent. Of all the interpreters within my recollection, Busoni alone could hold the attention continuously throughout. Unless this happens, length begins to tell and it becomes increasingly difficult to re-capture the main threads of the argument.

The public, which was slow in accepting Brahms's, opened its arms wide to Tchaikovsky's concerto ; it has the vigour, the high colours and the unbridled sentimentality of his symphonies. The art is a little crude, but sincere. There is less crudeness and also less sincerity in Tchaikovsky's more discreet heir and successor, Rachmaninov. Of the concertos that Rachmaninov has so far written, the second, in C minor, is most popular, the third most difficult and interesting, with intricate rhythmic patterns and a very exacting solo part. Frederic Delius's single essay in this form, the concerto in C minor, has not the charm of the best and most characteristic Delian music—a substantial, well written piece which must please best those who find the originality of the violin concerto a little too difficult.

Busoni's concerto for pianoforte, orchestra and male chorus, on the other hand, is thoroughly characteristic of the composer's style. It embodies every feature of his art— its detachment, nobility, mastery of the medium, delight in cold beauty of design, mystic feeling, striving after an impossible, inhuman perfection. We may well question whether this music can ever reach the public at large. The public is not easily attracted by solitary thinkers and Busoni was certainly that. Just because he had, as performer, to come in touch with every musical community all over the world, as composer he felt bound to vindicate his right to freedom of thought and action. There is pride as well as stern intellectual discipline in his aloofness. The Neapolitan Tarantella of the concerto is not really a concession ; its purpose is to mark one set of frontiers ; the mystic *cantico* marks another. Between the picturesque, spirited dance measure and the ascetic psalm the art of Busoni evolves easily with no human weakness and little human appeal. This music does not move us to a demonstration of pleasure and enthusiasm ; it does not go to one's head like the potent brew of the romantics, nor does it possess the clean outline of a classical work ; but it haunts the mind like the germ of an idea we know to be true and profound, even though it cannot find adequate expression.

In very recent years some composers have evolved a new theory which aims at making the most of the piano as an instrument of percussion and relegating to the second place its capacity for melodic expression. This notion permeates the concertos of Prokofiev and Stravinsky and also, it has been said, the concerto of a composer who elsewhere has shown his complete detachment from contemporary movements—Vaughan Williams. These experiments may be mildly amusing when undertaken in the light-hearted, irresponsible manner of Prokofiev. Their effect, however, is that of a stimulant, not of a tonic. An idea of their true musical worth may be formed by the fact that on one occasion when Stravinsky himself was playing the solo in his concerto, he missed completely some sixteen bars of his part. The omission passed unnoticed by all except the conductor who, of course, had to follow the soloist's performance on the score. The incident would seem to show that the new style possesses—for the player—advantages not to be found in the music of other ages. As can be expected in the case of a writer as earnest and sincere as Vaughan Williams, his concerto goes deeper than those of Prokofiev and Stravinsky, but it disappoints those who look to him for unconventional beauty of line and harmony.

An American, Edward Alexander Macdowell, wrote two concertos of which one enjoyed a brief popularity—facile, imitative, lively music of a Schumannesque cast. A deeper impression was made by Grieg's concerto, hailed at one time as a masterpiece. It is not that, but the freshness and unconventionality of national melodies and the deftness of their setting give it a right to a high place amongst compositions of a picturesque, popular type. Camille Saint-Saëns wrote five concertos, of which only one survives. Its form bears the impress of a distinguished mind ; its matter, of a particularly undistinguished creative faculty. The well-balanced periods of Saint-Saëns can show some of the worst characteristics of both the classical and the romantic eras. But Saint-Saëns is yet a model of neatness and polished elegance.[1]

[1] A friend of mine once said of Saint-Saëns that " he was the greatest composer that ever lived who wasn't a genius."—Ed.

## CHAPTER V

# FANTASIAS AND OTHER PIECES ; ARRANGEMENTS

### (a) BEFORE THE ROMANTICS

THE PIANOFORTE REPERTORY includes a number of compositions that are neither sonatas nor concertos, yet of vast importance both to the history of the instrument and to the history of music. If the composers who came before Beethoven contributed more or less directly to the creation of the sonata form, those who followed Beethoven found pleasure and scope in other forms—the Fantasia, the Rhapsody, the Étude, the Nocturne, the Ballad. The dance movements which, joined together, provided the elements out of which the sonata form evolved, re-asserted their independence as soon as the sonata had reached its fullest development. Waltz and Mazurka take the place of Minuet and Gavotte and become an essential part of the pianoforte repertory : the improvisations of the Prelude lead to the Fantasia ; the Prelude acquires a new character in the hands of Chopin.

These are mainly the products of the romantic era and especially of the three great romantic composers who made the piano their favourite medium—Chopin, Liszt and Schumann. Before we turn to them, it may be worth while to mention briefly a small but choice harvest to be gleaned by those who are not afraid to tread forgotten paths. A deal of old music remains unknown to-day which might usefully be employed to leaven the conventional repertory of average performers. It is impossible to do more than mention briefly the compositions of such composers as Carl Philip Emanuel Bach, whose works mark the transition from the contrapuntal style ; of Francesco Durante, more graceful than Domenico Scarlatti ; of Muffat, who anticipated Richard

Strauss in painting feminine coquetry by odd melodic intervals. All of these have written something that is worth preserving, even if it did not contribute to the making of history.

Some of the classical masters have also written admirable works in other forms than the sonata or the concerto. Haydn's Variations in F minor are better than his sonatas and Mendelssohn's " Variations Sérieuses " better than the concertos. The Fantasias of Mozart are delightful and Schubert's " Wanderer " Fantasia is a large canvas in which I, however, can take no pleasure.[1]

The bulk of piano works in forms other than classical comes from the three great composers who were born within a few years of each other—Liszt, Chopin and Schumann— who knew one another, contributed in almost equal degree to the technique of their instrument and are generally considered together as the standard-bearers of musical romanticism. Yet it would be difficult to find three contemporary composers as distinct in their style and manner as these. They are romantics, though each reflects but one facet of romantic feeling.

### (b) CHOPIN

The music of Frédéric Chopin has been called the music of lovers, possibly because of those sweet Nocturnes that may well fill with harmony a lover's Arcadia[2] or, perhaps, because of his well-known passion for George Sand. His music has also been said to voice national sorrow and the patriot's grief for a country rent and shackled ; and the chevaleresque element which undoubtedly permeates a

[1] Of this work it was once, rather unfairly, said that " the first hour and a half was very fine " !—Ed.

[2] Tausig declares the Barcarolle, Op. 60, to describe " a love scene in a discreet gondola. Dualism is pursued throughout ; all is two-voiced, two-souled." This would apply to many other compositions of Chopin equally " two-voiced." Tausig goes further : " At the modulation in C sharp marked DOLCE, SFOGATO, the lovers embrace and kiss." The last peremptory notes must stand for a rude awakening and a grasping gondolier.

good deal of it is said to prove it. He has been praised for felicity, fertility ; for the genius which revived and raised to higher status dance-rhythms and melodies; for the new and characteristic effects he contrived to obtain from the piano.

It may be admitted that there is much truth in all this ; but we must go further to discover the secret of the fascination he exerts over us. He has the gift of melody ; he has the gift of choice and effective harmonic combinations. More than any other pianoforte composer, excepting only the impressionistic Debussy, he has also the gift of suggesting in his music the light that never was on sea or land, the light of Turner's " Fighting Temeraire," the light that seems to have shone upon great deeds and great heroes. It is impossible to hear some of Chopin's ballads and impromptus without thinking of the " renascence of wonder," of the poetry imbued with mystery and its speculative interpretation in the revival of the past. The horn call which opens Weber's "Oberon " overture has often been quoted as a typical instance of a romantic atmosphere created by means of sound. There is a parallel for it in the four bars which preface Chopin's Étude in A minor.

Yet Chopin for all the immense variety and novelty of his idiom is essentially and exclusively a pianoforte composer. His finest effects are often of the simplest kind—a suspended resolution, a trick of rhythm, a pedal-note suffice him to work new wonders. The nine bars preceding the D major section of the F sharp major Impromptu represent no new harmonic adventure, yet the delayed close has the effect of a spell, of a silence full of portent. He can also give the piano a range the orchestra never had before Wagner. In the A minor Étude (Op. 25, No. 11) the left hand suggests a four part harmony while the right hand has just the kind of figure that corresponds on the piano to the descending scales of the violins in the " Tannhäuser " overture ; the entry of the long notes in the F sharp minor Étude (Op. 25, No. 10) recalls nothing so much as a brass entry piercing its way through the orchestral texture. It is one of the paradoxes of musical art that this composer who could be so orchestral when writing for the piano could only be the plainest of pianists when writing for the orchestra.

It is significant that the most illogical, most unreal of all the arts, the ballet, should find its most apt supporter in Chopin. Not the obvious polonaises, but the more delicate preludes and impromptus, when allied to fine miming and dancing show something of the romantic spirit at its best, as surely as Poe's " Annabel Lee " shows it at its worst.

Nothing in the great Chopin repertory is wholly negligible. He is never cheap. Nocturnes, Scherzos and Fantasias ; Concertos, Preludes, Studies ; an unrivalled collection of dances—with these he enriched the resources and the repertoire of the instrument.

## (c) LISZT

The contributions of Liszt are not less remarkable, although distinctly uneven in quality. Certainly it is impossible to appraise his genius by the examination of the piano music only. Liszt's finest music is to be found in his orchestral works. His transcriptions for piano, which sometimes surpass the original in sheer cleverness, those brilliant impressions of travel, published under the title of " Années de Pèlerinage," leave chiefly an impression of gifted improvisations—and Liszt was much more than an improviser in his orchestral work. But he was also too easily influenced by the mood of the moment. Anything and everything provided stimulus for composition—a page of Dante or a sonnet of Petrarch ; a visit to the chapel of William Tell ; a bell tolling at Geneva ; a sight of the cypresses at Villa d'Este. He appreciated Bach and transcribed six of the organ preludes and fugues, writing, besides, a set of variations on the prelude " Weinen, Klagen " ; but, apparently, he appreciated equally contemporary theatre music and wrote transcriptions from the operas of Wagner, Verdi, Meyerbeer, Halévy, Bellini, Donizetti, Auber and Gounod. He adapted for the piano songs of Mendelssohn, Mercadante, Rossini, Schubert and others besides. And from internal evidence alone it is impossible to discover which of these many composers was nearest to his heart.

In his admiration he was sincere—up to a point. He was, moreover, one of the great performers of an age that abounded in magnificent virtuosos and it is probable that, like a clever counsel for the defence, he delighted in all those things that gave him the best opportunity to display his own " slickness " and eloquence. It is said of Liszt that, when asked once what he would have liked to be if he had not been a musician, he replied : " the first diplomat in Europe." Certainly, if genius for appreciating foreign thought and ways is an important qualification for diplomacy, no one could have filled such a position with greater distinction. But there is in his music a lack of character and individuality that might have been even more serious in a diplomat. It is not exactly utter " want " of character ; there is character enough, but it is not robust nor defined ; it is not tempered by contact with hard realities. Fêted and applauded, greeted with processions, welcomed in all societies, Liszt never knew the struggle for recognition that has been the lot of so many other composers. Nothing came to hurt the artist's sensitive temperament. He passed through life in complete ignorance of its harder aspects. Even death was kinder to him than to most men. He was thus able always to make the best of two worlds, an abbé who had had a liaison with the Countess d'Agoult, a transcriber who applied his skill to " Robert le Diable " and " Parsifal," a composer who wrote mystic music and dashing rhapsodies, a Hungarian buried at one of the shrines of German art. An enviable life, but one unlikely to develop latent strength of character and now that his work is no longer backed by an irresistible personality the tendency is to scrutinise, perhaps too closely, his titles.

Modern organists ignore the work he did for them. He wrote for organ a number of arrangements from Chopin's Preludes, from Verdi's Requiem, from Wagner's " Tannhäuser " ; he wrote a fantasia and fugue on the Chorale in

Meyerbeer's " Le Prophète " and an Introduction, Fugue and Magnificat from his own " Dante " symphony ; an Andante Religioso and a fugue on the four note subject B–A–C–H. As a composer of symphonic music he is remembered as one who saw, but did not enter, the Promised Land. As a composer of pianoforte music he can never be set aside. He originated the pianoforte recital and as long as recitals continue to be given, the brilliance of his style and his masterly treatment of the instrument will make his music ever welcome.

### (d) SCHUMANN

Less accomplished but more human and more sincere than Liszt, Robert Schumann made his pianoforte music mirror all that delighted and troubled his own earnest, gentle soul—a composer versed in the subtleties of piano technique, profoundly influenced by the romantic thought of his time. Schumann once declared that he had learnt more music from Jean Paul Richter than from text books. Jean Paul could not teach him to write immaculate counterpoint but did impress upon him the value of free fancy, of humour, of a well designed organic whole. The inspiration of the " Carnaval " came from literary sources ; and in the finale he incorporated a scene from Jean Paul's " Flegeljahrë " ; " Kreisleriana " is also inspired by the fantastic tale written by another disciple of Jean Paul, E. T. A. Hoffmann. But he learned from Bach the art to devise a theme which represents the letters of a name as he did in the Variations Op. 1, where the name ABEGG is translated into the notes A–B flat–E–G–G, and, again, in " Carnaval."

The literary connection, however, neither adds to nor detracts from the intrinsic merits of his music. We do not like it the less when we have forgotten its source or even the meaning of its titles. Indeed we are warned that this is not programme music, that Schumann did not think of a pleading child and then write music, but that he wrote the music first and adopted a suitable title afterwards. The possibility of a subconscious idea, however, is always present. " The man and the musician," he said, " were always trying in myself to express themselves at the same time," which we may take to indicate the belief that music was for him inseparable from the spiritual experience that gave rise to a mood that, in its turn, found expression in music. He is at his best in small things, in graceful variations, in some melodic pieces that have at times a quiet, pensive charm all his own. In great things he is always sincere and even intimate, but sometimes, as for instance, in the Études Symphoniques, a little heavy-handed. " Kinderscenen," the slightest but not least delightful of the episodes collected under a common title, represents the musician's single tribute to the romantics' interest in child life and psychology.

## (e) BRAHMS, FRANCK, DEBUSSY, BUSONI, SCRIABIN, AND OTHERS

The great romantic era closes with Schumann, for in Brahms, who succeeded him, genuine romantic elements are bound up with a classical respect for form. The pianoforte pieces of Brahms, apart from the concertos and the sonata, are more romantic than classical and more completely satisfactory than the earlier essays. His rhapsodies have greater distinction than the brilliant rhapsodies of Liszt and represent the form at its best. The Intermezzos, Caprices and Ballads have taken their place by the side of Schumann's and Chopin's work. His great genius for variations is exemplified in a number of first-rate compositions— Variations on an original theme ; on a Hungarian theme ; on a theme by Schumann ; variations and fugue on a theme by Handel ; twenty-eight variations on a theme by Paganini. These are things of extraordinary mastery and ingenuity, essential to the student of the peculiarly substantial texture of his music. The expert pianist is seen in his arrangements of Gluck's Gavotte in A, of Weber's Moto Perpetuo and of Chopin's F minor Étude.

Brahms wrote also a few organ compositions. Eleven choral preludes are amongst his posthumous works ; a fugue in A flat minor and a choral, and a prelude and fugue in A minor were published as supplements to German musical journals. The more valuable contributions to organ literature, however, came not from Brahms but from Rheinberger and Merkel in Germany, from Widor, Guilmant and César Franck in France. The greatest of these is Franck. He was not as prolific as Rheinberger and his grasp of form was plausible rather than sure. The organ works are original and only a little less important than the Prelude, Choral and Fugue and the Prelude, Aria and Finale written for piano. These, if a little less imaginative and more dour than his best chamber music, are scholarly things that apply some new principles with complete success.

Franck's music is sometimes weak in harmonic modulations. His harmonic system has originality but, for all its richness, it can be nevertheless wholly artificial. A modulation is often made not because it is dictated by the composer's instinct but because it appears expedient. Some of his best themes are vitiated by an unnatural or commonplace harmonic change. Franck's weakness lay precisely where Claude Debussy found his strength. Debussy had no gift of lyrical expression but his harmonic system, which at first seemed obscure and even unreasonable, has none of the angularities of Franck's. Fully conscious of his strength and his weakness, Debussy did not attempt to vie with others where he was precluded by his temperament from meeting them on equal terms. He followed in his own way and with magnificent daring turned to impressionism, making music the rival of painting in re-evoking effects of light and colour, scenes from life touched and ennobled by the artists's vision, the shimmer of water, the pageant of clouds. " L'Isle Joyeuse," " Reflets dans l'Eau," " La Fille aux Cheveux de Lin," " La Cathédrale Engloutie "— these hold in music the place held by the works of Cézanne and Manet in painting.

Debussy has had but one successor, Maurice Ravel, whose

early works have a felicity of touch and a fertile imagination less surely revealed in more recent compositions. " Gaspard de la Nuit " and " Ma Mère l'Oye " are wholly admirable.

The original compositions and the arrangements of Ferruccio Busoni add to the difficulties we have in ascertaining the depth of this extraordinary musician's mind. Busoni was a pianist whose interpretations of any classical work were apt to vary according to the mood he happened to be in. Such was his power of suggestion that whatever view he chose to advocate seemed, for the time being, most desirable. Similarly in his compositions and arrangements he can convince us of the logic of his reasoning even when the weight of evidence would seem to point the other way. Carmen is a romantic subject matched, in the opera, by music picturesque and passionate. Busoni's own fantasia on Bizet's themes seemed, when interpreted by him, an irreproachable classic, cool, clean, dispassionate. It is difficult to say whether others will be equally convincing. His Bach arrangements have never seemed quite as happy interpreted by others—with the possible exception of the Chaconne. This adaptation of a violin piece for piano is admirable and of a piece with Bach's own arrangements of Vivaldi's concertos.

Scriabin, a contemporary of Busoni, is now paying the penalty for having exceeded the limits ascribed to him by nature. A talented musician and an excellent performer, Scriabin was allowed by the fashion of the time to place himself in the position of a prophet for the elect. The elect have now forsaken him and turned their backs also from the slighter, earlier works that have unquestionable merit, even though the undue influence of Chopin is frequently felt.

Richard Strauss's " Burlesque," ably scored and grateful for the soloist, draws out a genial idea to unconscionable lengths.

The shorter compositions for the pianoforte are innumerable. In every age performers have contributed their quota. The place vacated by Tausig, Thalberg and Henselt has

Uc

since been filled by Rubinstein, Godowsky, Paderewski, Sgambati and Rosenthal, every one of whom has some arrangements or original composition to his credit. Moreover, the pianoforte being a subsidiary subject with all music students, it is to the piano that they all turn in their salad days. Some of these modest, minor pieces have achieved some notoriety. Rubinstein's " Melody in F " was once a best seller ; Paderewski's Minuet was heard in every drawing-room and every parlour provided with a piano until it was evicted later by Rachmaninov's all too famous prelude.

More important than any of these are the short pieces of the Spanish composers Albéniz and Manuel de Falla who first revealed to us the full flavour of their national music, known to us before at second-hand through the versions of French composers. Original and striking are also the contributions of a number of contemporary British composers. Eugene Goossens, Frank Bridge and John Ireland have written a number of short pianoforte pieces of fine workmanship. Arnold Bax has covered a vast range which goes from a delicate Lullaby to the lively " In a Vodka Shop " and " Burlesque." These works can well stand comparison with similar continental productions ; they are not less musical for being technically adventurous, while whatever interest the work of Béla Bartók, the Hungarian composer, possesses is of a purely technical kind.

# B: PIANOFORTE AND VIOLIN SONATAS AND DUETS

## CHAPTER I

## THE CLASSICS

### (a) BACH AND HANDEL

NOT MANY SONATAS for piano and violin of the pre-Mozart age have survived. There are some fine things by J. S. Bach and one sonata (in E major) that stands above all the others and represents his genius in the art of instrumental writing at its best. It consists of four movements—two slow, alternating with two lively sections. The allegros have a sparkle that is not found in the allegros of the violin concertos ; nor is there any other single movement of his for violin in which slight, but effective, changes of melodic design are more happily exploited. The first adagio, somewhat florid and elaborate, serves well the purpose of an introduction ; the second equals the slow movements of the violin concertos in its exquisite tenderness of devotional expression.

Again, in Handel's sonatas for piano and violin one is found which overtops the rest. The sonata in A major has no real slow movement, its place, between the two allegros, being taken by a recitative-like passage only five bars long. Short as it is, it fulfils its purpose perfectly. The change from the preceding movement is complete ; the matter is so arresting that it takes away the mind entirely from all that went before it. The genius of Handel for dramatic expression, exemplified in the recitatives of " Messiah," touches here its greatest height. After the bustling energy of the first movement he conjures up in a flash an atmosphere of tense expectation ; in five bars he takes us to a tragic climax. When the last movement—a chaste Allegro of enchanting beauty—comes to unravel the plot, we experience a feeling of positive relief. Both *allegro* and recitative lose their qualities when the pace of the one and the sentiment of the other are not exactly measured by the interpreter. I have heard no completely satisfactory performance of this sonata since the death of its most understanding interpreter, Lady Hallé.

## (b) MOZART

Nothing written between Handel and Mozart for violin and piano need detain us, for the simple reason that nothing is ever heard. Even the sonatas of Mozart are seldom played in the concert room—much to our loss. For, indeed, while in the more favoured violin concertos there is occasionally alloy, at least two of the sonatas for pianoforte and violin are pure gold.

The sonata in B flat (No. 1 in Litolff's collection) has a rare wealth of characteristic Mozartian melody of the best kind. No other composer has joined the two instruments with greater skill or written music that so easily brings out their essential character. The *andantino*, dividing the brisk first movement from the third, deserves the closest attention. The part of the violin appears, at first, less important than that of the piano, for often its duty is that of a helper and supporter. As a matter of fact, the effect of the piece depends entirely upon the way in which the violin part is treated. The few notes that the violin adds to the pianoforte melody give it character, colour, eloquence. The tone of the piano, without them, would seem ineffective, unequal to the loveliness of the subject. The subsidiary rôle of the violin in the opening phrases makes its entry with the chief theme exceptionally striking. In the final Rondo is found one of those strokes of genius met only in the work of great composers. The subject in 3–8 time develops in the usual manner till an unexpected pause halts its progress ;

the 3–8 time changes to 4–4 ; violin and piano join in amicable gossip, chattering away till, recalled to their duty, they resume the main theme and conclude it in dashing style. The effect of the interruption is most delightfully new and surprising.

The second flawless sonata is in F major (Litolff's No. 8) and may well bear " L'Allegro " as its subtitle. I know of no other musical composition describing with such fine art jollity, high spirits, good humour. Every sentence in the opening movement has an upward sweep, as if cheerfulness could not be kept down. Scales and florid passages have lost all formality ; they rush up and down like things touched by the first sun of the spring. The second movement has all the Mozartian sweetness and proportions that cannot be admired enough—not a bar that is not inspired ; not a note that has not its purpose. The third movement, founded on one of those impish themes of which Mozart alone had the secret, takes us back to the happy mood of the first. Its quiet, strictly *a tempo* conclusion is a masterstroke and ends the sonata with a surprise ; it leaves the spectator with the impression of some good achieved and a delightful task accomplished.

In other sonatas Mozart uses freely the variation form. The second, fourth, seventh, eleventh and fifteenth sonatas of the Litolff collection have each one set of variations. These are all ingenious and, most of them, diverting. But ears accustomed to the complex variations of the moderns are apt to grow tired after a while of the rather too symmetrical diversions of the older composers.

Most of the other sonatas have at least one movement of exceptional beauty. The first movement of the A major sonata (No. 11) is almost a match for No. 8 in sparkle and liveliness ; the second movement of the E flat sonata (No. 14) has for its chief subject one of those broad, hymn-like melodies of the type found also in the finale of Brahms's first symphony and in his A major piano and violin sonata. Those who like Mozart best in a serious mood will delight in the second (G major) and fifth (E minor) sonatas. But, indeed, the whole collection deserves the admiration of every discerning musician. Their temporary eclipse can only be ascribed to the modern craze for a reckless pace not to be found amongst Mozart's tempos. Intelligent interpretation cannot fail to restore them to the affection of the public.

## (c) BEETHOVEN

Beethoven's sonatas have never known eclipse. Apart from the "Kreutzer," which has always been a favourite, they have all been fashionable at some time or other. Once the fifth sonata (in F major) held the lists together with the "Kreutzer"; then came the turn of the E minor, succeeded later by the first sonata in G major. Recently the second sonata in G major (Op. 96) has come to the fore and surpasses even the "Kreutzer" in popularity; the two sonatas together represent the two aspects of Beethoven's genius, the dramatic and the lyrical, as adequately as do the C minor and the Pastoral symphonies. The piano and violin sonatas, taken as a whole, resemble the symphonies in this, that the dramatic element predominates in the odd numbers.

The workmanship in the earlier sonatas is less certain than in the later, though even in the first sonata in D major there is much that only Beethoven could have written. The boldness of the opening already shows the force and energy of a Haydn raised to the square. The even melody opening the fifth sonata might have come from Mozart, but soon makes way for episodes instinct with a vigorous impulse Mozart never knew.

But the "Kreutzer" and the G major (Op. 96) undoubtedly stand at the head of the collection. All the most characteristic points of the earlier numbers are enhanced and developed in the "Kreutzer." Its violin part bears Beethoven's stamp in technique as well as in feeling. Every period seems to have been conceived while a special quality of violin tone was ringing in the composer's ear. The variations, which constitute the middle movement, would completely lose their character if played by any instrument other than the violin. It is not only that the prescribed bowing strokes are the prerogative of the string instrument ; the expression needed is what only a violin can give. The variations of the " Kreutzer " are the most notable things of the kind written before Brahms, mingling opportunities for *bravura* with expression of deep sentiment. After the theme we have a first variation in which the pianist has his chance, followed by a second in which the violinist alone matters ; then comes the variation in the minor, equalling in depth a noble *adagio* and the conclusion, in which grace-notes have the appeal of fine melody.

The sonata in G major (Op. 96) stands apart from the rest in being cast entirely in a mood of quiet, heart-easing, tenderness—an idyll in four movements. Even the frequent *sforzandos* of the scherzo are not the brusque jolts and jars so typical of Beethoven. They are but a foil to the fluent *legato* melody of the trio. This sonata enjoys over the " Kreutzer " the advantage of never tempting the pianist to exceed a volume of tone that the violinist can match. I cannot help feeling that the scant support given to recitals of piano and violin sonatas is due, in great part, to the failure of most executants to realise their responsibilities. The pianist cannot resist the temptation to assert his preponderance ; the violinist will not give in and tries to force his tone ; both of them incline to exceed the correct tempo ; the sonata loses its true character and becomes a mere show-piece.

The temptation to force tone and pace is great in the C minor sonata, which has an impressive first movement, an *adagio cantabile* that, rightly interpreted, becomes more " cantabile " than " adagio," and a very unequal last movement. On the whole I prefer to this the F major sonata, the short scherzo of which has more quips and pranks to each bar than any other scherzo in existence.

## CHAPTER II

# THE ROMANTICS AND THE MODERNS

### (a) SCHUBERT, SCHUMANN AND BRAHMS

THE CONTRIBUTIONS OF SCHUBERT in this field are disappointing. Best known are the three sonatinas, used generally to introduce young violinists and pianists to chamber music. They are of moderate difficulty but they have also the simplicity of heart that was Schubert's own. The very exacting " duos " for piano and violin can only be made acceptable by exceptionally finished playing. In the " Rondo Brillant " tunes of character and distinction are worked to excessive lengths. The " Fantasia " (Op. 159) and the " Introduction et Variations " are not exactly violin music and the last is significantly described as a composition for piano and violin or flute.

Schumann also could not quite get the measure of the piano and violin sonata. His themes are often very beautiful but not happily developed. The partnership of the two instruments is a casual meeting, not a solid union. The piano predominates and the violinist is expected to extract from his lower strings tone as clear as those of the E string.

The three sonatas of Brahms, on the other hand, are equally admirable and, together with the best examples of Mozart and Beethoven, show the form at its best. The first, in G major, has an opening movement in which romantic ardour is tempered by an instinctive regard for classical manner and order. The second subject, arresting when first played by the keyboard instrument, takes wings when heard on the violin, whose sustained warmth brings out fully its inherent, urgent sentiment. The last movement, embodying the melody of an earlier " Song of the Rain," gives an effect of cool, subdued light, such as that of a rainy day in spring.

The effect is not so much the result of material means (i.e. the semi-quavers representing rain-drops) as of the chaste, even mood which permeates it and turns the graver subject of the slow movement, when it re-appears, into something resigned, less poignant and more sedate. It ends with just such a dying fall as that which Orsino likened to the south wind breathing upon a bank of violets.

It has been noted that Brahms's second subjects are often more eloquent than the first. The second sonata in A major is a good example of this. The first subject of the opening movement—a solid, well-knit melody—represents a capital text to be commented upon and developed later ; the second subject is pure poetry. As in the first sonata, it is assigned first to the piano and then to the infinitely more eloquent voice of the violin. The second movement consists of two alternating, contrasting sections—andante and scherzo telescoped. The first section, comfortably settled in the key of F major, propounds a sentimental subject ; the second, "*vivace*" in D minor, answers with swift repartees. The *vivace* has the last word and wins the day. The broad, square theme of the last movement is of a piece with the finale of the first symphony. It is marked *alla breve*, which, however, does not refer to speed but to the nature of a melody that admits of two and not of four beats to the bar. Interpreters are frequently misled in such cases which, however, are common enough even in Bach. Schweitzer gives a much needed warning to the effect that an *alla breve* sign in Bach does not constitute a direction to double the pace.

The third sonata in D minor has been ranked by competent Brahmsians above the other two. It deals with lofty and beautiful subjects of a less lyrical and more dramatic cast than those of the G major and A major sonatas. There is, however, loss as well as gain. Lyrical phrases are more suited to the violin than to the piano ; they provide the violinist's special opportunities in the earlier sonatas. In the D minor, the pianist, except in the slow movement, is no longer a partner but a dictator. In the third movement the violin often can only fuss about, while the piano says all that really matters. This is a work of great thoughts and fine proportions which, however, only pianists can honestly and, indeed, inevitably prefer to the other two. But all three have their speciality ; the first is the most imaginative, the second the most lyrical and the third the most dramatic.

## (b) FRANCK, GRIEG AND SOME OTHERS

The only sonata of non-German origin that has a right to the first rank is the sonata of César Franck. The claims made for Franck in his adopted country have never been backed by foreign scholars. Except in France, only his chamber music appears to be highly valued, and the sonata for pianoforte and violin has been more warmly welcomed and more frequently performed than the quartet or the quintet. Franck's experiments in form are often but partially successful. In the sonata, however, he gives free rein to his fancy, with the happiest result. While in the classical form the first is the most important movement, Franck substitutes for it a very brief movement, in which there is no thought of development The last movement again is a brief canon in rondo form. Between these delightful short sections are found a piece of intense dramatic energy and one whose aim is explained by the title—Recitativo-Fantasia; this takes the place of the usual adagio and scherzo. Franck achieves thus a perfect balance, the comparative unimportance of the first and last movements finding compensation in the greater scope and length of the middle sections. Neither sense nor sentiment demand more. Within this framework there is music of aristocratic refinement, often exquisitely pathetic, sometimes simple to the verge of innocence, unworldly, very different from the more robust products of the German classics, very touching and sincere.

The progress of Franck's sonata was slow at first ; when recognition came its foundations were, however, truly laid. The three sonatas by Grieg on the other hand, immediately successful, have already seen the sun set on their glory. The folk-tunes on which they are founded have lost, by repetition, some of their wild flavour ; the impetuous rhythms that delighted us have palled in comparison with the still more impetuous energies of newer, more radical, more primitive nationalists ; the hard, rude framework begins now to be visible under the thin, picturesque material that covers it. The first sonata, in F, and the second, in G, conform more easily to accepted standards than the third, which yet surpasses them in boldness and originality. We must not look to Grieg for cultured wit and delicate fancy. His downright, plain phrases have nothing beyond elemental force and sentiment to commend them. The same is true of Sjögren, the best of his followers, whose single sonata makes up in high spirits what it lacks in distinction.

The influence of Grieg has been traced in the Belgian composer, Joseph Jongen. His piano and violin sonatas seem to me, if anything, nearer in style to Franck than to Grieg. At any rate they have a refinement wholly alien to the music of Grieg. The pace is a little slow ; the meticulous taste that cleared the music of all impurity has also weakened slightly its fibre. But there is no mistaking the high thought and the fastidious taste of their author.

The two sonatas by Anton Rubinstein and the many by Joachim Raff are now forgotten. Both Rubinstein and Raff had hands that were quicker than their wits. They had no difficulty whatever in devising plausible subjects ; training and experience had taught them how best to use them. It was all material labour, good and even excellent of its kind, which lacked the consolidating, inspiring force of mind and personality. Another sonata that created some stir when first heard and has now fallen into desuetude is Richard Strauss's. It is an early essay in an uncongenial form, whose idiomatic style has been much better exploited in opera and symphonic poem.

Neither Debussy nor Ravel has found the piano and violin sonata wholly congenial, and their attempts will not stand comparison with their best work. More grateful is the sonata by Ildebrando Pizzetti, who uses very deftly themes that bear the impress of Italian folk-song. The early piano and violin sonata by Paul Hindemith is free from the fuss and freakishness of his later work ; frankly and naïvely it acknowledges its debt to his great German predecessors. Stravinsky's " Duo Concertant " may conveniently be mentioned here, even though it is no sonata but a suite in five movements. It is said to represent an attempt to combine a modern technique with a romantic temper. Only the husks of romanticism can be found in it ; its heart and mind revolt against a mésalliance so clumsily urged. A genuine romantic feeling animates the two sonatas by Medtner—another Russian composer—who combines in a rare degree clearness of writing with felicity of expression.

### (c) ENGLISH COMPOSERS

There is true romanticism also in the sonatas of the English composers, John Ireland and Arnold Bax. The former has a firm grasp of every problem and a sure touch in the disposition of parts. Arnold Bax was inclined in the first sonata to pour out his ideas too lavishly and, perhaps, uncritically, so that its length seemed greater than its material justified. In the second and, still more, in the third the material is used more economically, giving an impression of increased strength and deeper emotion.

Two English works have not yet won the favour of the public to the extent the fame of their composers would have seemed to warrant—the sonatas of Delius and Elgar. The neglect of Delius's sonata is explained up to a point by a certain disregard of colour and movement ; this composition has yet all the elegance and fluency we expect from him. At present it is likely to delight the performer more than the listener, for only complete familiarity with every turn of phrase will yield its choicest flavour. Elgar's sonata still awaits the ideal interpreter. Experience seems to point to the fact that, while nothing is easier than the realisation of its most obvious features, such as the manly vitality of certain themes and the graciousness of others, it is extremely difficult to penetrate its subtler and rarer moods. Perhaps a more liberal and less literal interpretation of the composer's directions is needed before all its graces are set free.

# C: THE VIOLIN IN SOLO AND CONCERTO

## CHAPTER I

## THE STANDARD WORKS

### (a) BACH AND BEFORE

THE REPERTORY of the modern violinist includes nothing earlier than the works of the Italian masters of the seventeenth and eighteenth centuries. Even these have been but casually explored. Immediately after the World War, when national pride and susceptibilities were still on fire in every land, propaganda did useful work in searching out and seeking to revive old glories. One fruit of this work was the publication in Italy of a number of old sonatas by Veracini and other masters which, at the time, attracted considerable attention. When the political need for propaganda ceased, its value for purposes of information on artistic and other matters of general interest was lost sight of and its good deeds forgotten. The paintings of the old masters were sent abroad on loan ; the music of old masters remained at home unsung and unhonoured.

It must be admitted, however, that violinists have shown little desire to investigate for themselves, preferring the special editions prepared by players with a talent for adapting the sturdy art of the old masters to the supposed requirements of modern tastes. Perhaps the best known example of old Italian music is the set of variations by Corelli on " La Folia." It is never played in its original form, the favourite edition being one prepared by the Belgian violinist, Léonard. Léonard curtails the original somewhat but adds by way of a makeweight a cadenza of his own which is brilliant, not very difficult and wholly unnecessary. Another case in point is that of the Gavotte from Bach's unaccompanied sonata in E, a piano accompaniment for which has recently been added by a well-known violinist. The accompaniment, if superfluous, is ingenious. But the addition of a heavy bass to the concluding harmony translates old elegance into modern vulgarity.

Cadenzas have been written for most old compositions for the violin, for the sonatas of Tartini and for the concertos of Bach, as if to add another page or so to another man's music were an obvious, least responsible, task. Cadenzas are frequently at fault in that they introduce a technical style alien to the composition ; they also add to the length and alter the proportions of a concerto or sonata.

It is true, however, that the old Italians were themselves violinists who delighted in the display of their skill. There was then no such distinction as exists to-day between " real " and " virtuoso " music, since, apparently, the players known to us were equally skilled in playing and composing. It was natural for the composer to write in such a way that his abilities in the management of the instrument could find proper scope. It was the incompetence, as composers, of nineteenth-century violinists that gave virtuosity a bad name. But the compositions of Veracini, Locatelli, Corelli, Geminiani and Tartini were meant to be played with the utmost bravura—which does not mean that therefore anybody is entitled to add to them or curtail them. These old masters have nothing like the emotional force of later composers ; but their music has, within its limits, a rugged efficacy, a nobility of form and expression that modernisation can easily weaken but never improve.

Of Tartini's sonatas the best known is " The Devil's Trill," partly, without doubt, because of the fantastic story attached to it. I prefer the sonata in G minor, once known as the " Dido forsaken " on account of its dramatic expression. " The Devil's Trill " has nothing as intense as the first allegro of the " Dido," nor anything as finely sensitive as its concluding movement. A virile sonata in G major completes a trio that represents the music of the time at its highest.

Old French music is best represented by Rameau and Leclair whose debonair, genial compositions provide very pleasant diversion from more serious pursuits. Germany finds her champion in J. S. Bach, whose contributions to the violin are less numerous but not less beautiful than those for the organ and harpsichord. The present age is supposed to have re-discovered Bach, but there is at least one work of his that so far has escaped the notice of connoisseurs. This is the sonata in E minor which opens with a short prelude, passes on to one of the most delightful adagios in the whole Bach repertory and closes with a dance movement which, if less excellent than the rest, is still fully adequate. Considering the high qualities of the sonata and the crying need of variety in the average recital programme, the indifference of performers is difficult to explain. The loveliness of the adagio did not escape that incomparable interpreter of Bach, Hans Richter, who arranged it for string orchestra and incorporated it in one of the Brandenburg concertos.

The case is quite different in respect of the Bach sonatas for unaccompanied violin, which have reached just now the pinnacle of popularity. It is in every way right and proper that they should be carefully and thoroughly studied by every violinist, for there is no better foundation of taste or technique. Public performances by all kinds of violinists, on the other hand, are far from desirable. In the first place not every executant can give Bach all that he demands. The true Bach style is not more common than the true Mozart style. Again, discrimination in the choice of the sonata or excerpts is necessary, for not all the sonatas are equally interesting. There are numbers such as the adagio of the fifth sonata (in C major) and the andante of the third sonata (in A minor), where the uniformity of the melodic design becomes tedious, since the violin cannot match it with a sustained harmony. The G minor fugue of the first sonata is a more polished work of art than the C major fugue of the fifth sonata, because the latter lays bare the awkwardness of the violin as a medium for contrapuntal writing. The devices by which Bach overcomes the inherent weakness of the violin cannot be praised or admired enough ; but they still represent a compromise between what the composer wishes to do and what his medium allows him. For this reason a violin recital that includes two of the least happy sonatas is apt to be a trying experience. As a whole the collection is invaluable and includes some short, lively dance movements, like the Gavotte and Rondo in E major (sixth sonata) and the Bourrée in B minor (second sonata), slow movements of great dignity like the first adagio, and movements of incomparable grandeur like the famous Chaconne.

The two violin concertos by Bach in E major and A minor are amongst the best things in the whole repertory. The ornamentation of the quick movements is interspersed with flowing, beautiful melodies, spun with a touch that is at once light and sure. The two slow movements are typical examples of emotion recollected in tranquillity. Schweitzer tells us that Bach considered his concertos as pieces for a small orchestra in which one instrument or more are treated as soloists. In the violin concertos the orchestra is of great importance, even though it is, or should be, numerically small. Additional parts for organ have been added recently by scholars and conductors—not always judiciously. The additions to the E major concerto by Gevaert are unexceptionable.

### (b) MOZART AND SOME OTHERS

The close, happy relationship between soloist and orchestra in the old concertos has not escaped the attention of some contemporary composers who have sought to reduce the weight of the accompaniment. Vaughan Williams's " Concerto accademico " for instance, is accompanied by strings only. Paul Hindemith and other modern Germans have also reduced very considerably the size of the orchestra accompanying the solo instrument, in an attempt to revive the intimacy of these old " chamber " concertos. To this class belong also the violin concertos of Haydn, not specially important nor wholly negligible, though they have never won the confidence of performers, and the three concertos of Mozart (in E flat, G and A)—just now in great demand.

The best of Mozart's is the concerto in A major, in which melodies, fresh and heartfelt, abound. The concertos, however, are, as a whole, somewhat unequal. Even in the A major there are indications pointing to hasty writing, to the absence of a counsellor urging the composer to " load every rift of his subject with ore." The second movement is immaculate ; one could not praise too highly its refined sentiment, its virginal purity. But the third movement is far from unassailable. The minuet-like subject, graceful enough of its kind, has not sufficient life to balance the preceding sections and conclude effectively an important work. Moreover its even, not very eventful, course is arrested suddenly by the wholly unforeseen introduction of a Salzburg dance or Turkish march in A minor. What could have induced Mozart to interpolate such an irrelevant episode ? The desire to flatter Salzburg and please his father ? Did he feel that the minuet was inadequate ; did he mean to add with the Turkish music to its length and importance ? If this was his object, he failed to secure it, for minuet and Turkish music mix as well as oil and water. The interpolation remains a thing apart from the main scheme, unsupported and unsupporting, not a buttress but an excrescence. This is the blot in the concerto, whose first and, still more, second movements are, however, more than sufficient atonement for the sins of the third.

### (c) THREE MASTERPIECES ; AND SOME LESSER WORKS

We come now to the great violin concertos—great not only in violin music but also amongst the works of their respective composers. First of these, in order of time, is Beethoven's. Led by never failing instinct rather than by experience, Beethoven wrote for the instrument as no other composer had written before, discovering new possibilities, developing its capacity for expressing a very special and very fine type of emotion. A long succession of gifted interpreters has led us to expect at least adequacy in every performance of the concerto we hear. As a matter of fact, no piece of violin music is so exacting as this in its demands on the interpreter, and the success of every performance hangs by a thread. The florid, ornamental passages, the chief difficulty in older music, are never very difficult in Beethoven. The real difficulty is in finding the right quality of tone befitting musical ideas of an ethereal nature. Nothing can be taken for granted, not a single melodic bar can be entrusted with confidence to any but the most accomplished player. Only cultivated taste and intuition can teach us the way to its heart.

The writing is so simple that it crumbles into dust in the hands of the anatomist. No important lesson can be learnt by dissecting its component parts. The framework is of the lightest ; the harmonic changes are straightforward ; the melodies are not specially striking in their general design, and a little while ago a bold modernist declared them to be actually dull and commonplace. So they seem if they are separated from imagination and sensibility. So were the eyes that inspired Petrarch when the light had gone from them. The strength of Beethoven's concerto is not for the grammarian and the technician. It is wholly in the spirit of the music ; its supreme beauty is of the soul.

For many years the only concerto thought worthy to stand by the side of Beethoven's was Mendelssohn's. Certainly Mendelssohn's music lies even readier to the player's hand ; it is more brilliant than Beethoven's ; it offers a good harvest for technical research, for its effective " points " are many and obvious. It is also wholly material. The deep sources from which Beethoven draws his inspiration, the high altitudes to which his melody rises, are unknown to Mendelssohn. He is the picked craftsman who can paint superficial emotions with unsurpassed mastery.

His slow movements, including the Andante of the violin concerto, partake of the nature of the " song without words " he invented—pleasing, sensuous, fanciful melodies, devoid of spiritual appeal. But every stroke goes home ; the entry of the orchestra after the cadenza in the first movement, the short recitative introducing the third, the 'cello melody accompanied by the counterpoint of the soloist shortly before the coda of the finale—these are but some of the high lights in a piece abounding in happy ideas expressed always with elegance and ease.

In aim and outlook Brahms's concerto comes nearer to Beethoven's than to Mendelssohn's. The labours of composition are less effectively hidden ; we cannot but note the skill with which every problem is set and solved. The inspiration is not always maintained at the same height. The lay-out is not easy and does not look easy ; but Brahms has none of the snags of Beethoven and any interpreter of average intelligence and more than average mechanical skill is equal to it. The first movement, a noble conception, surpasses the other two. Felicitous scoring sets out well a solo part in which nothing is casually done, where the violin sounds a rich variety of tender and heroic feelings, rising to great intensity and giving an impression of audacity and vision. The second movement is introduced by a short prelude for woodwind, admirable melodically, objectionable in the instrumentation. The main theme is assigned to the oboe, chosen, no doubt, on account of its range and with the object of providing contrast for the string tone of the soloist. But the thin note of the oboe is completely over-balanced by the heaviness of the supporting harmonies ; nor is its uneven timbre suitable to the melody throughout its length. And so the entry of the soloist provides not only contrast but positive relief. The third movement introduces some manly music and some excellent writing. The only flaw here is in the use of an orchestra so full as to dwarf the soloist. There is too great a disproportion between the *forte* of the solo and that of the mass. In all other respects fertility of invention, loftiness of ideas, general lay-out—the concerto must be considered as the most remarkable contribution to violin music after Beethoven.

The third and last of the great concertos is, of course, Edward Elgar's. Some foreign critics, while acknowledging the very high quality of the music, have yet taken exception to its length, which they found excessive ; they have also pointed out that in the first movement the second subject is under-developed. Elgar, they said, having invented a very lovely melody, does little or nothing with it. Both charges may be admitted, but, far from diminishing, they enhance our admiration for Elgar's judgment. It is obviously true that the second movement could conveniently end some twenty or thirty bars before it does. Many another composer having gone as far would have written in the final chord conscious of good work well done. It is the measure of Elgar's genius that after doing so much he can take us still farther afield and discover other avenues of still greater beauty. As for the " development " of the second subject, only a hide-bound pedant could suppose a different treatment possible. Not all subjects can be subjected to the same processes. The composer alone is the proper authority in the matter ; against his decision no appeal can be entertained. The second subject of Elgar's concerto is perfect as it stands, and as anyone who listens with unbiased mind must acknowledge. It is poetry—not a text for a discourse. We feel its truth and depth ; an exquisite thought presented in exquisite form. It could not be subjected to any other treatment without outraging artistic sensibility. It is, in its way, as much a masterstroke as the cadenza of the third movement, the only excursus of the kind whose purpose is not solely to provide an opportunity for technical display or to bridge over a gap between the last section and its coda. Elgar reviews his materials for the last time and shows them no longer in the fulness of their life, but touched already with the pathos of past things. The resources of the soloist have here a real artistic purpose and become integral elements of the composition. The use of a full orchestra in the accompaniment is masterly and possible only to one who, having the genius of the violin in his very blood, knew instinctively how far it could hold its own against the orchestral mass.

British composers before Elgar had contributed little to violin music. Some eighteenth-century sonatas have been rescued from oblivion recently and one may find amongst them work of more than passing merit. The sonata of Thomas Vincent, for instance, can only disappoint those who judge every composer by the standard of another. It is true that Vincent has none of the qualities of old Italian masters, but he has a character of his own that is at least not less valuable. Gentleness, quietude of mind, a heart "fit for contemplation," may well console us for the absence of glitter and passion. The Largo of John Collett's sonata in A major is of a more emotional character. His finest work, is, however, in its two Allegros—sprightly, vivacious music, free from the obvious and the pretentious. A sonata in D minor by John Humphries makes a good third. These compositions are, unfortunately, too easy in appearance to tempt the expert, and require at the same time a stylistic distinction that only the expert can bring to them. The difficulties they present are not to be overcome by dashing, quick fingers. They need sound judgment of tempi and, still more, sympathy and understanding.

# CHAPTER II

# THE VIRTUOSO AS COMPOSER

Apart from the early sonatas and the finest concertos, the great bulk of violin music has been written by performers who sought to enrich their repertory to the best of their ability. There are innumerable concertos by such men as Kreutzer, Rode, Viotti, Lipinski and others, now used solely to supplement a lesson in technique. Most of these are negligible, but a great virtuoso can still extract from them something that is not wholly devoid of musical interest. The very bareness and gauntness of a concerto by Viotti or Rode could give an impression of austerity when galvanised into life by the bow of an Ysaÿe.

The larger vision of the romantic composers lured the virtuoso into unaccustomed and dangerous fields. As long as violinists kept to their own scholastic ideals they wrote what, at least technically, could never be wholly valueless. When they began to substitute emotionalism for scholasticism, the outcome was, sometimes, absolutely ludicrous. The concertos of Charles de Bériot present an array of platitudes with an air of pomposity that can be positively revolting ; at best they are fire and fury signifying nothing. More gifted than de Bériot, Henri Vieuxtemps wrote several pieces in which melodies are treated with great ingenuity and very effectively adorned by every trick known to the violinist. The Polonaise, Fantasia Caprice, Fantasia Appassionata and the Suite in the Old Style have positive merit. In the concertos he tries to be grandiose : the form atrophies his critical sense and the result is simply monstrosity, music that can only technically be described as violin music. There are passages in his D minor concerto that might be telling on some other instrument ; on the violin they give an impression of hopeless futility.

Ernst's F sharp minor concerto in one movement has greater sincerity and some of its florid writing is distinctly attractive. A bombastic main subject and the abuse of double stops weigh the scale against it. Ernst's once famous Elegy, supposed to have been written after the death of the woman he loved, does more credit to his heart than to his fancy. It is now as completely out of fashion as the Elegy by Bazzini (a better work) and Raff's Cavatina.

A more prolific composer, Louis Spohr, wrote, besides opera and oratorio, a number of concertos now used mainly to train young violinists in the way they should go. Spohr was a sturdy technician and no tutor can afford to ignore him. The chief weakness of his music lies in its heavy sentimentality, which soon surfeits the appetite. Let us, however, record the fact that the late Marshal von Moltke is reported to have preferred Spohr to all other composers. The best of his concertos is the Gesangsscene, not because it creates a new form similar to the " Recitative and Scena " of the opera singer, but because it consists of a number of sections too brief to cloy with their sweetness. Spohr is best remembered by his duets for two violins—clever compositions that explore effects of sonority in a way never before attempted. He shares with Paganini the honour of being the founder of modern technique.

It is still far from easy to ascertain exactly how much we owe to that violinist who easily surpassed all his contemporaries. Paganini introduced the double harmonics and the left-hand pizzicato—questionable legacy for his successors. The Moderns use them frequently without securing any real advantage over the old composers, who avoided them ; some have made them an excuse for trifles. Paganini's violin compositions—apart from the caprices—leave us cold, in spite of the frequent use of dashing effects of bow and left hand. There is no real " genius " in the concerto in D, in the many variations on well-known airs ; nor is there anything in the "Clochette" rondo, besides the talent of a clever, alert adapter. We know, from the record of competent musicians who heard him, that these compositions must have made a different impression when he himself played them. It is said that they drew tears and laughter from his hearers ; the most gifted modern violinists can, at best, make us gasp. If there was a touch of charlatanism in his playing, let us remember that the majority of public performers possess a degree of self-confidence that in other men would, to say the least, be deemed excessive. In any case, Schumann and Berlioz were not musicians likely to be deceived by a mere acrobat.

Paganini left also a set of twenty-four caprices that reveal a very different side of his character and, in spite of their admittedly technical purpose, subordinate technique to the requirements of essentially musical ideas that often have the severe simplicity of the old Italian music of Veracini and Vivaldi. Undoubtedly the man who wrote the caprices that Liszt, Schumann and Brahms applauded and adapted for their instrument had the composer's genius. Together with the caprices should also be considered the twelfth sonata, in which there are no harmonics and only a couple of left-hand pizzicatos that could just as well be omitted. In this strict, austere composition and in the caprices the real Paganini is to be found. The variations, which he would not allow to be published, are nothing more than brilliant improvisations whose effect varies according to the talent of their exponent.

Two names must be added to the record of the violinist-composers—Henri Wieniawski and Joseph Joachim. The former, a brilliant disciple of the romantic school, wrote effective fantasias, a couple of fiery " Polonaises," a Legend still heard at the less exclusive recitals and two concertos, of which the first was soon forgotten while the second, in D minor, is still remembered as one of the better examples of virtuoso music ; there are moments of some character in the " romance " and of hearty, breezy vitality in the finale. Joachim, on the other hand, was the champion of the classics, the best interpreter, in his day, of Bach and Beethoven and he is said never to have touched a composition by Vieuxtemps or Paganini. His compositions bear the stamp of a serious ideal and, although they are by no means free from bravura writing, claim to be considered solely as music. It is impossible to say that the whole of the Hungarian concerto is interesting—as music. The themes have not enough individuality to impress the listener and only just avoid being reminiscent. The slow movement surpasses the other two in richness of invention and genial warmth. A set of Variations for violin and orchestra, extremely well written for the instrument, are entitled to more generous recognition. Without resorting to virtuoso devices, they take us rapidly through a series of pleasing adventures in which sight is never completely lost of the main theme.

## CHAPTER III

# LESSER CONCERTOS.
# SOME MISCELLANEOUS WORKS

Composers of high standing have devoted their attention to the violin concerto, without quite winning the confidence of the performers or of the public. Goldmark's work, at one time a favourite with César Thomson, perhaps fails because of its ambiguous character, which is neither romantic nor definitely classical, and of melodies too smooth and unadventurous to hold the interest. The second movement, a well constructed Aria, will probably be remembered when the rest is forgotten. Of Dvořák's lean and muscular concerto, nothing derogatory can be said ; it is, indeed, a pattern of conscientious workmanship. But it is also singularly uninspired ; Dvořák gave his best to the 'cello, not to the violin. There is greater sincerity in the " Concerto Romantique " by Benjamin Godard—slight, unpretentious, melodious and also a little pompous.

More important than these is the unequal but deeply felt and, at times, very charming concerto of Tchaikovsky. Its inequalities are the result, partly, of an imperfect knowledge of what a violin can do to hold its own against an orchestra. The orchestration—heavy and sometimes clumsy —was, no doubt, the main cause why the concerto was rejected by the Vienna Philharmonic after being tried at a rehearsal. Some slight alterations were made with Tchaikovsky's approval by Brodsky, who sponsored the work and became its ablest exponent. " Poco Più Mosso," too rapid for clearness, became " Poco Meno Mosso," the mute which damped too effectively the solo in the slow movement was cancelled, a cut or two brought the work within more reasonable proportions and the concerto began to make its way. The scoring is still more befitting a pianoforte than a violin solo, but it is largely offset by the compelling qualities of the themes of the first and second movements ; the third degenerates into a Russian dance, far too noisy and exuberant to be congenial on the violin.

There is excellent material in the concerto by Glazounov which just misses the romantic tide—a better work than any by Max Bruch except his first concerto in G minor. Bruch could not write a first movement that was not perfunctory. But in the G minor concerto the mechanical first movement is followed by an adagio worthy of a greater composer. The allegro is infinitely more trilling and efficacious than anything he wrote later. A second concerto, in D minor, enjoyed a brief popularity, thanks to Sarasate, to whom it is dedicated, and to Ysaÿe. The rest—the Scottish Fantasia, the Serenade, dedicated to Willy Hess, the Swedish dances, —lingered during the composer's lifetime ; they have hardly been heard since.

The most attractive violin concerto of recent times is probably Jean Sibelius's, though it concedes nothing to tradition or popular taste. It exemplifies a new conception of the relations between soloist and orchestra, any failure of either being sufficient to wreck its effect completely. The art of music, as understood by classics and romantics, seems to have been reduced to its component elements, then moulded after a drastic purge of all that tended to undermine strength, to encourage loquacity or to lead to conventionality. The result is a little grim, but very bracing and tremendously exciting. Delius's temperament is not less distinct than Sibelius's, but it leads in the opposite direction ; his violin concerto is just an exquisite piece of lyricism as far removed from the gaunt, sinewy Sibelian ideal as well it can be. Too fine and delicate to impose its will, it expects the listener to bring to it concentration and an open mind. To the willing it reveals a heart of entrancing beauty. The " Concerto Gregoriano " by Respighi derives its character from the use of Gregorian melody. It has the merit of clever, distinguished craftsmanship and of an unusually effective solo part. Reger's single experiment has never reached England ; a loss, however, that can be borne without anxiety, for it sounds like nothing so much as over-ripe Brahms.

Stravinsky, according to some of his apologists, wrote a violin concerto to revive, *mutatis mutandis*, the old concerto form and style. The experiment, given the outlook of the composer, could only result in a hybrid that has neither the solidity of the old nor the piquant perverseness of the new. It babbles of things Stravinsky may like. There is no evidence of any ardent affection.

A number of compositions not strictly in sonata form can only be mentioned briefly. Lalo's " Symphonie Espagnole " does with ease what Bruch's "Scottish Fantasie" achieved not without dust and heat. It is picturesque music, requiring a deft and light touch. Chausson's " Poème " would be the better for an astringent ; its uncontrolled sentimentality quickly palls.

Some fantasias on operatic themes have also had a measure of success. Ernst's pot-pourri on Rossini's "Otello" was long a stock piece of the virtuoso repertory. Wieniaw-ski's clever arrangement of melodies from Gounod's " Faust " outlived Sarasate's essay in the same field. Ondricek's diligent fantasia on Smetana's " The Bartered Bride " is admirable, but too difficult to tempt the average performer. Short pieces for the violin have been written by Beethoven (two Romances), Wagner (Albumblatt), Sibelius (three pieces), Delius (Legend) and Ravel (Tsigane) —chips from great craftsmen's workshops.

# D: THE VIOLONCELLO AND THE VIOLA

## CHAPTER I

## THE 'CELLO CONCERTOS

### (a) HAYDN AND SCHUMANN

NOT MUCH MUSIC has been written for the solo 'cellist. Virtuoso concertos comparable to the pianoforte music of Liszt and Rubinstein do not exist ; nor is there anything to take adequately the place of the contributions to violin literature by Vivaldi and Tartini. But if great 'cello concertos are few in number, they are of considerable importance.

The earliest concerto known to the modern repertory is Haydn's. Not wholly without reason, its authenticity has been questioned by responsible scholars ; but there are pages which, if not written by Haydn, are certainly worthy of Haydn at his best. Only a Haydn or a Mozart could have written the second subject of the first movement, fresh as the dawn. The composition, as a whole, hangs well together and, whatever the truth about its authorship, provides no obvious evidence of a conflict of styles.

Schumann's concerto is far and away the best thing he wrote for a string instrument. His treatment of the violin in orchestral scores, as well as in the sonatas, shows so mean a conception of its capacity that his sympathy for and understanding of the 'cello appear almost miraculous. The exquisitely intimate slow movement is as native to the 'cello as Beethoven's adagio is to the violin. No other voice but that of the 'cello could give the right colour and expression to its gentle melancholy. The other movements do not rise to the same level of intensity but they never fall below the average of Schumannesque respectability and earnestness.

## (b) DVOŘÁK

Like Schumann, Dvořák wrote some of his worst music for the violin and some of his best for the 'cello. It is not too much to say that in richness and picturesqueness the 'cello concerto is equal to the symphony " From the New World." The orchestra is used with supreme skill, the greatest difficulty that confronts the 'cello composer, the low range of the instrument, being overcome with a never failing wealth of resources. The employment of the wood-wind, in particular, deserves the closest attention ; some of the most striking effects are obtained by contrasting their more or less fixed timbre with the subtle changes obtained from the string instrument simply by altering the pressure of bow or finger. The chief virtue of the concerto resides, however, in its themes and their development. Details of construction are skilfully hidden away ; melodies of Verdian warmth succeed one another in orderly fashion and give the work its pre-eminently lyric character. Dvořák himself must have loved it above others. He seems reluctant to come to the last bar and, before concluding, inserts a short epilogue that reminds one of the tears Dumas shed, when, having reached the last stage of the D'Artagnan cycle, he had to kill his beloved hero.

## (c) ELGAR, DELIUS AND BAX

The series of indisputably great concertos concludes with Edward Elgar's which, in some respects, surpasses them all. It includes a movement corresponding to the classical scherzo, generally avoided by concerto composers for the obvious reason that the necessarily light texture and brilliant colour cannot be easily secured when the predominance of a single instrument reduces the range of tonal values. Elgar's command of the more subtle shades of orchestral blends stands him in good stead. He sends the 'cellist off on a rollicking course with this or that orchestral instrument in hot pursuit ; it is a game in which all join in turn, all high spirits and good humour. The character of the movement is pre-eminently that of the scherzo, even though the rhythm is not the usual 3-4.

The other movements are not less distinctly original. The quasi-pastoral atmosphere of the first, one of Elgar's innovations, is alien to the music of the romantics and matched only by the somewhat more formal 6-8 or 12-8 movements of Handel and of the old Italians. It recalls slightly the quiet, even theme that opens the last movement of the sonata for violin and piano. It baffled the audience at the first performance (as real novelty invariably does), when the concerto had a lukewarm reception. The only movement that even then made its mark was the brief adagio. The 'cello, apparently, appeals to composers in particular as the exponent of long-drawn, lyrical phrases. Like Schumann and Dvořák, Elgar gives way entirely to lyrical instincts in the slower movement, and writes phrases of an intense beauty that take us to every source of emotion. The end is somewhat abrupt. Obviously the movement is not meant to stand by itself; it is but a part of the whole and the formal close comes at the end of the concluding allegro, which includes a section as grave as the slow movement. The subtle details of the orchestral score cannot be dealt with here. But it may be noted that Elgar uses the fortissimo chords of the full orchestra without embarrassing the soloist—something of a *tour de force*.

Two modern concertos, Delius's and Arnold Bax's, just miss the right to the first rank. The Delius work shares with the violin concerto refinement, reticence and individuality. But its vitality is slightly lower ; its graceful episodes are not knit together so closely ; there are moments when the progress halts—it is the work of a master craftsman in his less inspired hours.

Arnold Bax's concerto is so recent a production that one speaks of it with a certain diffidence, since it is possible that

further hearings may reveal something that at present
is still hidden from us. It is a work of great skill, most
convincing when the solo is allowed to sing out its fanciful
melodies while the orchestra, reduced to the position of a
junior partner, supports him with countless happy devices.
A clever piece of writing, but less completely convincing
than the same composer's sonata for 'cello and pianoforte,
which for close thinking, concentration, even distribution of
material and compactness bears comparison—and more—
with the best examples of its kind.

## (d) SAINT-SAËNS AND STRAUSS

The facile muse of Camille Saint-Saëns is seen in two
concertos (the favourite being in A minor) and an Allegro
Appassionato, which towards the end of the last century was
even more in request than the concertos. There is a certain
formal precision in his writing, which won the admiration
of so exacting a critic as Busoni. The modern musician finds
it a little too glib and, except in the neat workmanship,
almost casual. A revival is unthinkable ; but an occasional
dip into Saint-Saëns provides pleasant relaxation from the
study of sterner stuff. The concerto by another French
composer, E. Lalo, enjoyed at first a run of popularity that
has since waned. It shows in the best light the Gallic genius
for debonair thought cast in an elegant mould.

The very important part assigned to the solo 'cello in
Richard Strauss's " Don Quixote " may be mentioned
here, as it is as long and quite as difficult as some concertos.
The 'cello is intended to represent and express the thoughts
and sentiments of the Don, while his henchman, Sancho
Panza, is identified with the viola solo. The portraits have
both humour and pathos ; the dialogue between the two
adventure-seekers has points of a more subtle humour than
the Straussian portrait of Till Eulenspiegel and the characterisation carries a good deal further the precedent of
Berlioz's " Harold in Italy," where the solo viola is cast for
the part of Harold.

## CHAPTER II

# THE 'CELLO SONATAS AND OTHER WORKS

THERE ARE quite a number of old sonatas, available mostly in modern arrangements, by Italian and French composers. The sonata by Giuseppe Valentini is a fair specimen of its type. A better one is the A major sonata by Boccherini, for Boccherini could give musical value to a bravura turn. A fertile composer, Boccherini left, besides, four concertos, all of more than purely historic interest. The unaccompanied partitas by Bach take in violoncello music a position similar to that of the violin sonatas. Neither the partita in C nor the one in D minor—probably the most attractive of the set—hold anything as majestic as the chaconne or the C minor fugue, but the minuets of the D minor suite are more than the peers of the minuets of the E major violin sonata.

The sonatas for pianoforte and 'cello by Beethoven and Mendelssohn must take a second place in the works of their respective authors—pleasing, naturally fluent music that just falls short of excellence. Brahms, on the other hand, in writing for piano and 'cello quite rises to the level of the piano and violin sonatas. The sonata in F is finer as a whole than the sonata in E minor ; the second, however, has one or two moments more exquisite than anything found in the other. Grieg's sonata in A minor has characteristic colour but is slightly reminiscent of the corresponding work in C minor for piano and violin. A sonata by Ildebrando Pizzetti is less known than it should be ; judged by modern standards its texture is comparatively simple, but its direct-ness does not stand in the way of a beauty as true and un-affected as it is original. Until a few years ago, no 'cello recital was considered adequate which did not include some

Wc

example from the workshop of Popper and Davidoff, two 'cellists who did their utmost to supply the repertory with a number of long and short compositions and provide substitutes for the popular Variations Symphoniques of Léon Boëllmann. More earnest than these and quite as effective is Tchaikovsky's " Variations on a Rococo theme." Amongst the moderns Zoltán Kodály has shown a partiality for the 'cello, writing for it a duet with violin, an admirable sonata with pianoforte and an unaccompanied sonata. The last abounds in ingenious and happy touches and has a sense of measure and proportion not often found in un-accompanied string music. Debussy wrote an excellent sonata for 'cello and piano, Ravel one for violin and 'cello.

## CHAPTER III

# THE VIOLA WORKS

As Albert Tottmann's useful " Führer durch den Violin-Unterricht " shows, the only reputable composition for the viola, till recent times, was Berlioz's " Harold in Italy," which begins as a concerto and ends like a sym-phony. The rest of the repertory was made up of one or two original compositions by Vieuxtemps and Rubinstein and a certain amount of arias, romanzas and scenas from " The Huguenots," " Freischütz " and other operas.

" Harold," though not one of the best things Berlioz wrote, is yet by no means negligible. It was suggested to Berlioz by Paganini who, possessing a Stradivari viola, was anxious to have music worthy of the instrument. Paganini, however, never played it ; he fell ill and the first perform-ance was entrusted to another. In his memoirs Berlioz tells how in the Pilgrims' March the harpist lost his place and the conductor his head so that the situation was retrieved by the hasty order to play the last chord. " It was," says

Berlioz, " murder most foul." The reception was not unfavourable all the same. And it cannot be said that " Harold " is without sin. The Pilgrims' March is too long for the simple theme on which it is based ; the Brigands' Orgy has nothing like the fire and imaginative force of the Witches' Sabbath in the " Symphonie Fantastique." But the design is bold and original and the work lives up to the description given in the sub-title " Scenes of melancholy, happiness and joy."

There is nothing worth mention between " Harold " and the contemporary works of English and German composers. In Germany, Paul Hindemith, himself an admirable violist, quickly realised the opportunities offered by the employ-ment of an unusual medium. His viola music is not violin music transposed ; it takes into account the tonal charac-teristics, the peculiarities of the instrument. Æsthetically it embodies the curious doctrine of art for daily use, un-related to sentiment and experience.[1] In his earlier com-positions Hindemith shows the unmistakable influence of the great German tradition. The sonata for viola and piano, Opus 26, is free from that influence ; the composer rejects the stimuli that inspired his predecessors ; his refusal to be poetic, descriptive, or emotional is definite.

English composers of viola music are free from pre-conceived theories and prejudice. William Walton's con-certo for viola and orchestra is daring and original ; but there is no complete rejection of the past and the listener is not required to forget it before he can lay any pretensions to an understanding of the present. York Bowen has written a concerto of merit for viola and piano and Arnold Bax a phantasy for viola and piano. This, I imagine, to be a tribute to the talents of Mr. Lionel Tertis, a great violist, who has himself made a number of excellent arrangements, including a viola version of Elgar's 'cello concerto. Sir Granville Bantock's sonata for viola and piano makes us regret that the sonata form has not more often tempted so wise and melodious a composer.

[1] " Gebrauchsmusik." See also Book V, Part E, Chapter II, p. 564.

# E: TWO PIANOFORTES AND UNUSUAL COMBINATIONS

An unusual combination of instruments often acts as a stimulus on the composer's imagination. If there are additional instruments in the scheme, he will devise new ways to justify their employment ; if their number is reduced, he will seek to extract the utmost effect by a more discriminating use of the resources at his disposal. Most of the double concertos we possess are not oddities or *pièces d'occasions*, but masterpieces. Even the piano concerto for the left hand written by Ravel for the Austrian one-armed pianist, Paul Wittgenstein, is not a curiosity, but as good and eloquent a piece of music as Ravel ever wrote.

The earliest example of a double concerto known to modern performers is Bach's concerto in D for two violins. Scholarship and rich fancy have never been combined to finer purpose than in the lovely slow movement, where the two violins while acting with absolute independence are joined by identity of thought and feeling, sharing responsibilities, echoing each other's sentiments, neither sinking ever to the position of a mere auxiliary. The other movements in virility, directness, neatness of design are similar to the best introductory and concluding sections of Bach's concertos. A concerto for three pianos by Mozart is a *pièce d'occasion* and has little to commend it apart from its cadenzas which, contrary to the usual custom, are written out in full.

While the Bach double concerto has long been an accepted classic, the Brahms concerto for solo violin, 'cello and orchestra has been under a cloud that has not quite lifted, probably because Joachim was understood to profess but a cold admiration for this particular work of his friend.

Joachim's judgment may have been influenced by the circumstances in which the concerto was written. There had been a quarrel, in which Joachim had not shown the better side of his character. The double concerto, the eirenicon which brought the friends once more together, probably reminded Joachim of what he would rather forget. His attitude is also that of Richard Specht, who grows rhapsodical to the point of incoherence when other compositions of Brahms are in question. Specht admits the dignity of the main themes and praises the broad, sweeping lines of the andante, but objects to the composition as a whole, finding it sombre and artificial. The charge of artificiality is not completely without foundation ; but the double concerto is not alone in this respect, for traces of artificiality can be found in most of Brahms's compositions in classical form. Most of his development sections have a little more learning and a little less naturalness than Beethoven's. As for sombreness, nothing in the double concerto is as sombre as certain pages of the German Requiem or of the " Vier Ernste Gesänge." It is an austere work whose bold opening—a stroke of genius—is well matched by the typical Brahmsian tenderness of the second subject, more important than the first, as in other works. Its general tone is more sober than that of the violin concerto and its pace more sedate ; its melodies are not less gentle or less beautiful.

Brahms's variations for two pianos on a theme of Haydn have lost some of their attraction as piano music since they have become immensely popular in an orchestral setting. They remain, however, a worthy companion to the Schumann variations for two pianos, based on one of those themes that, once heard, can no more be forgotten than those famous lines of poetry good taste does not allow to be quoted.

Busoni's works for two pianos are exceptionally happy. The duettino concertante after the finale of Mozart's concerto in F major, the improvisation on Bach's chorale " Wie wohl ist dir, O Freund der Seele " are not arrangements in the usual sense. There is no difference in spirit between the work of Mozart or Bach and that of Busoni ; a composer carries on the labours of another composer. The pleasure we derive from the duettino is precisely that of a Mozart composition. Had he chosen to do so, Busoni could have written spurious Bach and spurious Mozart that would have completely baffled the critic. His "Fantasia Contrappuntistica," on themes from Bach's "Art of Fugue," written originally for one piano and rearranged later for two, is a vast and overwhelming work, held by many to be a modern masterpiece.

These and Arnold Bax's very remarkable "Moy Mell" are amongst the best things for two pianos. There exists also a number of neat arrangements. Humperdinck transcribed the harpsichord preludes and fugues of Bach ; Rheinberger did the same office for the Goldberg variation. Reger made a number of arrangements for two pianos, besides writing a very substantial "Introduction, passacaglia and fugue."

Delius's concerto for violin, 'cello and orchestra has the fine manner and poetry that make him so lovable a composer. But it lacks some of the vitality of first-rate music ; in this case the unusual medium does not seem to have led to unusual spiritual experience and the full range of the solo instruments is never thoroughly explored.

With the exception of the flute, wind instruments have not been used much as solo instruments by the older composers. Bach wrote sonatas for flute and violin with figured bass. But in the transition from the contrapuntal to the melodic style, colour and timbre acquired greater importance and wind instruments had to give precedence to the strings. Weber wrote concertos for horn, clarinet and bassoon—interesting enough musically but to be remembered only on very special occasions. Pepusch wrote a concerto for six bassoons and flute in which the bassoons represent six grunting pigs and the flute (included as a compliment to the heir to the throne) a sucking-pig. The concerto is now forgotten, but, somehow, composers of concertos for bassoon still remember its good-natured toleration of ridicule rather than the tragic mask the jester of the orchestra wears in the scores of great masters.

The oboe has been more fortunate. Two concertos written in recent times and suggested, no doubt, by the exceptional skill of Leon Goossens, are wholly musical in their effect. Eugene Goossens's is exceptionally brilliant and alive. Gordon Jacob's concerto for oboe and strings has fresh purpose and sober directness. A fantasia for oboe and strings by Benjamin Britten, successfully produced in London, was acclaimed again as a work of distinct originality at the International Society for Contemporary Music Festival of 1934.

Attempts have been made from time to time to write concertos for the horn. Schumann wrote one for a quartet of horns ; Ethel Smyth composed one for violin, horn and orchestra with consummate ingenuity. But, in the main, the available repertory for wind instruments consists of music of smaller dimensions. Arnold Bax has some charming things for flute ; Debussy a characteristic sonata for flute, viola and harp and a rhapsody for clarinet and orchestra. Stanford's concerto for the same instrument has a moving sincerity and depth not often met in the works of this scholarly but too facile composer.

In conclusion mention must be made of compositions for some unusual combinations of strings. Above all stands Mozart's " Symphonie concertante " for violin, viola and orchestra—masterly music of which it has truly been said that " it comforts the ear and the heart." Ferdinand David revised a sonata of J. M. Leclair for violin, viola and figured bass which, though pleasing to the ear, does not reach the heart. The less striking aspects of Mendelssohn's music are seen in the two " Konzertstücke " for violin, 'cello and piano accompaniment. Handel's " Tripelkonzert " for two violins and 'cello well repays the players' labours. Léonard's " Serenade humoristique à l'Espagnole " for three violins is a brilliant piece of work that had great success when first heard interpreted by Léonard, Alard and Sivori. It has proved almost equally effective in less competent hands.

Some light but delightful pieces for four violins have been composed by Josef Hellmesberger. The famous double bass virtuoso Bottessini wrote fantasias for his instrument and at least one concerto for violin and double bass.

# BOOK VII

## AN ESSAY ON
## PERFORMANCE AND LISTENING

*By* ERIC BLOM

# AN ESSAY ON PERFORMANCE AND LISTENING

## ❡ Of Performance in General and of Conducting in Particular

And now, what does all this reading about various aspects of music amount to for those who have sought enlightenment from this volume? The question is sure to be asked, for nobody can go on accumulating knowledge merely for the sake of keeping it in cold storage. The possession of facts means a craving for their application, even if only negative or amateurish, and I take my task to be, in this final summing-up, to give a series of indications to those who listen to music of how they may hear it to the utmost possible advantage, though without any professional insight on the one hand or professional detachment on the other.

I take it for granted that readers of this volume are all, in some way or another, listeners to music, and if any by some mischance are not, they will be people worth converting, or they would have no use for these pages at all. I shall therefore as a matter of course address those who have at least a mind to listen. How they do it is of no consequence to me, though I hope it will be to them by the time they have come to the end of this section. Every form of listening has its merits and its problems, and I can do no better than begin at once to deal with each in succession. As there can be no listening without performance, I shall have to discuss that too ; but as this is not a book for executive musicians nearly so much as for their audiences, the former's problems will never be touched upon here without reference to those of the latter.

Concert performance must come first. Despite the gramophone and the wireless it is still of the utmost importance; indeed more so than ever, precisely because of these inventions, as will be seen later. No doubt the most vital concerts nowadays—it was not always so—are the orchestral ones, not only in London, where three orchestras give extended series all through the winter season, but also in several of the larger provincial towns.[1] Symphony concerts without a soloist were unthinkable until not long ago ; now it is perfectly possible, thanks mainly to a vast improvement in the standard of orchestral playing, to give a whole programme without the assistance of any executive artist apart from the members of the band and the conductor.

It is true that the latter is often himself the star performer, which can on occasion be extremely annoying. A conductor like Sir Thomas Beecham without the genius of that supreme master of the orchestra would be a constant irritation. Beecham will do no music he feels to be uncongenial to him—to which one must add that he has vastly enlarged the range of his sympathies of late ; he conducts conspicuously and with some mannerisms that seem superfluous ; he sometimes exaggerates a tempo either on the slow or on the fast side ; occasionally he overpoints music that should be kept quite simple ; in short, he has his little perversities which are saved, which indeed can become fascinating, only because after all one knows from the intoxicating beauty of his musical shaping and phrasing that he is passionately interested in and in love with music as an art. He cultivates it as someone else might cultivate a vineyard that has the twofold value of growing an exquisite vintage and of being a precious family heirloom. Thus, in spite of occasional eccentricities, he compels one to listen to music, not to watch him. Only one other, Toscanini, can thus distil the very essence of a composer's meaning from the orchestra, unless Kussevitsky, whom I have heard only once in recent years, nowadays makes a third, as I suspected then—and of course no

[1] If I make conditions in England the basis of my discussion, much of it will, I think, be capable of a wider application.

conductor in the world can hope to achieve this at every performance.

To watch the conductor is dangerous, unless we have trained ourselves very carefully to be sure of listening to the music intently at the same time, which is not a natural thing to do or an easy thing to achieve. It is perfectly possible, unfortunately, to take the interpretation from the sight of a conductor who has the gift of gesture, instead of from the sound of the music. I remember a performance of Tchaikovsky's fifth Symphony a good many years ago during which I wished the conductor, who was that very Kussevitsky, had been placed behind a screen, for I felt certain that a stone-deaf man could have seen from his extremely telling antics exactly what the work was all about. But as stone-deaf people do not as a rule frequent concerts, the danger of Kussevitsky's method (which I found to have become much modified at his performance of the same work recently, while the musical effect remained as telling as ever) was greater than its advantages. The music was splendidly done ; the only trouble was that it was not at all necessary to listen to it, and I am certain that many people in the audience were so captivated by the conductor's extremely fine histrionic display that they really did not listen.

What is infinitely worse, of course, is to be engrossed by the sight of a conductor who merely attitudinises, without obtaining any convincing musical effect at all. This happens quite frequently, for orchestral performers, who are very shrewd people indeed, invariably play as badly as possible for a mountebank. They would rather turn out a pleasant performance off their own bows, so to speak, for a respectable dullard who merely beats time for them, and perhaps cannot even do that properly. In which case again the audience might judge badly by merely looking at the conductor, and so it might, once more, where the permanent conductor in charge of a rigorously governed orchestra—a man like Furtwängler, let us say—obtains with a minimum of outward show a variety of sensational effects that have been carefully drilled into the players beforehand. It is thus a good rule for concert-goers to beware of watching the conductor unless they are quite sure that they can listen intently at the same time.

## ¶ OF SCORES AND WHEN TO USE THEM

A sure way of keeping one's eyes off is to follow the performance with a miniature score.[1] However, whether from a purely musical point of view this is always to be recommended is debatable, to say the least. I think one may safely say : no, not always. It depends a good deal on how frequently a work is likely to be performed whether the acquisition of a miniature score of it is to be advised. A novelty or rarity that may not be heard again for years is on the whole better listened to without a score, unless a quick critical estimate has to be made of it, in which case it is undoubtedly easier to get hold of the more concrete aspects of the music at once by having it under one's eyes. But something of the general impression, of the mood, is apt to evaporate, and the average hearer is better left with that alone for a beginning.

On the other hand a library of classical works that are in the regular repertory is very much to be desired. The term " classical," in the sense in which I use it here, embraces, of course, such now established works as Debussy's " Prélude à l'après-midi d'un faune," or Strauss's " Till Eulenspiegel " or Elgar's violin Concerto, to give only three out of a hundred possible examples. Probably the best way of getting to grips with a repertory work and engraving it upon one's mind is to hear it the first time without a score, to follow it in print carefully the second, and then to go on as one feels inclined. There is no sense in laying down hard and fast rules.

One precept, however, should be heeded. Never try to follow a score you cannot be sure of reading reasonably well. I do not suppose that anyone nowadays would be

[1] See also Book I, Part A, Chapter IV, p. 43.

caught committing the classic blunder of the old lady who very carefully followed a performance of Berlioz's " Faust " with a vocal score of Gounod's : but the distracted roving of the eye up and down a page of full score and the desperate attempt at catching up a passage farther ahead after being left behind, snared in an entanglement of staves and notes, is a distressing spectacle that one is always sorry to witness at a concert. For in his frantic effort at seeing in print what is being played the earnest student quite forgets to listen to it.

## ℂ. OF SCORES AND HOW TO READ THEM

Perhaps the reader will ask what it is that constitutes fairly useful score-reading. Much could be said ; but as it will already have been gathered from other parts of this book, I will content myself with pointing to merely two or three accomplishments to be desired : the eye should be trained to take in the convergence of all the parts at any point from top to bottom of the page, with a certain amount of what is about to happen to each part farther on ; the reader should understand the nature of the transposing instruments and not be put off by their playing other notes than those written, remembering that relatively they follow the composer's intentions like the non-transposing parts ; there should be no feeling that the violas are playing at the wrong pitch merely because they do not happen to be written for in the familiar treble or bass clef.

The hearer should test himself with such things. If they are beyond him, score-reading at concerts had better be dropped for a time. It can, however, be learnt by anyone for whom the reading of a single instrumental part, or, better still, a work for piano, presents no difficulty. No teacher is needed. Self-instruction had best begin with a string quartet, or any not too complicated work ; the score should be taken to a performance and followed as closely as possible, unless the reader has the courage to worry it out at the piano until the parts in some of the easier passages fit together. The alto clef, in which the viola part is written, is learnt quite easily for reading purposes if it is remembered that it has middle C on the central stave and that the C's an octave above and below both look alike, as though one were the other's reflection in a mirror. The tenor clef, sometimes used for the 'cello, has middle C on the fourth stave from the bottom, which is less convenient, but not really difficult to learn.

From quartets it is advisable to go on to orchestral works with few wind parts, such as the first two of Bach's Brandenburg Concertos, and from those again to the more lightly scored symphonies of Haydn and Mozart. After that there will be no holding the reader until he has come to such lavish scores as that of Stravinsky's " Sacre du Printemps " or Holst's " Planets."

Score-reading quickly makes for instant recognition of the different qualities of sound produced by orchestral instruments, but such a knowledge, acquired first, also makes for greater ease in reading. The eye, which may be about to miss a phrase given out by the oboe, for instance, will quickly catch it if reminded by the ear where to look for it.

If a work followed with the score refuses to impress itself on the listener as a whole, he should not worry, unless it is one he is not likely to hear again for a long time, in which case he had better drop the music and listen. But in the case of a familiar composition, it will do him no harm for once to let go of the total impression and concentrate on details in the musical texture, perhaps one single strand throughout. It is excellent training to fix the eye entirely on the second violins and violas throughout a whole movement of a symphony, on the horns only during the next and on the clarinets and bassoons for another. That sort of thing should not be done habitually, of course, and never in the case of a work that is wholly new to the hearer ; but it will help much to train the ear to disentangle inner parts from the symphonic web.

## ¶ Of Hearing More Things than One

This brings us to an accomplishment even the most amateurish of music lovers must at all costs acquire if his love is to bring him reward. It is of the most vital importance to be able to hear a number of things going on simultaneously. When I say "going on," I mean it literally. Anyone, needless to say, hears the incidence of the notes of a static chord or of a series of chords in succession; but not everybody, I imagine, is able to make out several melodic lines played or sung at the same time. Several tests I recently made with myself have shown that it is quite possible to concentrate on a treble melody alone and to let all the rest recede into the background, and I do not doubt that this is the kind of way in which music is listened to by people who will tell you that much of Bach's work, or anything else of a polyphonic nature, has no "tune." If they hear a melody on the top, the music is tuneful for them; if a melody happens to be in a middle part, it is tuneless, because they never hear middle parts continuously. They are like shortsighted people who do not see the whole charm of the sight of a girl standing in a beautiful landscape, because they see only the human figure, and the rest is out of focus. If the girl happens to be pretty (i.e. if the tune pleases them) they are satisfied; if not, the beauty of the landscape (the rest of the musical fabric) fails to compensate for her plainness.

The easiest part to pick out, next to the treble, is the bass. Those who cannot do so had better make a point of listening to that first and see what melody they can find there—a great deal in some music (e.g. Bach and Handel). As soon as that becomes plain, without the top melody being lost to the ear, the inner parts should be concentrated on, still always with reference to the more obvious lines of treble and bass. Thus music will constantly gain in plasticity and life: orchestral concerts will become more and more of an adventurous delight. And almost the only thing that will become difficult about a big symphony concert will be to find it tiring or tiresome.

## ¶ OF SINGING TOGETHER

An excellent incentive to taking notice of the importance of hearing single strands in a polyphonic musical texture is, for those who can sing a little, to join a choral society. Even anyone who can sing more than a little has no business to assume a superior attitude which I am afraid is only too common among gifted amateur singers, and often not even gifted ones, who regard it as below their dignity and as possibly injurious to their precious voices to go and sing in a choir. Dignity can well survive such condescension, provided that it be there from the beginning, and a good voice is not harmed by being made to work. Even if there were some slight dangers of this kind, the positive gain in musical experience would still outweigh them enormously. Nothing cultivates musicianship, both practically and in the matter of taste, more markedly than taking part in a performance, and choral singing does so particularly in Britain, not only because it is generally on a high level of achievement, but also because the bad Continental habit of singing from chorus parts is rarely indulged in, the choristers reading nearly always from vocal scores and so having the work as a whole continually before their eyes.

Choral singing is almost a sport in this country, indeed wholly so where choirs take part in the competitive festivals, one or two of which are held at some town within reach of most choral societies. It may be debatable whether, from a purely æsthetic point of view, a sporting attitude towards music can ever be desirable ; but friendly competition is so natural to Britons that, so long as any kind of music-making remains a fit subject for contest, it is sure to show vitality and a considerable degree of skill.

Many of those who frequent choral concerts, and more especially the large festivals, do so in a sporting rather than a musical frame of mind. They may have friends or relatives in the choir, in which case that body of superlative musicians can do no wrong. Again, there may be some local axe to grind. I was once solemnly assured by a frequenter of the

Three Choirs Festival with plenty of county loyalty but no more than the haziest idea of how that venerable organisation was run, that the choir at Hereford was infinitely superior to those at Gloucester and Worcester.

Of all concerts, I am afraid, choral ones are most often attended for other than musical reasons. It is not merely a matter of limited taste, but a matter of indifference and utter lack of curiosity that at festivals and elsewhere the changes are eternally rung on " The Messiah " and " Elijah," though it must be acknowledged that in London at least choral enterprise has advanced greatly in recent years, not only thanks to the B.B.C. Chorus, the Bach Choir and a few other societies, but even through the astonishing rejuvenation of the Royal Choral Society, which until recently used to wade complacently through the same slough of stale performances of the same few favourite works year after year.

I have no wish to disparage " The Messiah " and " Elijah." They became standard works, in the first place, because they deserved it. But the concert-goer may just as well be recommended not to accept them uncritically merely for that reason. In the concert room, as in life, far too much is accepted simply because it is among the " things that are done." It is as well, while taking as much pleasure as possible in these two oratorios, to remember that Handel wrote many others containing an astonishing wealth of splendid music which are scarcely ever heard, and that Mendelssohn did better work in other musical spheres than even in his best choral composition, to say nothing of the desirability of hearing works by other composers, old and new. If choral concerts can teach us one thing more convincingly than another, it is the advantage of an open mind.

## ❡ OF RECITALS

While one may be glad that choral concerts have improved in quality, one need not be sorry that recitals have decreased in quantity, except in so far as this may be due to dire economic conditions generally. Artistically nothing is lost. Recitals used to be far too frequent, at any rate in London. Twenty-five of them in one week was once by no means an uncommon thing, and one has often felt this continuous parade of artists before the public to be a sort of grotesque tragedy on a gigantic scale. For alas ! to give a recital requires no artistic qualifications, or at any rate not more than can be comfortably eked out with self-confidence. It is only necessary to be able to afford the very considerable expenses, or, if not to afford them, at any rate to pay them somehow. So it comes about that week after week new artists appear in the smaller concert halls, performing generally to rows of yawning seats, which is only less bad than rows of yawning people, to be warmly applauded by a handful of friends, a little less warmly by a number of other deadheads, and benevolently but non-committally discussed by the Press, only to disappear again, more often than not, into heaven knows what limbo of dis-illusion. If now and then a young performer makes a recital pay, it is most likely thanks to an energetic mother who has sold tickets to reluctant but polite friends at tea-parties. Artistically the result is equally null. Occasionally an artist of quite exceptional gifts gets somewhere through that channel : she (it is more often " she ") would have done so in any case and less expensively.

So altogether the giving of recitals is hopeless. Our music lover may thus just as well make up his mind not to patronise them on an every-little-helps principle. The proverb is mis-applied here : it is the drop-in-the-ocean one that fits. Even a charitable principle to buy a ticket for every recital that is going would not help. If anyone wished to be really useful on a lavish scale, it would be far better to buy up the whole hall for one single recital by a really promising beginner ; but such a good deed would avail little in a naughty world in which there is so much talk, and talk too often justified, of " influence " and " push," unless it were done anonymously. That is being visionary. There are more recitalists than idealists.

Artists who have already made their names frequently give recitals that may be very much worth hearing. But let not the name alone be your attraction. It is always a good plan to look at the programme before one goes to hear any performer, however celebrated, and people who issue handbills of recitals without giving a fully detailed list of what they propose to do are to be invariably regarded with suspicion. A perfectly unknown artist who has the enterprise to give an unusual and exceptionally well planned programme is nearly always worth supporting, even if the performance itself should turn out to be far from satisfying. Those in search of guidance in the matter of musical experience cannot be strongly enough urged always to go and hear music, never, or only in quite exceptional cases such as the farewell appearance of a great artist, a performer, however eminent. Perhaps this is an austere view, but for anyone who professes a genuine interest in music as such it makes a perfectly good rule, the more so because it modifies itself automatically in the case of very great executive musicians, who invest a comparatively conventional programme with an interest that attaches legitimately to the hearer's expectation of a model performance on their part. Even if it turns out a disappointment, there is at least the satisfaction of seeing an idol tottering on its pedestal. That, too, is legitimate.

## ¶ OF SONG RECITALS

Much the most frequent recitals are those of singers, and it is here that one comes most often across more or less shocking exhibitions of incompetence. To go on a platform without some sort of an adequate technique is simply not possible for an instrumentalist, but a singer who has been complimented on possessing a beautiful voice often feels that to amount in itself to a vocation, which is almost as absurd as if I who, like the Irishman, have never tried whether I can play the fiddle or not, were to announce a recital merely because I happened to have become the owner of a Stradivarius violin. But then, I am afraid some singers *are* absurd.

All the same, song recitals can be very interesting indeed, and their programmes are worth watching. When all the feeble or pathetic upstarts and all the vain dabblers in and on the borders of the profession who misuse opportunities for public appearance have been discounted, there remain a number of highly intelligent vocalists, both British and foreign, capable of filling an evening unaided, except by an accompanist. (Of the latter, who is very important, more anon.) Singers who deserve the music lover's attention are those who do not merely throw together a number of songs which happen to exhibit their voices and natural capacities to the best advantage, but group their material in some order that presents the whole programme as a definite, shapely scheme. The plan may be historical and the order chronological ; the aim may be to show the differences between various national expressions through the medium of song ; there may be some literary unity, such as a whole evening of settings of Shakespeare or Goethe ; the development of a single school may be demonstrated ; and so on and on. Anything of this kind should be looked for as sure to yield an experience, and it may fairly be taken for granted that a singer who has had the intelligence to devise a programme of the sort will not be likely to present it in an entirely futile manner.

Songs, not arias, should as a rule be looked for at vocal recitals. Despised once by many of the most famous singers, who never dreamt of rendering service to music by submitting to the composer's requirements, but on the contrary expected it to provide them with material for their own display, songs in a programme are now to a great extent an index to the intelligence and artistic sincerity of a vocalist. A vocal recital is a matter of partnership between a singer and a pianist, and it follows that works written for voice and piano ought at least to predominate in its programme, if not to fill it exclusively. As to vocal pieces not originally so written, there is no need to proscribe them altogether and on principle. An aria from a Handel oratorio or a Bach cantata or a Mozart opera, or a group of such things, may serve two very good purposes at a recital. It may discipline the performer by a series of difficulties of a technical rather than an interpretative order, and it may be of such intrinsic beauty and so impossible to hear anywhere else as to make its performance, even in a makeshift version with a piano accompaniment, a true benefit for the hearer. What is undesirable is to feel that any and every recital must needs open with a set of classical arias as a sort of introductory rite demanded by a noble tradition. There is no noble tradition about this ; it is merely an ignoble convention, as may be judged from the disheartening monotony with which the same few arias are thrown together again and again for this ritualistic opening ceremony. There are still singers who have some obscure kind of hereditary notion that to begin a vocal recital without either Lully's " Bois épais " or Gluck's " O del mio dolce ardor " is among the things that are simply not done. Which is the more ludicrous because both these airs, more than worth doing, to be sure, for their exquisite beauty, are so difficult as to be quite beyond the powers of all but a dozen of the rarest vocal technicians, particularly at the start of a concert. A person who set out to perform a feat of mountaineering by first crossing the main street of Innsbruck or Zermatt high up on a tightrope would never reach the mountains at all, for he would either break his neck or be locked up as a lunatic first ; but foolhardy singers are still seen trying an exactly similar exploit without anyone in the audience turning a hair. Perhaps, though, that accounts to a great extent for the persistence of the bad habit of arriving late at concerts : people with nerves avoid the ghastly rope-dance in a sort of agony of artistic vertigo.

However, it all depends on the concert-giver. Most singers nowadays are better at interpretation, which indeed is an art that has vastly improved, than at technical accomplishments, which those who had the miraculous achievements of Patti and the de Reszkes and the rest from their own mouths, in one way or another, assure us have sadly deteriorated. Arias being, broadly speaking, vehicles for technical exhibition and songs for realisation as much by intelligence as by voice, it is generally safer to frequent recitals that lay stress on the latter.

## ¶ OF THE WORDS OF SONGS AND THEIR TRANS-LATION

Song recitals are not easy to listen to. More than anywhere else in the whole range of the singer's art is good enunciation wanted here. Not only is a song meaningless if its words are not caught ; a singer who does not make clear verbal articulation the first condition of its performance cannot possibly hope to be regarded as an adequate interpreter. Only in the shaping of the verbal phrases do the musical ones acquire their full meaning.

There is this to be said, though : song recitals are very rarely given in one language only, and that language the vernacular of the audience, so that even if the singer is thoroughly familiar with the three or four different languages represented in the programme, which is comparatively rarely the case, every member of the audience can hardly be expected to understand them all. Indeed, the more idiomatically they are sung, the harder they become to catch by the English ear. Some of the mediocre German, the dreadfully diphthongal Italian and the altogether atrocious French—to put them in order of difficulty—we are often condemned to listen to in our concert halls it would seem almost impossible not to understand, so considerably is it approximated to an English pronunciation ; but the real thing is a very different matter, and even that is rarely articulated so ideally as to be readily understandable by the initiated without artificial help.

Such help comes, with rare exceptions, from the programme book. The concert-goer may ask whether he is not likely to have his attention distracted from the music if he follows the printed words. Unfortunately, yes. It is much more difficult to lend an attentive ear if the eye is otherwise occupied at the same time. But since words are essential and yet cannot be expected to be always heard, it is better to follow them in the programme than to let them escape. Singers who give a recital and provide no printed words cannot eschew the reproach of dealing unfairly both with their audience and with themselves, unless they happen to sing a whole programme in the vernacular and have made quite sure by previous experience that their enunciation is wholly above suspicion.

These printed words must be really useful, though. For foreign songs the original is desirable, if not essential, and a translation into the audience's own language indispensable. These translations ought to be as good as possible. They need not be in verse ; indeed the turning of a fine poem into doggerel merely for the sake of versification is to be deprecated. Far better good prose versions, such as those made by Mr. Richard Capell for his book, "Schubert's Songs," or those by Miss Winifred Radford in the booklets accompanying the records of the Hugo Wolf Society and of Schubert's "Winterreise." For a great many classical German songs Messrs. A. H. Fox Strangways and Steuart Wilson have provided inimitable English versions, which might just as well be sung, not merely put into the programme to elucidate the originals. What should not be reproduced without careful thought are certain translations which paraphrase the original poem loosely in order to fit the music more or less faithfully. A bald literal translation is better than that, though it should preserve something of the spirit of the author, or at any rate his meaning. It will not do to pursue the line of least resistance quite so strictly and to be quite so scrupulously literal as was done on one occasion, when a famous German soprano sang an aria from Bach's " Phœbus and Pan " and gave in her programme a translation on the following lines : the opening words are " Patron, das macht der Wind," of which one of those free English versions which are no use for programmes begins " Yes, yes, just so." But in order to be quite faithful the translator simply said " Patron, that makes the wind," from which anyone not acquainted with the pitfalls of the business might have concluded that nothing was easier than the turning of German verse into English.

## ¶. OF PIANOFORTE RECITALS

This, however, as the observant reader will have noticed, is a digression. Let us return to recitals, with which we have not yet done. Instrumental executants require some consideration, in fact often deserve more than singers, their standards being higher all round. By far the most interesting, as a rule, are the pianists, not by any means because they surpass others in personal achievement, but because they have beyond all comparison the richest scope of music at their disposal. There is practically no limit to the number of things they can do in public, even if they made an organised effort never to duplicate each other's performances. It is the more distressing to find that every second manipulator of the keyboard must needs include Chopin's B flat minor Sonata in a recital programme, whether because it is regarded as an irresistible attraction or because each player thinks that he or she will at last give the exemplary reading, I shall not venture to determine. I will not lay myself open to the charge of Chopinophobia by suggesting that all public performances of any music by that composer ought to be forbidden for at least three years, though I do feel that the most hackneyed of his works, such as this Sonata and the first, third and fourth Ballades, all deserve a rest. The distressing fact is that precisely his best compositions, being ideal pianist's material, are apt to hang an atmosphere of staleness over a concert room, unless they happen to be played by a Paderewski or a Rosenthal, in which case it is the personality at the instrument rather than the composer who creates the spell. Through no fault of the composer's—no, curiously enough, rather owing to his peculiar merits—it has come about that Chopin recitals are generally better avoided and single groups of Chopin in a programme put up with only because they can be cut out by the hearer if the performance does not prove exceptionally good.

So much for the harm which the ordinary run of pianists must be said to have done to music. It is sad to think that they should have made some of the most congenial music for their instrument hard to listen to with patience—and by no means Chopin alone. Now let it be said that much gratitude is due to them also. Not only is their range of music as good as illimitable ; it gives them infinite chances for the exercise of personality. Interpretation may vary almost as much as the music itself, and there is endless fascination in following the play of the executant's imagination on the composer's invention, provided it be neither too feeble nor too perversely individual. Of all instrumental solo performers the pianist has much the greatest latitude here ; but questions of interpretation not being exclusively applicable to him, I will deal briefly with other instrumentalists' chances of public display first and then revert to matters of musical presentation.

## ❡ OF VIOLIN RECITALS, AND OTHERS

Violin recitals tend much more to become exhibitions of executive personality than of music as such. The repertory is surprisingly small compared with that of the piano and tends to be made to look even smaller than it is by a certain traditionalism that seems to be ingrained in most fiddlers, who would rather play Bach's Chaconne for the hundredth time than dig out an almost certainly less imposing but fresher work. And the Chaconne itself has often shown that violinists are too apt to expect their public to find fiddling interesting in itself, simply as a feat and a science, for they seem to be quite oblivious of the fact that unless this masterpiece is performed with the uttermost perfection it remains a lifeless abstraction and, it must be confessed, a sore trial to the mind and the ear alike. It is no less true that the numerous sonatas by the Italian violinist-composers of the seventeenth and eighteenth centuries, to which most recitalists almost invariably resort, are less interesting to those who have come for the sake of music rather than of fiddling, unless they are handled by a supreme master of style. They are only too apt to sound all very much alike, a fact which must however be attributed not so much to lack of personal enterprise in the composers themselves as to the disastrous shorthand system of thorough-bass which, too often imperfectly understood by modern editors, has caused the accompaniments to all these sonatas to be written out far too unenterprisingly and uniformly to bring the old music quite to life again. Italian sonatas and un-accompanied Bach are things to be avoided by all but master-performers, and generally by concert-goers too unless played by such performers. It is only kind, however, to bear in mind how limited violinists are in their choice.

'Cellists are even more so, though enough fine music is written for them to make a programme worth hearing, if they know how to find it. Even viola recitals are possible, as such a player as Lionel Tertis has shown, and can occasionally be attended for the music's sake, though the player will almost certainly have to fall back on a number of transcriptions. Other instrumentalists can hardly venture before the public with only an accompanist. Plenty of solo music is written for most of them, but nearly all of it is by specialists who know very well how this or that instrument should be played, but have too little taste and inventive power to give it something worth playing. The repertory of all wind instruments suffers from an astonishing pre-dominance of the most meagre fare, with perhaps a few exceptionally valuable things thrown in here and there. These are most likely to be found among French publica-tions, mainly for the reason that the Paris Conservatoire regularly encourages composers of some standing to turn out pieces for its competitive performances. Even there, however, too much of the music shows either a purely mechanical interest in the instrument or an impurely commercial one in the commission.

The nadir of ineptitude is probably a harp recital, partly because the instrument, unaccompanied by others, is too monotonous and insipid to make tolerable company for any length of time, partly because as a rule only those who have been trained to play it write really effectively for it, and they do not happen to be fertile as well as mechanically resourceful composers.

## ❦ OF ORGAN RECITALS

The organ, too, takes most of its repertory from performers who happen to compose chiefly for the sake of demonstrating its infinitely varied capacities and enlarging its library. Even the best of them, such as Guilmant and Widor in France or Rheinberger and Karg-Elert in Germany, remain almost unknown to lovers of music who do not happen to care for the organ. If it were not for the singular good fortune of organists that Bach happened to be one of them, and for a few composers of genius like César Franck and Max Reger, who really cared for and understood the organ, there would be extremely little in organ recitals to attract the musician. Isolated works of exceptional value written by composers who do not cultivate the organ particularly, but take it in their stride now and again, would be swallowed up in a spate of arrangements of music heard to better advantage in its original form and of pieces by organists more anxious to feed their instrument than to sustain the art of music.

Music lovers are well advised to look for Bach in an organ programme first of all, but not to give up an intended visit to a recital merely because he may happen to be absent. Some arrangements may be put up with as an unavoidable part-solution of the organist's dilemma, and the best of the specialist composers certainly deserve to be heard. The presence of a good composer's name should be regarded as an attraction even if he is not known particularly as a writer for the organ. For the rest, one may well go and hear a performer of repute in a spirit of adventure, always remembering that to listen to an organ must remain something of a matter of taste and its enjoyment to a great extent dependent on associations. It is a curious fact that numbers of people who would never think of going to any other concert will attend organ recitals with every outward sign of the most concentrated attention, which they will display even during a work like Bach's " Passacaglia " that taxes the hearer's musicianship to the utmost, though they may secretly much prefer a pretty Gavotte in which the organist will tickle the ear with the carillon stop. It is difficult to see what precisely it is that attracts crowds of undiscerning listeners to the organ. Perhaps some sort of exceptionally pleasant church-going that is all amenity and free from duty. The sheer sound of the organ may somehow make the listener satisfy his conscience about attending church without imposing on him the necessity of going through the service and being exhorted by a sermon. If so, this is rather touching in its ingenuous unconsciousness ; but it is hardly an attitude to be commended to those who frequent concerts for the pure love of music.

## ¶. OF PROGRAMME-MAKING AND THE CURSE OF ENCORES

Organists more than any other recitalists are faced with the difficult problems of programme-making, about which something may perhaps be said here in a general way, though I have already referred to it in passing, under the head of singers' recitals. How is the concert-goer to tell a good programme from a bad one beforehand, from the mere look of it ? Broadly speaking, he will make up his mind without difficulty as to whether it contains music worth hearing. But it is quite possible to make up an unsatisfactory scheme with nothing but fine music. A recitalist cannot simply throw together a number of songs or pieces that happen to be congenial. There must be contrast, but not confusion. A certain harmony in the composition of each group must be aimed at, and even the groups themselves must make some sort of shape between them. Styles should not be mixed too much, except possibly for certain purposes which may well disregard unity of period and possibly even chronological presentation. Again, a programme, like a single piece, should have a climax, or a series of graded climaxes, the placing of which ought to be very carefully considered. The most significant contribution may be gradually worked up to towards the end of the concert, or better still, since people so often discover that they have a train to catch or a supper to eat before the end, in the middle of the programme. In the latter case it is as well to observe the rule that the descent towards the close should be less steep than the ascent has been at the beginning, and it is also well worth the artist's pondering whether it ought to take him back to quite as low a level again as that from which the recital started. To end with a flashy group of show pieces seems to me the height of folly, for that is simply asking the most cultivated section of the public to depart early and only the indiscriminately omnivorous to remain to clear up the leavings of the feast, and rapaciously to demand more and more.

That brings me to the matter of encores. They are a ridiculous convention, and the artist who conforms to it too readily is to be regarded with suspicion. The abuse has grown so widespread that all programmes have nowadays to be deliberately shortened from the beginning in order to be afterwards artificially lengthened by these extras, which the public has come to expect as a matter of course, one hardly knows whether through its own exorbitance or through a particularly stupid mixture of vanity and compliance on the performers' part. The only sensible thing to do is to include everything in the printed programme that is really meant to be performed, even such displays of virtuosity for its own sake as may seem desirable. The public must know what to expect, or if it does not, be taught a lesson in moderation again and again until it has learnt to do so. This can be done quite graciously.

Instead of ruthlessly cutting out encores altogether, the artist may produce a sobering effect by the simple expedient of giving something short and quiet by way of an extra, instead of a gratuitous exhibition of brilliance that only excites a craving for still more. If a singer had the sense to show that no further adventures are to be expected, by merely adding such a thing of hearteasing simplicity as Bach's song, "Bist du bei mir," or a pianist by playing very calmly one of the gentle numbers from Beethoven's later sets of "Bagatelles," all would be over in a moment without any vulgar fuss, and sensible people would be able to go away refreshed. What is more, they would gradually learn that it is not necessarily degrading to stay to the end of a recital.

## ⓒ THE ACCOMPLISHMENT OF ACCOMPANIMENT

A word is due to the accompanist, of all executive musicians the most unjustly treated. He has in some respects to be more accomplished than a solo pianist ; yet he rarely gets his due. All those who go to recitals, and particularly recitals given by star performers who take all the efforts made on their behalf by the rest of the world calmly for granted, cannot be strongly enough exhorted to do justice, at any rate in their own minds, to the man " at the piano," as the programme has it. If they will only listen, they will find that this man very often is not merely at the piano, but actually plays it, and sometimes extremely well. Great deftness is expected of him, moreover, in various ways. If the soloist misses a bar or a page, he has to catch up with the offender without giving him away. He is expected to cover up a multitude of his more conspicuous partner's sins by a variety of subterfuges, and even to take them upon himself if they cannot be covered. Supposing a singer suddenly finds on the night of the concert that she cannot possibly produce that high B she sang so penetratingly at the rehearsal, he is asked at the last minute to transpose a possibly very difficult accompaniment at sight into E flat minor. And so on and on.

What is more, the accompanist sometimes improves out of all knowledge what without him would have been a thoroughly shapeless, flaccid performance. He can, if he is musician and man enough, be the real maker of a fine interpretation. This does not only mean an amount of moral courage for which a musical distinction equivalent to the V.C. ought to be specially created ; it is an uncommonly noble act of heroism, for it does not even draw attention to itself, but lets all the credit go elsewhere. There are songs—Schubert's " Erlking," for instance—of which even the finest singers can make nothing without an accompanist with the keenest sense of rhythm. Yet, if they have succeeded, who thinks of thanking the pianist ?

To ask concert-goers to make at least an attempt to recognise a good accompanist is to ask only for a simple act of justice. The difficulty is that it is often very hard to tell whether the merits of the performance are really his. It can sometimes be told only negatively, and listeners may well begin to train themselves by merely trying to determine whether this or that accompanist is bad or not bad. That will be something towards a discovery, for at least it will not take them long to know a bad one. We all know the type of accompanist of whom the critics say the next morning : " Mr. Timiddy Meek accompanied discreetly." Beware of that discretion which, whatever it may be the better part of, is certainly not that of a performance with rhythmic life in it. These good people have for years and years been so submissively following singers and players who have not a notion of what a rhythmic performance means, instead of imperceptibly leading them, that in the end they play with a lamentable flabbiness even when the artist they accompany happens to be gifted with a rhythmic sense.

## ❡ A Word about Rhythm and " Rubato "

That rhythmic sense, perhaps the rarest quality in performers, is nevertheless the one to be looked for first of all

Xc

by those who wish to become good judges. Rhythm is not mere time or metre. Jazz, popularly supposed to be much the most rhythmic music, is not rhythmic at all, but rigidly metrical. True rhythm has the fundamental regularity, but also the quick, responsive variability, of the human pulse, not the mechanically precise beat of the metronome. It feels time and goes in time, but not *dead* in time. Yet the jazz fever—if anything so cold-blooded and machine-pulsed may be called fever—has been allowed to invade the concert room. One has heard performances of Mozart concertos, particularly by one of the younger French pianists, sound as though their composer were indeed the " Austrian Gershwin."[1]

On the other hand, the fetish of the *rubato* is responsible for much ill-considered performing, especially piano playing. *Rubato* means literally "robbed"; but the wholesale pilferings that go on in the concert room are sheer wanton destructiveness that do music infinite harm. The true musician does not rob with violence, but rather in the spirit of Robin Hood, taking something from time in order to give it to rhythm, as it were.

## ❡ INTERPRETATION—AND THE VIRTUOSO

This is laying down no more than a broad principle. It cannot be uniformly applied. Mozart must be played much more strictly in time, for instance, than Chopin ; one modern composer may require the loosest treatment, another the most rigid. Still, a principle it remains, though subject to many varieties of style. Not style only, either. Everything does not depend on the composer in the ideal partnership of creator and executant that makes for a good performance. It is an exceedingly delicate relationship, the more so because the opinion of the hearer, who is a

[1] Mr. Ernest Newman's joke. Some musical patriot in the U.S.A. called George Gershwin the American Mozart, whereupon Mr. Newman ironically suggested that this was doing scant justice to the composer of the " Rhapsody in Blue " and that Mozart ought henceforth to be called the Austrian Gershwin.

kind of sleeping partner, carries some weight too. That is why it is so important that the hearer should understand the problem of interpretation which arises between the composer and his exponent. How much does the former impose or suggest ? How much may the latter assume and take upon himself ?

A great deal depends on the performer's individuality. An artist of strong personal convictions can read much more into a work without danger of warping it than one who is content to mirror the music as he sees it without holding very strong views of it. Many of Busoni's interpretations used to go to the very edge of perversity ; yet even while protesting with all one's might there was no helping one's admiration of such superb wilfulness. For in spite of his all-conquering technique Busoni was anything but a mere virtuoso. He was always felt to place himself at the service of the music, often wrongheadedly, but never without passionate sincerity. Thus one accepted all sorts of things from him which would have seemed alike repugnant in the virtuoso pure and simple—if purity and simplicity are not too fantastically inappropriate terms—and in the earnest interpreter of smaller mentality and weaker conviction.

Virtuosity in itself is one of music's curses. The sooner lovers of the art make up their minds to that the better. The artist who thinks only of personal display is an enemy to the fine things he does not even pretend to serve, but arrogantly takes to exist for his own glorification. He will sing or play bad music shamelessly, so long as it exhibits his technical attainments, and choose a good work only if by accident it lends itself to the same end. As a rule he will do his best to spoil it—yes, quite honestly what does happen to be *his* sort of best. Merely to bring his overweening mind to bear on the music is enough to warp it, ludicrously if not tragically. The one thing that redeems the out-and-out virtuoso is, to put it paradoxically, that he is doomed to perdition. He has his day, vanishes, and does not take long to fall into oblivion.

Fortunately the musician who is a virtuoso and nothing
else is comparatively rare. Although one would not go out
of the way to recommend an assiduous cult of the celebrities
who fill the largest concert halls, there are nevertheless few
of them who cannot be heard at any rate once or twice
without some profit. If there is no positive musical gain,
there is at least the general one of a new experience, of a
fresh exercise of the critical faculty. For the rest, there is
no need to fall into the inverted snobbery that insists on
discrediting any artist who has made a resounding name.
Even while fame is being exploited to the full, it is still possible to give a valuable performance, and indeed one may
often hear from artists who have attained to widespread
popularity the model performances their reputations would
naturally lead one to expect. They are at least worth trying. But if they are found supercilious in their attitude
towards music, they had better be dropped at once.

## ⁋ Liszt, Rubinstein, Paganini

The value of virtuosity thus remains disputable even after
its most self-centred representatives have been ruled out as
public nuisances. For that very reason, though, its possible
merits must at least be considered. A few typical figures of
the past may serve to show how the virtuoso may help
music, since to discuss living artists would be too uncomfortably invidious. Liszt as pianist is sufficiently distinct from
Liszt as composer to serve for a shining example of beneficent
virtuosity. In spite of the disconcertingly vulgar streak of
the showman in his oddly contradictory personality, he
made a vast amount of great piano music accessible to an
almost limitless public, and even his numerous arrangements did more good than damage to the music they
exhibited, for, shallow as they often were, they by no means
always betrayed the spirit of the originals. Another
composer-pianist who scarcely counts any longer as a
creative musician, but whose influence as an interpreter
has lasted, was Rubinstein, whose historical recitals did a

great deal to show younger players how to exercise virtuosity for the benefit of art.

Even virtuosi who dazzled the world by technique alone, or almost alone, contrived at times to advance music, at any rate as a medium for more lavish and varied writing on the composers' part. We may smile at the amazement of Paganini's contemporaries who thought that his tricks, which can nowadays be performed by dozens of virtuosi without turning a hair on their heads or ruffling one on their bows, were possible only because he was in league with the devil, who supplied him with strings made of human intestines, and whatever all the romantic stories are that circulated at the time ; it is nevertheless a fact that if he had not shown these apparently supernatural powers, it might not for a long time have occurred to anybody that they could ever become quite natural. Once it had become clear that undreamt-of things were possible for violinists to play, it also became habitual for composers to apply new technical acquisitions to their works.

Not only composers, but instrument, makers as well, advanced under the influence of virtuosi. Liszt, with his thunderously sonorous transcriptions of organ and orchestral works, demanded more of the piano of his time than it could give. The result was that piano makers, urged by these new requirements in the first place and by competition in the second, developed the instrument's power of sound to the utmost of which it is, and indeed need be, capable.

## ℂ Of Celebrities, and How One Hunts Them

As for the evils of virtuosity, it must be said quite brutally that they have sprung very largely from the public's attitude. The low sport of celebrity-hunting is responsible for the most appalling things that go on in the concert world. Unfortunately it is a kind of chase that has the peculiarity of being enjoyed as much by the hunted as by the hunters, which means that nobody, not even the tiny minority of humanitarians this wicked world contains, ever cries out vigorously against it. Critics, it is true, occasionally do so, being the only victims of this monstrous traffic in enslaved music ; but as in sheer self-defence they have to cultivate a blend of humour and resigned cynicism, their protests are apt to be somewhat ineffectual. The rest of mankind is divided into the indifferent and the enthusiastic. The latter, though very much in the minority, make up a public quite large enough to fill the biggest concert halls up and down any country which a musician who has somehow achieved celebrity may choose to visit.

No doubt that celebrity may have been legitimately gained by genuine musicianship ; still, it remains only too true that notoriety of one sort or another invariably affects the box-office returns to the concert-giver's advantage. Anything from spontaneous eccentricity (which soon enough loses its spontaneity and grows into a pose) to downright charlatanry will serve, and if only a performer who had murdered his wife and then bigamously married two others were allowed a concert tour before being forcibly seen off into the next world, he would without doubt depart on his last journey with the peculiar satisfaction of having first gained immense popularity and made a fortune.

Those who want to cultivate music sincerely for its own sake had better be warned to approach all but half a dozen of the popular virtuosi warily, and even the half-dozen with a mind unprejudiced by their reputation. It is always a good plan to judge for oneself. Even a Paderewski, a Gerhardt, a Kreisler, a Casals may not be to one's individual taste, in which case, though it will be impossible not to respect such artists' gifts, it is as well not to be guided merely by their fame, but to maintain a sturdy independence of judgment—that is, if one can be sure that there is a judgment. As for people of renown whom one has not previously heard, a trial may be made if curiosity is strong enough and sufficient cash is available. If not, one may safely make it a rule to distrust virtuosi about whom the more popular newspapers go out of their way to print what they call

" stories," in other words interviews by which they tell the world through the medium of a reporter exactly what they want it to know about themselves. For it is not unreasonable to expect of famous persons who are about to give concerts that they should be good musicians rather than breeders of dogs, lovers of parrots (three dozen of which are always taken about by special train), owners of racehorses, collectors of stamps, authorities on interior decoration or personal friends of exiled royalties.

However, some mild fun may occasionally be got out of the spectacle of celebrity-hunting by the mere onlooker. If a visit to one of the meets at the Albert Hall or elsewhere seems really indicated, it may turn out a success of sorts, even if the results are artistically too dreary for words. The levity with which great music is at times treated, equalled only by the solemnity with which these self-sufficient people dish up inferior pieces ; the ever-fresh surprise with which performing ladies greet a wholly unexpected floral tribute previously examined by them in the green-room, matched possibly by a perpetual grievance on the part of performing gentlemen at being by nature debarred from similar attentions (these vexing distinctions of sex have so far disappeared only at the Russian Ballet) ; the elaborately modest reluctance to give encores carefully prepared beforehand until the requisite amount of applause has been forthcoming ; the mechanical readiness on the part of the audiences to furnish such applause ; all this and much more should be enough to gladden the heart of anyone who has not been nauseated by the perennial repetition of these invariable manifestations. If it is, the quality of the actual performance is a matter of comparative unimportance.

## ❡ THE HAVEN OF CHAMBER MUSIC

Celebrity concerts are apt to be both arid and restless. In these turbulent deserts it is always refreshing to find an oasis of chamber music, and fortunately such rest for the nerves and food for the ear may be found frequently enough.

Not that public performance of chamber music is in itself the ideal way of presenting it. Greater intimacy and, so to speak, greater collaboration on the hearer's part is required to make it yield all its friendliness and emotional nearness. The finest works in its repertory do not seize upon the hearer with the pouncing effect that is characteristic of orchestral and choral works in varying degrees. They require more familiarity, more constant devotion. It is not enough to hear this or that Beethoven quartet once and then to go on to something else. Such a work wants to be sought out, pursued and wooed again and again before it will allow us to boast of its conquest. There is at once a coyness and a richness of feeling in the best chamber music which makes a kind of natural selection among its lovers, sifting out the cruder and more impatient ones, but retaining the finer and more discerning with an enduring hold that is unlike anything exercised by other species of music. Among those who are attached to the art, worshippers of chamber music are fewest, but also most constant.

They are a little shy about coming out into the open. The most devoted of them do not very much care to attend public performances. Still, these are to be welcomed as the only means whereby new attachments are to be formed, and anyone who has never been to a chamber music concert can be urged to attend one at the earliest opportunity. He may not find himself a case of love at first hearing, but if only the tiniest spark is kindled in him, it will be more than worth nurturing, since ere long it may warm his heart more steadily than he has ever found love for any other music to do.

Even so, he will have to regard public performance as more or less of a makeshift. It will never quite satisfy him. The more aware he becomes of the Muse in her most intimate moods, the more he will in fact feel the need of seclusion. He will want to offer her his home. In time even a gramophone record of a quartet will satisfy him more in his own room than a brilliant performance about town. Like a true lover, he will be far from sure whether he would not rather sit at his fireside and gaze upon a photograph of his charmer than see her out at a dinner or a dance, in the half-frivolous detachment which the world demands. It is such an attitude of correctness and unconcern that chamber music always seems to assume directly it is played in public. Half the charm of its true self is lost there.[1]

However, one may at least be introduced to it in the concert world and hope that such a meeting will be the first step to friendship, perhaps love. If only a grain of pleasure has been found in the first meeting, it will be well to cultivate the acquaintance assiduously. To drop all else in order to concentrate on chamber music is a good plan to adopt for a time, until one is fairly bitten by love of it. After that, it will keep its hold of itself. Indeed, it may then become necessary to beware of adoring it too exclusively. In this attachment, as in that to any other ideal, it is possible, dangerously possible, to become priggish. It will then be time to remember that to pride oneself upon an exceptionally select taste is itself a lapse from taste.

## ℂ, OF READING AND PLAYING FOR ONESELF

The habit of score-reading is especially to be recommended to those who have made up their minds to frequent chamber concerts. At least the current classical works should be listened to with their scores, which can be bought very cheaply and are, of course, comparatively easy to read, the parts being few and transposing instruments absent except in rare cases where wind parts are a feature of the music. It will be found that the standard works are absorbed by the mind and retained by the memory far more quickly if the music has been seen as well as heard.

[1] Many people find exactly the right sort of compromise in the informal chamber music concerts given throughout the winter every Sunday evening at the Conway Hall, Red Lion Square, by the South Place Concert Society, and at the Working Men's College, Camden Town, by the Sunday Chamber Music Society. Some of London's best musicians play the masterpieces of chamber music there—and there is no charge for admission and no reserving of seats !—Ed.

Another advantage of score-reading is that chamber music, thus listened to, greatly helps in the training of the ear to listen to single parts through the whole fabric of sound. Once a particular work has become fairly familiar as a whole, the eye should for once in a way be made to follow an inner part throughout and the ear induced to pick it out all the way. The second violin in a string quartet, being the part most likely to escape the ear, had better be chosen ; but in order to acquire the practice of reading the alto clef it is also advisable to concentrate on the viola part at some other performance.

Here is some sort of preparation for the home cultivation of chamber music—the true and final aim of its most ardent devotees. No musical pleasure is more enduring than that of playing this essentially domestic form of music in its proper environment. Even to hear it thus performed, if with no more than reasonable competence, is a treat of which a musical nature cannot soon weary. But the supreme joy is that of taking part in it. That is the natural thing to do, for chamber music, except in freakish cases, is written to be played rather than to be listened to passively. Anyone who can scrape a fiddle or strum on a piano should try to make something of a part in a quartet or trio or other combination. For it is an incontrovertible fact that this, of all musical delights, is the one not to be spoilt by incompetence. No doubt it is the charming domesticity of chamber music that makes it immune from blame even at its clumsiest. Affection sees only the attractions and fondly disregards the faults. As a cake over which a young wife has bungled hopelessly seems more delicious to the infatuated husband than the confection devised by a Brillat-Savarin, so lovers of music at home rejoice more over a Beethoven quartet mangled by themselves than over a crack performance of it by the finest quartet team in the world. And the wonder is that even those who are normally most inimical to amateurishness in music cannot but say that this is as it should be. Provided, it should perhaps be added, that they do not have to listen to these ardent fireside efforts. But that is not the point. The point is that such efforts should be made by all who can possibly do so. The more advanced amateur player of chamber music will find expert assistance in a short manual on the playing of chamber music, about to be published by the Oxford University Press ; it is written by George Stratton and Alan Frank.

## ⅌. Of Opera and the English

In England music lovers are perhaps more constrained to rely on their own resources at home than they are elsewhere. In London, it is true, there are more concerts than the public needs, and some of the larger provincial cities are well enough provided ; but concert-going is not for all moods of musical entertainment, and from one of the means of satisfying these moods, by far the most popular one in most other countries of any musical pretensions, we are all but cut off here. I need hardly say that I refer to opera.

Nothing could be remoter from the playing of chamber music at home than a more or less regular habit of frequenting opera. Nevertheless, there is no very great dissimilarity between these two forms of musical relaxation. For that is what they are. Neither is so strictly concerned with music for music's sake as concert-going is bound to be. In the former case sociability plays its part, in the latter the excitement of an evening out. The German, the Frenchman, the Italian who regards himself as a patron of music if he does nothing for it but visit the opera, more or less frequently and regularly, labours under one of the most agreeable self-complacent delusions it is possible for human vanity to discover, but a delusion without a doubt, and one of the easiest at that. It is perfectly possible to be very fond of opera without either knowing or caring more than two top notes about music. So long as one does not actually dislike it, there is enough going on in opera apart from the sound to engage all the attention there is to spare, during an evening following a busy day and a good dinner, for the spectator merely to regard it as a duck does water— a necessary and agreeable element, but one that leaves no mark on him.

No doubt there are differences. "Tristan," I suppose, attracts the better musician or the greater snob than "Tosca"; "Figaro" and "Falstaff" appeal to finer tastes than "Faust"; if a gorgeous spectacle be the main attraction, "Turandot" would still find a better audience than "Thaïs"; and if tense drama be the test, "Carmen" will have a more cultivated following than "Cavalleria Rusticana." However, it is certain that music alone is practically never the sole enticement of opera.

That being so, we may remain unmoved when a German writer with a keen gift for partial observation produces a book on England entitled "The Land without Music," since he quite obviously either takes this to be synonymous with "the land without opera" or else means nothing that is demonstrable at all. In any case his ignorance is too deliberate to carry the least weight. Having heard no music in England, he calmly takes it for granted that there is none, which is very much like asserting that there are no lunatics in Germany because you do not happen to have encountered any in the street.

Germany, all the same, has some right to talk. But the queer logic which first regards opera as being the whole of music and then asserts that opera-less England has no music whatsoever prevails all over Europe, and of course most generally in countries where opera really is the only music ever heard. I came across a comical example of this wilful obtuseness once at a dinner organised by I forget what club or society for the discussion of the operatic problem which does occasionally plague this country's artistic conscience. After a good deal of speechifying and discussion, a Roumanian gentleman at length rose and settled England's musical hash for good and all by declaring with a crushing finality that there was not the slightest hope for opera in this country for the very simple reason that it was not, and never had been, a musical country. It was far, far otherwise with Roumania, he more than implied, because, forsooth, Bucharest possessed a subsidised opera house. We were all much too humiliated, needless to say, to ask how many Roumanian operas that lavish establishment had ever produced. Much less did we inquire whether his country had ever given birth to a Byrd, a Purcell or an Elgar, whether a Billington or a Santley had ever risen from it, or whether it could point to such scholars as Donald Francis Tovey, Edward J. Dent and Charles Sanford Terry. Perhaps it was as well. No doubt the patronising patriot from Bucharest, still glowing with memories of the French and Italian operas he had heard there, would have given us a further proof of English musical obscurantism by demonstrating the insignificance of all these people with the assertion that they were totally unknown to him.

However, this is an almost Proustian digression—or should I say one like De Quincey's from the mail coach to the crocodile? Now that we have consoled ourselves with the welcome truth that opera is not the whole of music, and indeed a devotion to opera not necessarily a proof of musical intelligence, we may proceed to smite our breasts a little for not being in this matter as other nations are. To have no permanent opera houses in at least a dozen of the larger towns is decidedly a loss. To have a few popular works trotted round periodically by one or two travelling companies who cannot afford presentable productions even of these, let alone adequate revivals of operas off the beaten track, or indeed even those lying close within reach of it, is decidedly not good enough.

Occasionally a surprisingly sound and intelligent effort is made by these itinerant companies and they sometimes contain artists of exceptional gifts. Eva Turner, one of the greatest dramatic sopranos of the day, whom Italy treats like a queen, graduated from one of them. But the cramping effect of everlasting routine, of continual shortage of money, of makeshifts and half-hearted experiments is too much felt here ever to enable these companies to appeal to the public at large. Thus the curious, the ironical situation produces itself, which shows that in this country almost without opera, and therefore supposed to be without music, only people who really do love music as a rule go to hear an opera, people who for that love are willing to overlook hideous and shabby stage settings such as no other theatre-goers nowadays would tolerate for a moment.

## ¶ Of Opera Texts and the Language Problem

Here, at least, opera is heard in the vernacular, which is as it should be, if anything like a nationally established opera is aimed at. The foreign performances at Covent Garden are all very well in their place and at a certain time of the year, particularly if they can be regarded as models, which has by no means always been the case ; what is wanted regularly in England is, of course, opera in English. Not that anyone may hope ever to hear all the words. No country that has established opera in the vernacular expects that. At the Paris Opéra an old habit still persists— not the only one, by the way, in that fortress of traditions the very reason for some of which seems long ago to have been forgotten, though they are still kept up by a kind of custom-keeping mania—a habit of leaving a certain amount of light in the auditorium to enable people to cock one eye at the libretto while the other is fixed on the stage. Well, the French are a literary nation, and remain so even at their most august musical institution, indeed in the face of opera books which in some cases would seem to require a stoical humour.

English operatic translations, to be sure, are often better unheard. They are too apt to make one weep where all should be joy and laugh where one ought to remain serious. Consider this from " Il Trovatore " :

> *Soon to the dread stake*
> *(Beldam) they bound her,*

which raises the nice problem of singing a word in parentheses. Or this from " Tosca " :

> *Ah ! I have baulked them ! Dread imagination*
> *Made me quake with uncalled-for perturbation.*

No doubt life would have been sadder without these gems[1] ; but operatic performances would be less disconcerting.

Good translations of operas are very rare. Those by Francis Hueffer of Verdi's " Otello " and " Falstaff " have literary merit, if they are not always very singable, and that by the late Alfred Kalisch of Strauss's " Rosenkavalier," though it misses a good deal of the eighteenth-century flavour of Hofmannstal's original and naturally all of its Viennese tang, is effective in performance and contains many felicities. Dent's Mozart translations, though marred slightly by some modern colloquialisms for those who want the style of the words to match that of the music, are ingenious and witty, while Ernest Newman's versions of Wagner's music dramas are still neglected only, I fancy, because the older ones are even more difficult to forget than they must have been to learn. The majority of translations is indifferent to bad. Some of the Italian works are execrably done and both " Carmen " and " Faust " (" Loving smile of sister kind," &c.) cry aloud for new translators.[2]

## ⅠⅠ. Of Covent Garden

Whatever may be said about translation can be directed only against the practice, not the principle. It is obvious that only opera in the language of the country can be consistently well presented. Covent Garden can afford to remain aloof from the problem only because it is privileged to give special seasons of foreign operas in their own language with comparatively little financial embarrassment. Sometimes,

[1] And this from " Tristan " : " Bluish stripes are stretching along the west."—Ed.

[2] I understand that the former's call for help has been very ably answered by Mr. H. Procter-Gregg.

especially in the Italian season, a star or two is expected to shed enough lustre to dazzle us into overlooking, if possible, the dullness of satellites who can be wretched enough on occasion. Then again, there can be splendid performances, with singers whom Bayreuth and the Scala could not better, who indeed normally appear there. Moreover, the historic house has now taken on a new lease of life (it seems to be always involved in leases) and may well be expected to flourish exceedingly under the artistic directorship, and often the conductorship too, of Sir Thomas Beecham. Incredible as it sounds, that venerable repository of threadbare scenery and a switchboard that has been a standing joke has even gone in for new settings and for an up-to-date lighting plant.

Whatever the glory of the international season, however, it must of necessity remain exotic and, on account of its outrageous cost, exclusive. There is nothing English about it except the touching faith in the artistic superiority of foreigners that remains unshaken in a Covent Garden audience even after such a performance as a recent one of " Aïda," in which most of the singers disgraced themselves and which was saved only by the English conductor and English prima donna.

All the same, foreign models are immensely valuable, and in a negative sort of way foreign bad examples hardly less so. We have good reason to be thankful for Covent Garden, and more so now than ever since its almost legendary period of supreme glory, with its management being reorganised more satisfactorily than one had ever dared to expect.

But can Covent Garden, which does all sorts of things we are unable to do with English artists, and a good many also we ought never to aim at doing, really serve as a model for anything ? I think it can. It shows the value of specialising in opera by artists peculiarly gifted in that direction. It is perfectly true that, in the past, performances at the Royal Opera House were only too often the more or less haphazard results of people of varying degrees of genius and talent thrown together on the stage without any proper control, much less with any aim at unity. The point is, though, that without any intensive training at home they could not even have been thrown together. It was the experience of each individual that made some sort of adequate performance possible at all, from the point of view of stage-management. Even those singers who looked upon their appearances here as star turns, and were delighted to give a holiday airing to their autocratic instincts, had in their own countries to do very much as they were told, and the discipline they had thus acquired could alone save productions in which they were allowed to run wild on the stage. So that, although the lesson was an indirect one, they still taught us the immense value of team-work in opera.

Normally opera cannot get along with a star system, but only with team-work, just as any other repertory theatre gets along—and opera is, of course, always run on repertory principles. No wonder the only exception one can remember was a disastrous failure. It was the production of Sullivan's " Ivanhoe," which was put on for a run with a double cast without any provision for alternative works to be substituted in case of failure. The result was that the Palace Theatre, built as an opera house, became a music-hall. The only really serious trouble with English opera companies has always been that, being unsubsidised and consequently always short of money, the repertory could not be varied sufficiently to keep alert music-lovers continually interested, while the popular standard operas could not be put on in a sufficiently attractive way to appeal to the crowd.

## ℂ OF THE " VIC.-WELLS "

Who shall say, though, that we have no national opera on just such a repertory basis as is to be so much desired ? What about the Old Vic. and Sadler's Wells ? They do not, it is true, provide the country at large, for the company does not travel, and even London, characteristically enough, has to abandon the theatre world of the West End to hear the performances. However, as a first performance of anything of some out-of-the-way interest at one of Miss Lilian Baylis's two theatres has now come to be a fashionable event, that no longer matters. There is something to rejoice over even in the classically fatuous remark overheard at the Old Vic. : "Why doesn't one come here more often ? It isn't far from the Savoy." Perhaps Miss Baylis is at times dismayed by these smart invasions of theatres that were meant to give delight and enlightenment to the poor neighbourhoods of Waterloo and Islington (I have only lately discovered at last who the Angel of Islington is) ; but after all hers is a democratic opera, and true democracy goes from top to bottom.

The Vic.-Wells opera is an almost incredible achievement. It cannot do everything yet : the later Wagner seem to be still beyond it and so are musically and scenically elaborate works like " Rosenkavalier " or " Turandot." But one never knows. Astonishing things constantly happen, and anything may occur next. Already the orchestra has grown and vastly improved, and from the somewhat monotonous round of narrow repertory of safe box-office operas the enterprise has gradually encroached on rarer specimens. An impressive revival of Purcell's " Dido and Æneas " went hand in hand with the first public production of Arthur Benjamin's " The Devil take Her " ; Gluck's " Orpheus " has been adequately heard—and seen—in London after a lapse of two decades ; two of Rimsky-Korsakov's fairly-tale operas have been done for the first time in England, not only lavishly, but with charm. A very competent ballet is attached to the theatres, as it should be to any opera. Even current repertory works are well looked after and gradually furbished up in accordance with modern ideas of production. If " Traviata " is given anywhere with more style and atmosphere than at the Vic.-Wells, one would like to see it. I fancy it would take some travelling in Italy to discover anything like this.

It would be a poor sort of " musical companion " that did not urge the London reader to become a patron of the Old Vic. or Sadler's Wells, whichever happens to be the more accessible. This is not to suggest that everything is as good as one could possibly wish. The singing is not always first-rate and not all the productions of the more familiar works have been rehandled as yet. But what matters is that the conditions are wellnigh ideal, the potentialities endless. The problem is faced in a rational way, in fact the only right way. There are no selfish prima donnas and tenors, only a company of sincere artists always perfectly willing to submit to anything that will make a performance good as a whole. Music is looked after carefully by an enthusiastic and experienced staff, and at the same time production is faced seriously in all its aspects as far as funds will allow, and when they do not allow, a plan is dropped rather than insufficiently carried out.

## ❡ OF OPERA PRODUCTION

I have laid a good deal of stress on the importance of production in opera, though it is not strictly a musical matter. Production *is* vitally important. It is true that the complete musician who simply wants to hear the music of a great opera may be willing to shut his eyes to a hideous and incompetent setting and still able to enjoy himself. But if opera appeals to complete musicians only, it is doomed to failure, for there are not enough of them to keep it going. Even in Germany, where opera-going is a matter of course, immense stress has been laid of late years on production, so much indeed that an opera house like that of Cologne, after attaching a producer of genius, Hans Strohbach, to itself, was able to jog along quite successfully with a mediocre orchestra and an array of singers who were, to say the least, a mixed lot.[1]

That the general public in England will not go to " see "

[1] That was round about 1930. Strohbach has since been at Darmstadt and gone to Dresden.

operas, as it would certainly put it, unless they are beautifully and interestingly produced, may be taken for granted.
Modern theatre craft in the domain of the spoken drama,
though it may not have pampered us as much as it has the
audiences of some other countries, has nevertheless made
such strides in good taste and ingenuity that it is simply
ludicrous to expect the public to look without protest upon
such atrocities as Covent Garden itself has only just begun
to make up its mind to discard. On one occasion an opera
company started out brazenly with Wagner's " Ring " set
in the most ancient stock scenery, dug up mouldering from
some warehouse. No doubt people who wanted to hear the
tetralogy at all costs, even not any too well sung and played,
blithely enough disregarded these appalling settings, such
as the seared and yellowed second scene in " Rheingold,"
where a Valhalla of very doubtful architecture in the background had its roof cut off by a ragged strip of canvas
pathetically endeavouring to represent a glimpse of blue
sky. But that company badly wanted a large public, and
naturally enough, having once seen or heard rumours of
these ocular tortures, that large public politely but firmly
stayed away. And quite right too. I have no scruples in
asking even the most music-loving readers of these pages to
show no mercy and offer no patronage to any opera that
cannot, for no matter what reason, make a decent appearance. One is sorry for struggling companies, naturally ; but
opera as an art is of far greater importance, and it will
never become widespread in this country and grow to be
loved by the people at large as long as it cannot be relied
on for being at least adequately presented to the eye as well
as the ear.

## ❡ OF DEPORTMENT AT THE OPERA HOUSE

The potential opera-goer, having been told what he has
a right to expect at performances, may now without offence
be reminded of a few things that can be reasonably expected
of him. Some bad habits still prevail which, by eradicating

in himself, he may perhaps help to exterminate in others, though of course it remains true that, as Oscar Wilde said, " Vulgarity is the behaviour of other people." One of the most primitive and at the same time offensive is that of arriving late, a transgression equalled only by that of leaving before the end. It must be admitted that both are complicated by a tragic possibility of misunderstanding. It may well be that a late-comer, who tries desperately to present a brazen front before all the glowerings that assail him on all sides, is actually consumed with shame at making a disturbance and vexed at not being able to explain to everybody how his car was unexpectedly delayed by a policeman who may know all about point duty but has no regard whatever for opera. Those who leave early, too, may possibly have found that the performance is taking longer than they expected and that the last train on which they depend will be missed if the fall of the curtain is not.

With such cases one may sympathise theoretically ; but the fact remains that in practice late coming and early going are among the foremost things to make one hate mankind and all its blundering ways. Quite plainly, it is the duty of all who attend a musical function, a duty to art, to other people and not least to themselves, to be punctual. It is quite possible to make doubly sure about cars, trains, dinner and other nuisances of civilisation in planning an evening at the opera. Those who do not must be prepared to be looked upon, possibly unjustly, as among the barbarians who do not scruple to disturb a whole audience by turning up late and those who start that exasperating avalanche of early leavers—for there are always plenty of sheepish people ready to follow the bad example—merely because they cannot be bothered to get into a bit of a crush at the end of the performance. I verily believe that is the real reason for most of the early leaving that goes on in our theatres. It is not, I am sure, that people suddenly begin to be so intolerably bored by a performance that they cannot possibly endure another five minutes of it, after having sat through it for a whole evening. For are we not a nation of clubs and tea-parties and school sports and prize-givings and what not—a nation trained to the most stoical endurance of boredom in some of its most subtly cruel forms ?

Another trespass that is still too frequently committed at opera performances is that of creating disturbances in the middle by misplaced outbursts of enthusiasm or at least benevolence. It is true that this sort of annoyance used to be far more rife than it is nowadays. I shall never forget the horrors of a performance of " Don Giovanni " at Covent Garden at which not one of the wonderful instrumental postludes to the arias could be heard for the clapping that burst immediately upon the singer's final note. I remember reading in a paper the next morning that some sort of an extra, non-grand season was then in progress (it was about 1912 or '13, I fancy), and the rather snobbish assertion was that no doubt the kind of public present could not be expected to know any better, which did at least console one by showing that the riot of misguided applause was somewhat exceptional. Still, as Destinn and MacCormack were in the cast, with other distinguished people I have forgotten, the performance can hardly have been such a low one as all that.

Happily such atrocities seem to be a thing of the past. As a rule opera audiences have the good sense to wait at least until an aria they are aching to applaud is really finished, orchestra and all, and if the work happens to be one composed of a string of set pieces and of a lightish character—say " The Barber of Seville "—there is really no harm in a little demonstration of pleasure in the middle of an act, provided it be sincere and well-conducted. In fact I am not sure that it does not enliven the performance and put spirit into the singers. But where the music is continuous, any interruption before the end of the act is a lapse of taste, and it is always well to remember that an operatic act is not finished when the curtain begins to descend, but only when the music has stopped. You may find to your embarrassment—embarrassment, that is, if you have been clapping too rashly—that though the curtain may have dropped, the music does not stop at all, but leads on to the next scene, as in " Götterdämmerung," for example. Nothing could be more humiliating than to be found smiting one's hands together with a resounding smack while the rest of the audience gasps and glares, and then to look artificially unconcerned, as though the fly had been successfully killed at the first attempt. Therefore, if you do not wish to look like the abject hero of a *faux pas* in a Bateman cartoon, you will be well advised never to applaud at an opera until you are quite sure that the proper moment has arrived. There is not always a vainglorious singer present who will be prepared to acknowledge an encouragement at any stage of the performance, however inopportune.

## ℂ Of Deportment in the Concert Hall

It is perhaps needless to say that in the concert room too the attitude of an audience makes a great deal of difference to the impression made by the music. But although, as music is being taken more and more seriously by the public at large, concert manners are steadily improving, the behaviour of some people—invariably " other " people— still makes it desirable to advise all frequenters of concerts to make a firm stand against abuses, if not by protests, which unfortunately have a way of being at any rate as disturbing as the offences themselves, at least by example. Punctuality should be raised to the dignity of the first concert-goer's virtue and observed especially in cases of performances of long works at which late-comers cannot be kept waiting outside, as fortunately they almost invariably are nowadays at miscellaneous concerts.

That talk during the music is a bad habit hardly requires pointing out ; but it is perhaps worth remembering how difficult it may become at times to resist passing a remark to a friend if one is truly interested, keenly appreciative or passionately indignant. I am not so sure that in such cases a forcibly kept silence is always desirable. It is better that music should rouse feelings too strong for restraint than that it should leave us indifferent. If you cannot keep a remark to yourself without the danger of bursting, one can only say that to utter it will be less troublesome than to burst. To make an observation in an undertone during a not too quiet passage of music is not likely to be noticeably disturbing. Only let it *be* an undertone and on no account a whisper. Ordinary speech kept very low does not carry beyond your immediate neighbour's ear ; a whisper, with its sharply exaggerated sibilants, can cut through a concert room like a sudden gust of wind through the rigging of a ship. The historic remark of " we always fry ours in dripping " that is said to have once reverberated through the whole enormous nave of the Crystal Palace in the middle of the performance of some solemn classic was not delivered in a shout : it was a whisper.[1]

## ❡ OF APPLAUSE AND ITS ABUSE

The intelligent concert-goer could do much to help rescuing applause from the silly convention it has unfortunately become. One would think that applause ought to have something to do with the public's reaction to a performance, but only too often one suspects it to be a purely mechanical response. At certain concerts which attract a select audience—I mean musically, not socially select— differences in the quality of the applause may sometimes be detected which an analytical ear may bring into accord with the quality of the performance ; but too often the same thick, nondescript noise of hand-clapping greets any and every sort of music-making and induces one to ask despairingly whether audiences are really as dense as they seem or merely misguidedly kind-hearted.

Occasionally one has cause to suspect the latter more strongly. It is a psychologically interesting if artistically distressing fact that when for once in a way an audience in

[1] Mr. Blom has forgotten to protest against those who tap time audibly with foot, or even finger. There are few habits in the concert-hall more infuriating to other people whose rhythmic sense may need no such artificial inspiration.—Ed.

this country goes to quite extravagant lengths of generosity in the matter of applause, it is usually after some ghastly blunder on an artist's part, some accident too obvious to have escaped even the most impercipient listener. The British sporting spirit, admirable even where it is most grossly out of place, asserts itself on such occasions with a fervour that is humanly touching, but both ludicrous and exasperating from an æsthetic point of view. I shall be haunted to my dying day by a performance, I think it was of one of the Bach Passion, in which a singer who was more admired in fashionable drawing-rooms than in the concert world found himself a bar ahead in one of the arias. Found himself, that is, after jogging along out of step for a couple of pages and meeting frantic signs from the conductor with a stony stare of non-comprehension. When at last it began to dawn upon him that something was wrong, he attempted to fall in with the orchestra at the precise moment at which the conductor had succeeded in cutting out a bar of accompaniment, with the result that he was then a bar behind. Being by this time near the end, he appeared to regard any further adjustment as superfluous, if indeed he was not beyond noticing the necessity for it, and arrived at his final cadence too late, with excruciating effect.

Well, except perhaps at events like the farewell of Melba or the reappearance of Paderewski, I do not think I have ever seen an artist receiving such an ovation, or for that matter receive it with such condescending complacency. The sporting spirit was working at high pressure that evening. The singer had suffered a double accident and yet gone through his task without a breakdown, and so he had to be rewarded for his pluck and compensated for his misfortune, according to the ethics of the racecourse and the football ground. That a frank interruption and a clean new beginning would have been much more admirable did not occur to anybody, nor was the audience seemingly annoyed by the thought that more likely than not the singer really did feel as though he had performed a valiant deed and richly deserved this outburst of popular enthusiasm.

The whole incident was utterly absurd and I can only advise those who go to concerts to leave their sporting spirit at home if they do not wish to become involved in ridiculous demonstrations of this sort. Where sports and games are concerned nothing could be finer than the principle that approbation should be offered for an attempt rather than an achievement, and indeed such a principle may well be applied to musical performances by amateurs. But professional performers are to be judged only by the results of their work and on no account by shows of pluck. An attempt not properly carried out is simply a bad performance, and there is no excuse for applauding this from any consideration whatever. It is an excellent rule for any concert-goer to regulate his outward response entirely by the impression which the performance as such makes on him, not by the performer's personality. And really, he ought to take the trouble to train himself to measure his applause by what he feels about the music-making. If he is stirred to the point of wanting to shout for joy, let him shout by all means ; but if he is left cold, no mere sense of politeness should move him to stir a hand. Much less ought he to be induced to clap merely because others clap and it seems rather churlish not to join in. Enough goes on at concerts, goodness know, at which one *ought* to feel churlish. But there would probably be less of it before very long if only everybody were to learn to deal out applause according to feeling, and not merely for the sake of keeping up a stupid habit.

## ⁋ OF LIONS AND THE PRESS

Much of the emptiest and artistically most meaningless applause comes from the even worse habit of personality-worship. Indeed this amounts to a positive vice, which the lover of music cannot be strongly enough urged to shun. Although the cinema provides an excellent outlet for the shallowest seekers after entertainment, perhaps fortunately for music, there is no denying that the latter too suffers to some extent from the film-fan mentality of the less desirable of its patrons. There are people who will listen to anything from a prima donna who has to have half Scotland Yard on the stage of Covent Garden to watch her jewels, from a fiddler who has swum the Channel or from a pianist who has married first a peer and then a prize-fighter and is the mother of triplets. Beware of being caught by the glamour of such fascinating irrelevances.

Some newspapers, unfortunately, will do their best to spread what they call stories about an executive artist, particularly those who do not even pretend to take the slightest interest in their actual work. There are editors in Fleet Street who will welcome any indirect advertisement of an executive musician, provided only that it be sensational enough as news, while they will cut down the critic's notice of the same person's concert, supposing they do have a music critic at all and have not replaced him by a writer of musicians' gossip, to a minimum, if indeed he is lucky enough to escape having it reduced to nonsense for the sake of precious space, occupied more likely than not by the latest murder. Musical performers who are really anxious to endear themselves to the editors of the more popular and therefore presumably more useful Press might do worse than try their hands at some other than concert-room crimes. I would even go so far as to suggest to the most ardent seekers after notoriety among them that they might usefully put their own heads into the nearest gas-ovens. To people who do not perform, but who wish to show a sensitive appreciation of the best performers I can only recommend that they should take no notice whatever of newspaper and other stories circulated about artists, but try them for what they are worth as musicians and form an independent judgment from that.

## ⦿ OF PROFESSIONAL CRITICS

If anyone does not trust himself entirely, that judgment need not remain wholly uninfluenced, at any rate at first. There is something to be said for seeking guidance from professional criticism which, though variously competent, need not be despised on principle. Rather would it be advisable to determine for oneself whether it is despicable or not. The one way of reading it unprofitably is to make up one's mind to agree with it on the assumption, all too meekly made, that after all the critic, who is bound to have had some kind of training, naturally knows better. So he may ; but even the best critic sees things only from his own angle, and it is precisely the best who would not dream of asking anyone else to agree with him all the time.

What the reader of criticism should ask first of all is that it should be stimulating, not that it should be right. One critic may write brilliantly or entertainingly without being in the least convincing ; another may be judicious and informative but comparatively dull to read ; both will be worth attention, and if their views are diametrically opposed, all the more so. Even if the reader disagrees with either, he will still profit from his writing because he will have been compelled to articulate his dissension, if only to himself. In other words, he will have used his brains, which never does any harm.

Criticism, however, comes after the performance, which has the advantage of at least not sending anyone to a concert with a bias, but does not do everything for the listener that musical writers might do. Especially where it is desirable to read something about the music heard, rather than the way in which it is presented, it would often be a great advantage to do so beforehand. It is a pity that there is not enough opportunity of this sort. Newspapers are far too reluctant to help the musical public in this way. Only the few critics who are still fortunate enough to have a weekly column set aside for them in which they may deal with any subject they please are able to write an occasional article on an important work before its appearance or reappearance. Such articles ought to be eagerly looked for by the public and as eagerly read when found, unless they reveal themselves as mere pieces of news or propaganda. The latter shows usually more intelligence than the newspaper stories and it has at least the greater claim on our attention which the sincere passion for a cause confers. Nevertheless, propaganda in all its forms had better be distrusted. The hitherto obscure German professor who has suddenly been discovered by his countrymen as a great creative artist need not be taken on trust any more than the young English composer about whom another young English composer writes an enthusiastic article. It may only be, in the former case, that the professor happens to have shown himself a true-blue Nordic Aryan in full sympathy with the ideals of the Third Realm, and in the latter that both composers are entitled to wear the same public-school tie. Every interest, from politics to friendship, may be productive of propagandist writing on music, and at the slightest sign of it the reader had better desist from his perusal unless he scents some satisfaction to his sense of fun or feels in himself a firmer determination than ever to use his own judgment. In either of which cases propaganda may be quite a welcome stimulant.

## ℭ Of Programme Notes

One way of obtaining information about a work to be performed is to read programme notes beforehand. Unfortunately they are as a rule obtainable only too immediately beforehand. The Courtauld-Sargent Concert Club is, so far as I am aware, the only musical organisation that circulates its programmes, with excellent notes by Edwin Evans, a few days before the concerts—a procedure that might well be adopted by other institutions. The British Broadcasting Corporation publishes some advance literature in other forms. To scan programme notes hurriedly just before the music begins is not very helpful, and the sight of people reading them actually during the music is a distressing one. It is too obvious that they can take in neither the work nor the annotations properly, and certainly the musical impression cannot merge with the literary commentary. The temptation to do so much as glance at programme notes during the music should be firmly resisted. Even where a purely technical analysis with musical examples is given, no exception should be made, for although these quotations in music type are immensely useful to the analyst in his attempt to elucidate the structure of a movement, nothing could be worse for the listener than to glue his eye to the first example and wait until the theme shown duly pops out of the orchestra for the first time, then to lie similarly in wait for the next tune, and so to the end. He will be highly elated over the clever piece of detective work he has done, but he will certainly not have heard the music.

It depends, of course, very much on the quality of the notes whether they will do the listener a service or not. If he finds that they tell him nothing he needs, he may put them down without compunction and hope that the music may do without help. It must also be said, in fairness to the writers, that the best music does not by any means always call forth the best commentary. A symphonic poem that may be poorish music but is based on a good subject may be quite exciting to write about, whereas a great symphony, speaking for itself alone in terms of absolute music may yield nothing beyond a competent formal analysis. Sometimes notes on the most poetical music imaginable may positively have to make dull reading, because the poetry may not be interpreted in definite terms, lest they should fail to express the meaning of the composer, who may never have intended to be definite. It does not do to praise or condemn programme notes for their literary merits or shortcomings. They are not meant to be satisfying primarily as literature, but as signposts on a musical journey of adventure. Signposts are not expected to be beautiful in themselves ; they are prosaic objects showing the way into a land where one hopes to find poetry.

## ❡ OF GRAMOPHONIC AIDS

For a public hearing of the more familiar works the best preparation is, beyond a doubt, some kind of a hearing at home. Mechanical reproduction has made that not only possible, but often perfectly easy. Gone are the old times when one used to play through piano duet arrangements of orchestral and chamber music with an aunt or a sister, though let it be said quite firmly that this is still one of the ways of making its acquaintance most pleasantly and profitably, quite apart from the fact that the partner *need* not be an aunt or sister. All those who can play reasonably well and, what is more important, who can read at sight with some ease, must be urged most earnestly to play in duet form any mortal music they can possibly get hold of— and more particularly the immortal music. For the others there is the gramophone and the wireless, not to mention the pianola, which seems nowadays to have grown too much out of use to be discussed here more than casually. It does not in any case differ greatly in its merits and defects from other means of mechanical reproduction.

The gramophone, to deal with that first, can by this time hardly be said to have any defects at all, at any rate in itself. It may be productive of abuses, as I will show in a moment ; but the reproduction of the best discs on the best instruments may be said to have come as near living per-formances as one may well desire. A great deal of what is worth studying may be obtained, and the immense advan-tage of the gramophone over the wireless is that we may always make our own choice of the music we wish to hear and may repeat anything we want to know intimately as many times as we like. The difficulty is that records are still much too expensive and that therefore the accumula-tion of a library of respectable size is a slow business for most people. Until it has grown to a fair size the gramo-phone owner is in danger of either tiring of his stock of records or of limiting his musical experience unduly.

As few people can make endless purchases of discs, it is important to make a very careful choice. The quality of the records, which fortunately can be tested at most music shops, should be the first consideration. But only the very first. What should take much more thought is the music that is worth keeping at home. This matters far more than the quality of the performance, though naturally one will get the best singing and playing that is procurable, if one's resources run to it. I should certainly advise all those who buy records always to set out with the intention of acquiring this or that work, not such and such performers, however eminent. Even if Beethoven's B flat major Trio, let us say, were obtainable in a performance by the Archangels Gabriel, Michael and Raphael, it should still be bought for the sake of Beethoven.

What I have said earlier about the advantages of listening to music with the score applies even more forcibly to the hearing of gramophone records. Here, in fact, score-reading can be practised most usefully, so that full scores and records perform a kind of mutual service the twofold benefit of which goes to the owner of both. In following the music with the score, you will acquire a much more intimate knowledge of it ; at the same time you will almost automatically become an accomplished score-reader, or at any rate a follower of the printed music, which is not quite the same thing.

Now a word concerning the evils of which the gramophone, or rather the gramophone owner, may become guilty. I cannot urge passionately enough that the gramophone is not an outdoor instrument, though goodness knows it has been forced to become one against its nature and, what is worse, against the nature of music itself. The latter being sacred, the dragging of portable gramophones out of doors has become a heinous sin. It is hard to forgive manufacturers for having allowed an unreasonable demand to create an undesirable supply and to inflate both artificially by enticing advertisements of instruments which unfortunately happen to be the cheapest obtainable. The only consolation is that they punish themselves by the production of an article that does their latest researches and achievements anything but justice, for there is no getting away from the fact that even the best portable gramophone, at any rate heard out of doors, gives forth nothing but a miserable screech compared with the heavier models. If I were a member of Parliament, I should not rest until an Act were passed that forbade the manufacture of all gramophones of a portable weight, and if I had a voice in the Thames Conservancy, I should move with all the energy of which I am capable that every gramophone found on a river boat should be confiscated at sight and sunk at hearing. It may be as well for other reasons that none of these responsibilities fall upon my shoulders, but I will at least take this opportunity of impressing on any reader with a shred of artistic conscience that to take a gramophone on the river or anywhere else in the country where it can possibly be heard by other people is a gross breach of good manners, to say the least. It is in fact as unchivalrous and despicable as any other attack upon the defenceless, for there is no redress against the infliction of music in surroundings where it has no business to intrude.

## ℂ, OF BROADCAST MUSIC

As for the wireless, it has technically very much the same advantages and disadvantages as the gramophone. They vary somewhat according to conditions and the quality of the instruments used, but for the listener's purpose there is not much in these differences. When it comes to the question of usefulness, however, radio reproduction is quite another matter. A slight advantage lies in the fact that the performance is more direct, although still obtained at second hand by transmission, and consequently rather more alive and engrossing. One listens with a degree more of respect and less of detachment. Not that there is very much in it, for it still remains difficult enough to concentrate on a wireless hearing and to treat it really like a performance, not merely like a household commodity turned on like water or gas— sometimes, it must be confessed, gas without either light or heat, but merely a lethal element.

That music by wireless should be so easy to procure is something to think seriously about. Any quantity of it

Ya

obtainable at half a guinea a year : that cheapens it perilously. Of course, the best things in life being free, this
should not make us hold it in contempt ; but it would not
be like human nature to be able to think of it quite apart
from terms of cash. This is a pity. Those who wish to make
a companion of music, not a slave, must be enjoined to rid
themselves of this bad habit.

How is this to be done ? Most safely, I think, by making
up one's mind quite firmly never to have the wireless going
unless one means to listen. There is no harm, of course, in
tapping the supply idly, from mere curiosity to see what
happens to be " on," for there is always the chance of an
adventure. But there is no point whatever in keeping it
going if the adventure has not materialised. If what is
broadcast is not to one's liking, or if it is found to be something for which one has not time enough, it should be left
alone.

But even this adventuring is rather unprincipled, though
I would insist again that I have no wish to be so priggish as
to advise against it. What is to be viewed with disfavour is
only the probability that, if there happens to be something
going which one really wishes to hear, one may hit upon it
in the middle. Incomplete performances are always vexing,
and increasingly so in proportion to the rising value of the
music performed. This pecking and nibbling between meals
should therefore be reserved for occasional delectation, not
allowed to interfere with a regular diet, and the latter should
be worth some attention. Those who wish to make the best
of their wireless supply cannot do better than devise a programme for themselves. Let them sit down once a week with
the " Radio Times," or if their sets allow them to range
far afield, with " World Radio," and draw up a calendar
of what they intend to hear during the next seven days. If
other engagements interfere with something unusually enticing, they may be worth changing ; if not, then the music
may go. There is, it should always be remembered, too much
of it in the world to be absorbed, and the mere fact that an
only too plentiful supply now happens to lie to our hand is

not a good enough reason for us to plunge into a surfeit. If many interesting or thrilling experiences tempt us one week, it is as well to resist some of them. But they may as well be set down in the preliminary programme, provided that we can promise ourselves to cut them out ruthlessly if they will not fit in with whatever else is there to fill life. If we have work to do, or friends to see, or are perhaps only tired, then the music must withdraw. Nothing is worse than to listen with half our attention, unless it be to sample just a bit of some work or another and then cut off the rest.

## ⸿ Of Fixing the Mind

It is at the best of times not at all easy to listen to a radio performance with attention. In fact, speaking for myself, I find it amazingly difficult. I cannot tell what it is, but somehow it does not seem sufficiently absorbing just to sit there and let the music stream at you out of an apparatus. A score in my hand will help me to concentrate, it is true ; but without that I soon begin to grow restless, however compelling the music may be. I find myself looking at the clock, getting up to help myself to a cigarette, stretching out my hand for a book, only to withdraw it again with a sense of shame, stroking the cat, worrying over a word in that morning's crossword puzzle, discovering a subject for an article—I don't know what else. A hundred trivialities and irrelevances come into my head, until I feel as guilty as though I were eavesdropping and as often as not give up any attempt at paying attention, which for me is the same thing as turning off the music.

I speak quite personally for a moment because I cannot know whether many readers have the same experiences with wireless performances. From what various friends tell me about their own, I should imagine they do. What I am quite sure of is that nobody ought to keep the radio going unless he is really interested, or at least determined to be interested, in what it emits. To try and concentrate on a large amount of music each week simply because it is easily available is to be unnecessarily conscientious, not to say heroic ; to keep the wireless set always going, whether anybody heeds it or not, simply because it costs no more to let it yield a lot than a little, is downright vulgar. You may as well keep all the taps in the house constantly going for the sake of getting the most out of the people who make you pay water rate. In either case you gain nothing for yourself.

As an accompaniment to any other activity, except dancing, radio music is pernicious. Some people like to eat, talk, play cards or chess, even read to music, which means, of course, that they are incapable of giving their minds to anything properly. Nothing could be more deadening to the imagination and the intelligence than this duplicating of impressions on the mind, for it means not the redoubling of agreeable experiences, but the halving and thus utterly ruining of two of them that can be enjoyed only separately and whole. I have just said how hard it is in any case to give one's full attention to wireless performances ; there is no need, to be sure, to go out of one's way to train oneself to inattention.

## ¶. OF HEARING, OVERHEARING AND LISTENING

The larger question arises now how we do pay attention to music—not merely to mechanically reproduced music, from which it is time to get away, but to any sort of performance. Let us return to the concert room and see what happens there. Well, a great many things happen, perhaps as many different ones as there are people in the audience. For our present purpose they may, however, be reduced to three main categories, which I will for convenience call hearing, overhearing and listening.

The most primitive form is hearing ; but though primitive, it is also most common, as a glance round any concert hall will reveal in a moment. There are always numbers of people who yawn or cough, ladies who fidget with their handbags and fan themselves, gentlemen who read the advertisements in the programme or whisper to their friends, and so on and on. Within certain genteel limitations the possibilities for betraying a mere aural function unconnected with any mental process are infinite. For that is what hearing, in the sense in which I use it here, amounts to. It is a scientific fact that if the mental faculty is wholly engaged, such reflex actions as coughing or sneezing, are for the moment out of the question. People sometimes wonder what would happen if a singer or player were suddenly seized with a fit of coughing, sneezing or yawning in the middle of his performance. But this is precisely what cannot possibly happen. Or has anybody ever seen it happen ? If so, the performance must have been an extremely slovenly one.

Even a member of the audience who is entirely absorbed by the music cannot be caught doing anything of the kind. If he does, he has momentarily ceased to listen and taken, at the most, to overhearing, for it must of course be borne in mind that the three functions are very easily interchangeable. That is also why a careless performer *may* find himself caught in a coughing fit ; my point is that one who is anxious about his work cannot by any chance be so caught.

Listening, it will now have become obvious, is what I mean by a total absorption in the music, not merely a soaking up by the ear, but its penetration through that channel to the brain. While that process is going on, no other impression or reaction but that produced by the music can impose itself. The hearer, for instance, may think of a beloved person while receiving a separate aural impression of sorts that remains distinct from the fond recollections ; the listener will not be capable of thinking even of that person unless there is something in the musical impression as such to produce the thought and to make it commingle with what is being played.

It is much the same with reactions. A lady who is listening may still be seen waving her fan ; but she can do so only if she is impelled by the musical rhythm to wave it in time to what is being played. She will not, like the mere hearer, fan herself for the sake of coolness, for while she listens she will be conscious neither of heat nor of the effect of the fan. Here again, though, the interchangeability of the two functions must be remembered. It is always possible for the listener suddenly to become aware of intense heat in the room, the physical impression thus taking precedence over the musical one, and she will then begin to fan herself for coolness. But that will mean that she has ceased being a listener and become a hearer, if indeed she still pays any attention to the music at all.

Overhearing is more difficult to define and the definition, once made, more debatable. It may be said to take an intermediate place between hearing and listening. I do not, of course, take it in the sense of an apology for listening. I leave that to the person who tells you confidentially : " I could not help overhearing Mrs. Jones giving her husband a piece of her mind," which plainly means that she has been listening with strained ear and an unusually concentrated attention. Overhearing music is a kind of hovering on the brink of receptiveness, an absorption of the musical impression without any conscious effort. We may be keen, but tired. Nothing else will hold us more than the music, as it would a mere hearer, yet the music cannot quite move us out of our listlessness. But once the lassitude has worn off, we shall find that the impression has remained—nothing very definite, perhaps, only a sort of afterglow, but something compelling and endearing just the same. It is rather a blessed state to find oneself in at a concert, and afterwards the felicity, felt to be undeserved, is perhaps for that very reason the more welcome. The only trouble is that overhearing cannot be cultivated. It is a delight that comes rarely, a gift of the gods to accept thankfully, but it must not be expected too often. When most expected it will be least likely to produce itself. What can be cultivated is listening, and if that is done that delicious sense of effortless absorption which overhearing can give will now and again come as a reward.

Needless to say, there are different ways of listening. Let me mention two, both of which are valuable in their way. It is sometimes good to listen with complete emotional detachment, merely for the way in which things are done by a composer or for the place occupied by his work in the history of music. At other times passionate listening is indicated—indeed it should always come to that again. The charm or beauty, the emotional significance of the music, the composer's sensibility will then sway the listener : he will be in love with music.

It ought to be possible to mix these two attitudes to some extent ; but it is also very useful to be able to separate them and then to try and assume them in turn before different works which may at first seem to call exclusively for the one or the other. For instance, one would think it impossible, to begin with, to come to *love* an opera by Monteverdi or to take any real and detached intellectual *interest* in one by Verdi. Nothing could be more fascinating and revealing, however, than the discovery that in the former is, given an understanding of its period, a vast deal of sheer sensuous beauty, while the latter shows, apart from its fiery melodies, sumptuous harmony and dramatic aptness, a musicianly ingenuity that, studied quite dispassionately, yields a surprising amount of interest.

## ❡ Of Interest and Taste

Interest, yes. The listener must have that as well as a fund of affection for music. It will help him not only to discriminate and weed out inferior works, but also to add others to his store which he would never have discovered by mere loving. The great thing, then, is to listen with attention to anything that presents itself. Only so can an intelligent choice be made and a large stock of music of varied appeal accumulated. To hear everything with an open mind, to accept nothing too gushingly and dismiss nothing hastily, is to lay the foundation to a true musical culture. Taste is formed by browsing, and if a bad weed occasionally spoils one's digestion, there is no harm done.

By training a wide sympathy, by forming no prejudices, taste will be made comprehensive. For the lover of music must beware of acquiring too individual an outlook. To become so fastidious as to be able to tolerate only half a dozen composers or the music of only one period or one country is to become a bore to others and in the end a nuisance to oneself. On the other hand, it hardly requires saying, a taste that has no individuality at all, and no little spice of perversity, is too commonplace and dull for words. Only, if you do possess idiosyncrasies of outlook, beware of always indulging your peculiar taste, lest it should grow into a mere affectation. It must always remain possible to listen with interest even to distasteful things. If one truth is worth remembering more than another, where concert-going is concerned, it is that everything is worth hearing, at least once. It should be quite impossible to find any work intolerable to listen to the first time, however much one may wince at the bare idea of repeating the experience.

## ⓵ OF THE HISTORICAL SENSE

One way of acquiring a wider outlook is to cultivate the historical sense. There is much music, even great music, that does not become palatable until one has learnt the fine art of placing it mentally into a picture of its period ; and it is astonishing how much of the world's smaller music becomes delightful, at least temporarily, once it is perceived against its proper background. It is possible, to take a great instance, to regard much of Purcell's music as irritatingly florid and repetitive and stilted, though his supreme mastery could hardly escape notice. But it will be found that all vexation will vanish and give room to the keenest appreciation directly it has been realised that Purcell's music is the ideal expression of the baroque style in music. To this end it is obviously necessary to come to know something of baroque architecture and painting and sculpture, though there is fortunately no need to have seen Salzburg and Dresden or the work of Bernini in Italy, desirable as such experiences are in themselves. The study of a few monuments of the late seventeenth century, lovely examples of which can be found in almost every church of any importance in England, is sufficient to reveal the reason for the amusingly naïve over-ornateness, the graceful excrescences often found in Purcell's music and to show that, far from disfiguring it, they stamp it with characteristic features of its time without which it could not reveal the whole flavour of the man's personality. For great men express their time as well as their individuality, and only the perception of both emanations from their work can yield the fullest enjoyment.

Every time an old book is read, a picture gallery is visited, an ancient building is examined, a chapter of history or an essay is perused, in fact anything connected with any form of art is considered imaginatively, a richer store of musical experience is laid by for the future. For all æsthetic apprehensions hang together. Let me try to find another instance. I will create for myself an imaginary friend who is incapable of taking that keen-edged delight in Domenico Scarlatti without which any lover of music misses something in life. He may, for argument's sake, be made to object that Scarlatti's sonatas are merely the expression of a cynical swaggerer and give no emotional satisfaction. My answer to him would be that one should not invariably ask for emotional satisfaction, at any rate not without first inquiring whether the artist in question intended to give it. I should then recommend him to read one of the works of Smollett and to study the drawings of Rowlandson. When he had done so, I should invite him to lay his hand on his heart—his all too exacting heart—and swear that he derived no pleasure whatever from these deliciously stylish things merely because they left his emotions high and dry, as of course they would, and should. Having then, as I think he could hardly fail to do, admitted that he did find some enjoyment in them, I should ask him to go back to Scarlatti and say whether he did not now feel that there was some room in music for that master's particular brand of rather frigid and heartless but immensely vital and nimble wit. I should regard even the most grudging and fragmentary admission as a triumph and consider that my limited friend had made great *musical* profit from two enforced excursions into literature and graphic art which were, of course, beneficial in themselves as well.

## ❡ OF THE ECLECTIC IDEAL

Only the very greatest musical works stand, as it were, detached from time. Everything else has a period-value that requires appraisement by the listener, an appraisement that can be attained only by an understanding of artistic life in all its phases, not necessarily by profound study, but by a kind of casual, opportunist training of all one's faculties of perception. They can be exercised almost everywhere, not only in museums and theatres and churches, by the reading of books, and so on, but in the streets and in conversation with other people, who are as a rule more intelligent and critically alert than one would suppose from their preliminary remarks about the weather, which only too often are allowed to clog any further progress of the conversation.

Now it must be remembered that very great experiences do not come often. Indeed it is not desirable that they should. One neither can get, nor should one wish for, a Matthew Passion, a " Don Giovanni," a Beethoven quartet with an opus number in three figures, week by week any more than one wants to read nothing but the " Divine Comedy," " Paradise Lost " and the two parts of " Faust." The rarer the occasions are on which the most elevating artistic experiences come the better, for there must be plenty of time for the countless minor edifications and delectations which the exploring of the arts offer. A lifetime is not enough to encompass them all.

It is nevertheless advisable to husband one's opportunities

for artistic delight—or let me say musical enjoyment, since it is time to return to our immediate sphere. While as many different works as possible should be heard, it ought to be remembered that their enjoyment should never become a mere indulgence. It is good to listen to a great variety simply to satisfy one's curiosity, which again need not be extended to everything that is going in the way of new fashions and crazes. Curiosity being given its due, there must be room for that on which one can fasten a lasting affection. Have as many acquaintances as possible among composers, but be sure to retain a chosen number of them as friends. It is not worth while, however, to become attached to any of them simply from a sense of duty, because they happen to be universally recognised as outstanding figures. If you have no taste for Wagner or Brahms, for instance, do not pretend to any, though you will have to make quite sure of your disinclination by a most searching trial and a constant renewal of tests.

## ❡ OF HUMAN JUDGMENTS

To ask anyone to become an impartial listener would be absurd. Likes and dislikes add to the music lover's zest and interest, although it is true that there can be satisfaction both in the dismissing of the former and in the overcoming of the latter. It all depends on the quality of the music and on one's capacity of developing and refining one's taste. The great thing is to remain human in one's attitude to music, in other words not to come to imagine that there are any absolute values which one is in duty bound to learn to appreciate, perhaps against one's will. It may be admirable to attain to a kind of divine judgment of right and wrong by allowing no personal associations of memory, sentiment, historical knowledge, and so forth to interfere with a cool and collected appraisement ; but such utterly dispassionate listening is altogether too aloof to be desirable. Far better to be occasionally carried away by a second-rate work than to go about with an exalted air of one in a million who is always quite sure of what is good and what only seems so to the other 999,999 vulgarians.

That is speaking of works. In the case of performances it is as well to try and determine as positively as possible whether they are satisfactory or not. The only caution that must be offered here is that there are various kinds of satisfactoriness. It will not do to condemn a singer or player for not achieving something that was obviously not meant to be attempted, nor to praise another who may perform a work very pleasingly as far as sheer execution goes without entering in the least into the composer's mentality.

## ¶ OF PERSONALITY AND PERFORMANCE

This leads once more to the very difficult question of how far the performer may project his personality into the interpretation, and at the risk of repeating myself, I let it. Those who wish to answer that question for themselves will have to bear two things in mind : it depends, for one, on the magnitude and significance of the interpreter's personality and, for another, on how far the projection is consciously made. I have already dealt with the first point. Much wilfulness may be forgiven an artist of outstanding character, an interpreter of the type of which I have mentioned Busoni as being representative. As for the conscious or unconscious influence of the performer on the music, the attentive listener will not find it too difficult to learn to distinguish between them. Those who let their own character come through uncontrolled will invariably give a performance of a too plainly tell-tale badness. A careless or flabby pianist will make any music sound slovenly or flaccid ; a hectoring conductor will make Bach's B minor Mass or Delius's " Mass of Life " appear equally harsh and rigid ; a conceited singer will give a touch of arrogance to Mozart and Debussy alike. In all such cases it will require little training in listening to detect that it is hopeless to look for truth about the music. The facts about the performer are too glaringly revealed.

With the conscious obtrusion of personality it is quite otherwise. Here the finest judgment is needed, and a great fund of sympathetic adaptability. Values may temporarily alter and, what is more, be found to have been worth the change. It was all very well, for instance, to think of Chopin as one of the most feminine of composers ; but when a woman like Teresa Carreño came and made his music sound masculine, and doubly unexpectedly so, yet played it with superb conviction and persuasiveness, there was nothing for it but to capitulate admiringly. What was most amazing was that the music did not seem to have been in the least perverted. One simply felt that Chopin had facets that had remained unsuspected before. Thus does the great interpretative artist, in superimposing another individuality on that of the composer, often illuminate rather than obscure the latter's work. In fact, whenever that happens, the hearer may be sure that the interpretative personality really is a great one. Conversely, when the music does seem to have been wantonly perverted, the performer may be written down as inferior.

To draw the distinction here is not easy, as there are many borderline cases in which one cannot always immediately decide whether the performer belongs to the sheep or the goats. Short of discussing particular performers, for which this is not the place, I can only suggest as a general principle that the first test should be whether the artist delivers something that impresses one as being the truth— one of the many possible truths—about a composer and his work. If he does, the performance must be called a good one. Not necessarily a great one, though, which is another matter. Greatness comes in, I think it may be said, where the performer adds an imaginative quality that is quite his own and could not be reproduced just like that by anyone else, but does so—please remember—without in the least warping the aforesaid truth, but on the contrary enlarging and clarifying it.

Whether this happens in a performance or not must, failing actual examples that can be discussed on the spot, be left to the decision of each hearer, though I may perhaps add as a last warning that individual taste, let alone personal prejudice, should not be allowed a free rein here, if breadth of sympathy and sensitiveness of apprehension is aimed at.

## ❡ Envoi

And now I daresay that all readers of this book feel that they have been preached at quite enough, considering that what they are in search of is, I fancy, the acquisition of an independent judgment. I can only hope that the foregoing pages of this final Book may have helped a little to this end, if only by laying down a few principles, and I may perhaps be allowed to add on behalf of my colleagues, as I happen to be the last to address those in search of musical companionship, that we all trust to the whole of this volume or, more modestly put, to each other, for a certain amount of useful suggestion that shows music to be as approachable by all those who seek it sincerely, if not quite so cheap for those who regard it as a mere commodity, as modern conditions tend to show it.

# INDEX

# INDEX

With dates of the principal composers (*c.=circa*, indicating the approximate date of birth of a composer.)